THE LAST GREAT SENATE

THE
LAST
GREAT
SENATE

*Courage and Statesmanship
in Times of Crisis*

Ira Shapiro

PUBLICAFFAIRS
New York

PublicAffairs books are available at special discounts for bulk purchases in
the U.S. by corporations, institutions, and other organizations. For more information, please contact the Special Markets Department at the Perseus
Books Group, 2300 Chestnut Street, Suite 200, Philadelphia, PA 19103, call
(800) 810-4145, ext. 5000, or e-mail special.markets@perseusbooks.com.

Book Design by Timm Bryson

Library of Congress Cataloging-in-Publication Data
Shapiro, Ira S., 1947-
  The last great Senate : courage and statesmanship in times of crisis / Ira
Shapiro. — 1st ed.
    p. cm.
  Includes bibliographical references and index.
  ISBN 978-1-58648-936-6 (hardcover : alk. paper) — ISBN 978-1-58648-
937-3 (e-book) 1. United States.
Congress. Senate—History—20th century. I. Title.
  JK1161.S53 2012
  328.73'07109047—dc23
                          2011039314

First Edition
10 9 8 7 6 5 4 3 2 1

TO NANCY,

For your love and support in this venture, and all the others.

CONTENTS

1980

PROLOGUE

On February 15, 2010, Senator Evan Bayh of Indiana shocked his party and the political community by announcing that he would not seek a third term in the Senate. Fifty-four years old, Bayh had been Indiana's governor for eight years before being elected to the Senate in 1998. A respected centrist Democrat, he had briefly pursued a presidential bid in 2008 and was reportedly one of the three people most seriously considered by Barack Obama to be his running mate. Despite a tough political environment for Democrats nationally, Bayh had already raised $13 million for his campaign and seemed to be a solid favorite to win reelection.

But in an eight-minute announcement, Evan Bayh made it clear that he was fed up with the Senate. "There is too much partisanship and not enough progress—too much narrow ideology and not enough practical problem solving," he stated. "Even at a time of enormous challenge the people's business is not being done." Close friends noted that as a former governor, Bayh was used to "results, solutions and accountability" and found the Senate "frustrating."

Perhaps most important, it wasn't his father's Senate.

Birch Bayh, a lawyer, a farmer, and an Indiana state legislative leader, narrowly won election to the Senate in 1962. He was part of the memorable class of '62, which included Abraham Ribicoff, George McGovern, Gaylord Nelson, Daniel Inouye, and Edward ("Ted") Kennedy. These men arrived in the Senate at a unique moment of peace and prosperity when all things seemed possible in America.

Only thirty-four years old when he came to Washington, Bayh went on to participate quickly in the passage of two historic civil rights acts and the torrent of legislation that Lyndon Johnson rammed through the 89th Congress to build a "Great Society." He served through the national traumas of Vietnam and Watergate. He battled Richard Nixon and defeated two of his Supreme Court nominees. He authored constitutional amendments and was on the front lines expanding rights for women. His legislation to disseminate government-funded research to the private sector was described by *Economist Technology Quarterly* as "perhaps the most inspired piece of legislation enacted in America in the past half century," helping to create many of the companies listed on the NASDAQ. He chaired the newly created Intelligence Committee and investigated the connection between President Jimmy Carter's brother and the government of Libya. In the end, he was defeated in 1980 by a little-known Congressman named Dan Quayle and swept away by Ronald Reagan and the conservative political tide. Even so, Birch Bayh went down fighting for what he believed in. He left with a record of accomplishment and a reputation that still lives today.

That was a Senate career.

Is there any wonder then why Evan Bayh, a teenager during much of his father's Senate service, might conclude that the Senate of the 1990's and 2000's was a bad joke? No one had told him that his father's tenure precisely coincided with the eighteen-year period when the Senate was at its zenith.

This is the story of the final four years of that era of greatness—of the last great Senate. For nearly twenty years, from 1963 to 1980, the Senate occupied a special place in America. Working with presidents when possible, holding them accountable when necessary, the Great Senate provided ballast, gravitas, and bipartisan leadership for America during the crisis years of the 1960's and 1970's.

That Senate overcame our country's legacy of racism by enacting the Civil Rights Act of 1964, probably the most important legislative accomplishment in American history, and the Voting Rights Act of 1965. It attacked the premises of the Vietnam War, produced Democratic challengers to President Lyndon Johnson, and ultimately, on a bipartisan basis, cut off funding for the war. The Senate battled President Richard Nixon's efforts to turn the Supreme Court to the right, defeating two of his nominees in two years. Through its memorable televised hearings, the Senate made Watergate understandable to the nation and called Nixon to account. It conducted an extraordinary investigation into the abuses of our nation's intelligence agencies. And the Senate spearheaded new environmental and consumer protections and expanded food stamp and nutrition programs, as well as civil rights for minorities and women.

It all came to an end in 1980. Ronald Reagan's landslide election ushered in a new conservative political era, changing the Senate dramatically. On January 3, 1981, when the new Senate convened, fifty-five members had served less than six years. This represented much more than a change of party control. A basically progressive Senate had transformed into a basically conservative one.

The men who lost their seats—particularly Bayh, Frank Church, Jacob Javits, Warren Magnuson, Gaylord Nelson, and George McGovern, along with Abraham Ribicoff, who had retired, and Edmund Muskie, who had left the Senate seven months earlier to become Secretary of State—made an indelible mark in American political history. They were replaced by some of the least effective people ever elected to the Senate. Many arrived without any political accomplishments to speak of and left six years later with that record intact.

The election of 1980 shattered the Great Senate, and the Senate has never really regained its stature or reclaimed its special place in the life of our country. In the three decades since, the Senate, the proud "upper house," has become basically a third wheel in our political system, while Presidents Reagan, Clinton, and Bush did battle with the House of Representatives and its powerful Speakers, Thomas P. ("Tip") O'Neill, Newt Gingrich, and Nancy Pelosi.

The Senate's descent from greatness did not go unnoticed. In 2005, political historian Lewis L. Gould wrote that "a profound sense of crisis now surrounds the Senate and its members," and it would grow still worse. As Barack Obama took office in January 2009, with America facing its worst economic crisis since the Great Depression, the already diminished Senate became virtually dysfunctional: torn by partisanship, paralyzed by filibusters and holds, obsessed with fund-raising, the institution seemed frustrated by its lack of accomplishment but unable to change the situation. The once-proud Senate often seemed to be a parody of itself, or in the words of George Packer in *The New Yorker*, "the empty chamber."

In Washington, D.C., and across our nation, millions of Americans who first were drawn to politics because of John F. Kennedy, civil rights, or the Vietnam War remember the age when the Senate was great—the Senate of Hubert Humphrey, Everett Dirksen, Mike Mansfield, Jacob Javits, Howard Baker, Philip Hart, Sam Ervin, J. William Fulbright, Robert Byrd, Ted Kennedy, Abraham Ribicoff, Robert Kennedy, Wayne Morse, Henry Jackson, Albert Gore Sr., Edmund Muskie, Warren Magnuson, Paul Douglas, Walter Mondale, Robert Dole, Frank Church, Gaylord Nelson, John Sherman Cooper, Eugene McCarthy, George Aiken, Margaret Chase Smith, Birch Bayh,

Richard Russell, George McGovern, William Proxmire, Ed Brooke, and Barry Goldwater—names that still resonate in Washington and in their states.

The Great Senate was hardly perfect. The Senate gave Lyndon Johnson the Gulf of Tonkin resolution in August 1964 because the Democrats wanted him to look strong against Barry Goldwater in the presidential campaign. The Senate approved William Rehnquist's nomination to the Supreme Court in December 1971 because it was tired of fighting with President Nixon and wanted to adjourn for Christmas. But the Senate of that era remained both powerful and consequential in spite of its lapses. Dealing with civil rights, war and peace, and presidential power, the Senate seemed to have a special relationship to the Constitution. It had moral authority. It occupied a unique role in our country, just as the Founders had intended.

In the compromise that made possible the adoption of the Constitution, the Founding Fathers chose to create a bicameral legislature in which the Senate would play two central roles that the Framers saw as necessary. The Senate would serve as a check on executive power that the American people feared and detested, having just revolted against the excesses of the King of England. Consequently, the president could nominate cabinet members and judges, but the Senate had to approve them. The president could negotiate treaties, but the treaties became effective only after two-thirds of the Senate approved them.

But the Senate would also serve as a check on the political passions of the day, which the Founding Fathers believed might rip through the new republic and find expression in the House of Representatives, "the people's House." Thomas Jefferson had been abroad when the Constitution was written. He asked George Washington why he had accepted the idea of a Senate. Washington responded, "Why did you pour that coffee into your saucer?" Jefferson answered, "To cool it." Washington replied, "even so we put legislation into the senatorial saucer to cool it."

To discharge those responsibilities, the Constitution gave members of the Senate a six-year term, to give them more independence from the passions of the day. Senators were required to be at least thirty years of age, where House members could be twenty-five. In *Federalist Paper #62*, James Madison referred to "the nature of the senatorial trust, which requires great extent of information and stability of character." Senators were also appointed by the legislatures of their state, not elected by the people until 1913 when the Constitution was amended to require popular election of senators. Daniel Webster referred to "a Senate of equals, of men of individual honor and personal character, and of absolute independence." And each state would get two members of the Senate, regardless of their population (contrary to what Washington and Madison had originally envisioned), further ensuring extended debate and the ability to protect small states and different regional interests.

Around the world, there is no "upper house" comparable to the U.S. Senate. In other democracies, the "upper house" is either honorific, like the British House of Lords, or involved in legislation, but with constrained powers, like the upper house of the Japanese Diet. For that reason, the U.S. Senate has long been called the world's "greatest deliberative body."

Despite the accolades, the painful truth is that the Senate has failed to measure up to the challenges of the times for long periods of American history. In his 2005 book, *The Most Exclusive Club: A History of the Modern United States Senate*, Gould reached a depressing conclusion: "For protracted periods—at the start of the twentieth century, in the era of Theodore Roosevelt, during the 1920's, and again for domestic issues in the post–World War II era—the Senate functioned not merely as a source of conservative reflections on the direction of society but as a force to genuinely impede the nation's vitality and evolution."

The Senate of the 1960's and 1970's stands as an extraordinary exception to Gould's gloomy analysis. For a period of nearly twenty years, the Senate came closer to the ideal set forth by the Founding Fathers than at any other time in our nation's history. Men—and the Senate was at that time comprised of all men, other than Margaret Chase Smith of Maine, who was an independent stalwart for most of the period, and Nancy Kassebaum of Kansas, who arrived in 1979—of intelligence, experience, and genuine wisdom came together to help steer the ship of state during a perilous period.

What made that Senate great?

It started with a unique group of people at a unique time in American history. Tom Brokaw's *Greatest Generation* needs no postscript. But it is certainly true that the experience that many members of the Great Senate shared by serving in World War II profoundly influenced their lives and shaped their public service. Men who had fought at Normandy or Iwo Jima or the Battle of the Bulge weren't frightened by the need to cast a hard vote now and then. Seeing Paul Douglas or Daniel Inouye or Robert Dole on the Senate floor, living with crippling injuries or pain, and the other veterans fortunate to have escaped unscathed, set a standard of courage and character for those who followed them.

These men returned from the war with confidence in themselves and their country. They became party builders, and, for the most part, progressives. They believed in what America could accomplish, and most of them believed strongly that government had an indispensable role to play. Having seen America's strength, they were also willing to confront, and rectify, its weaknesses. They also got to serve at a time when America's economic prosperity was unquestioned, and its potential seemed unlimited. That allowed for ambitious legislative efforts to build the nation, expand opportunities, and right historic wrongs.

The Great Senate was also a magnet that drew talented, ambitious young men and women from all over the country, regardless of whether their fathers or mothers had been famous or obscure. They first came to Washington in the early to middle 1960's, attracted to Washington by the idealism and excitement of John Kennedy's presidency. Later, they came because of their commitment to civil rights, opposition to the war in Vietnam, or anger over Watergate. The Senate was the place to be: where a young man or woman could hitch their star to a major national figure, make a mark at a young age, and learn firsthand the skills needed to accomplish things in politics—above all, when to stand on principle, and when to compromise for the greater good.

It was no accident that the staff of the Great Senate included young men and women who would be future senators and congressional leaders: George Mitchell, Tom Daschle, Susan Collins, Mitch McConnell, Lamar Alexander, Fred Thompson, Tom Foley, Jane Harman, and Norm Dicks; future press and media luminaries: Tim Russert, Chris Matthews, George Will, Mark Shields, Jeff Greenfield, Colbert King, and Steven Pearlstein; and a future secretary of state, Supreme Court justice, and president: Madeleine Albright, Stephen Breyer, and Bill Clinton. As Justice Holmes once wrote about those who had been young during the Civil War: "In [their] youth, to [their] great good fortune, [their] hearts were touched by fire."

But it was not just the unique senators and staffers, nor was it the crisis times they faced that made the Senate great. It was a concept of the Senate that they shared.

Senators take the oath of office to "preserve, protect and defend the Constitution." But there is also an unspoken oath that many senators come to understand. The people of their states had given them the incredible privilege and honor of being U.S. senators. They had received the most venerable of titles that a democracy can bestow and a six-year term (usually leading to multiple terms) to serve. They would have the opportunity to deal with the full spectrum of issues, domestic and foreign, and they would develop expertise and experience valuable to the Senate and the country. In exchange, when they sorted out the competing, cascading pressures on them, they would serve their states and would not forget their party allegiance, but the national interest would come first. They would bring their wisdom and independent judgment to bear to determine what is best for the national interest.

And part of the unspoken oath was an obligation to help make the Senate work. As Mike Mansfield, the longest-serving Senate majority leader in history memorably noted: "In the end, it is not the individuals of the Senate who are important. It is the institution of the Senate. It is the Senate itself as one of the foundations of the Constitution. It is the Senate as one of the rocks of the Republic." The Senate was an institution that the nation counted on to take collective action. Understanding that brought about a commitment to passionate, but not unlimited, debate; tolerance of opposing views; principled compromise; and senators' willingness to end debate, and vote up or down, even if it sometimes meant losing.

Those qualities characterized the great Senate and its members. Hubert Humphrey and Barry Goldwater were poles apart politically, but no one doubted that they were both committed to the national interest and to the Senate as an institution. Because of those overriding commitments, in the Great Senate, the members competed and clashed, cooperated and compromised, and then went out to dinner together. The Great Senate worked on the basis of mutual respect, tolerance of opposing views, and openness to persuasion in the search for bipartisan solutions. The Senate has often been described as a club, but at its best, the Senate actually functioned more like a great team, in which talented individuals stepped up and did great things at crucial moments, sometimes quite unexpectedly.

All of those qualities are missing from today's Senate, and they have been missing for a long time. When senators see the Senate as simply a forum for their own talents and interests, when they see their own views as so important or divinely inspired that compromise becomes unacceptable, or when they regard the Senate as merely an extension of the battle between the political parties, the Senate can become polarized and paralyzed, on the path to irrelevance and decline.

The story of this book begins in January 1977, as Senators Robert Byrd and Howard Baker become the new majority and minority leader, and the Senate prepares to deal with the newly elected president, Jimmy Carter. Some of the most iconic figures in the Senate—Sam Ervin, J. William Fulbright, Mike Mansfield, Philip Hart, George Aiken—are gone: retired, defeated, or passed away. But the core of the Great Senate, the liberal Democrats and moderate to progressive Republicans who created a legacy of bipartisan accomplishment, seems to remain intact. Moreover, the veteran senators have been joined by talented new arrivals in both parties such as Gary Hart, Dale Bumpers, John Danforth, John Chafee, Paul Sarbanes, Richard Lugar, Joe Biden, and Daniel Patrick Moynihan.

Reacting to the "imperial presidency" of Lyndon Johnson and Richard Nixon, the Senate and the House have reasserted Congressional prerogatives and given themselves powerful new weapons for holding the executive branch accountable, such as the War Powers Act, the Budget Control and Impoundment Act, the Freedom of Information Act, and the Privacy Act. There are good reasons to believe that this would be a workmanlike period for the Senate, and a period of renewal for America, which had come through the crisis years of Vietnam and Watergate to celebrate a joyful bicentennial, despite the economic challenges looming since the 1973 OPEC oil embargo.

Within three years, America has plunged back into crisis. The economy has been savaged by a combination of inflation and stagnation, prompted by soaring oil prices and a surge of foreign competition that catches our industries unready. A tax revolt, starting in California, has swept across the country. A series of disasters—Love Canal, Mt. St. Helens, Three Mile Island—has rocked the country. Americans are being held hostage in the U.S. embassy in Tehran. Soviet tanks have rolled into Afghanistan, setting relations between the United States and the Soviet Union back to the darker days of the Cold War.

Ronald Reagan rides the tide of anger and rising conservatism to a landslide victory in the presidential election, winning forty-four states. The Reagan landslide is probably worth five to seven points to every Republican challenger in the country, bringing in a dozen new Republican senators, and with them, an end to the Great Senate.

An important part of the story will be, as it must, the transformation of the Republican Party. Looking back, it is evident that what made the Great Senate possible was a bipartisanism that is no longer present in our political system. That bipartisan spirit came in part from senators exercising independent judgment and being devoted to making the institution work. They loved the Senate, and they recognized the need to reconcile diverse viewpoints in order for collective action to be possible. But bipartisanship was also possible because many Republican senators were at least moderates, or even progressives. In the search for a working majority, the leaders of the great Senate had a large field of Republican senators who were willing to come together with their liberal Democratic colleagues, to overcome the opposition of the southern Democrats opposed to civil rights and Republican conservatives generally opposed to federal spending and social legislation.

In the late 1970's, most of the Senate Democrats remained progressive (even "liberal"!) although they trimmed their sails somewhat, moving toward the center, as the economy weakened and antigovernment sentiment crested. The Senate Republicans, however, began their inexorable move to the right, particularly the newly elected senators from the mountain west and the south. Some of the leading Republican progressives or moderates retired, but others, such as Clifford Case (R-NJ) and Javits (R-NY), were defeated by right-wing challengers in Republican primaries. The rightward movement continued and accelerated through the 1980's, 1990's, and the last decade. Today, too often, the field of Republican moderates seems to begin with the senior senator from Maine, Olympia Snowe, and end with the junior senator from Maine, Susan Collins, although Richard Lugar continues to show the foreign policy leadership and vision that has characterized his long career.

During most of the 1960's and 1970's, the Senate, although a political institution, was surprisingly free from partisanship. The herculean effort to give civil rights to black Americans, the tragedy of Vietnam, the crisis of Watergate, checking the imperial presidencies of Johnson and Nixon—these were not partisan issues, and the Senate responded in a bipartisan way. Moreover, a commitment to pursuing the national interest and making the Senate work acted as powerful constraints on partisanship.

Of course, elections came every two years, and political campaigns went on around the country, but the Senate stayed somehow separate, almost a demilitarized zone where partisan politics were concerned. That began to change in the late 1970's, with the rise of the New Right and single-issue politics, marked by negative advertising and fiery grassroots campaigns around emotional issues such as abortion, guns, and the Panama Canal. The Great Senate, in those last years, held together, still capable of subordinating partisanship to accomplish the nation's business. But the seeds of destruction were being planted. The high walls that separated the Senate from raw, endless partisan politics started to come down thirty years ago; today, the Senate often appears to be just another arena for what has been called the permanent campaign, where the Democrats and Republicans struggle for advantage, more like scorched earth than hallowed ground.

I began working on this book in the spring of 2008. The excitement of the presidential campaign had caused a group of old friends from the Senate thirty years before to get together monthly for breakfast to talk politics. Inevitably, the talk also turned nostalgically to the great days when we worked in the Senate. We were amazed at how the Senate had been missing in action throughout the presidency of George W. Bush: rolling over for the Bush tax cuts, the Iraq war, and the Supreme Court nominations that had cemented the conservative majority that had been the goal of the right wing for forty years. We reflected on how the Senate had become so partisan and ineffectual that it was barely recognizable to us.

All of that was before 2009. Any hope that a new president, a wave of public excitement and interest in politics, and an unprecedented economic crisis would prompt the Senate to rise to the occasion was quickly dashed. By the end of 2009, senators still went on the Sunday talk shows in great numbers, but the once-proud Senate, a crown jewel of our Constitutional system, had become the clearest example that our political system had broken down. As Senator Olympia Snowe (R-ME), one of the most serious and capable legislators, put it sadly: "We have been miniaturized."

The Senate's deterioration affects all of us, but it has a special poignancy for those who worked there during its great period. I came to the Senate as a summer intern in 1969, one day after graduating from college. That summer changed my life, causing me to go to law school in the hope of returning to work in the Senate. I came back in 1975 and worked there through 1987, in a range of senior positions—personal staff, committee staff, leadership staff. I worked for veteran senators Gaylord Nelson, Abraham Ribicoff, Tom Eagleton, Robert Byrd, and then a newly elected senator, Jay Rockefeller. I participated in many legislative accomplishments—domestic and international—and made lasting friends on both sides of the aisle. Every staffer's career is unique, but what many men and women shared during that period was a sense of joyous excitement, purpose, and fulfillment.

I anticipate that some readers will conclude that the author thought the Senate was great when it was Democratic and progressive, because he himself is a progressive Democrat. It is undoubtedly true that as a progressive, believing in the necessity of a positive government action in many areas, I am more concerned about the decline of the Senate than someone whose objective is to stop the government in its tracks. But I have a long record of working successfully with Republicans while in the Senate and in the Clinton administration and have great admiration for many Republican senators, including several currently in the Senate. Readers will make their judgments about my analysis, but it is a fact that many distinguished Republicans put the blame for the condition of the current Senate squarely on their party.

As far back as 1996, several notable Republican senators chose to retire from the Senate, because of the increasingly strident right-wing position of the Republican caucus and the insistence on party unity by the Republican leader. Former Senator John Danforth has written that the Republican Party was completely taken over by the Christian right. Former senator Alan Simpson of Wyoming, still prominent because of his co-chairmanship of the National Commission on Deficit Reduction, has said that the Senate changed when "the battered children from the House came over, led by Trent Lott." The current Senate Republican leader, Mitch McConnell, has said that his overriding objective is to defeat Barack Obama, rather than making the Senate work for the good of the country.

This book attempts to help fill a large void in understanding of the Senate. Those writing critically about today's Senate often jump back to Lyndon Johnson's time as majority leader to show how the Senate worked in its best days. In truth, and in spite of Robert Caro's brilliant portrayal of Johnson's career, the Senate's most consequential period came after Johnson left to become vice president in 1961. As Gould has written: "For the Senate, Lyndon Johnson was a noisy summer storm that rattled the windows of the upper chamber and then moved on, leaving few traces of its passing. . . . He seemed a towering figure at the time, but his essential lack of vision about the Senate limited his impact."

The Senate's most historic legislative accomplishments—the Civil Rights Act of 1964 and the Voting Rights Act of 1965—certainly could not have occurred without Lyndon Johnson's inspired leadership from the White House. But 2011 marks a half century since Johnson left the Senate, and it seems timely to recognize that the Senate became great only after he departed. Mike Mansfield, who followed LBJ as Senate majority leader, served much longer (sixteen years, as compared to Johnson's six), accomplished much more, and left behind the legacy of a democratized Senate, in which every senator could potentially play an important part. Robert Byrd and Howard Baker, the new leaders who play a central part in this book, were working with the opportunities and challenges of the democratized Senate that Mansfield created.

In my epilogue, I attempt to connect with the current debate about the Senate by offering a view of what has happened in the thirty years since the Senate shattered in 1980. In essence, although the Senate made a seemingly solid comeback in the mid-to-late 1980's, after that, the continuous movement to the right by the Republican Party caused a downward spiral for the Senate that has lasted twenty years, accelerating over time. But this book is, first and foremost, my effort to recapture and celebrate the accomplishments of the great senators and the Great Senate of the 1960's and 1970's. I hope that the book will remind readers what they should expect from, and demand of, their Senate. I also hope that it will help inspire the new generation of senators and their staff members about what they can accomplish in Washington.

In his recent memoir, former vice president and senator Walter Mondale described the Senate as the "national mediator," debating issues at length, educating itself and the country, balancing and resolving ideological and regional differences. To be sure, today's intensely vitriolic political culture makes being a senator harder than ever before. The endless demands for fund-raising required for increasingly expensive campaigns drain the time and energy of senators and expose them to the ceaseless demands of a vast corps of organized interests and lobbyists. The air travel that makes regular trips home routinely possible diminishes the time that senators and their families once spent together. The impact of the twenty-four-hour news cycle, the blogosphere, and the tendency of Americans to choose the news they want to hear has changed the public debate profoundly.

But these changes in our political culture make it even more imperative that we have a Senate of wise men and women, bringing experience, wisdom, and independent judgment in their collective responsibility to determine the national interest. Commentators now focus on the possible changes in the

Senate rules, and some changes are indeed needed, particularly with respect to the pernicious impact of "holds," by which one determined member can paralyze the Senate. However, what is most urgently needed is for senators to act like senators, not partisan operatives. They should not mirror, and even exacerbate, the nation's divisions. They were sent to Washington to overcome them. In another difficult era, this is how the Senate worked to do so.

1977

chapter 1

THE
GRIND

EXCITEMENT AND HAPPINESS PERMEATED THE COLD AIR ON CAPITOL Hill on January 4, 1977, the day that the 95th Congress would be sworn in. With the holiday season over, members of Congress were gathering in Washington, D.C., from all over the country. Most were returning veterans, but there were also seventeen new senators and sixty-seven new House members among the crowd on what was always a festive day. Those who had lost their seats or retired were long gone; only the winners remained.

At 2:00 p.m., they would enter their separate chambers to take the oath of office. In the House chamber, all the members had been elected for a two-year term. They would take the oath of office together. In the Senate, only one-third of the seats are contested every two years, so a third of the members had just been elected for a six-year term. They would be sworn in, usually four at a time. Accompanied by their wives and children (for the crowd of new Senators and Representatives was overwhelmingly male), the first-timers would stand, speak their vows, and then accept the congratulations of returning members. It was the one day on Capitol Hill that traditionally blended pomp and circumstance with informality and family joy. The ceremony would last less than an hour, to be followed by celebrations with friends and supporters in the Senate and House office buildings on the opposite sides of Capitol Hill.

Many of those swarming toward Capitol Hill came from Union Station. The long-awaited Washington Metrorail system had finally opened the previous

March, with Union Station being one of the first five stations in operation. A ride on the beautiful, futuristic system was an attraction that none of the out-of-town visitors wanted to miss. Even the jaded K Street lobbyists flocking to the Hill were still excited about riding Metro. Those who emerged from Union Station could see the Capitol, the most familiar and iconic symbol of American democracy, looming in the distance.

As they approached the Senate office buildings on foot along Constitution Avenue, they could also see workers constructing a platform off the east side of the Capitol for the inauguration of Jimmy Carter as president on January 20. Carter would take the oath of office in the same place as every president elected since Andrew Jackson. The continuity of the peaceful transfer of power was one more reminder that America, having celebrated its bicentennial the previous July, had been a democracy for two centuries. But it also served as a reminder of the volatility of American politics. Just four years before, Richard Nixon had been on that same platform after winning reelection by a historic margin but only nineteen months later he became the first American president to resign from office.

It was a singular moment in Washington. The polls said that the American public wanted change; the election of Carter, a virtual unknown when 1976 began, dramatically signaled that desire. But Congress faced major changes of its own. For the first time in the twentieth century, there would be new leadership on both ends of Pennsylvania Avenue and on Capitol Hill: a new president, new Senate leaders, and a new Speaker of the House. Whether the new leaders could make the executive and legislative branches work together effectively after the celebrating was done was an open question.

Before the afternoon ceremonies, important work remained to be done. In his Capitol office, Robert Byrd of West Virginia, the second-ranking Senate Democrat, was taking the last steps to ensure that he would become the new majority leader by acclamation. A dedicated and meticulous vote counter, Byrd had long ago locked up enough support within the Democratic conference to become majority leader. Weeks before, his elevation already seemed so inevitable that two potentially formidable challengers, Edmund Muskie of Maine and Ernest "Fritz" Hollings of South Carolina, had withdrawn in the face of Byrd's overwhelming strength. But as the moment of his triumph drew near, Byrd faced a delicate political conundrum: what to do about Hubert Humphrey.

Ranking among the most brilliant of senators between 1949 and 1964, and one of the best loved, Humphrey had been a liberal icon before he became Lyndon Johnson's vice president in 1965. But the war in Vietnam took its toll on his reputation, just as surely as it consumed Johnson, the Democratic Party, and the country. Humphrey had offered up his unstinting support for Johnson's course in Vietnam, thereby winning the Democratic presidential nomination in 1968. But that support cost him the respect of millions of Americans, and ultimately, the presidency itself.

Humphrey regained his Senate seat from Minnesota in the 1970 election. But when he returned to the Senate in January 1971, it was a different place. The Senate's central focus was now on ending U.S. involvement in the war he had supported. His colleagues no longer responded to him with their customary warmth. They treated him like a freshman, rather than restoring him to senior positions on his committees. Undaunted, Humphrey had run again for president in 1972. But with antiwar sentiment cresting in the Democratic Party, Humphrey failed to win the nomination, managing only to damage George McGovern, the eventual nominee, in a bitter California primary.

With the Vietnam War now over, some of the wounds between the liberals and Humphrey had healed—and Humphrey sought to reclaim his leadership position in the Democratic Party by ascending to majority leader. However, Byrd knew, even if Humphrey didn't, that Hubert could count on only a handful of votes in the Democratic conference. Byrd had been seeking and locking up commitments from Democratic senators since the previous summer. As if that were not enough, Humphrey was battling a recurrence of the cancer that had been in remission for several years. Despite his jaunty spirit and customary enthusiasm, Humphrey was visibly weak and frail.

Byrd understood that many of the senators still genuinely loved Humphrey, while some of the liberals harbored serious doubts of their own about Byrd. Byrd's first step to becoming Mike Mansfield's successor would be to win the position without humiliating Humphrey and antagonizing his supporters.

On the evening of January 3, with the conference vote scheduled for the next morning, Byrd took a call from Humphrey. Humphrey said he would withdraw from the race if Byrd were willing to make him the chairman of the Democratic conference. Byrd was not surprised; some of Humphrey's supporters had suggested that same solution. But Byrd was not prepared to relinquish power in this way. He would not agree to any arrangement that suggested that Humphrey would be the policy leader, leaving him to make the Senate trains run on time. Reluctantly, but firmly, Byrd declined Humphrey's offer.

Humphrey relented at last. At eight o'clock in the morning of January 4, three hours before the conference was scheduled to meet, Humphrey called Byrd to say that he was withdrawing. Obviously pained and distracted, he did not extend the same courtesy to his supporters. When the Democrats convened in meeting room S-207 of the Capitol, Ed Muskie put Humphrey's name in nomination and was startled when Humphrey moved for Byrd to be chosen by acclamation.

Byrd rose to accept the position. Seeking to soothe the hurt feelings of Humphrey and his supporters, Byrd told his sixty-one-member conference that the Minnesotan did not need any title to denote his importance to the nation: "He is a national leader, he has been a national leader, and he will always be a national leader." But Byrd knew that more than words were required.

He announced that he was appointing a three-member ad hoc committee, chaired by Senator Abraham Ribicoff of Connecticut, to make recommendations for special recognition of former presidents or vice presidents who become senators—in this case, a class of one. The next day, the Democratic conference accepted the recommendations of Ribicoff's ad hoc committee: Humphrey would be given a salary equal to the majority leader's, as well as a chauffeured car, additional staff, an office in the Capitol, and the title of deputy president pro tempore of the Senate. Humphrey was delighted, and his supporters were pleased. Robert Byrd had made a strong and dexterous start, unifying the Democrats and placating liberal critics. It was the culmination of a truly remarkable rise to power by Robert Byrd.

THE U.S. SENATE HAS always had more than its share of very wealthy members, and in later years, it would come to be increasingly comprised of millionaires and "legacies," the children of politicians whose names were already famous. But the Senate still made room for those who came from ordinary circumstances, sometimes even grinding poverty, rising to prominence on the basis of ability and energy, luck and timing, but above all a fierce determination to succeed.

None of these senators had come further or worked harder than Robert Byrd. Byrd was born in North Carolina in 1917 as Cornelius Calvin Sale. He was the fifth child born to a woman who died in the great influenza epidemic within a year of his birth. Before her death, she asked her husband to give the infant to one of his sisters, Vlurma Sale Byrd, and her husband, Titus Dalton Byrd—a couple who had no children of their own. In accordance with her wishes, the Byrds adopted the child, renamed him Robert Carlyle Byrd, and took him to Bluefield, West Virginia.

Robert Byrd's father worked in the coal mines. Byrd would grow up moving from one mining community to another. Barely a step above abject poverty, he was educated in a two-room schoolhouse without electricity. As a teenager, he worked in a gas station, as a produce boy, and as a butcher; eventually he ran a grocery store.

In his late twenties, Byrd taught Sunday school, attended college part-time, and became active in local politics. Hard working and attentive to his community, Byrd was elected to the West Virginia House of Delegates in 1946. In his first speech, on Workmen's Compensation legislation, the newly elected delegate said: "To me, the dollar is secondary; human misery and suffering, and the welfare of dependent children, come first."

Robert Byrd's work ethic and his thirst for knowledge were awesome. Embarrassed that he had not finished college, he earned his law degree by taking classes at night for ten years after reaching Capitol Hill. His commitment to West Virginia was total, and the people of his state felt a deep bond with him. With their support, he never lost an election, reaching the State Senate in 1950, the U.S. House of Representatives in 1952, and the U.S. Senate in 1958, defeating an incumbent Republican senator. His constituents rewarded him with increasingly lopsided victories in 1964 and 1970 over token opposition. By 1976, in the campaign he had just finished, Byrd had been completely unopposed.

Byrd could easily have been dismissed as a parochial politician. For years, he single-mindedly channeled money to his impoverished state, using his mastery of the legislative process and his increasingly powerful position on the Senate Appropriations Committee to earmark funds to improve West Virginia's infrastructure, particularly its roads, bridges, and airports. "No item beneficial to West Virginia," Byrd would write, "was too large or too small for me to give my close attention to." But his timing was good. West Virginia was the state where John F. Kennedy learned about American poverty, where he saw with his own eyes what he had previously only read about in Michael Harrington's *The Other America*.

When he became president, Kennedy did not forget West Virginia. His legislative record during his first two years was unimpressive, but his first major legislative victory in 1961 had been the enactment of the Area Redevelopment

Act (ARA), legislation labeled S.1 in the Senate. The ARA channeled public works money into economically depressed regions of the country, particularly Appalachia, to help close the gap between the region and the rest of the United States by investing in water and sewer construction, education and workforce training, small business startups, and above all, highway construction to break down the isolation of the mountainous region. "Appalachia" included parts of thirteen states, but only one state was entirely within Appalachia—West Virginia. From the beginning of his Senate career, Robert Byrd had good reason to believe that alleviating West Virginia's poverty was a national priority, and he never changed that view.

In 1967, Byrd saw an opportunity to move into the leadership of the Senate Democrats. George Smathers of Florida had decided not to seek another term as Secretary to the Democratic conference, the number three position in the Democratic leadership. Liberals predominated in the Democratic caucus, and when two of the most liberal Democrats threw their hats into the ring simultaneously, Byrd saw an opening. He quickly and quietly gathered the support of all conservative Democrats, particularly the Southern bloc. Capitalizing on the split within the liberal camp, Byrd won handily, and jumped on to the first rung of the leadership ladder.

Almost immediately, he parlayed that minor post into real power, becoming, according to the *Washington Post*, "the man who runs the Senate during most of its nine-to-five hours. . . . He's made himself 'the indispensable man.'" He spent so many hours on the Senate floor that some new staffers thought he was the Senate sergeant at arms, and not a senator. He developed an extraordinary knowledge of the rules of the Senate but also an innate feeling for its rhythms. In 1971, after the accident at Chappaquiddick had disgraced and distracted then-Democratic whip Ted Kennedy of Massachusetts, Byrd mounted a swift and stealthy campaign to defeat Kennedy for the position. For the next six years, Byrd lived up to the *Post*'s description, effectively running the day-to-day operations of the Senate and taking advantage of his new power to accrue experience and stature, as well as the opportunity to do countless favors for his fellow Democrats.

Byrd chafed at the widespread idea that he was simply a Senate mechanic—a grind—but in the end, his love of the Senate, his mastery of its rules, and his passion for detailed work paved his way to the position of majority leader. Moreover, if he had not been viewed as the man who could make the Senate do its work effectively, his conservative views might have disqualified him, particularly in light of his history with racial issues.

As a young man starting out in West Virginia politics, Byrd had been a member of the Ku Klux Klan. He had long ago resigned his membership, which he had regarded as necessary to advance in local politics, yet remained vehemently opposed to advances in civil rights that were the moral cornerstone of the Democratic agenda during the 1960's. Byrd conducted an all-night filibuster against the Civil Rights Act of 1964 and opposed both the Voting Rights Act of 1965 and its extension in 1970. He opposed Lyndon Johnson's 1967 nomination of Thurgood Marshall to be the first African American to serve on the U.S. Supreme Court. He waged a harsh campaign against the District of Columbia's home rule government, which struck many observers as tinged with racism. Byrd proved so conservative that in 1971, after the Senate had rejected two Republican nominees to the Supreme Court, an incensed Richard Nixon gave serious thought to nominating Byrd, taking pleasure in the notion that the Senate would have no choice but to confirm one of their own, despite his hard-line views on race and crime.

But Byrd benefited from passing time. His views on civil rights became muted and more moderate. Moreover, although racial issues would remain difficult for America, the historic civil rights legislative battles had been won. Even Richard Russell, the Georgia Democrat who was the formidable leader of the Senate's segregationist bloc, recognized "the Southerners' time had passed." The Great Senate was a progressive one, and the nation had moved on.

By 1977, the Senate Democrats could justify making Robert Byrd their majority leader because of his selfless, unending efforts to make the Senate work. In the decade since he had joined the Senate leadership, the idea of Robert Byrd as majority leader had shifted from inconceivable to inevitable.

Robert Byrd was not a hail-fellow-well-met. He was a serious, almost severe, man. He had narrow eyes and rarely smiled. He dressed in a three-piece suit, often with an incongruously flamboyant red vest. He had few close friends among the senators and made no real effort to cultivate them. He preferred to be called "Robert" but was uncomfortable correcting his colleagues, so he would almost always be known as "Bob." To his chagrin, his hands frequently trembled. He occasionally surprised visiting groups from West Virginia by suddenly veering off into an unexpected discourse on the inevitability of death.

Yet Byrd also had an unexpected joyous side. His staff members remember being summoned to the majority leader's office on Friday afternoon at 4:30. They anticipated having to brief Byrd for his Saturday morning roundtable with the reporters covering the Senate. Instead they were ushered into his room that held several rows of folding chairs. A moment later, Senator Byrd would appear, with his fiddle in hand, and would happily play for thirty minutes, taking particular joy from his favorite, "Turkey in the Straw."

Byrd had a considerable ego and in January 1976 had declared for both his fourth term in the Senate, where he was unopposed, and the presidency, thinking that the battle for the Democratic nomination might deadlock. But his presidential bid was not taken seriously, and Carter ran away with the nomination. Byrd quickly shifted his attention back to his effort to become majority leader.

He was lucky. If the Republicans had held the White House, the Senate Democrats might have opted for a more charismatic figure to serve as their national spokesman. But with a new Democratic president in the public spotlight, a capable mechanic was needed to ensure that the Senate ran smoothly. Byrd's colleagues did not pretend to understand him fully, but they respected him. They knew that he was absolutely committed to the Senate's place in the constitutional system and making it work. They expected that the Senate would run effectively under his leadership and that each of them would be treated fairly. He seemed to be the right steward for the Great Senate, though few expected him to live up to the standard set by his predecessors.

FOR DECADES, THE SENATE was controlled by a powerful combination of southern Democrats and conservative Republicans. Mainly the product of small states and sparse populations, they maintained a stranglehold on the Senate due to the Founding Fathers' decision to give each state two senators regardless of population. For this reason, even during the liberal presidencies of Franklin D. Roosevelt and Harry S. Truman, the Senate stood as an obstacle to progressive legislation that would have benefited the nation's cities and minorities, particularly black Americans. As William S. White observed in *The Citadel*: "The Senate was the only place in the country where the South did not lose the [Civil] War . . . the South's unending revenge upon the north for Gettysburg."

But by the late 1950's, even the conservative Senate could not stand immune from the winds of change sweeping the nation. In 1954, the Supreme Court, under the leadership of a new chief justice, Earl Warren, had handed down the unanimous, landmark decision in *Brown v. the Board of Education*, establishing that "separate but equal" schools were unconstitutional. President

Eisenhower had been forced, against his instincts, to send U.S. troops to Little Rock, Arkansas, to integrate the schools. The movement for civil rights was building, foremost among black Americans but also among the white liberal intellectuals and the labor unions that provided much of the political power of the Democratic Party.

Paradoxically, Lyndon Johnson was the ideal man to bring these changes to fruition. Narrowly elected to the Senate from Texas in 1948 at the age of forty, he became minority leader just four years later, and then majority leader two years after that. Johnson was a southerner, but one with national aspirations and gut liberal instincts, which had made him an early supporter of Franklin D. Roosevelt. Though deeply rooted in his region, he was embarrassed by its bigotry, poverty, and backwardness and determined to overcome them. Earthy and forceful, Johnson had a lust for power and used it to advance the South, the nation, and himself.

He transformed the role of Senate leader, utilizing committee assignments and office space to favor those senators that he liked and punish those that he didn't. He expanded the use of unanimous consent agreements to drastically limit serious debate, shifting the real action from the Senate floor to the cloakroom or the leader's office. He worked his will through matchless powers of persuasion, including a ruthless knowledge of each member's priorities, needs, and weaknesses. In the words of Robert Caro, Johnson used "every carrot, no matter how small and unappetizing, and every stick, no matter how thin and seemingly fragile, to create his own 'special powers.'"

Using Hubert Humphrey as his liaison to the liberals, Johnson acted as a bridge between the old conservative Senate and the more progressive institution that would emerge. As Caro has famously recounted, Johnson demonstrated his leadership most brilliantly by surprising his southern colleagues and spearheading the passage of the first civil rights legislation in a century. The Civil Rights Act of 1957 was a relatively modest measure, watered down by the need for compromise, but it represented the first breach in the dam of Southern obstructionism.

Yet, even as Johnson bullied, badgered, and cajoled the Senate into the mid-twentieth century, the forces of change were moving too quickly even for him to control. The election of 1958, which brought Robert Byrd to Washington, marked a turning point in the history of the Senate. The Eisenhower administration, after six years in office, was running on fumes. America was in recession, and it was in shock as well, still reeling from the stunning news that the Soviet Union had launched *Sputnik* into space. The 1958 election was a rout in which the Democrats won three open Senate seats and defeated ten Republican incumbents. Gaining new seats in every part of the country, the Democratic majority became more geographically diverse, more urban, and more liberal, with a commanding margin of 65–35 over the Republicans.

The 1958 Democratic landslide left Johnson with a new challenge from restive liberals, such as Albert Gore Sr. of Tennessee, Joseph Clark of Pennsylvania, and William Proxmire of Wisconsin. These men rebelled against his heavy-handed leadership, and they could increasingly count on support from the newly elected senators. In one telling incident, Bobby Baker, the wheeler-dealer secretary of the Senate Democrats who was Johnson's right-hand man, told Johnson that he had to discipline Clark for voting against him. Johnson agreed and buttonholed Clark on the Senate floor. The two men were seen arguing angrily. When Johnson came back he said to Baker plaintively, "He told me to go to hell. Now what do I do?" Plainly, a new Senate was stirring.

In July 1960, at the Democratic convention in Los Angeles, Lyndon Johnson stunned most political observers by jumping at the vice presidential nomination when John Kennedy offered it to him. He saw it as the only possible road to the presidency for a southerner. He had relished being Senate majority leader with a Republican president, but found he had no real interest in the position when a Democratic president would dominate the spotlight. Not only that, he also understood that his power over the Senate was ebbing. Though he had been extraordinarily effective, Johnson had just about worn out his welcome. Most of the senators were ready to see him on the other end of Pennsylvania Avenue.

THE ELECTION OF 1958 had poured the foundation of the Great Senate. But the next off-year election, in 1962, completed the edifice that was the progressive Senate of the 1960's and 1970's. In most off-year elections, the president's party loses seats in Congress. But 1962's election came just days after President Kennedy had successfully defused the Cuban missile crisis. National adulation of Kennedy provided a lift to Democratic candidates across the country and likely tipped the scale in several close races. (Republican Senator Barry Goldwater observed: "We were Cuber-ized.")

Eight new Democratic senators were elected in 1962, and they proved some of the most effective and liberal senators of their time. Their number included Abraham Ribicoff of Connecticut, Gaylord Nelson of Wisconsin,

George McGovern of South Dakota, Birch Bayh of Indiana, and Daniel Inouye of Hawaii. The youngest man elected in 1962, barely thirty years old, with minimal qualifications, and riding on his brother's name, was Edward M. Kennedy. The twenty-one Democratic senators elected in 1958 and 1962 formed the heart and soul of the Great Senate.

No group in Senate history ever had a run like those elected in 1962. The fourteen years they had served in the Senate had been, to use Doris Kearns Goodwin's famous phrase, "no ordinary time." To be sure, it was also turbulent, emotional, and often disheartening—an era marked by assassinations, war, urban unrest, and political scandal. Four presidents—Kennedy, Johnson, Nixon, and Ford—had left or come to office in extraordinary and heartbreaking circumstances. The senators elected in 1962 had ridden the roller coaster of American history, shaping events, yet often being buffeted by them.

They had come to the Senate at a moment of profound hope and optimism, thanks to Kennedy's popularity and the end of the missile crisis. In their first year in the Senate, 1963, they had the opportunity to vote for the Limited Nuclear Test Ban Treaty and watch President Kennedy respond to the violence in Montgomery, Alabama, by making the moral case for landmark civil rights legislation. They suffered with their new Senate colleagues and the country the devastating news from Dallas that the president had been assassinated.

In their second year, 1964, they participated in the Senate's most towering accomplishment, breaking the southern filibuster to enact the Civil Rights Act. Just weeks later, they participated in the Senate's great abdication of responsibility, the Gulf of Tonkin resolution, which Johnson used as the justification for his disastrous escalation of the war in Vietnam. In 1965 and 1966, they were part of the historic 89th Congress, which worked with President Johnson to shape the landmark Great Society legislation, a progressive outpouring of laws that touched and improved almost every facet of life in America.

In 1967 and 1968, they formed an important part of the growing Senate opposition to the Vietnam War, worked to respond to the anger and fires in American cities, and battled for one more landmark civil rights law to combat discrimination in housing. They watched with amazement as their enigmatic colleague Eugene McCarthy from Minnesota, a gifted politician and a cynical intellectual who often seemed uninterested in the Senate, mounted the "kiddie crusade" that drove Lyndon Johnson out of the presidential race. They mourned the deaths by assassination of another Kennedy, their friend and Senate colleague Robert Kennedy—to them, always "Bob"—and the Reverend Martin Luther King Jr.

In 1969 and 1970, they took on President Richard Nixon, rejecting two of his Supreme Court nominations, and spearheaded the rising environmental movement. In 1971 and 1972, even as Nixon moved toward a landslide re-election, the senators helped abolish the draft, gave eighteen-year-olds the right to vote, and added Title IX to the Civil Rights Act, expanding opportunities for women in college sports.

In 1973, the hearings of the Senate Watergate Committee riveted the nation, exposing the abuses of power in Nixon's White House and creating the path that led inexorably to his resignation. In 1973 and 1974, they played important parts in enacting the War Powers Act, the Freedom of Information Act, the Privacy Act, and the Budget Control and Impoundment Act, a burst of legislation intended to redress the constitutional balance of power by cutting the "imperial presidency" down to size. In 1975 and 1976, they participated in the unprecedented investigation of the abuses of the intelligence community conducted by the Select Committee on Intelligence Activities, chaired by Senator Frank Church of Idaho, and the resulting creation of a new permanent Senate Intelligence Committee in September 1976.

By 1977, the senators who had been elected in 1962 were now serving their third terms and had become well-known national figures: Ribicoff, for denouncing the "Gestapo tactics in the streets of Chicago" during the 1968 Democratic convention; Bayh, for leading the successful fights against the Supreme Court nominations of Clement Haynesworth and G. Harrold Carswell; Nelson, as the father of Earth Day in 1970; McGovern, as a leading dove and Democratic presidential nominee, crushed by Nixon in the 1972 election; Inouye, for his impressive work on the Watergate Committee; and Kennedy, the last brother, an increasingly influential senator, and still a potential president despite the Chappaquiddick incident. Byrd counted on them as strong assets; each of them would be a committee chairman either in this Congress or by the start of the next one. What remained to be proven was whether they would find him to be an asset as leader, and how effectively he could follow in Mansfield's footsteps.

Mike Mansfield was in every way the polar opposite of his flamboyant predecessor, Lyndon Johnson. Born in New York, Mansfield moved to Montana to live with relatives after his mother died when he was seven. As a young man, Mansfield served in the army, navy, and marines and developed a fascination for Asia where he had served after World War I. He returned home to become a university professor of political science and history, but his deep interest in world affairs took him into politics. His intellect, honesty, and humility appealed to Montanans, and he was elected first to the House and then to the Senate in 1952.

Perpetually sucking on a pipe, Mansfield was a man of few words, laconic in his personal style. He did not believe in the theatrics that had characterized LBJ's Senate leadership. Unlike his predecessor, he did not believe in midnight Senate sessions liberally lubricated by alcohol. Nor did he believe in a Senate where seemingly impossible deadlocks were broken by covert deals in the cloakroom for which the majority leader took all the credit. He certainly never relied on arm twisting or abuse.

Even more fundamentally, Mansfield did not believe in a Senate dominated by the majority leader or a handful of senior senators. He believed in a democratic, small-d, Senate, where all senators were adults, elected by their constituents, and all senators were equal. In fact, he treated even the senators in the minority as his equals. To a degree that stunned the senators, Mansfield believed in the "golden rule" and acted accordingly. He treated each senator the way he wanted to be treated himself and expected reciprocity.

Most senators, starting with Minority Leader Everett Dirksen, doubted that Mansfield could possibly run the Senate according to the standard he envisioned. Under his leadership, the one hundred senators, not the majority leader, were responsible for making the Senate work. By 1963, his democratized Senate had become newly paralyzed. Very little legislation was moving, and absenteeism among senators was on the rise; they saw no reason to come to the Senate floor. Mansfield seemed unable to rouse the Senate from its torpor and made few efforts to do so. He faced intense criticism in the press, led by the reporters and columnists that Johnson had cultivated. Meanwhile, he contended with a virtual rebellion inside the Senate, led by Democrats Russell Long of Louisiana and Thomas Dodd of Connecticut, who publicly pined for a return of a strong leader.

On Friday, November 22, 1963, Mansfield announced that on the following Monday, he would deliver a speech on the Senate floor addressing the questions that had been raised about his leadership. He gave the Senate advance notice because he wanted to ensure that a quorum—at least fifty-one senators—would be in attendance for his speech.

The speech that Mansfield prepared for delivery was remarkable for its clarity and candor:

> Descriptions of the majority leader, the senator from Montana, have ranged from a benign Mr. Chips, to glamourless, to tragic mistake.... As for being a tragic mistake, if that means that I am neither a circus ringmaster, the master of ceremonies of a Senate night club, a tamer of Senate lions or a wheeler and dealer, then I must accept too that title.... But as long as I have this responsibility, it will be discharged to the best of my ability by me as I am ... I shall not don any Mandarin's robes or any skin other than that to which I am accustomed in order that I may look like a majority leader or sound like a majority leader....

He closed with an eloquent explanation of how he viewed the Senate:

> The Constitutional authority does not lie with the leadership. It lies with all of us individually, collectively and equally.... In the end, it is not the senators as individuals who are of fundamental importance. In the end, it is the institution of the Senate. It is the Senate itself as one of the foundations of the Constitution. It is the Senate as one of the rocks of the Republic.

We will never know how the Senate would have reacted to hearing this extraordinary speech—it was never given. It had to be inserted in the *Congressional Record*, because it was early on November 22, 1963, that Mansfield had informed the Senate about his upcoming speech. Several hours later, the Senate received the news of President Kennedy's assassination in Dallas.

Mansfield's leadership was never seriously challenged again. Galvanized by the tragedy of Kennedy's assassination, the leadership of President Lyndon Johnson, and the moral imperative of action on civil rights, Mansfield's democratized Senate met the challenge of history. So it was that in the summer of 1964, with the country and the rest of the world watching, the Senate broke the filibuster of the southern bloc to enact the most important piece of legislation in the country's history.

The Senate was no longer the graveyard of progressive dreams. It would become the place where those hopes and dreams were translated into legislation, carried forward with presidents where possible, and, where necessary, despite them. The Great Senate would extend the "liberal moment" of 1963 through 1966, and even the "liberal hour" of the 1960's, well into the 1970's.

Respectful of all senators, whether Democratic or Republican, senior or freshman, without flamboyance, letting others take the lead and the credit, Mansfield managed to play a central role throughout the period. He combined what his principal aide and biographer Francis Valeo called "awesome patience" with utter honesty and straight dealing.

Mansfield had given private advice to Presidents Kennedy, Johnson, and Nixon about Vietnam. His numerous memos were heartbreakingly prescient about the folly of escalation. It was Mansfield who gave up on Nixon's commitment to ending the Vietnam War, after the invasion of Cambodia in 1970, and encouraged senators, on a bipartisan basis, to finally cut off funding for the war. It was also Mansfield, angered at the evidence of "dirty tricks" and illegal practices in Nixon's reelection campaign, who announced in October 1972 that the Senate would investigate these abuses. Only Mansfield could have had the stature and credibility to pick Sam Ervin of North Carolina, a former state supreme court justice who had emerged as one of Richard Nixon's fiercest opponents, to chair the Senate Watergate committee, enlist the cooperation of the Republicans, and launch it on a bipartisan basis, just two months after Nixon had won a forty-nine-state landslide.

Most recently, Mansfield, who had been calling for stronger oversight of the intelligence community for twenty years, created the Church Committee to investigate and illuminate the abuses of America's intelligence agencies. The establishment of the Senate Intelligence Committee in September 1976 was one of Mansfield's crowning achievements and a fitting coda to his extraordinary service. His decision to retire, announced without fanfare on March 4, 1976, was typical of the man. "There is a time to stay and a time to go," Mansfield told a stunned Senate. "Thirty four years [in the House and Senate] is not a long time, but it is long enough."

Robert Byrd, the most conservative of the Democrats elected in 1958, would be the majority leader of the Senate in 1977, elevated by a Democratic conference generally more liberal than he. Byrd would have to lead the democratized Senate created by Mansfield, which Gary Hart, the young senator from Colorado, would describe as "a kind of controlled madhouse," presenting great opportunities and its own special set of challenges.

EVEN AS HE ACCEPTED congratulations for his triumph, Byrd's mind was, undoubtedly, on Senate business. Byrd sought the position of majority leader because he thought that it was the most important and difficult job that his country had to offer (with the possible exception of the presidency). He may well have been right. He would face multiple challenges: leading the Senate Democrats; dealing with the new president and the White House; working with the Republican minority whose partisanship was intensifying; and ensuring that the Senate, with its tradition of unlimited debate, would do the nation's business and avoid paralysis by filibuster.

The Senate Democrats had recently lost some of their greatest members— Philip Hart, Sam Ervin, and J. William Fulbright, not to mention Mansfield himself. Nevertheless, its members still constituted a very strong caucus. Byrd could rely on a powerful core group of experienced men who had been crucial parts of the Senate for twenty or even thirty years, such as Warren Magnuson and Henry "Scoop" Jackson of Washington, Russell Long of Louisiana, Frank Church of Idaho, John Stennis of Mississippi, and William Proxmire of Wisconsin. There were also potential bright new Democratic stars who had been elected in the 1970's, such as Lloyd Bentsen of Texas, Dale Bumpers of Arkansas, Dick Clark and John Culver of Iowa, Sam Nunn of Georgia, and Joseph Biden of Delaware. There were some great legislators among the veterans, but their past achievements had come at a time when the strength of the U.S. economy seemed beyond question. A growing economy created the budgetary resources and the political support needed to start and sustain ambitious legislative undertakings. But times were changing.

Ever since the 1973 OPEC oil embargo, the U.S. economy had been hammered by a severe recession, which was only just ending, and a more challenging future characterized by rising energy costs and intensified foreign competition. Polls, press reports, and the recent presidential campaign showed that the economic pressures felt across the country had begun to produce a new reluctance to support "big government" programs. The younger Democratic senators entered their new offices with an understanding that the weakening economy created new political imperatives. Gary Hart, elected in 1974, had been widely quoted: "We're not just a bunch of little Hubert Humphreys." Time would tell if the veteran Senate Democrats could adjust to a new situation.

They would also have to simultaneously adjust to a new president. Naturally, Byrd and the other Senate Democrats were excited about having a Democrat in the White House, but they were genuinely uncertain what Jimmy Carter cared about and what he stood for. When John Kennedy became president sixteen years before, many of the senators had known him personally. More important, when Kennedy said that it was time to get the country moving again, they understood what he meant: respond to the Soviet challenge—at that time, scientific and ideological as much as military—and start passing the progressive legislation needed to complete the New Deal and Fair Deal agendas. By contrast, all they knew about Carter was that he wore his religion on his sleeve and talked about "a government as good as the American people." The Democratic senators believed in progressive policies; Carter seemed to believe in purifying politics.

Carter had told Byrd that he was strongly committed to strengthening ethics in government. The Senate Democrats thought that they had taken the most important step to cleaning up government by helping to drive Nixon from office. But reports of illegal campaign contributions had touched congressional leaders on both sides of the Hill, so Byrd was determined to get out ahead of the issue. He had already spoken to the incoming House Speaker, Thomas P. ("Tip") O'Neill, and they had agreed that each house would move rapidly to adopt an ethics code, long before Carter would be able to move his own ethics legislation through Congress. The first two items of Byrd's agenda would therefore be the Senate ethics code and completing the committee reorganization that had been in the works for several years.

Byrd already knew to anticipate a feistier Republican minority. The Senate Republicans were principally angry at Richard Nixon, who had tarnished the Republican brand, cost them the White House, and thrown away their majority support across the country. But their resentment toward Senate Democrats was also building. The 1974 New Hampshire Senate election between Democrat John Durkin and Republican Lewis Wyman, the closest Senate election in history, had left deep scars. After New Hampshire's election authorities had certified the Republican Wyman's election by two votes, Durkin had petitioned the Senate to declare him the winner. It was expected that the Senate, with its Democratic majority, would do so. But the Senate deadlocked for months, unable to resolve the issue. Senate watchers were treated to the spectacle of Durkin and Wyman each maintaining desks in the rear of the Senate, until Durkin won the seat by reelection, ten months after the initial battle. Democrats won the seat, but Senate Republicans may have won the larger battle. They came away much more unified and with significant, tactical experience for dealing with the Democratic majority. They also came away from the experience, fairly or unfairly, seeing Byrd, who had taken the lead for the Democrats, as more partisan than Mansfield had ever been.

For Byrd, who revered the Senate and its traditions, the right of extended, even unlimited, debate was the main cornerstone of the Senate's unique place in the Constitutional system. In Byrd's view, that right justified occasional use of the filibuster, and of course, he had resorted to this mechanism himself in 1964. Traditionally, however, a Senate vote by super-majority to invoke cloture produced an expeditious end to debate. But James Allen, a staunch conservative Democrat from Alabama and a formidable parliamentarian, had developed a new and ingenious version of the filibuster—the post-cloture filibuster. This technique enabled a single senator, using the one hour to which he was entitled after cloture was invoked, to tie up the Senate for days through dilatory tactics: calling up amendment after amendment, requesting the reading of the amendments, asking for roll call votes, suggesting the lack of a quorum. Because the time consumed by all those activities was free time, not chargeable to the senator, the process could theoretically last indefinitely.

Allen had demonstrated the lethal potential of the post-cloture filibuster by preventing the passage of the Hart-Scott-Rodino antitrust legislation for weeks. Byrd and Mansfield had ultimately secured passage of the legislation, but Byrd knew that they had prevailed only because the Senate wanted to pass the bill to honor Phil Hart, who was dying of cancer. If not for that, Allen might be holding the Senate hostage still. The nightmare scenario of a paralyzed Senate was never far from Byrd's mind.

The convening of a new Senate, and the passing of the torch to Byrd from Mansfield, made it a natural moment to reflect on the nature of Senate greatness. Just one week before the day's festivities, on December 28, 1976, 1,200 solemn mourners had gathered in St. Matthew's Cathedral to celebrate the life of Phil Hart, who had succumbed to cancer two days earlier. "The rich and the powerful were there, dressed in tailored suits and fine furs," observed a reporter. "So, too, were the poor and powerless, dressed in jeans and parkas."

It was a modest ceremony. "The Hart family wanted everything very simple," said the funeral director. But it was not just because of Phil Hart's personal modesty. Hart's Antitrust and Monopoly Subcommittee had once investigated the high costs of funerals, and Hart was appalled to find that funeral homes were taking advantage of people in their hour of utmost grief. "If I die in office and you spend more than $250 on my funeral," Hart told his wife, Janey, "I am going to get up and walk out." Janey Hart had done her best to comply with his wishes, arranging for a simple pine coffin that cost only $150.

Phil Hart was a World War II veteran and a man of uncommon courage. He had been seriously injured during the D-Day invasion, when shrapnel from an exploding German artillery shell severed the main artery of his right arm. Despite the seriousness of his injury, from which he had not fully recovered, Hart refused to return to the United States and rejoined the army in time to be involved in the Battle of Bulge in December 1944. After the war, he returned to Michigan and became a leading figure in the group of liberals that helped the Democratic Party take power in the state. Hart came to the Senate in the Democratic landslide of 1958. Of all the liberal senators, Hart may have been the most liberal.

Throughout his eighteen-year Senate career, he provided unflagging leadership to advance civil rights, battle poverty, improve conditions in the nation's cities, and challenge U.S. business when it overreached. Soft-spoken, unassuming, gentle, and fair-minded, Phil Hart was universally loved. In June 1975, Hart inserted a statement in the *Congressional Record* announcing that he would not seek a fourth term. It was consistent with his long-held view that there should be a mandatory retirement age for members of Congress. Hart believed it would be far better to have younger members coming to Capitol Hill who thought they could change the world and had the energy and stamina to do so. His decision to retire came long before the detection of the cancer that would kill him. As his strength ebbed away, Hart agonized about the future of Detroit, which was wracked by the related problems of poverty, crime, drugs, and race.

Phil Hart would not be forgotten in Washington. In August 1976, the Senate paid their dying colleague the highest tribute by naming the third Senate office building, which was just starting construction, after him. The Hart Senate Office Building would rise on Constitution Avenue, just east of the two current Senate office buildings—the "old" Senate office building, named for Richard Russell, Democrat of Georgia, and the "new" Senate office building, named for Everett Dirksen, Republican of Illinois.

These were striking choices. The Senate could have named its buildings for the famous senators of the nineteenth century, Henry Clay, Daniel Webster, and John C. Calhoun. Instead, it opted for three Senate giants of its own period, men of absolutely different ideologies and temperaments.

Richard Russell towered over the Senate through the 1940's and 1950's, revered by senators of both parties for his intellect, integrity, and absolute commitment to the institution. He was probably the foremost advocate of American military strength throughout World War II and the Cold War. In the spring of 1951, President Harry Truman fired General Douglas MacArthur for exceeding his authority to wage war in Korea. "It is doubtful that there has ever been in this country so violent and spontaneous a discharge of political passion as that provoked by the President's dismissal of the General," Arthur Schlesinger and Richard Rovere wrote. At that moment of crisis, Russell chaired a series of public hearings that calmed the nation and reasserted the importance of civilian control of the military. Russell's greatness as a senator was so universally acknowledged that the first Senate office building was named for him despite the fact that he was also the most effective opponent of civil rights that ever served in the Senate.

Everett Dirksen came to the Senate as a Midwest isolationist and a tough partisan whose hard-line position on the threat posed by communists in government was not much different from that expressed by Senator Joseph McCarthy of Wisconsin. When he became Republican leader, Dirksen was noteworthy mainly for his unruly shock of white hair—Bob Hope once described Dirksen as looking "like a man who had been electrocuted, but lived"—and his mellifluous speaking voice and theatrical style. But Dirsken evolved into a statesman who worked closely with President Kennedy to ensure Senate approval of the Limited Nuclear Test Ban Treaty in 1963, and then with President Johnson to enact the landmark Civil Rights Act of 1964. He would be remembered for transcending partisanship when the national interest required it.

And Phil Hart would be honored for the consistency of his views and, in Reverend King's famous words, "the content of his character." Columnist Coleman McCarthy wrote that "it was not an accident that he was the most trusted man in American politics. He fronted for no one. His alliances were to timeless ideals, not upstart lobbies. As though he were the wildest of gamblers, he bet that the common vanities of hack politics—images, smiles, calls for brighter days—counted for little. Instead, he wagered that conscience and persistence could matter." It would be a long time, editorialized the *Washington Post*, "before anyone in the Senate matches his integrity, diligence and compassionate humanism."

It would fall to others, starting with Robert Byrd, to fill the large holes left by the departures of Mike Mansfield and Phil Hart. Knowing Senate history as well as any person living, Byrd understood that being majority leader did not guarantee his place as a great senator. Who remembered Ernest McFarland or Scott Lucas or William Knowland, several of the majority leaders before Johnson? Great senators needed another dimension, and Byrd quickly signaled his priorities and aspirations. Hoyt Purvis, one of Fulbright's most respected staffers when he chaired the Senate Foreign Relations Committee, had left the Senate to teach at the LBJ School of Public Affairs at the University of Texas. Purvis was stunned to get a call from the majority leader's office, inquiring whether he would consider returning to the Senate as Byrd's chief foreign policy adviser. Purvis had never realized that the dedicated West Virginian had any interest in foreign policy. But he came to Washington for an interview and went away convinced that the new leader wanted to be a forceful player on foreign policy and national security. Purvis soon returned to the Senate and would provide exactly the expertise and credibility that Byrd was seeking. For Byrd, a growing personal interest in international issues combined perfectly with his view that the Senate needed to reassert its Constitutional role in foreign policy.

Eighteen years—three terms—was a full Senate career for many men. But Robert Byrd, who had completed three terms, was just getting started.

chapter 2

THE NATURAL

BYRD'S TRIUMPH MAY HAVE BEEN HISTORIC, BUT ON THE MORNING OF January 4, the real drama was taking place on the Republican side. With the Senate Republicans scheduled to meet at 10 a.m., Howard Baker, one of the most gifted politicians of the era, remained unable to decide whether to run for Senate minority leader.

As soon as the previous Republican leader, Hugh Scott, had announced his intention to retire, Baker's key supporters, led by Robert Packwood, assumed it was a given that he would run. Liberal Republicans Ed Brooke and Charles McC. Mathias, who formerly supported Scott, promised to be with him. The likeliest other challengers—Robert Dole, John Tower, and Barry Goldwater—had each decided against making the race. But Baker, although intrigued by the possibility, had refused to commit.

The heir apparent for the job was Robert Griffin of Michigan. Griffin had come to the Senate in 1967 at the same time as Baker and had rapidly risen to become Republican whip. A tough partisan and formidable politician, Griffin was well respected in Senate Republican ranks, and his rise to minority leader seemed to be going smoothly.

Yet the stars were not aligning for Griffin the way that they had for Byrd. Jimmy Carter's victory ensured that the Senate Republican leader would become the most visible Republican in the country. Griffin had many talents, but charisma was distinctly not one of them. Baker, on the other hand, had become a household name as vice chairman of the Watergate Committee.

Boyishly handsome with a reputation for fair-minded independence, he was by far the most attractive face that the Senate Republicans had to offer. Still, Baker hesitated.

When the incoming Republican senators met for breakfast on January 3, Harrison Schmitt, the former astronaut who was New Mexico's new senator, called Pete Domenici, his senior colleague, to tell him that Griffin was about to speak, but that Baker was a "no show." Domenici called Baker at home. "You just have to go over there," Domenici pleaded. "And you can't just say, if I run, I want you to know what I'm like if you decide to vote for me."

Baker went to the breakfast and declared his candidacy. When asked whether he simply planned to use the minority leader position as a platform for a presidential race, Baker acknowledged that the presidency was among his ambitions but said his principal goal would be to strengthen the badly weakened Republican Party. The new senators seemed impressed by his remarks and his candor. But what was truly amazing was that even after the breakfast, Baker *still* remained undecided. A series of repeated, large disappointments had taken a toll on his confidence.

By 1977, there was no denying that Howard Baker was an extraordinarily gifted politician. If Robert Byrd was a grind, Baker was a natural. His father, Howard Henry Baker Sr., became a Tennessee congressman, and his stepmother, Irene Baker, had also served in Congress, after his father's death. In 1951, Baker married Joy Dirksen, a congressional staffer who was the daughter of the eminent Republican from Illinois, Everett Dirksen. These family ties played an important part in Baker's rise to power. But Baker's blend of intelligence, temperament, and political skill meshed so well that there sometimes seemed to be no limit to his future. It was frequently said that if the senators chose the president by secret vote, Baker would have been in the White House by a wide margin.

Friendly and seemingly easygoing, Baker had reached the Senate a decade earlier in 1967, a young man in a hurry. Many observers thought he would be a good soldier for his father-in-law, dismissing him as a "junior grade Everett Dirksen." Baker quickly dispelled that notion. The Supreme Court had handed down its landmark decision in *Baker v. Carr,* ruling that the Constitution required states to apportion legislative districts on the basis of population—"one man, one vote." Dirksen, fearing that the decision could dilute the power of the Republican Party in many states, opposed rapid compliance. Baker did not agree. He surprised Dirksen with the firmness of his position and then crossed the aisle to work with Ted Kennedy on legislation to preserve the newly mandated doctrine of "one man, one vote."

In September 1969, Dirksen suddenly succumbed to lung cancer. A group of young senators, led by Packwood, who had just been elected, urged Baker to run for minority leader—and Baker was willing. Yet in stepping forward, Baker was seeking to become Senate leader faster than anyone in the history of the Senate, even faster than Lyndon Johnson. This act of chutzpah exceeded the amount of ambition that most senators recognized as acceptable, and Baker was defeated by Hugh Scott, who had already served eleven years in the Senate after sixteen years in the House. To underscore the point, the Republicans also rejected Baker's bid to become whip, choosing Griffin instead. Apparently unfazed by these setbacks, Baker surprised everyone by challenging Scott again two years later, another unusual step: at least in the previous race, the leader's position had been open. Satisfied with Scott's leadership, the Republican caucus rejected Baker once again.

Yet these political setbacks seemed to do Baker no lasting damage, because his talents were so universally acknowledged. In 1971, President Nixon, casting about for a southerner who could be confirmed by the Senate, had offered Baker a seat on the Supreme Court just four years after he was elected to the Senate. Baker gave it serious thought, frustrating Nixon with his indecision, but eventually concluded that he was much too young for the cloistered Supreme Court. "Funeral homes are livelier than the Court," he later told Orrin Hatch, the young Republican senator from Utah.

When the Senate decided in January 1973 to appoint a select committee to look into the abuses generically known as "Watergate," only three Republican senators volunteered to serve—Ed Gurney of Florida, regarded as a knee-jerk defender of Nixon's; Lowell Weicker of Connecticut, seen as headstrong and fiercely independent; and Baker, known for his steadiness and moderation. Viewing Baker as "the best television personality in the Senate," Scott made his former opponent the vice chairman of the Watergate Committee.

Scott's decision made Howard Baker a household name in America. In the summer of 1973, millions of Americans, riveted by the Watergate hearings, saw Baker, day after day, sitting next to Sam Ervin, persistently but nonabrasively pursuing the truth wherever it led. Baker's famous question—"what did the President know and when did he know it?"—was not only a memorable moment in the hearings; it would become a virtual axiom, dusted off and reused in almost every scandal for the next thirty years. Baker's skill in navigating the difficult cross-pressures of Watergate earned him an assignment to the Church Committee investigating the abuses of the U.S. intelligence agencies; he was, in fact, the only senator to serve on both select committees, an indicator of his unique stature in the Senate.

Yet despite his rapid rise and formidable accomplishments, 1976 had been a terrible year for Baker. He had harbored high hopes that Gerald Ford would pick him as a running mate. When Ford chose Bob Dole instead, Baker left the Republican convention wounded. Ford's decision probably cost him the White House. In opting for the ultra-partisan Dole, to placate the Republican right, Ford solidified his support only in Farm Belt states, which were already in his pocket. The more independent and moderate Baker would have enhanced Ford's appeal, particularly in the South and border states. This was cold comfort to Baker. Still hurting, he gave serious consideration to running for governor of Tennessee, thinking it might make for a better platform to the White House. But he loved the Senate, and realizing that he would be bored in Nashville, he stayed put.

Now, just months later, a third chance to be the Republican Senate leader had presented itself. But Baker, his confidence frayed from previous disappointments, and fearing the impact another defeat could have, still wavered.

Remarkably, even as the Republican senators gathered to make their choice, Baker remained undecided. "I don't have the votes," he told Domenici, Mathias, and Packwood, and he considered withdrawing from the race that he had just entered. "You can't do that," Packwood said, "and Bob [Griffin] probably doesn't have the votes either." With Packwood's tally showing six members still undecided, Baker agreed not to make up his mind until he reached the caucus meeting.

Entering the high-ceilinged meeting room in the Russell Senate Office Building, Baker encountered Griffin, whose confidence had undoubtedly been shaken by Baker's sudden appearance at the breakfast the previous morning. "Bob, I've got 17 votes, and I don't know what the hell to do," Baker candidly stated. "Well," Griffin replied nervously, "good luck if you win." Sensing Griffin's fear, Baker signaled to Mathias to nominate him. Leadership contests, because they are secret ballots, are often difficult to predict, and Baker's last-minute entry made this one truly uncertain. Moments later, Baker had won by a margin of 19 to 18.

Third time was the charm, and by one vote, at the age of fifty-one, Baker was finally to be the Senate Republican leader. Griffin generously broke the tension, shaking Baker's hand and opening a bottle of champagne that he had brought to celebrate his expected victory. In politics, the smallest margin can be world changing. Griffin, stung by his unexpected defeat, promptly lost interest in the Senate. Baker would become the most visible Republican in the country, the Senate minority leader, and, very possibly, a future president.

AS HE PREPARED TO deal with his new responsibilities, and a new occupant of the White House, Baker's model for a great Republican leader was his father-in-law. Everett Dirksen would always be remembered for transcending partisan politics to accomplish great things in the national interest. His support for President John F. Kennedy's Nuclear Test Ban Treaty in 1963 had made Senate ratification possible. Most famously, Dirksen's support for the Civil Rights Act of 1964, when he borrowed Victor Hugo's words to endorse "an idea whose time had come," had made possible the Senate's greatest accomplishment and secured Dirksen's place in history. But Dirksen had been leader in a different era, when the Republican conference gave him many more progressives and moderates to work with. Baker would preside over a Republican caucus that had begun moving rightward.

The Republican Party was gradually shedding moderates. In addition to Hugh Scott's departure, two of the unsung Senate giants, George Aiken of Vermont and John Sherman Cooper of Kentucky, had retired at the end of the two previous Congresses. Aiken, rock-ribbed and independent, had breakfasted with Mike Mansfield every morning. Americans of all ages could recite Senator Aiken's four-word plan for ending the Vietnam War: "declare victory and leave." Cooper had played a major role in formulating and carrying out the bipartisan foreign policy of the years following World War II. He had been appointed by President Truman to be a delegate to the United Nations, served as special assistant to Secretary of State Dean Acheson, been deeply involved in the reconstruction of Germany and the formation of the North Atlantic Treaty Organization, and served as ambassador to India and Nepal. Cooper's knowledge of the world and his reputation for absolute fairness made him influential with many of his colleagues; he had joined Democrat Frank Church in the successful, bipartisan effort to cut off funding to military operations in Cambodia in 1971. These were not senators easily replaced, and their departures changed the Republican caucus.

But beyond that, the Senate Republicans were in a testy mood. Many had defended Nixon, thinking that the Democrats were trying to make something out of what Ron Ziegler, Nixon's press secretary, had dismissed as a "third rate burglary." They now knew that Nixon had lied to them, and worse, he had thrown away his 1972 landslide victory that could have cemented the Republican majority for a decade or more.

By 1977, a new group of Republican senators was coming to prominence. These men combined strident right-wing views with an intolerance of compromise. An increasing number of the Senate Republicans had come to oppose Nixon's policy of détente toward the Soviet Union that he and Henry Kissinger had carried out. Those Republican senators reflected the right wing of the party, had never embraced Gerald Ford's presidency, and were angry that Kissinger was still on the scene. This wing of the GOP had supported Ronald Reagan's challenge to Ford's renomination, a hard run and bitter contest. Hammering away at détente and the Panama Canal treaty, Reagan had almost seized the nomination from Ford. The Republican right had forced Ford to jettison Nelson Rockefeller, his chosen vice president, whose liberal views were anathema to them. The intensity of the Republican right had been one important factor in Ford's choice of Dole over Baker. Compromise was the lifeblood of politics, and particularly necessary in the Senate, where so much business was conducted by unanimous consent. Howard Baker would lead the Republicans at a time when, for some members of his caucus, compromise was beginning to be a dirty word.

SENATE LEADERS WORKED TOGETHER, so Baker's largest challenge would be one that Byrd would share: the personification of hard-right intolerance, Jesse Helms of North Carolina. Helms had won election to the Senate in 1972 as the first Republican senator elected in North Carolina since Reconstruction. His election was a byproduct of Richard Nixon's landslide over George McGovern, representing a triumph for Nixon's southern strategy, by which the Republicans would seize the south, and therefore, the nation, by deliberately polarizing the country over a range of issues that centered on race.

Helms had followed a unique path to the Senate. He returned from World War II where he had worked as a military recruiter, to a career in journalism, first in newspapers, then in radio. He served for a brief time on the city council in Charlotte, North Carolina, and eighteen months as administrative assistant to Senator Willis Smith, a North Carolina Democrat. After Senator Smith died unexpectedly in 1953, Helms, then thirty, returned to North Carolina to become the principal lobbyist for the North Carolina Bankers' Association (NCBA).

While he worked with the NCBA, WRAL, a television station in Raleigh, invited Helms to broadcast a weekly news commentary, *Facts of the Matter*. Starting in 1957, Helms's weekly program allowed him to take on the "liberal establishment." Helms's main themes included opposition to the growth of federal power, skepticism about an internationalist foreign policy, and, above all, support for separation of the races.

In 1960, Helms became the full-time executive vice president of WRAL, with responsibility for operations and programming. A. J. Fletcher, the right-wing owner of WRAL, wanted to make the station a beacon for conservatives and break the liberal monopoly that he believed was controlling North Carolina media. Fletcher asked Helms to expand *Facts of the Matter* to a new series of daily television editorials, known as *Viewpoints*, which would be broadcast twice a day, five days a week. Helms received carte blanche to choose his themes, and between November 1960 and February 1972, Jesse Helms broadcast 2,732 viewpoints.

Helms's very first viewpoint, on November 21, 1960, was an attack on president-elect Kennedy, and throughout his viewpoints, Helms assaulted liberalism. He stressed the dangers posed by an ever-growing government and the threat of socialism to freedom. The "sacred cows" of "subsidies, controls and federal aid" all consumed freedom. He expressed strong anti-communism, weaving his hatred of the Soviet Union into his oft-repeated refrain that liberals were diminishing freedom for Americans. He became one of the most prominent voices attacking liberalism, and radicalism, in universities, using the free speech movement at Berkeley to support his attack on the liberal administration of the University of North Carolina in Chapel Hill.

Strongest of his viewpoints was his vehement opposition to the civil rights movement, which was gaining strength in North Carolina and elsewhere in the South. His broadcasts gave him hundreds of opportunities to attack and attempt to discredit the civil rights movement, and on the air, during those years, Helms formulated many of the themes that would later resonate from Ronald Reagan and other conservative politicians, including attacks on "forced integration," "welfare handouts," and "radical agitators," who were disrupting what Helms portrayed as the otherwise fine relations between whites and blacks in North Carolina. Helms denied the existence of discrimination against black Americans; in his view, the real problem was the failure of black Americans to take responsibility for the breakdown of the structure of black families and communities.

Helms worked hard to link "liberalism, subversion and perversion," attacking Reverend Martin Luther King Jr. for sexual immorality and Bayard Rustin, a distinguished civil rights leader, for being a known homosexual and an avowed Communist. Helms sought to rally his audience around a radical new conservatism that rejected interventionist government, resisted integration, ridiculed student protestors and campus activism, and opposed societal changes in morality and sexuality.

By the late 1960's, Helms had become the leading voice of the conservatives in North Carolina. He had always been politically ambitious, and when he glimpsed an opportunity to run for the Senate, he jumped at it, even though the Democratic incumbent senator, B. Everett Jordan, was an old friend of his. In the 1972 Democratic primary Senator Jordan was upset by the liberal Congressman Nick Galifianakis, setting up a classic confrontation between the ideological opposites that made up the two increasingly disparate strands of North Carolina politics.

Running statewide for the first time, Helms was not a particularly effective campaigner, but he was well financed, already well known, and running on Richard Nixon's ticket. His opponent found himself on a ticket headed by George McGovern, who would be routed nationally and in North Carolina. On election night, Jesse Helms's victory may have taken Washington by surprise, but the people of North Carolina knew what they were getting. By a narrow margin, the majority of the voters in the Tar Heel State wanted what Jesse Helms was offering, and in the coming decades, they would return him to office, time and again.

When Helms arrived in the Senate in January 1973, he encountered a discouraging environment. Despite Nixon's landslide victory over McGovern, the Democrats remained in firm control of both houses of Congress. The Republicans had been in the minority in the Senate since 1955, and for the most part, had grown both accustomed and comfortable with it. As Helms confided to a friend shortly after arriving, the Senate GOP was "almost as lib'rul" as the other side." He was right; the Republican ranks contained many senators who were moderate to liberal. They took pride in their role in the enactment of the 1964 Civil Rights Act and the 1965 Voting Rights Act, the Great Society legislation, and in their growing opposition to the Vietnam War. In short, many of the Senate Republicans, and the overwhelming majority of the Senate, stood for everything that Jesse Helms came to Washington to stop. But in some ways, this was Helms's ideal moment. Nixon had won by a landslide; his southern strategy was working; the "liberal hour" of the 1960's was approaching its end—and Helms would do everything he could to hasten its conclusion.

The Senate had changed a great deal in the two decades since Helms had briefly worked there—but some things hadn't changed. Helms understood that the Senate, a pillar of the Republic, was also a delicate institution that relied on comity because it operated by unanimous consent and offered the opportunity for unlimited debate. Consequently, the Senate could be diverted, derailed, and even driven by a handful of senators—and often just one—who had an agenda and was willing to incur the wrath of the other senators.

When Helms arrived in the Senate in January 1973, Jim Allen, the Alabama Democrat who was a master of parliamentary obstruction, made it a point to be the first senator to greet him. Soon, Helms was seeking out Allen as a mentor, and they met twice a week in Allen's office on the 6th floor of the Dirksen Senate Office Building. Jesse Helms planned to be an insurgent, and for an insurgent, knowing the Senate's byzantine rules was important for driving an agenda to frustrate the majority.

Within weeks of arriving in the Senate, Helms had made himself a force to be reckoned with. He quickly began making the Senate consider one controversial amendment after another—"throwing legislative smoke bombs, amid dozing senators in the near empty chamber." In his first two months, Helms had sponsored or cosponsored seventeen bills and four resolutions. His two most prominent proposals were constitutional amendments to permit school prayer and end school busing.

He virtually never won, but winning was not the point. He wanted to force senators to make controversial votes, making them vulnerable to attack at home, and he wanted to disrupt the Senate's bipartisan comity. He was also seeking to build a national "conservative" constituency. "Defeats don't discourage me," Helms told an interviewer in 1976. It was "good to get people on the record," to make his fellow senators "feel the heat so they would see the light."

Just as Jim Allen had invented the post-cloture filibuster, Jesse Helms had invented a powerful new political weapon. The votes that senators cast, of course, had always been fair game for their opponents in political campaigns. But those votes arose in the course of normal Senate business. Using the Senate to raise issues for the purpose of making Democrats cast painful votes that could be used against them in campaigns—this broke new ground.

Helms also began regularly to resort to the filibuster. He filibustered a compromise between the Nixon administration and Congress on legislation to establish the Legal Services Corporation, saying that it would "contribute to social disruption and serve to encourage would-be rioters." He filibustered a Senate campaign finance bill that eventually passed by a vote of 88–1. He filibustered a bill that would have strengthened the government's antitrust powers, and after a cloture vote presumably ended the filibuster, he conducted a post-cloture filibuster, offering amendment after amendment until the managers of the bill made concessions to him, changing its character in order to secure Senate passage. To Helms, the filibuster was "the only way a minority has to work its will." Whether, in a democracy, the minority should be able to work its will, was a problem for others to consider—namely, the majority whose will was being thwarted.

January 1973 also proved to be a historic moment for Helms to arrive in the Senate. On January 22, 1973, the U.S. Supreme Court handed down its decision in *Roe v. Wade*, holding by a 7–2 vote that the Constitution established and protected a right to privacy that enabled a woman to choose an abortion in the first trimester of her pregnancy. Years earlier, Helms had already begun to add the "social issues," such as school prayer, to the more traditional issues of opposition to civil rights and communism that were standard fare on the right-wing agenda. But no social issue would be more central to Helms's agenda, and to the rise of the right wing as a national movement, than opposing the Supreme Court's decision in *Roe v. Wade* and championing the rights of the unborn.

Helms's "take no prisoners" style was not just directed at Democrats. He had been friends with Richard Nixon since 1951 when he worked in an office down the hall from Senator Nixon's. Although he still admired Nixon's early anti-communism and recently benefited from Nixon's southern strategy, Helms believed that Nixon had become much too liberal on domestic issues and far too willing to spend the taxpayers' hard-earned money. Moreover, Helms despised Nixon's approach to foreign policy, judging his policy of détente toward the Soviet Union as weak and immoral. Helms was appalled when Gerald Ford picked Nelson Rockefeller to be his vice president and decided to keep Henry Kissinger, the architect of détente, as his secretary of state. When Ford, acting on the advice of Kissinger, refused to meet with Aleksandr Solzhenitsyn, the dissident Russian author and Nobel Prize winner, Helms had had enough. He gave serious thought to leaving the Republican Party to form a new right-wing party. But when Ronald Reagan challenged Ford for the Republican presidential nomination, Helms saw a better path for changing the Republican Party, and the country. He became one of Reagan's most ardent and effective supporters.

Helms would continue using the Senate to hold the feet of the "lib'ruls" to the fire, forcing painful votes at every turn. He would work tirelessly with a collection of loosely connected outside groups to build the "New Right" across the nation, in the hope of making Reagan president in 1980.

DESPITE THE CHALLENGES HE would face, Baker had understandable confidence in his ability to navigate difficult currents. He had seen his father-in-law support Kennedy and Johnson on issues of overriding importance, while keeping his Republican bona fides by uniting his party and confronting the presidents on lesser issues. Baker had an exceptional ability to bridge seemingly irreconcilable views through a disarming and conciliatory brand of bargaining. Lisa Myers would write: "To hear [senators] talk, Howard Henry Baker could bring together a boll weevil and a cotton planter." His stepmother, a distinguished politician in her own right, once said, "Howard is like the Tennessee River. He always runs right down the middle." If there was a middle to be found, Baker would find it.

Baker quickly moved to share the leadership responsibilities with a large group of ideologically diverse Republicans. Ted Stevens of Alaska, a thoughtful moderate, would be Republican whip. Stevens would keep a foot in each camp of the Senate Republicans, breakfasting with both the liberal Wednesday Group and the conservative Steering Committee. John Tower of Texas, a hard-liner on defense issues and conservative on economic policy, would remain as chairman of the Republican Policy Committee, with enhanced resources. Conservatives Carl Curtis of Nebraska and Jake Garn of Utah would chair the Republican Conference and the Committee on Committees. Bob Packwood, perhaps the strongest defender of abortion rights in the Senate, would chair the Republican Campaign Committee. Jacob Javits of New York, generally regarded as the most liberal Republican and the smartest senator, would head an economic policy task force; Clifford Hansen of Wyoming would head the energy policy task force. Baker planned for the Republicans to emerge as a counterforce in the Senate, and he wanted them to have coherent alternatives to offer in contrast to the new Carter administration.

Baker faced one other problem that Dirksen had not when he became leader. Howard Baker hoped to be president someday. So, in addition to the multiple pressures that pull on a Senate leader, Baker would always have to be weighing whether his actions furthered or undermined his presidential ambitions.

The incoming Senate would have sixty-one Democrats, thirty-eight Republicans, and one independent, Harry Byrd of Virginia—virtually the same balance as the previous one. This was surprising, given the supposedly strong national tide favoring the Democrats after Watergate. But the status quo result was deceptive, because the incoming Senate would include seventeen new members, the largest turnover since the historic 1958 election. Mostly, it was a generation shift; more than half of the changes resulted from the retirement or defeat of veterans who had served three or four terms. But to the extent a political message could be discerned, it was that the West was becoming more conservative, as Republicans defeated Democrats in Utah, Wyoming, New Mexico, and California.

The new senators promised to be a diverse and interesting group. Paul Sarbanes, Democrat from Maryland, was a Rhodes Scholar well known on Capitol Hill for his impressive work on the House Judiciary Committee, which voted out the articles of impeachment against Richard Nixon. Don Riegle, Democrat of Michigan, was a young (thirty-eight), charismatic, driven politician who had already switched parties after being elected to the House as a Republican and written an exposé of Congress. John Danforth, Republican of Missouri, was his state's attorney general, an ordained minister, and the scion of the family that controlled Ralston-Purina. S. I. Hayakawa, Republican of California, was a professor of linguistics who had risen to prominence as president of San Francisco State, taking a hard line against campus demonstrators.

The most famous member of the entering senators was undoubtedly Daniel Patrick Moynihan, Democrat of New York, former U.N. ambassador; adviser to four presidents, Democratic and Republican; Harvard professor and author, provocateur, and disturber of the intellectual peace. Moynihan's work in the Nixon White House, including his frank assessment that the Negro family in America was disintegrating, had earned him the enmity of many liberals. His assertive stance at the UN in support of Israel and in opposition to America's enemies had won him a huge following in New York and around the country. Moynihan knew the Senate well, having crafted Nixon's Family Assistance Plan that had been killed in the Senate by Russell Long, the chairman of the Finance Committee. The Senate prided itself on being a place for large men, and Moynihan, wearing his trademark bow tie, stammering with a distinctive British accent, and constantly writing his next book, certainly promised to fit that bill.

The Democrats might be riding high in January 1977, but only four years before, the Democratic presidential nominee had lost forty-nine states, winning only Massachusetts and the District of Columbia. American politics had been volatile since John Kennedy's death. As 1977 began, the Democrats, as well as the Republicans, had a great deal to prove to a skeptical populace. And as the two parties sought to sharpen their separate appeals to the American people, the Senate would be the place where they would have to work together most closely.

chapter 3

GREAT EXPECTATIONS, DIFFERENT AGENDAS

SIXTEEN DAYS AFTER THE SWEARING IN OF THE NINETY-FIFTH CONGRESS and the election of its majority and minority leaders came the inauguration of America's thirty-ninth president, James Earl Carter of Plains, Georgia.

A year earlier, Carter was still a virtual unknown, and perhaps the longest shot in a large Democratic presidential field. But Carter had grasped several fundamental political realities. He understood that the Democrats who voted in caucuses and primaries were open to new faces; George McGovern had demonstrated that in seizing the Democratic nomination four years earlier. He also saw that the Iowa caucuses could be a springboard that could propel the winner to national prominence. Jimmy Carter had the patience and persistence to meet every active Iowa Democrat—in their kitchens if necessary—and he gave himself the time to do it. He also had a huge advantage that in retrospect would seem obvious: unlike his fellow candidates, he had the freedom to run for president full time, and he did exactly that.

In the aftermath of Watergate, 1976 promised to be a Democratic year, and a large field of contenders entered the presidential fray. Four senators ran in the primaries. Birch Bayh of Indiana, handsome, likeable, and genuine, had become one of the country's most effective liberal forces in his two terms in the Senate. Bayh had taken the lead in the Senate's rejection of two of

Richard Nixon's nominations for the Supreme Court, building deep friend-ships with unions and the civil rights and other liberal organizations that constituted the established strength of the Democratic Party.

Frank Church of Idaho was a leading opponent of the Vietnam War, and he had recently captured the nation's attention by chairing the select com-mittee investigating the abuses of America's intelligence agencies. Henry Jack-son of Washington, better known as "Scoop," was one of the Senate giants. A New Deal liberal on domestic issues and a hard-liner on foreign policy and defense, Jackson had earned the strong support of the AFL-CIO and the Jew-ish community, powerful forces within the Democratic Party. Senator Fred Harris of Oklahoma was the populist candidate for the nomination, directing his campaign to "the little people."

Bayh, Church, Jackson, and Harris quickly discovered what many senators had found out before them: you could be a very good senator and still be an awful presidential candidate. Bayh's liberal supporters split in too many di-rections, and he never won a primary. Church started much too late. Jackson, extraordinarily effective on Capitol Hill, was simply unable to communicate on television or in speeches. As one humorist noted, "If Scoop Jackson gave a fireside chat, the fire would go out." After Harris was crushed in the crucial New Hampshire primary, receiving less than 1 percent of the vote, he ex-plained: "The little people couldn't reach the levers."

In July 1976, Jimmy Carter accepted the nomination of the Democratic Party for president. Carter was a truly unknown quantity when the Demo-crats nominated him. A political cartoon in the *Washington Post* by Herblock, which showed the Democrat Party as a nervous bride at the altar waiting for a groom who was a complete stranger, captured the moment. The Democrats drew some comfort from Carter's choice of Walter F. ("Fritz") Mondale, a popular Minnesota senator with strong ties to labor and the liberal commu-nity, to be his running mate.

As the general election campaign started, Carter appeared certain to be the next president. He had captivated the country and captured the public mood after Watergate with his promise of "a government as good as the American people." America had initially been grateful to Gerald Ford, for the calm and assured way that he had ended the "long national nightmare" and stepped into the presidency. But Ford had made the difficult decision to pardon Richard Nixon, enraging much of the country. Moreover, America's economy had been going through a serious downturn, featuring high unemployment and soaring inflation, triggered by the 1973 Arab oil embargo. Ford's efforts to provide economic leadership were often painful to watch. When he put on a WIN button—"whip inflation now"—he was widely ridiculed for offering slogans and gimmickry, rather than real leadership. After the Democratic convention, national polls showed Carter with a thirty-point advantage over Ford, who was still struggling to fend off Reagan's challenge. The only unelected president in American history looked to have no chance of winning in 1976.

And then, suddenly and surprisingly, the national mood began to change. July 4, 1976, was America's Bicentennial. All across the country, people participated in a national celebration of the historic occasion. They thrilled to the image of the "tall ships" coming into the harbor of New York City. The Vietnam War, the longest in U.S. history and the most divisive since the Civil War, had ended badly, but it was finally over. Anger about the Nixon pardon began to fade as more Americans concluded that Ford had made a courageous decision to put an end to the national crisis. The U.S. economy was recovering from the deep recession. For the first time in many years, Americans just felt better.

Ford managed to outlast Reagan to win the nomination. His convention speech was undoubtedly the best he had ever given. Meanwhile, Carter seemed to be squandering his advantage. He gave an interview to *Playboy* magazine in which he confessed to have "lust in his heart" many times, which jolted the many Americans who were previously attracted by his piety, and others who questioned his political judgment. As voters grew uneasy that they really did not know Jimmy Carter, Gerald Ford came to seem comfortable and familiar, rather than boring or incompetent.

The race tightened steadily, and on Election Day, 1976, Jimmy Carter won, but in one of the closest elections in American political history. His mandate was uncertain. Americans said they wanted change, but the change they seemed to want was a period of calm after the crisis years that began with the Cuban missile confrontation in 1962 and ended, apparently, when the last Americans went to the roof of the U.S. embassy in Saigon to leave Vietnam.

Although Carter's margin of victory had narrowed dramatically, other Democratic politicians were increasingly confident as they added control of the presidency to significant majorities in both houses of Congress. They had prevailed over Richard Nixon, a longtime adversary whom many senators had personally despised. Watergate had tarnished the Republican brand,

and the party itself had split sharply during the contest between Ford and Reagan, the type of division that was usually confined to the Democrats.

But below the placid surface ran deeper and more ominous currents. Carter's outsider campaign had resonated with Americans who were angry at Washington, and angry at government as usual. The Democratic Congress seemed not to recognize that, fairly or unfairly, it personified government as usual. Polls and press reports indicated that the country was becoming more conservative, less inclined to be supportive of government programs as they perceived the U.S. economy to be weaker than it had been. As the Democrats congratulated themselves on their victory, looking out at a seemingly prostrate Republican Party, they would have been wise to recall the last time the Republicans had been pronounced dead, after Lyndon Johnson's 1964 landslide victory over Barry Goldwater. Four years later, Richard Nixon was elected president.

ON JANUARY 20, 1977, Jimmy Carter became the first president to walk down Pennsylvania Avenue after his inauguration. Expectations for his presidency ran high. Although only eight years had passed since a Democrat had occupied the White House, it seemed much longer. In 1967 and 1968, as America's cities erupted into flames and violence and the Vietnam War tore the country apart, Lyndon Johnson's presidency had crumbled. More than ten years had passed since a Democratic president had the political support needed to take meaningful action for the country.

From FDR to Harry Truman to John Kennedy to Lyndon Johnson, Democratic presidents come to office to "get the country moving again," using an activist federal government to expand economic opportunity and advance social justice. Democrats expected Carter to assume their mantle and fall into line—but it was an open question how a neophyte like the new president would work with his legislative counterparts.

The interest groups that were the most influential forces in the Democratic Party wanted action. During the presidential campaign, they had run phone banks, gone door to door, and mobilized supporters to help Carter win his narrow victory. Experienced in the ways of Washington, they understood that the legislative victories they sought would not come easily. In the historic Eighty-ninth Congress, Lyndon Johnson, at the height of his power, secured passage of eighty-four out of the eighty-seven pieces of legislation he proposed. But one of the three failures was labor's highest priority: rolling back the 1947 Taft-Hartley Act, which allowed states to pass "right to work" laws disallowing exclusively union shops and prohibiting contractual agreements that required employers to hire only union members. The labor movement would not rest until it achieved its key objectives in this Democratic administration—and other Democratic constituencies felt the same urgency.

The labor unions, led by George Meany and the AFL-CIO, wanted legislation that would make it easier to form unions in order to reverse the long decline in union membership. Consumer groups, led by Ralph Nader, wanted legislation to create a Consumer Protection Agency, which would establish a consumer representative in agency proceedings to offset what the consumer groups saw as the disproportionate power of corporate America. A constellation of organizations representing the interests of minorities and the poor wanted action to create jobs and strengthen the social safety net in response to what had been the worst recession since the Great Depression. These groups would make their case directly to the incoming administration, and they would pressure the administration by enlisting their longtime allies in the Senate and the House.

The relationship between the new president and the Democrats on the Hill would be crucial, and yet Hill veterans were already growing anxious. Jimmy Carter had campaigned as a liberal while preserving as much maneuvering room as he could. Political Washington looked carefully for telltale signs of Carter's true interests and beliefs, above and beyond faith in himself and a desire to purify politics. He remained inscrutable.

During the transition, president-elect Carter invited a number of leading Democrats to Plains to discuss administration appointments. Those invited came eagerly, anxious to begin forming the relationships needed to help Carter govern successfully. They came back stunned.

For three hours, Jimmy Carter had presided over a meeting with leading Democrats on steel folding chairs, without food or drink or even a bathroom break. Vice President–elect Mondale, still getting to know Carter, said to a Carter aide, "I learned three things about Carter today. First, he has a cast-iron rear end. Second, he has a bladder the size of a football. And third, his idea of a party is a half glass of scotch."

It would become clear soon enough: the new president disliked political small talk, disliked politicians, and liked politics least of all. He thought that the interest groups who had worked to elect him were selfishly pursuing their own narrow agendas at the expense of the national interest. He saw members of Congress as either complete captives of the interest groups or too quick to bend to their views. The only politician he had faith in was Jimmy Carter. Principled compromise was the heart and soul of the legislative process, but Jimmy Carter was not a believer in compromise.

Carter's training as an engineer, coupled with his inordinate self-confidence, convinced him that there was a right answer to every problem that he could find if he studied it carefully. By contrast, Congress seemed to crave endless consultation—before he was even president, no less. Meeting their demands, if that were even possible, would take Carter away from what he really wanted to do: study problems, decide what was in the national interest, and pursue a solution irrespective of the political fallout.

The Senate Democrats were potentially Carter's strongest allies. Their experience was broad and deep, and although they had forged close friendships with the Democratic interest groups, they were, for the most part, astute, independent-minded politicians with a keen sense of what was possible. Most of them understood that the winds had begun to shift in American politics. They recognized both the fiscal constraints imposed by a weakening economy and the growing doubt around the country that federal programs were being run successfully or effectively. John Kennedy had once described himself as "an idealist without illusions," and his description fit many of the senators. They wanted to be partners with the new president—but if he chose not to cultivate their friendship, they could also be very tough adversaries.

The Founding Fathers built tension into the Constitutional system, dividing and checking power between the legislative and executive branches. Advocates of congressional power noted that it was no accident that the Founding Fathers had specified the powers of Congress, rather than the presidency, in Article I of the Constitution; their experience with England had left them fearful of a strong executive. At the same time, the Constitution created a president, and separated the powers of the two branches so that our democracy would not be a parliamentary system.

The power of the executive had generally increased over time. Starting with Franklin D. Roosevelt, when America desperately needed strong leadership to battle the Depression and win World War II, power had tilted dramatically toward the presidency and away from Congress. The Cold War and the threat of nuclear war had further strengthened the hand of presidents that followed Roosevelt.

But the tragedy of Vietnam and the abuse of power that was Watergate had provoked a powerful reaction on Capitol Hill. Congress had brought the Vietnam War to an end and forced Richard Nixon out of office. It had also made far-reaching institutional changes designed to allow Congress to reclaim its authority in major areas, particularly the budget and the power to declare war. Jimmy Carter would be the first elected president to deal with a Congress that had reasserted its authority.

As professor Nelson Polsby memorably observed, the president and the Congress were like "two gears, each whirling at its own rate of speed." American presidents live in the shadow of FDR's first one hundred days. They are expected to put together their administration during the ten-week transition, inspire the nation in the inaugural address, go to the Hill for the first State of the Union, and put forth a program. In general, presidents are expected to fire out of the box and create movement and a sense of change immediately.

Alternately, the Congress has its own pace, particularly the Senate. Relatively little gets accomplished in the early weeks of the session. Senators and Senate committees take their time studying, critiquing, and improving the president's proposals. Their leaders think not in terms of three months, but of what can be accomplished during the two-year Congress. The Senate does not like to be rushed, and its leaders would not hesitate to let the president know when his expectations are unreasonable.

Jimmy Carter had campaigned for president almost nonstop for two years. His campaign had certainly included significant study of the issues facing the country. But actually making decisions on a legislative program requires a much different type of preparation—in fact, just the type of preparation that Carter liked best. At home in Plains, he immersed himself in the issues, reading briefing paper after briefing paper, meeting with his transition staff, who would become his key advisers. These meetings seldom included members of Congress. By the week before his inauguration, Carter had already decided on the key initiatives for the early months of his presidency. And, for the most part, he had already decided to leave the Senators, and their repeated pleas for consultation, out.

CARTER AND HIS ADVISERS confronted a complicated economic picture. The economy had begun to recover from the severe recession of 1973–1974 triggered by the OPEC oil embargo, but unemployment still stood at an unacceptably high rate of 7.8 percent. The nation's output of goods and services had increased only a disappointing 3 percent in the last quarter of 1976, the lowest since the spring of 1975. Fortunately, inflation had come down from 12 percent in 1974 to about 6 percent by the end of 1976, but by historical standards, that number was still very high. The American public listed job creation as its number-one priority, and that certainly was true for key Democratic constituencies.

Carter's hope was to stimulate the economy without kicking off another ruinous round of inflation. He proposed to do so by keeping tight control of the tools of fiscal policy—most notably, spending. In spite of his efforts, before too long, it would become clear that the economic challenge was not just complicated, it was unprecedented: what Bruce Schulman would describe as "the disintegration of the long sweet summer of post-war prosperity." Economic policy would prove a continuous battleground between the president and the Hill for the four years to come.

On January 17, Carter and congressional leaders came together for an announcement. Carter would kick off his presidency by offering an economic stimulus package to give the sluggish economy a moderate, and hopefully noninflationary, boost. Carter proposed to cut corporate taxes by $900 million and called for modest increases in public works and other job-creating programs. The most visible feature of the proposal would be a tax rebate of $50 for each taxpayer and for those on Social Security. Michael Blumenthal, the new secretary of treasury, testified that the rebate would "provide a quick injection of spending into the national economy." As far as tactics were concerned, the White House hoped to secure a quick legislative victory, both to stimulate the economy and to establish political momentum for subsequent initiatives. But a quick victory without early congressional buy-in would be almost impossible, and the new administration had not made an effort to work out the economic package with the Hill.

The rebate came as a surprise to the Senate, and the initial reaction to Carter's initiative was ominous. Blindsided by the announcement, Democrats struggled to be supportive of the idea, even though many of them thought it strange. For the first time in almost a decade, Senate Republicans seized the advantage that comes from being in the opposition. They felt no compunction to support the president's proposal. Moreover, thanks to the work of Howard Baker, John Tower, and Jacob Javits, they swiftly assembled a credible alternative to put forth.

Within a week, the thirty-eight member Republican conference offered a $26.2 billion plan to compete with Carter's $30 billion stimulus. The Republicans sought to replace the one-time rebate, which they called a "temporary gimmick," with "sizable, permanent" tax cuts. The Republican plan would lower tax rates on the first $18,000 of gross income. They also proposed an employment tax credit, a home insulation credit, an increase from $400 to $600 on the amount of dividend income taxpayers could exclude from taxes, and an exclusion of $100 for interest income. For good measure, they also threw in a jobs training program for young unemployed people. It represented the first Republican effort to become the party of tax cuts, and it certainly would not be the last.

With competing proposals in hand, Senators busied themselves arguing over their respective ideas to stimulate the economy. Unbeknownst to them, Carter was moving ahead with an entirely separate initiative that would prove to be the centerpiece of his domestic program: energy.

On February 2, Jimmy Carter delivered his first televised "fireside chat" to the country. Wearing a cardigan sweater and a tie, sitting by a fireplace, the president laid out the grim facts. The United States was using far too much energy. Production could no longer keep up with consumption. The nation was becoming increasingly and dangerously reliant on imported oil. In response, he sketched a program that would include conservation, increased coal production, increased emphasis on solar and other alternative and renewable forms of energy, and a recommendation that Americans lower thermostats to 65 degrees during the day and 55 during the night. He asked Congress to consolidate the energy programs split among fifty government agencies by creating a new Department of Energy, and stated that he had asked James Schlesinger, the former secretary of defense in the Nixon and Ford administrations, to take the lead on a comprehensive energy plan to be prepared in the next ninety days.

If the tax rebate had rattled the senators, Carter's fireside chat now came as an utter shock. During the campaign, Carter had placed no particular emphasis on energy. After the election, his study of the issues convinced him that America was facing a crisis that necessitated immediate action. Characteristically, Carter and his White House team had done very little, if any, consultation with Capitol Hill, and the frosty reaction from many members reflected not only the difficulty of the issues, but how unhappy they were about being blindsided.

Now they were being asked to expend political capital of their own to support economic and energy initiatives that they felt had been foisted upon them. This rankled many of the Senators, such as Ernest F. Hollings, a Democrat from South Carolina and one of the most forceful and caustic personalities in the Senate. At a Budget Committee hearing on February 4, Hollings referred to Carter's call for Americans to make sacrifices during the fireplace chat: "While he's asking us for sacrifice, his team is up here asking us to give everyone 50 bucks."

Despite mounting and widespread doubts about whether the rebate would be effective, the economic stimulus package, including the rebate, inched forward in the Senate Finance and House Ways and Means committees. Democratic Senators and Congressmen were unenthusiastic, but they wanted to be supportive of their new president. That is, until a few weeks later, when Carter dropped a brand new bombshell.

During his private study of domestic issues during the transition, Carter had become incensed about the wasteful, pork-barrel spending attached to water projects in the south and west of the United States. He saw them as "worthless dams" that caused more harm than benefit. Characteristically, Carter had reviewed each project personally and made the final decision alone.

On February 19, without previous consultation, the White House began notifying members of Congress that it intended to cut off funding for nineteen projects that had been previously approved by Congress, the Army Corps of Engineers, and the Interior Department. The projects were in various stages of construction and had been championed by senators for years, disproportionately from the West and Louisiana. Political candidates routinely promise a break with "politics as usual," but Carter really meant it. The water projects had strong support from Scoop Jackson, chairman of the newly constituted Energy and Natural Resources Committee, and Russell Long of Louisiana, chairman of the Finance Committee, who would inevitably be the two most influential senators in determining the fate of Carter's energy and economic programs. No president other than Carter would have picked a fight with Jackson and Long over the Corps of Engineers water projects.

Russell Long was one of the Senate's most formidable and remarkable figures. His father, Huey Long, the legendary "Kingfish," had risen to power in Louisiana and Washington, as governor and then senator, on the radical ideas of "share-our-wealth" and "every man a king" before being assassinated in 1935. Russell Long had been elected to the Senate in 1948 one day before his thirtieth birthday. He had arrived in the Senate with a memorable freshman class that included Lyndon Johnson; Hubert Humphrey; Paul Douglas, the liberal lion from Illinois; and Robert Kerr of Oklahoma, the oil magnate who had founded Kerr-McGee Corporation. Now, only Long remained, having spent nearly half his life in the Senate.

Short and doughy-faced, often stuttering and hard to understand, Long could be easily underestimated—but only at one's peril. By any measure, Russell Long was one of the most formidable legislators ever to serve. He had chaired the Finance Committee since Kerr's death in 1963, and as Bill Proxmire once said admiringly: "He knows the tax code as thoroughly as the Pope knows the Lord's Prayer." Armed with great substantive knowledge, he was also an absolutely superb negotiator, who regularly outsmarted and outmaneuvered his House counterparts. He was a master of building consensus in his committee, treating his members generously and fairly. Utterly straight with his colleagues, he would often warn them against voting for amendments that he was offering. "No question about it," one of his liberal colleagues commented, "next to Hubert Humphrey, [Russell] is clearly the most congenial man in the Senate."

He formed great friendships with even those liberals, like Walter Mondale and Gaylord Nelson, who came to the Finance Committee dedicated to eliminating the oil depletion allowance. The liberals were charmed by Long's uncanny ability to zealously defend the oil and gas industries while channeling his father's populism. Long championed the concept of employee stock ownership programs (ESOPs) and in 1975 had been one of the architects of the new program to give an Earned Income Tax Credit to the working poor. At one time, Long had suffered from alcoholism, which contributed to his being replaced as Democratic whip in 1969, but he had stopped drinking years ago. The year 1977 found Russell Long at the peak of his skill and at the pinnacle of his career.

Jimmy Carter would face the challenge of seeking to legislate a national energy policy when the Finance Committee chairman was an extraordinarily effective defender of the oil and gas industry. Carter would compound that challenge by not understanding Russell Long. The president expressed confidence that he could handle the Louisiana senator. He would learn the hard way that his confidence was misplaced.

BY MARCH, EMOTIONS WERE running high in the Senate, as the Democrats unenthusiastically continued to push Carter's economic agenda. On March

10, the rebate barely survived two party line votes (10–8) in the Finance Committee. Long then demonstrated the dexterity that made him such a formidable legislator. He helped the administration prevail on the rebate but went to the Senate floor to say that the water projects would do far more good for the economy than the rebates would. Abe Ribicoff concurred, stating that he would support the administration on the rebate "with a great deal of skepticism. In all the years I've been on the Finance Committee, I've never known a group of economic advisers to any president to be correct." But he concluded: "This is a new administration, and they ought to be given a chance"—presumably, to make their own mistakes.

Resistance was building. Byrd had expressed his unhappiness with the failure of the Carter administration to consult as early as January 26, less than a week after Carter was sworn in. Now, the handling of the water projects had infuriated him afresh, and he decided it was time to act. On April 5, after meeting with the president and congressional leaders, Byrd told the press that the rebate was doomed unless Carter compromised on the water projects. Jody Powell, Carter's press secretary, responded to Byrd: "We've indicated what our position is on the water projects." The president was as little interested in compromising as he had been in consulting in the first place.

Two days later, Carter made a special appearance in the White House press room, stepping up the pressure on Congress for the rebate and stating that he would not trade water projects in order to get it. On April 11, columnists Rowland Evans and Robert Novak reported that Senator Lloyd Bentsen had urged Carter to walk away from the rebate altogether, as the economy was now showing signs of improvement. Many administration officials privately agreed, but Carter remained firm. A presidential aide opposed to the rebate said that surrender on the rebate "just isn't Jimmy's style." Instead, the administration doubled down, raising the stakes ever higher. On April 12, Secretary of Labor Ray Marshall gave a major speech in Michigan where he said that if Congress did not approve the rebate, it would hurt consumer confidence and make it impossible for the administration to bring unemployment below 7 percent that year.

Yet on April 14, in a stunning reversal, the president announced in the White House briefing room that he had decided to abandon the rebate proposal. Carter based his decision on the evidence that the economy was improving and no longer needed the jolt that the rebates would have provided. He also noted his concern that his upcoming energy proposals would be costly and could have a potentially inflationary effect. He also acknowledged that winning the Senate vote would have required a "bruising battle" and that he did not want to spend his political capital on the rebates when he wanted to focus on other priorities, including the energy plan. Carter noted that he had consulted with congressional leaders and it was "a mutual decision." Byrd called the retreat "a wise decision," though the reaction on Capitol Hill was mixed.

Edmund Muskie, the first chairman of the Senate Budget Committee, had worked to defend Carter's $50 rebate proposal, and now found that the president had abruptly cut him off at the knees. "What kind of fucking fiscal policy is this, Charlie," Muskie raged to Charles Schultze, the chairman of the Council of Economic Advisers. Calling Carter's decision "a disappointment" and a "breach of promise to the people," Muskie ridiculed the lack of "steadiness" in economic policy: "We cannot allow our policies to be dictated by every small movement of the economic statistics. Should we propose stimulus during the slowdown, oppose it when Christmas sales turn up, propose it again when the severe winter descends, and once again oppose it when spring raises the temperature and our spirits?" Muskie also charged that Carter "did not consult with us adequately, gave us no warning [and] retreated from a program that was a month in the making." In a stroke, Carter had angered one of the most formidable members of the Senate, and perhaps his most important potential ally.

ED MUSKIE HAD COME to the Senate in the large Democratic class of 1958, after being a popular and effective governor of Maine. From the beginning he was proud, principled, and prickly. Arriving in the Senate in January 1959, he quickly managed to get on the wrong side of Senate Majority Leader Lyndon Johnson. In their first meeting, Johnson, in a patronizing tone, had advised Muskie not to commit his vote too quickly, but to wait until "the roll call came to the M's." Shortly thereafter, Johnson was counting votes on a motion to change the cloture rules, an issue of critical importance to him. When he approached Muskie, seeking his vote, the new senator responded dryly, "Well, Lyndon, I think I'll wait until the M's are called."

Johnson began to refer to Muskie as "chicken shit," his all-purpose term for those he felt were disrespecting him. When the new Democratic senators received their committee assignments, Johnson denied Muskie a seat on any of the three committees that he requested. Instead, he gave Muskie the least attractive set of committee assignments that he could put together: Banking, Government Operations, and Public Works.

Muskie initially sulked, but then threw himself into his committee work. Before long it became clear that Johnson had inadvertently done Muskie a real favor. After publication of Rachel Carson's *Silent Spring* in 1962, almost overnight, the environment became an important concern for Americans from coast to coast. Muskie became the chairman of the public works sub-committee dealing with environmental pollution. Starting in 1963, and continuing for the next decade, Muskie became the principal author and architect of the Clean Air Act and the Clean Water Act, far-reaching and creative legislation mandating industry to make dramatic improvements in their operations to improve America's air and water quality. Muskie's efforts derived strength from a great staff led by Leon Billings, a passionate liberal from Montana, who would become known throughout Washington as the power behind the chairman and a major force in his own right.

By 1968, Muskie had achieved enough prominence to be chosen by Vice President Hubert Humphrey to serve as his running mate against Richard Nixon and Spiro Agnew. Against the backdrop of the turbulent events of that year, Humphrey lost narrowly, but Muskie, by all accounts, acquitted himself extremely well in the national spotlight. He emerged as a leading contender for the Democratic nomination in 1972 and solidified his position with a calm, statesmanlike response to Nixon's "law and order" campaign on the eve of the 1970 off-year election.

Muskie entered the 1972 Democratic primaries as the clear front-runner. However, his campaign proved to be top-heavy and slow-moving, far too Washington DC–oriented, and his previous ties to Humphrey, a defeated Democratic nominee still linked to Vietnam, were unhelpful to say the least. It is unlikely that Muskie could have defeated McGovern, whose campaign was powered by the energy of the activist Democrats who opposed the Vietnam War. But the Muskie campaign also melted down because of "dirty tricks" orchestrated by the Nixon reelection campaign, including a fabricated letter, leaked in New Hampshire, which accused Muskie of insulting French-Canadians by calling them "Canucks." Muskie's campaign dissolved in the snows of New Hampshire, at an extraordinary press conference in which the press reported, inaccurately, that the angry candidate had broken down in tears.

Muskie returned to the Senate, understandably embittered. He became increasingly active on foreign policy issues, as opposition to the Vietnam War intensified. The subsequent revelations of the Watergate Committee that he had been one of the victims of Nixon's dirty tricks further enhanced his stature. By 1977, Muskie had become one of the most influential of senators, respected for his accomplishments, his intellect, and his rectitude. He had played a key role in enacting the Budget Control and Impoundment Act in 1974, which legislated a complex process through which Congress would reassert its power over the federal purse. It seems extraordinary in retrospect, but prior to the Budget Act, Congress enacted the thirteen appropriations bills separately, without making any attempt to monitor or manage the overall federal budget. Muskie became the first chairman of the new Senate Budget Committee, which gave him a unique responsibility for making the new legislation work and reining in Congress's free-spending ways and the chance to think broadly about the budget, federal priorities, and overall economic policy.

Muskie welcomed the challenge; he had given notable speeches in 1975 and 1976 about the importance for Democrats to discover fiscal responsibility and make sure that important government programs ran well, messages not usually heard from liberal Democrats. He even sponsored "sunset" legislation, which required all existing federal programs go out of existence unless periodically reauthorized—a position that labor and other liberal Democratic constituencies hated. Deeply respected, authentically liberal, but fiscally tough-minded, Muskie was the Budget Committee chairman from central casting: the perfect choice for a thankless job that would pit him, at one time or another, against most of his Senate colleagues—and the president, as in the case of Carter's flip-flop on the rebate. But Muskie was also a potential bridge between Carter and the liberal wing of the Senate.

In truth, with respect to the rebate, the circumstances had left Carter no good way out. He would have been (and in fact, was already) condemned for his rigidity in pushing a bad idea, or for his fecklessness in walking away from it. The *Washington Post*, in a scathing editorial, wondered whether the Democratic senators who had supported the rebate despite their reservations would support the president on a tough issue next time around, after he had left them hanging. It was a good question, and how it was answered would go a long way to determining the success of the Democratic administration. The ill-conceived rebate would soon be forgotten, but the clash of styles and perspectives between the president and the Senate would be a constant problem in what would prove to be the defining issue facing the country on the domestic front.

JAMES SCHLESINGER HAD COMPLETED his work to formulate a comprehensive energy package, and Jimmy Carter was prepared to stake his presidency to the issue that threatened the security and economic prosperity of the United States. On April 18, in a twenty-minute televised talk, President Carter described the energy crisis as "the greatest challenge our country will face during our lifetime. . . . If we fail to act soon, we will face an economic, social and political crisis that will threaten our free institutions." He set forth new goals for the nation: reduce gas consumption by 10 percent; cut oil imports to 6 million barrels a day; establish a 1 billion barrel strategic petroleum reserve; increase coal production by two-thirds; insulate 90 percent of American homes; and expand solar energy to 2.5 million homes.

It was only the beginning of what would be a sustained campaign for a signature issue. On April 20, Carter sought the largest audience possible, going before a joint session of Congress to propose a response to the energy crisis. The pomp and ceremony were briefly disrupted at precisely 9 p.m. when the great doors of the House chamber opened, but instead of President Carter, a confused and somewhat disheveled Schlesinger rushed in, looking for his seat. The address itself, however, contained no levity.

Carter called the United States "the most wasteful nation on earth," wasting more energy than we import. Without the ability to substantially increase production domestically, Carter warned that the United States was on track to becoming perilously dependent on imported oil. Carter also predicted that without immediate action, there would be pressure "to plunder the environment" in a crash program to expand nuclear plants, strip mining, and drilling offshore wells. Regions within the United States would compete with each other for supplies; "inflation will soar, production will go down, people will lose their jobs."

He set forth his plan: let domestic oil prices rise to world levels, increase prices of newly discovered natural gas by 20 percent (to approach oil prices), place a 5 cents per gallon tax on gasoline each year if conservation goals were not met, and use tax penalties on gas guzzlers and rebates on small cars to encourage purchasers to select energy-efficient autos. He held out the possibility of gasoline rationing as an alternative solution if conservation goals could not be met. The president also noted that he had the authority to impose rationing without congressional approval by declaring a national economic emergency.

Jimmy Carter's address to Congress laying out his energy program brought his sometimes rocky first one hundred days to an extraordinary conclusion.

He had challenged the nation in a way that it had seldom been challenged before, certainly not since *Sputnik*, and perhaps not since World War II.

Some critics suggested that the magnitude of his program did not approach the magnitude of the crisis that he described. Humorist Russell Baker noted that Carter's "moral equivalent of war" equaled MEOW. Tom Quinn, special assistant to California Governor Jerry Brown, said that "large Chevy owners will have to switch to small Chevies . . . not much of a sacrifice."

But polls showed that Americans were responding positively: 69 percent of Americans approved of Carter's presidency; 86 percent agreed with him that the energy situation was serious. By large margins, Americans supported most of the proposals in his plan. But there were dark clouds as well. The public disapproved of the standby gas tax by 54 percent to 39 percent, and 62 percent of those polled said the program lacked "equality of sacrifice" because people feared it would have a disproportionate impact on the poor.

Congressional leaders recognized the difficulties ahead. Setting aside their gripes about the abortive rebate, they expressed admiration for Carter's courage and determination to see his legislation through. Byrd said, "This is a supreme test and it requires a supreme effort. Yet I think that there is a reservoir of courage and strength and patriotism here that will respond." House Speaker Tip O'Neill predicted that the passage of the president's program would involve "the toughest fight this Congress has ever had." Lloyd Bentsen, the Democratic senator from Texas, expressed admiration: "The president is doing what has to be done. He has proposed a broad national energy program." Anticipating the problems ahead, Bentsen added: "It should be given a fair hearing, not nibbled to death."

O'Neill quickly announced the formation of a thirty-seven-member, special ad hoc committee to handle the energy legislation. Byrd made it clear that the Senate would use its regular committee process, which had been recently reformed.

The real question now would be: was Congress capable of considering a comprehensive energy program, without nibbling it to death?

THE ENERGY LEGISLATION WOULD pose the first serious test of the committee reorganization that had been completed by Byrd and Baker in the first weeks of the session. They had moved quickly to address a festering problem that had produced increasing frustration in the Senate through the 1970's. In the old Senate, dominated by the southern barons, senior senators chaired the committees, held the disproportionate number of slots on the most powerful committees, and limited the number of subcommittees to ensure that there would be no competing power centers. Mansfield's democratized Senate had gone the other way, and had eventually—perhaps inevitably—produced a proliferation of subcommittees.

Mansfield's Senate also saw a rapid expansion of staff. The Senate would grow from 4,100 employees in 1971 to more than 6,900 a decade later. Burned by its experience with the imperial presidencies of Johnson and Nixon, the Senate felt the need to "staff up," arming itself with additional expertise needed to deal effectively with the executive branch. A larger staff expanded a senator's reach, enabling him to get involved in more issues. But it also required a senator to spend more time supervising his staff members, or, more likely, giving many of them broader discretion than previously given. Senators often complained about the size and hyperactivity of their staffs, but almost all of them maximized the size of their staffs to the fullest extent possible.

The explosion of staff in the 1970's opened the Senate, for the first time, to professional women. Traditionally, the Senate had been, in the words of Daniel Patrick Moynihan, "a male preserve," and that extended from the senators themselves to the most influential committee and personal staff members. There were plenty of women staffers, but virtually all of them performed clerical or administrative tasks. Many were chosen on the basis of physical attractiveness, rather than professional competence. By the 1970's, it undoubtedly occurred to senators who were advocating the Equal Rights Amendment and Title IX of the Civil Rights Act that they were working in an environment where women had been largely deprived of equal opportunities. Beginning in that decade, some of Washington's talented women would make their mark in the Senate.

There were some awkward moments as the Senate adjusted to a changed environment. Joseph Biden, the thirty-year-old senator from Delaware who had taken office immediately after the tragic death of his wife and daughter in a car accident, interviewed Paula Stern for a position as his foreign policy adviser. Biden was impressed by Stern's academic and journalistic credentials. But he reluctantly decided against hiring her, telling her that he was afraid that there would be rumors about them if they traveled together. Stern took a job with Gaylord Nelson.

Robert Byrd was horrified when Mary Jane Checchi, the staff director of the Democratic Policy Committee, rushed into the Democratic cloakroom looking for a member. "Mary Jane," Byrd said, "women aren't allowed in the cloakroom." "Senator," Checchi responded, "I can't do my job if I can't go into the cloakroom." Byrd relented, accepting that times had changed.

Ed Muskie hired Madeleine Albright, a Georgetown professor, to be his senior legislative assistant. Several years later, Albright left his staff to work in the White House for National Security Adviser Zbigniew Brzezinski. At her farewell party, Muskie expressed pride that "Madeleine brought sex into the office." As those attending the party roared with laughter, Albright drily corrected him—"I think you mean 'gender,' Senator."

In contrast, Scoop Jackson had been far ahead of his time, entrusting Dorothy Fosdick with great authority in the area of defense and foreign policy beginning in 1954. In 1978, Jackson and Fosdick traveled to Saudi Arabia with a group of senators including Ted Stevens, and Susan Alvarado, a young legislative assistant. When the Saudis informed Stevens that the women would not be allowed in their meetings, Stevens shrugged his shoulders and told Alvarado: "When in Rome, do as the Romans do." When Jackson heard the Saudi position, he told Stevens that if the women were not allowed in the meetings, there would be no meetings. The meetings took place, with Fosdick and Alvarado included.

Even Lyndon Johnson's Senate had been slow-moving, quiet, often sleepy. The new arrivals—men and women—transformed the pace. Mostly young, ambitious, and policy-oriented, they were determined to serve the country and make their mark. The Senate office buildings grew crowded and crackled with energy, as the young lawyers, economists, and reporters who arrived competed to advance the interest of their bosses through new policy initiatives, and press releases and floor statements on the business of the day.

Useful as the expanded staff was, the Senatorial apparatus was becoming unwieldy. New senators, such as John Culver, who moved from the House in January 1975, were amazed by the chaos that greeted them. Starting in 1971, senators, led by Adlai Stevenson III of Illinois and Charles McC. Mathias Jr. of Maryland, had begun to complain about the proliferation of committee and subcommittee assignments, the irrationality of the committees' jurisdiction, and the bias against newer members. Stevenson pointed out that the lack of jurisdictional realignment meant that "we sometimes end up reinventing the wheel simultaneously in different subcommittees. And we often end up dealing with parts of an issue with no mechanism to put the parts together." Mansfield and Scott had established a select committee to study the problem, chaired by Stevenson, with Bill Brock of Tennessee as the ranking member. Hammering away at jurisdictional overlap, wasteful scheduling, and poor organization, Stevenson and Brock emphasized the fact that the average senator served on twenty committees, subcommittees, boards, and commissions.

In July 1976, the Stevenson Committee set forth recommendations for a major reorganization of the committee system. By prior arrangement, the recommendations would go to the Rules Committee, rather than directly to the full Senate, and it was in the Rules Committee that the ambitious proposals would collide with the realities of the Senate. While senators constantly complained about the committee system and their schedules being out of control, they also hated to lose power and influence over issues in which they were deeply invested, intellectually and emotionally.

For example, the fiercest fight within the Rules Committee broke out over who would have jurisdiction over the oceans. In recent years the crisis conditions of the oceans had emerged as a huge issue. Jacques Cousteau, the famed ocean explorer, had testified in 1971 that life in the sea had diminished by 30 to 50 percent over the last twenty years. Cousteau argued passionately that unless action was taken to combat pollution, the oceans would be dead in the next thirty to fifty years.

The Stevenson Committee had recommended that oceans be shifted from the Commerce Committee to a new Environment and Public Works Committee. That might make sense on an organizational chart. But Fritz Hollings had spent the summers of 1939 and 1940 when he was in college working with the Army Corps of Engineers on a project in Charleston Harbor. Thirty years later, as a senator, he had become chairman of the Oceans and Atmosphere Subcommittee of the Commerce Committee. In eight years in that position, he had become an expert on the problems of the oceans. He had spearheaded such landmark legislation as the Ocean Dumping Act, the Coastal Zone Management Act, the Marine Mammals Protection Act, and the creation of the National Oceanic and Atmospheric Administration (NOAA). Along with the popular and powerful Warren Magnuson, who chaired the full Commerce Committee, Hollings pushed back fiercely, and the Rules Committee reversed Stevenson's recommendation, leaving oceans in Commerce. For good measure, the Commerce Committee also expanded its reach by acquiring jurisdiction over the science and technology functions of the government, including the space program, which had previously been handled by a separate committee on Aeronautical and Space Sciences.

The new Energy and Natural Resources Committee was intended to have the broad jurisdiction needed over production and conservation needed to address the nation's problems. The Post Office and Civil Service Committee would be abolished, its functions to be handed over to an enhanced Governmental Affairs Committee. George McGovern's high-profile Select Committee on Hunger and Nutrition would be folded into the Agriculture Committee, which would become Agriculture, Nutrition, and Forestry. Gaylord Nelson, chair of the Small Business Committee, indicated a willingness to support his own committee being abolished—but the small business community pushed back so hard that the Senate reversed Stevenson's recommendation and preserved it.

Finally, reorganization had been talked about long enough. Byrd and Baker had made it the first order of business for the new Senate. On February 4, the Senate approved S. Res. 4, the reorganization that had been negotiated by the Stevenson Committee, the Rules Committee, and the Senate leadership. The number of committees did decrease by 23 percent and the number of subcommittees decreased by 33 percent. Senators would have fewer assignments by about one-third. Younger senators were major winners; they would be able to serve on two major committees plus a minor committee if desired; they would receive improved choice of subcommittees and more and better chairmanships. The minority party would be guaranteed a bigger share of the committees' budgets. Stevenson described the result as "incremental idealism." The new leaders Byrd and Baker could take satisfaction in the fact that they had delivered quickly on the promise to reorganize, without much blood being spilled. Far more difficult battles still loomed, however.

JIMMY CARTER'S ENERGY PROGRAM would have to be shepherded through the Senate by Scoop Jackson, the chairman of the new Energy Committee. Jackson was a masterful legislator who shared Carter's belief that America's energy dependency was an urgent problem. Jackson also had a strong relationship with Schlesinger, whom he greatly respected. But the personal chemistry between Carter and Jackson was terrible. Carter had crushed Jackson's hopes of being president, and he and his people had gone on to rub salt in Jackson's wounds. (Hamilton Jordan, one of Carter's closest aides, had observed that they didn't need to cultivate Jackson because "we whipped his ass in the Pennsylvania primary.") Jackson also disliked Carter's penchant for wearing religion on his sleeve and maintained grave doubts about his capacity to govern.

The relationship was fraught with danger, and it would have to carry a lot of weight if Carter's presidency was to succeed. Carter's best hope was that Jackson was a patriot who could rise above his personal feelings. The energy challenges would be hard enough—but in the end, Henry Jackson had another overriding priority. He planned to be Jimmy Carter's most formidable adversary on issues of national security.

chapter 4

HAWK
AND
DOVE

WHEN GERALD FORD ASSUMED THE PRESIDENCY AFTER RICHARD NIXON'S
resignation, his first words to the nation were his most memorable: "Our long
national nightmare is over." And yet, eloquent as Ford's formulation may have
been, it was fundamentally inaccurate—at least from the Senate's perspective.
For the senators, nothing had ever been more intriguing, enthralling, dramatic, and ultimately satisfying than Watergate. The Senate Watergate Committee played an extraordinary role in holding Nixon accountable. Its
hearings revealing the sordid nature of the Nixon White House captivated
the nation in the summer of 1973. The press, courts, special prosecutor, and
the House Judiciary Committee also played key parts in exposing Nixon's
abuses of power and ushering him offstage. With the stakes very high, the
American system of government came through with flying colors.

In contrast, for the Senate and for America, Vietnam had been the true
national nightmare.

The Senate had focused on the unfolding debacle in Vietnam since 1965.
Many had to live down the mistake of putting their trust in Lyndon Johnson
when they gave him the Gulf of Tonkin resolution in August 1964, which he
twisted into a virtual declaration of war, justifying a rapid and open-ended
escalation that put more than 500,000 American military men in Vietnam
and tore the country apart.

Numerous senators, among them Mike Mansfield, Frank Church, Wayne Morse, Albert Gore Sr., Stuart Symington, Richard Russell, John McClellan, and J. William Fulbright, all tried privately to convince Johnson that he was pursuing a disastrous course. Although haunted by doubts about the course he had chosen, Johnson rejected the senators' advice. He mocked Mansfield as a weak-kneed professor and described Fulbright as a racist who didn't care about Vietnam because the people were not white.

Fulbright would never forget the day in late July 1965 when he brought an impressive group of senators to the White House to implore Johnson to stop the escalation. Johnson coldly told the senators that the situation in Vietnam was deteriorating, the decision had been made, the war would last six or seven years, and there was no turning back.

Democratic senators soon became increasingly public in their opposition to the president of their own party. As chairman of the Foreign Relations Committee, Fulbright convened a major set of hearings in February 1966, which laid bare the weakness of the rationale for the Vietnam War. The hearings produced an indelible image: Fulbright had to wear sunglasses to shield his eyes from the phalanx of television lights. And Fulbright's hearings marked the moment that opposition to the war began to move from the students on college campuses to their parents in middle-class America. But Johnson's escalation continued.

In late 1967, Senator Eugene McCarthy decided that the war could be stopped only if Johnson were driven from office. He challenged Johnson for the Democratic nomination, and his improbable campaign, fueled by the passions of antiwar opponents including thousands of college students, caught fire. Senator Robert Kennedy of New York, also an opponent of the war, belatedly joined the Democratic contest. The combined challenge of McCarthy and Kennedy succeeded. On March 31, 1968, Johnson shocked the nation by announcing he would not seek reelection and began to explore a negotiated settlement. Yet the Vietnam War raged on, proving far more difficult to stop than it had been to start.

Richard Nixon took office in January 1969, having promised a "secret plan" to end the war. After a few months, it was clear that Nixon's plan—"Vietnamization"—by which South Vietnam would gradually assume the responsibilities for the war as Americans came home—had flaws of its own. The leaders of South Vietnam, and its military, had no interest in stepping up to the responsibilities Nixon envisioned for them; the war was likely to continue for years unless Congress intervened.

In one of its defining moments of greatness, the Senate stepped forward, becoming the cockpit of national opposition to the Vietnam War. Just as Democrats had to lead opposition to Johnson, Republicans now assumed leadership roles in opposing Nixon's stewardship of the war. Starting in 1969, Republicans John Sherman Cooper, Clifford Case, Mark Hatfield, Charles Goodell—just appointed to fill Robert Kennedy's seat—and Jacob Javits worked hand in hand with Democrats Frank Church, George McGovern, and Tom Eagleton on legislation to cut off funding for the war and reassert the constitutional role of Congress in declaring war. For almost four years, the quest to stop the war became the Senate's raison d'être.

In 1971, five years after his first set of hearings had questioned the rationale for the war, Fulbright convened a new series of hearings, providing a forum for a new group of opponents to the war. On April 22, 1971, a riveted nation heard the eloquent testimony of navy veteran John Kerry, one of the leaders of Vietnam Veterans Against the War. Testifying for two hours, Kerry brought the human costs of the war home and demolished the intellectual arguments of those who defended the war. "It was the moment," Kerry remembered, "that the soldiers tried to stop the war."

That same week, Jacob Javits hosted a dinner for Secretary of Defense Melvin Laird. Eight Republican senators and House members came to the dinner with one message. "You don't see any hawks around here," Senate Minority Leader Hugh Scott told Laird. "The hawks are all ex-hawks. There's a feeling that the Senate ought to tell the President that we should get the hell out of the War."

By late 1972, Congress was prepared to pass the Church-Case amendment, which would cut off all funding for the war, excepting those funds needed to withdraw U.S. forces from Vietnam. The Nixon administration temporarily forestalled that action by seeking a little more time to negotiate. On January 27, 1973, the Paris Peace Accords ended U.S. involvement in Vietnam and temporarily stopped the hostilities between North and South Vietnam. These accords were a direct response to the Senate's pressure.

Two years later, North Vietnam invaded the South and overran Saigon, the South Vietnamese capital. Americans were left with the indelible image of U.S. embassy personnel escaping by helicopter as Saigon fell on April 30, 1975. The United States had suffered its first military defeat, but the war had finally ended.

Along with Watergate, the tragedy of Vietnam was certainly a major factor in Jimmy Carter's unexpected race to the White House. The effects of Vietnam would ripple through American life for decades; its lessons for policymakers would be debated endlessly. For the senators, the Vietnam experience taught one lesson with brutal clarity: no president could be fully trusted, so the Senate must play a major role in shaping national security policy. Although he was no dove, no one held that view more strongly than Scoop Jackson.

HARD WORKING, HONEST, AND deeply committed to public service and the country, Henry "Scoop" Jackson was at least as much of a straight arrow as Jimmy Carter. Having reached Washington thirty-six years before Carter's election, he had been on Capitol Hill since Carter was fifteen years old. Even if they had not run against each other for president, tensions were probably inevitable. Their personalities would clash, and so would their worldviews.

The fifth child in a Norwegian family, Jackson grew up in Everett, Washington, a rough-and-tumble lumber town of 30,000. From the beginning, his parents, teachers, and friends found him uncommonly serious and hard working. One of his closest high school friends later commented: "[Scoop] had a fixidity of purpose, received good advice and uniquely followed it. He never took the detours that others of us took. . . . He was a very honorable man."

Those qualities were in short supply in Everett after Jackson graduated from law school. Prohibition had come to America, and Everett became a center for bootlegging; corruption spread to the local law enforcement officials. When the state attorney came under suspicion of corruption, the twenty-six-year-old Jackson sought the office and won handily. After several prominent prosecutions earned him significant publicity and a fine reputation, he ran for Congress two years later. He arrived in Washington in January 1941, aged twenty-eight, the youngest member of the House of Representatives at a moment of great national and international stress. By the end of the year, the United States would be plunged into war against Japan and Germany.

The threat posed by the Soviet Union to the United States would become the central focus of Jackson's career. After spending twelve years in the House, Jackson won election to the Senate in 1952. Once there, he educated himself about national security issues, serving on the Joint Atomic Energy Committee at precisely the time when the Soviet Union exploded its first atomic bomb. Jackson saw the United States as being in an arms race with the Soviet Union, but also in a moral and ideological struggle. He believed that the Soviet Union could be deterred only through evidence of overwhelming U.S. military strength. He mistrusted arms control negotiations, doubting that the Soviets would adhere to any agreement they signed. He had only contempt for those who believed that restraint exercised by the United States in defense spending would be reciprocated by the Soviets.

Jackson built a network of defense experts and scientists who ensured that he would be the most informed member on the issues that mattered to him. He benefited from the extraordinary talents of Dorothy Fosdick, who came to work for him in the Senate in 1955, after being the first woman ever to hold high-level positions in the State Department, on the Policy Planning Staff and as a member of the U.S. delegation to the newly created United Nations. Fosdick stayed with Jackson for twenty-eight years as his principal foreign policy adviser. Secretaries of State and Defense—not to mention presidents—came and went, but Jackson and Fosdick stayed on, relentlessly pursuing the issues of national security that mattered most to the senator. In 1969, Richard Perle joined Jackson's staff and quickly became a Senate legend in his own right, exerting more influence on U.S. foreign and defense policy than most senators.

The depth of Jackson's knowledge and his relentlessness made him a feared adversary in Senate debates. Forty years after it happened, Bob Packwood still spoke in awe about the greatest debate he ever heard in the Senate, when Jackson had squared off against Stuart Symington, a former secretary of the Air Force, and Fulbright in a rare closed debate of the Senate over the Anti-Ballistic Missile (ABM) system in 1969. Packwood recited from memory Jackson's devastating rebuttal of Fulbright's naïve assessment of Soviet intentions.

The peak of Jackson's power came during Nixon's presidency, which saw the most successful Cold Warrior of his era change course, working to defuse tensions with the Soviet Union. Commentators often observed that only Nixon, whose anti-Communist credentials were beyond question, could have opened the door to China, or sought détente with the Soviet Union.

Jackson had adamantly opposed Nixon's policy of détente. He deplored Nixon's willingness to overlook the Soviet regime's abuses of human rights and mistreatment of dissidents. And, initially with very few allies, Jackson found a legislative instrument that made it possible to elevate human rights as a major objective of U.S. foreign policy and to block Nixon's effort to promote détente. Along with House member Charles Vanik, Jackson wrote legislation to condition trade benefits for the Soviet Union on the willingness of the Soviet leaders to allow Jews to emigrate freely.

Throughout the mid-1970's, Jackson virtually stymied the Nixon-Kissinger policy of détente with the Soviet Union. Kissinger ruefully recognized Jackson to be his most effective and persuasive critic. It is possible that no single senator had wielded as much power over U.S. foreign policy since Henry Cabot Lodge blocked President Woodrow Wilson's League of Nations from being approved by the U.S. Senate in 1919.

Jackson sought the Democratic nomination for president in 1972 but did not make it to the first tier of candidates. After George McGovern was crushed by Nixon in the 1972 election, Jackson's admirers concluded that the moment was at last right for Jackson. They believed that the combination of Jackson's domestic liberalism and his hard-line foreign policy views made him an ideal Democratic candidate against Gerald Ford, an unpopular president who was continuing Kissinger's policy of détente. They were quite certain that the Democratic Party had learned that weakness on national security issues was politically disastrous, and they saw Jackson as the natural candidate of the labor unions and the Jewish community, which were powerful pillars of the Democratic Party. Jackson hoped that the end of the Vietnam War "would mollify the bitter hostility that antiwar activists felt toward him."

It was wishful thinking. While the Democrats would probably not nominate anyone as dovish as McGovern, "the Democratic party primary voters were not going to elect an anti-Soviet hardliner in 1976," as Senator Daniel Patrick Moynihan later observed. Carter not only had the advantage of being able to run against Washington; he had benefited during the campaign from leaving his views on foreign policy and defense somewhat undefined. Jackson lost the nomination, and had to console himself with an easy, virtually unopposed, reelection to a fifth term in the Senate.

When Jackson met with Carter during the transition, he still maintained some hope that Carter could be brought around to his more hawkish point of view. The president-elect was a Naval Academy graduate and a protégé of Admiral Hyman Rickover, the father of the nuclear navy—not a resumé that indicated adherence to the McGovern wing of the party. Carter also had a close relationship with Schlesinger, President Ford's secretary of defense, whose views were close to Jackson's. The Coalition for a Democratic Majority, a group of hawkish Democrats focused on the Soviet threat, cochaired by Jackson and Moynihan, suggested no fewer than fifty-three right-thinking candidates for positions in the new administration. And Carter had seemed to listen attentively to Jackson when they met. But Jackson's hopes were dashed as soon as the president-elect announced his national security team.

First of all, Jackson shared the general amazement that Carter had chosen Theodore Sorensen to be the director of the Central Intelligence Agency. It wasn't that he was an unknown quantity—Jackson had known Sorensen since the mid-1950's when Sorensen had chosen to work for Jack Kennedy, the rising star in the Senate with presidential aspirations, instead of Jackson. In fact, Jackson would have enthusiastically supported Sorensen for a position like attorney general—he was more than qualified for that—but he found nothing in his background to suggest that Sorensen could take on the leadership of the troubled CIA. Jackson's instinct was sound. Sorensen's nomination was withdrawn very quickly, after the revelations that he had registered for the draft as a conscientious objector and removed classified information without proper authorization when serving in the Kennedy White House. It was an early embarrassment to the new president.

But Jackson was much more dismayed and angered by Carter's choices regarding the issues that mattered most to him: arms control negotiations and the threat posed by the Soviet Union. Every one of the Coalition for a Democratic Majority's choices were rejected. Instead, Carter had chosen to name the same person to two jobs simultaneously, filling the position of director of the Arms Control and Disarmament Agency (ACDA) and chief negotiator on U.S.-Soviet arms limitations in a stroke. Unlike Sorensen, the nominee was undoubtedly qualified; but from Jackson's standpoint, Carter had chosen perhaps the most wrong-headed person imaginable for dealing with the intentions and capabilities of the Soviet Union.

Paul Warnke epitomized the views and sensibilities of the Democratic doves that Jackson detested. He had served as the principal adviser to Senator George McGovern in his 1972 presidential campaign, and in 1975, Warnke highlighted his availability for a cabinet position in the next Democratic administration by writing a major article published in *Foreign Policy*, entitled "Apes on a Treadmill." In his article, Warnke described the United States as the principal culprit in the perpetuation of an arms race that left both superpowers armed to the teeth and feeling more insecure. Warnke believed that "the superpower aping has meant the absence of restraint," but the United States could "present a worthier model. . . . We can be the first off the treadmill."

If Warnke saw the Soviet Union as "aping" the behavior of the United States, Jackson imagined the Soviet Union as a burglar, going house to house, eager to take advantage of vulnerabilities anywhere they presented themselves. He believed that the Soviet Union was aggressively moving forward to capitalize on U.S. weakness and uncertainty after the Vietnam debacle, and that the Soviet Union could not be trusted to adhere to any agreement that it signed. Where Warnke envisioned the superpowers working in tandem, restraining themselves and reducing arms, Jackson's overriding interest was ensuring the superiority of U.S. military strength. In short, as far as Cold War and arms race strategy was concerned, Warnke and Jackson were polar opposites, and Warnke's nomination was a harbinger of the new president's aggressive approach to arms control.

Jimmy Carter assumed the presidency with the historical legacy of the arms control efforts of Presidents Richard Nixon and Gerald Ford and Secretary of State Henry Kissinger. A central aspect of the Nixon-Kissinger policy of détente with the Soviets had been the Strategic Arms Limitation Talks (SALT). In May 1972, Nixon and Soviet Premier Leonid Brehznev announced, with great fanfare, that the United States and the Soviet Union had reached historic arms control accords. SALT I was a five-year, interim agreement, specifying the number of intercontinental ballistic missiles (ICBMs) and submarine-launched ballistic missiles (SLBMs) that each country could have, while imposing no restrictions on strategic bombers. SALT I actually allowed the Soviet Union a greater number of ICBMs and SLBMs than the United States, but the Nixon administration argued that those numerical advantages were more than offset by the technological advantages that the United States had, particularly with respect to MIRV missiles, a collection of nuclear weapons carried on a single ICBM, each of which could be independently targeted.

SALT I was accompanied by an Antiballistic Missile (ABM) Defense System Treaty, which allowed the United States and the Soviet Union no more than two ABM sites, with one hundred interceptors each—one deployed around the nation's capital and one deployed to safeguard a limited portion of the nation's ICBM launchers. The theory behind that ABM Treaty was that nuclear war would be more likely if either side thought it could put in place a comprehensive missile defense system, because it would embolden that country to consider a first strike since the other country could not effectively retaliate.

On June 1, 1972, Richard Nixon told a joint session of Congress that the SALT I Interim Agreement and the ABM Treaty represented a historic turning point, ushering in a new era of international relations. By giving up missile defense, Nixon contended, the United States and the Soviet Union had accepted the same basic premise of mutual assured destruction, so that both countries had the same interest in preventing a nuclear war. Henry Kissinger described the summit as "one of the greatest diplomatic coups of all time." Kissinger, of course, was hardly objective, but Congress, the press, and most Americans responded enthusiastically to the SALT accords reached in Moscow. It was the high-water mark of détente between the superpowers.

Henry Jackson, however, had not been caught up in the general euphoria. He disliked the limitation on the number of ABM installations, believing that it constrained the United States from using its technological superiority to build a comprehensive missile defense. He contended that SALT I had not allowed the United States enough launchers to prevent a Soviet first strike. He ultimately gave his support to the Interim Agreement, but conditioned it on the Senate adoption of a Jackson amendment, in September 1972, stating that the future treaty (SALT II) had to assure the United States of parity in levels of intercontinental strategic forces. It also expressed the sense of Congress that a more permanent and comprehensive agreement was dependent on "the maintenance of a vigorous research and development and modernization program" of America's nuclear arsenal.

Two years later, in November 1974, President Gerald Ford and Brezhnev reached the Vladivostok Agreement, their framework for a SALT II treaty. That agreement posed equal ceilings of 2,400 intercontinental delivery vehicles and limited each side to 1,320 MIRV vehicles. It placed no constraints, however, on Soviet heavy missiles, forward-based systems, or missile modernization.

Jackson condemned the results of Vladivostok, arguing that it sanctioned a massive Soviet arms buildup because of the "astonishingly high" level of MIRV missiles that were permitted. He also objected to the exclusion from coverage of Soviet Backfire bombers and any constraints on the number or range of U.S. cruise missiles. Jackson's bottom line for SALT II was equal ceilings at sharply reduced levels, rather than consenting to "an arms buildup agreement." James Schlesinger, then Ford's secretary of defense, shared Jackson's opposition to Vladivostok, which further strengthened the friendship between the two men, but also led to Schlesinger being fired from his post as Pentagon chief. Opposition to the Ford-Kissinger approach to SALT II became one of the central arguments made by Ronald Reagan in challenging Ford for the Republican nomination in 1976.

Against this background, Jimmy Carter came to office intensely committed to seeking a new approach to arms control negotiations. He wrote to Soviet General Secretary Leonid Brezhnev on this subject less than a week after his inauguration. Six days later, he invited the longtime Soviet Ambassador Anatoly Dobrynin to the Oval Office and startled the wily and experienced Russian by combining a commitment to continuing the SALT II talks with an outline of a dramatically different set of proposals. Carter envisioned establishing prior notification of any test missile launchings, a comprehensive test ban, demilitarization of the Indian Ocean, and, most sweepingly, deep cuts in total nuclear weapons with exact confirmable equality of strength. Carter's goal was to complete the SALT II treaty, a daunting task in itself, in order to move on to even larger reductions in nuclear arsenals.

At first glance, Jimmy Carter's commitment to deep reductions in nuclear arsenals seemed to parallel Scoop Jackson's call for sharply reduced levels of nuclear weapons. It was an illusion; the distance between Carter and Warnke, on the one hand, and Jackson on the other, was an unbridgeable chasm. The new president believed that meaningful and verifiable arms control agreements could be negotiated with the Soviet Union, and that the national security of the United States, and world peace, depended on doing so. Jackson didn't share any of those beliefs. He and his allies believed that Carter's approach to the Soviet Union was naïve and dangerous—"McGovernism without McGovern." There would be no honeymoon on foreign and defense policy for the new president.

UP UNTIL THIS POINT, new presidents had always received great latitude to make their key appointments. In fact, the Senate had never in its history rejected a cabinet-level appointment by a new president. Scoop Jackson determined that where Paul Warnke was concerned, it was time to make history. Jackson's formidable staff would prepare him to go after Warnke fiercely.

The Foreign Relations Committee, which had jurisdiction over Warnke's nomination, held the first hearings on his nomination on February 7 and 8. Warnke glided through the dovish committee, despite some serious contradictions between his testimony and some of the positions that he had taken earlier. Even so, Paul Nitze, who had resigned as the country's SALT I negotiator and was known for his hard-line position, testified strongly against

Warnke. The Coalition for a Democratic Majority, a neoconservative group with close ties to Jackson, began circulating a memo accusing Warnke of favoring unilateral disarmament.

Prior to the Foreign Relations Committee, Robert Byrd had seen no reason that Warnke would not be confirmed. But following the hearings, Byrd's comments were much more negative. Noting that he was keeping "an open mind on the nomination," Byrd acknowledged that "many senators think he is too soft to negotiate with the Soviet Union." Howard Baker, impressed by Nitze's testimony, said that Warnke had "been damaged by it. I have grave doubts that he can do the job." With Jackson and other hard-line senators already opposed, a nominee without support from Byrd or Baker was a nominee destined to crash and burn.

Typically, Carter wasn't easily deterred. Over the next few days, the Carter administration scrambled to make the case for Warnke even more strongly. Just a week later, on February 18, Byrd reversed himself, now predicting that Warnke would be confirmed by a wide margin. He elaborated that "it would be bad to send a man over there who is just confirmed by a vote of 60–40. If we're going to confirm him, we ought to confirm him with the kind of support that will let the Soviets know that we . . . intend to back up a strong negotiator. As of today, I'd say he should be confirmed by a substantial majority . . . over ⅔."

Byrd was plainly struggling to balance his loyalty to the Democratic president, his leadership of the Senate, and his own tough views about the Soviet Union. His argument why a strong Senate vote on Warnke was important was much better suited to quiet lobbying of undecided senators than to public musing. By predicting an overwhelming victory, Byrd was actually setting a standard that would be difficult to reach. Jackson and other Warnke opponents were doubtless quite pleased by this statement.

The stage was set for a bruising hearing in the more hawkish Armed Services Committee. Because it did not have primary jurisdiction over the nomination, the committee would not vote on Warnke's confirmation, but the committee Republicans were hitting Warnke hard, charging that he had opposed virtually every weapons system modernization of the past decade. Of course, no Republican made the case as powerfully as Jackson.

During a long line of tough questions, Jackson endeavored to obliterate the nominee. He named thirteen missiles systems and weapons upgrades, then asked Warnke to confirm that he had opposed every one of them.

Warnke admitted that he had, but claimed that he had since modified many of his positions because the superpowers had subsequently proceeded with new weapons deployments.

Jackson and the Republicans had the advantage. There was sufficient ammunition to charge that with his nomination in jeopardy, Warnke was walking back from many of his positions and describing himself as more hawkish than he had been. "I don't think there were 25 votes against him three weeks ago," Jackson said on the eve of his confirmation vote, but now many additional senators had come to doubt his intellectual honesty.

Yet the nominee's fate was not quite sealed. Many Democrats had already committed to Warnke. Others, whatever doubts they might have, were deeply concerned that rejecting the nominee would be a devastating blow to President Carter, who had already suffered the humiliation of Sorensen's withdrawal as the nominee for CIA director. Despite his opposition, Jackson would not filibuster the Warnke nomination. He felt that he had made his point powerfully enough and guaranteed that any arms control treaty negotiated by Warnke would be highly suspect in the Senate.

On March 9, after four days of sometimes acrimonious debate, Paul Warnke's nomination to be the head of ACDA was confirmed by a 70–29 vote. However, he was confirmed as SALT negotiator by only a 58-40 vote. President Carter and Vice President Mondale lobbied intensively for the nomination, convincing at least a dozen senators that confirmation was crucial. It was a solid majority but far from a strong vote of confidence, given the fact that the SALT II treaty, his principal negotiating responsibility, would require a two-thirds vote of the Senate for confirmation.

Jimmy Carter would have his nominee, but the president and Warnke had been put on notice by Scoop Jackson and the Senate. Ideas that sounded good in the McGovern campaign in 1972 or *Foreign Policy* magazine in 1975 were not likely to cut it in the U.S. Senate in 1977 and onward.

THE BATTLE OVER WARNKE and the coming clashes over arms control treaties both pivoted on one crucial fact: Jimmy Carter had a deep abhorrence of nuclear weapons. He envisioned a world free from nuclear weapons and was anxious to reach an agreement with the Soviet Union where both countries actually made deep cuts in their nuclear arsenals. Carter thought he saw an opportunity to gain Jackson's support by going far beyond the Vladivostok formula reached by Ford and Brezhnev in 1974.

In March, shortly after Warnke's confirmation, Carter sent Secretary of State Cyrus Vance to Moscow carrying two alternative proposals. Carter's principal proposal departed radically from the Vladivostok formula to include (1) substantial reductions in the number of strategic weapons on both sides; (2) a freeze in the number of MIRV missiles; and (3) a moratorium on the development of new missiles. Vance, who had never met Brezhnev, was put in the position of making the strongest SALT demands ever made, amidst a negotiation that Kissinger had claimed was "90% complete." Vance's backup proposal simply embodied the Vladivostok limits in a treaty and deferred action on the Backfire bomber and the Cruise missile.

It was a bold bid to break with the Nixon-Ford-Kissinger approach to arms control. It was probably the only way to unify the U.S. arms control advocates and the U.S. hard-liners because it represented real reductions and would have prevented either country from developing a missile force that could destroy the other country's ICBMs. But Moscow flatly rejected it. Observers speculated that the proposals were turned down because of the new administration's criticism of the Soviet Union on human rights, or the fact that the proposals were put forth in detail publicly before being presented to the Soviets.

Jackson later told a breakfast meeting of reporters that Carter had "taken a giant step in cutting back on arms levels." But he questioned whether springing the proposals on the Soviets was a good idea, noting "frankly, I would not have gone public on this. . . . You never want to push them into a corner in public," Jackson commented. The Soviets "are accustomed to negotiate under the rules of privacy." But now, "everything is in the sunshine."

Perhaps a bit wiser for its early missteps, the administration bent over backwards to share information with the Senate. On May 27, Vance had a two-hour meeting with Senate leaders on both sides of the aisle. Jackson characterized it as a breakthrough on information sharing with the Senate. On May 30, the *Washington Post* observed that "Carter may have invested as much effort clearing the Capitol Hill path for continuance of new arms talks as he did for the actual Geneva negotiations." The *Post* went on to say that "each of them carries almost equal priority for administration strategists. And both are tenuous."

It was not long before Carter realized that pursuing Jackson was futile. Any agreement that the Soviet Union might sign was anathema to Jackson, and vice versa. An editorial in *Pravda,* the Soviet government organ, slammed

Carter's proposal, in large part because, as one Soviet analyst put it: "Anything that Jackson likes so much has to be bad for us."

It would soon become clear that Jackson and other hard-liners would use the administration's proposal as a benchmark against which they could attack the less comprehensive agreement that would ultimately emerge. Moreover, Jackson's brilliant and hyperactive staff members did not hesitate to use the administration's briefings to sharpen their criticisms of Carter's efforts, subjecting them to withering attacks through favored news outlets, particularly the widely read columns of Evans and Novak.

JACKSON WAS NOT THE only senator determined to play an important role in foreign policy. Immediately after the 1976 election, twelve senators, led by Abraham Ribicoff and Howard Baker, had spent eighteen days visiting Israel, Egypt, Jordan, and Iran. They had focused principally on the prospects for peace in the Middle East, pending nuclear power reactor sales in the region, and U.S. policy toward Iran. Codel (short for "Congressional Delegation") Ribicoff issued its report on the prospects for peace in the Middle East and U.S. policy toward Iran on February 10, three weeks after Carter's inauguration.

The Codel's s report on meetings with the leaders of Israel and Egypt combined familiar observations with interesting insights. "The predominant apprehension in Israel," the report noted, "is a sense of insecurity and fear of continuing hostility and attack from terrorists or from Israel's neighbors." Yitzhak Rabin, the Israeli prime minister and a renowned general, told the Codel grimly that no Arab nation had shown a willingness to deal directly with Israel or acknowledge Israel's right to exist. But the Codel had also reported that Anwar Sadat had stressed that "1977 must be a year to reach a peace settlement." Sadat had said that Egypt would start peace negotiations without preconditions. Most importantly, the Codel reported that "for the first time Arab leaders are willing to recognize the right of Israel to exist as an independent and secure Jewish state."

The five days spent in Iran warranted special attention. The fortunes of the United States had been tied to Shah Mohamed Reza Pahlavi for nearly a quarter century, since the U.S.-backed coup in 1953 that toppled Premier Mohammed Mossadegh, who had expressed determination to nationalize oil production in Iran. Pahlavi, then only thirty-three, but handsome, fluent in English and French, educated in Switzerland, and dedicated to the Westernization of his country, became the leader of Iran. Every president since

1953 had regarded him as an ally and a friend. U.S. reliance on the shah only intensified after the 1973 Yom Kippur War and the OPEC oil embargo, which made it clear just how precarious western oil supplies were.

The Codel report noted that "strategically, Iran is an important friend in a critical and unstable part of the world. Iran needs support to maintain its integrity free of Soviet influence." Moreover, the United States and its allies had an enormous stake in protecting "the oil lifeline from the Gulf oil producers through the Straits of Hormuz." The report noted that while 18 percent of U.S. oil came through the Straits, Europe depended on the Gulf for 52 percent of its oil; Japan for 75 percent. Since Britain had withdrawn from the Gulf in 1971, the United States had relied on Iran for the defense capacity to ensure that the Straits stayed open and had sold arms to Iran accordingly. By 1976, Iran had become the leading recipient of U.S. arms sales, with a long list of requests for advanced weaponry still in the pipeline, including a request for the Airborne Warning and Control System (AWACS).

The delegation intentionally avoided staking a position on the merits of any particular arms sale. But it clearly and repeatedly characterized Iran as "an essential ally" and "important friend," and that the requests should be evaluated in light of Iran's crucial role in the Straits and its vulnerability to Soviet pressure, either directly or through Iraq, a Soviet client state.

Of late, human rights groups had been increasingly critical of conditions in the shah's Iran, focusing particularly on allegations of torture committed by SAVAK, Iran's security police. The senators took up the human rights issue with the shah and other officials. "Recent developments give cause for both optimism and dismay," the report noted. "The Government and the Shah himself appear receptive to international concern." On the other hand, reports of torture by SAVAK continue to be reported in the press. Detailing advances in education, health care, literacy, land reform, and voting rights, including voting rights for women, the report concluded that "the 'Shah-people' revolution of the past two decades has involved extensive and basic changes in all aspects of life. . . . Through a considerable social change a middle class is emerging. Many of the positive goals of human rights movements are being reached through the rapid development of Iran."

This view of the situation in Iran was much too optimistic for two Codel members, Thomas Eagleton of Missouri and John Culver of Iowa, two of the Senate's most liberal Democrats, both well known for straight talk. They exercised their right to file separate views from the majority. Eagleton and

Culver contended that the new administration "should consider the risk that massive arms sales may not contribute to regional stability and the continuing flow of oil—if such sales increase rivalries and instability within or among nations of the area or if they lead to conflicts which halt the flow of oil." They stated their basic concern emphatically: "Our relations with Iran are far too dependent on a highly personalized relationship with the Shah."

The Iran we visited, Eagleton and Culver wrote, "is a society slowly emerging from extreme underdevelopment. Despite a high degree of social and economic activity, Iran is still decades away from acquiring the infrastructure necessary to absorb the influx of foreign ideas and technology." They reviewed the specific requests made by Iran for F-14s and the AWACS and concluded that Iran could not use either effectively without massive assistance from the U.S. military and Boeing Corporation.

Eagleton and Culver disagreed with the majority of the delegation on Iran's progress: "On the evidence available to us, we believe that Iran is an authoritarian nation whose internal policies often appear antithetical to American values." They concluded: "We should therefore act according to our own interests. . . . We cannot subordinate our disagreements to ritual demonstrations of friendship or declarations of 'special relationships.' Arms sales, for example, must not be taken as tokens of commitment or proof of close relations, but rather only when both sides benefit."

Jimmy Carter's foreign policy views were premised on a deep commitment to human rights. But in Iran, plainly, where human rights were concerned, even experienced senators could disagree on whether the glass was half full or half empty. As a candidate, Carter had sharply criticized America's emergence as the world's leading arms supplier. Now, however, focused on economic and energy issues, SALT II, and his first steps toward bringing Israel and Egypt together, Jimmy Carter chose to be optimistic about Iran. He noted in his diary that he would continue: "as other presidents had before me, to consider the Shah a strong ally." Consequently, his administration would continue major arms sales to Iran. It was an understandable decision—and one he would come to greatly regret.

THE DISSENTS FROM CULVER and Eagleton presaged a problem for the president altogether different from the likes of Scoop Jackson and his hawks. As it turned out, Carter would also face a serious threat from the liberal wing of the Democratic Party, especially with respect to his domestic program.

His commitment to combating inflation by balancing the federal budget threatened cuts in programs favored by many Democratic constituencies. The liberal groups could issue their own critiques, but they also could rely on leading senators whose views would command widespread attention.

With the possible exception of Ted Kennedy, George McGovern was the best-known representative of the liberal wing of the Democratic Party. McGovern had always doubted Carter's liberalism and was appalled at how long Carter had supported the Vietnam War. Wanting a Democrat in the White House, he encouraged the party to unify behind Carter, offering an unusual endorsement at the 1976 Democratic Convention: "If any of us have disagreements with Governor Carter, let us save them for President Carter."

He did not hold back long. After Carter was in office less than one hundred days, in April 1977 McGovern "suggested that the Carter administration was trying to balance the budget on the backs of the poor and the jobless; that our great cities were deteriorating while the Administration held back on public investment and the reform of our tax, welfare, health and railway systems." Carter responded, perhaps reasonably, that it was too early for that type of judgment, but McGovern's experiences during the Johnson and Nixon presidencies had convinced him that it was preferable to speak out strongly, early, rather than wait until it was too late.

Of the extraordinary group of Democratic senators elected in 1962, George McGovern's trajectory had been the most remarkable. Ten years before coming to the Senate, McGovern, the son of a Methodist minister from Mitchell, South Dakota, and a World War II bomber pilot, had been a thirty-year-old professor of political science and history at Dakota Wesleyan, just completing his Ph.D. at Northwestern University. With an earnest demeanor, ordinary looks, and reedy voice, McGovern seemed more naturally suited to the pulpit or the campus than the political world. But politics was his chosen realm. He was a liberal and an idealist inspired not only by the eloquence of Adlai Stevenson but by the activism and policy entrepreneurialism of Hubert Humphrey from the neighboring state of Minnesota.

After the 1952 election of President Dwight D. Eisenhower, the Republicans held every major office in South Dakota. In the state Senate of thirty-five members, no Democrats had been elected. The seventy-five-member state House was slightly better; there were two Democrats. McGovern saw the chance to build the Democratic Party in South Dakota, and he did not have much competition for the dubious honor of trying to do so.

McGovern began driving across South Dakota. He met with Democrats in all sixty-seven counties and found men and women whose liberalism, in his words, "had been refined in the fires of opposition, ridicule, and in some cases, the penalty of social and professional discrimination." Within a few years, McGovern built the state Democratic Party from nothing to a competitive position. His intellect, energy, and unmistakable decency helped him get elected to the House of Representatives in 1956. After his reelection in 1958, he immediately started planning a Senate race against Republican Senator Karl Mundt, an affable and adroit campaigner, who played effectively on the fears of communism in his state. McGovern proved to be a strong candidate and came within a point of upsetting Mundt.

Ironically, his defeat could be traced to the fact that South Dakota went overwhelmingly for Nixon over Kennedy in 1960. South Dakota wasn't ready for a liberal, New England, Catholic president. John F. Kennedy understood as much. After a campaign appearance with McGovern in South Dakota, Kennedy said to his brother, Robert: "I think we just cost that nice guy a Senate seat."

Perhaps partially out of guilt, President Kennedy tapped McGovern to be White House director of the Food for Peace effort—a great match for his energy and idealism. But when the other South Dakota Senate seat came up for election in 1962, McGovern plunged into the race against the respected Senator Francis Case. In the midst of the race, Case died suddenly and was replaced by Lt. Governor Joe Bottum. This should have guaranteed McGovern's victory, but weakened by hepatitis, he had difficulty campaigning in his own right. McGovern seemed destined for a second, heartbreakingly narrow defeat. But President Kennedy was far more popular in South Dakota in 1962 than he had been two years earlier, and his surge of popularity after the resolution of the Cuban missile crisis helped all Democratic candidates. On Election Day, George McGovern won the South Dakota Senate seat by 200 votes; a recount increased his margin to 597. On these few hundred votes, McGovern's career—and American political history—would turn.

In the Senate, McGovern demonstrated a passionate commitment to feeding the hungry, in the United States and around the world. He focused a spotlight on hunger in America, which led to enormous media attention and a great increase in understanding about the shocking scope of the problem. McGovern's tireless efforts also led to the creation of the Select Committee on Nutrition and Human Needs, of which he became the first chairman. The new committee spearheaded the dramatic expansion of the Food Stamp Program and the School Lunch Program. The number of Americans receiving food stamps increased from three million in 1968 to twelve million in 1972 to nineteen million in 1975, as unemployment increased. The children receiving free or reduced-cost school lunches more than doubled between 1969 and 1972.

His singular accomplishments in the area of food and nutrition reflected his compassion, idealism, and political ability. When Robert Dole came to the Senate in 1969, McGovern was not immediately drawn to him. He regarded the acerbic Dole as a "cheap shot" artist; once, when invited to go on *Meet the Press* with Dole, McGovern declined, offering to appear with anyone else. But within a short time, having joined the Agriculture Committee, Dole saw the advantage to Kansas farmers of the food stamp program, because it increased the demand for the full range of agricultural products. He was also genuinely moved by the plight of those suffering from hunger and malnutrition. McGovern and Dole were both World War II veterans. McGovern admired Dole's great courage and fortitude in dealing with the crippling injuries that he had sustained in the closing days of the war. Dole admired the courage McGovern had shown in flying more than thirty-five bombing missions over Europe, winning the Distinguished Flying Cross. Despite their differences, McGovern and Dole forged a bipartisan alliance that made a series of great legislative accomplishments possible.

In the Senate, McGovern was best known for his opposition to the Vietnam War. He expressed his opposition to war in September 1963, earlier than anyone else. He became one of the Senate's leading doves, and when Robert Kennedy was assassinated in June 1968, McGovern made himself a candidate for the Democratic nomination for president, so that the followers of Robert Kennedy would have someone to rally behind, although he had no chance to seize the nomination from Hubert Humphrey.

After Richard Nixon's election, McGovern escalated his opposition to the Vietnam War, teaming with Republican Mark Hatfield of Oregon in one of the leading efforts to cut off funding for the war. In September 1970, with a bitter off-year election campaign under way and opposition to the war cresting, McGovern made one of the most memorable speeches in the Senate's history. "Every senator in this chamber is partly responsible for sending 50,000 young Americans to an early grave," McGovern intoned, to a somber Senate and packed gallery. "This chamber reeks with blood." He also chaired the Democratic Party's commission to change the party nominating rules to ensure that no one would ever again secure the nomination the way Humphrey had—without running in primaries and caucuses, essentially selected by the party bosses.

Moved by the continuing war in Vietnam and the failure to deal with the problems of America's cities and poor, McGovern sought the Democratic nomination for president a second time in 1972. Muskie was the frontrunner; Humphrey, seeking a rematch with Nixon, was also in the race. Nevertheless, Humphrey was not going to be nominated by the Democratic Party in 1972 because of his association with Johnson and the war. Muskie chose to run a campaign based principally on seeking endorsements of party officials and Washington power brokers. McGovern understood the intensity of the new Democrats around the country, fueled primarily by their opposition to the Vietnam War. He also understood the new party rules that his commission had designed and the need to win delegates from primaries and caucuses all around the country, from the grass roots.

McGovern ran a brilliant insurgent campaign, sounding the theme of "Come home, America." Like Adlai Stevenson twenty years earlier, McGovern brought a new generation of activists into the party, including recent Yale Law School graduates William Clinton and Hillary Rodham, and the Denver lawyer who ran his campaign, Gary Hart. McGovern won the Democratic nomination at a tumultuous convention in Miami, where the new Democrats took great pride in ejecting Mayor Richard Daley from the convention and distancing themselves from other traditional powers like AFL-CIO President George Meany.

Yet seizing the nomination in 1972 proved to be McGovern's peak. The general election campaign proved to be an unmitigated disaster, starting with the revelation that Senator Thomas Eagleton, McGovern's choice for vice president, had been given electric shock therapy for depression. McGovern reacted indecisively, first endorsing Eagleton "1000%" and then, flip-flopping, asked him to leave the ticket. It was only downhill from there.

The Republicans effectively used the words of Democrats to paint the straitlaced McGovern as the candidate of "acid, amnesty and abortion," and weak on national defense, despite his heroic service in World War II. Meanwhile, Nixon skillfully wound down the war and pumped up the economy. Blockbuster *Washington Post* articles by Bob Woodward and Carl Bernstein linking the break-in at Democratic National Committee headquarters in the

Watergate office complex to the Nixon reelection campaign came too late to affect the election. In November, George McGovern suffered the worst loss in the history of presidential elections, winning only Massachusetts and the District of Columbia.

American politics is a tough and unforgiving business. Many people of South Dakota, who had been proud that a native son had been nominated for president, were now criticizing McGovern for having "gone national." McGovern focused his energies on rebuilding his ties in the state, which he described as "bending over and letting everyone kick me in the ass." He did so with sufficient grace that he was reelected to the Senate in 1974 and rekindled his enthusiasm for the Senate when he got a coveted seat on the Foreign Relations Committee. As the full scope of Watergate emerged, many of his supporters saw McGovern as vindicated. He received a rousing reception at the Democratic mid-term convention in 1974, which buoyed his spirits.

George McGovern recognized the brilliance of Jimmy Carter's campaign early on, because Carter had taken McGovern's playbook, both in terms of grassroots effort and in terms of his message. Imitation is a high form of flattery, but McGovern remained hostile to Carter. After his early criticisms of Carter he decided to spell out his concerns with a "memo to the White House," and it came in the form of an article in *Harper's* in October 1977.

McGovern's article was a blistering assault on Carter's first eight months in office, but it went even further, claiming that Carter had "already set the priorities that will determine policies for the next four years." The overriding priority to Carter, McGovern charged, was balancing the federal budget by 1981. McGovern was not against a balanced budget "if that be accomplished on a foundation of full employment, a prosperous urban and rural economy, and substantially reduced military spending." But because Carter had committed to an increased military budget, his balanced budget "would weigh most heavily on the 10 million unemployed and underemployed Americans, on the minorities trapped in decaying central cities, and on the majority of Americans who need health insurance, decent housing, and efficient transportation." McGovern criticized Carter for using "obsolete economics, or a misreading of present economic conditions, or both." To drive the point home, the article harkened back to Herbert Hoover's pursuit of a balanced budget in 1931.

McGovern several times suggested that Carter could learn about economic policy from President John Kennedy and called for an attack on concentrated economic power, especially in the oligarchies that controlled the steel and energy industries. He offered one word of praise for Carter—the decision to cancel the B-1 bomber—but then condemned him for using the savings to fund other weapons programs, rather than needed domestic investments. McGovern wrote his bottom line on Carter's balanced budget idea: "thus the tight circle around needed public investment closes: a balanced budget, increased military spending, and tax cuts leave only a trickle of dollars for the programs that the President promised the Urban League." Having already invoked the specter of Hoover, McGovern also compared Carter to the disgraced Nixon and his "secret plan" to end the Vietnam War. "It is not 'too early' to decide that there is no secret plan for social justice."

McGovern focused his fire mainly on Carter's budget proposals and what he regarded as misallocated funds and mistaken priorities. But he also criticized Carter's emphasis on human rights as selective, and likely to be seen in the Soviet Union as a "reincarnation of John Foster Dulles' attempt to bring Communism down by encouraging dissent and revolt in Eastern Europe." He charged that SALT II "has been delayed at best, and the Carter rhetoric has revived a Cold War psychology among Americans."

It was a powerful critique, particularly on the domestic issues. Coming from one of the most prominent Democrats, who had been the party's standard bearer just five years earlier, it was potentially far more damaging than any criticism that the Republicans could mount. For many years, liberal Senate Democrats had worked closely with the labor unions, the consumer groups, the environmental movement, civil rights organizations, antiwar activists, and those battling poverty. McGovern's speech reflected the concerns of those groups, reinforced them, and legitimized them.

There was no longer any doubt: Jimmy Carter would have his hands full, dealing with a wily and increasingly effective Republican opposition; Scoop Jackson, a power unto himself; and the Democratic liberals.

chapter 5

THE
APPEARANCE
OF IMPROPRIETY

STARTING WITH HIS WALK DOWN PENNSYLVANIA AVENUE ON INAUGURA-
tion day, Jimmy Carter had surprised the Senate repeatedly in the early weeks
of his presidency. The content of the economic package, the retreat on the
rebate, the attack on the water projects, the new approach to arms control,
and above all, the overriding emphasis on breaking America's energy dependency—all had been unexpected. No one, however, could claim to be surprised by his emphasis on ethics in government.

Carter had presented himself as the antidote to the corruption of Richard
Nixon and scandal of Watergate. In this role, he had been convincing enough
to be elected president. He pledged that his administration would observe
an unprecedented level of ethical behavior—a "government as good as the
American people." Reasonable people could disagree about how good a government that standard might require, but no one doubted that Carter took
his commitment seriously.

When Carter's administration put together its legislative package of ethics
proposals, it was able to borrow liberally from Democratic ideas labeled "Watergate reforms" dating back to the previous Congress. The centerpiece was
legislation to establish a mechanism by which a temporary special prosecutor
would be appointed to investigate high-ranking executive branch officials,
when necessary. The package also included a requirement of public financial

disclosure by high-level executive branch officials, as well as prohibitions against executive branch officials accepting gifts.

Carter was successfully tapping into a widespread feeling that corruption was rampant in America. The 1970's marked a period in which Americans had lost confidence, not only in their political leaders, but in their institutions in general. Watergate was the most visible manifestation, but the public was bombarded with seemingly endless news of corruption in state and local governments, in the police departments, and even a cheating scandal at West Point. In 1976, polls suggested that just two out of ten Americans trusted the government.

Many in Congress felt that both the Senate and the House had performed with distinction in responding to the abuses of Watergate. They had already legislated significant reforms in its aftermath. But there had been highly visible scandals on the House side of the Capitol, with the sexual peccadillos of powerful chairmen Wilbur Mills, who had been involved in a drunken incident with Fanne Foxe, an Argentine stripper, and Wayne Hays, who had hired Elizabeth Ray on his staff even though she had no noticeable clerical skills. Moreover, Senate Minority Leader Hugh Scott had completed his distinguished career under a cloud, having accepted an illegal contribution from Gulf Oil Corporation. With Carter putting so much emphasis on ethics, the new congressional leaders really had no choice. Consequently, Tip O'Neill and Robert Byrd determined to beat Carter to the punch.

IN MID-MARCH, THE WORD spread rapidly that two of the Senate's most respected members, Gaylord Nelson and Ed Muskie, the two leading environmentalists in Senate history, were going to square off in a debate. Unfortunately, the highly anticipated debate would have nothing to do with the environment. Nelson and Muskie would clash on "honoraria," the question of how much outside income senators could earn from making speeches.

Gaylord Nelson was known for his wry wit and ability to find the humor in any almost any situation. But on that day, as he took the subway that connected the Russell Senate Office Building to the Senate chamber in the Capitol, he saw little to laugh about. Nelson was about to defend the central provision of the proposed Senate ethics code—a sharp limitation on the outside earned income of senators—against some of his best friends, who were infuriated. They could not understand why Nelson advocated taking away the income they needed to put their children through college.

Nelson was beginning his fifteenth year in the Senate, having been elected with the great class of 1962. He came to the Senate after serving two terms as governor of Wisconsin, and few, if any, of the governors-turned-senators had a record of accomplishment equaling Nelson's. Raised in Clear Lake, Wisconsin, Nelson was deeply touched by the natural beauty of Wisconsin's forests and lakes. He forged his identity as the "conservation governor" several years before the release of Rachel Carson's *Silent Spring* and the consequent launch of the environmental movement in the United States.

During Nelson's tenure, Wisconsin enacted a series of path-breaking conservation measures, including legislation to control billboards, acquire more wetlands, and establish conservation easements to expand the number of state parks, fish and wildlife habitat, and state forests. Nelson was probably the most innovative governor in the country, and his popularity in Wisconsin showed that people understood the need for action to preserve the state's natural beauty against the pressures of growing population, automobile traffic, and industrialization. Nelson ran for the Senate to take the lessons of Wisconsin's experience to the nation.

In the spring of 1962, President John Kennedy came to Milwaukee to speak at a Jefferson–Jackson Day dinner. Riding together to the event, Kennedy told then-governor Nelson that most government issues had become too complex for people to grasp; except for Medicare, there were no easy issues to explain. Nelson disagreed. There was at least one other significant issue that resonated with people from all walks of life—conservation of natural resources. He urged Kennedy to make conservation a priority. Maybe it was important, Kennedy admitted, but since he'd been born and raised in a city, and despite his love of sailing, he hadn't really given it much thought.

In November, Nelson won a comfortable victory over three-term senator Alexander Wiley. After his election, undeterred by Kennedy's initial reaction, he pressed the issue again with White House staffers. Finally, Kennedy agreed and on September 24, 1963, the president embarked on a five-day, eleven-state conservation tour. Nevertheless, Kennedy had no real interest in the environment. He never issued a dramatic warning that the country's natural resources were imperiled, using the trip to emphasize other issues of greater interest to him. The *Wall Street Journal* observed that Kennedy was "rather bored with the whole subject of conservation." The *New York Times* editorialized that Kennedy seemed "more interested in conservation of the Democratic Party than in conservation of America's natural resources." Nelson was bitterly disappointed that a great opportunity to educate the country about protecting the environment had been lost. He would not make the same mistake.

Freshman senators were expected to settle in slowly, hire staff, set up offices, and learn about the Senate by spending time in the cloakroom and seeking advice from the veterans. The Senate made it easy to settle in gradually. A senator was emphatically not a governor or a mayor. There was no budget to prepare, no state legislature or city council to battle, and virtually no defined responsibilities at all. Moreover, every two-year Congress began slowly. Its pace intensified before recesses, but most major legislative accomplishments occurred only in the second year of the session.

In many ways, Nelson was content to accept the role of a freshman, adapting to the Senate's unique mores. Engaging, relaxed, possessed of a wonderful sense of down-home humor, he truly enjoyed other politicians, irrespective of where they stood politically. He made friends in the Senate almost immediately. He and his irreverent wife, Carrie Lee, were at the center of a bipartisan group of senators and their wives who ate dinner together regularly. As the years went by, the Nelsons' home became one of Washington's most popular dinner places.

But there was nothing easygoing about Nelson's passionate commitment to environment. Long before others, he saw the peril the planet was in. He became the first member of Congress to propose a ban on DDT. He offered six pieces of legislation on water pollution in 1966, the most comprehensive program ever suggested. He battled to clean up the Great Lakes and prevent ocean dumping. He would tell a United Auto Workers convention that the internal combustion engine had "powered Americans to unparalleled affluence, but now may drive it to unprecedented environmental disaster." Shortly thereafter he proposed banning the internal combustion engine altogether. Starting from conservation and constantly broadening his field of vision, Nelson was one of the nation's first and greatest environmentalists.

Nelson's first year in the Senate, 1963, would prove to be a historic year in terms of environmental legislation. Muskie, who was chairman of the subcommittee with jurisdiction over air and water pollution, had collaborated with J. Caleb Boggs of Delaware to write the Clean Air Act, the first serious attempt to grapple with the pollution of an industrial age. Nelson was the visionary whose radical proposals created space for Muskie's progressive legislation. But for Nelson, even the enactment of enlightened legislation wasn't enough. He wanted the legislative equivalent of a long pass, while the Senate tended to operate day by day, issue by issue—grinding matters out three yards at a time.

On April 22, 1970, Nelson's effort culminated in the first Earth Day. Twenty million people—fully 10 percent of the country—mobilized to show their support for the environment. They planted trees and picked up tons of trash. They attended marches, rallies, concerts, and teach-ins. They confronted polluters, held classes on environmental issues, and lobbied politicians. Philip Shabecoff, a longtime *New York Times* environmental reporter, called it "the day environmentalism in the United States began to emerge as a mass social movement."

The environment was Nelson's passion, and Earth Day would be his legacy. But the best senators recognized the opportunity to range wide across a wealth of issues, and Nelson did so as well. He waged a private war against the powerful, distrusting concentrated power whether held by corporations or by presidents. Nelson successfully pushed legislation to give Congress a veto power over foreign arms sales. He battled the pharmaceutical companies on behalf of consumers and attacked them for "the circle of death" by which they sent unsafe drugs into foreign countries. He conceived and spearheaded the legislation to make the tapes and papers of Richard Nixon's presidency the property of the federal government; before that time, presidential papers were treated as private property of the president. And, in January 1977, when asked by Majority Leader Byrd, he took on the challenge of producing a Senate code of ethics.

I WAS NELSON'S LEGISLATIVE counsel at the time, and on January 18 he told me "Byrd has asked me to write the God dam ethics code." He initially seemed pleased with the assignment. It was something of an honor to manage such a delicate assignment. Producing an ethics code by April 1, the deadline set by the leaders, was going to be a real challenge. But Nelson felt reassured that the House effort, already under way, was being chaired by his close friend, Representative David Obey, also of Wisconsin. "Obey's smart as hell," Nelson said. "We will be able to borrow some of the work that he has already done."

Nelson understood that most of his colleagues resented the idea that the Senate needed an ethics code. He firmly shared their view that ethical standards in government were at least as high, if not higher, than in any other walk of life. And he certainly believed that the situation had improved from when he had arrived in the Senate, when one of the most powerful senators had been the flamboyant oil man, Robert Kerr, the Oklahoma Democrat, who was known as "the senator from Kerr-McGee." The line between public service and private gain was crossed far less often than it had been in the past. But for Nelson, the bottom line was clear: "The Senate's concern should be the current period of deep disillusionment and cynicism. . . . If restored public confidence demands a strong code, the Senate should adopt one. There is no arbiter of right or wrong in this arena; there is only the overriding question of whether the people trust their government."

Yet the task quickly proved even more difficult than anticipated. The cornerstone of the ethics code being drafted in the House, which Nelson's Special Committee on Official Conduct would parallel, was a straightforward deal: the members would receive a much-needed pay increase, from $42,500 to $57,500, in exchange for limiting their outside earned income to 15 percent of their new salary. Nelson and his staff soon discovered that this approach, generally acceptable in the House, would be extremely controversial in the Senate. Most House members were not wealthy, and they did not receive much outside earned income. They needed the pay raise and would not be sacrificing much to get it.

In contrast, the Senate was filled with wealthy men who received income from investments and did not need honoraria from speeches. On the other hand, those of more modest means who gave a lot of speeches for money regarded outside earned income as essential to maintaining two residences and putting children through college. Additionally, the Senate had considered requiring senators to disclose their finances as early as 1965. Most of the senators hated the idea then—and shot it down quickly. Now, despite the public mood after Watergate, and the pressure created by Carter's emphasis on ethics, many still hated the idea. The Nelson Committee was heading straight into a buzz saw.

The Special Committee on Official Conduct brought its proposed Senate code of ethics to the Senate floor on March 17. Nelson and his staff anticipated three or four days of floor debate; they had underestimated the Senate's rising anger. For eleven days, the Senate debated its ethics code with an intensity usually reserved for war or taxes; the ethics code hit senators where they lived, affecting their personal finances and intruding on their privacy.

On the day that Nelson and Muskie were set to debate, the Senate chamber was fuller than usual, and the press gallery was packed. Nelson was relaxed, his sparkling blue eyes gleaming with good humor. Dressed in blue slacks and a blue and gray sports jacket on the Senate floor, he looked more like a pharmacist from a small town in Wisconsin than a U.S. senator. It was all part of his charm. From the "well" of the Senate, where the senators managing legislation hold forth, Nelson explained the need for a limitation on outside earned income. Honoraria for speeches provided interest groups an unacceptable opportunity to influence senators. What was the point of limiting campaign contributions if affected groups could simply channel money directly to senators through honoraria?

Several of the opponents of the honorarium limit had indicated their intention to speak, including Bob Packwood, Birch Bayh, Bob Dole, and Fritz Hollings. If nothing else, the anger was bipartisan. But Muskie had taken the position as the leading opponent to the honoraria limit; he and George McGovern had even gone to the Common Cause office, to tell the organization's leaders just how unfair they thought the honoraria limit was. And Muskie's opposition would count for a great deal.

From the back row of the Senate, he sought and received recognition from the chair. Muskie then launched a passionate attack on the outside income limitation. Muskie was 6'4", and he had a fierce temper. His face got redder and redder as he spoke. The Senate chamber is gently banked, with the back rows higher than the front, and Muskie seemed to grow taller as he got angrier, looking down at Nelson from the Senate's commanding heights.

Muskie recounted that when he was Maine's governor, he had refused to supplement his income by staying in law practice, although that was commonly done at the time, because he believed that it would inevitably present blatant conflicts of interest. But the governor's salary was a pittance, and Muskie had small children, so he needed to supplement his income. To stay afloat, he had chosen to give speeches for honoraria.

Muskie reminded the Senate that political speechmaking was a great American tradition. He recounted tales of speeches given on the Chautauqua circuit. He was enraged at the implication that receiving honoraria for speeches was in any way corrupt or corrupting. "You're throwing us to the wolves," Muskie shouted. "The senator is putting a cap on my income, and he doesn't give a damn what the consequences are for my family."

As Muskie continued, Tom Eagleton entered the Senate, flopping down next to Nelson. Eagleton had agreed to speak in favor of the outside income limitation. But after hearing a few minutes of Muskie's speech, he whispered to Nelson, "Jeez, Gaylord, he's killing you. I don't want any part of this issue." Then Eagleton threw back his head and laughed raucously. He later gave a powerful speech opposing Muskie.

Muskie was approaching his climax. "I have looked everywhere for an explanation of why the committee is taking away my livelihood," he boomed. "I have read the legislation and found no explanation. I have read the committee report and found no explanation. But finally, in today's *Washington Post*, I got an explanation. An aide to Senator Nelson is quoted: 'We can't do anything about outside income from investments, but we can limit outside earned income to prevent conflicts of interest.'"

Nelson turned to me and whispered "Did you say that?" Embarrassed, I shrugged sheepishly and nodded. Nelson rose, turned to Muskie, and sought permission to respond.

Nelson was as unflappable as Muskie was furious. "Let me say to my friend from Maine: I don't know if one of my staff members said that or not," Nelson observed. "But if he did, it was actually a statement of uncommon wisdom and insight." Then Nelson restated his argument about the fundamental differences between outside earned income and investment income, in terms of potential conflicts of interest.

When Nelson finished his comments, Muskie, still steaming, stormed down the Senate aisle to confront his longtime friend. Nelson suggested the lack of a quorum, the clerk began calling the roll, and Nelson, seemingly without a care in the world, left the Senate floor before Muskie could reach him. Further infuriated, Muskie approached me. I jumped up to greet him, and in the process knocked a glass of water all over the senator. Muskie, already enraged, was now both startled and soaked. I imagined the Wicked Witch of the West shriveling up at the touch of water. Muskie stalked off the Senate floor, still searching for Nelson and, perhaps, a towel.

Byrd had no sympathy for Muskie' argument. He believed that senators were obviously profiting from their positions when they accepted honoraria; "I don't think any group of citizens would pay me $2,000 to play my fiddle for 15 minutes if I were a meatcutter or working in a shipyard or practicing law." Byrd saw the limitation on outside earned income as the centerpiece of the ethics code, and worried that the Senate would look bad if Muskie's amendment prevailed. Howard Baker also supported the limit on outside income, even though most of his Republican caucus opposed it. Both of the leaders worked hard to line up votes against Muskie.

On March 22, the Senate defeated Muskie's amendment by a vote of 62–35. Muskie angrily commented: "There is every indication that the Senate is panicking, and will vote for anything in the name of ethics." He said that he might have to sell one of his houses in order to make up for the lost honoraria income and finish his term.

Several days later, on April 1, 1977, the Senate enacted the ethics code by a vote of 86–9. Common Cause, the citizens' lobby, and editorial writers around the country praised the Senate's action. But the overwhelming final vote masked how angry many senators were about the outside income limit, the new requirement that senators and senior staff members publicly disclose their finances, and the basic implication that the Senate needed an ethics code to behave ethically. Abraham Ribicoff, a key member of the special committee writing the code, said in a committee meeting: "I hate this code. I *hate* this code." And he was a stalwart supporter of it.

In the closing hours of the debate, the Senate offered something of a compromise to the code's opponents, accepting an amendment that delayed the effective date of the honorarium limit until January 1, 1979, giving the senators two more years to supplement their incomes.

Meanwhile the Carter administration pressed forward on government-wide ethics legislation, which would require public financial disclosure by all high-ranking officials, slow the "revolving door" between government and the private sector, and create a mechanism to trigger the appointment of a temporary special prosecutor to handle investigations in cases involving high-level executive officials close to the president. The legislation would take almost eighteen months to work out. But long before it was complete, Carter and the Senate would face a full-blown ethics crisis.

BY LATE JULY, SIX months into the Carter presidency, Hill Democrats had grounds for cautious optimism about their new president and their work together. Congress had enacted the Carter tax cut and put together legislation to raise the minimum wage, a cherished Democratic goal. Carter's ambitious energy program was rolling forward much faster and more favorably than expected. In late July, he had signed legislation creating a Department of Energy, the first new cabinet-level department since the Department of

Transportation in 1966. In early August, the House of Representatives had passed his entire program virtually intact, less than four months after the president introduced it.

Carter had met with Egyptian president Anwar Sadat in April and Menachem Begin, the new Israeli prime minister, in July as part of a bold initiative to bring about Middle East peace. In a speech at Notre Dame, he had committed the United States to a foreign policy focused on human rights, rather than an "inordinate fear of Communism," strong words at a time when the Cold War was very real and the war in Vietnam a recent memory.

The White House seemed at last to be playing the Washington game. Against his nature, Carter even seemed to have accepted the senators' preferred role as advisors in large decisions. In June, Carter faced a major decision on whether to fund the B-1, a new generation of bombers. George McGovern and John Culver had collaborated masterfully the previous year to prevent the Ford administration from approving the B-1. McGovern had proposed to kill the program, a move that could not have prevailed in the hawkish Senate, but then allowed Culver to offer a moderate, compromise amendment to defer the decision on the B-1 to the next president. As Carter considered the future of the B-1 bomber program, he invited supporting and opposing senators to debate the issue at the White House on two consecutive evenings. His ultimate decision to kill the B-1 elated some senators and angered others, but the decision-making process augured well for the future.

To be sure, the White House had taken some losses. The Senate Republicans had won a significant victory by blocking legislation expanding the rights of unions to picket at construction sites. The several-year effort to create a consumer protection agency went down in flames, adopted in neither house. The Senate Republicans had also successfully filibustered Carter's legislation for public financing of elections, after Howard Baker had made an extraordinary plea for party unity against a "lousy bill" aimed at helping Democrats win elections. Still, the overall record was positive, and the trend was encouraging. Tip O'Neill, who had complained early on that "Carter thought Congress was like the red necks in the Georgia legislature," was now more optimistic. "He may not be able to balance the budget," O'Neill said, "but he will have a stable government."

The Speaker had spoken too soon. Ironically, and painfully, the Senate committee that most respected and admired Jimmy Carter would play a central role in an enormous setback for the Carter presidency.

THE GOVERNMENT OPERATIONS COMMITTEE had a long history of high-profile investigations. These dated back to the 1950's when Senator John Mc-Clellan, an Arkansas Democrat, and his chief counsel, young Robert Kennedy, had investigated Jimmy Hoffa and racketeering in labor unions. However, Byrd and Baker's committee reorganization had given "gov ops" new jurisdiction over postal and civil service issues, and a new name—"Governmental Affairs." Along with its mandate to investigate and provide oversight, Governmental Affairs now had broad legislative jurisdiction over the operations of the federal government: its organization and reorganization, management and mismanagement, ethics and lack of ethics—all issues that Jimmy Carter cared about deeply.

The committee's leaders—Abe Ribicoff, the chairman, and Charles Percy of Illinois, the ranking Republican—worked in close harmony. Percy, the handsome former CEO of Bell and Howell, had been elected to the Senate in 1966, riding a strong white backlash against civil rights in Chicago's ethnic neighborhoods and suburbs to defeat the liberal lion Paul Douglas. But despite the political currents that helped carry him to victory, once in the Senate, Percy proved to be quite independent and moderately liberal—pro-business, an internationalist, supportive of civil rights and most domestic legislation. He was very much a Rockefeller Republican, and therefore destined to be estranged from the Republican right that had recently succeeded in forcing Gerald Ford to drop Nelson Rockefeller as his running mate. Naturally comfortable with the Senate tradition of working across party lines, Percy was an ideal partner for Ribicoff.

In 1977, Ribicoff was in his fifteenth year in the Senate. He was one of a handful of people in U.S. history who had been a governor and served in the House, the Senate, and the cabinet as well. He had been one of John Kennedy's earliest supporters when Kennedy ran for president and was a close enough friend that after Kennedy won, he asked Ribicoff to be his attorney general. Ribicoff declined, telling the president-elect that he did not need a Jewish attorney general when civil rights legislation was going to be a pressing national concern. Kennedy then asked Ribicoff to become secretary of Health, Education and Welfare, a cabinet post that seemed ideal for a man so deeply committed to each of those major issues.

It was a heady time in Washington, especially for members of Kennedy's New Frontier, but Abe Ribicoff, like many ambitious politicians before him and since, wanted to be a senator. He had reached for the Senate unsuccessfully in 1952, losing to Republican Prescott Bush (the father of one president and the grandfather of another). But ten years later, a Senate seat opened up again, and Ribicoff, at the peak of his popularity in Connecticut, won handily.

The Senate suited Ribicoff. He had wide-ranging interests in domestic and foreign issues, and he worked very well with other senators of diverse viewpoints. When Howard Baker made his first foreign trip as a senator, he criticized President Johnson's foreign policy. Ribicoff, on the same trip, told Baker quietly that U.S. senators did not criticize the president—any president—while on foreign soil. Baker understood his error, and appreciated the way Ribicoff had offered the advice. They went on to form one of the closest friendships in the Senate.

Ribicoff's greatest moment of fame occurred at the tumultuous Democratic convention in Chicago in 1968. There was violence in the streets of Chicago, as the police moved against the antiwar protestors. There was bedlam on the floor of the convention, as the delegates favoring Eugene McCarthy or George McGovern tried to get a plank in the Democratic platform expressing opposition to the Vietnam War. And with the bedlam reaching a peak, the convention floor in near chaos, Ribicoff took the podium to place McGovern's name in nomination. Glaring down at Chicago Mayor Richard Daley less than twenty feet away, Ribicoff said that "with George McGovern, we wouldn't have Gestapo tactics in the streets of Chicago." The national television cameras captured the moment when Daley cursed out Ribicoff with a derogatory reference to his religion. "How hard it is to accept the truth," Ribicoff responded. He acquired an admiring national following.

In 1977, Ribicoff was sixty-seven years old and in good health. He dressed impeccably, usually in well-tailored gray suits, blue shirts with white banker's collars, and an expensive watch that he would check frequently during committee meetings. "Ribicoff and his people exuded class," recalled Tom Daffron, chief of staff for Senator William Cohen and later Fred Thompson. Younger senators, such as Gary Hart and John Danforth, admired Ribicoff as a mentor. Through and through, he was a Senate man and a pillar of the establishment. Ribicoff and his elegant wife, Casey, were popular figures on Washington's social scene.

But Ribicoff's deep concern about the condition and direction of his country was unmistakable. In 1972, he had written a small book entitled *America Can Make It!*, which included some of the most sweeping proposals for legislative change ever suggested by a sitting senator. Ribicoff's basic assertion was that "our new domestic priorities must focus on the problems that divide this nation and threaten the fabric that holds our society together: the problems of black and white, rich and poor, the working class and the health of our economy." Ribicoff talked straight about some of the toughest social issues facing the country, offering far-reaching solutions, including legislating metropolitan school desegregation over a twelve-year period, a guaranteed annual income for the poor, national health insurance, and a housing policy designed to match people with jobs and "head off fleeing suburbanites at the pass."

In 1971, Ribicoff offered an amendment that would have required schools in northern metropolitan areas to end their *de facto* segregation within ten years by mixing suburban and inner-city pupils. Jacob Javits opposed Ribicoff's amendment, arguing that *de jure* desegregation practiced in the South could be distinguished from the de facto desegregation that was created by white flight to the suburbs in the north. Ribicoff, always a gentleman on the Senate floor, lashed out at Javits, accusing him of "hypocrisy" for being "unwilling to accept desegregation for [New York] though . . . willing to shove it down the throats of the senators from Mississippi." If that was not clear enough, Ribicoff declared: "I don't think you have the guts to face your liberal constituents who have moved to the suburbs to avoid sending their children to school with blacks." Ribicoff edited his remarks so they did not appear in the *Congressional Record*, but they left an indelible impression on the senators and reporters who had heard them.

Ribicoff was delighted to have a Democrat in the White House again. He had no ambitions for higher office, and he was eager to help make the Carter presidency successful. But Ribicoff was no rubber stamp for anyone. Respected as he was, he had the capacity to be a formidable opponent, as Carter would soon find out.

DURING THE TRANSITION, THE Governmental Affairs Committee's energetic and activist staff worked happily and closely with Carter's White House team. Their collaboration produced one of Carter's earliest victories: expanded authority to reorganize executive agencies. Midway through Carter's first year, the committee staff, led by Richard Wegman, a nine-year Senate staff veteran, was working overtime on legislation to form the Department of Energy, reform the civil service reform, promote government-wide ethics reform, and a host of other "good government" initiatives. They saw the opportunity for major legislative accomplishments and wanted to seize the moment. However, there was one cloud in the committee's otherwise blue sky: lingering concern about the Senate's confirmation on January 20 of Bert Lance to be the director of the Office of Management and Budget (OMB).

Bert Lance, president of the National Bank of Georgia (NBG), was Carter's first cabinet appointment. Carter's decision to nominate his best friend for OMB Director initially won praise from Republicans and some conservative Democrats, who wanted a businessman at Carter's side to temper his supposed liberal instincts.

Even during the Governmental Affairs Committee's very brief investigation, it quickly discovered some disquieting facts about Lance. The U.S. Attorney's office in Atlanta had closed an investigation of Lance's banking practices one day before Carter announced the nomination. The investigators also found that Lance's bank had allowed family members to overdraw their accounts to the tune of several hundred thousand dollars, and that Lance's gubernatorial campaign still had an unpaid overdraft of $250,000 with his bank.

Though the Senate had the constitutional responsibility of confirming cabinet appointments, presidents had traditionally been given broad latitude to choose their team. Indeed, the Senate had never previously rejected a cabinet nominee proposed by a new president. Ribicoff and Percy raised their concerns in questions at Lance's confirmation hearings. Lance assured them that the Atlanta investigators had closed their probe of overdrafts properly and that all the overdrafts had been repaid. Both claims were supported by the acting comptroller of the currency, Robert Bloom, who called Lance "well-qualified" to be OMB Director and stated that Lance "enjoys a very good reputation in the banking community." Ribicoff, Percy, and the staff remained uneasy but concluded that the committee could not justify delaying Lance's confirmation. The Senate confirmed Lance on January 20, Inauguration Day, along with Carter's other major nominees.

Consistent with Carter's pledge to bring about a new ethical standard in government, Lance had pledged to divest his bank stock by December 31. Unfortunately, the bank stock was sinking in value, and Lance faced the possibility of an enormous loss. Moreover, it soon became clear that the high-flying banker was already deeply in debt because of loans taken to buy the controlling shares in the National Bank of Georgia when he bought it.

After conferring with Lance, Carter asked the committee to release Lance from his pledge to divest by year's end. At a July 15 hearing, the committee agreed to do so, after Lance pledged to steer clear of banking policy issues. But Lance's unusual request opened Pandora's box with respect to his banking practices, and a series of damaging stories quickly followed.

It soon became clear that Lance had engaged in a range of improper banking practices, including receiving favorable treatment from various banks that was based on his friendship with the Democratic nominee for president. William Safire, a *New York Times* columnist and a former Nixon White House staffer intent on holding the new administration to high standards, wrote a damning column entitled "Carter's Broken Lance," charging that "the man in charge of the nation's books" was "deeply, dangerously in hock," and deeply involved with the controversial Teamsters' pension fund "just as Mr. Carter's star began to rise." Other bombshells quickly followed, as the investigative reporters competed to unearth stories in what was becoming the first post-Watergate scandal. The new comptroller of the currency, Robert Heinemann, pledged a full investigation that would be "neither a witch hunt nor a whitewash."

Ribicoff convened another hearing on July 25 to allow Lance to defend himself. Either operating on faith or doubling down on the committee's original gamble, Ribicoff told Lance: "There isn't a thing that has been uncovered that impugns your integrity. . . . You have been smeared from one end of the country to the other, in my opinion, unjustly."

A month later, Ribicoff spent a good part of his vacation reading the 394-page first installment of the report by the comptroller of the currency. The report cleared Lance of any criminal wrongdoing, but severely criticized many of his actions as "unsound" and "unsafe" banking practices. The report found most troubling the fact that Lance had established a correspondent relationship for his bank with another bank at the time he was receiving a personal loan from the other bank, a clear violation of federal banking law.

Wading through the evidence, Ribicoff regretted his earlier rush to judgment. He concluded that Lance could no longer serve credibly. If he remained in office, it would do untold damage to the Carter White House. After returning to Washington, Ribicoff conferred with his staff and Percy, then requested an appointment with President Carter, which was set for Labor Day.

That day, Ribicoff and Percy entered the White House to meet President Carter. There was only one issue on the agenda. Ribicoff was certain that Carter would understand their message that Lance had to go, for the good of Carter's presidency. But Carter's response stunned the senators.

Carter expressed the view that Lance had been victimized by a press eager to show that the president and his "Georgia mafia" were not equipped to run the country. He insisted that Lance had done nothing wrong and made it clear that he thought the senators had rushed to judgment. Lance had vowed that he would not resign without having his "day in court," and Carter agreed. He asked the senators to hold another hearing so Lance could respond to the comptroller's report.

Ribicoff emerged from the Oval Office tight-lipped and somber, Wegman recalled. The White House staff directed Ribicoff and Percy away from the back of the White House where their cars were waiting to the front lawn where the press was already assembled, an ill-advised and amateurish decision by the White House staff after a presumably private meeting. "I think it would be wise for Bert Lance to resign," Ribicoff told the press. "I don't think [Lance] can be an effective OMB Director pending the outcome of these hearings and investigations."

Ribicoff's statement sparked a public firestorm. No experienced Washington hand could recall a situation where an executive branch official had stayed the course when the Senate committee chairman and ranking member were both calling for his resignation. As long as Lance lacked Ribicoff's support, Senator Clifford Case of New Jersey noted: "This guy is going to go, no question."

Lance's situation had already proved an embarrassment for Carter. Ribicoff had tried to limit the damage by setting their confrontation for Labor Day to keep it a summer storm, burying the news as best he could. However, Carter's decision to stand by Lance compounded the damage in a crippling way. For two long weeks, the Lance fiasco was front page news as the Governmental Affairs Committee held a remarkable series of hearings, with the most media coverage of any hearings since Watergate.

Lance offered a full-throated defense, attacking Ribicoff and Percy for "bringing in a verdict of guilty before I have been given the opportunity to present my side of the case." Clark Clifford, the legendary lawyer and an original Washington "wise man," served as Lance's counsel, ensuring that Lance would get excellent advice—though his very presence in the hearings signaled for anyone who doubted it that he was in very serious trouble. Officials from the U.S. attorney's office and the comptroller of the currency's office left no doubt in their testimony that they had gone easy on Lance for their own personal reasons, because his best friend was going to be president, or simply to keep their jobs and their pensions. The committee's usual bipartisan and collegial atmosphere broke down. Lance had several Democratic defenders on the committee—Lawton Chiles of Florida, Sam Nunn of Georgia, Jim Sasser of Tennessee, and Tom Eagleton—and they went at other senators, particularly Percy, quite heatedly. They also insisted that Ribicoff call an unprecedented hearing so that they could interrogate the staff members who had interviewed Lance. "It was like the committee eating its young," Wegman recalled ruefully.

The Carter administration seemed unable to stay quiet on the matter, further damaging its case. At one point, the *Chicago Sun Times* reported that White House Press Secretary Jody Powell leaked a false story charging that Senator Percy had flown on a corporate jet without making the necessary payment and used campaign funds illegally. Powell first denied leaking the story, and then admitted it, describing the leak as "inappropriate, regrettable, and dumb."

Ultimately, Jimmy Carter faced an unavoidable and excruciating choice: cutting his friend loose, or allowing continuing damage that could erode his standing with the country and undermine his entire agenda. Percy could be discounted as a Republican with his own presidential aspirations, but Carter knew that Ribicoff was a stalwart Democrat who fervently wanted his presidency to succeed. He sought Byrd's advice, more than once. Byrd predicted intense partisanship if Carter hung tough. He also reminded Carter that he had campaigned on ethics in government, and people expected higher standards from him than from previous presidents. His bottom line: Lance had acquitted himself as much as he could, to no avail, and now it was time for him to give up.

Jimmy Carter finally bowed to the inevitable. On September 21, Bert Lance resigned. The president made no effort to hide his pain. No one could "replace Bert Lance" who would be "as competent as strong, and decent, and as close to me as a friend and adviser."

Most senators praised Lance and Carter for doing the right thing for the country. Lance's defenders praised him as well, but expressed unease at the powerful machinery unleashed during the investigation. Sam Nunn warned that the presumption of innocence had been eroded by the ceaseless investigations of "five government agencies," "hundreds of bureaucrats stumbling over themselves to see and possibly leak information," and "scores of investigative reporters nipping at [Lance's] heels."

It is possible to recognize the force of Nunn's concerns without sharing his conclusion that Lance was mistreated. Ribicoff plainly had lapses of judgment, which he deeply regretted. Safire, who won the Pulitzer Prize for his columns, obviously relished the chance to hold the Carter White House to the same tough standards by which he thought Nixon had been crucified. Certainly, many reporters competed to bring out the story, hoping to become the next Woodward or Bernstein. Multiple agencies with jurisdiction over banking practices joined in as well, feeling obligated to get involved. Lance would not have been confirmed if all the facts had been known, but time did not permit a full investigation; the Senate wanted to follow tradition and allow the president the right to pick his full team.

But none of these facts alters the fundamental problems: Lance's improper banking practices and precarious financial situation and his failure to make full disclosure to Carter. Lance took advantage of his friendship with the president-elect and Carter's own strong desire to have his friend in the cabinet. Lance should have never been nominated, and he certainly should have resigned in July. When the scope of the problems came to light, Ribicoff's committee had no choice but to pursue them, which it did, thoroughly and transparently. It was Lance's insistence on staying on to fight, and Carter's unwillingness to remove his friend, that precipitated the media spectacle of the extended hearings and deepened the damage to Carter.

Lance's departure deprived Jimmy Carter of more than his closest adviser and best friend. The facts that emerged from the investigation of Lance made the Carter administration look newly tawdry, engaged in cronyism, self-dealing, and dirty tricks. In his memoirs, Carter wrote: "It is impossible to overestimate the damage inflicted on my administration by the charges leveled against Bert Lance."

The Lance experience brought about a major and lasting change in the relationship between the Senate and the executive branch. The powerful presumption that a president was entitled to the team that he wanted had blown up in the face of a Senate committee, and almost all the committees of the Senate changed their processes of investigating executive branch nominees so as to prevent the possibility that they would be similarly embarrassed. Every president after Carter would have at least one of his cabinet nominees rejected or withdrawn because of the newly vigilant Senate. Some improvement in the confirmation process was needed, but over time, the Senate's handling of executive branch nominees would become both increasingly politicized, and delayed and diverted by issues that can only be described as trivial.

But those consequences would be in the future. Now, in September 1977, having promised the American people a new standard of ethics, Carter had been hoisted on his own petard. The Senate had not always distinguished itself, but it had always proven capable of recovering. Less than a year into his presidency, it would remain to be seen if Carter could do the same.

chapter 6

THE LIBERAL FILIBUSTER

SIX MONTHS AFTER JIMMY CARTER, IN A CARDIGAN, HAD GIVEN THE NA-tion the hard truth about America's energy dependence, his energy plan emerged from the House of Representatives largely intact on August 5. Tip O'Neill's ad hoc committee had done its work well, turning Carter's ambitious program into legislation and enacting it in less than four months. Everyone knew that Senate passage would be more difficult. What no one anticipated was just how difficult it would be.

Carter's program was both complex and multifaceted. It sought to raise the price of energy to reduce consumption, while at the same time shielding consumers from most of the adverse effects of higher prices by returning the money to them through various rebates. One key provision imposed a well-head tax on oil, designed to cut fuel consumption by lifting the price of U.S.-produced crude to the price of OPEC-produced oil. The House had agreed to Carter's proposal to rebate the revenue raised from the tax to consumers. But it swiftly became clear that many senators, led by Russell Long, would not support a wellhead tax unless the revenues raised were returned to the oil and gas companies to fund additional energy production, either through increased drilling or the development of new sources, such as gasification of coal. This would pose a substantial problem, to be sure. But it would be an altogether different issue, however, that would ultimately take center stage and determine the fate of Carter's energy plan.

Natural gas pricing had been a contentious issue since 1954 when the Supreme Court had ruled that gas piped across state lines was subject to federal control. By 1977, with the price of producing gas steadily rising, artificial price ceilings had created a distorted "dual market." The price of gas was so low in some regions that it was not worth shipping across state lines. Heavy gas-consuming northern states were subject to shortages, while gas-producing states like Texas paid bargain prices for intrastate gas.

Carter proposed to end the dual market and control all new discoveries of natural gas (interstate and intrastate) at a higher price. This would apply to new wells found at least 2.5 miles from or 1,000 feet below existing reservoirs, so as to avoid producers merely digging new wells right next to the existing ones in order to exploit the higher prices.

The Senate was traditionally a much friendlier forum for the oil and gas industry than the House. Producer interests had traditionally dominated the Finance Committee, causing despair and anger for great liberal senators of the 1950's and 1960's such as Paul Douglas (D-IL) and Albert Gore Sr. (D-TN). Although many things had changed about the Senate since the 1950's, the basic orientation of the Finance Committee wasn't one of them.

The oil and gas industries were not impressed by Carter's complex proposal. Any continuation of price controls on natural gas would put them at a disadvantage. They had a counter-proposal—one that could upset all of Carter's carefully laid plans for energy policy. The Senate had endorsed complete deregulation of natural gas two years earlier, approving an amendment offered by Texas Democrat Lloyd Bentsen and Kansas Republican James Pearson. That remained the answer that the oil and gas industries wanted.

Carter's intense focus on energy had heightened public awareness about the magnitude of the energy problem and given his proposals some credibility. He could count on strong liberal support for continued price regulation, including Jackson, the chairman of the Energy Committee. As the time for Senate floor action approached, the advocates of deregulation seemed to have the upper hand by a narrow margin, but the ultimate outcome was truly too close to call.

Byrd called up the energy legislation for Senate consideration on September 22. Fierce resistance from the oil and gas industries was to be expected. But Byrd and Carter would face an unprecedented problem from an unexpected corner. The next day, two of the Senate's most liberal members, Democrats James Abourezk of South Dakota and Howard Metzenbaum of Ohio, announced their intention to filibuster to prevent a Senate vote in favor of deregulating natural gas.

Abourezk and Metzenbaum had previously numbered among the Senate's least consequential members. Just elected in 1976, Metzenbaum had made millions by building a successful parking garage empire and was now known principally for the visible animosity that characterized his relationship with John Glenn, Ohio's other senator. Abourezk, elected in 1972, had already decided that the Senate was much too confining for a free spirit like his and had announced his intention not to seek reelection earlier that year. He was increasingly seen in western garb, rather than a business suit.

The whole scenario seemed incongruous. The southern bloc filibustered; James Allen, Jesse Helms, and their fellow opponents to civil rights filibustered; liberals did not filibuster. In fact, the liberal senators had worked for years to make it easier to invoke cloture—cut off filibusters—and had finally succeeded in 1975, led by then-senator Walter Mondale, in reducing the number of senators needed to cut off debate from two-thirds of those "present and voting," which could require as many as sixty-seven votes, to three-fifths of the Senate, sixty votes. Neither Abourezk nor Metzenbaum seemed to have the gravitas or the knowledge of the complex Senate rules needed to maintain a filibuster concerning legislation that was President Carter's highest domestic priority.

Byrd, Baker, and Jackson responded to Abourezk and Metzenbaum's announcement by filing a cloture petition, signed by twenty senators, which would come to a vote on September 26. It seemed odd to file a cloture petition before a filibuster had even begun, but it had become a common tactic in dealing with Allen or Helms. Once cloture was invoked, debate would be limited to one hour per senator.

Conventional wisdom held that only a parliamentary wizard like Allen could pose a real danger to a rule-master like Byrd. Yet a great myth about the Senate was about to be shattered.

SENATE RULES WERE AND are arcane. The precedents can be mind-numbing in their complexity, to be sure. However, a few basic tenets could be easily grasped. Abourezk and Metzenbaum had learned that any amendment filed before a cloture petition would have to be considered and voted upon.

Consequently, their staffs labored through the weekend to prepare more than 500 amendments which the senators filed before Byrd's cloture petition.

Abourezk and Metzenbaum did not feel like lonely soldiers when they began their filibuster. They rightly believed that their opposition to deregulation had the support of President Carter, the House, and a significant number of senators. Speaking at a rally in Virginia, President Carter had already affirmed that he would veto the Bentsen-Pearson bill if it reached his desk: "I hate to veto a bill that a Democratic Congress passes, but you can depend on it—I'll protect your interests." And so, on September 26, after the Senate voted to invoke cloture, the two senators began calling up their amendments, demanding fifteen-minute roll call votes on each of them, and frequently asking for quorum calls as well. Byrd's fear of a paralyzed Senate seemed very real. And it would be a Senate paralyzed not by a substantial minority, but by two senators.

When the Senate convened the next day, Byrd grimly noted that no progress had been made on the bill. He warned that he was prepared to keep the Senate in all night if the filibuster didn't end. He also filed a motion to suspend the rules and bundle the 508 amendments together into one, which would require a two-thirds vote.

Abourezk responded plaintively:

> We are acting in the tradition of the Senate. Are we here to follow rules or ask questions and act in the best interests of our constituents? Senate rules are devised to let one man object as long as he physically can. It is not very pleasant to be put in a position of protest. There are all kinds of peer pressures. I want to say to the leader and the membership that there are a number of us who feel the natural gas deregulation issue is the most important economic issue of the last three decades. I apologize to my colleagues for inconveniencing them. Someday perhaps you will have an issue that strikes you so hard you will want to do the same thing.

In fact, Byrd was torn. He revered the Senate's tradition of unlimited debate, but as the majority leader, he wanted the Senate to remain a strong and credible legislative body. That meant vigorous debate leading to action, within a reasonable period of time. He also knew that many senators, however aggravated by the current filibuster, agreed with Abourezk's penetrating observation. They could envision a time that an issue would matter so much to them that they might resort to a filibuster. Consequently, they might balk if Byrd cut off debate prematurely.

Instead of seeking to dismiss the amendments by bundling them, Byrd made good on his threat to keep the Senate in session through the night. The scene was sometimes humorous, painfully exhausting, and borderline surreal. Fritz Hollings walked on to the Senate floor in a bright green jogging suit, which he said made comfortable pajamas. Barry Goldwater padded around in stocking feet. Jackson was heard to mumble "excuse me" after bumping into a wall. Senators began joking that someone might die of exhaustion.

Unlike earlier filibusters, when one senator or a handful held the floor all night, often reading hundreds of pages of legislation into the *Congressional Record*, this filibuster by amendment featured roll call votes throughout the night. Eighty-eight senators came to the floor to vote on one meaningless amendment at 2:15 a.m. A vote at 3:15 a.m. brought eighty-six senators to the floor. The Senate broke its all-time record by holding thirty-eight roll call votes during this session (which lasted thirty-seven hours). Muskie called the process "silly," while Baker described it as "barbaric." The senators' anger, initially focused on Abourezk and Metzenbaum, was increasingly directed at the majority leader. Dale Bumpers sharply criticized Byrd's tactics for dealing with the filibuster, saying "I don't believe that we have to prove our masculinity to the American people."

Tempers began to fray. When Ted Stevens defended deregulation as "restoring the free enterprise system of the United States," Hollings ripped into him, averring that "the issue is greed. The [energy industry] is like a sheepdog. . . . They have tasted blood."

At the night's end, Byrd decided against extending the session to the next night as well, but advised senators to be prepared to work late and return early. Abourezk and Metzenbaum, challenging "the forces of deregulation," said they were "fresh and prepared" to go another twenty-four hours. Even so, behind the scenes, things were moving in a more positive direction.

Although the public face of a filibuster, or any extended debate, may seem to be of intractable conflict, in truth the maneuver prompts senators to search for common ground, even giving them a sense of where a majority can be gathered. What is happening on the Senate floor is thus much less important than the alternatives being drafted and redrafted in the cloakroom or around the leaders' offices. September 28 saw that type of movement. Backstage, Byrd offered a compromise that raised the price ceiling still further, offering concessions to the oil industry, while stopping short of deregulation to please the liberals.

Abourezk and Metzenbaum were satisfied. Though the price of gas would increase, it would remain controlled. Even so, the advocates of deregulation opposed the compromise. John Tower called it "a concession to the filibusterers." And the deregulators weren't finished yet.

Undeterred, Bentsen and Pearson now circulated a revised version of their deregulation legislation, which would retain controls for two years, with a ceiling of $2.48, before deregulating. Byrd was frustrated: "We've debated this bill for nine days," he snapped. "I've heard that the world was created in seven."

In agreeing to support Byrd's compromise, Abourezk and Metzenbaum had left open the possibility of resuming their filibuster if a deregulation amendment passed. That position enraged Long. The Finance Committee chairman said he was willing to let the Senate choose between regulation and deregulation, but he would not accept a situation where one side could prevail with a majority, while the other would need a supermajority. "If the other side wants to be a poor loser," Long said, "I'll be a poor loser. I have as much capability as the average senator to engage in a filibuster." No one doubted Long's ability as a legislative strategist, his parliamentary expertise, or his commitment to deregulation. After a few encouraging hours, the situation already seemed to be slipping back toward paralysis again. That night, Jimmy Carter noted in his diary: "The influence of the oil and gas industry is unbelievable . . . Scoop Jackson and Bob Byrd are doing the best they can, but Russell Long and others plus the lobbyists are prevailing."

On September 30, in a critical test vote, the Senate refused, by a vote of 50–44, to table the deregulation legislation. In essence, Bentsen-Pearson seemed to maintain the support of the majority of the Senate. Neither the filibuster nor the intense lobbying by Byrd, Jackson, and the Carter administration had shifted many senators. Asked if the vote meant that the administration could not prevail in the Senate on this issue, Jackson acknowledged: "I don't think we can." Byrd spent the day in meetings with the various combatants, particularly Abourezk, Metzenbaum, and Long, trying in vain to get them to agree to an up or down vote. President Carter kept lobbying a handful of senators who were regarded as "gettable," but no one ever seemed to be gotten. The fate of the energy legislation was in serious doubt.

By October 3, Byrd decided that the filibuster had to end. He thought the compromise he had offered was a good one, but it did not seem to command a majority of the Senate. He knew that the Senate—and its leader—was already being ridiculed in the press for its inability to complete action. Abourezk and Metzenbaum had said they would stop the filibuster if Carter requested it, and that was certainly a possible option. Although the White House opposed deregulation, at a certain point, the best strategy for Carter might be to have the Senate pass deregulation legislation, putting the issue into a conference with the House. But Byrd saw the prospect of White House intervention as undercutting his leadership. This was a Senate problem to be dealt with by the Senate leader. Byrd determined to take care of the filibuster his own way.

In his arsenal of parliamentary tools, Byrd found only one: the right of the majority leader to obtain recognition from the chair before other senators. He could seek recognition of the chair, call up the remaining 300 amendments, and ask the chair to rule them dilatory and out of order. Byrd shared his plan with a small group of senators including Alan Cranston of California, the Democratic whip; Baker and Stevens, the Republican leaders; and Long and Wyoming Republican Clifford Hansen. All endorsed the strategy. The group also agreed that Vice President Walter Mondale should be in the chair, presiding over the Senate and making the rulings from a prepared script. It made sense; Mondale was not only vice president; he was a former senator, well liked and respected by his colleagues, and an avowed enemy of the filibuster. If the senators trusted anyone, it was Mondale.

BY LATE 1977, FRITZ Mondale could fairly be described as the most successful and luckiest member of the Great Senate. Ever since John Kennedy had pointed the way to the White House from the Senate, many senators had sought the presidency; all had gone down in flames. Only two senators had made it to the other end of Pennsylvania Avenue as vice president: Mondale and his friend and mentor, Hubert Humphrey. Humphrey was elevated by Lyndon Johnson, a man he had known well and worked with closely since 1949, when they first entered the Senate together. Mondale had been chosen by Carter, a man he barely knew but greatly impressed in his two-hour interview. Johnson humiliated Humphrey, and his vice presidency proved to be the death knell of his presidential hopes, although it helped him get the 1968 presidential nomination. In contrast, Carter accepted Mondale's vision of a vice president as a senior adviser, gave him an office in the West Wing, and made him probably the most influential vice president in history up to that time and a model for future vice presidents.

It was one more piece of good fortune for Fritz Mondale. His meteoric political rise had combined hard work and keen intelligence with an uncommon ability to win the respect and affection of other politicians, while always managing to be at the right place at the right time. Mondale had been appointed attorney general of Minnesota at the age of thirty-two, appointed to the Senate (to fill Humphrey's seat) at the age of thirty-six, and chosen to be vice president at forty-eight, after dropping his own presidential campaign in late 1974. His often-quoted observation that he "didn't want to spend two years of his life living in Holiday Inns" had allowed him to make an early and classy exit from the 1976 Democratic race. If he'd stayed in, the contest would have pitted him against four other senators and certainly would have ended as badly for him as it did for his colleagues.

Other politicians envied his rapid rise, his timing, and his luck. But it had come with a price. Mondale had co-chaired Humphrey's presidential campaign in 1968, even though he harbored grave and growing doubts about the Vietnam War policy that Humphrey continued to support. It was agonizing for Mondale to find himself defending the Johnson-Humphrey policy on the war against a new generation of Democrats energized by their opposition to the war. Mondale had advised Humphrey to break with Johnson on the war and was gratified that Humphrey did eventually call for a pause in bombing and a negotiated settlement.

Mondale had been an impressive senator in his own right. He had a fine legal mind, loved to legislate, and got along well with colleagues in both parties. He spearheaded the enactment of the Civil Rights Act of 1968, legislation designed to end discrimination in housing, an extraordinary legislative achievement for the Great Senate during a year when American cities were in flames and the politics of the country had shifted sharply to the right. Mondale had worked with Robert Kennedy and Cesar Chavez to protest the terrible conditions of migrant workers. After RFK's death, Mondale had become the most visible senator addressing the plight of the underprivileged. In 1975 and 1976, outraged by the FBI's domestic surveillance program, Mondale played a powerful role on the Church Committee, rolling up his sleeves and working "like a staff member" to hammer out guidelines that would constrain the bureau's rampant wiretapping and infiltration of domestic groups.

Now, as Vice President, Mondale was the administration's natural liaison with the Senate. Starting in the very early weeks of the presidency he frequently fielded complaints about Carter's political ineptitude and tendency to overload the legislative circuits. Moreover, labor and the other liberal interest groups saw Mondale as their man in the White House, and given his background and political philosophy, they were not mistaken. Mondale frequently raised concerns with Carter that his focus on balancing the budget was inflicting collateral harm on the people who could least afford it, who also happened to be the political constituencies most important to the Democratic party. Carter listened intently and respected Mondale's views, though he did not usually follow them.

So Mondale's charmed political career came with its own challenges, which were about to intensify. On October 3, Mondale arrived at the Senate at 11 a.m. In Byrd's office he learned what the senators had in mind. It must have been a painful moment—Mondale had thought he had succeeded in disciplining the use of filibusters less than three years before by lowering the requirement for cloture to sixty votes. But the need for further action was clear, and he voiced no objection.

Abourezk had gotten wind of a rumor that the vice president was going to crush the filibuster. He brushed it off saying, "Nah, he wouldn't do that." Ted Kennedy, who had known Mondale much longer, assured him that it was not possible. Mondale understood the traditions and rhythms of the Senate; he would recognize the anger that such an action would produce. They would soon find out otherwise.

When the Senate convened, Byrd took the floor, sought recognition, and read from a prepared script. He announced that the chair was "required to take the initiative under Rule 22 to rule out of order all amendments which are dilatory or which are on their face out of order." The vice president, also plainly reading from a script, responded that "the point is well taken, and the chair will take the initiative." Byrd moved in for the kill, calling up amendment after amendment, and Mondale, just as rapidly, ruled each amendment out of order. In nine minutes, thirty-three amendments were rejected.

Instantly, the Senate turned to bedlam. Dozens of senators leaped to their feet to protest this unprecedented procedure. Mondale continued to recognize only Byrd. When Ed Muskie finally got recognition, he charged that the vice president was arbitrarily creating "a new order of things, a change in the rules." Gary Hart charged that "the Senate has seen an outrageous act." Jacob

Javits had to be dissuaded from offering a resolution condemning Byrd's action. John Culver criticized Byrd himself in harsh, personal terms.

Byrd, flushed with anger at the criticism, responded furiously: "I have not abused the leadership's prerogatives. I am trying to keep senators from abusing the Senate." He acknowledged that he had taken advantage of his leadership position but insisted that "one has to fight fire with fire where necessary." He noted with some bitterness that he had done many favors for those who were criticizing him.

At that point, Byrd backed off. The filibuster could have been resumed, but Abourezk and Metzenbaum, shocked by Mondale's involvement, concluded that the Carter administration had sold them out, even after tacitly encouraging them to mount the filibuster. They lost heart and ended their effort. The next day, by a vote of 50–46, the Senate passed legislation deregulating natural gas within two years. In Ribicoff's words, the Carter administration energy program was "in shambles."

Publicly, Byrd was philosophical about what had happened. "The Senate is very much like a violin," he noted. "The sound will change with the weather, the dampness, the humidity. The Senate is a place of great moods. It can shift quickly, very quickly." But it had been a searing experience, with disturbing implications going forward.

Filibustering senators had found new methods to paralyze the Senate. The leadership, in turn, had acquired a new tool for suppressing dissent. Most of the Senate had been angry at Abourezk and Metzenbaum for abusing the Senate rules and exhausting them. But when Byrd took strong action to end the filibuster, the Senate had turned its wrath on him. As much as the senators were frustrated by the filibuster, they disliked Byrd's power play even more. Mondale would always contend that after cloture had been voted, he was obligated to rule dilatory amendments out of order. But Carter, not known for his concern about congressional sensibilities, thought that Byrd and Mondale "had used the wrong tactics; a little too abrasive. The Senate's not accustomed to that."

Byrd's mistake was not parliamentary, but political. Abourezk and Metzenbaum believed they were protecting Carter's energy agenda. Rather than passing a watered-down bill, they had chosen to snarl Senate business and enrage the deregulators. It would have been natural for Byrd to seek White House help in lobbying Abourezk and Metzenbaum, but he had shown excessive pride and exercised bad judgment. As a result, he had ended up with nothing. In attempting to reassert leadership he had simultaneously failed to get Carter's energy program through the Senate and made the Senate itself look ridiculous.

Even so, Byrd had taken precautions that protected him from lasting damage. He had enlisted the support of Republican leadership, moved against two of his own Democratic members, and made it crystal clear that his overriding interest was ensuring that the Senate could conduct the nation's business. It all went with the responsibility for being the Senate leader, and ultimately, most of the senators would accept it and respect him for it. And most important, his observation about the Senate was completely accurate. It was a place of great moods, which often changed quite rapidly.

ALL YEAR, JIMMY CARTER had made energy legislation the centerpiece of his domestic agenda. Now, he raised the stakes again. Barnstorming through Michigan, Iowa, Nebraska, and California, Carter put his prestige on the line, saying: "I have equated the energy policy legislation with either success or failure of my first year in office." It was a bold statement that proved very costly. The Senate's vote on the natural gas legislation came on October 4. In most cases, that would have left enough time for a conference to resolve differences between the House and Senate so that final legislation could be written, approved by both houses, and sent to the president for signature. But the differences between the Senate- and House-passed energy legislation were truly monumental. It soon became clear that the issue would not be resolved until the next year.

The American public had taken Carter at his word, and now passed negative judgment on his presidency. His approval ratings, which had been astronomical after one hundred days and very respectable after six months, came crashing down with the failure of the energy legislation and the Lance debacle. Other substantial achievements, such as an increase in the minimum wage, creation of the Energy Department, halting production of the B-1 bomber, and new curbs on strip mining, were swiftly forgotten. Although Carter had worked ceaselessly on efforts to further Middle East peace, he received no political benefit from the historic visit to Israel by Egypt's President Anwar Sadat in November. Even relatively robust economic growth did not seem to matter. Overall, barely 50 percent of the American people approved of his performance as president. The bright promise of his unique presidency seemed to be slipping away.

Most presidents stayed close to home for the holiday season, either in the White House or Camp David. Jimmy Carter certainly deserved some down time, but that wasn't his nature. He ended the first year of his presidency with a whirlwind foreign trip. New Year's Eve found him in Tehran, where he toasted the shah for making Iran "an island of stability in one of the more troubled areas of the world." No one could not have anticipated that Carter would finish each year of his presidency consumed by events in Iran.

It would have been difficult for the Democratic Senate to look good at a time when the Democratic president was staggering. Sure enough, on December 18, David Broder, one of Washington's most respected political columnists, offered a withering indictment of the Senate. Broder rejected the widely held notion that "Congress is the lion act and the President's job, as the lion-tamer, is to turn those brawling 'cats' into a disciplined troupe of performers." He pointed out that the members of Congress "collectively had thousands of years of working experience in the federal government" and should be helping educate Carter on how to get things done.

After giving Tip O'Neill conditioned praise for his efforts, Broder sharply criticized Byrd for his constant "one note warning of dire catastrophe around the legislative bend." Noting that several of the senators were "tinged with bitterness" that Carter, not they, were in the White House, Broder slammed the Senate for a series of failures: rejecting the Sorensen nomination, nearly sabotaging the Warnke nomination, reacting like "Tammany aldermen" to Carter's threat to cut off dam projects, and for demonstrating, for eight months "that it lacked the will, the skill or the expertise to resolve its own differences on the energy issues."

"Carter and his aides bear full responsibility for the many errors of judgment and tactics they made in dealing with Congress," Broder concluded. "But they were acknowledged novices. The Senate has no such excuse."

For Robert Byrd, a man both proud and sensitive, Broder's judgment would come as a painful holiday greeting. The Senate had demonstrated its ability to act as a check on imperial presidents, particularly Nixon, in the crisis times of Vietnam and Watergate. But now the Senate still had to demonstrate that it could work with a nonimperial president to accomplish things in the national interest. The Senate's second session in the Ninety-fifth Congress would have to be far different, and far more productive, than its first.

1978

chapter 7

A YEAR
OF LIVING
DANGEROUSLY

FOR THE SENATE, 1978 BEGAN WITH THE LOSS OF AN ICON. ON JANUARY 13, Hubert Humphrey, aged sixty-six, died after a valiant battle against cancer. Humphrey had fought the disease with characteristic energy, courage, and optimism since its initial appearance in 1973, and then its reappearance, in invasive form, in September 1976. While battling the disease, he had introduced the Humphrey-Hawkins full employment act, become chairman of the Joint Economic Committee, issued a major assessment of China's future, fended off supporters who wanted him to run for president for a fourth time, and sought the position of majority leader, before concluding that he had no chance against Byrd. His friend and protégé, Vice President Mondale, spoke memorable words at Humphrey's funeral service in the Capitol Rotunda: "He taught us how to hope and how to love, how to win and how to lose. He taught us how to live and, finally, he taught us how to die."

For two generations of Americans, it was impossible to remember politics without Humphrey, the Happy Warrior. He would always be associated with the greatest triumph of his generation, the battle for civil rights. His brilliant speech at the 1948 Democratic convention stirred the nation and lifted him to national prominence, and his superb leadership in the Senate helped bring about the 1964 Civil Rights Act. Unfortunately, he would also always be associated with the greatest tragedy of his era, the Vietnam War, which prevented him from becoming president just as surely as it destroyed Lyndon Johnson's presidency and his dream of a Great Society.

In late 1977, the *Washington Post* had asked a thousand people on Capitol Hill to name the greatest members of Congress. Their choice for greatest House member was Speaker Sam Rayburn; the greatest senator was Hubert Humphrey. As political scientist Nelson Polsby observed: "Humphrey, more or less, invented the modern senator as we know him: creator, innovator, educator, using his place and prominence to define issues for the wider public—and, ultimately, through mastery of the interminable process of committee, cloakroom, and floor maneuver, translating those issues into law." Humphrey might advise new senators, like young Joe Biden of Delaware, that he should pick an issue and become an expert—he suggested housing for Biden—but the range of his interests, the depth of his understanding, and the wellspring of his energy and creativity were astonishing. "I like every subject!" Humphrey once exclaimed.

When he first came to the Senate in 1949, the southern club, led by Richard Russell, shunned him for his passionate commitment to civil rights and for his exuberant, talkative style. Close enough so Humphrey could hear him, Russell once asked caustically: "Can you believe that Minnesota would send such a fool to the Senate?" Virtually ostracized during his first years in the Senate, which he described as the worst of his life, Humphrey decided that he would learn to do it the Senate way. He became a pragmatic progressive and served as Lyndon Johnson's bridge to the liberals. Through the warmth of his personality, his commitment to poor and working people, and his willingness to learn, he won over those who had opposed him.

Russell came to describe Humphrey as one of the most attractive personalities he had ever met. One evening in the late 1950's, as he was leaving the Senate, Russell heard Humphrey speaking passionately about the hard lives that farmers faced, given the harsh agriculture policies of the Eisenhower administration. Riveted, Russell stayed, and with two other southern senators, became a virtual "amen chorus" for Humphrey, beating out a rhythm on their Senate desks. Humphrey once said: "I knew every senator better than I knew anybody in my family," and they were deep, friendly relationships, animated by humor. Barry Goldwater liked to joke about Humphrey's rapid-fire speaking style, 250 words per minute with occasional gusts up to 300. Humphrey would respond by telling Goldwater that he was handsome enough to be a movie star—for Nineteenth Century Fox.

But there was Vietnam: the tragedy for Humphrey, Johnson, the Democrats, and America. When Johnson finally offered Humphrey the vice presidency in 1964, after dangling it in front of him for weeks, he warned Humphrey that he would not have the independence that he had as a senator; he would have to be a loyal soldier. Nonetheless, Humphrey jumped at the vice presidency. After Johnson trounced Goldwater in the 1964 election, Humphrey wrote Johnson a private memo, giving the president his best advice that the administration was on the wrong course in Vietnam. Johnson promptly froze Humphrey out for nearly a year. Humphrey regained the president's confidence only when he showed a willingness to travel to Vietnam and become a leading cheerleader for the war. It reduced Humphrey in the eyes of millions of Democrats and contributed to his defeat by Nixon in 1968.

For the senators, Vietnam had taught other lessons. Watching Johnson misuse the Gulf of Tonkin resolution, they learned that no president could be fully trusted. Seeing him ignore the prescient, private counsel of Humphrey, Mansfield, Russell, and Fulbright, they decided that it was necessary to go public with their opposition to a president's foreign policy. They concluded that because of World War II and the constant threat of the Cold War, the balance of power in the constitutional system had shifted too much power to the "imperial presidency." Because of Vietnam, the Senate enacted the War Powers Act, created the Intelligence Committee, and adopted the Budget Control and Impoundment Act and the Freedom of Information Act.

Jimmy Carter might think that the Senate was intruding on his foreign policy because they did not respect him or trust his judgment. And of course, many of them did not respect or trust a neophyte outsider where national security was concerned. But the Senate had reasserted its role in the foreign policy area because of their searing experiences with Johnson and Nixon, the most experienced Washington insiders imaginable. Now, the senators insisted on being partners with the president in shaping the country's foreign policy. They would get their chance soon enough.

Humphrey was such a large figure in Senate history that his death overshadowed the passing, six weeks earlier, of John McClellan, the dour Arkansas senator who chaired the Appropriations Committee. Twenty years earlier, McClellan had been among the most influential and famous senators in the country, having chaired the remarkable hearings into labor racketeering and organized crime that became for many Americans their first memory of the Senate on television.

But by the time of his death, McClellan had become a relatively minor figure in the Senate, despite the powerful committee post. He typified the conservative southerners who had run the Senate in an earlier era, and he was increasingly out of step with the progressive Senate, which he accommodated by allowing the Appropriations Committee to be controlled by subcommittee chairmen and ranking members, who were much more progressive than he. He had endured a tragic personal life, dealing with the deaths of his wife and three sons. In 1973, McClellan would meet Joe Biden, just elected to the Senate and trying to cope with the loss of his wife and daughter in a car accident. Bury yourself in work, the old man told the new senator—it's the only antidote.

The new appropriations chairman would be Warren Magnuson of Washington, serving his sixth term at the age of seventy-two. "Maggie," as he was universally known, walked slowly, with a painful shuffle, perpetually hampered by a weakened foot resulting from diabetes. He was not a forceful speaker, and he sometimes appeared shy. But in this case, appearances were deceptive; Maggie was one of the most accomplished and powerful senators in history. A prodigious worker in what he called the "legislative kitchen," Maggie had done large things for his state, bringing military contracts for Boeing in Seattle, protecting Puget Sound, and spearheading the electrification of the Pacific Northwest. But he had also done large things for the country, negotiating the public accommodations section of the Civil Rights Act, reorganizing the nation's railroad system, and spearheading the creation of the National Institutes of Health (NIH) and the National Cancer Institute (NCI).

Unlike McClellan, Maggie had been perfectly in tune with the progressive, activist Senate of the previous fifteen years; in fact, he epitomized it. Under his leadership, starting in 1963, the Senate Commerce Committee had spearheaded the nation's growing commitment to protect consumers. Maggie hired and empowered a brilliant and entrepreneurial staff led by Michael Pertschuk; they worked in close harmony with Ralph Nader and "Nader's Raiders" and investigative reporters, led by Jack Anderson and Drew Pearson, to spotlight corporate abuses and enact remedial legislation. Maggie and Pertschuk had become a legendary combination, protecting consumers and changing the relationship between government and business in the United States. In 1977, Jimmy Carter had nominated Pertschuk to chair the Federal Trade Commission, to implement the many laws that he had helped put on the books. Pertschuk would find himself at the pinnacle of the government's consumer protection effort at precisely the moment when the tide was shifting against it. The Republicans and the business community had already succeeded in scuttling the proposed Consumer Protection Agency, the consumer movement's highest legislative priority.

Magnuson had already been de facto chairman of the Appropriations Committee as McClellan's health had declined, so his new chairmanship would not change the Senate significantly. But two of the best-known senators had kept a relatively low profile in 1977, and that was about to end. The Senate needed more intellectual and political firepower to deal with the second session's overwhelming agenda, and two of the Senate's leading liberals were ready to provide it: Frank Church and Ted Kennedy.

FRANK CHURCH, ONE OF the most admired and reviled men in the Senate, spent the opening weeks of 1978 preparing for the battle that was likely to end his career.

Church was the second-ranking Democrat on the Foreign Relations Committee, and John Sparkman of Alabama, the committee's chairman, aging and in poor health, could not handle the enormous burden of bringing the controversial Panama Canal treaties to Senate ratification. The Carter administration had asked Church to take the lead on the treaties, which were absolutely hated in Idaho, arguably the most conservative state in the nation. His staff implored him to let this dubious honor pass, and keep a low profile. But Church had spoken for twenty years about changing U.S. foreign policy toward the developing world. It was at the core of all that he stood for. Frank Church could no more walk away from leadership on the Panama Canal treaties than Hubert Humphrey could have walked away from leadership on civil rights. He would take on the challenge, even if it was likely to cause him to lose his Senate seat in 1980.

Church had risen to fame as a youthful debater, known as the "boy orator of the Snake River." Cancer almost took his life in his twenties, but Church beat the disease. That brush with death fired his ambition and pushed him to take risks. He was elected to the Senate in 1956 at the age of thirty-two, one of the youngest senators in American history.

Church quickly established himself as an independent mind capable of forging tough compromises. Within a few months of entering the Senate, he helped smooth passage of the 1957 Voting Rights Act by brokering a compromise on how voting rights violations would be prosecuted. Impressed,

Majority Leader Lyndon Johnson gave Church a coveted seat on the Foreign Relations Committee, and in 1960, Church made the keynote speech at the Democratic National Convention when John Kennedy was nominated for president.

Church had been an intelligence officer in the China-Burma theatre during World War II and came away deeply opposed to the imperialism of Great Britain and France. He feared Cold War paranoia was driving the United States on its own imperial course: one that was overly reliant on military force, ambivalent about the hopes of developing nations for self-determination, and dangerously detached from American ideals.

He became one of the earliest and most eloquent critics of the Vietnam War. In a December 1964 magazine interview, he argued the increasing U.S. commitment in Vietnam was "fighting the tides of history." Asians will quickly forget our honorable motives, he said, and see nothing more than "another white, western nation using force to get its way." In February 1965, as the Johnson administration intensified air attacks on North Vietnam, Church's article, "We Are in Too Deep in Africa and Asia," appeared in the *New York Times Magazine*. That same week, on the Senate floor, he said: "we have plunged into these former colonial regions as though we had been designated on high to act as trustee in bankruptcy for the broken empires."

On June 24, 1965, Church was traveling with Johnson on Air Force One when a young lieutenant reported that a plastic bomb had killed several soldiers and two American women in Saigon. Johnson turned to Church and challenged him: "What would you do? Turn the other cheek?"

Incensed, Church shot back: "We're the ones who sent them there. And we did so knowing the dangers, the risk. Plastic bombs are terrible things, but that's all the Vietnamese have to fight back with. They don't have big bombers to drop napalm on villages from 35,000 feet." Johnson stormed off in a rage.

Church deepened his critique of the war in late 1965 and 1966 through articles in the *Washington Post* and *New York Times*. Americans could not understand the transformation that was sweeping the postcolonial world, he argued, because of our obsession with communism and because we were such a wealthy nation. "Sober and satisfied and comfortable and rich," the United States was close to being "the most un-revolutionary nation on earth."

On February 21, 1968, Church went to the Senate floor to deliver a speech entitled "Torment of the Land." He argued that "the nation's marathon dance with war" was taking a terrible toll. The conflict in Vietnam "pervades and brutalizes our culture," he said, and is circling back to our own streets, as returning veterans "transferred the arts of guerilla war" to the festering slums. He quoted a returning veteran looking at the streets of Detroit in flames: "It's here, man, that the real war is."

In the early years of the war, Church's liberal views caused a harsh reaction in Idaho. He might have been defeated for reelection if forced to run in 1965 or 1966. But by 1968, when he sought his third term, the public was turning against Vietnam. Church's earlier criticism seemed prescient. After he was reelected, ending the war in Vietnam became Church's principal focus in the Senate. With Republican John Sherman Cooper, he offered legislation to prevent Nixon from expanding the war into Laos and Cambodia and supported legislation to cut off funding for the war entirely.

When the U.S. involvement in Vietnam finally came to an end in January 1973, most Senate doves took a much lower profile, but Church became even more prominent. In 1972, he successfully urged the Foreign Relations Committee to undertake an in-depth study of the role of multinational corporations and their relationship to U.S. foreign policy. The investigation was spurred by accusations that the International Telephone and Telegraph Company (ITT) had offered the Nixon administration a contribution of "up to seven figures" in exchange for a CIA plan to undermine Chile's president, Salvador Allende, at the polls after Allende had threatened to nationalize ITT's 60 percent interest in the Chilean telephone company.

Church had always distrusted big corporations, which he equated with the lumber and mining companies that came into Idaho to extract its natural resources. By 1972, Church had been a critic of U.S. multinationals' activities in the developing world for almost two decades and as subcommittee chairman, he pursued the investigation aggressively, despite intense pushback from the Nixon administration, the U.S. business community, and the CIA.

The ITT-CIA investigation showed Church at his best, relentlessly exposing government abuse and corporate greed. A major U.S. corporation had tried to rig an election in a friendly country and enlisted the CIA in its efforts. The CIA, in turn, had encouraged ITT to damage Allende by creating economic chaos in Chile. Church ridiculed the argument that Allende's election posed a threat to U.S. national security, joking that Chile was "a dagger pointed at the heart of Antarctica."

Church's subcommittee tackled an even more explosive issue when the Organization of Petroleum Exporting Countries (OPEC), the cartel of Arab oil exporters, cut off U.S. oil shipments in retaliation for U.S. aid to Israel during the October 1973 Yom Kippur War. In the months that followed, oil prices tripled, gas shortages were common, and long lines at the pump became part of daily life. Meanwhile, oil company profits soared by 50 to 70 percent above the previous year. Economists said these profits simply reflected higher prices caused by a shortage of supply, but Church spoke for many Americans when he attacked the oil companies for "profiteer(ing) upon the present adversity." He announced his subcommittee would investigate and expose the complex relationships between the Arab governments and U.S. oil companies. "We Americans," Church declared, "must uncover the trail that led the United States into dependency on the Arab sheikdoms."

Church's subcommittee staff, led by its crusading chief counsel Jerry Levinson, made public thousands of previously classified documents that drew a picture of increasing U.S. dependence on oil companies, and oil companies' increasing reliance on Middle East crude. The U.S. government had given oil companies credit for taxes paid to Arab governments. More importantly, the CIA had aided the companies by sponsoring the overthrow of Iranian Prime Minister Mohammad Mossadegh's government after he nationalized the holdings of the Anglo-Iranian oil company.

Church was reelected to a fourth term in 1974. Spurred on by public outrage over Watergate and other government abuses, his subcommittee plunged into an investigation of bribes offered to foreign governments to obtain defense contracts, focusing particularly on Northrop and Lockheed Martin. The subcommittee found evidence of bribes paid by Northrop to Price Bernhard of the Netherlands and by Lockheed to top government officials in Japan and West Germany. The report ultimately found that officials in more than thirty countries had received payoffs from Lockheed, Northrop, and other corporations. In response to the subcommittee findings, the Netherlands and Italy opened their own investigations. "Lockheedo," as the Japanese press referred to the scandal, led to the arrest of former Prime Minister Kakuei Tanaka, and Robert Waters, Lockheed's fifty-four-year-old vice president, committed suicide with a hunting rifle as a result of the revelations.

In late 1974, a series of articles by *New York Times* reporter Seymour M. Hersh accusing the CIA of illegal intelligence operations against antiwar activists and other dissidents had captured the attention of a country already made distrustful by the excesses of Watergate. On January 27, 1975, just one month after Hersh's first bombshell story, the Senate created a Select Committee on Intelligence Activities, by an 82–4 vote, charged with investigating the CIA, FBI, and other intelligence agencies.

Majority Leader Mike Mansfield had long been concerned about the lack of congressional oversight of the intelligence community. When Phil Hart turned down the select committee's chairmanship, Mansfield offered the job to Church. As a former intelligence officer, Church recognized the need for the United States to gather intelligence abroad, but his investigation of the CIA role in overthrowing Allende had helped convince him such activities often proved counterproductive and were contrary to American ideals.

Church had a daunting and delicate assignment. His committee was charged with investigating, and perhaps making public, decades of previously secret intelligence activities that could have a profound effect on U.S. foreign policy and U.S. standing in the world. There was a fundamental divide on the committee between senators like Church who believed the United States would be better served by airing these abuses, and those, like Republicans John Tower and Barry Goldwater, who believed publicizing previous covert operations would damage the intelligence agencies going forward.

The Church Committee doggedly pursued CIA attempts to assassinate foreign leaders, notably Fidel Castro, and battled the Ford administration to increase what could be disclosed. The committee held 21 public hearings and 250 closed ones and gathered over 110,000 pages of documentation. The committee issued an extensive report on the FBI's domestic counterintelligence programs (COINTELPRO), which had focused on civil rights groups, antiwar activists, and Native Americans. The committee also revealed a special unit within the Internal Revenue Service (IRS) that had "politically harassed" thousands of activists and disclosed that, for thirty years, companies such as ITT and RCA had routinely provided the CIA with telegrams Americans sent abroad.

Church's critics believed he was using the committee as a springboard for a presidential run, and there was some truth to that. However, he vowed to Mansfield he would finish the committee's work before announcing his candidacy. Consequently, he did not enter the race until March 18, 1976, by which time Jimmy Carter had been campaigning for more than a year and was close to locking up the nomination. Although Church won several late primaries, he was too late to derail Carter's march.

Almost every candidate who loses an election comes away thinking he could have won had he done certain things differently. In Church's case, those "what ifs" were well justified. Church had been ideologically well positioned to seize the nomination. He was a true dove, at a time when anti-Vietnam fervor still mattered. More important, four years of high-visibility investigations had given him enormous public exposure. He was fifty-two years old, still telegenic, and, after twenty years in the Senate, a masterful orator. When Jimmy Carter spoke of the need for "a government as good as the American people," he was sending a message that Church had been using for years. He had become the Senate's foremost moralist in a post-Watergate period when the country was troubled by the lack of morality in its government and business leaders. He compared himself to an evangelist, preaching Justice Brandeis's admonition that "sunlight is the best disinfectant." He had reason to think it was his moment to be president, and reason to be disappointed, even bitter, that he had missed it.

So Church was subdued, even depressed, for much of 1977. But his energy and enthusiasm returned in August when he made a remarkable trip to Cuba, at the invitation of Fidel Castro. Acting as an emissary for the Carter administration, Church won concessions from Castro allowing the families of U.S. citizens to leave Cuba with their savings and personal possessions. Castro also agreed to review the cases of Americans imprisoned in Cuba. Church subsequently recommended to the Foreign Relations Committee that the United States should respond to Castro's gestures by easing the trade embargo against Cuba, stopping U.S. anti-terrorist activities against the Castro regime, and increasing cultural and other exchanges with Cuba.

The trip was vintage Church: walking his own path, inspiring his admirers, and enraging his opponents. The year 1978 found him reinvigorated, with a renewed commitment to putting U.S. foreign policy in the hemisphere on a higher moral plane. Soon he would have an historic opportunity to do so.

ON JANUARY 31, 1978, Senator Joe Biden visited Jimmy Carter in the White House. One of Carter's strongest supporters, Biden told Carter that Ted Kennedy was going to run for president and was already lining up support. Carter was surprised; he had seen no evidence of it. But Biden—young, handsome, brash, and ambitious—had keen enough political instincts to anticipate the decision long before Ted Kennedy had actually made it.

A crucial year for the Senate and for Jimmy Carter, 1978 would also be a decisive year for the last of the Kennedy brothers. Through the first year of the Carter presidency, Edward M. Kennedy, having weathered some terrible personal storms, charted his distinctive course almost below the radar. He planned to be more visible in 1978, sometimes tacking left, sometimes right, racking up large legislative accomplishments, and leaving the ultimate question even more present in the minds of many Democrats: would he pick up the mantle left by his fallen brothers?

Ted Kennedy had been elected to the Senate when he was barely thirty, arriving with the great class of 1962. He seemed to have minimal qualifications for the office. Reportedly, even John Kennedy expressed doubt that Teddy was ready for the Senate. But Joseph Kennedy, the family patriarch, wanted Teddy to take Jack's seat in the Senate, and that ended all discussion. The family united in support of the race, and that was probably enough to ensure victory for Ted Kennedy in Massachusetts.

However, even in that first race, after a hesitant start, he found his footing and proved himself to be an attractive candidate: handsome, energetic, the most outgoing and engaging member of the family, armed with a self-deprecating sense of humor to disarm those skeptics.

He never tired of telling the story of his encounter with a Boston longshoreman. "Kennedy," the man said, "is it true you've never worked a day in your life?"

Ted sheepishly acknowledged there was some truth to the charge.

"Kennedy," the man responded, "you haven't missed a thing."

He arrived in the Senate in January 1963, the brother of the president and the attorney general, movie star handsome with a beautiful wife. It was the peak of the New Frontier. Nuclear disarmament and civil rights were the leading issues. In such an environment, Ted Kennedy became instantly one of Washington's most watched celebrities.

From the beginning, Ted Kennedy found the Senate both challenging and collegial. Humbled by the opportunity that he had been given and fully aware of his limited experience, he gravitated to experienced senators who could teach him the ropes. Adam Clymer, the *New York Times* reporter and Kennedy biographer, would describe him as the "lion cub of the Senate" in his early years.

Of course, his life would be touched repeatedly by tragedy. Less than a year after he came to the Senate, his brother was assassinated. The next year, after the Senate had passed the historic civil rights legislation, a small plane carrying Kennedy and his friend Birch Bayh crashed in Massachusetts. Bayh dragged Kennedy to safety, but Kennedy's broken back condemned him to live with chronic pain. In November 1964, Robert Kennedy was elected to the Senate from New York, and Teddy had the joy of being "senior senator" to his older, hard-driving brother. But less than four years later, in 1968, the worst of years, Bobby, too, died at an assassin's hand. Ted Kennedy, only thirty-six, was now the patriarch of the family. For many people who wanted a restoration of the Kennedys, he was the last hope of the Democratic Party and the country.

There are those who believe that Kennedy could have been nominated in his brother's place at the 1968 convention in Chicago if he had indicated any interest. But numb with grief over Bobby's death, he held back. At the beginning of 1969, however, Kennedy channeled his energy and his growing comfort in the Senate to mount a challenge against Senate Democratic whip Russell Long. Long was a wily and gifted legislator, but his drinking problems were well known, sometimes causing embarrassing incidents in the Senate. Ted Kennedy was popular within the Senate, and revered by Democrats around the country as "the last Kennedy." Richard Nixon had just become president, adding to the luster of a Senate leadership position. Kennedy defeated Long handily, and his increased visibility prompted the Washington press (and Richard Nixon) to see him as the Democratic front-runner for 1972.

Six months later, the car accident on Chappaquiddick killed Mary Jo Kopechne, a former staffer of Robert Kennedy, and plunged Ted Kennedy back into personal crisis. Shaken to the core, Kennedy declined to take the leadership role in the Senate battles against Nixon's Supreme Court nominees Clement Haynesworth and G. Harrold Carswell and generally withdrew from his responsibilities as Senate whip. In January 1971, Byrd ousted Kennedy from his leadership position, just as Kennedy had ousted Long two years earlier.

Kennedy's family and friends, personal resilience, and love of the Senate saved him. With the presidency out of the question in 1972, Kennedy threw himself back into his Senate work. He was already on the way to becoming a respected legislator, playing a leadership role on immigration and health-care issues, particularly the federal government's newly launched War on Cancer. As evidence mounted of abuses of power in connection with Nixon's reelection campaign, Kennedy's Judiciary Subcommittee on Administrative Practice and Procedure ("Ad Prac") plunged into investigating the Justice Department's role, connecting the strands of fund-raising abuses and political dirty tricks. The subcommittee investigation developed significant evidence that it was able to turn over to the Watergate Committee, established in January 1973.

In April 1973, Kennedy played a crucial role in conditioning Elliot Richardson's nomination to be attorney general on his willingness to appoint Archibald Cox, Harvard Law professor and former solicitor general, to be the special prosecutor investigating Watergate, ensuring that Cox would have the necessary independence to do the job. Richardson agreed to Kennedy's insistence that the special prosecutor could only be removed for "extraordinary improprieties." When Nixon, feeling the heat from the special prosecutor's investigation, fired Cox in what became known as the "Saturday Night Massacre," it was a step that led inexorably to his resignation from the presidency ten months later.

Richard Nixon's crimes and abuse of power helped put Kennedy's very personal failing at Chappaquiddick in perspective. By late 1974, public opinion showed Senator Kennedy running ahead of the new president, Gerald Ford, in a hypothetical matchup. But with his family responsibilities compounded by another tragedy, his son's cancer, Kennedy made an unequivocal statement on September 23, 1974, that he would not seek the presidency in 1976, and focused intently on his work as an increasingly influential senator and creative policy entrepreneur.

Kennedy had always benefited from an excellent and aggressive staff, anchored by Paul Kirk, his administrative assistant; Carey Parker, his legislative director; Tom Susman, his staff director on the Ad Prac Subcommittee; and Larry Horowitz, a physician who moved into the policy arena to lead Kennedy's health-care efforts. All were attracted by the magnetic combination of working in the Great Senate, being part of the Democratic government in exile, fighting Richard Nixon, and working for the last Kennedy.

In early 1974, Kennedy invited Stephen Breyer, a Harvard Law professor specializing in administrative law, to dinner at his home. During their dinner, Breyer cited the Civil Aeronautics Board as a clear example of a regulatory agency that had been captured by the industry it was supposed to regulate—airlines—stifling competition, subjecting consumers to higher fares, excluding new airlines from the industry, and limiting access to profitable routes. Kennedy, intrigued by the merits of the issue and its potential political appeal, asked Breyer to come to work for him.

Breyer agreed, taking a sabbatical from Harvard Law School, shocking his faculty colleagues. It was a time-honored tradition for Harvard Law professors, going back to Felix Frankfurter, to spend time in Washington, but only in the solicitor general's office or other high-level executive branch positions.

The Harvard Law faculty regarded working in the Senate as a "political" job that marked a clear step down from Cambridge.

The Harvard Law faculty was wrong. Breyer soon discovered that being staff director and chief counsel to a Senate subcommittee, particularly one chaired by Kennedy, provided an endlessly fascinating opportunity to shape public policy. Once he had the chairman's trust, which happened almost immediately, Stephen Breyer had broad license to advance the issue of airline deregulation and get legislation enacted. He had the opportunity to solve the problem intellectually and present it in a way that was politically attractive. He crafted Kennedy's statements. He scheduled the hearings and picked the witnesses so as to illuminate the issue: embarrassing the Civil Aeronautics Board, having the airlines lay out what deregulation could mean to consumers. He briefed the press so as to ensure their understanding of the issue and maximize the attention it got. He ran the process of committee consideration, educating and persuading the staff of other committee members, negotiating changes in the bill, where needed, to address problems or win additional support. Inevitably, in what Eric Redman called "the dance of legislation," Breyer would confront challenge after challenge, and find ways to overcome them. Sometimes he would call on the chairman, but mostly, he and his staff would solve the problems and make sure the chairman was informed of what had been done in his name.

Congress had long believed that it needed more resources to match up against the executive branch. In the foreign policy area, that was generally true (although the State Department often felt overmatched against Scoop Jackson). But on domestic issues, even one of far-reaching importance like airline deregulation, Senate committee staffers stood at the major intersection where the policy and the politics came together. Hundreds of executive branch officials might be involved in airline regulation and deregulation. But ultimately, it was Congress that funded their activities, and it was Congress that enacted, changed, or killed legislation. To get what they wanted, the executive branch officials had to convince the committee of jurisdiction, which meant convincing the chairman, which started with convincing his staff director.

Like many committee staffers before him, Breyer would discover one of Washington's realities: on the issues within his jurisdiction, nobody wielded more power. That made it crucial that he knew the chairman's thinking, stay within his mandate, build trust, and deal with others in a way that reflected well on Kennedy. Breyer did it so well that he was able to overcome tensions arising from the fact that the Commerce Committee, not Judiciary, actually had primary jurisdiction over the issue. By the beginning of 1978, the airline deregulation bill was moving toward passage by the full Senate—a substantial legislative accomplishment. Breyer had returned to Harvard Law School after his leave, but would soon be drawn back to the excitement of the Senate.

In 1975, Kennedy moved aggressively into the complex and politically charged issue of crime. A national commission had recommended that federal criminal law should be codified for the first time. Kennedy worried that the Senate consideration of a federal criminal code would be dominated by hard-liners John McClellan and Roman Hruska, the Nebraska Republican who was notoriously uninterested in civil liberties. But at the same time, liberal Democrats were being hammered as being "weak on crime." Kennedy wanted to combine strong law enforcement with his unquestioned commitment to civil liberties. The Kennedy network recommended that he interview Kenneth Feinberg, an assistant U.S. attorney from New York, who had successfully prosecuted John Mitchell and Maurice Stans, Nixon's attorney general and chief fund-raiser. At the end of their meeting, Feinberg thanked Kennedy for his time, but expressed doubt that their views were compatible. "Don't be too sure," Kennedy responded to the prosecutor, who had greatly impressed him. "I'm not sure what my views are on criminal justice."

Feinberg joined Kennedy's staff in October 1975. Shortly thereafter, Kennedy made a far-ranging speech on crime in which he called for gun control, efforts to relieve the burdened federal courts, and minimum two-year imprisonment for violent crimes. Kennedy plainly sought to bridge the chasm between liberals and conservatives on the volatile crime issue. He criticized "eight years of federal efforts to reduce crime by talking tough." But he also talked straight to liberals by saying, "Nor can we counter law and order slogans with arguments that crime can only be controlled by demolishing city slums, ending poverty and discrimination and providing decent health and education to all of our citizens." Kennedy said, "let us not confuse social progress with progress in the war on crime. . . . We fool ourselves if we say 'no crime reform until society is reformed.'"

Such a speech may sound like common sense to contemporary readers. But in 1975, where the debate over crime was poisonous, for a liberal like Kennedy to sound tough on crime was a dramatic departure. Feinberg went to work on the herculean task of trying to write legislation to codify the federal criminal laws, reaching so many agreements with the staffers of McClellan and Hruska that the Washington director of the American Civil Liberties

Union wrote to Kennedy that "Feinberg was out of control." In response, Kennedy called Feinberg into his office, and said "good job."

Ultimately, the task of writing a new federal criminal code proved too ambitious and was never completed. But the work done by Kennedy and Feinberg provided the basis for a new set of sentencing guidelines adopted by the federal judiciary, reducing the range of judicial discretion. Kennedy and Feinberg also began working with the Carter administration to spell out the circumstances in which wiretapping to gather foreign intelligence could occur. This effort, which Kennedy had begun during the Ford administration, required a delicate balancing between national security needs and civil liberties concerns. Like airline deregulation, this initiative broke new ground for Democrats, moving a considerable distance from traditional liberal concerns. Both the senator and the White House saw 1978 as the year that these initiatives would become law.

At the same time, Kennedy maintained a laser-like focus on his highest priority—health care for all Americans. He had become chairman of the Health Subcommittee in 1971. He had begun his subcommittee chairmanship by fighting to increase funding for cancer research but had gone on to broaden his concern to providing national health insurance, which he would call "the great unfinished business on the agenda of the Democratic Party." In May 1977, when Carter had been in office just four months, Kennedy had sharply criticized him at the United Auto Workers convention, saying that "health reform is in danger of becoming the missing promise in the Administration's plans." Kennedy regarded the issue as his life's work and the true litmus test of what the Democratic Party stood for. His critique of Carter was far more focused than McGovern's blasts had been. He would keep up the drumbeat, despite Carter's determination to proceed piece by piece, in an effort to keep health care costs down.

Seeking new ways forward for the Democrats and the country, Kennedy had found important issues on which he could work comfortably with the Carter administration. But it was his move to the left—insisting that the moment to realize the dream of national health insurance had come—that fueled excitement among liberal Democrats and fed their growing dissatisfaction with Carter.

FOR THE SENATE, A year of living dangerously was about to begin. Robert Byrd wanted to prove himself a great majority leader and statesman, rather than a mechanic who made the Senate trains run. Howard Baker wanted to be a minority leader like his father-in law, Everett Dirksen, who put the national interest first and worked with presidents to accomplish great things. Frank Church wanted to transform the relationship of the United States to the developing world, particularly Latin America.

Jimmy Carter would give all of them the opportunity they sought, when he committed his presidency to addressing the festering sore between the United States and Panama: control over the Panama Canal. Baker and Church would soon ruefully recall the admonition "Be careful what you wish for."

chapter 8

THE
PANAMA
CANAL FIGHT

THE PANAMA CANAL HOLDS A SPECIAL PLACE IN AMERICAN HISTORY.
President Theodore Roosevelt ordered the gunboat *Nashville* to help secure
Panamanian independence from Colombia in 1903. Within days he secured
a treaty giving the United States full rights over the land to build the canal
and to control it "in perpetuity." Cutting through one of the narrowest points
of Central America, it offers ships passage from the Atlantic to the Pacific
Ocean.

Over time, though, the ten-mile-wide, American-controlled Canal Zone
became a bitter source of frustration to the Panamanian people. This frustration escalated in the wake of World War II, when a wave of African and
Asian nations won independence from the war-scarred and bankrupt old
powers. The Canal Zone began to look more and more like a relic of an old
imperial era. Successive Panamanian presidents won office with stridently
anti-American rhetoric and the canal's future became a contentious issue between American presidents and Congress.

On Panamanian Independence Day, November 3, 1959, Panamanian students tried to force their way into the Canal Zone to tear down the American
flag at the U.S. embassy and replace it with the flag of Panama. Thirty people
were injured in the riots that followed. President Eisenhower, who had served
in the Canal Zone in the 1920's, sympathized with the Panamanian position.

Attempting to cool tempers, he ordered the Panamanian flag flown along with the U.S. flag in a prominent corner of the Canal Zone despite a House resolution that attempted to stop him.

Anti-U.S. rioting broke out again in 1964 after another flag-raising incident. This time, thousands of Panamanian students poured onto the streets. Four Americans were killed and twenty-four injured in the ensuing chaos. Panamanian President Roberto Chiari suspended diplomatic relations with the United States in retaliation.

Lyndon Johnson, just six weeks into his unexpected presidency, had insisted that President Chiari restore calm before he would discuss any other issues. At the same time, he began informally polling the Senate about the possibility of a new treaty. There was certainly a base of potential support: Mansfield spoke for many when he observed that "our national interest is in a trouble-free water passage, not the safeguarding of an outdated position of privilege." Hawks like Richard Russell and Everett Dirksen took the opposite position. Russell opposed voluntarily giving up U.S. power under any circumstances, while Dirksen believed rewarding the protesters' violence would set a bad precedent for U.S. relations with other small nations. It was far too early to assess how the full Senate might respond to a treaty, though it was certainly not too early to sense that it would be controversial.

Johnson committed to negotiating a new treaty with Chiari in December 1964. However, by the time that treaty was completed in June 1967, Panama's new president, Marcos Robles, caught in a tough reelection battle, was unwilling to fight for it. With Robles's subsequent defeat in 1968 and Johnson's decision not to seek reelection that same year, the treaty was orphaned, and the issue continued to fester.

Richard Nixon largely ignored Panama during his first term, focusing instead on the more pressing foreign policy issues of ending the Vietnam War, seeking an opening with China, and pursuing détente with the Soviet Union. In March 1973, Panamanian president Omar Torrijos, installed in a 1968 coup, forced the issue. He called a United Nations Security Council meeting in Panama at which the United States was forced to veto a resolution calling for a new "just and fair" treaty that would "guarantee full respect for Panama's effective sovereignty." That summer, Nixon and Secretary of State Kissinger chose Ambassador Ellsworth Bunker, one of the country's most distinguished diplomats and former ambassador to South Vietnam, to begin negotiating a new treaty with Panama.

By February 1974, Kissinger and Panamanian Foreign Secretary Juan Antonio Tack had signed a set of "principles" that could form the bases of a new treaty. The principles included the United States' use of "lands, water and airspace" necessary to operate and defend the Canal but set a fixed date for the return of the Canal Zone to Panamanian sovereignty. Senate conservatives soon shot back. A resolution sponsored by Strom Thurmond, the arch-conservative Republican from South Carolina, "in support of continued undiluted United States sovereignty over the United States–owned Canal Zone" won thirty-four cosponsors—enough to defeat any treaty. Nixon's presidency was soon crippled by Watergate and, while negotiations continued, the Panama Canal became a low priority once again.

As negotiations dragged on, Panamanian frustration grew. As the 1976 presidential election neared, many feared renewed violence, perhaps even a seizure of the Canal. General George Brown, chairman of the Joint Chiefs of Staff, reassured the country's leader, General Omar Torrijos: "General, you have my word as a soldier that we will work for a fair and just treaty . . . I am asking you to be patient a little longer and keep things under control until we can move ahead."

For many Americans in 1976, the Panama Canal issue struck a deep and emotional chord. Troubled by the weak economy and humiliated by America's loss in Vietnam, many voters saw challenges to American control over the canal as evidence of a country in retreat. They believed maintaining control over the canal showed American strength and purpose. The simplicity of the issue also made it an ideal political football. Ronald Reagan, challenging President Ford for the Republican nomination, trailed badly until he began attacking the "quiet, almost secret, negotiations to give away the Panama Canal." The Reagan-allied American Conservative Union ran 33 newspaper ads and 882 radio spots on the issue in the North Carolina primary, helping deliver Reagan an upset victory. A Ford organizer later said the North Carolina campaign turned on "Sally Jones sitting at home, watching Ronald Reagan on television and deciding that she didn't want to give away the Panama Canal." It provided the momentum for Reagan to continue his challenge all the way to the Republican convention.

Jimmy Carter had said very little about the Panama Canal during his presidential campaign. But during the transition, Robert Pastor, his foremost Latin American expert, warned that unless a treaty was negotiated and submitted to the Senate in 1977, "violence in Panama is virtually inevitable, and the repercussions for the U.S. will be widespread." Kissinger briefed Carter on the state of negotiations, underscoring Pastor's message, noting that if violence broke out again, Mexico might send troops to back Panama, leading to unprecedented regional instability.

While previous presidents had favored a new treaty because of concerns about canal security, Carter also saw it as the cornerstone of a new relationship with Latin America. He hoped it would signal a powerful step toward a new, liberal internationalism, one pillar of which was promoting equitable relationships with smaller countries.

It would not be easy. Smaller than South Carolina in size, and smaller than Houston in population, Panama would soon loom very large in American politics.

THE SENATE PLAYS A special role in foreign policy. As far as treaties are concerned, its constitutional responsibility is to advise and consent. The reality is often far less constructive. John Hay, secretary of state to President Theodore Roosevelt, reflected on bitter experience. "A treaty entering the Senate is like a bull going into the arena," Hay wrote. "No one can tell just how or when the final blow will fall—but one thing is certain—it will never leave the arena alive." It was the Senate that ultimately shattered President Woodrow Wilson's dream of a League of Nations, a United Nations precursor that might have stemmed Hitler's rise. More recently, several important treaties, including the Law of the Sea Treaty, the Kyoto Protocol, and the Framework Convention on Tobacco Control, were not even submitted to the Senate because they were clearly doomed to failure.

Nevertheless, there were some reasons to be optimistic at the outset of the Panama Canal battle. Many of the Senate veterans in 1977 had just arrived in the Senate during the last major treaty considered there, the Limited Nuclear Test Ban Treaty struck by President Kennedy and Soviet Premier Nikita Khrushchev in 1963. In that case, early opposition from Republicans and Democratic hawks, including Scoop Jackson, Richard Russell, and John Stennis, was worn down by Kennedy's strong, patient advocacy, resulting in the treaty being ratified by an 80–19 vote. After the Cuban Missile Crisis, Minority Leader Everett Dirksen observed, Americans trusted Kennedy's leadership and wanted desperately for the superpowers to move away from the nuclear abyss. However, it was doubtful that the Senate in 1978 would ever trust Carter the way they trusted Kennedy, and the Panama Canal clearly presented a "hot button" political issue. Would the senators, particularly those seeking reelection, be able to get past the politics and focus on the substantive issues?

The negotiators were working on two treaties. One would set forth new terms for the joint operation of the canal for the rest of the century, at the end of which Panama would assume total control. The other would guarantee the permanent neutrality of the canal and the right of the United States to defend it.

In the beginning, Byrd was ambivalent about the treaties. By background a hawkish, proud patriot, he had been a cosponsor of Strom Thurmond's resolution three years earlier committing the United States to continued sovereignty over the canal. As he had begun to play an increasingly influential role in foreign policy, his views had become more nuanced. He was also a pragmatist who wanted to help a struggling Carter to a foreign policy victory if possible. All these factors made Byrd open to weighing the case for the treaties. His first step would be to ensure senators would be fully educated about the treaties and he loaned out his inner office, just off the Senate floor, as a classroom.

Over the next few months, Ambassador Bunker and White House Latin America Specialist Sol Linowitz led at least half a dozen seminars on the treaties to more than seventy senators. Byrd attended several sessions, sitting in the back, taking extensive notes on a yellow pad, and occasionally interjecting a pointed question. The diplomats impressed him with the case they presented, but Byrd kept his powder dry, not yet ready to commit.

In mid-August, as the diplomatic process had moved forward to the point where the basic principles of the treaties were settled, Carter invited Byrd and his wife, Erma, to a private White House dinner. Carter knew Byrd's support was indispensable for getting the treaties ratified, and he took care not to pressure the proud majority leader too much. At the same time, he wanted Byrd to know the treaties were close to completion, and that the Senate would not be able to escape debating them. Byrd made no promises but underscored for the president that the treaties "had an uphill road to travel."

As negotiations neared completion, senators began traveling to Panama themselves. Ernest Hollings was recognized as one of the smartest, toughest, and most independent thinkers in the Senate. A graduate of the Citadel, a lawyer and former governor, Hollings had opposed a new treaty when Johnson put forth the idea. Now, however, Hollings approached the problem with an open mind. He grilled Panama's President Demetrio Lakas and U.S. Lt. General Phil McAuliffe of the Southern Command, focusing sharply on whether the new treaties would strengthen or weaken U.S. access to the canal. A few days after returning to Washington, Hollings sent a newsletter to South Carolina with a ringing defense of the new treaties "as the only reliable and fair way for the United States to keep the Canal in use."

Not all the Panama visits turned out so well. Strom Thurmond, Jesse Helms, and Orrin Hatch, all openly opposed to the treaties, traveled to Panama in August 1977. They rejected most of the meetings that the U.S. ambassador tried to arrange for them, instead secretly recording a meeting with Lakas and turning the tape over to an anti-treaty newspaper columnist—an outrageous breach of diplomatic protocol. The right-wing Republicans' action signaled just how hard, and how partisan, the fight over the Panama Canal would become.

CARTER AND TORRIJOS ANNOUNCED the completion of the Panama Canal treaties on September 16, 1977. Ten days later, the Senate Foreign Relations Committee began hearings in room 318 of the Russell Senate Office Building, a room used only for the most important hearings. Over three weeks, the committee would hear testimony from seventy-nine witnesses and accept countless written statements. The committee was working in the best tradition of the Senate, delving deeply into important and emotional issues, educating the public and educating itself.

Early questioning focused on what rights the United States would have to protect the canal once it had been turned over to Panama and whether U.S. warships would have priority over commercial vessels going through the canal. Statements by Panama's chief negotiator, Romulo Escobar, most likely made for domestic consumption, had raised doubts that Panama shared the U.S. understanding on these issues, and senators wanted assurances. U.S. Ambassador to Panama William Jorden, appointed by Nixon in 1974, had been retained by Carter for the duration of the treaty fight. He testified that for Panamanians the issue was "not (about power over) the canal at all," but about "the presence of a slice of territory (in Panama) in which the country on both sides has absolutely nothing to say about what goes on."

On the issue of a U.S. right to intervene in the Canal Zone, he argued Panamanian and U.S. interests were not fundamentally different, but that Panamanians opposed the term "intervention" because of the legacy of colonialism. According to Jorden,

"Intervention" in Panama and in the minds of Latin Americans has a very special meaning. When Latin Americans think about "intervention," they think of foreign troops coming in, killing their people, removing their government, taking over and running the show. . . . They remember the Spanish, they remember the French in Mexico, they remember Haiti and Nicaragua, and all the rest of it. When they talk about "intervention" that hits a very sensitive nerve, and it is bloody difficult for any Panamanian to say: "Yes, we have given the United States the right to intervene."

Perhaps the most crucial testimony came from the Pentagon. General Brown had been working on the treaty for four years. He made it clear that the U.S. national security interest was in using the canal, not owning it. "Our capability to defend the Panama Canal will be enhanced through cooperation with the government of Panama," he said.

Howard Baker was a member of the Foreign Relations Committee and participated extensively in the hearings. Like Byrd, Baker had been a cosponsor of the Thurmond resolution. Also like Byrd, Baker wanted to bide his time and make a considered decision. But Baker faced a much more complicated political calculus. He was up for reelection in 1978. He was the Republican leader, and an emboldened far-right faction of his party vehemently opposed giving away the Panama Canal. Unlike Dirksen dealing with the Test Ban Treaty, Baker would not be able to deliver many Republican votes under any circumstances.

Perhaps most importantly, Baker understood that supporting the Panama Canal treaties would likely end his hope of gaining the Republican presidential nomination in 1980. Howard Liebengood, Baker's most senior legislative adviser, called the decision "a confrontation between statesmanship and politics" and said it "lends a chilling quality to the 'Would you rather be right than President?' cliché." Many years later, Baker would remember his reaction to Jimmy Carter's call in August 1977 asking for his support. "I wished he hadn't asked," Baker said. "It was an unwelcome challenge." At the time, he wondered: "This has been kicking around for years. Why now, and why me?"

Baker was especially troubled when Panamanian negotiator Escobar questioned the U.S. right to defend the canal under the treaty and priority passage for U.S. warships. In Baker's judgment, there was no way the Senate would advise and consent to a treaty unless those uncertainties were laid to rest. In October he told Carter as much with a dozen senators in tow. Carter got the message. He invited General Torrijos to Washington and after several hours of negotiation, the two issued a joint "statement of understanding," which stated that American warships would be allowed to go to the head of the line of ships transiting the canal and that both Panama and the United States had the right to defend the canal from aggression. The statement clarified that this right to defend the canal did not create a U.S. "right of intervention" into Panamanian affairs, which was necessary to assure Panamanian passage of the treaties in an October 23 plebiscite.

Baker and Byrd both applauded the Carter-Torrijos statement but continued to withhold their endorsements. On November 9, Codel Byrd arrived in Panama City. The delegation included six other Democratic senators—Howard Metzenbaum, Paul Sarbanes, Walter "Dee" Huddleston of Kentucky, Donald Riegle of Michigan, Spark Matsunaga of Hawaii, and Jim Sasser of Tennessee. Codel Byrd also included three members of Byrd's staff and, in a remarkable sign of cooperation between the two leaders, two of Baker's most senior advisers, William Hildenbrand and Howard Liebengood.

On their first night in Panama City, the visiting senators dined with a cross-section of leading Panamanians from government, the business sector, and academia. Responding to the ambassador's welcoming toast, Byrd gave the group a thoughtful description of the American political landscape. "What you have to understand," he told them, "is that any senator voting for these treaties will pay a high political price. He will gain absolutely nothing personally by doing so. Therefore, you have to be tolerant and patient in bringing people around to understanding these problems and to taking this difficult decision." It was an honest and important message that the audience needed to hear. Undoubtedly, though, the Panamanians thought they had been patient long enough. They had been waiting to redress the inequities of the 1903 treaty since the Eisenhower administration.

Codel Byrd had come principally to take the measure of General Torrijos. The Panamanian leader defied easy description. Critics attacked him as a "dictator" and a "tyrant," and many Americans feared his ties with Castro. But American diplomats also praised his moderation in office and many believed he could be a trusted partner. Among Panamanians, Torrijos was a hero who was alleviating poverty in the countryside and making Panama a player on the world stage.

Torrijos impressed the senators on the second day of the tour, which they spent in San Blas territory, on the northeast coast of Panama, home of the

Cuna Indians. The senators' small plane landed on a dirt airstrip; they climbed into small boats to cross the lagoon to their island destination. Once there, Torrijos, who was acting as guide, presided over a meeting where a Cuna leader ran through a catalog of complaints about the Panamanian government, from an unreliable water supply to poor child health care. When Torrijos tried to offer explanations, the tough-minded woman cut him off. The senators, all veterans of town meetings, had never expected to see this type of grassroots democracy in the remote parts of Panama, with the dictator they had expected to meet having to struggle to make his points.

The next day, Codel Byrd flew to Los Santos on the Azuero Peninsula, southwest of Panama City. It was cattle and farm country, and the people were celebrating the 156th anniversary of Panama's independence from Spain. As the people of the town drank beer and danced to the music of a local band, Torrijos walked through the crowds, without a car or bodyguards, shaking hands, hugging women, and picking up children. The senators followed in his wake, admiring a natural politician at work.

Many senators and representatives had visited Panama in the previous months, but this delegation was the toughest. They asked Torrijos about his relations with Castro, why he had sent some of his people into exile, when he was planning to have elections, and whether he would step down. Riegle, Metzenbaum, Huddleston, and Sasser asked the harshest questions, often surprising Ambassador Jorden with their rudeness. But Torrijos responded calmly and patiently to even the most incendiary questions. Whatever he really thought of the senators—the phrase "ugly American" occurred to Ambassador Jorden—he understood that these visitors held Panama's future in their hands.

As the delegation left a seaside resort, one senator told a CBS news reporter: "It was one of the toughest interrogations that could be made of any man." Metzenbaum, who had been among the most insistent questioners, offered an important verdict: "I feel it is just to say that General Torrijos has impressed all of us favorably, particularly by his honesty and frankness." If the final meeting went as well as the one just completed, Metzenbaum went on, "I would not have any difficulty in confirming that I would vote for the ratification of the treaties."

Back in Washington, despite his considerable patience, Baker was getting increasingly irritated by cheap shots from his Republican colleagues. Helms, speaking to the Florida Conservative Union in mid-September, had said

Baker was "squirming like a worm on a hot rock." Dole, back in the Senate after his failed vice presidential bid, was also speaking out against the treaties and subtly suggesting Baker was weak for his refusal to take a stand. Mary McGrory, the acerbic columnist, described Baker as "the Republican Hamlet on the Potomac." Now, Baker received a full briefing from Hildenbrand and Liebengood about Codel Byrd. The report left little doubt that Byrd would fully support the treaties, as would the other senators. Moreover, Baker's staffers came away with the same positive reaction. Baker decided it was time for him to visit Panama.

Over lunch at Torrijos' seaside villa, Baker laid out the political realities. The treaties in their present form would not be ratified by the Senate. He insisted that the treaties must explicitly incorporate the clarifications that Torrijos and Carter had agreed to in October. "There can be no doubt about our right to use force to protect the canal," Baker stated. "And in time of emergency, our navy ships have to be able to get through the canal as fast as possible." Torrijos agreed, provided the Senate insisted on no changes that would require him to resubmit the treaty, which had already won a two-thirds majority in a countrywide plebiscite, to another majority vote.

Torrijos's commitment settled it for Baker. He had already decided that if these crucial principles were incorporated into the treaties, he would support them. He would be able to show that he had closed the loopholes and addressed the most crucial concerns, insulating himself from criticism and making the treaties something the Senate could responsibly ratify. There was an embarrassing moment when Torrijos told the press he had won Baker's backing. Baker, who preferred to announce his own positions, said flatly that he had not made a commitment, which caused Torrijos to walk away angrily. Sensing Torrijos's embarrassment, Baker softened his point, saying appropriate "modifications" might satisfy him and might also win the necessary backing of two-thirds of the Senate. The atmosphere eased, the two men shook hands, and the visit ended successfully.

The next day, Torrijos sent a clear signal to Baker that he had gotten the minority leader's message. An editorial in one of the government-directed newspapers was headlined: "I am not dogmatic, gentlemen of the Senate." The editorial acknowledged that senators had some "reasonable objections" to the treaties and stressed Torrijos's flexibility. Before leaving Panama, Baker told waiting reporters he was inclined to support the treaties if the changes he had suggested could be worked out. Byrd, who had not yet announced his intentions, decided it was time to declare his support. First, he called Baker, who was in Brazil, and the two leaders decided to work together to obtain ratification. It would prove to be a historically important decision.

On January 13, 1978, Byrd announced his decision to support the treaties at his weekly news conference. Repeating the arguments of the Joint Chiefs of Staff, Byrd said "the treaties are the best means of continued access to the canal." He said he was "cautiously optimistic" that the Senate would ratify the treaties but admitted there would be a "difficult battle" ahead.

Thanks to Byrd and Baker, the second year of Jimmy Carter's presidency was starting on a promising note. Byrd had captured the central truth quite clearly several months before when speaking to administration officials. "You're not going to get a treaty without me, and you're not going to get a treaty without Senator Baker," he said. "If you have both of us, you might get a treaty."

The Panama Canal issue provided a stark reminder that politics entails courage, risk, and, sometimes, sacrifice. Baker's support went a long way to ensuring that he would not be the Republican presidential nominee in 1980. Frank Church's support made it quite likely that his distinguished Senate career would come to an end. Church had supported a new Panama Canal treaty as far back as 1967. Redressing the injustice of the 1903 treaty was completely consistent with his world view. He was the Senate's most eloquent critic of "Yankee imperialism" in Latin America. Unfortunately, that view had little support in Idaho, one of the most conservative states in the country. Perennial right-wing suspicion about Church had already intensified as a result of his historic investigation into the intelligence community. Now, thanks to New Right opposition to the Panama Canal treaties, the political atmosphere in the country and in Idaho was coming to a boiling point. By 1977, 78 percent of Americans wanted to maintain control of the canal. In Idaho, it was slightly higher.

Church saw the political writing on the wall. His staff told him the treaties were like "dynamite" and a leadership role in supporting them would ensure his defeat in 1980. When Ambassador Sol Linowitz approached him about floor managing the treaties, because of Foreign Relations chairman Sparkman's failing health, Church told him that he would prefer to back the treaties as quietly as possible. Ultimately, though, Church realized that he could not avoid acting on his convictions—he would take the lead on the floor. Paul Sarbanes, a freshman senator who chaired the Subcommittee on Western

Hemisphere Affairs, would be Church's deputy. Sarbanes had won plaudits during the House Judiciary Committee hearings on Nixon's impeachment in 1974. He was already regarded as a likely star in the Senate.

BY FEBRUARY 1978, THE stage was set for a historic debate. Most Americans still opposed the treaties, but supporters were prepared to do what they thought was in the national interest, irrespective of the consequences. Even such prominent conservatives as William F. Buckley and George Will supported the treaties, suggesting the national security benefits of compromise on the canal, argued by every president since Eisenhower, were visible to anyone who looked for them. John Wayne, the legendary actor who personified cowboy ruggedness, had been married to a Panamanian woman, and had visited the country many times. He sent a three-page letter endorsing the treaty to all the senators.

By this time, there was evidence the pro-treaty forces might be gaining the upper hand. The Foreign Relations Committee had opted not to formally include the Carter-Torrijos understandings when they passed the treaty out of committee, instead recommending their inclusion later. This was part of a Church-designed plan to avoid tempting fate before the Panamanian plebiscite. When Byrd and Baker introduced the Carter-Torrijos amendments now, they had seventy-six cosponsors.

But the growing, populist right wing of the Republican Party opposed the treaties ferociously. To be sure, many opponents were sincere in their positions, but they were also taking a position that had been carefully road tested for political advantage. Richard Viguerie, the leading right-wing political direct mail guru at the time, called the treaties "an issue conservatives can't lose on. If we lose the vote in the Senate, we will still have had the issue for eight or nine months. . . . We will have rallied many new people to our cause. . . . [Conservative activists] can go to the polls, look for a person's name on the ballot who favored these treaties and vote against him." Paul Laxalt of Nevada, who was leading the Senate opposition and serving as liaison between New Right conservative leaders and Senate treaty opponents, told the California Republican convention: "This is the best political issue that could be handed to a party." The personally genial Laxalt was well liked in the Senate, but he was no less opposed to the treaties than Helms, Hatch, and Thurmond.

On February 8, 1978, the Senate debate began. This was the first time a Senate debate would be aired live on radio by the Public Broadcasting Corporation—a promising development, but one that was immediately dashed by James Allen, who refused to grant the "unanimous consent" necessary to expedite any Senate business. So listeners were forced to listen to Senate debate each article of the treaty with yea or nay votes on any proposed changes. The debate would be protracted, and there would be no place for senators to hide.

Like so many Senate debates, the real action in this case was not on the floor, but in the cloakrooms and the leaders' offices. Byrd and Baker, thoroughly committed and communicating regularly, needed time to identify undecided senators and to find the combination of appeals that would sway them. The opponents were doing the same. But for them, wooing individual senators was less important than the fire they were lighting at the grass roots.

The battle over the Panama Canal treaties broke new ground in the use of direct mail and grassroots lobbying. The opponents were borrowing Helms's favorite strategy: "make them see the light by making them feel the heat." The Carter administration had launched its own extensive public education effort, spearheaded by Anne Wexler, the White House's talented and hard-driving director of public liaison. Within weeks, Wexler had convinced America's elites that the new treaties were in the national interest. But polls and the mail flooding into Senate offices showed that most Americans had not yet been convinced.

Struggling for every vote, the Carter administration soon discovered the downside of Mansfield's democratized Senate in which limited deference was given to seniority, expertise, or committee jurisdiction. Dennis DeConcini was a freshman Democrat from Arizona, a conservative state where sentiments against the "canal giveaway" were running high. For a brief time, it appeared DeConcini would have the best possible political cover. Arizona's senior senator, Barry Goldwater, the first hero of the New Right, had given serious thought to supporting the treaties, concerned that guerilla warfare might break out if the canal was not returned to Panama. Carter talked to Goldwater and several times expressed great hope that Goldwater might be with them. Yet ultimately Goldwater decided he could not go against so many of his strongest supporters.

DeConcini, stuck in a politically difficult position, decided the Byrd and Baker amendments were too weak. In his view, there should be no uncertainty about the United States' ability to intervene if unrest in Panama threatened canal operations. He introduced an amendment on February 9, which stated that if the canal was closed or its operations interfered with, the

United States could take "such steps as it deems necessary" to reopen or restore operations.

Many treaty supporters believed the DeConcini reservation was necessary to secure key votes. But the Carter administration, which was beginning to earn grudging respect from the Senate for its improved congressional relations, now failed to check its other flank. Reassured by Deputy Secretary of State Warren Christopher that the reservation would be acceptable to Panama and nervous about the future of his signature foreign policy initiative, Carter agreed to the amendment on March 15.

Neither Christopher nor anyone else had checked with Torrijos. Panamanian leaders were enraged by the news. They had accepted many amendments and reservations to win Senate votes, but DeConcini's language undermined the basic idea of the treaty. It re-enshrined the 1903 concept of "perpetuity." Ambassador Jorden told Washington the DeConcini reservation was flatly unacceptable to Panama, and "if adopted, could cause rejection of the treaty."

Every difficult negotiation has its crisis points, when the possibility of failure becomes vividly real, and everything thereafter rides only on cool judgment and improvisation. This was one of those moments.

The White House and Senate worked frantically to explore whether another reservation could be added to undercut the impact of DeConcini's language. Byrd was seething at DeConcini but cautious about trying to find consensus on new language at the eleventh hour, fearing he would lose DeConcini's vote and several others. Consultations with Sarbanes and Vice President Mondale reached the same conclusion: changing the DeConcini reservation was impossible at the moment. The only realistic course, they decided, would be to convince Torrijos to stay calm, pass the Neutrality Treaty, and find a way to fix the problem during consideration of the second treaty. Torrijos and his advisers, despite their anger, agreed to go along for the moment.

On March 16, just before the conclusion of debate, DeConcini rose to offer his reservation. Metzenbaum and Kennedy spoke strongly against it, calling it a throwback to the attitudes of the 1903 treaty and completely contrary to the new partnership with Panama that the current treaties sought to build. But most treaty supporters assumed the DeConcini reservation was a necessary evil, which had been fully vetted and discussed with Panama. The Senate approved the reservation 75–23.

The historic debate had finally reached its conclusion. The majority leader had the last word. Byrd began by quoting the words Shakespeare gave Brutus before the Battle of Philippi:

> There is a tide in the affairs of men,
> Which, taken at the flood, leads on to fortune,
> Omitted, all the voyage of their life
> Is bound in shallows and in miseries
> On such a full sea are we now afloat.
> And we must take the current when it serves,
> Or lose our ventures.

Byrd acknowledged to those who supported the treaties, "your badges of courage may be the dents in your armor." But "nothing can be politically right if it is morally wrong. In my judgment, it is not only economically right, not only commercially right, not only right from the standpoint of the security interests of our country, not only politically right, but it is morally right that we vote to ratify these treaties, and thus live up to the principles that we have so long espoused among nations."

The vote was finally called. Vice President Mondale instructed the gallery to be silent. Every senator was in his seat for the vote, which happens only under extraordinary circumstances. The Senate voted 68 to 32. Byrd and Baker had the votes, with one to spare, and with two-thirds of the senators present and voting, the Neutrality Treaty was agreed to.

A historic victory in a legislative battle of this magnitude would ordinarily trigger a night of celebration for the White House and its Senate supporters, before exhaustion set in. But this time, the elation was short-lived.

WITHIN HOURS, THE WHITE House began to understand that the "DeConcini fiasco" had caused a poisonous backlash in Panama. Hamilton Jordan, Carter's chief of staff, lamented not having recognized the danger posed by the reservation and reported that Carter was berating himself as well. Sarbanes, who had been steadfast and near-brilliant in his responsibilities as a floor manager, was incensed by the administration's poor planning. Exhausted from the all-out effort to win passage of the first treaty, the White House had no strategy for neutralizing the DeConcini amendment, but officials desperately tried to reassure Torrijos, mostly on the basis of faith, that the problem could be rectified in the second treaty.

By April 6, while the Senate was debating the second treaty, the administration and State Department had still not found a way to solve the problems created by the first. The Panamanians were pressing for strong language making it clear that the DeConcini reservation was overruled by the Organization of American States charter and the Charter of the United Nations, which prohibit armed intervention by one state in another's territory. The Panamanians' harsh language was straining treaty supporters and giving right-wing opponents a public relations bonanza. Several liberals, some of them among the treaties' strongest advocates, were threatening to pull their support altogether, and Baker warned Panama on *CBS News* that "just the twitch of an eyelid, just the slightest provocation or expression that these treaties, or this treaty in this form, is not acceptable to Panama, and this whole thing could go down the tubes."

Remedying the impact of the DeConcini reservation should have been a manageable problem. But the key senators and the White House had very little room to maneuver. If they went too far in providing reassurance to Panama, they ran the risk of looking weak and losing the votes of DeConcini and others who had been hesitant to come on board. Relations between the Panamanian government and the Carter administration were deteriorating rapidly. The White House and the State Department seemed unable to admit the magnitude of their error, and therefore could not rectify it. The senators would have to devise a solution.

The senators found an important ally in Mike Kozak, one of the State Department's legal advisers. Kozak had devoted himself to the Panama Canal treaties for several years and was determined to not let them go down the drain. He wrote a tightly reasoned statement any senator could deliver to show the DeConcini reservation did not provide a license for the United States to intervene in Panama's internal affairs and shared it with Hoyt Purvis, Byrd's chief foreign policy adviser. Purvis told Kozak he had been thinking along the same lines, but that Byrd would not want to be out in front of the movement to modify DeConcini. He suggested giving the language instead to Church, who had devoted all his energies to the treaties for months, exposing himself to Republican vitriol at home.

Church read the statement and quickly embraced it. He went to the Senate floor, and won recognition from the chair.

"It is highly regrettable," Church stated, "that in the course of strengthening the Neutrality Treaty—by removing the ambiguities that we found in it—we appear to have introduced a new ambiguity which is causing grave concern among the people in Panama."

Church argued that "the U.S. policy of intervention is long gone." He cited the U.N. Charter and other international agreements that prohibited interference in the internal affairs of other countries and quoted Senator DeConcini himself saying: "It is not our expectation that this change gives to the United States the right to interfere in the sovereign affairs of Panama."

Church allowed that the Panamanians might be "overreacting" or interpreting the reservation "out of context." But given the history of U.S. interference in Latin American countries, he said, Panama's reaction was "not so inexplicable." Church urged the Senate to find "an appropriate way to reassure the people of Panama that our intention was not to nullify the specific pledge of non-intervention" that had been incorporated in the first treaty. He closed eloquently: "Let us find a way to tell all the nations of this hemisphere that we have not in one afternoon nullified the last 40 years in the history of United States–Latin American relations. Let us make clear to the world that we are not seeking for ourselves the kind of rights the Soviets claimed in Czechoslovakia in 1968."

When Church finished, Daniel Patrick Moynihan took the floor to congratulate him for "what in history may prove to be the critical address in this long, crucial debate." Moynihan's praise was justified. Church had laid the problem before the Senate frankly and eloquently. He had shown an understanding of Panama's anger and frustration, but he had also been careful to give DeConcini room to claim Panama had misunderstood his intent.

On April 13, the *Washington Post* ripped DeConcini and the Carter White House in a hard-hitting editorial. Referring to future historians, the *Post* wondered: "How was it, they may ask, that the treaties, with their immense diplomatic and political freight, came to hinge on the ill-informed whims of a 40-year-old freshman senator of no previous renown, of no known international awareness, or little experience of any kind beyond minor administrative posts in Arizona?" The editorial criticized Carter, saying he had "blundered sorely in failing to anticipate the explosive Panamanian reaction" to the reservation and called on him to impress on DeConcini that "if he persists in his ways, the wreckage will be on his hands and on the hands of those other senators so cynically playing his game."

Jimmy Carter knew that if the Panama Canal treaties failed, no one would remember DeConcini very long; the "wreckage" would belong to the president, causing incalculable damage. Carter told Hamilton Jordan he wanted to go on national television that evening, to urge the Senate to adopt a resolution reaffirming the longstanding U.S. policy of not intervening in other countries' internal affairs. The response from Byrd, Church, and others was harshly negative. Many of the senators supporting the treaties were being savaged politically in their home states. Carter going on television to reassure the Panamanians would be very damaging to the senators already under political fire from the right. Moreover, they said, the president and his administration had mishandled DeConcini long enough. They should stand aside now and let the Senate solve the problem. Carter quickly agreed to drop the idea.

AS THE LONG SENATE debate finally neared a conclusion, Byrd, Church, and Sarbanes shuttled between the majority leader's office and the vice president's, hammering out a new resolution that would neuter the DeConcini amendment without angering its author or his supporters. The language also had to be strong enough to mollify a half-dozen treaty supporters, led by Democrat Mike Gravel of Alaska, who were prepared to bolt unless the interventionist language was modified. Gravel was not a Senate heavyweight, but he had studied the canal treaties diligently and was deeply offended by the DeConcini reservations, even to the point of advising the Panamanian ambassador to "stick to (his) guns," because Gravel and other supporters would kill the treaty if the problem was not solved to Panama's satisfaction.

Byrd recessed the Senate on Thursday night, to give himself and the others until Monday, April 17, to find a satisfactory solution. Several versions of the resolution were drafted and tried out on DeConcini and his allies, but the senators also maintained close contact with the government of Panama, through its Washington counsel, William Rogers, a former undersecretary of state. Byrd, Church, and Sarbanes were very careful not to make the same mistake the Carter administration had. They would not lose touch with Panama.

On Saturday, April 15, Panamanian Ambassador Gabriel Lewis and Rogers were ushered into the Capitol and taken to S-208 where Senators Byrd, Church, and Sarbanes and Deputy Secretary Christopher were waiting for them. It was 11 a.m., and they were scheduled to meet with Vice President Mondale at 12:30 p.m. Every successful negotiation must have a deadline. This one was strict. They gave themselves ninety minutes to finally solve the DeConcini problem.

Ambassador Lewis was under instructions to insist on language in the second treaty to protect his country's "political independence" and "territorial integrity." So far, the resolution was not sufficiently explicit on those points, he said, and was therefore unacceptable.

Ambassador Jorden vividly described the scene in his memoir. Byrd put a copy of the resolution on the coffee table and, running his hand two-thirds of the way down the text, said: "We're in agreement down to here." Lewis said that was correct. "And you want to change the rest?" Byrd asked. Lewis again said yes. Byrd knelt on the floor beside the low table and began questioning Lewis, crossing out some words and adding others. Church and Sarbanes crowded around the coffee table, while Christopher and Rogers stayed in the background.

They worked through the paper, making changes to win Lewis's approval while staying as close to the compromise language they had shown to other senators as possible. The senators and the ambassador reached one last temporary impasse. Lewis wanted an explicit reference to Panama's "territorial integrity." The senators thought it was sufficient to refer to Panama's "sovereignty," which subsumed "territorial integrity" and would be less of a red flag to DeConcini and his supporters. Byrd finally agreed to the phrase "sovereign integrity," which the lawyers insisted had no real meaning, but had the value of being reassuring to Panama.

When Byrd rose from his awkward kneeling position his back and shoulder were cramped. Church had to apply a hasty massage to help the majority leader stand up. Byrd told Ambassador Lewis the newly agreed language might encounter some resistance in the Senate, but assured him it would not be changed. Lewis said he would send the language to General Torrijos with the recommendation that it be approved and he had no doubt it would be.

The final drafting session was both substantive and symbolic. Byrd, Church, and Sarbanes had not only moved mountains to meet Panama's concerns, but they had treated Panama as a full partner in the effort. Shortly thereafter, Lewis received word from Torrijos that the wording was acceptable. "Tell the senator and the White House," Torrijos said, "we think this is a dignified solution to a difficult problem." Torrijos warned, though, that there could be "no surprises at the last minute."

At noon on Monday, the last day of the historic Panama Canal treaties debate, Byrd summoned Senators Patrick Leahy of Vermont and Kaneaster Hodges of Arkansas, two close friends of DeConcini's. He explained the new language and, with Byrd's encouragement, they went off to discuss the new resolution with DeConcini. Soon after, Byrd told a group of reporters he planned to introduce a reservation to "clarify" U.S. rights to protect the canal. He also disclosed the language was acceptable to Panama. The news traveled fast through the Senate.

The final, decisive meeting was with DeConcini himself. Byrd and others met with him in the leader's office. Seemingly undaunted by the criticism that had rained down on him, DeConcini was still trying to get wording closer to his own, including the damaging reference to "the use of military force." Byrd looked at DeConcini with cold eyes. "It has to be like this, Dennis," he said grimly. "I will not accept any changes." DeConcini quickly considered what his future in the Senate might be like with the majority leader as an implacable enemy and concluded that the language was acceptable. On the Senate floor, he later described himself as "amazed," "puzzled," and "shocked" that his reservation had generated so much controversy. He volunteered to cosponsor the new amendment.

On April 15, at 6 p.m., the Senate cast the final vote on the second Panama Canal treaty. The result was 68 to 32, precisely the same as the vote on the Neutrality Treaty a month before. This time, however, the celebration in Washington and in Panama City was heart-felt, authentic, and unalloyed. The United States and Panama had transformed their relationship, transcended their history, and changed the relationship of the United States to the rest of the hemisphere.

Jimmy Carter deserved great credit for staking his presidency on an issue so contentious that five previous presidents had failed to resolve it. But the Senate deserved extraordinary praise, too. The New Right, spearheaded by Richard Viguerie and his allies, had broken new ground in grassroots lobbying and single-issue attack politics; the assault had been multifaceted and brutally effective. As a result, many senators had supported the treaties because they were in the national interest, but at very high personal political cost. Baker's bipartisanship and political courage would go down in Senate history. Church's eloquence and tenacity in the face of potential political suicide would be long remembered. Sarbanes had as much impact in his first sixteen months in the Senate than any freshman in memory. And Byrd, who had been steadfast and brilliant throughout the long battle, would no longer be thought of as a Senate mechanic. He had proven himself a statesman and "the Leader." The Senate had reminded the country what political courage and statesmanship was about.

chapter 9

VENTURING INTO THE MIDDLE EAST

THE PANAMA CANAL FIGHT HAD BEEN A LONG, BRUISING HISTORIC BAT-tle—probably the most bitter foreign policy fight since the Senate had re-jected the League of Nations in 1919. In ordinary times, the Senate would have returned immediately to routine business, allowing itself some time to recover. But pressing matters did not permit the Senate that luxury.

Just days after completing the Panama Canal treaties, the Senate would plunge into three more major battles. It would have to approve or reject the sale of F-15s to Saudi Arabia and Israel, consider major changes in the na-tion's labor laws, and determine whether to offer loan guarantees to New York City. Little surprise that one senator, perhaps the foremost legislator of his era, would play a central role in all three issues, as he had done countless times over the past two decades.

On most afternoons when the Senate was in session, Jacob Javits sat at his desk in the Senate chamber, paging through a thick file of memos and press articles provided by his staff as he listened to the flow of Senate debate. Most senators came to the floor only to vote, speak, or wrangle over the few matters that were most important to them. In contrast, Javits regularly stayed on or near the Senate floor for hours on end. Virtually all the Senate's deliberations were important to him. He sought recognition to participate regularly, al-ways going right to the heart of the matter. When he got impassioned about a subject, as he frequently did, he would prowl all over the Senate chamber, the clarity of his voice matching the clarity of his reasoning.

A liberal Republican from New York, Javits was first elected in 1956. By 1978 he had served twenty-one years in the Senate. During that time, he had never once been in the majority. Until his third term, he was denied committee assignments on the Foreign Relations Committee and Judiciary Committee that he sought. Some of the southerners never warmed to the Jewish senator from New York City. In the early years, when he rose to speak in the Senate, Javits encountered a "chill of hostility." James Eastland once stared coldly down a committee table and said: "I don't like you—or your kind." But nothing could deter Javits from becoming a force in the Senate out of sheer will and ability.

He once described his principal interests as "anything that affects New York City or America's place in the world." He was involved in almost every legislative matter because he added value in every legislative situation. Universally recognized as the Senate's best lawyer and its foremost debater, he had a gift for brokering compromise. He was also a master of the committee process, which he saw as "a stimulating forum for individual creativity." He frequently attended three committee hearings in a morning, requesting his time to be heard no matter how late he had arrived and cutting right to the heart of the issue at hand.

Besides possessing a superb intellect, Javits always seemed to operate at top-speed. He was always walking faster than anyone around him, playing tennis regularly, and swimming laps daily in the Senate pool long before exercise became fashionable. His wife, Marion, was an artist who lived in New York City, and Javits would take the shuttle to New York once or twice a week, catching the last flight back to Washington at night. In the days before airport security, Javits insisted on leaving the Capitol no more than fifteen minutes before the Eastern Shuttle was scheduled to take off from National Airport. He never missed it.

Javits extended his influence by hiring and retaining superb staff members. It seemed quite natural to Javits that lawyers from Harvard, Yale, or Columbia or top-flight journalists or economists would want to work in the Senate and love working for him, and they did. He had a soft spot for his staff members, whom he regarded both as his protégés and his children. "Take a chance on the young," he would tell them, "like I did with you."

Above all, Javits loved being a senator. In his autobiography, he wrote of the Senate:

The United States Senate was my home. I know its rules and traditions and moods, and I could often sense what action it was about to take. My seat on the aisle in the Senate chamber became as agreeable to me as a favorite living-room easy chair, and I was familiar with the voices, the quirks, the foibles and inclinations of the ninety-nine other senators. I was thrilled when a team of senators enlisted in a cause worked smoothly, like a well-drilled football backfield, each senator knowing the others' moves, and communicating by a sixth sense based on shared knowledge and skill. I was stimulated by the ebb and flow of debate and the philosophic tensions of the work we did—balancing lofty principles against sectional or selfish interests, welding together antagonistic human and economic and ideological forces into the coherent schemes of government that we call laws.

In the spring of 1978, Javits was nearing age seventy-four, serving out his fourth Senate term. His legendary energy and focus were beginning to flag. The ceaseless work of the Senate, its annual authorizations and appropriations, was becoming repetitive. He was also beginning to experience a weakening of his abdominal muscles, which doctors would later diagnose as the onset of motor neuron disease. In time, he would have to give up tennis and take breaks while climbing stairs.

To be sure, the demands of being New York's senator took a toll; no senator from the Empire State had ever served in that position as long as twenty-four years. At the time, Javits planned to finish his term, set a state record for longevity, and then return to his beloved home city. His record spoke for itself. He had been one of the major players in enacting the Civil Rights Act and had been the principal architect of the War Powers Act and the Employee Retirement Insurance Savings Act (ERISA). Virtually every piece of social legislation had his fingerprints on it somewhere.

But now, even with his energy diminished and the twilight of his career approaching, the Senate needed Jack Javits more than ever.

JIMMY CARTER HAD PUT his presidency on the line for the Panama Canal treaties. For once, the gamble had paid off. But his overriding preoccupation with foreign policy, even more than the quest to reduce nuclear arms, was the effort to make peace in the Middle East.

He was not the first president so inclined. Beginning with Harry Truman, who pushed successfully for the recognition of the state of Israel in 1948, every American president had become deeply involved in the effort to secure Israel's defenses against its Arab enemies, particularly Egypt, and to work for peace in the region. But no president had embraced the intractable issues posed in the Middle East as vigorously as Carter. "Looking back," Carter would write in his 1982 memoir, "it is remarkable to see how constantly the work for peace in the Middle East was on my agenda, and on my mind." This was no understatement.

Carter had entered office in a moment of relative regional calm. The Yom Kippur War in October 1973 had ended without either side losing. Israel had prevailed militarily, but only after recovering from Egypt's successful surprise attack. The performance of the Egyptian military, under the leadership of President Anwar Sadat, had shattered the Israeli euphoria, hubris, and complacency that had resulted from routing Egypt, Syria, and Jordan in the Six Day War in 1967. It had also allowed Egypt to recover its pride and reinforce its standing as the leading nation in the Arab world. But despite the temporary calm, the intense enmities in the region remained, as did the untenable U.S. dependence on Middle East oil.

Jimmy Carter first met with the Israeli Prime Minister Yitzhak Rabin on March 7, 1977. Carter described the meeting as "a particularly unpleasant surprise." He found Rabin "timid, stubborn and somewhat ill at ease." Rabin offered nothing when Carter asked whether there was anything he could convey to Sadat. In contrast, Carter's first meeting with Sadat on April 4, 1977, was much more encouraging. Sadat impressed Carter as being "a very strong and courageous leader who has never shrunk from making difficult public decisions." Carter noted that Sadat had moderated Egypt's position significantly on "the nature of permanent peace" as well as how soon open borders and diplomatic relations might be established. This was an opening to further discussions, if Carter could only bring Israel on board.

Within a few hours of Sadat's return to Egypt from Washington, stunning news came from Israel that Rabin had announced his withdrawal as a candidate for reelection because of irregularities related to a bank account in New York. Rabin's decision dramatically transformed the political situation in Israel. Within a few weeks, Menachem Begin, who had been a leader of Israeli resistance to British rule before the founding of the Israeli state, became the first prime minister from the Likud party. Begin's background and Likud's stridency made it likely that he would be even tougher than Rabin in considering peace with the Arabs. He would be particularly adamant about returning any of the West Bank areas captured in the 1967 war, which Likud regarded as part of Judea and Samaria—biblical Israel.

Nevertheless, in April and May 1977, after meeting the leaders of Jordan, Syria, and Saudi Arabia, Carter concluded that the Arab nations could be convinced to recognize Israel. Any peace agreement could occur only if there was a Palestinian state, linked to Jordan, and Israel was prepared to relinquish occupied territories as part of the peace agreement. His optimism about certain leaders, notably President Hafez Assad of Syria, would soon be proven misplaced, but at the time, it was enough to begin renewed efforts toward peace.

Carter's aggressive outreach to Arab leaders was beginning to disconcert many leaders in the American Jewish community. He realized he would need to seek support from well-known friends of Israel in the Senate. On June 16, 1977, flanked by Vice President Walter Mondale and National Security Adviser Zbigniew Brzezinski, Carter met with Senators Abe Ribicoff, Hubert Humphrey, Ed Muskie, and Scoop Jackson. Regarding the meeting as "constructive," Carter continued meeting with key Senate and House members. Only Javits remained unpersuaded by Carter's approach to peace. Yet everyone would soon have to reexamine their assumptions, as one of the most electrifying reversals in modern history was about to take place.

On November 19, 1977, Anwar Sadat travelled to Israel in pursuit of peace. Sadat stated to the Knesset, in direct, forthright terms, the Arab requirements for peace. As Carter would note, "he was standing there alone, before his ancient enemies, holding out an olive branch. The Israeli welcome to him was truly remarkable. The Israelis were also facing *their* ancient enemy."

This being the Middle East, Sadat's extraordinary and courageous bid to overcome the region's hatreds thrilled many people but enraged many others. Assad promptly broke off relations with Egypt, while high officials of the Syrian, Iraqi, and Libyan governments openly called for Sadat's assassination. In the wake of such furor, the prospects for serious peace talks in the region seemed as distant as ever.

To keep the hope of peace from withering on the vine, support from other powerful forces in the region would be necessary. No nation held more sway than Saudi Arabia, the world's leading oil producer and the location of Mecca and Medina, Islam's holiest places.

On January 3, 1978, Carter met with Crown Prince Fahd of Saudi Arabia. Fahd told Carter that Saudi Arabia privately supported everything Sadat was doing, but was not willing to make that known through public statements, for fear of antagonizing more militant Arabs who might threaten his rule. Fahd expressed a strong view in support of an independent Palestinian state, which Carter termed a dangerous idea. But despite his disappointment that the Saudi leaders would not be more publicly supportive, Carter came away convinced, again, of Saudi Arabia's central importance in the region and the need to bolster the U.S.-Saudi relationship. He chose to make a bold move.

ON FEBRUARY 14, 1978, the Carter administration announced that it would seek congressional authorization to sell fighter planes to Israel, Egypt, and Saudi Arabia. Though Israel had been the recipient of U.S. fighter planes for years, this was the first time that an American administration was offering to sell advanced arms to Arab nations. The administration requested approval to sell sixty F-15s, the most advanced U.S. fighter, to Saudi Arabia, while selling only fifteen F-15s, along with seventy-five F-16s, to Israel. Israel already had twenty-five F-15s. The administration's request for Egypt was for fifty F-5Es, a plane considerably less advanced than the F-15 or F-16.

Such a decision could not be made without congressional support or at least acquiescence. In 1974, as a major step to reasserting its role in foreign policy, Congress had enacted the Nelson-Bingham Amendment giving itself the authority to block any arms sale by passing a concurrent resolution of disapproval within thirty days of formal notification. The congressional leadership and the White House had agreed that formal notification of this proposed sale would be given right after the Panama Canal treaties were resolved.

In the Senate, the prevailing reactions to the proposed arms sales package were marked by dismay, mystification, and anger. Daniel Patrick Moynihan, a stalwart champion of Israel while serving as U.N. Ambassador, blasted the proposal as "an ill-timed intrusion into the Middle East peace process." Frank Church, who had long deplored the emergence of the United States as the world's leading arms merchant, pointed out that we were yet again potentially arming both sides of a conflict.

The American-Israeli Public Affairs Committee (AIPAC) announced its vehement opposition to Carter's proposal. AIPAC argued that selling advanced weaponry to Saudi Arabia and Egypt was a mortal threat to Israel, justifiably increasing Israel's insecurity and making it less willing to compromise. Since its inception in 1953, AIPAC had never lost a vote in Congress, and at the outset, it seemed that AIPAC's winning record would stay intact. The Senate Foreign Relations Committee, which would consider the arms sale package, appeared overwhelmingly opposed to it.

Javits would play a central role in the coming battle. He had been deeply involved with Israel since 1946, when, as a newly elected member of the House, he had made a ten-day trip to Palestine. Javits saw British tanks rolling through the streets as the British searched for the Irgun, Jewish freedom fighters, whom the British regarded as terrorists. He walked through refugee camps in Europe and returned home to sponsor legislation calling for the United States to press Britain to lift its limitations on Jewish refugees coming to Palestine. In years since, he had personally known every leader of Israel starting with its founder, David Ben-Gurion.

Javits was one of the first members of Congress to articulate the view that supporting Israel, the only democracy in the Middle East, was not just a moral imperative; it was in the security interests of the United States. Further solidifying his beliefs on the subject was the fact that one of his foreign policy advisers, Hal Rosenthal, had been killed by a terrorist bomb in Istanbul airport in 1971.

Although elated by Israel's victory in the Six Day War in 1967, Javits was sobered as the Soviet Union openly sold arms to Egypt and Syria to rebuild and strengthen their military capabilities. With Scoop Jackson's help, Javits led the fight to convince the Nixon administration to sell more planes to Israel, eventually overcoming the reluctance of Nixon and Kissinger.

Javits was no blind advocate of Israel's policies—he expressed early frustration about Israel's expanding settlements. But he firmly believed that Israel needed advanced weaponry from the United States, particularly aircraft, to maintain its qualitative edge, deter its Arab enemies, and provide the security needed to negotiate with its enemies.

Javits watched dynamics change in the region following the Yom Kippur War of 1973. Israel had been stunned by the surprise attack by Egypt and Syria and the courage and new capabilities demonstrated by their adversaries. After a period of days in which serious defeat seemed likely, Israel had rallied, with the support of American arms, and was on its way to victory, having encircled 20,000 troops of the Egyptian army. Israel then made the hard choice to release the Egyptian forces, prodded by Nixon and Kissinger, enabling the war to end. The Yom Kippur War allowed Anwar Sadat to erase the humiliation of Egypt's defeat six years earlier. It gave him the stature, confidence, and impetus to make his historic trip to Jerusalem in November 1977.

Now, just a few months after Sadat's trip, the Senate would consider President Carter's request for advanced weapons for Saudi Arabia, Egypt, and Israel. Javits was impressed by Carter's sincere commitment to seeking Middle East peace but worried that Carter's approach may be naïve. The aircraft for Egypt did not trouble him much—the F-5Es were not very advanced and posed little threat. It was Saudi Arabia that bothered him, in large part because Saudi Arabia's blanket embargo of Israel extended to even American Jews who worked for U.S. companies doing business in Saudi Arabia. But he had made his first trip to Saudi Arabia in early 1977 and came away impressed with the unexpected openness of the Saudi royal family. They seemed much more concerned with external threats such as Iraq, rather than Israel or the danger of internal dissent.

With the sands seemingly shifting in the Middle East, Javits decided that he could support selling airplanes to Egypt and even Saudi Arabia. But he opposed Carter's decision to package the arm sales to the three countries together. To Javits, as well as to other senators, the decision undermined the special relationship between the United States and Israel, which could only weaken Israel's security and confidence. Javits couldn't help but wonder if Carter was attempting to send a message not to the Arab nations but to Menachem Begin that the United States was moving to a more evenhanded policy in the Middle East that would no longer favor Israel. Until Carter could convince him otherwise, Javits remained opposed.

Another key player in the legislative battle would be Scoop Jackson, who supported Israel as fervently as he opposed the Soviet Union. He had great stature in Israel because of his untiring efforts to help Russian Jews to emigrate from the Soviet Union. He was dead set against Carter's proposal. Meanwhile AIPAC was gearing up very effectively to lobby against the package, using both direct lobbying and grassroots efforts to generate communications from concerned Jews all over the country. The battle promised to be a fierce and uphill struggle for Carter and the supporters of the proposed arms sales.

IT WAS DIFFICULT TO see how the Carter administration could possibly convince the Senate to give the green light to the arms sale package in view of the combined opposition of Javits, Jackson, and AIPAC. Carter remained adamantly opposed to separating the arms sales into three separate deals, and with his characteristic doggedness, certitude, and aversion to compromise, he also opposed changing the package to make it more salable. However, the Panama Canal battle had given at least some members of the Carter White House team valuable lessons on how to deal with the Senate. Despite the president's reluctance, his administration began communicating with the three senators who had been most decisive in the Panama Canal fight: Byrd, Baker, and Church.

Baker again played a critical role. His former Senate colleague from Tennessee, Bill Brock, now chairman of the Republican National Committee, believed that opposing the arms sale was best for the security of Israel, as well as good politics, because Jewish voters, thinking that Carter had endangered Israel, might start voting Republican. Bob Packwood, who chaired the Republican Senate Campaign Committee, felt the same way. Baker, however, feared the Saudis would abandon their presently moderate position, and that America would be breaching a trust with Sadat, who had repeatedly shown his commitment to peace. Baker made it known to the White House that he would support the arms sale, but only if it contained some concessions to Israel.

Baker was also talking with Ribicoff. Not only were they close friends, they had also traveled to the Middle East together in November 1976. At the request of the White House, Ribicoff had made a quick trip to Saudi Arabia to assess the importance of the arms sale, its impact on U.S.-Saudi relations, and the prospects for Middle East peace. Upon his return, based on his trip, Ribicoff found himself in agreement with Baker's approach. Once they had agreed upon principles, they approached Church and Javits, asking them to reconsider the matter.

Baker took soundings in the Republican caucus, and found that the majority would support the arms sales package if changes were made. He informed President Carter that the sale would not be approved in its original form but told the president: "If you want to work this out, I'm willing to try." While reaching out to the White House and his Senate colleagues, Baker also enlisted Henry Kissinger, to gain his support for a modified package. Although out of power, Kissinger maintained great credibility with respect to the Middle East because his shuttle diplomacy had helped conclude the Yom Kippur War in a way that allowed all combatants some modicum of face-saving success.

On May 9, Secretary of Defense Harold Brown sent a seven-page letter to the Foreign Relations Committee, setting forth important changes in, and clarifications to, the arms sales package negotiated with Baker. Brown stated that Saudi Arabia had agreed that it would not add special auxiliary fuel tanks to expand the range of its planes; would not transfer the planes to any other nation or permit any foreign national to be trained to fly the planes; and would use the planes only for defensive purposes. The Saudis also specifically committed that the F-15s would not be kept at Tabuk, the airfield in northwestern Saudi Arabia only 250 miles from Jerusalem, from which the F-15s could carry large bomb loads over most Israeli territory, including the port of Eilat on which Israel depended for oil imports. Brown also pledged that Israel would receive twenty additional F-15s. The changes Brown outlined addressed most of core concerns of Senate opponents to the arms sales package.

Church, who had agreed to see if a consensus could be found on the committee, began lobbying his colleagues vigorously on behalf of the package with Brown's amendments. He convinced McGovern, who had started out strongly opposed, that if Carter's proposal was rejected, Saudi Arabia would simply buy advanced aircraft from France, without any limitations on their use. Israel would be less safe, and the U.S. relationship to Saudi Arabia would be greatly damaged.

On May 11, the Foreign Relations Committee met in its hearing room on the fourth floor of the Dirksen Building. There is always excitement and anticipation when a committee meets on an important issue. Reporters buttonhole senators as they arrive, while staffers confer with one another, waiting for their principals to come to the table. Church and Javits whispered to each other about the recent developments. The atmosphere surrounding this markup was particularly electric because most of the committee had been so strongly opposed to Carter's proposal; Brown's letter was so recent that the outcome was still uncertain. Baker believed that there were eleven votes in the committee for the modified proposal, and Moshe Dayan, the legendary war hero who was Israel's Foreign Minister, conceded the restraints offered by Secretary Brown furthered Israel's interests. Experienced Senate hands expected that the package would win.

They were wrong. After a passionate debate, the committee stunned the Senate and the president by deadlocking 8–8, offering no recommendation to the full Senate. Three votes that Baker had counted on had disappeared. Church's reversal of position was most shocking. One senator described himself as "flabbergasted by that switch. One day he was lobbying people hard to go with the Administration. The next day he waltzes in and does a 180 degree turn." Baker ruefully smiled after the surprising vote and commented: "I have a chilling feeling that this may be the start of my troubles."

It would be up to the full Senate to resolve the issue. White House Press Secretary Jody Powell grimly commented: "We had hoped to spare [the Senate] this ordeal." Certainly the senators would have strongly preferred not to choose between a vote for Israel or the moderate Arab countries, which was how the vote would be portrayed by AIPAC even if the White House sought to frame it differently. But the arms sales package presented the most important Middle East vote in many years and could stand as a new beginning for the United States' relationship with Egypt and Saudi Arabia. It was fitting that the Senate, which had fought so long to reestablish its role in major foreign policy decisions, would not duck the issue.

EMOTIONS RAN HIGH AS the Senate met four days later. Debate began over a resolution disapproving the arms sales package, offered by Joe Biden, ordinarily one of Carter's strongest supporters. The foreign policy issues posed by the Middle East arms sales package were serious enough, but the debate would also carry with it an ugly overtone about the role of Jewish lobbying. Gravel criticized AIPAC for turning the vote into a "litmus test" by which members would no longer receive support from Jews even if their previous voting record had been impeccable: "This vote, if it is not done properly, kisses away in the future all kinds of financial support that would inure to a candidate for office."

Packwood defended AIPAC's lobbying with considerable heat, noting that Jews had the same understandable interest in the homeland of their forefathers as do "Poles, Greeks and blacks." Packwood went on to say, "It is with sorrow and disgust, therefore, that I hear the State Department time and again refer to the Jewish lobby or the Israeli lobby in a tone suggestive of a group which puts the interests of another country ahead of the United States."

But the Senate focused mainly on the difficult questions about what substantive U.S. policy was best suited to advancing American interests in the security of Israel and peace in the troubled region. Javits, who had signaled a willingness to consider a compromise if the number of planes sold to Israel was dramatically increased, came out strongly against the package. Calling it "the wrong issue, at the wrong time, for the wrong reason," he added emotionally, "What do we want to do with the Israelis? Sap their vitality? Sap their morale? Cut their legs out from under them? Is that what this is all about?"

Only a senator with both stature and a proven commitment to Israel could debate Javits and the other opponents of the arms sale. This senator was Abe Ribicoff. In an extraordinary two-hour closed session, Ribicoff took on the opponents' arguments forcefully. "We must have the courage, we must have the guts to face a changing world," Ribicoff intoned. "The fact is that without a stable, predictable supply of oil from Saudi Arabia . . . the West would face the worst depression of the industrial era." Ribicoff also pointedly defined the standard that senators should use in casting their vote: the national interest of the United States, not the national interest of another country, even if it was Israel, one of our closest friends and strongest allies.

There were larger geopolitical currents to take into consideration as well. Lloyd Bentsen noted that the Saudis had been moderate on oil prices and had been branded as "American lackeys" as a result. The Saudi government needed to show the region that it was gaining some benefit from its moderation in the area of international economic policy as well as its political and military policy course. A Senate decision to disapprove the package would have grave consequences for the relationship with Saudi Arabia going forward. Moynihan countered, saying that, in essence, the aircraft sale was a rationalization of "American nervelessness."

Tom Eagleton, another strong supporter of Israel, captured the painful difficulty of the choice facing the Senate. Serving his tenth year in the Senate, Eagleton said that he had "agonized over the decision which is thrust upon us more than any I can recall." He concluded that it was "better to give the Saudis a means to defend against attacks on their vital resources," rather than send in American forces to do it.

The debate was deeply emotional. When the ten hours that had been set aside for debate ended, the Senate voted 54 to 44 to defeat the Biden resolution of disapproval. The arms sale would go through intact. AIPAC had lost its first vote.

The process of approving the arms sale had been a wrenching experience for the Senate and the Carter administration alike. Paul Sarbanes, who had earned great respect for his work on the Panama Canal treaties, sharply criticized the Carter administration's "skill and competence in the art of government" in the way the package had been handled.

In retrospect, this criticism seems unjustified. If the Carter White House had agreed to separate the arms sales, Congress would have quickly ratified the sale to Israel, approved the sale to Egypt after some consideration, and, quite possibly, rejected the proposed sale to Saudi Arabia. Instead, the Carter administration made changes in the unified package and won an extraordinary and unexpected victory. The Senate, which had fashioned the arms sales legislation that would give Congress a role in this important area of foreign and defense policy, had stepped up and played that role.

Those who believed that U.S. foreign and defense policy would be more effectively shaped by cooperation between the executive and legislative branches could derive satisfaction from the collaboration between the administration and Senators Baker and Ribicoff. The issue was hard-fought, but not on partisan lines. The White House got the votes of twenty-six Democrats and twenty-eight Republicans, while losing thirty-three Democrats and eleven Republicans. Leading Democratic doves split down the middle. Eagleton, Muskie, and McGovern supported the president; Church, Cranston, and Kennedy went the other way.

Some issues simply present an agonizing and uncertain choice, yet despite the difficulties and intense political pressure, the senators faced the issue squarely, refusing to engage in obstruction or seek partisan advantage. It was neither easy nor expected that strong supporters of Israel would come down against AIPAC and favor Carter's proposal. They did it because they were persuaded that it was the right course for the United States, at a time of great fluidity in the Middle East. For these reasons, the arms sales debate showed the Senate at its best. And Jimmy Carter's position would be vindicated soon enough.

Just four months later, at the Camp David presidential retreat, Carter would successfully mediate between Prime Minister Begin and President Sadat to bring about the Camp David Accords, which led to peace between Israel and Egypt and the return of the territory that had been captured by Israel from Egypt in the 1967 war. It is impossible to say that the rejection of the F-15 sale by the Senate would have prevented the Camp David accords. However, there is little doubt that the decision of the Senate to support Carter gave a major boost to the president's stature and credibility as a mediator and peacemaker in the world's most intractable conflict.

chapter 10

AN EPIC BUSINESS-LABOR CLASH

THANKS TO THE SENATE'S HEAVY LIFTING, THE CARTER ADMINISTRATION had cobbled together an unlikely winning streak: historic foreign policy victories in Panama and the Middle East, and an airline deregulation bill that came to represent a key plank in Carter's new centrist economic agenda. Now, one of the most contentious domestic issues facing the Senate could no longer be put off. Byrd informed the White House that the Senate intended to take up labor law reform. A third major battle was in the offing.

Since the time of Franklin D. Roosevelt, the American labor movement had been a central force in the Democratic Party. FDR had successfully fought for the Wagner National Labor Relations Act, the passage of which in 1935 had secured the right to organize unions and bargain collectively. In the period after World War II, the Republican drive to curb the rising power of unions became a central political issue. In 1948, union support played a critical role in Harry Truman's stunning upset victory over Republican Thomas Dewey. Labor's political power later boosted John F. Kennedy to his narrow victory in 1960, and all-out union support nearly rescued Hubert Humphrey in the turbulent year of 1968, despite considerable rank-and-file sympathy for George Wallace. The time had come for that relationship to be reaffirmed.

George Meany, the president of the AFL-CIO, had not been enthusiastic about Jimmy Carter, who had defeated two labor favorites, Scoop Jackson and Birch Bayh, on his way to winning the Democratic nomination. Nevertheless labor had played a strong role in securing Carter's narrow victory over Ford. The unions provided generous funding and manpower to the campaigns of numerous congressional Democrats as well. Any Democratic administration would have to make time for the priorities of Meany and the union movement. And given the size of the Democratic majorities in both houses of Congress, labor had every reason to believe that its highest priority, labor law reform, would become law in the Ninety-fifth Congress.

Labor needed a helping hand from the Congress for, strong as it was as a political force, there were cracks in the foundation. The AFL-CIO was suffering significant setbacks in the workplace. Organized labor's share of the workforce had fallen steadily—from 34.5 percent in 1956 to 25.1 percent in 1978. Some of Meany's critics blamed him personally for the decline in union membership. When the AFL and CIO had merged in 1955, union leaders expected that the end of bickering between the two rivals would result in increased organizing. But Meany, a plumber who had never walked a picket line in his life, seemed uninterested in putting labor resources into funding organizing drives.

Labor's precipitous decline in the 1970's also reflected a fierce and concerted campaign waged by the business community. The company most notorious for anti-labor tactics was J. P. Stevens Company, which, by tough and clever legal tactics had blocked the unionization of its textile plants in the south for more than a decade. Farah, a pants manufacturer in Texas, had endured a very long strike by hiring consultants who specialized in defeating union organizing efforts.

More and more companies intimidated workers by firing union organizers among them. According to National Labor Relations Board (NLRB) statistics, the number of employer unfair labor practice charges tripled between 1960 and 1980, and the number of workers ordered to be reinstated because they had been fired illegally increased fivefold.

To block these tactics and to reverse the decline of labor organizing, the AFL-CIO, led by Meany, sought a labor law reform bill that would increase the penalties on companies that violated the law. Labor also wanted to expedite the arduous appeal processes that companies were using to avoid holding or accepting the results of union elections. The House of Representatives had passed the legislation the labor movement was seeking in October 1977, by a comfortable vote of 257–163. It was now the Senate's turn to act, and it would be walking into what would prove to be an epic legislative battle between the Democratic majority and an uncommonly unified Republican minority. Meanwhile, the traditional lobbying power of the union movement would have to contend with a new force in American politics—a mobilized, unified business community, armed with innovative political tools and vast financial resources.

At the outset, the chances of Senate passage seemed good, if not quite assured. Its resolve would be tested if cloture, which required sixty votes, became necessary. And in the coming battle, labor's supporters would discover that their most tenacious opponent was a new Republican political star by the name of Orrin Hatch.

HATCH'S UPSET VICTORY OVER three-term Utah senator Frank Moss had been one of the bright spots for the Republicans in the otherwise bleak 1976 elections. Moss, a western liberal from the class of 1958, had long been a bête noir for the business community, as a champion of consumer protection legislation throughout the 1960's and 1970's. Hatch, a self-styled citizen politician, running for office for the first time, was firmly positioned at the leading edge of the New Right conservatism that Ronald Reagan would come to epitomize—vehemently anti-government, strongly pro-business, and anti-labor to the core.

On arriving in Washington, Hatch quickly became one of the favorites of the right wing and the business community. Still, he was startled at being asked to lead the opposition to the labor law reform bill. The business community had approached other Senate Republicans but had not found anyone who would assume the leadership in this tough, uphill fight. Hatch agreed to take on the challenge, but stipulated two conditions. First, the business community would have to stay united: companies could not make separate deals on the legislation with the unions. Second, if he was going to be the public leader of the effort, the business community would have to agree to follow his leadership and his leadership alone, rather than debate competing strategies.

This was a moment when the U.S. business community was spoiling for a major fight. The 1950's and 1960's had been great decades for American business. Rising economic prosperity had produced a broad middle class and rising demand for all types of products and services. American corporations became global icons, finding markets for their products across Europe and Asia. Certainly, there was some acrimony between labor and management, and corporations could point to plenty of government regulations that they disliked. But generally, shared prosperity made possible a comfortable consensus during the Eisenhower, Kennedy, Johnson, and early Nixon years, in which the interest of corporations and the public were in reasonably good balance. Many leading corporations had no quarrel with the emerging environmental and consumer movements; their corporate CEOs served on the boards of the Ford Foundation and Brookings Institution and looked kindly on collective bargaining.

The situation changed rapidly in the 1970's. Energy prices rose following the first oil embargo imposed by the Organization of Petroleum Exporting Countries (OPEC) in 1973. Rising energy costs ripped through the U.S. economy, straining U.S. consumers and reducing profits for business. Additionally, U.S. manufacturing companies faced the first onslaught of intense foreign competition. The great U.S. auto companies of Detroit were abruptly losing customers and market share to small, improbable, previously laughable Japanese cars made by Toyota, Nissan, and Honda. Previous decades' pattern of comfortable prosperity had come to a swift end. In such an environment, the cost of regulation and labor's wage demands, previously nettlesome but manageable, were becoming serious problems.

Major U.S. companies had been engaged in Washington legislative battles for years, pursuing their own company or industry interests. Now, in what they perceived to be an anti-business environment, the business community saw a broad common interest in uniting to achieve its goals. The National Association of Manufacturers (NAM) and the Chamber of Commerce, which had become weak and ineffectual during the 1960's, refocused their efforts in Washington and expanded their staffs and budgets. In 1972, at the urging of senior Nixon administration officials, a small group of CEOs formed a new organization called the March Club, soon to drastically expand and rename itself the Business Roundtable.

Lobbying groups weren't enough, however—business interests needed ideas to power their crusade. At the urging of two powerful intellects, Lewis Powell, the distinguished Virginia attorney soon to be elevated to the Supreme Court, and Irving Kristol, the editor of *Public Interest* and generally regarded as the godfather of the neoconservative movement, the business community began to fund the activities of a network of policy think-tanks and institutes, of which the American Enterprise Institute and the Heritage Foundation were most prominent.

By the time Jimmy Carter became president, the business community had put in place a network of alliances that could bring powerful unified lobbying efforts to bear, coupled with formidable intellectual firepower to make such initiatives credible. From the think-tanks, policy groups, and academics funded by the business community and the right wing, a concerted message, and new ideology, emerged. In essence: government was responsible for America's ills. Inflation resulted from government deficits, not from the whims of OPEC. Slow growth did not reflect overcapacity, lack of demand, or the recent surge of tough foreign competition. Rather, the growth-killers were government regulations, which increased business costs, government spending, and taxes, depriving the private sector of funds. There was a path to faster growth; all that was needed was rolling back environmental, workplace, and product regulations, slowing wage increases, and above all, cutting taxes.

This "supply-side" message did not exist in 1971 when Powell and Kristol urged the business community to mobilize. By 1978, it had become pervasive. It reached the academics from the think tanks; the elites through the *Wall Street Journal* editorial page, *Forbes,* and *Fortune*; the public through articles in *Readers' Digest.* As Murray Weidenbaum, one of the leading supply-side thinkers said: "We knew we scored when we got into comic strips. You change public understanding that way. Broom Hilda did five comic strips in a row showing OSHA penalizing her for her broom."

Nothing reflected the changing political currents more clearly than the shifting fortunes of Mike Pertschuk. For more than a decade, as Commerce Committee staff director, he had been one of the most powerful people in Washington: the embodiment of consumer protection, entrepreneurial policymaking, and liberal activism. Now, as chairman of the Federal Trade Commission, Pertschuk found himself under siege, as the surging business community painted him as the symbol of the intrusive, costly "nanny state," and Congress tore into virtually every rule that the FTC proposed. Pertschuk would later write ruefully about the golden days: "We did not appreciate the uniquely benign political environment within which we had the good fortune to operate.... We neither contemplated the severely circumscribed, inherent limits to our strategies, nor took adequate note of the lowering clouds of gathering business concern and mobilization."

A series of national Gallup Polls registered just how effectively the new conservative supply-side message was being disseminated. Gallup asked whether "you have been better off or worse off as a result of government control and regulation of the business practices of large corporations?" In 1970, 43 percent answered "better off" and only 15 percent "worse off," with the rest saying "no difference" or "don't know." In 1977, the same question produced a response of 28 percent "better off" and 26 percent "worse off."

The pro-business message proved particularly successful because the other side, starting with Jimmy Carter and the Democratic Congress, offered no compelling counter-narrative to explain the weakening economy or how it could be improved. The upshot was that the Democratic Senate and the Carter administration would be fighting for labor law reform at a time when public attitudes were moving emphatically in the opposite direction.

Byrd and his colleagues were certainly aware of the changing climate. In the early months of the Carter administration, one of the AFL-CIO's other priorities, making common situs picketing legal, had been emphatically rejected on the Hill. A long and bitter strike by the United Mine Workers during the winter of 1977–1978 had made President Carter look indecisive and ineffectual, eroding his public support. But the labor law reform legislation had overwhelming committee support and the support of the majority of the Senate. Moreover, Byrd was never one to duck a legislative battle—indeed, he relished the chance to demonstrate his parliamentary mastery—and his home state of West Virginia had a long and proud tradition of support for a strong labor movement. He did not intend to be beaten this time.

IN JANUARY 1978, THE Senate Labor and Human Resources Committee approved the labor legislation by a 16–2 vote. The legislation expanded the NLRB from five to seven members to expedite the processing of unfair labor practice cases. It mandated elections within thirty days after a union presented membership cards signed by a majority of employees. It granted back pay of up to 150 percent for workers illegally fired for union activity. Union organizers would be allowed equal time to address any workers forced by management to attend anti-union meetings. Companies found guilty of violating labor laws would be denied federal contracts. And if the NLRB found that a company refused to negotiate in "good faith" with a newly certified union, its workers would receive back pay. This was the strong bill that the

AFL-CIO wanted. But the overwhelming committee vote did not guarantee success in the full Senate; the Labor and Human Resources Committee probably had the most liberal makeup of any Senate committee, attracting members who were pro-labor as well as deeply committed to federal spending on education and health. Byrd, and the floor managers, Harrison Williams, the New Jersey Democrat, and Javits, would have their work cut out for them passing it through the full Senate.

On May 16, Byrd called up the legislation and announced that the Senate would not be operating on a "two-track" system by which other Senate business could be conducted at the same time. Labor law reform would be the only issue before the Senate. If opponents wanted to filibuster, they would have to be on the Senate floor, actually talking, rather than simply threatening to do so.

Byrd made it clear, however, that the opponents of labor law reform would have plenty of time to make their case. There would be no justification for claims that the legislation had been "rammed down their throats." He would not keep the Senate in session, day and night, and he already foresaw multiple cloture votes, of which the majority would lose at least the first two. Furthermore, Byrd promised that there would be no cloture votes until after the Senate returned from its Memorial Day recess. That would give the unions a chance to lobby members directly and personally while they were at home. Of course, the opponents would have the same chance, and they planned to make good use of it as well.

Hatch, the leader of the opposition to the labor bill, was still a neophyte at Senate procedure. He certainly was not yet a match for Byrd, the ultimate master of the Senate rules. To make up for this deficit, Hatch received regular counsel from Jim Allen, who, despite being in failing health, was the one person who could equal Byrd in thinking up, anticipating, and countering games on the Senate floor.

Hatch also benefited from having Democrat Fritz Hollings strongly in his camp. He was a strong intellect and a powerful debater and orator whose outspokenness frequently led to outrageous remarks. But in a battle where Democrats troubled about labor law reform were reticent to offend the unions, Hollings's habit of speaking out fearlessly was very helpful. From the beginning of the debate, Hollings made it clear that he thought "big labor" was engaged in a "power grab." With Republican Richard Lugar of Indiana, a freshman senator who had made it to the Senate despite the handicap of having been known as "Richard Nixon's favorite mayor," serving as his lieutenant, Hatch organized the labor law opponents into rotating teams of five or six senators to man the floor and keep talking and to protect against the possibility of unexpected motions by Byrd to cut off debate.

For ten days, speeches as long as four hours were commonplace. Substance mattered less than endurance. The debate droned on, with everyone knowing that only a handful of conservative to moderate Democratic senators would decide the eventual outcome: Russell Long, Dale Bumpers, Lawton Chiles, John Sparkman, and Edward Zorinsky of Nebraska. Across their states, and throughout the country, supporters and opponents of labor law reform worked intensively to ratchet up the pressure on the key senators.

The AFL-CIO had years of experience in lobbying Capitol Hill. But Hatch and the business coalition allies had built a formidable lobbying machine, and they were breaking new ground in lobbying. The very idea of "grassroots lobbying" was still relatively new, and the opponents of labor law reform were developing it with great skill. They launched a letter-writing campaign to help local businesses contact their representatives and senators. They conducted countless meetings with newspaper editorial boards around the country; when local business leaders, armed with the strongest arguments possible, visit their hometown newspaper, the effect can be very powerful.

When reports emerged of a senator's indecision, the opponents were able to mobilize the grass roots to flood his office with more than 50,000 letters and telegrams in a day. The senators were not just hearing from Washington organizations; they were hearing from small businessmen and women whom they knew from the "main streets" of every community in their state. Together, the NAM, the Chamber of Commerce, and the construction industry action associations set up a National Action Committee that ran ads and distributed editorials. They also orchestrated eight million letters and telegrams reaching the Senate. In the last week of the debate, 97 percent of the mail that came to the Senate opposed the labor law reform legislation.

The opponents decided early on that the way to defeat the bill was to energize small business by frightening them about its consequences. The opponents made the survival of small business the key issue even though small business was exempt from the provisions of the bill. Making small businessmen feel that they would be the victims of "big labor" was a key theme of the battle.

Byrd was an unparalleled master of the inside game, and the Senate had very recently demonstrated its ability to act in the national interest even when the congressional mail and public opinion was running strongly the other way. But labor law reform was different than the Panama Canal treaty. Senators and their staffs knew the difference between post cards ginned up by a few right-wing groups and an authentic grassroots opposition to a piece of legislation. Senators were impressed when small businessmen who seldom lobbied for anything came to Washington to express their concerns. "It's a different type of lobbying," said an aide to an uncommitted Senator. "I'm seeing people on this bill that I wouldn't ordinarily see."

The battle was heating up. The labor side sought to convince companies that were unionized to break from the business community coalition. Some issued threats that powerful Democrats would retaliate. But the opponents would brook no dissent. When Hatch heard that one company was prepared to leave the coalition, he called a meeting the next day at the National Association of Manufacturers. Without singling anyone out, Hatch noted that he had heard that companies might be considering leaving the coalition for fear of angering Democrats, particularly the powerful Senator Long. "Senator Long may be chairman now," Hatch said, "but I'm going to be here for thirty years or more, and whoever does that will be one sorry company." The coalition held firm. If Hatch could continue to keep the opponents together, Byrd's mastery would be put to the ultimate test.

The Senate returned from its Memorial Day recess ready to begin the series of cloture votes that Byrd had promised. On June 1, however, the Senate was stunned by the news that Jim Allen had passed away. The Senate delayed the first cloture vote until June 7, so that senators could attend Allen's funeral the day before. It was well known that Senator Allen had been ill, but his death was not anticipated. It was the second time a senator had died in six months, and a vivid reminder of the impact that one senator could have on the institution, and the course of history. Hubert Humphrey, passionate advocate of civil rights, had been the single person most responsible for transforming the Senate into a progressive institution. Jim Allen would be remembered as the person who first cracked the code of Senate rules and precedents, inventing the post-cloture filibuster to frustrate the will of the majority and paralyze the institution. In the long run, Allen would not compare to Humphrey in accomplishments or stature. He would be less famous than others who shared his views, such as Jesse Helms or Strom Thurmond.

But the tenacious obstructionist would have a powerful, lasting impact on the operation of the Senate.

WHEN THE TIME CAME to vote, the first cloture motion failed, by a vote of 42–47. Hatch and his colleagues had mastered the procedural lessons taught by Allen well. On this first vote, they had made a surprisingly strong showing, though both sides knew that some of the votes cast against cloture were no more than a courtesy to the minority—the real battle was still to come.

On June 8, the second cloture vote failed, 49–41. It was commonplace in the Senate when deadlocks arose for key participants to leave the floor, moving to the office of one of the leaders, or Vice President Mondale's Capitol office, returning with a compromise that could resolve the situation. In this case, although the ideological lines were rigidly drawn, Javits, Williams, and Byrd put forth a compromise that softened several of the most controversial provisions, without changing the basic thrust of the legislation. Hatch and the other leading opponents labeled the changes "cosmetic," and the fight continued. They would not be satisfied until the legislation was dead.

On June 12, Russell Long approached Hatch on the Senate floor. From his position as Finance Committee chairman, Long had frequently made Carter's first year a living hell: slicing, dicing, and generally savaging his economic, tax, and energy proposals. Washington Star columnist Mary McGrory had written just before Christmas, "Russell Long appears to be running the country. It must occur to Carter that the senator from Louisiana has found a way to be president without being elected to the job." In a relatively rare moment of public humor, Carter had joked that he had arrived in Washington, proud that a southerner would be taking the reins of the federal government, and "found that Russell Long had filled that position for a long time." But Long had been a decisive vote in support of the Panama Canal treaties, and he was looking for an opportunity to help Carter and Byrd on labor law reform.

Now, Long repeated an offer he had made to Hatch a week before: in exchange for an end to the filibuster, the Democrats would modify several provisions of the bill. That way, everyone could win. George Meany would get the legislation he needed; President Carter would avoid embarrassment, and Hatch could claim credit for making the legislation more even-handed. Long left unspoken the tacit threat that if there was no compromise, the Democrats could unite behind the bill and invoke cloture, and the opportunity for changes to the bill would be lost. It was a classic Long compromise, but Hatch was not in a compromising mood. He told Long that a few amendments would not change the labor law reform bill from being terrible legislation.

After more than a month of debate and relentless lobbying, exhaustion was setting in among the senators. Hatch could barely speak from the strain that the six-week debate had placed on his voice. Tempers were short. Hollings sat close by John Sparkman, who was still uncommitted, to ensure that no one persuaded the aging Sparkman to vote for cloture. Byrd approached Sparkman on the floor, hoping to convince him to change sides. Before he could even begin, however, Sparkman pushed him away, telling the majority leader to leave him alone.

Several moderate Republicans—Lowell Weicker, Ted Stevens, and John Heinz of Pennsylvania—announced that they would vote for cloture. These defections were anticipated, but it was the defection of Chuck Percy, a former CEO, that jolted the business coalition. After the vote, Hatch caught Percy on the floor, unable to mask his anger. "I thought you promised to be with us," Hatch said. "I did promise to be with you," Percy snapped, "but I didn't promise to be with you forever." The fourth cloture motion produced fifty-eight votes, bringing labor's advocates tantalizingly close to victory. A fifth cloture vote—already the most that had ever been taken on a single piece of legislation—produced fifty-eight votes as well.

When Byrd announced that there would be a sixth cloture vote on June 22, everyone knew it would be the last. Bumpers, Chiles, and Sparkman had decided to stay on the side of business. Long had not yet disclosed his intentions, but Hatch and Hollings expected him to be the fifty-ninth vote. Zorinsky, an obscure, first-term senator from Nebraska, was the last possible vote to break the filibuster, and the majority leader and other Democrats were working hard to bring him around.

The Democrats' efforts seemed to be working. Journalists were already openly predicting a Democratic victory. Hatch came to the Capitol on the morning of the vote only to find Long just emerging from the minority leader's office. "Orrin, you know you're going to lose today," Howard Baker said to him. Long had just revealed that he was going to change sides in exchange for a number of amendments to the bill. Baker, who had stood by Hatch throughout the long battle, plainly hoped that he would go along with the compromise. Hatch again refused, saying it remained a terrible bill. If the Senate passed it, he wanted it clear who was responsible. Baker appeared disappointed, but did not push him further: Hatch was still in charge.

Hatch had another reason to stand firm: Long may have been influential, but he was still only the fifty-ninth vote. Hollings had been doing some discreet lobbying of his own. He had discovered that the father of one of his friends from Greenville, South Carolina, Freddy Collins, had been in business for years with Zorinsky's father in Nebraska. Hollings had urged Collins to ask his father to call Zorinsky's, and he had done so. Still, Zorinsky's vote remained in doubt.

As the final cloture vote started, Hollings voted and raced over to Zorinsky's office in the Russell Senate Office Building. He caught Zorinsky coming down the hall and said, "Ed, I really need your help on this one. This is a big issue back home, and if you can vote my way, then I'll be your man on something you need." Zorinsky gave Hollings the high sign.

The vote was very close when Zorinsky entered the Senate chamber. No one was certain how he would vote. Zorinsky was plainly torn; he disliked the bill, but as a freshman Democrat, he had to be particularly nervous causing a defeat for the president and the majority leader. At the same time, demonstrating independence would add to his stature and certainly strengthen his standing with Nebraska's small business community. Hatch caught Zorinsky's eye, and Zorinsky, face expressionless, nodded. Hatch knew that he had his forty-first vote.

Byrd rose on the Senate floor, to begin the parliamentary theater that would give Long the opportunity to change his vote. He asked unanimous consent to return the bill to committee, with instructions to report it back with a few minor changes. The changes were intended to allow the last few senators to shift their votes. After speaking for a few minutes, Byrd asked for unanimous consent, but Hollings objected. Long leaped to his feet, attacking the opponents for frustrating the will of the Senate. Long said that he was so angered by these tactics that he was going to vote for cloture.

"Well, the distinguished senator from Louisiana has always been the fifty-ninth vote for cloture, and we have always known it," Hollings said. His comment left unspoken the question: where was the 60th? Without Zorinsky, the pro-labor forces had fallen short.

Stevens, the Republican whip, had voted for cloture, but he had tired of the long debate and the gamesmanship. "If Senator Long is going to cross over, then I'm crossing back," Stevens announced.

The battle was over. The sixth cloture vote produced only fifty-three votes as Byrd freed some of the Democrats who had committed to him. The AFL-

CIO, the Senate Democrats, and White House had suffered a stunning defeat at the hands of the Republicans and an energized and unified business community.

Javits considered the outcome a tragedy. He judged the legislation necessary, securing for labor the Wagner Act's right to organize, which had been undercut by corporate tactics in the previous decade. In Javits's view, relatively amicable labor relations had been a crucial element of America's prosperity since World War II, and he feared that the legislative battle was the harbinger of a much more contentious period. Javits undoubtedly shared the frustration expressed by Secretary of Labor Ray Marshall, who observed, "we have the only labor movement in the world that embraces capitalism and [the business community] is trying to kill it."

The battle over the Panama Canal treaty had been historic, but the battle over labor law reform showed that the tectonic plates of American politics were shifting. The AFL-CIO would never get the labor law reforms that it sought in 1978—not during the remainder of the Carter administration and not during the eight years of the Clinton administration. In 2009, Barack Obama came to the White House, with strong Democratic majorities in both houses of Congress, having committed to push labor's highest priority, the Employee Fair Choice Act, better known as "card check," which made it easier for workers to form a union in the plants. The labor movement continues to await a debate and vote.

chapter 11

SAVING NEW YORK

JACK JAVITS'S LOVE FOR THE SENATE WAS MATCHED ONLY BY HIS LOVE of his birthplace, New York City. He saw New York as the most vibrant city in the world: a center of commerce and finance, the media, the arts and culture, and an unsurpassed melting pot that represented America's commitment to diversity and immigration. To Javits, New York was a place that "always had the luster and magic of a new town, with an adventure around every corner and behind every window, with human energy, ingenuity and inventiveness coursing every street, changing every moment . . . the most exciting city in modern civilization."

Javits gave serious thought throughout his career to leaving the Senate to run for mayor of New York. As Javits put it, "the temptation to seek the mayoralty ran like an underground stream throughout my career." He saw himself as perhaps the only public official who could stand up to the demands of the municipal unions. Although he was a strong supporter of unions, Javits maintained a tough-minded independence. When Walter Mondale was a young senator, Javits warned him: "Fritz, if you start whoring for labor, you'll never stop."

In early 1978, Javits was focused like a laser on the problem that had preoccupied him for the past several years: saving New York City from financial disaster. Beginning in the 1950's and continuing throughout the 1960's, the city's financial situation had spiraled out of control. Its manufacturing base was weakening; its middle class was heading for the suburbs. Successive mayors gave in to the wage demands of strong municipal unions. Tourism suffered from fear of crime. The city's liberal social programs and generous benefits drew in poor people from within the United States and around the world, causing a demand for public services that the city could not provide.

In 1975, after an intense and acrimonious debate, Congress had sought to convince President Gerald Ford that New York City, facing bankruptcy with incalculable consequences for the city and the nation's economy, had to be thrown a financial lifeline. It was a tough sell. Ford, in the White House less than a year, had adamantly opposed federal help for New York City. Even the lobbying of Nelson Rockefeller, Ford's chosen vice president and the former New York governor, could not convince Ford that New York City—fiscally out of control, dominated by public employee unions—deserved the help. Ford's initial opposition had yielded an infamous front page headline in the *New York Daily News*: "Ford to City: Drop Dead."

Ultimately, the Ford administration went along with a strictly limited three-year program of direct aid to New York City, in the form of seasonal loans to be paid back in full with interest at the end of each year. It was an unprecedented step made necessary by a deep recession sweeping across the country. In such a situation, the collapse of the nation's largest city could have incalculable consequences. The seasonal loan authority would expire on June 30, 1978—and the Ford administration had intended that it would never be repeated.

By May 1978, even New York City's toughest critics acknowledged that the city, responding to Congress and the strong leadership of New York governor Hugh Carey, had taken major steps to improve its financial management and get on a more sustainable course. As a condition of receiving the seasonal loans, New York City had gone into virtual receivership, with a state-established Emergency Financial Control Board making its fiscal decisions. To close the budget deficit, the city had slashed it spending, reduced the number of city workers, and its new Mayor, Edward Koch, had taken on the public employee unions, negotiating the least generous contract in many decades. Meanwhile, the economic recovery under way in the country buoyed New York City's economy. New York's advocates believed that if a second round of loans were extended, the city had a strong chance to not only survive, but prosper. Without a second round of loans, however, New York City's future remained in peril.

Banking Committee Chairman William Proxmire and Ed Brooke of Massachusetts, the committee's ranking Republican, saw the situation differently.

In February 1978, the Banking Committee had issued a unanimous report on the city's financial condition concluding that if the interested local parties—city and state employee pension funds and the New York financial institutions—would agree to provide reasonable amounts of aid to the city there would be no need for continued federal assistance.

The committee report came as a shock to the advocates of New York City, led by its senators. Javits believed that New York City's recovery was fragile, and its fiscal problems still cried out for a more permanent fix. He said that "the report of the Committee, if literally taken, is a prescription for disaster." Daniel Patrick Moynihan observed bitterly that those who had regarded the Banking Committee as "a sympathetic friend of the city" had been disabused of that notion; "the tone of this document is—put plainly—hostile and adamant."

The lack of sympathy for New York's fiscal woes reflected a burgeoning ideology sweeping the nation—one that reviled government assistance, programs, and bailouts, instead preferring tax cuts as the solution to virtually every problem. In the words of Bill Brock, the former senator chairing the Republican National Committee, "The American people are just plain fed up. They are sick to death of government and taxes, and the Democrats have imposed them both. They are looking for alternatives."

Bill Roth, the Republican senator from Delaware, thought he had such an alternative. Elected in 1970, after several terms in the House, Roth was a low-key, intelligent lawyer, absolutely lacking in charisma. But Roth combined legal ability with a keen sensitivity to the impact of taxes on individuals and businesses. Roth understood that American middle-class families were not feeling prosperous. As a result of the inflation that had dogged the economy since 1973, they simultaneously paid higher prices and found themselves forced into higher tax brackets. To distinguish itself from neighboring states, Delaware had made itself the headquarters of most corporations in the nation and sustained a vibrant business climate by having no state income tax whatsoever. Roth recognized that the federal government had responsibilities that made it impossible to eliminate taxes, but Delaware's experience convinced him that substantially reducing taxes would spur the economy, by providing individuals and companies with additional capital to spend and invest.

As the U.S. economy began to falter under the pressures of rising energy prices and tough foreign competition after the 1973 oil embargo, Roth began to "noodle" with his staff and a group of outside advisers about the potential impact of reduced taxes. In early 1976 Roth found a House Republican counterpart. Buffalo Congressman Jack Kemp, the former professional quarterback, and far more charismatic, was equally enamored of tax cuts.

Together, the two men introduced legislation to cut individual rates 30 percent across the board. Kemp and Roth became a political odd couple, explaining to reporters the "Laffer curve," the work of economist Arthur Laffer, which purported to prove that increasing tax rates beyond a certain point became counterproductive, because it diminished the incentive to work. Consequently, cutting taxes would produce more economic activity and more revenues. In some respects, that was a common-sense notion, and Republicans would often point to President Kennedy's 1963 tax cut as evidence for their supply-side arguments. The real question was how the Laffer curve, or the nation's needs, could justify the deep slashes in tax rates proposed by Roth and Kemp. According to Neil Messick, Roth's longtime chief of staff, "no one in Washington took them seriously." But at precisely the same time, the anti-tax, anti-government message was taking hold in dramatic, long-lasting ways on the west coast.

On June 7, 1978, California voters, enraged by soaring property taxes, approved Proposition 13, with 65 percent of the vote. Slashing revenues from existing property taxes by 57 percent, and then forbidding property taxes from being raised unless approved by two-thirds of the electorate, it would be the most famous proposition in American history. Its impact is still being felt today in California's ongoing fiscal crisis.

Prop 13 wasn't the only barometer of the public mood. On the same day, Ohio voters turned down 86 out of 139 proposed school bonds, including those needed for emergency relief for Cleveland and Columbus school systems. In New Jersey, Jeffrey Bell, an unknown professor who had moved to the state two years earlier, shocked the political world by defeating Clifford Case in the Republican primary basically running on a single issue—tax cuts. The people had spoken. In three major, bellwether states in different parts of the country, the message was loud and clear. Although the deep recession of 1973–1975 was over and relatively vigorous economic growth had resumed, inflation was taking a severe toll on the economic well-being and the confidence of Americans. They were stretched thin, and angry at all levels of government. They were not interested in waiting for the next election to choose new leaders. They wanted to do the one thing that would improve their situations immediately: pay less taxes.

Overnight, Proposition 13 became the talk of Capitol Hill. Members of Congress, of course, could not reduce property taxes, but they could demonstrate their political awareness to an angry public by cutting federal spending and moving toward a balanced budget. Within a week, the House of Representatives voted to ban cost of living increases for members of Congress, federal judges, and high-ranking officials of the executive branch. The House also demonstrated its newfound frugality by voting to stop the use of public funds for free distribution of calendars, almanacs, and similar items by members of Congress, although distribution of American flags would still be permitted.

William Proxmire, a noted pinch-penny, suggested a $3.5 billion cut in the budget of the Department of Housing and Urban Development (HUD), as "an acid test of whether this Congress is willing to take Proposition 13 seriously and cut its budget." Brooke, who was the only African American in the Senate, advised Proxmire that "we ought not come in here and panic under Proposition 13. It's not some magic word." Five months later, the Senate would have no African American members. Brooke would have personal problems arising from an ugly divorce, but his distinguished career ended in part because he had underestimated the power of Proposition 13 and the anger of the tax revolt.

In such an environment, it was little wonder that extended financial assistance for New York City appeared such an unappealing, and in fact politically dangerous, prospect.

Nevertheless, some were still willing to go to bat for New York City. In March, in an act of considerable political courage, Treasury Secretary Michael Blumenthal had put the Carter administration on record in favor of federal guarantees for New York bonds. But the Senate Banking Committee appeared unmoved. Now, less than four months after its unanimous report, and less than thirty days from the end of the seasonal loan program, the Banking Committee was considering legislation introduced by Javits and Moynihan, reflecting the urgent request from Mayor Koch and Governor Carey to provide new federal loan guarantees for New York City–related securities. Despite the assurances given in 1975, New York City was asking the Senate to save it again. The Senate would have to decide the future of the nation's premier city.

As of the first week of June 1978, the fate of New York City could no longer be avoided. Proxmire brought the Banking Committee together for hearings to consider New York City's request for federal loan guarantees. As opponents of the city went, he would be formidable indeed.

Bill Proxmire had come to the Senate in 1957, winning a special election to fill the Wisconsin Senate seat left vacant when Joseph McCarthy died. Proxmire had won the seat after years of relentless campaigning, having lost two previous bids for the Senate. Educated at Yale and Harvard, he had never before held elected office. Proxmire was the original maverick, long before the term became fashionable. He campaigned for reelection to the Senate without raising any money. His gaunt appearance and passion for exercise—he ran five miles to work in the morning, and home in the evening—caught the attention of many people. As a *New York Times* profile put it, Proxmire's "highly-ordered life included 5,669 consecutive roll call votes, three millions hands shaken, the first Senate hair transplant and face lift, and vacations hauling garbage, and living in fire houses."

Proxmire's fame dramatically expanded when he conceived of the idea of the "Golden Fleece" award, which he handed out, with great fanfare, to the federal government program he considered the biggest waste of taxpayer money. Proxmire took special delight in going after wasteful Pentagon expenditures, although he never hesitated to subject domestic programs to ridicule as well, including a famous NIH expenditure of $84 million to study the physiological effects of love.

In 1971, Proxmire pulled off a genuine political miracle when he led a successful coalition to the first great legislative victory by the environmental movement, defeating a program for Supersonic Transport (SST), which was heavily supported by the Nixon administration, Washington's powerful senators Magnuson and Jackson, and the AFL-CIO. No one questioned Bill Proxmire's brains, independence, tenacity, or guts—for Javits and Moynihan, the problem was that he now strongly opposed helping New York City.

Ed Brooke, the first black American ever to be elected to the Senate by popular vote, was a liberal Republican who took pride in being a member of the party created by Abraham Lincoln. He championed civil rights legislation and demonstrated his independence from his own party by being the first senator to call for Richard Nixon's resignation in 1973. During the hearings, Brooke was campaigning for his third term in the Senate, facing a formidable challenge from Congressman Paul Tsongas. Nevertheless he seemed likely to win reelection. Senator Brooke cared deeply about America's cities, and he was not a skinflint like Proxmire. But he shared many of the chairman's concerns about the wisdom of extending further federal support to New York City.

On June 6, Proxmire gaveled the hearing to order, glared down at the contingent from New York City, and made his position clear: "It troubles me greatly that the committee will be confronting . . . the same pleas for financial aid that we heard 3 years ago in 1975—and from many of the same people as well. But 1978 is not the same as 1975."

Proxmire stated that the loans had only been granted out of concern about a ripple effect that would be heightened by the Arab oil embargo. Because of the extraordinary circumstances, Proxmire said that Congress had granted seasonal loans to New York City, but with a clear understanding that it was a "one-time thing." The mayor and governor had given their assurances to that effect. Proxmire was not pleased to see the New Yorkers returning for more.

Proxmire promised that the committee would give full consideration to the case presented by New York City and New York State, but he left no doubt about the depth of his "grave misgivings" about giving further federal financial help to New York City. He suggested that New York's banks and pension funds had ample resources to do more for the city. He rejected the notion that they would be permitted to sit on the sideline and watch New York City go under. A modest increase in investment by the New York banks would go a long way to meeting New York City's needs. A similar small increase by the massive New York City pension funds could do the rest. "It amazes me to hear that these local parties are offering so little—the banks a measly $500 million, the pension funds nothing without a federal guarantee," Proxmire concluded. "Does this show a lack of confidence in the city, or more nearly a lack of desire to do themselves what they think they can lay on the back of the Federal Government?"

The chairman had set the terms for the debate. The burden on New York City's advocates was now heavy. Senators, and virtually everyone else, knew Proxmire to be fanatically opposed to wasteful government spending. He would be tough to persuade. New York City advocates could only hope that there would be some relent from Brooke, a champion of cities. But Brooke's opening statement came as a cold splash of reality. Noting the Banking Committee's unanimous conclusion in February that no further federal support was needed, Brooke stated, "I do not believe that providing Federal guarantees will solve New York City's problems and in fact providing such guarantees on obligations to be purchased by New York banks and pension funds seems to me to represent a step backwards from 1975 when those parties agreed to buy such obligations without guarantees."

Brooke noted the civic pride of New Yorkers, captured by the "I Love New York" buttons that had appeared throughout the city, and assured those listening to the hearing that "members of this committee are not without affection for New York and are concerned about the city's future." Given his stated position, Brooke's attempt to conclude on a warm note provided cold comfort to New Yorkers, who had a general suspicion of those from Boston under any circumstances.

Speaking in defense of New York City was Daniel Patrick Moynihan—a recent arrival to the Senate, though not every senator started equal. Past accomplishments counted, and very few people in American history, if any, had come to the Senate with more accomplishments than Moynihan. After earning his Ph.D. at Tufts, he had joined the Harvard faculty, where he wrote a stream of notable books and articles. He had been a wunderkind in the Kennedy administration, stayed to help Lyndon Johnson, became ambassador to India, returned to Washington to be White House domestic adviser to Richard Nixon, and then became a national figure as a combative ambassador to the United Nations, fighting off the attacks of the developing nations critical of the United States and Israel.

Moynihan had broken the hearts of many New York Democrats by narrowly defeating liberal Congresswoman Bella Abzug, one of the nation's best-known women in politics, to seize the Democratic nomination for the Senate. Now, color and controversy followed Moynihan everywhere, but no one questioned his credentials as an expert on urban problems, or his love of New York, where he had grown up in East Harlem and gone to college at City College of New York (CCNY).

Moynihan loved to speak, and he almost always brought a different slant to whatever issue he was addressing. Now he spoke somberly: "For two generations representatives of New York have been coming to the Congress, from the time of Franklin D. Roosevelt proposing ways to help other parts of this Nation and the world and now we have to ask help for ourselves, and it's not easy. It's never easy. It's not been made easier."

He quoted an editorial from the morning's *New York Times* on the brutal steps that New York City had taken to pull its act together. He urged the committee to remember that there's not one thing the matter with the city of New York that could not have been avoided if we had chosen to treat the poor of the rest of this nation who came to us the way the rest of this Nation in the main has treated its poor, all but driving them to us, where we have looked after them for two generations, and in the process we have indeed near bankrupted ourselves. It is not something to be ashamed of, sir.

Javits was up next, and duly picked up on Moynihan's theme and delivered it straight from the shoulder:

We are where we are because New York is the central city of this country and probably the world and because the demography of this country has chased three million taxpaying middle-class citizens out of New York and substituted for them another 3 million desirable persons who one day, and I hope soon, will be just as good taxpayers, but right now are tax receivers. Now that's a national problem because it was caused by the great civil rights revolution of the 1960's, but there's no national way to account for it except for this.

Javits did not excuse the liberal contracts that past mayors had negotiated with New York City's powerful public employee unions. He had long believed that the city's mayors had been too weak in their dealings with the unions, but he attributed only 10 to 15 percent to "corruption and inefficiencies." The welfare problem represented the principal cause of New York City's perilous financial condition: "most of our troubles were attributable to the fact that we are where we are and what we are."

Javits recounted the help that the government had extended to others in the past, "Our government has guaranteed District of Columbia bonds for a stadium. Our government guarantees hundreds of billions of dollars for new communities . . . billions by which we guarantee everything and everybody—farmers, people who transport by water, builders, truckers and everybody else," Javits observed. "Why suddenly is it a big shattering blow or precedent if the Secretary of Treasury tells us if you want to redeem New York in the national interest, this is the way to do it." He set forth the standard by which the Senate should judge its action: "The national interest of the United States—nothing else—and the national interest of the United States demands as a paramount matter that New York be saved."

Thanking Proxmire for holding the hearing, Javits remarked, "You helped save us once before . . . and I think you will again. I have not lost hope at all." His heartfelt comments went beyond the usual courtesy that senators extended to each other. A committee chairman could kill legislation that he opposed, simply by inaction. Proxmire was giving New York City's advocates a chance to make their case. They might not convince them, but even if they could not change his mind, they might affect the intensity of his opposition. Javits loved what he called the "woof and warp of the legislative process." Many things could happen between now and June 30.

Now the committee turned to its principal witness. Ed Koch had been mayor of New York City for only six months, moving into Gracie Mansion, the mayor's residence, after nine years of representing New York's silk stocking district in the House of Representatives. Koch's predecessor as mayor, Abraham Beame, a former city comptroller, had been hammered down by the enormous burden of the city's financial problems. Koch, a politician with a large ego and enthusiasm, had brought new energy to Gracie Mansion, attacking the problems, showing up at all hours of the day or night around the city, constantly asking New Yorkers "how'm I doing?" He came before the Banking Committee sleep-deprived, having just completed negotiations of a new labor contract with the city's municipal unions. Proxmire greeted Koch, noting "what a good strong job you're doing as Mayor of New York." The senators respected Koch for taking on one of the toughest jobs imaginable.

Koch submitted a sixty-page written statement and probably would have delivered it all if he had been allowed. After presenting the actions he had already taken to rescue the city's finances—including getting tough on unions and enacting austerity measures—Koch outlined the comprehensive plan that he formulated for the city's financial future, involving a partnership by the federal, state, and city governments and with the private sector. It included a reduction of 20,000 employees over four years, a 12 percent reduction in real purchases of materials and supplies, and a continued reduction of the welfare rolls, which were already at their lowest point since 1970. Koch embraced the Emergency Financial Control Board—"I have the same sense of fiscal integrity"—although his predecessor Beame had said he could not live with its edicts. He also expressed pride in landmark legislation that he had been able to get through the state legislature, changing the arbitration system so that an arbitrator's award could be challenged at every stage by the Emergency Financial Control Board on the basis that the city did not have the ability to pay.

Koch implored the Committee to provide the federal loan guarantees that the Treasury Department was supporting. "We are on the edge of a renaissance," Koch predicted. "If we are able to pull this together, the city of New York will once again be the premier city in the world." He described the grim alternative: "The cost to the federal government of not helping the city will be greater than the cost of helping. If the City does not rehabilitate itself, it will decay and slowly die, becoming a ward of the state and the Federal governments. In these circumstances, denying the City's request for financing assistance today will prove costly tomorrow. It is being penny-wise and pound-foolish on an incredible scale."

During questioning, Proxmire asked again and again why New York City should receive special treatment. "We have problems in Milwaukee, there are problems in Boston, Detroit, and Pittsburgh, and so forth," he noted. "So where do we draw the line? Why shouldn't we do it for everyone?" At one point, he quoted a "splendid analysis" by economist Herbert Bienstock, who had predicted New York City's decline in the 1960's but was now much more optimistic about the city's future. Moynihan said he had great admiration for Herb Bienstock, "who reported to me when I was Assistant Secretary of Labor under President Kennedy," but that if Bienstock were testifying: "He would tell you the one thing New York City needs is a dependable fiscal future for its government."

On the second day of hearings, Proxmire and Brooke showed a new willingness to support seasonal loans. It would not be enough for New York, but it represented movement from their adamant starting positions. Felix Rohatyn, the brilliant investment banker from Lazard Freres who had been instrumental in the 1975 rescue of New York and a moving force in the proposal for loan guarantees, responded: "The city can live with it, but the city cannot get well with it. Seasonal loans will postpone the return of the city indefinitely." Governor Carey, greatly admired for his steadfast leadership in meeting the city's financial crisis, sounded the same theme in his forceful testimony.

Javits hoped that the hearings had accomplished their purpose. A month before, he and Proxmire had exchanged views on the Senate floor. "There are some things that lean on each other," Javits noted. If the federal government committed to helping New York, the unions, the pension funds, the banks and the State would all come forward and contribute. "That is the cement that is going to put them together." Proxmire could be the "principal architect. . . . If you take it in hand, it will happen. If you don't take it in hand, I have grave doubts about it."

Proxmire would later say that "Jack Javits and Pat Moynihan did more to change the Banking Committee from 'no' in January 1978 to 'yes' in June 1978 than any two senators I have ever seen operate on any issue in all my career." And with the hearings over, White House lobbying efforts began in earnest. But Senate action to help New York City would also require a strong advocate from the Banking Committee to overcome Proxmire's continuing opposition.

Richard Lugar had missed most of the hearings, because of his intense involvement in the filibuster against the labor law reform legislation. A moderate conservative, Lugar had expressed his opposition in principle to further federal assistance for New York City. But Lugar came to the problem from his experience as an innovative and successful mayor of Indianapolis. His leadership of the city, coupled with his remarkable leadership to forge a metropolitan solution to problems of finance and school desegregation, made his a strong and credible voice on helping New York City if he chose to be involved. He had become very familiar with New York's problems in 1975–1976, while serving as the president of the National Conference of Mayors.

Briefed on the hearings, Lugar concluded that the federal government had no choice but to help New York City. However, the help would have to come with such stringent conditions that other cities would be deterred from seeking assistance. Working with the Banking Committee staff, Lugar drafted and circulated a compromise proposal. It included $1.5 billion in federal loan guarantees, limited to $500 million a year, and a requirement that the State of New York had to maintain its level of effort, coupled with strict controls and requirements, such as the continuation of the Emergency Finance Control Board, that would make it virtually impossible for other cities to seek similar relief.

Lugar's proposal became the legislation that the Banking Committee would consider. This well-crafted, "tough love" compromise, and the fact that Lugar had been opposed to helping New York but switched positions, had transformed the situation. Javits and Moynihan continued to lobby fiercely. President Carter called three undecided Banking Committee members, and Vice President Mondale called two others. Proxmire ruefully gave credit to an extraordinary lobbying effort on behalf of New York City. Calling it "wholly unnecessary legislation," Proxmire, still opposed, nonetheless predicted the committee would approve it by a vote of 12–3, and he was right on the mark.

On June 29, less than four weeks after the committee hearings, the New York City Loan Guarantee Act of 1978 came before the Senate. In most cases, legislation opposed by a chairman never makes it to the full Senate. In those relatively rare cases when the committee overcomes a chairman's opposition, the chairman would usually ask another committee member to manage the bill. In this case, however, Proxmire chose to manage the bill, saying that he had an obligation to work for its passage in the form approved by the committee.

On the Senate floor, Proxmire gave an extraordinary, perhaps unprecedented, performance, alternately as the bill's strongest supporter and its toughest critic. He told the Senate that the committee bill represented a distinct improvement over the administration bill and the substantially more generous House bill. "If there are to be long-term guarantees," Proxmire stated, "the committee has come up with a tough, responsible bill—a bill that can do the job intended, and with minimal risk to the Federal government."

To make it absolutely certain that other cities could not seek the same deal, the guarantees would be available only for loans made by pension funds, and no other city had pension funds large enough to provide funding of the scale contemplated. Proxmire also noted the continuing requirement that the Emergency Financial Control Board be in operation, and the stringent cost controls and expenditure limits it had imposed; "this is not just a little patsy that was put in just to reassure people. This is a board that has force and has demonstrated that it will use it to keep expenditures down."

At the same time, he "continued to disagree with its fundamental premise. I do not believe that New York City needs or should get more financial aid from the Federal government." He repeated his view that the New York City banks and pension funds had ample resources to save the city, saying "one of the most frustrating experiences that I have had in my years in the Senate is that nobody answers that argument. We give them the arithmetic over and over." He expressed fear that:

> We are setting a number of undesirable precedents. We are relieving a
> major state of its responsibility for the financial soundness of one of
> its cities. We are relieving some of the biggest banks in the country
> for seeing that the city they live in and do business in remains solvent
> and returns to fiscal responsibility.... Above all, and most disturbing
> of all, we are setting the precedent of providing long-term Federal

guarantees to a municipality to meet its basic financing needs. Despite the efforts made in the committee's bill to limit the scope of the guarantees and confine them to the rather singular conditions prevailing in New York City, there is no way to get around the fact that the Federal Government is now going into the business of guaranteeing municipal bonds. Once we get in, I see no way of getting out, no way in fact to get anywhere but deeper in. . . . "The richest city in the country has a guarantee. Why not us?" Where will be the grounds to deny to Los Angeles, Cleveland or Oshkosh what we just gave to New York?

Taking the floor, Javits expressed the hope that "New York day in the Senate" would be "a day of realism." He argued that "no precedent is set by this loan guarantee legislation. Indeed, the precedent, if any, was established in 1975" and contrary to the predictions of critics, no other cities had come forward to seek relief. He commended Proxmire, Brooke, Lugar, and Don Riegle for a "brilliant and exacting cross examination," thoroughly examining the case; they had produced a bill that was both constructive and strict, which would put New York on the "road to viability" so it could go into the public markets as any city must. In his view, the country had come to understand that New York City's bankruptcy could be prevented and "that is a national blessing, not a national disaster."

Moynihan injected an extraordinary personal note. He told the Senate that in May 1976, he had intended to leave the United Nations to return to the university; "I had been in the Cabinet or Sub-Cabinet of four presidents. I wanted to go back to a quiet corner." But on that day, Moynihan read that the Emergency Financial Control Board had decided to close the City College of New York. Moynihan had attended CCNY; it was the first free urban college in the world, created in 1847, and it had educated hundreds of thousands of immigrants and produced extraordinary graduates who helped build New York City and the country. The decision to close CCNY shocked New York, and it convinced Moynihan to run for the Senate.

Howard Baker had come on to the floor to speak. With a mischievous smile, Baker observed wryly that having known Moynihan for some years, "I feel compelled to say that whatever place he occupies is not likely to be quiet." Then Baker offered his support, praising the committee and particularly Lugar for the legislation that had resulted.

The hour for decision had come. John Tower, a leading opponent, closed with resignation, nominating Proxmire for the Golden Fleece award, for having "apparently taken leave of his earlier good judgment, and succumbed to the plaintive cries, please and entreaties of those who would feed at the public trough." Shortly thereafter, the Senate approved the legislation to provide federal loan guarantees to New York City by a vote of 53–27, with 35 Democrats and 18 Republicans voting in favor.

The emphatic vote came just weeks after it had appeared that aid to New York City was a lost cause. The absence of twenty senators from the final count provided a reminder that coming in the immediate aftermath of Proposition 13, it was still a politically difficult vote. But New York and its advocates had made a compelling case. And the city's progress under Koch's leadership, perhaps coupled with the successful Democratic convention in 1976 and the memory of America's Bicentennial when the tall ships sailed into New York harbor, had softened people's attitudes toward the Empire City, and not a moment too soon.

Proxmire pledged to fight for the tougher provisions in the Senate bill in conference with the House. As always, the conference committee's legislation took some features from each bill, but generally favored the tougher Senate approach. On July 28, 1978, the Senate approved the legislation that the conference committee had produced. Flinty as he was, Proxmire nonetheless seemed to be in good spirits. He rhapsodized about the greatness of New York, from the magnificent skyline to its legendary characters like Damon Runyan and Walter Winchell. "But," Proxmire concluded, "if New York has one quality above all, it is that fantastic brass, the ability to con you into a $1.65 billion loan guarantee when . . . this is the credit capital of the world. . . . It's a wonderful city, and it's a great privilege to be conned by the city."

LOOKING BACK ON MAJOR historical moments, it often seems as though their outcome was inevitable. Yet in fact, at crucial moments, the outcomes are usually very uncertain. Unlike the Panama Canal treaties, the vote in favor of loan guarantees for New York prevailed by a wide margin, but the battle was much closer fought than the margin reflects. Jimmy Carter, Treasury Secretary Blumenthal, and others in the administration deserved enormous credit for their political bravery; they saw the national interest, and they acted on it.

The Senate proved to be a harder sell, particularly after the unanimous report of the Banking Committee opposing further federal help for New York. But at this crucial juncture, the Senate fortunately included Javits and Moynihan, two passionately committed natives of the streets of New York, and Lugar, a conservative, midwestern Republican freshman, who had been the nation's finest mayor. They stepped up to the challenge, just as Byrd, Baker, and Church had stepped up in the Panama Canal debates. At times like these, the Senate lived up to its reputation as being "the world's greatest deliberative body." But it also resembled a championship sports team. In the big games, people came forward and made the big plays.

In the 1980's and 1990's, New York City ultimately did indeed experience the renaissance that Mayor Koch predicted. Prosperity returned to the city, and crime diminished. The city was again the magnet for ambitious, talented people from all over the country and the world. Many people, such as Mayor Rudy Giuliani, played an important part in New York City's resurgence, and the strong national economy certainly helped. But there is little doubt that the foundation for New York's revival was laid when the Senate, despite the tax revolt that was sweeping the country, stepped forward with a rescue package in 1978. The Senate's action was reminiscent of a famous statement by Mark Twain: "Do the right thing. It will gratify some people and astonish the rest."

chapter 12

CLOSING
DAYS

THROUGHOUT 1978, THE SENATE HAD BEEN FIRING ON ALL CYLINDERS.
Historic accomplishments—the Panama Canal treaties and the rescue of
New York City—were joined by major legislative actions such as approval of
the F-15 sale to Saudi Arabia and landmark legislation to deregulate airlines.
Civil service and ethics reform were moving forward toward enactment. Yet,
even so, month after month, the natural gas nightmare continued.

The failure to enact legislation in 1977 had damaged Jimmy Carter greatly.
In an effort to show confidence and encourage Democrats, Robert Byrd had
expressed optimism that the legislation could be finished in early 1978. This
prediction, like a second marriage, proved to be a triumph of hope over experience. It also served to highlight, yet again, Carter's failure to achieve his
highest domestic priority. The hard truth was that no matter whatever other
legislative accomplishments occurred, Carter's second year would likely be
judged by the same criterion as his first.

By the fall of 1978, Congress appeared much closer to adjourning than to
passing natural gas legislation of any kind. Senators and staff took long meetings with industry and consumer advocates, and staff dutifully noted down
any number of new ideas for breaking the deadlock. But for months, despite
intense effort and perpetual activity, everyday was Ground Hog's Day—nothing ever changed. Advocates of the oil and gas industry favored deregulation
of natural gas. Consumer advocates preferred the continuation of price controls on gas. James Schlesinger, Carter's secretary of energy and architect of

the administration's energy plan, described the negotiations with the Senate as a "descent into hell." Both sides seemed beyond compromise. Experienced Washington hands could remember nothing like it.

And yet the pricing of natural gas had originally been only a minor part of Carter's energy program that Schlesinger had prepared. In April 1977, when Carter declared the energy crisis to be "the moral equivalent of war," he had unveiled a plan to reduce U.S. oil consumption, and thus oil imports, by increasing energy prices by a new tax on domestically produced crude oil and a series of measures to encourage industry to switch from oil and gas to coal. The administration estimated that these measures could save 4.5 million barrels of oil daily by 1985. However, the Senate buried the crude oil tax, which had been passed by the House. The Senate also weakened the coal conversion measures. With its hands tied, the administration was now forced to trumpet the energy savings that could result from a change in natural gas pricing. The resulting compromise legislation, starkly different from the original proposal on gas, had somehow become the less-than-inspiring centerpiece of Carter's energy policy.

Carter's original plan had been to continue controls on gas consumed in the state where it was produced, but to raise the price ceiling and then let it rise with inflation. The House had passed this version, but the Senate, after Byrd crushed the filibuster by Jim Abourezk and Howard Metzenbaum, had voted to decontrol all natural gas in two years, and the conferees had thrown up their hands and gone home without agreement in 1977.

Finally, after eight more months of haggling, the conferees had struck a deal to end controls on new gas by 1985, but to allow the president or Congress to reimpose controls for one eighteen-month period that could run through 1988. The ceiling would then rise about 10 percent per year, assuming 5 percent inflation. The Senate staff report said that this would increase producer revenue by not more than $9 billion, or 6 percent, by 1985. The report also predicted that the compromise would lead to additional production of 700,000 barrels a day, by 1985, about 10 percent of current imports. However, a Department of Energy analysis of the compromise concluded producers would gain $28.5 billion over the next six years.

A *Washington Post* analysis commented: "This legislation is much closer to what the president once denounced as 'war profiteering' than it is to the administration's original gas plan." But the administration's change of position made sense. America's gluttonous use of energy reflected the artificially low prices of oil and gas. If the administration wanted to reduce the use of oil and gas and provide incentives for increased production, price increases, however distasteful, had to play a fundamental part in the strategy.

The compromise quickly produced a remarkably diverse coalition of opponents. On August 1, Abourezk and Metzenbaum held a news conference to denounce the compromise as "total surrender" to the oil and gas industry and said they were ready to filibuster once again. A coalition of unions and citizens' action groups claiming to represent 20 million people pledged an "all out" campaign against the compromise. This time, however, they could count on some allies from Senate champions of the oil and gas industry, who opposed the delay in deregulation. Champions of the energy industry, such as Jim McClure, Republican of Idaho, worried that the annual price increases would not raise the price of natural gas to free-market levels by the time of deregulation and threatened to join in a filibuster.

On August 11, Bennett Johnston, a key architect of the compromise, had announced that he could not support it. In Johnston's view, the compromise had changed significantly when it was written down, which was certainly conceivable in an issue of this complexity where negotiators may have been stretching to find common ground. Russell Long said the conference report could not pass unless it was renegotiated. Byrd said that "the bill is still alive. It would be absolutely ridiculous, after 14 months of working, not to produce a bill." He promised to push ahead "until it is absolutely and obviously and indubitably impossible to think about getting a bill."

Scoop Jackson had worked tirelessly for this legislation, despite the fact that he opposed it philosophically and disliked Carter personally. Now he was facing the strong possibility of its failure. Jackson compared seeking a compromise at this stage to "negotiating with the Russians," which, given his view of the Soviet Union, was the harshest characterization he could summon up. He looked exhausted, visibly aging, causing his staff real concern for his health. "We are either going to do it in this Congress or it's dead," Jackson warned. "We will not have this problem again."

Seeing that the situation was becoming dire, Carter finally overcame his aversion to getting his hands dirty. On August 18, he met with key conferees in both houses, and his efforts produced majority votes on both sides. He won over Jim McClure by agreeing to a compromise to move forward with the Clinch River Breeder reactor, a project that Carter had vehemently opposed, and won over Pete Domenici of New Mexico cheaply by promising to work very hard for passage of the bill when it hit the Senate floor.

A week later, the political roller-coaster ride continued, turning downward once again. On August 24, Long confirmed that he would vote against the conference bill. Dale Bumpers and Mark Hatfield, both conferees who had voted in favor, now reversed their positions because of their opposition to the breeder reactor compromise reached with McClure. The White House seemingly had no margin of error; concessions made to gain one senator's vote often caused another senator to become an opponent.

Carter tried to elevate the argument. On August 31, he invited the critics of the legislation to the White House and urged them "to put aside any reservations [they] might have about specific details" to support the "critical measure." He told business leaders that defeat of the bill would have a devastating impact on U.S. world standing, affecting the value of the dollar, trade balances, and inflation—an impact even more important than the bill itself. Administration leaders all admitted that the bill had faults, but argued that it was crucial to pass it, because nothing better would come along for years.

Finally, sensing that the senators' resolve seemed to be softening after the intense lobbying, on September 8, with the lawmakers back from a brief recess for Labor Day, Byrd announced that the Senate would take up the legislation beginning September 11. Byrd had no assurances from the other side that a filibuster or other delaying tactics could be avoided. However, good news emerged when Ed Muskie, previously an opponent to deregulation, announced that he would support the compromise. Aides said Muskie had been swayed by the argument that defeating the bill would have negative repercussions internationally and by a Congressional Budget Office report that the bill would not cause excessive inflation or unfairly gouge homeowners.

Muskie's stature in the Senate helped ensure that liberal opponents of deregulation would give the bill further serious thought. Nevertheless, opponents remained undaunted. Long and Clifford Hansen sent a mailgram to 110 CEOs criticizing the bill: "It does no honor to our national will to adopt a bad bill."

The White House countered the opponents' grassroots efforts with intensive lobbying and outreach of their own. On September 9, the bill received endorsements from the National Council of Mayors, the National Conference of State Legislators, and the Solar Energy Industries Association. The administration's position was strengthening, but the opposition, coming from both consumer and oil and gas interests unwilling to compromise, remained fierce.

Byrd now predicted a week to ten days of debate, with periodic efforts to kill the bill by recommitting it to committee, and possible filibusters. He said his personal contacts with seventy senators, including those in the uncommitted bloc, had left him increasingly optimistic. "Seventeen months ago, I said this would be a ball game that would go into extra innings—we are now in those extra innings," Byrd commented—not exactly an accurate recollection, given his repeated predictions of early victory.

On September 12, the Senate debated for a second day, and the outcome remained too close to call. Roughly forty senators were committed on each side, with a bloc of twenty undecided senators to determine the bill's fate. Howard Baker said that he expected the motion to recommit to fail, and the cloture to fail, meaning that the bill would die in a filibuster. Jackson, who was managing the bill on the Senate floor, expressed confidence that cloture would pass because senators would want to give Carter's priority legislation an up or down vote. Bumpers veered back to supporting the bill, saying he would take his fight against the breeder reactor to another piece of legislation. Gary Hart expressed a willingness to support another bill if the opponents could come up with one, but said that the compromise "does what needs to be done."

Vice President Mondale practically moved to his Capitol office for the week, lobbying continuously for the administration, while President Carter was at Camp David mediating between Anwar Sadat and Menachem Begin. Reporters could see Mondale going over vote counts with Jackson in the back of the Senate chamber. Six liberal Democrats who had previously opposed deregulation agreed to sign on: Adlai Stevenson, Tom Eagleton, Tom McIntyre, Pat Leahy, John Culver, and Dick Clark. They seemed to accept the argument that the bill would bring more gas into interstate markets, reducing shortages, and that gas prices were going up regardless, but that the bill would provide some protection for homeowners. The supporters were clearly gaining ground, and seemed close to having a majority, but certainly could not guarantee the votes to end a filibuster.

Byrd continued to work tirelessly on the delicate parliamentary situation. He desperately wanted to avoid a filibuster, which could kill the bill, and he continued to offer the opponents—on both sides of the spectrum—ample time to make their arguments in the hope that they would agree to proceed without a filibuster. On September 14, he engineered a breakthrough agreement. Opponents would be allowed to offer numerous motions to recommit the bill, with the first coming on September 19, but in exchange for the extended debate time, opponents agreed not to mount a filibuster. If none of the motions to recommit succeeded, the Senate would vote up or down on the legislation on September 27. Byrd's patience and persistence had produced the agreement that was needed. In his memoir, Carter would describe Byrd's work on the natural gas legislation as "prodigious."

On September 19, Jackson, Byrd, and the supporters of the bill defeated the first motion to recommit by a vote of 50–39. Jackson was exuberant, finally seeing the light at the end of the tunnel in which he had been stuck for fourteen months. "They made their maximum effort [on recommittal] today," Jackson said. "They even threw in the Alaskan pipeline to try to get votes. We won't get 59 votes for the conference report, but we will get a majority." Metzenbaum vowed to continue the fight, trying to fashion a motion to recommit that would achieve broader support, but the end was finally in sight.

On September 27, the Senate approved the natural gas compromise legislation by a vote of 57–42. President Carter said of the Senate vote: "I think it proves to our nation and the rest of the world that we, in this government, particularly Congress, can courageously deal with an issue and one that tests our national will and ability." Byrd called the bill "a legislative milestone." Abourezk called it "a lousy, stinking bill." On October 15, Congress finally adjourned after staying in session all Saturday and through Sunday evening. The Senate had to break another Abourezk filibuster at 1 a.m., and at last passed the conference bill 60–17.

After eighteen months, Jimmy Carter could finally claim significant, if incomplete, progress on a national energy plan. The natural gas legislation, which ended a thirty-year debate on the pricing issue, was a notable accomplishment. The Senate had fulfilled its role as a "national mediator," reconciling the differences between consuming and producing interests. Several of Carter's less controversial measures, dealing with appliance efficiency standards and tax credits for energy conservation measures, became law. But the plan as enacted did not include several important measures, including proposed taxes on gasoline, "gas-guzzling" autos, and industrial users of oil and gas. Most significantly, a tax on oil, to be rebated to consumers—a centerpiece of Carter's program—had not come close to enactment.

Carter noted in his diary that the energy legislation that he signed on November 9 would deliver 60–65 percent of the energy savings that he had sought. That estimate, if public, would have been subject to intense debate. What was certain, however, was that Carter and the Congress would have to face the brutally difficult energy issues again—very soon.

LONG DAYS AND NIGHTS, suspense, and adrenaline mark the closing week of any Congress. In tense, crowded rooms throughout the Capitol, conferees meet to hammer out final agreements, then rush to the floor to memorialize them before they could fall apart. The Ninety-fifth Congress was no exception, as the senators and their staffs worked virtually nonstop to finalize other major legislation. Congress approved the first overhaul in forty-four years of the laws regulating grazing on public lands. It also enacted legislation that, for the first time, would charge fees to commercial users of inland waterways. Unable to override Carter's veto, Congress gave him a sweet victory by agreeing to legislation that met his specifications for funding water projects.

The Airline Deregulation Act and the Foreign Intelligence Surveillance Act were completed, major accomplishments for Kennedy and his staff. The Civil Service Reform Act, the Ethics in Government Act, and the Presidential Records Act—all products of Abe Ribicoff's Governmental Affairs Committee—also reached the finished line successfully. Once the committee members put the rancor and divisions of the Lance hearings behind them, the committee went on to have a banner year.

Legislation to establish inspectors general (IG) in twelve major departments and agencies, to consolidate the audit and investigative functions, was a key piece of the Democratic effort to combat fraud, waste, and abuse. The legislation originated in the House; as one of the staff counsels to the Governmental Affairs Committee, I became responsible for shepherding it through the committee and the Senate and reconciling it with the House version.

Tom Eagleton had taken the lead on the bill. A former prosecutor and hardnosed investigator, he also had a strong sense of the political appeal of the idea. After two days of hearings, he told me that we should strengthen the independence of the IGs by giving them a direct line reporting to Congress. He also told me to prepare a hearing on the Defense Department, which was not covered in the House bill. A member of the Defense Appropriations Subcommittee, Eagleton hated the amount of waste and fraud at DoD that he had seen as a member of the Defense Appropriations Subcommittee.

The hearing on the Defense Department had been illuminating; there was no doubt that DoD could do a great deal to improve its audit and investigative functions. But the military had had inspectors general for decades, and they performed different functions than what we were proposing for the civilian agencies. Moreover, each service had its own audit and investigative units. Getting an understanding of everything they were doing would be difficult, and forcing the Pentagon to accept the same model as the civil agencies would be impossible. I spent many hours late at night writing a committee report on the IG legislation, including a section on DoD. The Armed Services Committee staff spent only minutes advising me that if Governmental Affairs wanted to include DoD in the legislation, we could forget about passing an IG bill.

I went to Eagleton's office to tell him the bad news. I was sure he would see the wisdom of backing off and getting the legislation to cover the twelve civilian agencies. He didn't.

"The legislation isn't worth a damn if it doesn't cover the Pentagon," he said angrily. "That's half the government and most of the waste, fraud, and abuse." He told me that there would be no bill without the inclusion of DoD.

Shaken by his reaction, I walked back to my office, trying to figure out how I would explain it to my House counterparts. I took the cowardly way out and delayed calling. Fortunately, Eagleton called and asked me to come back to his office. Recognizing the realities, he instructed me to get the legislation done without DoD in the bill. But he started calling me "Neville," for "Neville Chamberlain," the disgraced British prime minister who had tried to appease Hitler. "Where's your umbrella, Neville?" Eagleton would ask me the next few times we saw each other. Fortunately, his cleverness on the subject only lasted a couple of days.

With that problem resolved, the inspectors general legislation appeared to be sailing through to enactment. I had worked out an agreement with the House committee staff; the Senate would pass the legislation with certain changes, and the House would accept the changed bill, eliminating the need for a conference. Still, in the frenzied closing days of a Congress, nothing is over until it's over. One morning, my assistant, Grace Allen, a grey-haired woman who always radiated calm, came into my office looking very worried.

"Ira, Chairman Brooks is on the phone for you," Grace said.

"You mean Brooks' staff?" I responded.

"No," she said, "it's the chairman himself."

I only knew Jack Brooks, the chairman of the House Government Operations Committee, by reputation. An experienced and savvy legislator, Brooks was a bald, beady-eyed Texan who had fought in the Pacific in World War II and was one of the few southerners to support the Civil Rights Act and the Voting Rights Act. Brooks was legendarily tough; he probably flossed with barbed wire. His calling me could not be good news.

"Hello, Mr. Chairman," I said, trying to sound calm and upbeat.

"Shapiro, how are you, boy?" Brooks rasped.

"Good, Mr. Chairman," I responded. "How are you?"

"Not good, son." Brooks snapped. "The CIA amendment is screwing up the IG bill. You need to fix it." He hung up the phone.

I had been working on the IG bill continuously for months. I knew every word of it, and every contentious issue. I had no idea what Brooks was talking about.

The phone on my desk rang. It was Eagleton.

"Ira, I just got off with Jack Brooks," Eagleton boomed. "He's furious about the CIA amendment. Says it will sink the bill. You have to fix it."

I reached for courage to tell Eagleton that I had no idea what Brooks was talking about. But the phone line went dead as he hung up.

My Senate career, which had seemed so promising just a few minutes ago, flashed before my eyes. I didn't know what to do. Somewhat numb, I started flipping through my files, looking for a file labeled "CIA amendment," which I knew didn't exist. I went down the hall to the men's room to throw cold water on my face.

When I returned a few minutes later, Grace seemed close to panic.

"Ira, it's Chairman Brooks again," she said, with an alarmed look. "He wanted to hold for you."

I picked up the phone. "Hello, Mr. Chairman."

"Shapiro, where you been, boy?" Brooks inquired.

"Just down the hall, Mr. Chairman, in the men's room," I stammered.

"Shapiro," Brooks continued, "The CIA amendment? Forget it, son. Wrong bill." And he hung up the phone.

As suddenly as I had been condemned, I was spared. I called Eagleton to give him the good news, but his assistant said he was on the Senate floor. I rode the subway to the Capitol, went on the floor, and found him. In front of the couches where the Democratic staffers watched the Senate action, I recounted the call.

Eagleton literally fell over laughing. He crashed on to the Senate staff couch, almost landing on a startled woman staff member. Thirty-two years later, I can see it as vividly as if it happened yesterday.

On the evening of the closing day of the Ninety-fifth Congress in October 1978, I went looking for Senator Eagleton to tell him that the Inspectors General Act had passed both houses of Congress and would be sent to the president for signature. I found Eagleton in the Monocle restaurant, with Muskie. The two men were eating steaks, drinking wine, and relaxing from the rush of the closing day of a Congress, when the fate of many pieces of legislation gets resolved.

Eagleton, with an impish grin, asked me to join them. Then he said, "Ed, I believe you know Ira Shapiro. He and Gaylord took away your income from making speeches."

Muskie gave me a sharp look. "You were wrong about that issue," he said. "And so was Gaylord. There's nothing wrong with giving speeches at colleges." Then, suddenly, Muskie relaxed and smiled. "Still, I'll admit that I had to pause when John Tower came by and said, 'great speech, Ed.' I knew that Tower would go downtown at lunch for an hour, give a speech to some group of bankers, and come back with $2,000."

IN REMARKS TO THE press, Byrd gave the Ninety-fifth Congress a grade of "A," saying that it had dealt with more major legislation than any Congress he could recall. He was probably overstating the case, since no Congress could match the record of achievement of the historic Eighty-ninth Congress when President Lyndon Johnson drove through a raft of Great Society legislation. But Byrd could take pride in the record of the Senate in his first two years as majority leader. The Ninety-fifth Congress had compiled a remarkable record of achievement, facing one major domestic or foreign policy challenge after another. The Panama Canal treaties, the energy legislation, and the loan guarantees to New York City constituted major achievements, and in each case, the outcome had been in no way assured.

The Senate had met the challenge time after time. On the Panama Canal treaties, many senators, particularly Democrats, had cast votes that were clearly dangerous for their own political well-being. They had also voted against the interests of some of their strongest constituencies on the natural gas legislation. But if the Senate Democrats deserved credit for political courage, the Senate Republicans deserved praise for political restraint. They had successfully employed the filibuster on labor law reform but had not resorted to it again, allowing the Senate to work its will on important issues by majority vote. The nation's politics were moving to the right. The political currents were swirling and complex. But the Senate had managed to transcend politics to produce landmark achievements. It was not yet political scorched earth; it remained an arena where ideas were debated at length, persuasion still counted, compromise was valued, and the national interest prevailed.

On September 26, Jimmy Carter claimed the greatest achievement of his presidency, and a truly historic accomplishment. After twelve days of direct and unprecedented presidential mediation, Carter succeeded in helping Israel's Prime Minister Menachem Begin and Egypt's president Anwar Sadat reach an agreement by which Israel returned to Egypt large parts of the Sinai Desert captured in the 1967 war in exchange for Egypt making peace with Israel. Polls showed overwhelming public admiration for Jimmy Carter's accomplishment and public confidence in Carter at its highest level since the early months of his presidency.

Unfortunately for Democrats, in political terms, the legislative accomplishments and Carter's historic peace making did not matter. In off-year congressional elections, voters almost always inflict losses on the party in power. In 1978, with public anger cresting, incumbents were extremely vulnerable. Despite Carter's accomplishments, the Republicans had the momentum. Their troops were already energized by the Panama Canal treaties, the labor law reform fight, and the abortion issue, which Jesse Helms and pro-life forces had been pushing relentlessly around the country. Now thanks to Proposition 13, they were surfing the biggest political wave in many years. A *New York Daily News* poll, asking its readers to mark a "ballot" on taxes, got the largest response in its history, with 117,000 readers favoring slashing all taxes—property, sales, and income.

The Republicans continued to ratchet up the pressure, using the Kemp-Roth tax cut proposal as a weapon to put Democrats on the record. On September 20, the GOP launched a seven-state campaign in support of Kemp-Roth in a Boeing 747 nicknamed the "Republican tax clipper," featuring Reagan, Ford, and Baker. Baker, simultaneously running for reelection in Tennessee, gauging his presidential chances, and trying to atone for the Panama Canal treaties, told a cheering crowd: "It's time to get the federal government off your back and out of your hair. . . . The Republican tax proposal may be the last chance for the free enterprise system in the United States." Roth observed: "We have helped the rich, we've helped the poor, but we've ripped off the middle class. We have to change the country in a new direction and help our working people."

Democratic Senate candidates who were not burdened by past voting records moved rapidly to catch the tax-cut wave. In Minnesota, where two Senate seats were being contested because of Hubert Humphrey's death, Robert Short, the conservative multimillionaire owner of the Minnesota Twins, seeking office for the first time, proposed slashing the federal budget by $100 billion. In a stunning upset, Short won the Democratic primary, defeating Representative Donald Fraser, a liberal stalwart of the Democratic-Farmer-Labor (DFL) party. In November, Short would lose to Republican David Durenberger. Rudy Boschwitz, a little-known Republican, would win Minnesota's other seat by defeating Wendell Anderson, the former governor who had appointed himself to the Senate to fill Humphrey's seat. In Illinois, attorney Alex Seith ran a tough, anti-tax campaign against Charles Percy. Percy's campaign consultants had warned him for months that tax-cut fever was in the air. Percy, who did not believe in "meat axe tax cuts," had brushed aside their concerns. But with his Senate seat suddenly in danger, Percy became a born-again tax cutter, publishing a "taxpayers' agenda" brochure and endorsing Kemp-Roth. In his television ads, Percy told the voters of Illinois that he had "gotten the message"; they wouldn't have to worry about Chuck Percy being a liberal Republican. Percy was not planning to go the route of Cliff Case, and he moved quickly and adroitly enough to win reelection.

Republican political assets extended far beyond the tax revolt and the newly engaged business community. They also benefited from the 1976 Supreme Court decision in *Buckley v. Valeo*, which had upheld the limits on political contributions, while concluding that limits on expenditures infringed the First Amendment. The decision opened the door to a flood of unrestricted donations to parties and an explosion of independent and corporate political action committees (PACs). The number of corporate PACs exploded from 139 in 1975 to 1,710 in 1985. Independent PACs, first counted in 1977, rose from 110 to 1,003 in eight years. "An unprecedented opportunity was created for the Republican Party by the 1974 Federal Election Campaign Act," Republican operative Lee Atwater later wrote. It was a seminal moment, a true turning point in American politics.

By the 1978 election, conservatives controlled the five best-funded independent Political Action Committees: Ronald Reagan's Citizens for the Republic, the National Conservative Political Action Committee (NCPAC), the Committee for the Survival of a Free Congress, the American Medical Political Action Committee, and Gun Owners of America. Only the American Medical PAC had existed five years before. These PACs funneled significant financial resources to Republican Senate candidates. The Republicans also benefited from the small contributions resulting from the direct mail genius of Richard Viguerie, who built a mailing list of millions of names when he worked to retire George Wallace's debt from the presidential campaign of 1972. These PACs formed so rapidly and raised money so quickly that the Democrats never really knew what hit them.

ON ELECTION DAY 1978, the voters across the country signaled to the Washington Democrats that despite their efforts, the public mood remained angry at the federal government, deficit spending, and the level of taxation. The Senate Democratic majority was reduced by three. The House Democrats lost fifteen seats. Just on the numbers, this was not a bad result for the president's party in an off-year election. But the evidence of a stronger tide and an uglier mood came through clearly.

Dick Clark's defeat shocked the Democrats most. Clark had come to the Senate in 1972, in an upset victory over the incumbent senator. He had captivated Iowans by walking the state and won by a large margin in the face of Nixon's landslide victory. By all accounts, Clark had made a strong start in the Senate. He became a favorite of Common Cause by championing the Senate ethics code. He chaired the Africa Subcommittee of Foreign Relations, an important assignment as the Soviet Union extended its reach into Africa. Nor did he neglect home state interests.

A week before the election, a poll by Peter Hart, the Democrats' most trusted pollster, showed Clark with a twenty-point lead. On Sunday, two days before the election, Clark's brother-in-law called him with a "heads up." He and Clark's sister were Catholic and had come out of church to find a pamphlet on their windshield that pictured a fetus and attacked Clark for favoring abortion. Every car in the parking lot had the pamphlet, and that was the case at Catholic churches all over the state. The race turned in the last forty-eight hours; Roger Jepsen, a seemingly weak candidate, stormed from behind to upset Clark.

In Colorado, Floyd Haskell, a solid if undistinguished liberal, went down to William Armstrong, a talented arch-conservative, whose election continued the pattern of an increasingly New Right wave in the Mountain West. In New Hampshire, Tom McIntyre, a more formidable and accomplished liberal, lost to Gordon Humphrey, an airline pilot with no previous political experience. Humphrey was the darling of William Loeb, the strident right-wing editor of the *Manchester Union Leader*. Gun control proved to be a decisive issue, and Loeb had been gunning for McIntyre since the senator's notable speech attacking the scorched earth tactics of the New Right during the Panama Canal debate.

The national mood was clear. The New Right had succeeded in purging Case and scaring Percy. In Minnesota, the unconquerable Democratic-Farmer-Labor party, whose senators had included Hubert Humphrey, Walter Mondale, and Eugene McCarthy, lost both Senate seats. In Massachusetts, liberal governor Michael Dukakis lost the Democratic primary to his conservative challenger, Ed King. In the Atlanta suburbs of Georgia, a young firebrand Republican, Newt Gingrich, won a congressional seat, launching a career that would help shape the next three decades in American politics.

Jesse Helms was reelected by a comfortable margin in North Carolina, raising a record $7.7 million, which gave him a 30:1 funding advantage over his opponent. Helms had brought about a significant change in the operation of the Senate, repeatedly offering amendments to put "lib'ruls" on the record on sensitive social issues. At the same time, he created a new model for a senator: national political organizer and fund-raiser. Along with his aide, John Carbaugh, Helms had launched the Conservative Caucus in 1974. He helped create NCPAC, which historian Allan J. Lichtman called "the first all-purpose Political Action Committee of the right." Describing itself as a "gut cutting organization"—and run by Charlie Black, a former Helms staffer, and Terry Dolan, two of the New Right's most effective political operatives—NCPAC targeted and slammed Democratic senators relentlessly. Helms also formed his own PAC, the National Congressional Club, run by Tom Ellis, his leading political ally in North Carolina.

Virtually single-handedly, Jesse Helms was bringing down the high wall that had separated the Senate from the outside world of partisan warfare and what would become known as the "permanent campaign," where politics never stopped long enough to allow for the responsibilities of governing. In retrospect, it is now evident that the toxic politics that we live with today began in 1978. That was the moment that political action committees proliferated and that single-issue politics became commonplace. It was also the moment when legislative issues no longer found final resolution in Congress, but rather became ammunition for political campaigns. A strong Senate, with members of both parties whose roots were in the Great Senate of the 1960's and earlier 1970's, would work to resist the dangerous changes that had been unleashed. In later years, a weakened Senate would not be as successful.

In 1964, Senate Minority Leader Everett Dirksen had led twenty-seven out of thirty-three Republican senators to support the 1964 Civil Rights Act, at precisely the same time that his party was getting ready to give its presidential nomination to Barry Goldwater, an opponent of the Civil Rights Act. The right wing thought there was a "hidden majority" in the country that favored its position. Goldwater would, of course, be crushed by Lyndon Johnson. Dirksen and the Senate Republicans were out of step with the GOP's rising right wing, but they understood the mood of the country.

Now, fourteen years later, senators, Democratic and Republican, had worked effectively to make hard choices and accomplish things that were in the national interest. But unlike 1964, they would find that their legislative accomplishments were often out of touch with the mood of the country. The single-issue voters motivated by their intense feelings about abortion, guns, and the Panama Canal; the energized business community; and many members of the broad middle class, hard-pressed by inflation and seeking tax relief—this time, the "New Right" was getting closer to finding that majority; it was no longer well hidden.

While the American people were moving to the right, liberal Democrats, frustrated by a series of administration decisions and failures, increasingly felt that Carter was not standing firm on the issues that mattered most. Byrd might have given the Ninety-fifth Congress the highest marks, but George McGovern denounced it as "the worst Congress in memory for working people."

Ted Kennedy had successfully spearheaded major legislation—the Foreign Intelligence Surveillance Act and the Airline Deregulation Act—but his mind was on the unfulfilled agenda. As part of its reform program, the Democratic

Party had committed to holding its first off-year "mini-convention." On December 9, in Memphis, Tennessee, speaking to 2,500 Democrats and reporters gathered for a workshop on health care, Kennedy delivered one of the most memorable speeches of his career. Proclaiming that "national health insurance is the great unfinished business on the agenda of the Democratic Party," Kennedy evoked a memorable nautical image. "Sometimes a party must sail against the wind. We cannot afford to draft or lie at anchor. We cannot heed the call of those who say it is time to furl the sail."

The crowd went crazy, and the chairman of the workshop, Bill Clinton, the young governor of Arkansas, pounded Kennedy on the back as the ovation continued. Hamilton Jordan, the White House chief of staff, turned to Patrick Caddell, the president's pollster, and said angrily, "That's it. He's running."

In fact, Kennedy had not yet decided to challenge Carter for the Democratic nomination for president. But his Memphis speech laid bare the fissure in the Democratic Party. As Carter struggled against an energized right wing, with the country moving in a conservative direction, he could not count on support from the liberal wing of his party. Carter and most of the Senate Democrats were working to find the political center of the country. It remained to be seen whether the center was no man's land.

IRONICALLY, WHILE LIBERAL DISSENT was rising on domestic issues, and while Democratic senators were licking their wounds, Carter was earning the admiration of many Democrats by his willingness to take on the toughest foreign policy problems. On December 15, he surprised the country, and shocked the Senate, by announcing that the United States would establish diplomatic relations with the People's Republic of China and break its diplomatic ties with the Nationalist Chinese administration on Taiwan on January 1, 1979—in two weeks—and terminate its defense treaty with Taiwan a year later. After taking on the Panama Canal treaties, Jimmy Carter was walking into another foreign policy minefield and a likely battle in the Senate in the coming year.

At the same time, a potential foreign policy disaster loomed as events began to spiral out of control in Iran. Shah Mohamed Reza Pahlavi's program of land reform and economic modernization had antagonized the traditional clergy. The actions of the security police, SAVAK (an acronym for the Persian "National Intelligence and Security Organization") and his reduction of the parliamentary process to a one-party system had cost the shah the support of secular democrats. By the spring of 1978, crackdowns on both groups inevitably created an expanding cycle of opposition.

On September 8, Iranian troops had fired on a crowd of demonstrators in Jaleh Square, killing between 700 and 2,000 people, depending on which press reports were reliable. The next day, Tehran oil workers issued a call to strike in solidarity with those who had been killed and in protest against the shah's imposition of martial law. In November, gangs of young men rampaged through Tehran, setting fires to banks, movie theaters, and liquor stores and shouting "Allah is great!"

The Ayatollah Ruhollah Khomeini, exiled in Paris, provided leadership to the rising opposition, spurring them to a near frenzy. In the last week of November, he called upon his followers to take action during Muharram, the first month of the Islamic calendar. "This is the month that blood will triumph over the sword . . . the month the oppressors will be judged and the Satanic government abolished. . . . The Imam of the Muslims has taught us to overthrow tyrants. You should unite, arise, and sacrifice your blood." On December 10, a crowd estimated at 1 million gathered around the Shayad Monument in Tehran, chanting "Death to the American cur."

The crisis in Iran hit Washington without warning. In August, the CIA had reported to Carter that "Iran is not in a revolutionary or even a pre-revolutionary situation." The Defense Intelligence Agency analysis predicted the shah's rule was stable for at least a decade. The United States had relied on Iran as a listening post to gather intelligence on the Soviet Union. But the United States seemed to have no listening post to understand what was going on in the shah's Iran. The Carter administration offered the shah support, but without understanding just how fragile his position was. In late October, one comprehensive Department of State memo outlining the dire situation facing the shah and the grim alternatives for U.S. policy never made it to the president or for discussion in the National Security Council.

William Sullivan, the U.S. ambassador to Iran, understood the severity of the situation and tried to force high-level consideration of the problem but could not break through Zbigniew Brzezinski, Carter's national security adviser, who downplayed the urgency of Sullivan's cables. When the Carter administration did fully focus, it found itself fundamentally divided. Secretary of State Cyrus Vance wanted the shah to introduce more democratic reforms and expand his political base. Brzezinski believed that the shah's only option was to install a military government, which would be willing to use force if necessary to put down the resistance.

One result of the Senate's string of legislative accomplishments was that Jimmy Carter had begun to rely intensively on Robert Byrd's counsel and judgment in foreign policy issues. At the president's request, Byrd undertook a major trip to the Middle East, meeting with the leaders of Saudi Arabia, Jordan, and Syria to support the breakthrough agreement negotiated at Camp David. But with the situation in Iran confused but clearly deteriorating, Byrd decided to go to Tehran as well. Even above and beyond the potentially enormous national security implications of the shah's situation, Byrd had a personal interest in Iran; his daughter had married an Iranian physician.

Before leaving Washington, Byrd met with Brzezinski, who told him that the State Department was preventing the shah from taking the strong action needed to deal with the dissidents. He urged Byrd to help stiffen the shah's spine, by telling him to use whatever means he thought were necessary to stay in power.

Byrd arrived in Tehran on November 26. A curfew was in effect, and security conditions were very tight. There was practically no traffic on the road from the airport to the U.S. embassy, but bonfires could be seen, and military troops were in evidence. A car was turned on its side, burning near the gates of the embassy.

Byrd, accompanied by his chief foreign policy adviser, Hoyt Purvis, met for five hours with Ambassador Sullivan. The grim conversation through the long evening persuaded Byrd that urging the shah to crack down on the dissidents could lead to many deaths. Byrd came away from the meeting with a strong sense that the shah was not likely to stay in power very long.

When Byrd met with the shah, he found him dispirited, preoccupied, and very much adrift. Byrd could only conclude that the situation was deteriorating rapidly, probably irreversibly. At the end of his trip, the Carter administration asked if Byrd would make a statement expressing confidence that the shah would be on the throne for a long time. Having concluded that the shah's days were numbered, Byrd refused.

Ambassador Sullivan had recognized the urgency of the situation facing the shah. But he had also advised U.S. officials that Khomeini and his supporters were anti-Communist and anti-Soviet and predicted that "Iranian economic ties with the West could continue" and that the Iranian military could preserve the nation's integrity. These wildly inaccurate assessments showed just how little anyone knew about the Islamic militant revolutionary forces at work. But Sullivan was right on the mark with another observation: "A single misstep could produce unforeseeable consequences."

An eventful year, 1978 would come to an end with the bright promise of peace between Israel and Egypt, the hope for a new relationship between the United States and China, and deep uncertainty about the future in Iran.

Majority Leader Mike Mansfield (D-MT) greets five of the eight Democrats elected to the Senate in 1962, the election that cemented the progressive Senate of the 1960's and 1970's. From left to right, Thomas McIntyre (NH), George McGovern (SD), Ted Kennedy (MA), Daniel Inouye (HI), and Abraham Ribicoff (CT).

Credit: © Bettmann/CORBIS

Robert Byrd (D-WV) and Thomas "Tip" O'Neill (D-MA) become Senate majority leader and Speaker of the House as the Ninety-fifth Congress begins in January 1977.

Credit: U.S. Senate Historical Office

Howard Baker (R-TN) (right), during the Watergate hearings that made him a household name, along with Fred Thompson, the Republican chief counsel. Baker becomes Senate minority leader in January 1977. Thompson is elected to the Senate in 1994, also representing Tennessee.

Credit: U.S. Senate Historical Office

Byrd and Baker, here huddling with principal aides Joseph Stewart and William Hildenbrand, worked together closely as Senate leaders.

Credit: U.S. Senate Historical Office

Three iconic senators serving together on the Foreign Relations Committee: from left to right, Edmund Muskie (D-ME), Jacob Javits (R-NY), and Hubert Humphrey (D-MN).

Warren Magnuson (D-WA) and Bob Packwood (R-OR) led the Commerce Committee in a bipartisan way characteristic of the Great Senate.

Gaylord Nelson (D-WI), the father of Earth Day, and one of the greatest environmentalists in American history.

Credit: U.S. Senate Historical Office

Two of the most influential senators ever to serve: Ted Kennedy (D-MA) and Henry "Scoop" Jackson (D-WA). Jackson supported Kennedy's challenge to Jimmy Carter for the Democratic nomination in 1980.

Credit: AP Photo/Harvey Georges

Veteran senator John Tower (R-TX) provided leadership on defense matters, while freshman senator Orrin Hatch (R-UT) led the newly mobilized business community against labor law reform.

Credit: U.S. Senate Historical Office

Jesse Helms (R-SC), the "righteous warrior," played a determined and effective role in obstructing the work of the Senate and the will of the majority, while lowering the wall that separated the Senate from partisan politics.

Credit: U.S. Senate Historical Office

Robert Dole (R-KS), seen here with Marshall Matz, from George McGovern's staff. Usually a tough partisan, Dole began working with McGovern and Matz in a historic forty-year alliance to fight hunger in the United States and globally.

Frank Church (D-ID) (right) and Paul Sarbanes (D-MD), floor managers of the Panama Canal treaties, meet with Jimmy Carter in the Rose Garden in the spring of 1978.

Credit: Boise State University

Democratic senators Daniel Patrick Moynihan (NY), Russell Long (LA), Byrd, Ribicoff, and Bill Bradley (NJ) savor a long-awaited victory in the three-year fight over energy policy.

Credit: U.S. Senate Historical Office

Key senators on foreign policy issues—Javits, Baker, Church, and Byrd—with Deng Xiaoping, leader of the People's Republic of China, as the United States moves forward with recognition of the PRC in 1979.

Credit: U.S. Senate Historical Office

Freshman Carl Levin (D-MI) (right) meets with Vice President Walter Mondale during the effort to prevent Chrysler from going under in 1979. Young senators played increasingly prominent roles in the democratized Senate of the 1970's.

Joseph Biden (D-DE) with Ted Kaufman, his administrative assistant. In 2009, when Biden became vice president, Kaufman was appointed to his Senate seat.

Richard Lugar (R-IN) (right), seen here with Baker, played an indispensable role in rescuing New York City in 1978 and Chrysler the next year.

Birch Bayh (D-IN) and Strom Thurmond (R-SC) led the inquiry into the connection between Billy Carter and the government of Libya, exonerating the Carter administration just weeks before the 1980 election.

Credit: Photo by Charles Geer. Image provided by the U.S. Senate Historical Office

Byrd, Bayh, and John Stennis (D-MS) (left) coming from the Capitol after the failed mission to rescue the hostages held in the U.S. embassy in Tehran.

Credit: AP Photo/Harrity

1979

chapter 13

BEFORE
THE STORM

THE SENATE THAT CONVENED IN JANUARY 1979 INCLUDED TWENTY NEW senators, a record number of new members. As always, the group represented a broad spectrum of experience and ideology. The celebrities included Virginia Republican John Warner, a former secretary of the navy better known as Elizabeth Taylor's husband; Maine Republican William Cohen, who had distinguished himself as a member of the House Judiciary Committee during Nixon's impeachment proceedings; and New Jersey Democrat Bill Bradley, a former Rhodes Scholar from Princeton, who had deferred his entry into politics until after completing a great career in the National Basketball Association, where he was a cornerstone of two champion New York Knicks teams. Several other newly elected members seemed destined to become solid senators: Democrat Carl Levin, a thoughtful, intense lawyer from Michigan, who had ended Bob Griffin's Senate career; Democrat Howell Heflin, a Supreme Court justice from Alabama, who reminded many Senate watchers of a younger Sam Ervin; Paul Tsongas, a cerebral, "new Democrat," from Massachusetts who had upset Ed Brooke; and Alan Simpson, a Republican from Wyoming, elected to a seat that his father had held, who soon became known for speaking his mind in salty, unpredictable ways.

The new class of eleven Republicans and nine Democrats represented a group large enough to be noticeable. During the transition period, the newly elected senators bonded, and they decided to continue meeting for lunches, on a bipartisan and nonpartisan basis, when they arrived in Washington.

These lunches continued for several months, and led to some lasting friendships across party lines. Neither Robert Byrd nor Howard Baker ever became comfortable with the bipartisan lunches, regularly asking, in all seriousness, what was going on. Before too long, the new senators had discontinued the lunches.

Any election that brought Bradley, Tsongas, and Levin to the Senate could not be portrayed as a Republican landslide, and even the Republicans Cohen, David Durenberger, and Rudy Boschwitz seemed likely to be moderates. But the nature of the 1978 campaign, with its unprecedented focus on single-issue politics—particularly, the Panama Canal, guns, and abortion—changed the mood of the Senate and left a palpable sense of a move to the right. The Republican caucus was only slightly larger, but seemed more significantly changed, with Ed Brooke and Clifford Case, two liberal lights, gone, and Chuck Percy back only because he trimmed his sails dramatically. William Armstrong's election from Colorado, following the arrivals of Orrin Hatch (Utah), Malcolm Wallop (Wyoming), and Harrison Schmitt (New Mexico) two years earlier, reinforced the impression of a strong New Right Republican wave in the western states. Ted Stevens, the Republican whip, had been a regular participant in the Wednesday Club, a breakfast group of the moderate-to-liberal Republicans. Before long, Stevens stopped attending the group's breakfasts, shifting his allegiance to the much more conservative Senate Steering Committee. The Wednesday Club shrank dramatically after that.

At the same time, Baker and Bob Dole were beginning to lay the groundwork for seeking the Republican presidential nomination in 1980. Dole had already shown little moderation in 1978, particularly during the Panama Canal debates. Baker would, predictably, be tacking to the right to catch up with the shifting center of the Republican Party, and to make up for his heresy—supporting the Panama Canal treaties—if it was possible to do so.

In his own way, Carl Levin represented the new political mood in the country. Educated at Swarthmore and Harvard Law School, the son of a respected Michigan Supreme Court justice, Levin vaulted from the Detroit City Council to the Senate by upsetting Bob Griffin, who never recovered from having remarked that he did not want to run for reelection and then changing his mind. On issues of war and peace and constitutional rights, Levin looked to be every inch a liberal. But what animated his campaign, and his first years in the Senate, was a passionate commitment to reining in the federal bureaucracy.

Levin came to Washington to impose a legislative veto on federal regulatory agencies to bring the bureaucratic "monster" to heel. As a Detroit city councilman, he had battled with the Department of Housing and Urban Development (HUD), which in the mid-1970's refused to either repair or demolish thousands of empty, federally owned houses in Detroit. At one point, frustrated to the limit, and politically aware of what made good local television, Levin rented a bulldozer and went to a vacant house with the intent of demolishing it. As a new Senator, Levin warned that if well-intentioned federal programs were not run more effectively, they would lose public support. His message differed somewhat from the antigovernment rhetoric of Ronald Reagan and other right-wing conservatives intent on dismantling the federal government, but sometimes one had to listen very carefully to make the distinction.

The 1980 Senate campaigns started almost immediately. Paul Brown, the leader of Life Amendment PAC (LAPAC), took aim at what his group called the "deadly dozen." Boasting that his group had been instrumental in defeating pro-choice senators Dick Clark, Floyd Haskell, and Tom McIntyre, Brown said: "We've proven our point. There's a pro-life vote. We've come of age as a political force." Birch Bayh headed the group's "Deadly Dozen" list, followed by George McGovern, Frank Church, and Representative Morris Udall. Also targeted were John Culver and Patrick Leahy, and, for good measure, one Republican—Bob Packwood, who had been the most outspoken Senate advocate of abortion rights.

Birch Bayh, facing tragic circumstances, probably didn't even notice his LAPAC ranking. His wife, Marvella, one of Washington's best-liked and most impressive women, had been diagnosed with breast cancer in 1971, at the age of thirty-eight. Marvella Bayh battled the disease and had become a full-time advocate for the American Cancer Society, giving more than 175 speeches about cancer and its prevention. But her cancer had returned in 1978, in an invasive form that was in her bones. Her doctors had said it was inoperable, but that she might live five or six years. On March 28, she was scheduled to receive the Hubert H. Humphrey Inspirational Award but could not appear because she was hospitalized. Accepting the award for his wife, Birch Bayh, near tears, had to struggle to regain his composure. Marvella Bayh died on April 24 at the age of forty-six.

For Senate Democrats, one exciting transition took center stage: Ted Kennedy's long-awaited ascendancy to the post of Judiciary Committee chairman. The symbolism of Kennedy, the Democrats' best-known liberal, taking the gavel from the reactionary James Eastland was a profound political and ideological transition, even though Eastland had maintained his power by providing generous budgets over the years to support the liberal activities of subcommittee chairmen Kennedy, Bayh, Phil Hart, John Tunney, and Joseph Tydings. Kennedy would take on the full spectrum of the Judiciary Committee's responsibilities, which included the volatile issues of civil rights, criminal law, gun control, and proposed constitutional amendments relating to busing, abortion, and school prayer. He had just captured the attention of all Democrats, with his full-throated defense of liberalism and critique of Carter at the Democratic midterm convention in Memphis.

Speculation that he would challenge the president for the Democratic nomination was rising. Suddenly, seemingly every ambitious Democratic lawyer wanted to be part of the powerhouse Judiciary Committee staff. Before long, Kennedy's team included staff director Stephen Breyer, a future Supreme Court justice; Chief Counsel David Boies, who would later become the most famous litigator in the United States; Ken Feinberg, who would become the country's leading mediator, specializing in the handling of mass torts; Ron Brown, later the chairman of the Democratic National Committee and the secretary of commerce during the Clinton years; and Susan Estrich, who combined a great legal mind with impressive effectiveness as a political operative. Kennedy was building a powerhouse Judiciary Committee staff, which could also bolster his presidential campaign, if he made the decision to challenge Carter.

With the retirement of John Sparkman, Frank Church finally achieved his long-awaited dream of being chairman of the Senate Foreign Relations Committee. "Congratulations on your chairmanship," said a note supposedly from William Borah, the long-deceased senator and former chairman of the Foreign Relations Committee, who had been Church's boyhood idol. "What took you so long?" In the four years since the departure of its famous chairman, J. William Fulbright, the Foreign Relations Committee had lost some of its influence—it had become considerably less prominent than the Armed Services Committee and even somewhat supplanted by the new Intelligence Committee. Church sought to restore the committee's luster, by getting it to focus on issues of long-term importance, rather than just responding to the crises of the day. He planned to do so in part by bringing back the staff resources that had been dispersed to the subcommittees, in large part because of his own relentless lobbying for the Subcommittee on Multinational Corporations. Unfortunately for Church, the subcommittee chairmen had grown accustomed to their power and resources and fought against returning them to the full committee. Within a short time, Church's effort to claw back the resources had antagonized several committee Democrats. He and John Glenn were barely on speaking terms.

An increasing partisan divide on the committee posed a more serious problem. The committee had traditionally been more liberal than the Senate as a whole, and it had been remarkably bipartisan, operating with a unified professional staff. Now, however, Dick Clark and Clifford Case were gone, and Baker and Percy seemed determined to make up for their votes for the Panama Canal treaties. For the first time, the Republicans pressed for, and secured, a separate minority staff. New to the committee, Jesse Helms seized upon a provision in the Senate rules by which a majority of the minority could demand a budget and office space. Over the objection of Jacob Javits, the ranking Republican, Helms prevailed. Although Javits kept his own staffer, Peter Lakeland, as the minority staff director, Helms and his conservative allies exercised more influence within the committee. Later in 1979, as the Foreign Relations Committee considered the SALT II treaties, the atmosphere was so adversarial as to remind observers of a court proceeding.

The 1980 presidential race heated up early. Eight Republican presidential hopefuls were moving around Washington in advance of Jimmy Carter's State of the Union speech. Ronald Reagan led by a wide margin in the early going, but neither he nor any other Republican came close to Carter in the polls. On January 20, 1979, Carter led the former California governor 57–35, according to Gallup. However, those poll numbers would change dramatically within a short time, as the situation in Iran forced itself to center stage for Jimmy Carter, the Senate, and the American public.

On January 16, the shah of Iran bowed to what Robert Byrd had seen to be inevitable. He and his family boarded a Boeing 707, ostensibly for a vacation but never to return. On February 1, the Ayatollah Ruhollah Khomeini returned to Iran, ending fourteen years of exile in Turkey, Iraq, and France. His supporters greeted him with a tumultuous reception. By February 11, it was clear that the military would support the government run by Khomeini. The U.S. attaché in Tehran concluded his report for the day with the words, "Army surrenders; Khomeini wins. Destroying all classified."

Neither the Carter administration nor the leading foreign policy experts in the Senate understood the intentions of Ayatollah Khomeini. But they were not the only ones. Even those closest to Khomeini, such as Abolhassan

Bani-Sadr and Sadegh Ghorbzadeh, who would have key roles in the new government, completely misread their spiritual leader. Bani-Sadr expressed astonishment after the Ayatollah's speech at the Cemetery of Martyrs on February 1, 1979: "It was the speech of a politician more than the speech of a religious leader." As Carter historian Betty Glad has written, Khomeini's goal was "to establish an Islamic Republic in which he retained final authority in both religious and political matters. The moderate politicians who had joined him in an anti-shah operation would last only as long as they served Khomeini's political purposes."

MORE THAN A YEAR had passed since the natural gas filibuster by Jim Abourezk and Howard Metzenbaum, but Byrd continued to brood about it. He passionately respected the Senate's tradition of unlimited debate, but he had learned just how easily the Senate could become paralyzed. Byrd could not crush every filibuster by abusing the Senate rules and precedents; it would embitter the Senate and antagonize his colleagues. He needed to convince the Senate to change its rules so that filibusters would go back to being extraordinary—not everyday features of Senate life. In November and December 1978, Byrd spent many hours talking with the Senate parliamentarians, Murray Zweben and Robert Dove, assessing possible responses to the filibuster problem.

On January 15, Byrd went to the Senate floor to propose a sweeping set of changes to the filibuster rules. He had alerted the Senate two days earlier, outlining the proposals to the press. Now he spoke directly: "I dare to say that it cannot be challenged that I have stayed on the floor more than any other Senator since the first Senate met in 1789. I know pretty well what the Senate rules and precedents are. No man ever becomes a master of them. But I know something about them. Having been in the leadership for 12 years, I know what the difficulties are for having to lead the Senate."

Byrd described the deteriorating situation, in terms that are strikingly similar to those used thirty years later as the Senate confronted paralysis in 2009: "The Senate is continually being faced with a filibuster threat. The mere threat of a filibuster, these days, is nearly as bad as the filibuster itself. We have seen, in the last 9 years since 1970, more filibusters than occurred in the previous 30 years."

For many decades, he noted, there had been one or two filibusters per year. But, "we have reached the point now where every year we can expect 4, 5, 6 and as many as 10. . . . In 1975, there were 12 filibusters. We are becoming more and more the victim of this ingenious procedure that allows, first, a filibuster threat; second, the filibuster on the motion to proceed; third, the filibuster on the matter itself; and fourth, and finally, the most cataclysmic and divisive filibuster of all, the post-cloture filibuster."

Byrd recalled the Abourezk and Metzenbaum filibuster in a defensive tone: "Some senators were outraged at the procedures that I used to save that bill. . . . This post-cloture filibuster is the kind of thing that creates ill feelings and deep divisions in the Senate. It is fractious; it fragments the Senate, it fragments the party on either side of the aisle." And most important for Byrd, "It makes the Senate a spectacle before the nation. It is not in the national interest."

He laid out a guiding principle that seemed like eminent common sense: "One filibuster is enough. If a minority of the Senate has enough votes, 41, to kill a bill, it should allow the bill to at least be brought up for debate on the merits." He offered a set of rules changes to solve the problem. He proposed to end filibusters on motions to take up an issue by limiting debate on such procedural motions to thirty minutes. He proposed to end post-cloture filibusters by strictly limiting debate to one hundred hours once cloture had been invoked, including time for amendments and roll call votes, and allowing the one hundred hours to be reduced to as few as twelve with sixty votes. A motion to limit debate could not be offered until at least ten hours of debate had passed. Byrd's package also included changes to allow sixty senators to limit amendments to those that were germane; allow a motion to suspend reading of the Senate journal to be passed without debate; and allow a simple majority to waive reading of an amendment or committee report if it is available in a printed form. But ending the ability to filibuster the motion to proceed and resort to the post-cloture filibuster constituted the heart of Byrd's far-reaching proposals.

Byrd left no doubt of his determination to make changes. He even expressed a willingness to resort to what decades later would be called the "nuclear option," the Senate's right to change its rules by majority vote on the first day of a new Congress. "We are at the beginning of Congress. This Congress is not obliged to be bound by the dead hand of the past." Vice presidents of both parties (Nelson Rockefeller in 1975 and Walter Mondale in 1977) had made such rulings, angering many senators. Byrd admitted that he had not always supported those rulings but had come to see the wisdom of them.

Yet he reassured his colleagues that he would not press for a vote until members of both parties had been given a chance to work out a resolution. He wanted to change the rules in an orderly fashion, after ample consideration and with a time agreement on debate. He would recess the Senate in order to preserve the fiction that it was still the opening legislative day when the Senate returned. Byrd closed with great emotion:

> If these post-cloture filibusters continue, the day will come when the majority of the Senate will rise up and will strike down that rule and will change it . . . I may not be around here when that happens, but a majority of the Senate and the Nation is not going to stand for government by post-cloture filibuster on the part of one, two, three or a small majority of the Senate, flaunting and defying the will and thwarting the will of the majority of senators who have voted to invoke cloture on a given matter.

Minority Leader Baker took the floor to respond. He complimented Byrd for visiting him to explain the proposal, and noted that during the natural gas filibuster, the majority leader and the vice president had "managed to establish a line and series of precedents that created the possibility to at least accelerate the disposition of the controversy and conflict."

Baker described the challenge with characteristic diplomacy: "How can we avoid reiterating an unfortunate precedent, meet the procedural challenge of these times, and promote the best interchange of ideas between us to create a new rules situation with which we all can live, whether we are in the majority or the minority, now and in the future?" Baker advised Byrd and the Senate that he was appointing an ad hoc committee to be chaired by Stevens, which would include Javits, Helms, Jim McClure, and John Chafee from Rhode Island, a group that spanned the full spectrum of the Senate Republicans, to study Byrd's proposal and propose a Republican reaction.

More than two weeks later, the Senate remained on the first legislative day. Discussions had continued within the groups and between them, reaching a "concept" but no details. Traditionalists insisted that Byrd's changes would wrest power away from the whole Senate, bestowing it on the leadership.

On February 7, another long day of talks failed to reach a compromise. Byrd indicated that he was prepared to force through changes with a simple majority; he issued the threat, in all likelihood, to bring things to a negotiated resolution.

But the next day, Baker expressed optimism that a compromise would be reached as soon as the Senate returned from its Presidents Day recess.

Indeed, the Senate reached its resolution of changes in the filibuster rules. On February 22, by a vote of 78–16, the Senate voted to restrict the use of the post-cloture filibuster. Byrd did not get everything he had asked for. He had previously agreed to allow the post-cloture debate to be extended, not just limited, by sixty votes, and raised the floor of post-cloture filibuster debate, after sixty votes, to thirty hours rather than twelve. Republicans agreed to let the issue come to a vote only after Byrd agreed to drop his demand that sixty votes could limit post-cloture debate at all beyond the strict 100-hour limit (including amendments and roll-call votes). Byrd also agreed to give up his effort to limit filibusters on the motion to proceed, which had become known as the "pre-filibuster filibuster."

After the vote, Byrd adjourned the Senate, rather than recessing it, to signal the end of the fight. It was no longer the first legislative day, removing the threat of changing the Senate rules by a majority.

The resolution represented the third time in history that the Senate had acted to make it easier to break a filibuster. The southern Democrats, who had used the filibuster in previous decades to thwart civil rights legislation, became supporters of Byrd's initiative. They had always accepted cloture as final and believed the post-cloture filibuster threatened the Senate's ability to function.

Baker's sense of the Senate had proven unerring once again. The compromise tracked closely with his opening statement on January 15. The Senate recognized the need to rein in the post-cloture filibuster. The Senate could not accept a situation where Metzenbaum and Abourezk, or Helms and Hatch, could thwart the operation of the body. But the minority leader, and the minority party, was not going to accept a solution that allowed key decisions to be made by fewer than sixty senators. The Republicans were not willing to allow a unified Democratic majority—if such a thing were possible—to determine what legislation would be considered on the Senate floor.

The 1975 change in Rule XXII had established that sixty votes were required to cut off debate. It was a result that the Republicans could live with, particularly now that they had forty-one senators among their number. But they held firm on another very important issue: it would also require sixty votes to *start* debate, allowing a unified minority to filibuster the motion to proceed. Thirty years later, the Senate would struggle to overcome paralysis, and commentators would wonder when we became a country where the "minority rules." The well-intentioned changes in 1975 and 1979 would have unanticipated effects as comity eroded.

CHINA HAD LOOMED LARGE in the minds of legislators for some time. In 1971, Richard Nixon had electrified the nation by revealing the secret talks between Henry Kissinger, his national security adviser, and the People's Republic of China (PRC). Nixon's visit to Peking in 1972 and his meeting with Mao had been a major historical event, capturing the fancy of Americans and people all around the world.

To most Americans, it made very little sense that the United States would have no relationship with a regime that had ruled the Chinese mainland since 1949 and represented 900 million people, one-fourth of the world's population. But at the same time, strong support remained for the island of Formosa, later known as Taiwan, where the nationalist Chinese had fled from the Communists to build their own country. Full normalization of relations with Communist China had not moved forward because of the U.S. commitment to Taiwan. Nixon and the Chinese leaders had signed the Shanghai Communiqué, which deferred the problem of diplomatic relations and Taiwan for the sake of working together on the basis of common Sino-American strategic interests in Asian and world affairs, particularly a shared interest in checking Soviet expansionism.

Starting in 1972, Peking's leaders were consistent in their demands that the United States withdraw military forces from Taiwan, break diplomatic relations with the government of Taiwan, and terminate the U.S.-Taiwan defense treaty. Only after these conditions were met could normal relations be established.

On December 15, 1978, the Carter administration announced that, in effect, these three conditions would be met. The mutual defense treaty would end in a year, though the United States would honor commitments already made to Taiwan for military equipment. Even after the defense treaty ended, the United States would continue to make available to Taiwan "selected defense weaponry" on a "restricted basis."

A political firestorm swiftly ensued. Barry Goldwater, the father of the surging right wing of the party, called the move "one of the most cowardly acts ever performed by a President of the United States" and "a stab in the back" to Taiwan. Helms charged that Carter "proposes to sell Taiwan down the river . . . in order to involve the United States in a conflict between two communist regimes"—the People's Republic of China and the Soviet Union.

Ronald Reagan's presidential campaign, already gearing up for 1980, recognized a red-meat issue when it saw one. Reagan attacked the administration for having "abandoned Taiwan to the Red Chinese" providing yet another example of "Uncle Sam putting his tail between his legs and creeping away. . . ." He also cabled an apology to the Taiwan government. Clearly, the Republicans saw the "sellout" of Taiwan as a rallying cry for their political base, continuing the themes of weakness and retreat that they had sounded during the Panama Canal fight.

A number of Senate Democrats expressed anger as well. Six months earlier, the Senate had voted 94–0 in a nonbinding resolution asking that Carter not alter the treaty's status without "prior consultation" with Congress. John Glenn and Richard Stone of Florida, members of the Foreign Relations Committee, charged Carter with failing to meet the "prior consultation" obligation. "Calling a few of us in one hour before he goes on television doesn't seem like much consultation," Glenn snapped.

Carter could still count on at least some support. Byrd called normalization of relations "a natural and positive advancement . . . that will contribute to our national interest and aid the stability of world peace." Kennedy, too, applauded the move, saying that "normal and enduring relations with 900 million people on the mainland" was fully compatible with "assuring the peace and prosperity of the people on Taiwan." Church was delighted. He had criticized for years the "absurd" policy of viewing mainland China as a nonentity. He praised the administration for having finally brought "American policy into line with Asian realities."

Baker, as always, would play a key role. His diplomatic instincts would again be in conflict with the prevailing anger in his party and his own hopes of winning the Republican nomination. He had gone far out on a limb politically to help Carter on the Panama Canal treaties, but that had been a long process in which he had been given a central role and consulted constantly. On Taiwan, the White House had surprised him, adding an angry Senate to the right-wing rage in the country. Baker called Carter's decision "a mistake" and said, "We owe the Taiwanese more than this." He sent a telegram to the president urging him to delay beginning to dissolve the mutual defense treaty until the Senate reconvened in mid-January. Carter quickly and publicly rebuffed Baker's request during an interview with Walter Cronkite—not the best way to deal with the minority leader who had been an indispensable ally.

A fierce battle seemed inevitable. On December 22, Goldwater and fourteen other conservative lawmakers had filed suit in U.S. District Court, contending that Carter had overstepped his authority in abrogating the pact. Calling it "one of the worst power grabs in history," Goldwater contended that the president could not repeal a treaty, any more than he could repeal a law. The brief argued that the president had to seek Senate approval before abrogating a treaty, because the Senate had been a partner with him in ratifying the treaty. If Carter's action stood, Goldwater argued, countries would have no faith in treaties with the United States because there was no assurance that a treaty will last "any longer than the whim of a single person who happens to sit in the Oval Office at any given moment of history."

The administration hit back forcefully, responding with a nine-page memo and a thirty-five page historical index created by the State Department: "The Senate's role is in giving advice and consent to the making of the treaty is made. Thereafter execution and performance of its terms relating to its duration or termination are delegated by the Constitution to the nation's chief executive."

Speaking on his own, Jimmy Carter continued to make clear his view that no Senate help was needed: "I really don't believe that any resolution is needed. I think our legislative proposal and the announcement made about normalization—the combination of those two—is adequate." Carter's willingness to pursue the national interest irrespective of political consequences represented one of his greatest strengths. But his insensitivity to politics often endangered some of his most important undertakings. In this instance, the Senate Foreign Relations Committee would be crucial in deciding the issue.

Taiwan posed the first major issue for Church as Foreign Relations Committee chairman. The Panama Canal fight had shown that he brought legislative experience, knowledge of the world, and eloquence to the major fights. Despite his initial approval of Carter's decision to recognize the People's Republic, Church thought Carter had badly mishandled the Taiwan part of the problem. He characterized the administration's recent agreement as "woefully inadequate to the task, ambiguous in language, and uncertain in tone." The political pressure on Church from home was severe; both Houses of the Idaho legislature had already petitioned Congress and the president "to maintain diplomatic relations and the mutual defense treaty with the Republic of China." Church set out to rescue the China agreement, knowing it would require building a broad consensus in Congress and the country.

Javits was the ranking Republican on the Foreign Relations Committee. He and Church had come to the Senate in the same year, worked on many crucial issues together, from civil rights to war powers, and maintained great mutual respect for each other's abilities. They approached the problem from the same starting point, because Javits also favored recognizing mainland China, but thought that Carter had seriously shortchanged the U.S. commitment to Taiwan. Javits always relished tackling the toughest foreign policy and legislative issues, and the Taiwan issue fell decisively into that category.

ON FEBRUARY 5, CHURCH banged the gavel to begin the Foreign Relations Committee's hearings on Taiwan. Twelve senators, seven Democrats and five Republicans, attended the hearing, underscoring the importance of the moment. Church laid out the key issues concisely. President Carter's action in extending diplomatic recognition to the People's Republic of China "gives long overdue acknowledgement of one of the central realities of Asian affairs, the existence of the government which actually exercises jurisdiction over the most populous and second largest nation on Earth," Church noted. But "we must also face another reality: The importance the United States must attach to the future security and well-being of the people of Taiwan. . . . The task of embracing China without deserting Taiwan will require a high order of diplomatic skill and legislative ingenuity."

In his opening statement Javits dismissed the notion that Carter had exceeded his authority in terminating the mutual defense treaty. He disassociated himself from the senators angry about insufficient consultation, noting his understanding that the People's Republic had accepted the American proposition more rapidly than expected, leaving the Carter administration with little time to consult. He repeated his view that the administration had not gone far enough in proposing how we would take care of Taiwan's security. And he noted that a congressional judgment was plainly required.

Speaking for the administration, Deputy Secretary of State Warren Christopher reminded the committee that our NATO allies and more than 100 other nations had already recognized the People's Republic of China. He reviewed assurances by Chinese Vice Premier Deng Xiaoping that China intended to resolve the Taiwan issue peacefully. In response to Church's questions,

Christopher noted that the issue of China renouncing force had been explored at the time of the Shanghai Communiqué, and the best that could be
done—then and now—is that the United States would make a statement that
it expected the Taiwan matter to be resolved peacefully and the People's Republic of China would not contradict that statement. To Church, that background made it even more important for Congress to state the American
view and its expectation that there would be no resort to force in resolving
the Taiwan issue.

Church and Glenn, surmounting their personal differences, were working
on a statement that affirmed America's "deep and abiding concerns for the
people of Taiwan" and asserted the United States' determination to maintain
good relations with Taiwan, to continue to sell them defensive weapons, and
to act appropriately in the event of an attack. Church stated that Carter's legislation would be "substantially revised. Ambiguities in the bill leave far too
many questions unanswered." Reacting, however, against some of the hawkish
rhetoric being used, Church observed that some proposals being floated
would have committed the United States to Taiwan's defense even more explicitly than the mutual defense treaty that was being abrogated.

As in the earlier fights over the Panama Canal and the F-15s to Saudi Arabia, the negotiations were intense and marred by occasional miscommuni-
cations. On February 8, Church endorsed a Javits resolution that would have
labeled an attack on Taiwan "a common danger to the peace and security . . .
of the United States." This language came directly from the old mutual defense treaty. The Javits draft pledged that the United States "would maintain
its capacity in the Western Pacific to resist armed attack and other forms of
external activities that would jeopardize the territorial and functional integrity of Taiwan." After strong opposition from the Carter administration,
expressed by Christopher, Church withdrew his support, saying that "this
was a tentative proposition. It was hastily drawn up." When Javits pointed
out that Church had approved circulating the draft, Church said that didn't
mean that he was "bound to it." This irritated Javits and reminded people on
the committee of Church's on-again, off-again approach to the F-15s the previous year. But they kept working away, seeking language that would achieve
a broad consensus.

World events threatened to derail the effort. On February 17, China
launched a major cross-border attack into Vietnam, plunging six miles deep
into Vietnamese territory with air support. That Chinese action, coming at a

crucial juncture in Congress's deliberation, troubled many members. Percy noted that "the Chinese invasion of Vietnam has made it even more imperative that the Chinese understand . . . our concern for Taiwan." But notwithstanding China's incursion, Church and Javits, working continually with their staffs and consulting with the administration, agreed on legislative language.

On February 22, the Foreign Relations Committee unanimously approved a statement of support for Taiwan and the legislation establishing a new basis for Taiwanese relations. The Church-Javits language stated that the United States "will maintain its capacity to resist any resort to force or other forms of coercion that would jeopardize the security or social or economic system of the people of Taiwan." It also stated that any use of force against Taiwan would be "a threat to the peace and security of the Western Pacific area and of grave concern to the United States." Previously, the committee rejected a Percy amendment that stated "any effort to resolve the Taiwan issue by other than a peaceful means" would be considered "a threat to the security interests of the United States." The differences between the Church-Javits and Percy formulations seemed small, but they were enormous. Church-Javits was a strong statement of U.S. policy and concern, but it did not continue to language of the mutual security treaty or constitute a commitment by the United States to go to war over Taiwan. The Carter administration could accept Church-Javits, and both Peking and Taipei could live with it.

The formulation met the high standard that Church had set at the beginning of the hearings—"diplomatic skill and legislative ingenuity." Immediately, it gained the same broad support in the full Senate that had it received in the Foreign Relations Committee. Helms had threatened to filibuster the nomination of Leonard Woodcock, the former president of the United Auto Workers, to be Ambassador to China. But now, Helms folded his tent quickly, and the former UAW president was confirmed by an overwhelming 82–9, which included such staunch conservatives as Goldwater and Strom Thurmond. Even Helms had kind words for the committee's language. It was a stunning turnabout.

On March 13, the Senate approved the Taiwan bill with the Church-Javits language by a vote of 90–6. The House adopted a similar bill by a vote of 345–55. The Senate approved the final conference report on the Taiwan Relations Act by a vote of 85–4. President Carter wavered before signing it, because some of his advisers wanted him to veto the bill lest the PRC leaders conclude that he had negotiated in bad faith. But on April 10, he signed the legislation. Later that year, Goldwater's legal challenge to the President's termination of the 1954 treaty failed.

The Carter administration's recognition of the PRC, combined with the Taiwan Relations Act, constituted what Harvard's John K. Fairbank called "a great diplomatic achievement." Fairbank, the dean of China scholars in the United States, believed that the results far surpassed anything that China experts had anticipated: "Since Peking now has latent sovereignty, we need not confront Chinese nationalism. Since Taiwan will be defensible, we have not 'abandoned' it."

Although PRC officials objected to the Taiwan Relations Act, they went along with it. When Church and four other committee members visited China in mid-April, Deng told them that the act had almost derailed the normalization process. But Deng's comments took up only a few minutes of an otherwise positive meeting that focused on the long-term interest of the United States and China in establishing good relations. In Taiwan, initial rage about the U.S. decision to recognize China gave way to reluctant acceptance. When Carter first announced the agreement, angry demonstrators had taken to the streets, breaking the windows of a car containing Deputy Secretary of State Christopher. The enactment of the Taiwan Relations Act calmed the situation by placing the United States and Taiwan in "a unique relationship," which managed to maintain a significant level of U.S. commitment to the island, even while fundamentally altering it. Church received expressions of "deepest appreciation" from the Republic of China's premier and "profound gratitude" from Taiwan's Deputy Representative in the United States.

The Taiwan Relations Act constituted a remarkable legislative and political accomplishment. At the outset, it had appeared that the China/Taiwan debate might be prolonged and bitter. Within a period of weeks in early 1979, the Senate, led by Church and Javits, had completely transformed the political environment. The committee's hearings had educated the Hill and the country, and the senators' determination to find a way to embrace China without abandoning Taiwan had managed both to reflect the public mood and calm it. The American people basically supported the position of Church and Javits, rather than the position of Reagan, Helms, and Dole.

The United States would no longer ignore the reality of China. Nor would we pretend that there were two Chinas. Our policy would be to recognize China and continue to support Taiwan. Thirty years later, both China and Taiwan are prospering, and Taiwan has become a vibrant democracy. China has made no moves to forcefully incorporate the "renegade province" into China. In fact, political and economic relations have deepened between China and Taiwan.

Of course, it was a different time. This was how the Senate worked in the era when it was still great. Issues were taken on the merits, and faced, no matter how tough they were. Nominees got judged on their merits, irrespective of partisan politics. The national interest dictated the result. It was the last great Senate, and it would not last much longer.

chapter 14

ENERGY BATTLES AFTER THE IRANIAN REVOLUTION

IN THE SEA OF PROBLEMS CONFRONTING CARTER AND THE CONGRESS from 1977 through 1979, healthy economic growth had been the Democrats' lifeline. The U.S. economy was in its fifth year of expansion since the deep recession triggered by the OPEC oil embargo of 1973. Manufacturing employment had reached an all-time high, employing 19 million Americans. Industrial capacity was beginning to be strained, causing inflation to rise to 9 percent, with food prices rising especially quickly. But oil prices had been stable for a year.

The Iranian Revolution ended that stability, changing the economic picture almost overnight. After the revolution, Iranian oil production virtually stopped. Global oil production at the beginning of 1979 was down 2 million barrels a day from the last quarter of 1978. OPEC members used the tight world oil market created by the loss of Iranian production to raise the price of oil 17 percent. A week later, OPEC announced another 9 percent increase. Shortly thereafter, the cartel hit the world's oil-consuming nations with its largest increase yet. Gasoline prices rose 55 percent in the first three months of the year. Carter's economic advisers estimated that the inflation rate in

America could reach 15 percent. Within weeks, the American economy slowed dramatically. The country faced the specter of energy shortages, soaring inflation and a looming recession. Theodore White wrote: "There was a contagion of fear."

Jimmy Carter had devoted the first two years of his presidency trying to convince America that its increasing dependence on foreign oil threatened our country's future. As memory of the 1973 OPEC embargo receded, the public's intensity of concern had eased, and energy legislation bogged down in acrimonious debate. Now, as oil prices skyrocketed and produced long lines at gas stations across the country, the energy crisis was no longer abstract or somewhere in the distant future.

If the powerful reverberations from the Iranian Revolution were not bad enough, on March 28, a pump failed at Three Mile Island, the nuclear power station near Harrisburg, Pennsylvania, and emergency crews had to rush to shut down the plant before its overheated core could melt down. One hundred thousand residents fled their homes, while across the country, Americans fearfully hoping for the best quickly lost confidence in nuclear power as an alternative to dependency on foreign oil.

Carter and the Congress now plunged into a third consecutive year of grueling battles over America's energy crisis. On April 5, saying "the future of the country we love is at stake," Carter announced a three-pronged strategy for building energy security. He called for a massive effort to develop synthetic fuels as an alternative to oil. He advocated the creation of an Energy Mobilization Board, which would be able to cut through federal, state, and local regulation in order to expedite the building of synthetic fuels plants, to replace fossil fuels and enable American energy independence. And he proposed the gradual decontrol of oil prices and other measures, aimed at forcing Americans to "use less oil and pay more for it." Because loosening controls on oil prices would primarily benefit the oil industry, Carter also asked Congress to create a windfall profits tax, with the proceeds going to an Energy Security Fund.

The debate over the windfall profits tax would soon take center stage. The administration estimated that decontrol would raise gas prices by 5 cents a gallon by 1982 and reduce foreign oil imports by 600,000 barrels a day, mostly from stimulated domestic production following higher prices. The administration officials also estimated that oil company revenue would jump $10.7 billion in 1981 if the windfall profits tax was not imposed. They indicated that the tax proceeds would go to credits for low-income homeowners, expanded mass transit, and development of synthetic fuels.

Scoop Jackson, the chairman of the Energy Committee, strongly supported Carter's proposal for an Energy Mobilization Board to expedite the production of synthetic fuels. He saw it as a big proposal, appropriate for the magnitude of the threat from OPEC. The EMB reminded Jackson of the World War II Defense Production Board, which cut through red tape and helped make possible the rapid buildup of the war effort. The Defense Production Board, however, had done its work during a national war effort and before the enactment of environmental laws and regulations. More fundamentally, the United States knew how to build planes and tanks. No one knew how to build synthetic fuels plants, and whether, or how quickly, synthetic fuels could be made an alternative to oil.

The Senate had already consented to lifting price controls. Its fiercest debate would be about the windfall profits tax: its size and what the money would be used for. Chuck Percy gave an early indication of the direction of the debate, saying that "if a windfall profits tax on oil company profits is necessary . . . then full credit should be given to oil companies for plowing back profits into discovery and development of new energy sources."

In the crisis atmosphere, the issue heated up quickly. Russell Long and other members from oil states had promoted the idea of a "plowback," giving a tax break for any oil profits spent on new exploration. On April 26, the administration estimated that its proposed windfall profits tax would require oil companies to pay back only $1.7 billion in 1982 out of an estimated $14.5 billion in extra profits. Carter was not supportive, protesting that any additional "plowback" would be a travesty. Carter would recall in his diary: "Everyone was trying to demagogue decontrol and windfall profits tax." He decried the irresponsibility of Congress in refusing to give him authority to ration gasoline and impose conservation measures in an emergency. "Congress is disgusting on this particular subject," he wrote.

ON MAY 3, ABE RIBICOFF jolted the Senate by announcing that he would not seek reelection in 1980. Ribicoff was sixty-nine but in excellent health and at the peak of his power and influence. But in a short statement that left his staff as stunned as his colleagues, Ribicoff observed that "a man who has held power needs to know how to step aside and open up the political process." In recent years, Ribicoff had confided to friends and colleagues that the Senate had begun to change in ways that he did not like: "there were few real states-men left." But he made it clear that he had actually decided not to seek a fourth term in 1974, just after being reelected for his third. "No one should feel indispensable," Ribicoff added.

Jack Javits was shocked by his friend's announcement. "He must really be sick of the place," Javits said to Alan Bennett of his staff. "He's younger than I am." Javits had not announced his intention to retire at the end of his term but continued to plan on it.

Ed Muskie, too, was stunned by Ribicoff's announcement. Muskie had just completed twenty years in the Senate. He was tiring of the Senate, feeling like he often stood alone in the battles for fiscal responsibility while fighting to preserve important government programs. The disappointment of not reach-ing the presidency had taken some toll. Muskie had begun to consider what life after the Senate might be like, but the private sector held little appeal for him. Leon Billings, his administrative assistant who had sparked Muskie's environmental accomplishments, had become close friends with Frank Moore, Carter's congressional liaison and a member of the Georgian inner circle. Billings asked Moore what he thought of the idea of Muskie becoming Secretary of State in Carter's second term. Moore liked the idea quite a bit, and promised to check it out.

Any seeds that Moore could plant would fall on potentially fertile ground. Muskie had become an indispensable ally for a president increasingly beset on all sides. As Carter tried to control the budget in a futile effort to curb in-flation, Muskie was a tower of strength. Working closely with Henry Bellmon of Oklahoma, the ranking Republican on the Budget Committee, Muskie took on Senate liberals trying to restore cuts that Carter proposed in urban and social programs and then wheeled to take on Bill Proxmire and others who were trying to balance the budget, warning that they would throw the economy into recession with their proposed draconian cuts. No one enjoyed fighting the popular and powerful Warren Magnuson, but Muskie insisted that Maggie's Appropriations Committee come up with the cuts that Budget Committee required for reconciliation. "We don't need fiscal handcuffs to wipe the deficit out," Muskie said. "We need fiscal discipline."

On April 26, Carter expressed his gratitude: "The Senate did a superb job yesterday in protecting our budget. I thanked Ed Muskie, who has become perhaps the foremost statesman in the Senate." Carter reached that judgment despite the fact that Muskie had recently ripped Carter's environmental regulatory council, calling them "anti-regulators" and the "principal threat to the environment as we close the environmental decade of the 1970's."

THE ENERGY BATTLE CONTINUED to rage. Russell Long had done about as much for Jimmy Carter as he could in 1978, standing with him on the Panama Canal treaty and the Labor Law Reform bill, while not blocking a natural gas compromise that he hated. Long had already signaled that Carter could not count on as much support from him again. On May 7, at a Senate Finance Subcommittee hearing, he ripped into the Carter administration officials. "Under your program," Long thundered, "industry can raise enough money to stay at the mercy of the Arabs as long as you remain in government . . . which may not be that long."

Arguing that the current oil shortage required that the energy industry should be more profitable than any other industry, in order to expand production, Long asked whether the administration realized it was "flirting with the survival of freedom in this nation and on this planet?" Other senators from oil-producing states agreed. Mike Gravel, the subcommittee chairman, said he saw "really no need for a windfall tax." Emil Stanley, the deputy assistant secretary of Treasury, coolly responded to Long's tirade, telling him that Carter's plan essentially did what Long wanted by decontrolling oil prices, but that the windfall tax was "the price of entry."

Just as in 1977, the House moved forward rapidly on Carter's energy proposals and was far more sympathetic to the consumer interests, working to increase the windfall profits tax. The Senate, characteristically, worked on a slower track. Long refused to commit to the House approach of handling the windfall profits tax before taking up other elements of the package. He said he would explore the possibility of a filibuster to prevent all elements of the bill being combined but kept his options open.

Carter simultaneously faced a changing political atmosphere. Kennedy's intensified rhetoric, ripping Carter's proposal as a giveaway to the oil industry, caused Washington Democrats to reconsider the possibility that he would challenge the president. One Hill Democrat said: "I used to think there was no way Kennedy was going to try to run against Carter in 1980—until I heard what he had to say about Carter's energy plan. Now I don't know what to think." Tip O'Neill told Kennedy that he would make a lot of his friends look foolish if he decided to run for president after saying for so long that he would back Carter. Kennedy responded that he still expected Carter to be nominated and planned to support him. O'Neill responded: "Well, you're sure picking a funny way to do it." Kennedy replied: "Well, I think the liberals need a voice—and besides, I'm enjoying it."

On June 22, the Americans for Democratic Action (ADA), a leading liberal group, committed to creating "an irresistible national mandate" to make Kennedy a candidate in 1980. The ADA political commission issued a statement saying: "Carter has given us conservative domestic policies and Republican party economic programs. Jimmy Carter is a one-way ticket to defeat and a trip to a party bankrupt of principles and devoid of officeholders in 1980."

By late June, anger and frustration had gripped the country, as the gasoline shortages produced long lines at the gas station. The American Automobile Association reported that 58 percent of the nation's gas stations were closed due to lack of supply. Returning from an economic summit in Tokyo, Carter, on the advice of his aides, requested television time for a July 5 speech on energy. On July 3, however, the White House abruptly notified the networks that the time would not be needed. Carter, on the advice of pollster and political adviser Pat Caddell, whose memos described a crisis of the American spirit, had decided to retreat to Camp David to reflect on the nation's problems more broadly. For eleven days, the president stayed at Camp David, meeting with a broad range of visitors invited to express their views about the state of the nation. Rumors swirled about the president's lengthy and unexpected absence, further eroding public confidence that had already frayed.

Walter Mondale had served Carter superbly, virtually reinventing the vice presidency to become the president's principal adviser on domestic and foreign policy issues and his most valuable liaison with Congress. Caddell's psycho-babble was too much for him to take. Mondale told Carter that people's problems weren't in their heads—their problems were real, felt everyday. People's paychecks were getting smaller; they couldn't feed their families or pay for gasoline. He warned Carter not to blame the American people for the problems. It was the only time in the four years that he exploded at Carter, who described him as "distraught."

On July 15, Carter returned from Camp David to deliver one of the most unusual presidential speeches ever given. While his speech contained still more new energy proposals, it focused mainly on Carter's view that the nation faced "a crisis of confidence" concerning "the meaning of our own lives" that was "striking at the heart and soul and spirit of our American will." He focused on fundamental moral and spiritual issues, such as the country's soulless materialism and the growing disrespect for schools, churches, and other institutions.

It was an astonishing speech, remarkable for its candor and anguish. It would always be remembered as the "malaise" speech, even though Carter never used the word. The polls indicated that the American people reacted positively to it. But not for long—to politicians, pundits, and ultimately the public, even as Carter worked to provide leadership on a full range of issues, he seemed to be abdicating responsibility, blaming the American people for their current problems. And Carter followed the speech by firing or accepting the resignations of five cabinet officials: Treasury Secretary Michael Blumenthal, HEW Secretary Joseph Califano, Attorney General Griffin Bell, Transportation Secretary Brock Adams, and the long-suffering Secretary of Energy, James Schlesinger. The public seemed stunned by the mass exit. According to one poll, approval of Carter soon plunged to 23 percent.

As Carter reeled, Howard Baker refused to pile on. Speaking to the National Association of Counties, on July 17, Baker said that Carter deserved strong, bipartisan support for his energy programs and that "this is not a time to nickel and dime these programs to death." Still, despite Baker's support, Carter found Congress newly skeptical about his energy proposals and his political viability.

For Kennedy, Carter's malaise speech and the cabinet firings were the last straw; it was the moment when he decided to challenge Carter for the Democratic nomination.

It was the last straw for Jackson as well. On July 29, in an extraordinary press conference, Jackson gave lip service to praising Carter for being a persuasive, one-on-one communicator and then blasted him for running a failed administration that had created the crisis of confidence across America. Jackson also said that Kennedy would only enter the race if Carter stepped aside and then predicted that Kennedy would enter the race, and win. Two days later, George McGovern, another constant thorn in Carter's side, gave a speech to a group of Hill interns at the Library of Congress. Unlike Jackson, McGovern did not even pretend to find anything positive to say about the president. Saying Kennedy was "the most logical candidate" for 1980, McGovern accused Carter of "moral posturing, public manipulation, and political ineptitude."

"We can recover from our present malaise by setting the stage now for a presidential election in 1980 that is equal to the ideals and hopes of a great nation," McGovern told the interns. "We do not know whether Senator Kennedy will respond to the public opinion polls indicating that he is the popular Democratic choice for the presidency in 1980," McGovern continued. "I agree with Senator Jackson that our Massachusetts colleague is the most logical candidate for our party. If he decides to run, I believe that he can be nominated and elected and would be an inspiring president. If he declines to run, the Democrats must field a strong alternative."

Other prominent Democrats, in Washington and around the nation, began clamoring for Kennedy to run. Despite the strong action by the Carter administration to rescue New York City the previous year, Senator Daniel Patrick Moynihan and Governor Hugh Carey told Kennedy that they would support him.

MEANWHILE, CARTER'S ENERGY PROPOSALS continued to move forward, in stutter steps. On July 26, the Senate Energy Committee, led by Jackson, voted 14–1 to approve the general structure of the Energy Mobilization Board that Carter had proposed, without defining its scope or power. The lopsided vote was misleading, however. The Energy Committee quickly made it clear that it planned to move more slowly on both creating the EMB and providing aid for synthetic fuels. The committee gave general approval to Carter's goal of producing 2.5 million barrels of synthetic fuel a day but pushed the deadline out to 1995, instead of Carter's goal of 1990.

The committee staff proposed a two-stage solution. The first would involve the government helping create at least one "synfuel" plant for each major process, including extracting oil from shale and converting coal to oil or gas. After congressional review of the first stage, the second stage would ramp up spending to Carter's proposed $88 billion. Paul Tsongas said it made no sense for government to pay to build more than one of each prototype plant until the processes had proved feasible. Jackson agreed, saying "we shouldn't go off the deep end." Turning to the EMB, the committee rejected a proposal to allow the federal government to override state and local laws after congressional and presidential review. Instead, the committee voted in favor of having the EMB negotiate with state and local governments to fix deadlines for projects. If agreement could not be reached, the EMB could set a deadline that would need approval from both Houses of Congress.

Even that cautious approach went too far for Gary Hart, who chaired the "Synfuels" task force within Muskie's Budget Committee. Hart was hearing testimony from several synfuels consultants questioning whether Carter's plan was flexible enough for later plants to learn from earlier plants' mistakes to improve the chances of commercial viability. One of the consultants expressed doubt that we would get much production, even ten years from now, with a crash program. Initially, Hart took the view that investing in prototype plants made sense and estimated that the operating cost of each plant would be about $2 billion. The more Hart studied the issue, the more skeptical he became.

Senate Finance Committee members, heavily lobbied by the oil industry, said that they hoped to widen the categories of exempted oil to include all new discoveries and all Alaska oil. Senate sources said that if the Finance Committee approved all the amendments before it, it would wipe out nearly all the expected $142 billion in new revenue that the tax would bring in by 1990. Carter charged that the Finance Committee was seeking to "gut" his windfall profits tax.

Baker's support for Carter's energy proposals carried no weight with his Republican colleagues and proved to be short-lived. A week after his positive statement, the Senate Republicans announced plans to try to tack a general tax cut on to the windfall profits tax when it reached the Senate floor. The Republicans had unveiled a massive "Economic Program for the Decade," calling for phased, across-the-board income tax reductions, a limit on federal spending, and new tax incentives. The Republican senators charged that Carter "seems to lack either the ability or the will or both" to address America's worsening economic problems. It had become a familiar scenario: the Democrats, with the responsibility to govern, battled among themselves about the issue at hand, while the Republicans, luxuriating in being in the minority, played a separate, longer game.

Rising oil prices raised the economic stakes and added to the political pressure. When Carter first proposed the windfall profits tax, estimates said that it would raise $20 billion by 1990. But oil prices had risen 25 percent since April, and the likely revenues from a windfall profits tax were now projected to be $146 billion. This was real money, sparking a fierce battle between conservatives, liberals, and energy interests about how the revenues should be spent and what new finds of oil should be exempt. Initially, when the bite of the tax had seemed relatively small, the oil industry had not been vocal. Now it was fighting back fiercely, and gaining surprisingly strong support within the Finance Committee.

Carter had hoped that the windfall profits tax would be passed before the August recess. Long had told him not to expect action before October, and Long, as usual, had been more accurate, since the chairman held most of the trump cards. As the Senate prepared to recess, Vice President Mondale chided Congress for its failure to complete action. "As the gas lines have receded and the inevitable interest group pressure has mounted," Mondale observed, "Congress has failed to make adequate progress on the president's proposals." The endless Senate consideration of energy legislation during the previous two years remained sharply etched in everyone's memories.

WHEN THE SENATE RETURNED in September, the dealing began in earnest. Carter had hoped to use $88 billion in revenue from the windfall profits tax to invest in synthetic fuels production, ideally reducing foreign oil consumption by three million barrels a day by 1990. Bennett Johnston, a supporter of "synfuels," thought the administration was wildly unrealistic about the amount of revenue it would receive from the windfall profits tax as well as the pace that synfuels production would come on line. Johnston also objected to making the synfuels program dependent on the windfall tax, which he opposed.

Facing the realities of the Senate, the administration began to give ground, lowering its expectations to production of about 1.75 million barrels of synfuels production per day, more likely by 1995. Carter also told state and local officials that he would not insist that the EMB be allowed to override state and local regulations. But Carter still envisioned a $20–30 billion first phase to build a dozen plants, and then a course correction, and a second phase leading to 80–90 plants. It was an uncommonly grandiose vision for Carter, who prided himself on his engineering background and his realism.

On September 18, Senate Finance unanimously approved a proposal by John Danforth to provide synfuels producers a tax credit of $3 per barrel of the equivalent amount of oil, adjusted by inflation. The next day, the Finance Committee voted unanimously to double the existing tax credit for installation of residential solar energy equipment and to extend it to cover adjoining buildings and residential homes. This was just one of a string of proposals approved by the Finance Committee as part of the windfall profits tax, even though it had not yet decided on how high the new tax would be. The day after, the committee tripled the tax credits for installing home insulation, storm windows, and weather stripping and provided new breaks for replacing furnaces and buying wood-burning stoves.

The measures were approved "in principle only," because committee members realized that they were promising credits without having addressed the revenue source to fund them. Long warned the members that they would have soon given away all the new revenue they were considering, even before they decided on the level of the tax. Some observers concluded that Long appeared to be using tax credits to prod committee members to vote for the windfall profits tax. It was also possible, given Long's dislike of the windfall profits tax, that he was just waiting for the whole scheme to sink of its own weight.

On September 22, Jimmy Carter told a group of out-of-town editors that it was "almost impossible" for a president to maintain high approval ratings, given the state of the world and the economy. Carter expressed pride in making tough decisions to pursue the Panama Canal treaties and a balanced national energy policy, even though they were "patently a losing political proposition." "Most of the decisions that have to be made by a president are inherently not popular ones," Carter observed. "They are contentious."

Even Republicans were beginning to agree. Danforth for one could no longer abide the amount of abuse being heaped on Carter. In a speech in Columbia, Missouri, Danforth suggested that "we let up on President Carter." Saying he was "terribly concerned about the incessant drumbeat of criticism directed at the president," Danforth argued that "we have overdone the criticism, it has become too unrelenting and it has impaired the man's capacity to fulfill his responsibilities." This was a highly unusual speech for a Republican senator to give then; it would be inconceivable now.

On September 25, Senate Finance voted 13–0 to exempt all new finds from Carter's windfall profits tax and broadened the definition of new oil to include anything not in production in 1978. This move cut an estimated $14 billion in profits by 1990. Observers calculated that the Finance Committee had stripped about $20 billion from the $104 billion in estimated revenue, and already approved $63 billion in tax credits, while preparing to consider $62 billion more. Danforth warned that the committee must begin comparing revenues with credits, or "we will end up with a tax of zero and expenditures of $200 billion."

The next day, the Finance Committee had made more cuts to, and credits from, the windfall profits tax than the tax would raise: $117 billion to $104 billion. The round of credits included a 40 percent break for businesses that explore unconventional energy, such as solar and geothermal. Danforth expressed his view that it would be necessary "to make a choice between the Energy Security Trust fund and these energy tax credits. There is no way you can have both." Ribicoff suggested a solution to the dilemma, proposing a 25-cent-per-barrel tax on all oil used in the United States, but got little support. As the committee gave out credits far beyond the revenues it would raise, one Senate observer commented: "It was just like a bunch of college kids drinking beer. It didn't matter how much they'd drunk before. They just chug-a-lugged it all."

Long had given the Finance Committee wide latitude, and most of the members recognized that the result had been massive overreach. On September 28, the chairman told the committee that they had voted too many credits, versus revenues, and that they should start over. The members agreed, and the staff was asked to prepare several alternative plans for the committee to consider in the following week. Committee members would face the challenge of dealing with the magnitude of the credits, and the exemptions that they had carved out.

On September 28, Hart's subcommittee issued its report, pouring cold water all over Carter's synfuels program. The report said that synfuels were not likely to become a major alternative to dependence on foreign oil and that Carter's plan could not be justified on economic grounds. The report recommended instead a greater emphasis on conservation by businesses and homeowners, and a quick conversion by many utility plants from oil to coal. The report estimated that such an intensive effort could save 5.5 million barrels of oil a day by 1990, and that full decontrol of oil prices could save another 2.4 million barrels a day.

With the enthusiasm for synthetic fuels waning, on October 3, Long put forth a compromise to cut the revenues in the House-passed version by about one-third (through exemptions) and split the remaining revenues between synfuel production and credits to homeowners and businesses that take energy-saving measures. The committee tentatively rejected Carter's idea of an energy trust fund, but reversed itself the next day. Ribicoff, who had tried to be responsible during the committee's feeding frenzy, persuaded the members that the trust fund provided the only assurance that the money would be used for energy conservation or production and not go into the general treasury.

The Finance Committee bill would capture 29 percent of the new oil revenues, a solid amount, but far less than the 43 percent that the House bill would capture. It was still an open question how the Senate as a whole would respond.

ON OCTOBER 2, LEGISLATION to create an Energy Mobilization Board reached the Senate floor. The novel idea had come to divide the Democrats sharply. Jackson and Johnston favored the powerful EMB originally proposed by the White House; ideally, they wanted a board that could override state and local environmental regulations to speed the construction of synthetic fuels plants. But the vehement opposition of state and local officials, supported by a strong environmental lobby, forced them to scale back their ambitions. They proposed instead that the board could set a two-year deadline on projects and make a decision itself if the deadline was not met. They also wanted approved projects to be "grandfathered" into future environmental laws.

They encountered formidable opposition from Muskie and Ribicoff. Muskie, with his customary passion, told his colleagues that waiving future laws would "make it impossible to protect people from chemical poisons produced by the new energy facility if those poisons are discovered after the facility is built and make it impossible for the government to correct its mistakes. Under the committee bill, we would be literally and dangerously helpless."

Jackson responded vehemently, saying that the Muskie-Ribicoff substitute "guts" the bill, does "nothing to help expedite the time schedule, puts another layer of bureaucracy in and injects the court into it too." Jackson hammered on the basic justification for the EMB: "The energy mobilization board offers the best hope in the short term for reducing our dependence upon OPEC oil. The nation is now paralyzed by a bureaucracy that can delay vital energy projects for months and even years. . . . We should either give the board the power to get the job done or not create a board at all." Jackson had his own strong environmental record, but argued that "the environment and state's rights have dominated this debate . . . many of us seem to have forgotten that our future is at stake."

The next day, the Senate rejected the Muskie-Ribicoff substitute by a 58–39 vote. Pete Domenici said that the defeat of Muskie-Ribicoff "clearly indicates the Senate is ready to make some major energy decisions." But Jackson and the administration, seeking to build a strong consensus and undercut the opponents, reached out to Muskie and Ribicoff, agreeing that the secretary of interior or the EPA director could veto any board decision to waive a state or local law. Muskie was not placated; he predicted that the legislation would face court challenges that would slow energy progress rather than speeding it. "If they think they are short cutting anything with this," he argued, "they could not be more wrong." But the EMB legislation passed the Senate on October 4, by a strong 68–25 vote.

Building on the momentum, on October 10, the Senate Appropriations Committee approved $20 billion for synfuels development funds, even though the synfuels projects had not yet been authorized. Lowell Weicker, among others, argued against this novel approach: "What kind of legislating is this," Weicker asked, "when we just put out on the table $20 billion?" Stevens argued that the money was essential, even if it only sent symbolic help to those Americans stuck in long gas lines. Vermont Democrat Patrick Leahy retorted that "$20 billion is a lot of symbolism." But Robert Byrd's argument—"the money will be there; we won't have to wait. . . . If we reject this, we're put in a position of turning down synthetic fuels"—helped carry the day.

On October 17, the Committee decided to scale back the tax credit package by scrapping the increase in the insulation tax credit it had previously adopted. The money saved was committed to energy aid for the poor and a tax credit for families earning $20,000 or less.

Despite the intense flurry of action on so many fronts, the Senate had not met Carter's deadlines or Long's. Now presidential politics began to intrude. On November 4, at a rally in Buffalo, Kennedy called on Carter to issue an ultimatum that if Congress did not impose a windfall profits tax of 50 percent, he would veto the measure and reimpose price controls. He also called on Carter to issue a moratorium on new nuclear plants.

TED KENNEDY WAS SCHEDULED to announce his presidential bid on November 7 in Boston, at historic Faneuil Hall. But on the evening of November 4, CBS televised an interview of Kennedy done by Roger Mudd, which would go down in the annals of disastrous political appearances. Kennedy failed to respond adequately to tough, but fair and predictable, questions from Mudd about the state of his troubled marriage and the Chappaquiddick tragedy. (Tip O'Neill had warned Kennedy in September that he was greatly underestimating the impact of the "moral issue" and urged him not to run.) When Mudd served up a softball, asking Kennedy why he wanted to be president, the senator offered a rambling, stammering answer that was as nonsubstantive as it was incoherent. Kennedy's performance shocked the national political community. Despite his gaudy poll numbers, his impressive Senate record, his magnetism, and the memory of his brothers, Kennedy was about to launch a presidential campaign without being ready. Some of his closest friends wondered whether the weak interview reflected lingering doubts about whether to run.

The Roger Mudd interview was major political news, but it was quickly overshadowed by dramatic events in Tehran on the same day. For months, the Carter administration had been grappling with the question of whether to admit the shah to the United States. Henry Kissinger and David Rockefeller, the chairman of Chase Manhattan Bank, had been lobbying the White House on the issue, pointing to the shah's decades of support for the United States. Zbigniew Brzezinski strongly supported their argument, and over time, Vice President Mondale and Secretary of State Cyrus Vance also supported the recommendation, on humanitarian grounds because the shah, suffering from potentially fatal lymphoma, could not get first-class medical care in Mexico, where he was currently living.

At an October 19 meeting of his national security team, Carter asked: "What are you guys going to advise me to do if they overrun our embassy and take our people hostage?" Carter's concern may have reflected the warning of Ibrahim Yazdi, the foreign minister in the Barzagan government, who, upon hearing of the idea of letting the shah into the United States, had told U.S. policymakers: "You're opening Pandora's Box with this." Despite his reservations, on October 20, Carter agreed to admit the shah into the United States for medical treatment in New York City.

Two weeks later, on November 4, several hundred militant students stormed the lightly guarded U.S. embassy in Tehran on a rainy Sunday morning. By the afternoon, more than sixty U.S. diplomats and embassy personnel had been taken hostage. The original idea, according to the leader of the students, was to seize the embassy for "forty eight or perhaps seventy two hours—unless the provisional government evicted them earlier." The ordeal of the hostages, which would last for 444 days, doom Carter's presidency, and introduce the United States, and the world, to militant Islam, had begun.

CARTER WAS CLEARLY FEELING the political pressure from the Northeast and aggrieved consumers around the nation. Speaking to a conference of northeastern state officials, Carter lashed out at the Senate Finance Committee, saying that its efforts to reduce the proposed windfall profits tax "could become a trillion-dollar giveaway to the oil companies." Administration officials scrambled to correct the president's recklessly inaccurate statement. Unperturbed by the criticism, Long commented: "When people campaign for office, they tend to make controversial statements."

Carter was in a political vise. The middle ground that he sought seemed to be shrinking daily. Kennedy was attacking him for "surrender to the oil companies and OPEC." Oil company executives were accusing him of stretching the truth and unfairly bashing the industry. The general political climate on the Hill had shifted against him. In July, legislators had applauded Carter's statement that he would use quotas to ensure that the United States would never import more oil than it did in 1977. Now, four months later, the Senate voted to give Congress the power to restrict any future presidential move to limit oil imports.

On November 5, the Senate began floor debate on competing versions of the synfuels legislation. Jackson and the Energy Committee pushed the administration's proposal to create a Synthetic Fuels Corporation, to distribute $20 billion. Proxmire offered the Banking Committee alternative, providing $3 to $10 billion for synfuels and another $11 billion on solar power, conservation, and gasohol. Proxmire, a notorious skeptic about big government projects, argued that his bill limited federal government involvement, while the Energy Committee version involved the federal government "up to their eyeballs."

Proxmire had some strong arguments, but he was offering them on the wrong day. Bennett Johnston retorted that "as of yesterday, there was a cutoff of oil delivered by Iran"; passage of the Banking Committee's "puny" bill would send the wrong message about America's determination to fight OPEC and become energy independent. The Senate rejected Proxmire's version, 57–37, and the next day approved the Energy Committee version, with additional conservation measures that the administration had not sought, by a 65–14 vote.

On November 7, a *Washington Post* article by Mary Russell presented a caustic analysis of the progress on energy so far. "Congress' pattern of response to the national energy problem had become fairly clear," Russell wrote. "It is to give money to people and sometimes create new agencies but not to take chances or inflict pain. It is all strained carrots and no sticks." Reviewing the bidding, Russell noted that the Senate had taken away part of Carter's power to impose oil import quotas; refused to give him clear authority to ration gasoline; "flinched" when asked to set demanding fuel economy standards for new cars; and refused repeatedly to take other steps that would have restricted consumption. "The chosen congressional weapon to fight the oil cartel is—," Russell concluded, "storm windows."

The only possible meaningful action that remained under consideration was decontrol of oil prices coupled with a stiff windfall profits tax—and any decision would require much wrangling.

ON NOVEMBER 16, THE Senate finally began floor debate on the windfall profits tax. The Finance Committee version of the bill recaptured $138 million from the oil industry, only half of what the House-passed bill had done. Long, speaking in support of the bill, called it "the largest tax increase ever levied on a single American industry," but went on to describe it as "a compromise between revenue considerations and the need to provide the proper production incentives." Howard Metzenbaum, in his customary, self-assigned role of protector of consumers, called the bill "by far the biggest giveaway in American history." Bill Roth endorsed the bill, which found the middle ground "between those who want to kick the hell out of Big Oil and those who want to get in bed with Big Oil." Days and nights of debate remained ahead, with possible pitfalls on the left and right.

On November 19, Dale Bumpers introduced an amendment to substitute the House bill for the Senate's. Like Metzenbaum, Bumpers believed that the oil companies were getting away with murder. So did Muskie, who argued passionately: "We have mortgaged our future. Without a more productive windfall profits tax, we just can't make the payments." Bumpers's amendment would go down to defeat, but so would an amendment by Bob Dole that would have further reduced the windfall profits tax.

On November 27, the Senate voted, 53–41, to exempt most independent producers from the windfall profits tax. Lloyd Bentsen, a longtime champion of the independents, who drilled 98 percent of the nation's exploratory wells, offered the amendment to exempt the first 1,000 barrels a day that they produced. Bentsen argued that the exemption was needed to ensure that they would keep drilling at full tilt. Moynihan led the fight against the exemption. Calling Bentsen's amendment "legislation for a privileged thousand firms," he argued that the independents were rich enough and that the exemption would not produce any more oil. Several Democrats expecting hard races in

1980, including McGovern, Bumpers, Frank Church, Birch Bayh, and Ernest Hollings, voted for the exemption even though they traditionally opposed the oil industry.

Byrd's role as majority leader required him to harmonize the White House agenda, what the country expected of the Senate, and what traffic would bear within the Senate. In Byrd's estimation, the Finance Committee had already reduced the windfall profits tax too much, and now Bentsen's amendment had reduced it by $10 billion further. On December 1, Byrd said he favored raising the windfall profits tax in the Senate bill to $190 or $200 billion and that Long was willing to work with those numbers. If a "fair tax" isn't passed, Byrd said, Carter should reimpose price controls. Bill Bradley, in his first year in the Senate, took the lead for those pressing for an increased tax. Stevens, Dole, and Bellmon represented the pro-producer Republicans. A possible compromise was coming into view.

On December 4, the Senate voted 58–35 for a Bradley-Chafee amendment to add $22.5 billion over the next decade by raising the windfall tax on oil discovered between 1973 and 1979 from 60 to 75 percent. Then, in a surprising move, the Senate approved a Metzenbaum amendment to extend the tax for six years, into the mid-1990's, producing a total revenue of $214 billion. This was too much for the pro-producer Republicans and the talks stalemated again.

The Republicans rarely missed an opportunity to put the Senate on record on the subject of tax cuts and balanced budgets, and this was a natural moment. On December 5, the Republicans offered a plan to force a major tax cut in 1981 by capping the amount of GNP that the government could take in tax revenues, at 20.5 percent in 1981, 20 percent in 1982, and 19.5 percent thereafter. They took pleasure in pointing out that Jimmy Carter had endorsed a tax ceiling as part of his 1976 campaign. They were forcing the Democrats to oppose a simplistic, but appealing, scheme. Muskie and Moynihan argued against it, saying it would interfere with the government's budget process and produce deficits at least through the mid-1980's. The amendment went down on a virtual party line vote; and the Republicans had put the Democrats running for the Senate in 1980 on record with a very unpopular vote.

Nevertheless, the Senate seemed to be moving toward a compromise that would allow the windfall profits tax to pass, until a new amendment nearly derailed the entire process. Danforth offered a plan to tax some of the oil royalties that state and local governments would derive from decontrol of profits on state-owned oil lands. He reasoned that if there was going to be a windfall profits tax, it should apply not only to private producers but to states fortunate enough to be in coastal areas with oil deposits. Danforth estimated that state and local profits from decontrol would reach about $138 billion, and his proposed tax would capture about $10.5 billion of that.

Danforth's amendment constituted a major attack on four oil-producing states, including Louisiana, and Long set out to crush it. In Danforth's view, the senators from forty-six other states had good reason to support him in trying to tax part of the royalties from the producing states. But, as Danforth would write almost thirty years later, his belief in the righteousness of his cause blinded him to the political realities of the fight.

On December 12, the Senate plunged into a filibuster over stiffening the windfall profits tax. Byrd urged the senators to cancel all engagements and ordered that cots be set up outside the Senate chamber. The filibuster began after Byrd and other administration allies blocked a move to table an amendment to add $31 billion worth of tax revenue to the current $151 billion in estimated revenues. But Long's anger over Danforth's amendment made the filibuster far more serious. Long said that he would oppose cloture until the Danforth amendment was resolved. He produced 300 amendments, almost all technical or trivial, to delay consideration of the bill if needed. Long told Danforth: "In about 15 years, I think you'll be a great senator, but right now, you're the biggest horse's ass that I've dealt with in 30 years here."

On December 14, the Senate ended a three-day filibuster, voting 78–13 for a deal between producing and consuming state senators that would raise $178 billion by 1990. The compromise included a 10 percent minimum tax on newly drilled wells and a 20 percent tax on "heavy oil" and oil produced by chemical methods. Danforth's amendment became the last serious hurdle to completing the bill.

Long spoke for hours in opposition. In a folksy and selective recounting of American history, Long said that Missouri had only been admitted to the union because President Thomas Jefferson had wanted Louisiana, so Danforth was being pretty ungrateful. He accused Danforth of advocating "a land and resources redistribution scheme by plundering the states of their own natural resources." With historical analogies flying, Bennett Johnston ranged further afield, saying it was unfair to pick on states like Louisiana that are only now "climbing out of the economic bondage of Reconstruction." Danforth went down to a sound defeat, by a 65–28 margin. (Years later, the humiliating defeat stayed with him, and he would mistakenly recall that he only got 18 votes.)

On December 17, the Senate gave final approval to a $178 billion windfall profits tax, by an overwhelming 74–24 vote. Three days later, the House and Senate split the difference, settling on $227 billion. Impatient to recess for the holiday season, after a long and difficult session, the conferees decided to wait until January to figure out the details of where the $227 billion would come from. ("The details" were not that easily worked out. It was not until February 26, 1980, that conferees approved the compromise windfall profits tax.) Ironically, after months of intense debate, the windfall profits tax became the first part of Carter's 1979 three-part energy plan to be approved. It was, as Long had predicted, the largest tax ever levied on one industry, and many people in the oil industry in Louisiana were embittered that Long had agreed to it. But Long believed in principled compromise and had seen that a fair trade was possible: enormous profits in exchange for somewhat higher taxes.

The conferees agreed on the main points of the synfuels bill—$20 billion and the creation of a corporation to administer it—in March 1980. But it took until May 21 for the conferees to reach a compromise agreement on a long list of conservation measures that the Senate had included. The synfuels goal had become 500,000 barrels a day by 1987, with the next $68 billion installment to be approved sometime in the mid-1980's. The legislation finally reached Carter's desk at the end of June.

Of the objectives that Carter had set out to accomplish in April—price decontrol, a windfall profits tax, support for synthetic fuels, and an Energy Mobilization Board—he received most, but not all, of what he had sought. In a surprising development, the House refused to approve the Energy Mobilization Board even though the conferees had earlier agreed. The once-exciting idea had long ago ceased to create excitement, and it died, never to be resurrected.

JIMMY CARTER WOULD later write:

> The struggle for a national energy policy had been an exhausting fight
> involving almost every federal agency, all state and local governments,
> every member of Congress, dozens of interest groups and hundreds
> of billions of dollars. It had spanned more than three full years of my

administration. The total energy package did not please anyone completely, but overall it was a good compromise, and I knew that the final result was well worth all our efforts.

Carter's assessment was basically accurate, although describing the struggle as "exhausting" may qualify as an understatement. Legislating a national energy policy may well have been the most complex undertaking in the history of Congress. The legislation that resulted balanced the interest of consumers and producers from throughout America. It affected the cost of energy for everyone—and if that didn't make the undertaking complex enough, formulating a national energy policy required working with scientific, engineering, and political uncertainties. Who really knew whether synthetic fuels would be viable, and on what scale, ten years down the line? How much oil remained to be tapped, and would new drilling techniques greatly expand the potential supply? What were the auto companies really capable of, in terms of fuel economy, once they stopped resisting? Would the United States overcome its fear of nuclear energy after Three Mile Island, and even if so, would Congress ever agree on an appropriate place to store spent nuclear fuel?

One thing was certain: the price of energy in the United States had to rise, as an incentive to both increased production and conservation. Carter's energy program caused the price of oil and gas to rise, for consumers and businesses. It represented a serious effort to raise those prices as equitably as possible. The Senate was the forum in which the extended and hard negotiation took place, to reach a series of principled compromises. The resulting legislation succeeded in reducing U.S. oil imports from 8.7 million barrels per day in 1977 to 4.3 million barrels per day five years later—a reduction of more than 50 percent. The legislation also included strong commitments to increase the use of renewable energy and mandatory improvements in the efficiency of buildings, industrial equipment, and transportation. Assessing Carter's quest for a national energy policy, John C. Barrow wrote in 1998: "Carter's conservation policies would contribute to an energy glut in the mid-1980's." Tragically, these strong gains would be lost in the coming years, as subsequent presidents, starting with Ronald Reagan, would again adhere to the view that cheap energy was something of an American birthright.

Thirty years would pass until Congress again undertook, and enacted, legislation as complex and far-reaching as Carter's energy program—Barack

Obama's health care legislation. Jimmy Carter, in his recently released *White House Diary*, would note that "in dealing with Congress, I had one presidential advantage that no longer exists: cross-party support when it counted. . . . The bipartisanship that I enjoyed has now almost disappeared." Carter faced enormous problems, at home and abroad, but unlike Obama, he had a great Senate with which to work.

chapter 15

FIGHTING THE ECONOMIC TIDE

THE U.S. ECONOMY MAINTAINED ITS STRENGTH THROUGH 1978, DESPITE mounting inflation. The American job creation machine seemed to be recovering from the deep recession of 1973–1975 that followed the first Arab oil embargo. But in 1979, the OPEC oil increases, sparked by the Iranian Revolution, plunged the U.S. economy into a new and disturbing phenomenon known as "stagflation."

Previously, inflation had almost always occurred at the same time as low unemployment, while the damage caused by high unemployment was at least mitigated by prices that were not rising. Now the old economic rules seemed to no longer apply. The economy slipped rapidly back into recession, while inflation surged toward double digits, wreaking havoc for people on fixed incomes and outrunning wage increases for the vast majority of workers. By mid-1979, "it's the economy, stupid" aptly described the challenge for the Senate. Fortunately, some of its finest legislators had been thinking about these issues for a long time.

Abe Ribicoff had been one of the first senators to show an understanding that American economic strength was beginning to weaken. In his 1972 book, Ribicoff pointed out that the U.S. economy, while still the strongest in the world, had begun to show serious strain in the face of intense foreign competition from Europe and Japan.

On a trip to Europe Ribicoff found "geo-politics," such as military pacts, treaties, and balance-of-power diplomacy, being replaced by "ecopolitics"—or, "developing international trade and investment policies to achieve economic prosperity and a higher standard of living." He decried the willingness of the U.S. government to stand aside while the governments of our competitors were working hard to help their businesses compete. He called on the U.S. government to concentrate its efforts "in those areas where we can hope to achieve a superior competitive position." He called for a major increase in government research and development and "the creation of a new permanent board which would select areas of national priorities, make long-range plans and then actually design possible government-industry programs to be funded."

Ribicoff's message had not resonated in 1972 when the U.S. economy still seemed strong. Seven years later, his insights reflected a fundamental challenge facing the president and Congress—how to overcome a deeply ingrained assumption that American economic prosperity would continue forever without an active, focused government role.

The economic prosperity that extended from the end of World War II into the early 1970's had touched nearly every American. It had stimulated the poorer regions of the country, lifted blue-collar workers and their families into comfortable middle-class homes, and provided wide-ranging opportunities to high school and college graduates. This boom generated growing tax revenues that in turn funded social programs. Belief in a perpetually growing economic pie created a widespread willingness to help the poor and to extend opportunities to bring them into the economic mainstream. Among other things, this prosperity powered the liberalism of John Kennedy's New Frontier and Lyndon Johnson's Great Society. Confidence in America's unparalleled economic might also created a willingness to help rebuild Europe and Japan and then to tolerate trade arrangements that were less than balanced in order to help other countries prosper.

For decades, American prosperity was a core assumption. Economic policy was therefore an afterthought, at best, to the Senate led by Mike Mansfield, Everett Dirksen, and Hugh Scott. Through the 1960's and into the 1970's the Senate focused instead on extending opportunity to the poor, dividing the economic pie more equitably, and regulating business, confident that America's companies could handle any additional costs. Absolute confidence in America's economic strength shaped the way the Congress did business; it allowed Congress to pass separate appropriations bills without even calculating the total cost, until the enactment of the Budget Control and Impound-ment Act of 1974. But, as Ribicoff had foreseen, the economic ground was shifting under America. When the OPEC oil embargo of 1973 ended what Bruce Schulman described as "the long, sweet summer of post-war prosper-ity," the economic situation of Americans changed dramatically—and sena-tors would have to reexamine their core assumptions about the condition and direction of the American economy.

JIMMY CARTER HAD COME to office an avowed free trader. He also thought that the United States, Europe, and Japan should stimulate their domestic economies to become the "locomotives" for the global economy. However, soon enough it became disturbingly evident that Europe and Japan hoped to grow through exports, rather than domestic demand, and that those ex-ports were heading, disproportionately, to the United States.

By 1978, the American steel industry was facing an acute crisis. The open-ness of the U.S. market, combined with the aggressive subsidies of Europe, Japan, and other countries, had turned the United States into the dumping ground for the world's excess steel. Carter's focus on fighting inflation, which led him to see lower-cost imports as attractive, only exacerbated the problem.

Ribicoff chaired the Subcommittee on International Trade of the powerful Finance Committee. From that position, he worked to fashion new rules of trade, to govern the relationship between the United States and its leading trading partners, Europe and Japan, and to begin bringing the developing economies into the global system. He worked closely with Robert Strauss, the U.S. Trade Representative and a Texas lawyer who had chaired the Dem-ocratic National Committee and helped Carter to the presidency. Strauss was a consummate dealmaker, and he was proving that international negotiation drew on the same savvy, charm, and brass that had made him so successful in Texas and Washington.

On April 12, 1979, thanks in large part to Strauss's canny leadership, 102 nations announced the completion of the multilateral Tokyo Round, launched by the Nixon administration in 1973. Previous multilateral "rounds" had focused only on cutting tariffs. In contrast, the Tokyo Round went fur-ther to establish six agreements, known as codes, which attempted to impose discipline on the array of nontariff barriers that prevented U.S. exports from reaching their potential in foreign markets. The codes addressed government procurement, technical barriers to trade, customs valuation, import licensing, antidumping, and countervailing subsidies.

Trade agreements would later become extraordinarily controversial, but in 1979, the Tokyo Round results were universally regarded as beneficial to the United States. With Strauss and Ribicoff working together smoothly, the Senate passed the Trade Amendments Act, implementing the Tokyo Round results, by an overwhelming vote of 90–4, on July 23, 1979—virtually record time. The completion of the negotiation and the congressional endorsement of the result were two bright spots during a period that was becoming quite bleak for Jimmy Carter.

Birch Bayh focused on a different economic problem. Through the work of his Judiciary Subcommittee on Patents and Copyrights, Bayh had become fascinated by the issue of American innovation. The United States still seemed to be leading the world in advances, measured in terms of patents filed. But somehow those breakthroughs were not making it into the commercial marketplace. As Bayh and his staff probed the issue, they discovered that 28,000 patents earned as a result of research done in American universities were gathering dust, not shared with the commercial world. Bayh started working on legislation to address the problem. He found that Bob Dole, shopping for economic ideas to use for a potential presidential run, shared his interest and would be willing to collaborate on the effort.

Gaylord Nelson meanwhile used his chairmanship and energetic staff with increasing effectiveness to address the concerns of small business. Aware that small businesspeople were reacting strongly against the regulatory burden they faced, Nelson, along with John Culver, introduced the Regulatory Flexibility Act, which would require agencies to develop less burdensome regulations on small business. Nelson had also worked to persuade the White House to convene the first national conference on Small Business, scheduled for January 1980. Nelson would always be on the union side when labor and business collided, but he nevertheless saw this as a way to broaden his appeal to the business community and respond to some legitimate concerns.

Given the tax-cutting fervor that was sweeping the nation, taxes were also on Senators' minds during this troubled economic period. Lloyd Bentsen was a rising Democratic star. A World War II bomber pilot of great distinction, Bentsen served three terms in the House of Representatives before leaving Congress to start a successful insurance company. In 1970, Bentsen had defeated George H. W. Bush for the Senate seat after ousting the incumbent senator, Ralph Yarborough, a liberal Democrat, in a bruising primary. Now, Bentsen—moderate, thoughtful, and business-oriented—shared the Republican view that America needed a tax cut, but he disagreed with Kemp-Roth and the suggestion that personal tax rates instead be slashed 30 percent across the board. Bentsen thought a reduction in business taxes would be more appropriate. Bentsen was serving as chair of the Joint Economic Committee (JEC), a committee without legislative jurisdiction that functioned more like a high-visibility think tank and research arm of Congress. He pressed the staff to consider whether there were measures that would appeal to both Democrats and Republicans and could bolster the "supply side" of the economy.

Together, all of these senators were generating a number of good ideas that could provide foundation blocks for a new economic agenda. All, however, would take time to develop into legislation, and then even more time to impact the economy. But the senators, and the Carter administration, did not have the luxury of time to wait for results as the economic downturn accelerated. They were about to face a dramatic example of economic distress and the need to make hard and historic choices rapidly, with an election year looming on the horizon. These choices became concrete with the near-collapse of an iconic American corporation.

ON MAY 29, 1979, Chrysler Corporation announced that it was closing its most storied auto plant—"Dodge Main" in Hamtramck, Michigan. In the late 1970's, 5,000 workers assembled Dodge Aspens and Plymouth Volares in that plant. Dodge Main had weathered hard times before, and the workers had become accustomed to threats of closure. But this time, the threat was real; the last car would roll off the line at Dodge Main in January 1980.

The fate of Chrysler Corporation, the nation's tenth-largest company, would soon hang in the balance. Chrysler had major manufacturing facilities in St. Louis, among other places—its rescue would require the combined talents of a group of younger senators, of which the most senior was Tom Eagleton of Missouri.

Eagleton was a terrific politician: informal, likeable, a fine lawyer, and a rousing speaker and debater. His father had been St. Louis's finest trial lawyer and counsel to the St. Louis Cardinals. Eagleton had grown up going to spring training every spring and remained a great baseball fan. But his true passions were American history, politics, and government. Eagleton had a rumpled appearance, with his shirttail often out. Many people detected a marked re-semblance to Jack Lemon. He was customarily a whirling dervish of activity: chain smoking, racing from meeting to meeting, tearing articles out of news-papers and magazines, dashing off irreverent notes to staff members and friends, sometimes on note paper with the heading "Dear Fuckface."

He was known for his sense of humor and comic timing. Once, in the sen-ators' elevator crowded with members going to vote, Eagleton started loudly telling a new Polish joke that he had heard. From the back of the elevator, Ed Muskie, who was Polish, growled, "I'm here, Tom." "That's all right, Ed," Ea-gleton shot back, "I'll speak slowly." He took great joy in retelling the story of the time when Admiral Hyman Rickover, the father of the nuclear navy, came to his office. Rickover had dressed him down, turned smartly, and walked into the closet. Years later, Eagleton would act out all the parts, his body shak-ing with gales of laughter.

Eagleton's rise through Missouri politics was meteoric. He moved from circuit attorney to state attorney general to lieutenant governor, reaching the Senate at the age of thirty-nine. He had never lost an election and had im-pressed enough experienced Washington political figures to be considered for vice president less than four years after reaching the Senate. When George McGovern, having finally clinched the 1972 Democratic nomination for president, turned to choosing his running mate, his disorganized and hurried search led him to choose Eagleton, who was young, appealing, and Catholic, with strong ties to the labor movement McGovern's insurgent campaign had alienated. But McGovern and his advisers, exhausted by the final push for the nomination and a chaotic convention, made the vice presidential choice in haste, with virtually no vetting of the prospective candidates.

Almost immediately after the convention concluded, press reports re-vealed that Eagleton had a history of depression and had been treated with electroshock therapy. The ensuing national media frenzy overwhelmed Mc-Govern's general election campaign before it even got started. McGovern an-nounced his intention to stand by Eagleton "1000 %," and then reversed himself, asking Eagleton to leave the ticket. Many Americans sympathized with Eagleton and felt that his past medical history was not relevant, given his strong performance as a senator. Others, however, thought that Eagleton should have disclosed his past history to McGovern, letting the nominee de-cide how much weight to give it. Eighteen days after being selected, Tom Ea-gleton was off the Democratic ticket, and George McGovern, already facing an enormous uphill struggle, was on the way to a landslide defeat at the hands of Richard Nixon.

The whole experience might have broken a lesser man, and Eagleton lived with the possibility that no matter how much he accomplished, he might only be remembered for leaving McGovern's ticket due to his past mental illness. But the voters of Missouri then stood by him in 1974, reelecting him by a wide margin. Eagleton had been on the way to being a great senator before the vice presidential debacle. He had been one of the leading opponents of the Vietnam War and one of the foremost advocates of reasserting Congress's power to declare war. He had helped Muskie and Howard Baker fashion innovative provisions of the Clean Air Act. Eagleton was even proud of his work as chairman of the D.C. Subcommittee, although it was a thankless task and a political millstone. He had been instrumental in the legislation giving the District of Columbia "home rule" in 1973. He remained determined to be a great senator. And if Chrysler, the employer of so many of his fellow Missourians, was in jeopardy, Tom Eagleton would make rescuing it his highest priority.

CHRYSLER WAS FOUNDED BY Walter Chrysler in 1922. It played a major part in the U.S. effort during World War II, deftly switching from the manufacture of automobiles to airplanes. During the postwar period, although it was the smallest of the "Big Three" auto companies and constantly battling to hold its ground against GM and Ford, Chrysler had become the tenth largest U.S. corporation.

The U.S. auto industry had boomed along with the postwar prosperity and an expanding middle class with suburban lifestyles. But the auto industry's situation changed abruptly in 1973 when OPEC embargoed oil shipments to the West, punishing the United States for its support for Israel. Suddenly, the Big Three auto manufacturers faced intense competition from Japanese companies that had manufactured small, fuel-efficient cars that previously lacked appeal to Americans. What Robert Reich would later describe as "the peculiar post-war preeminence by default" of American companies seemed to disappear overnight.

The U.S. economy entered a severe recession. Unemployment reached 9.2 percent by 1975, and auto sales shrank. At the same time, the auto industry was coping with an array of new regulatory requirements dealing with safety, emissions standards, and fuel efficiency. These requirements imposed billions of dollars in additional costs just as the industry was facing a recession and intense foreign competition. Chrysler, the smallest of the companies, would have the hardest time meeting the regulatory requirements.

The company seemed snake bit. It had restyled its large cars at precisely the moment when the oil embargo made them unappealing. Its new small cars, Aspen and Volare, earned *Motor Trend*'s car of the year award in 1975; eighteen months later, the Center for Auto Safety labeled them "the lemons of the year" after a series of safety recalls. Chrysler laid out a $7.5 billion modernization program, but in 1978, despite an expanding U.S. auto market, Chrysler lost $159 million. The banks that funded Chrysler's debt were showing increasing impatience and decreasing confidence in the company.

In December 1978, John Riccardo, Chrysler's CEO, had come to Washington to alert Stuart Eizenstat, Carter's chief domestic policy adviser, about the company's deteriorating financial situation. He lamented the double whammy of a crumbling auto market and looming capital requirements. Fully half of the cost of the retooling that Chrysler was doing came from complying with new government regulations issued between 1971 and 1977. Despite a determined strategy of divestiture, consolidation, and layoffs, Riccardo said that Chrysler could fail to meet its capital requirements by one billion dollars in 1979 and 1980.

Riccardo asked Eizenstat for temporary relief from certain federal regulations. He made it clear that Chrysler did not want a "Lockheed-style" loan guarantee, which had saved the aerospace company in 1971. In his view, the publicity surrounding such a loan guarantee would hurt Chrysler more than it helped. Eizenstat listened, but made no commitments, and Riccardo left empty-handed.

Now, in 1979, Chrysler's losses mounted ominously. By the end of June, Riccardo returned to the White House as Chrysler was about to lose $230 million in a single quarter. Treasury Secretary Michael Blumenthal and Eizenstat listened attentively to Riccardo's presentation and promised to keep an "open mind" about granting relief to Chrysler. They agreed to review all the options, including special legislation and even federal aid, although one official described that option as "very unlikely."

Chrysler knew what it wanted from the federal government: two years of relief from federal regulations and an advance refund against federal taxes that the company would pay when it returned to profitability. But Treasury Department officials were adamantly opposed, calling it "a complete nonstarter." Chrysler's struggle to convince policymakers became even harder when Carter replaced Secretary Blumenthal, who was regarded as sympathetic to the company's plight, with G. William Miller, the Federal Reserve Board chairman, who had been outspoken in his opposition to providing help for Chrysler.

On August 3, Miller advised President Carter that Chrysler and its congressional advocates (foremost among them Eagleton, Don Riegle, and Michigan House member Jim Blanchard) were running around Washington making the argument that the government had created their problems and that the solution was a large advance against future taxes. The Carter Administration was trying to hold the line on the federal budget, and it certainly did not want to do anything that would further intensify the anti-tax, anti-regulatory fervor that was sweeping the country. Miller recommended that Chrysler's proposal should be knocked down before it developed any momentum. The president agreed: "You're absolutely right, put it any way you like, we're not going to do it."

Secretary Miller quickly disabused Chrysler of any illusions about tax relief. According to Wendell Larsen, Chrysler's vice president for government relations, "Miller just blew us out of the water." Larsen recalled Miller saying: "'If you're going to get anything, it's going to be loan guarantees, and even then you'll only get seven hundred fifty million dollars, and it's going to be tough to pass, and even if it passes, it's going to be so awful you'll wish you never brought the whole thing up.' . . . He was vicious."

Only a year had passed since the Senate's hotly debated decision to offer loan guarantees to New York City. But ultimately, the Senate had accepted the arguments of Jacob Javits, Daniel Patrick Moynihan, Governor Hugh Carey, and Mayor Ed Koch that the bankruptcy of the nation's leading city would be damaging to the national economy and America's place in the world. The American public seemed comfortable with that reasoning; there was no obvious buyers' remorse coming from the taxpayers.

In comparison, Chrysler was a leading U.S. company, an employer of 140,000 people directly, whose failure would have a major effect on suppliers throughout the Midwest. But it was not New York City. Many senators were already expressing concern about the precedent to be set by bailing out a private company. Bill Proxmire, the Banking Committee chairman, and Jake Garn, now the ranking Republican after Ed Brooke's defeat, had led the opposition to helping New York City. It was safe to assume that they would be adamantly opposed to helping Chrysler. But other committee members, generally moderate to liberal, including John Heinz, Lowell Weicker, and Adlai Stevenson, were also expressing opposition. The early headcount looked very bad for Chrysler. Russell Long, however, said that it was too early to predict how Congress would ultimately react. "We did save Lockheed," Long noted, "and we made money. The alternative is the company going out of business."

JIMMY CARTER HAD FRUSTRATED many members of Congress with his regular lack of sensitivity to *their* politics. But the Carter White House understood presidential politics and the dynamics of the Democratic Party. Rebuffing Chrysler in late 1979 would be very damaging to Carter in Michigan, Missouri, and throughout the industrial Midwest. Saying no to Chrysler meant saying no to the United Auto Workers (UAW), which occupied a special place in the Democratic Party. Douglas Fraser, the UAW president, had earned great respect from Democrats; he followed in the great tradition of Walter Reuther and Leonard Woodcock. Fraser had a longstanding and close relationship with Vice President Walter Mondale, but his friendship with Ted Kennedy was even deeper. It was not difficult to envision the UAW playing a powerful part in a Kennedy challenge to Jimmy Carter for the Democratic nomination. Ideology might have dictated the federal government standing aside rather than helping Chrysler; politics surely dictated the ultimate decision to find a way to help.

Chrysler recognized that in order to win the assistance of the U.S. government it would need to present a new face to the Congress and the country. Riccardo agreed to step aside as CEO to be replaced by Lee Iaccoca, a blunt-spoken engineer who had built a brilliant career at Ford but had been bypassed for company leadership by Henry Ford. ("I just don't like you" were Ford's last words to Iaccoca when he fired him.)

Iaccoca met with Treasury Secretary Miller on September 7 and advised him that Chrysler's losses had doubled each quarter and would exceed $700 million for the year. Iaccoca asked Miller for $1.2 billion to save the company. Miller immediately responded that "was way out of line" and that the administration would support a move for $500 to $700 million in loan guarantees. Iaccoca knew that wouldn't be enough. The task of bridging the gap would therefore fall to the Congress, particularly the Senate.

Further bad news was on the way. On October 31, Chrysler reported a staggering $460 million loss for the third quarter, compared to $150 million the year before. The company was hemorrhaging money. Seeing the political and economic necessity of action, Carter finally waded in.

On November 2, the *Washington Post* reported that the Carter administration had decided to provide $1.5 billion in federal loan guarantees to Chrysler, backed by $1.5 billion from other sources. That package would constitute the largest bailout ever provided to a private company. The administration had raised its ceiling because it had become convinced that Chrysler would fail if the rescue package was any smaller. Secretary Miller stated that the aid program should "be sufficient to achieve the purpose" of keeping Chrysler in business, rather than just postponing "the day of reckoning." He observed soberly that the collapse of America's tenth-largest corporation could trigger "substantial unemployment and economic disruption" with costs "more onerous to our country than the risk of loan guarantees."

In six weeks, the administration's commitment to Chrysler had tripled. This happened in part because the UAW demonstrated its readiness to play an important part in rescuing Chrysler. On October 17, the union announced that it would make concessions to Chrysler that it would not make to GM and Ford—a break from its usual negotiating approach. On October 19, Doug Fraser told a House subcommittee that the UAW would loan Chrysler $850 million from its pension fund if the federal government would guarantee Chrysler against default. Within the White House, Vice President Mondale and Eizenstat had taken the lead in educating administration officials to the urgency of Chrysler's situation and the political realities facing the president. Mondale, for one, got an earful from Coleman Young, Detroit's charismatic mayor who was also vice chairman of the Democratic National Committee. The economic health of Michigan, Missouri, and much of the Midwest hinged on the survival of the American auto industry, to be sure. But administration officials also acknowledged that presidential politics played a key role. No one in the Carter administration wanted to be the reason that Doug Fraser and the UAW threw their great weight to Kennedy and against the president. Economic realities and political realities coincided.

IT WAS NOW UP to the Senate. As chair of the Banking Committee, Proxmire would face the situation the same way he had approached the New York City challenge the previous year. Although vehemently opposed, he would hold hearings to allow Chrysler to make its case and the Senate to fully consider the issue.

On November 14, Proxmire gaveled the Banking Committee hearing to order in a hearing room packed with reporters and television cameras. After noting the urgency of the problem, he promptly ripped into the idea of providing relief to Chrysler. He disputed the contention that the cost of a Chrysler bankruptcy would be astronomical, or that hundreds of thousands of jobs would be lost. "No one wants to see jobs lost. And no one likes to see companies fail," said Proxmire. "But why should some companies be worthier than others? We let 7,000 companies fail last year; we didn't bail them out. Now we are being told that if a company is big enough, if it's the 10th largest corporation in the country, we can't let it go under. Then how big is big enough to not be allowed to fail? Where do we draw the line?"

Proxmire saw the precedent as a dangerous path to follow: "We must face the possibility, even the probability, that if we give loan guarantees to Chrysler today, we may well have Ford on our doorstep tomorrow." Proxmire kept his statement brief, saying that he wanted the committee to hear from the other senators; this was not a "routine situation" and these were some of the best statements on both sides of the issue that he had read in a long time.

Garn, the ranking member, further proved Proxmire's point. Although stating a strong philosophical opposition to "government bailouts of business," Garn expressed concern about the costs to the government, in terms of unemployment and pension benefits, if Chrysler were to fail. Garn committed to keeping his mind open, exploring all key issues, including the need for federal assistance; Chrysler's business plans and prospects for the future; the union, dealer, and supplier efforts to keep Chrysler viable; and the cost to Chrysler from "unnecessary government regulations."

John Heinz, bearer of one of the most famous corporate names in America, prided himself on his business acumen. He, too, expressed profound reservations about bailing out Chrysler, predicting "the precedent for bailing out a single business could well come back to haunt us." Heinz also expressed a fundamental concern that the calls for sacrifice to save Chrysler had so far asked a great deal from Chrysler's management, employees, suppliers, and creditors, but nothing from Chrysler's stockholders, who stood to receive "the biggest windfall of all times" if the federal government bailed out Chrysler.

Lowell Weicker had earned a reputation for fiercely independent judgment, and he hated bailing out failing companies. He expressed anger about the unfairness of helping Chrysler when thousands of small businesses were allowed to fail each year without any hope of government help. "I am not going to stand by and watch inefficiency rewarded while thousands of other businesses go down the tubes," Weicker warned. "More jobs will be lost if the Government hands out money to every Lockheed, Wheeling Pittsburgh, or Chrysler that comes along."

The task of making the case for helping Chrysler and changing the tenor of the debate in the Committee fell to Don Riegle, who had already been close to the center of the effort to save Chrysler for months. He had earned some credibility with the Banking Committee the year before by actively supporting the loan guarantees to New York City. At that time, he had expressed pessimism about his city of Detroit and the health of the auto industry. Now he termed Chrysler's situation a "danger signal" for the rest of the country:

> In industry after industry, the United States today is encountering increasingly tough and sophisticated competition from foreign firms. This is no accident. Many of those firms are part of a modern industrial base that was built after World War II, unlike ours, and they have benefited from supportive policies of their governments. Japan, West Germany, France and almost every other nation have mechanisms for charting the development and if necessary the redevelopment of major sectors of their economy. Government, industry and labor in those countries have cooperated to influence how major industries affect the national interest. The flow of capital, tax policy, import and export policy, government regulation and other public action are often coordinated in a coherent strategy to modernize major industries, increase their international competitiveness, and stabilize employment.
>
> But what of the United States? Unfortunately—and with a few notable exceptions such as agriculture—the United States has not thought to develop national policies and strategies for its major industries. Instead, government, labor and industry are often adversaries. We have moved into a full-blown world market situation and yet our national economic mentality is still largely geared to insular notions and strategies that really do not properly fit today's new circumstances.

It was an early, cogent statement in the debate over trade, competitiveness, and "industrial policy" that the United States would conduct over the next decade.

Riegle then turned to the plight of the auto industry. Unlike its competitors, the United States kept gasoline prices artificially low, producing a market for large cars that could not be exported. After decades of inattention, fuel conservation was then imposed through government regulations. The cost of complying with these regulations was staggering, hitting the auto manufacturers at precisely the time when foreign competition was most intense and the demand for their cars was crumbling.

Riegle noted that two years before, Chrysler had embarked on a massive revitalization program that would allow it to produce fuel-efficient cars with four-cylinder engines and front-wheel drive, which could compete with foreign imports. But now that revitalization program was in jeopardy. He outlined his assessment of the grim consequences that Chrysler's failure would have: Chrysler's assets tied up in court for years; 600,000 workers out of jobs, at least temporarily; disproportionate damage to the inner cities where Chrysler was a major employer; 20,000 suppliers, many well managed and technologically advanced, also driven to the wall.

"So Chrysler would not be just another bankruptcy," Riegle concluded, "any more than a nuclear explosion would be just another bomb going off, and no intelligent and responsible Government should permit the unleashing of such a devastating, uncontrollable and far-reaching chain of events."

Testifying in support of helping Chrysler, Eagleton honed in on the critics' concern about the precedent being set. "What is the precedent," he asked, "of standing rigidly on some supposed principle while one of our major auto makers, and perhaps the entire U.S. auto industry, is overwhelmed by foreign competition which finds itself particularly well served by our energy crisis?" Eagleton contended that in our mixed economic system, he could find a precedent for almost any action. The genius of America's system was adaptability to problems at hand, and in this case, federal guarantees, however risky, were far preferable to letting Chrysler go under.

Robert Byrd was not on the committee, but had been following the situation closely and asked to testify. Two weeks earlier, he had expressed the view that "Chrysler must exhaust all self-help possibilities before the Government could properly offer assistance." He was not sure that test had been met but was pleased that Treasury's loan guarantee proposal would require the company to raise additional unguaranteed capital. But Byrd's principal point was Chrysler's employees should receive a substantial part of Chrysler's stock as a condition for federal help to Chrysler. By creating an employee stock ownership plan (ESOP), "Chrysler's work force would be offered a tangible financial incentive to make the sacrifices which the Treasury plan would require." Byrd made it clear that he meant "blue collar employees," since Chrysler's white-collar employees already held a significant amount of stock.

Moreover, Byrd argued that "the bitter medicine" of requiring Chrysler to provide its employees with one-third of the stock would deter other companies from seeking federal help. "Diluting existing shareholders' ownership, together with the inevitable election of employee representatives to the board of directors, will discourage all but the most desperate companies from approaching the Government for help," Byrd observed. "To authorize federal assistance without this disincentive would pass an unacceptable windfall from the Federal government to Chrysler's financiers."

ON NOVEMBER 15, THE more liberal House Banking Committee approved the Chrysler bailout by a vote of 24–17. The next day, the Chrysler workers voted to approve the three-year contract negotiated by Fraser and the other union leaders. It broke with UAW's long tradition of "pattern bargaining" by getting a less generous deal from Chrysler than from GM and Ford. But the rank and file accepted their leaders' view that the terms were necessary because Chrysler was "on the brink" of going under.

Nevertheless, several Senate Banking Committee members condemned the action by the House Committee. Former commerce secretary Peter Peterson, who had significant stature on the Hill, told the Banking Committee that he would reluctantly rather let Chrysler fail than set a precedent. After testifying himself on November 19, Doug Fraser told the press that based on the attitudes of the Senate Banking Committee, he felt less optimistic that Congress would bail out Chrysler. "After listening to some of the comments in there," Fraser said, "I began to wonder."

Opposition from staunch free-market advocates was expected. But the idea of rescuing Chrysler was also under assault from the left. By 1979, consumer advocate Ralph Nader had been a national icon for almost fifteen years. Since he burst into the public consciousness in 1965 with his book *Unsafe at Any Speed,* no one had played a larger role in forcing change on the reluctant auto companies. On November 20, Nader testified in vehement opposition to saving a company "with a two decade pattern of mismanagement, which includes . . . the production of too many of the wrong kind of vehicles at the wrong time and the production of too few of their better selling vehicles at the right time." Nader ripped Chrysler for opposing every effort to improve fuel economy and auto safety, including the installation of seat belts, and urged that as a condition for any federal aid, Chrysler should be required to manufacture only safe and fuel-efficient cars, and mass transit equipment.

Jake Garn injected a note of humor, saying that Nader's testimony disturbed him because he found himself agreeing with so much of it. But Garn quickly went on the attack, ripping Nader for being one of the "toughest arm-twisting people that come around this Hill" and for "being anti-business, anti-profit, pro-government" in virtually every case. Garn went on to say that if the American consumers knew what Nader was costing them, through excessive government regulation, "they would have run you out of the country."

The exchange became unexpectedly infused with emotion when Nader noted that Garn's wife had been killed in a car accident in 1976:

> Nader: I suspect, Senator Garn, that some senator's personal tragedy might not have occurred if the auto industry had listened to some of us in the early years to build safer cars.
> Garn: I think that is one of the cruelest comments that you have ever made. Yes, my wife died in an auto accident.
> Nader: And she could have been saved. She could have been saved with cars that should have been built 20 years ago.

After an angry exchange about the details of the accident, Garn exploded:

> Garn: That's a personal tragedy of losing my wife of 19 years, to interject that into a hearing. What kind of a human being are you?
> Nader: A human being who is working to save lives on the highway. Don't try and over-emote. I'm saying that safer cars would have saved many Americans, including people in a crash of that kind. And for you to try to pillory me because I am trying to say that your wife could have been saved in a casualty of that kind is irresponsible.

The next day, Citicorp Chairman Walter Wriston testified against the bailout, and the President of Manufacturers Hanover Trust, John McGillicuddy, said that Chrysler's creditors might not approve new loans. Opposition to helping Chrysler was producing strange political bedfellows, from Nader to the nation's leading bankers, from arch-conservatives like Barry Goldwater to neo-liberals like Gary Hart and Adlai Stevenson. With Thanksgiving imminent and the year-end coming fast, Chrysler, its future uncertain, hung by a thread.

IT WAS TIME TO fish or cut bait. At the heart of the effort, working every day to put together an acceptable compromise, were the key senators. Eagleton and Riegle were joined by Carl Levin from Michigan and Bill Roth and Joe Biden from Delaware, because of their deep interest in the fate of Chrysler's plant in Newark, Delaware. These Chrysler advocates would turn to Richard Lugar and freshman Paul Tsongas from Massachusetts, Banking Committee members who were positioned to cut the deal in committee.

The senators could use their positions to negotiate with all the key players, from the White House and Treasury Department, to Chrysler and the United Auto Workers, to the banks on Wall Street and Main Street. They had the credibility that came from their commitment to rescue Chrysler if at all possible. They had the ultimate authority because they were producing the legislation that would authorize the loan guarantees and set the conditions that had to be met before Chrysler would receive any money. They had the vantage point and the political acumen needed to assess what package could command congressional and public support. They rolled up their sleeves and worked tirelessly in a desperate effort to stave off Chrysler's collapse.

Anyone who has been involved in a high-stakes, multiparty negotiation will recall that there is a time, often late at night, when you are exhausted, when differences seem unbridgeable and failure appears likely, if not inevitable. But very often, the feeling of likely failure signals a prelude to the final negotiations and the concessions that everyone must make to reach an acceptable result. Although Proxmire was a political maverick, he had keen insight, and he had been through the New York City experience just eighteen months before. He predicted that despite his opposition, his committee would report a favorable loan deal for Chrysler before Christmas.

ON NOVEMBER 27, JUST after Thanksgiving break, Lugar, a key architect of the New York City loan guarantees, once again stepped forward with a crucial contribution to a possible compromise. He proposed a "pure" $4 billion bailout with only $1 billion coming from the government. His proposal would freeze UAW wages, freeze management wages, and require Chrysler to sell $50 million in stock in 1980 to dilute the value of the stock held by the current Chrysler shareholders. "This plan is based on the principle that taxpayers should help save the Chrysler jobs," said Lugar, "but only after driving a reasonable bargain in terms of real sacrifice by the workers, management, stockholders and bankers who are asking for the help." Tsongas, who had been previously on the fence, expressed his willingness to support a package based on shared sacrifice.

On November 29, the Senate Banking Committee, by an emphatic 10–5 vote, approved the bailout for Chrysler that had seemed impossible just a few weeks before. Lugar and Tsongas, sitting at far ends of the committee dais (Proxmire referred to them as his "wide receivers"), produced the near-final bill.

"Shared sacrifice" had become the watchword of the day, and the bill certainly took pains to dole out misery for many. Chrysler stockholders would give up 40 percent of their shares to employees; banks, which had $400 million in outstanding loans to Chrysler, must lend $400 million more. Most tellingly, the Lugar-Tsongas bill required the UAW to give up the modest wage increases it had just negotiated with Chrysler for the next three years. A wage freeze for three years, at a time when inflation was running at 13–14 percent, could mean a 40 percent reduction in earning power. The freeze would save a potential $1.3 billion.

But negotiations were not quite finished. In fact, the bill inflicted too much misery for the UAW to accept. Its lobbyist, Howard Paster, who had worked for Birch Bayh and was widely respected on the Hill, called the proposed wage freeze "so unfair as to be unacceptable." Paster said "anti-union" senators "are laying the burden on us for saving the company. . . . If the price of preserving the company is not to feed their families and give up their homes, it may not be worth paying." On December 4, Doug Fraser termed the three-year pay freeze "unacceptable." On December 6, Chrysler issued a formal announcement denouncing the Senate banking bill as "unworkable because it would impair worker productivity and would cause a serious loss of highly skilled design, engineering and technical workers so essential to the company's future success."

Auto sales continued to plummet, increasing the precariousness of Chrysler's position. Chrysler said that without an interim loan, by January it would run out of money. The vise was tightening on all the key players.

On December 14, Mondale, speaking for Carter, said that it was essential for Congress to act immediately. Lugar said that he might bend on the wage freeze, if the UAW would make other concessions. "I'd rather see a demonstration of people trying to save their jobs rather than negotiate a figure," Lugar commented. "The wage increases are only increases if you have a job, if there is a wage at all." Tsongas reluctantly indicated that he would compromise further, but expressed doubt that a reduced package—$3.3 billion rather than $4 billion—would be enough to save Chrysler.

On December 18, both the House and Senate took up the Chrysler loan guarantee bill. Quick approval seemed certain in the House. The Senate outcome remained in doubt as the debate began. Roth argued that the wage freeze was too much to ask; many of Chrysler's best employees would leave for other jobs. Lugar responded strongly that "the brain drain argument is specious from beginning to end." He described himself as being "weary of those who are serving as champions of Chrysler and of the workers trying to diminish any potential success of this package." Off the Senate floor, the key senators negotiated to find the delicate balance: inflicting enough pain on Chrysler and the UAW to win Senate support, without pushing the company and the union into outright opposition.

Riegle held the Senate floor for hours, rebutting every attack on Chrysler's plan, warning that the Senate bill asked too much of the UAW, and chiding Proxmire for his earlier support for assistance to American Motors. It soon became clear that he was stalling for time. He wanted the House bill to pass first, with its $400 million contribution by the UAW. When the House passed the legislation at 7:30 p.m., by a vote of 271–136, it seemed to have the effect sought by the UAW's supporters.

Byrd called a brief recess and again summoned the key senators to his office. They emerged with a deal: the final vote would be postponed until the next day, and Eagleton, Biden, and Roth offered a new version of the legislation cutting the UAW contribution to $400 million. Despite the opposition of Proxmire and Lugar, the Eagleton-Roth-Biden amendment passed the Senate by a 54–43 vote. Chrysler supporters were jubilant. The final vote seemed close, and the outcome assured.

Just as swiftly, a furious Lowell Weicker punctured the celebratory atmosphere with the promise of a filibuster. "I assure the Senators that I and many others on their side of the floor now feel it is the worst of all worlds," Weicker boomed. "I suspect there would be no great difficulty in assuring that debate will be thorough, very thorough." Weicker would use the filibuster to delay, and Chrysler, with cash evaporating, needed the legislation quickly.

No one doubted Weicker's seriousness. Byrd summoned the key senators into his office again, where they were joined by Fraser, and they produced a new compromise. Labor's contribution was set at $525 million, and the government's loan guarantee figure was increased to $1.5 billion to match the House legislation. Levin attempted an amendment that would have granted Chrysler $500 million of the $1.5 billion as "interim financing," to be granted immediately while the overall package was being worked out. Proxmire, and many other senators, adamantly refused. Weicker called Levin's bridging loan "the wickedest part of the proposal" and threatened to filibuster again. Levin and Riegle went to Gerald Greenwald, Chrysler's chief financial officer. "They told me 'pick your poison,'" Greenwald later recalled. "We could either have no act at all, or an act without interim financing. I took about three minutes to call Lee [Iaccoca] and told them to do what they had to do." Supporters of the amendment staged a tactical retreat, and the Levin amendment was defeated.

Byrd went the extra mile to ensure that the debate would finish. Byrd did not have a close relationship with Weicker, and he rarely left the Capitol when the Senate was in session. But this time, Byrd startled Weicker (and the receptionist in Weicker's office) by coming to see Weicker unannounced. He reviewed the situation with Weicker, including the fact that the legislation had been rewritten to meet some of Weicker's objections. They met for a short time, and Byrd went back to the Capitol. Weicker made his forceful arguments against the bill but did not filibuster.

Neither did anyone else, despite the intensity of many senators' feelings about the issue. Goldwater said of the bill that it was "probably the biggest mistake Congress has made in its history. I think future historians will register this as the beginning of the end of the free market system in America." Within a few years, the absurdity of this prediction would be quite clear as America embarked upon a period of cowboy capitalism.

The Senate passed the Chrysler Loan Guarantee Act 53–44 and sent it to conference with the House. The legislation passed without a filibuster, and it passed without a 60-vote majority. Although Democrats made up most of the majority, with Republicans most of the opponents, the vote did not break on absolutely partisan lines. Supporters of the Chrysler loan guarantee included liberal Republicans Jack Javits and Mac Mathias, but they also included Bob Dole, Ted Stevens, John Tower, and Harrison Schmitt, along with Lugar and Roth, Republicans who had played a key role. Democratic opponents included Dale Bumpers, Gary Hart, Adlai Stevenson, and Abe Ribicoff. The unprecedented issues produced some senatorial judgments that could not have been predicted.

In conference, the Senate and House split the difference on most of the key issues, including the UAW contribution, which was set at $462 million. When the legislation returned from conference, William Armstrong, the freshman conservative Republican, carried on a "mini-filibuster," pointing to the working copy of the bill with its "chicken scratching and underlinings" as evidence of the Congress's "unseemly haste." But in time-honored Senate tradition, Byrd had made the legislation the last bill to be considered before the senators could leave for Christmas. Armstrong ultimately stopped talking, and the Senate approved the conference report by a vote of 43–34. Again, support for the bill fell well short of the 60 votes that would later become the standard requirement for doing anything in the Senate.

The year 1979 had been a brutal year for America, marked by a deepening recession, soaring inflation, energy shocks and gas lines, foreign competition of surprising and sudden quality, and a palpable threat to Chrysler, the U.S. auto industry, and the industrial heartland. Given those realities, most Americans did not want lectures about the workings of the free-enterprise system. They wanted evidence that the U.S. auto industry and the Midwest had an economic future. They wanted their government to take action to save jobs and keep Chrysler in business, while exacting enough pain to ensure that other companies would be very reluctant to approach the government to be bailed out. Goldwater's dire prediction seemed far less relevant than the heartfelt words of Tsongas. Describing how his hometown of Lowell, Massachusetts, had been crushed by the decline of the textile industry, Tsongas declared that he "did not want to do to Detroit what others have done to my city."

Just as it had done the previous year with New York City, the Senate struck the right balance to make legislation possible. It accomplished that in weeks, rather than months or years. It did it by majority vote, not super-majority. Chrysler survived, returned to profitability quickly, and the federal government ultimately came out ahead. No other corporation stepped forward to get the same help, administered as the same bitter medicine. The Senate had come through again, as it did on other big issues, with different senators stepping forward to take the lead, and opponents making their case strongly, but allowing the Senate to conclude the debate and reach a result. It was the way the Senate worked when it still worked.

Less than two weeks later, in a low-key White House ceremony, Jimmy Carter signed the Chrysler Loan Guarantee Act of 1979 while Douglas Fraser and Lee Iaccoca looked on. After the ceremony, Fraser, who had asked to see the president, was escorted into the Oval Office. He advised Carter that despite the administration's support for Chrysler's rescue, the UAW would be supporting Ted Kennedy against Carter. Perhaps the rescue had taken too long; perhaps the legislation demanded too much of the UAW members. But, more likely, one of the most liberal forces in the Democratic Party had simply chosen to support the most liberal Democrat running for president. Whatever the reason, Carter must have been bitterly disappointed.

chapter 16

SALT II

Death by a Thousand Cuts

IN LATE 1979, CARTER WAS STRUGGLING TO COMPLETE HIS SIGNATURE energy legislation, rescue Chrysler, and cope with the hostage situation in Tehran. Still unresolved was the fate of SALT II, a treaty that Carter fervently hoped the Senate would approve. Along with Middle East peace, nothing mattered more to Carter. Yet the Senate's ratification remained uncertain, seemingly always just beyond his reach.

Carter had hoped to restructure the SALT II negotiations to seek deeper reductions in nuclear arms, but after the Soviet Union rebuffed his initial bold proposals, the administration essentially returned to the complex SALT II framework that had been under negotiation by the Nixon and Ford administrations. Carter certainly expected the completion of the treaty negotiations and Senate approval no later than by the end of his second year. After that, he hoped to pursue deep nuclear arms reductions separately.

However, the relationship between the superpowers was deteriorating. The administration was deeply mistrustful of Soviet activities in the Horn of Africa and elsewhere. Carter continued to hammer the Soviet Union on human rights violations. His commitment to human rights was deeply felt, and it was good politics in the United States, but it enraged Leonid Brezhnev and other Soviet leaders.

By the spring of 1978, the Soviets were punishing dissidents at home, and the United States responded with economic sanctions. W. Averill Harriman, ambassador to the Soviet Union during World War II and the American diplomat most respected in Moscow, advised Carter that Brezhnev was very emotional about the deterioration in the relationship, calling it the worst it had been since the Soviet invasion of Czechoslovakia a decade before. The two countries often seemed much closer to rekindling the Cold War than reaching a SALT II treaty.

Nevertheless, despite the rising tensions, the SALT II negotiations continued to move forward, if fitfully. Carter remained deeply committed, and the Soviet Union, facing the strain of enormous defense expenditures, had incentives of its own for reaching a treaty. By the end of September 1978, with the Camp David talks behind him, Carter, pleased by an excellent meeting with Soviet foreign minister Andrei Gromyko, authorized Cyrus Vance to explore a summit meeting with Brezhnev at which the treaty would be signed.

But the road to the summit contained unforeseen potholes. Carter's surprising decision to recognize the People's Republic of China infuriated the Soviets, particularly when the final communiqué between Carter and Chinese Vice Minister Deng Xiaoping suggested that the two countries would cooperate in opposition to "hegemonic powers," a term the Chinese often used to describe the Soviet Union. By February 1979, the State Department, which had previously focused its concern on whether the Senate would ratify the SALT II treaty, was worried that there would be no treaty to ratify.

Still, throughout this turbulent period, Secretary Vance and Soviet Ambassador Anatoly Dobrynin had not given up. They met more than twenty-five times to keep the treaty alive. In February, Carter met with Dobrynin and made it clear that he still wanted a treaty. Impressed with Carter's determination to improve U.S.-Soviet relations, Dobrynin noted that, for the first time in their meetings, Carter had not mentioned human rights.

Finally, after more than two years of negotiation against the backdrop of a turbulent relationship, Jimmy Carter and Leonid Brezhnev met in Vienna on June 15, 1979. The leaders exchanged views on the full range of issues in their relationship. Carter outlined his hopes for future limits on nuclear arms and told Brezhnev that the United States had vital interests in the Persian Gulf and the Arabian Peninsula that the Soviet Union must respect. Brezhnev responded that the Soviet Union was not the source of instability in Northern Africa or the Persian Gulf and expressed unhappiness at the casual way that the United States defined remote regions of the world as being in its vital interests. Plainly, notwithstanding the treaty that had brought them together, the leaders would continue to disagree about almost everything.

Nevertheless, after resolving the last major treaty issue, related to the limitation on the Soviet production of Backfire bombers, the mood lightened and became celebratory. Carter conceded that the elegance of the dinner at the Soviet embassy surpassed that offered by the United States the previous night. Brezhnev observed that the American dinner had menus only in English, while the Soviet dinner menus were printed in both languages. Finally, on June 18, in Vienna's famous Hofberg Palace, Carter and Brezhnev signed the SALT II treaty, which they sealed with a formal embrace and a kiss.

The SALT II treaty that they signed was a far cry from the ambitious arms reduction agreement that Carter had initially hoped for. It provided for modest cuts in major delivery systems. The limits on all missiles for each side was capped at 2,400, though that number would be slightly reduced by January 1, 1981. Submarine and land-based multiple independently targetable reentry vehicle (MIRV) missiles would be counted in a subtotal of 1,320 on MIRV launchers; no missiles could have more than 10 warheads. The United States agreed to place no limits on Soviet heavy missiles or the Backfire bomber, a concession that would give the treaty opponents a major point to attack, even though an addendum to the agreement limited the Soviets to producing no more than 30 Backfire bombers each year. Heavy bombers were counted against the total number of launchers permitted and against the subtotal for MIRV launchers.

The arcane provisions of the agreement brought to mind a candid admission made by Sam Nunn during the Warnke debate that it was almost impossible to grasp the mind-numbingly complex details of arms control. But ultimately, the fate of SALT II would inevitably turn on more fundamental issues—namely, senators' views of the value of arms control agreements, their assessment of Soviet intentions, and the overall state of the relationship between the superpowers.

Fundamental disagreements between the SALT II advocates and the treaty opponents remained. The treaty advocates believed that arms control agreements were essential to maintaining a positive relationship between the two superpowers and were therefore too important to be linked to other Soviet activities around the world. Moreover, they believed, as Warnke had written, that the Soviet Union would respond positively if the United States showed a willingness to get off the arms race treadmill.

The opponents believed that any arms control agreement should be conditioned on improved treatment of Soviet dissidents and a cessation of aggressive

Soviet actions in the Third World. Treaty opponents were deeply mistrustful of Soviet intentions. They believed that the Soviets were working to achieve nuclear superiority to tilt the balance of power to ensure that the United States and their allies would have to stand by and accept their aggressive actions in the developing world. The opponents also had deep doubts about President Carter's commitment to a strong defense. Carter had cancelled the B-1 bomber and the neutron bomb, increasing the fears of treaty opponents that he was allowing U.S. defenses to be weakened.

Détente between the United States and the Soviet Union had been on the skids even before Jimmy Carter became president, and the Senate and public mood toward the Soviet Union had further deteriorated during Carter's time in office. Carter had been shocked in January, in a meeting with senators mostly presumed to be SALT II supporters, to find how hostile they were toward the Soviet Union. Abe Ribicoff said that the Soviets did not understand the Senate; Henry Bellmon said they were two-faced; Jack Javits expressed the view that the Soviets were not willing to give up anything for a SALT treaty. Others were similarly negative. Perhaps the fact that a treaty had been signed would change their views, but significant residual distrust remained. Moreover, the Senate's consideration of the SALT II treaty would take place in the long shadow cast by the Iranian Revolution.

Treaty opponents, led by Scoop Jackson, had been gearing up for a long time, and the bleak public mood, marked by a lack of confidence in Carter and a fear of America's declining power, ensured that the struggle to get the treaty ratified would be clearly uphill.

JIMMY CARTER LANDED AT Andrews Air Force Base on June 18, 1979. Two hours later he was addressing a joint session of Congress, urging support for the treaty he had just brought back. Carter emphasized that the SALT II treaty was not a favor that the United States was doing for the Soviet Union; it was in the national security interest of the United States. Arguing that our economic and military power surpassed that of any other nation, Carter reminded the Congress that "a nuclear war would bring horror and destruction and massive death that would dwarf all the combined wars of man's long and bloody history."

Understandably, Carter seemed tired. His speech received a lukewarm response. In the coming days, he would find that his Vienna triumph had generated no groundswell of public support in a country preoccupied with the price of gasoline. To the extent that Americans were thinking about foreign policy, anti-Soviet sentiment in America had risen during the past year, probably in part because Carter had harshly criticized the Soviet Union in the Horn of Africa as an atheistic nation and a strategic threat to the United States.

In the Senate, the initial signs were ominous. Alan Cranston of California, the Democratic Whip, was perhaps the most passionate Senate advocate of the SALT II treaty. Cranston had been a foreign correspondent for two years before World War II. When an abridged version of Adolf Hitler's *Mein Kampf* was published, sanitizing Hitler's anti-Semitism and martial intentions, Cranston published an unabridged and annotated version to make Hitler's full message clear to the public. A committed believer in world government, Cranston authored a book on America's failure to join the League of Nations and became president of the World Federalist Association. His path to political power came through the peace movement and the creation of the California Democratic Council, which unified the Democratic clubs throughout the state. Cranston was a practical politician and a supremely successful fund-raiser, but he was also a deeply idealistic opponent of nuclear weapons. After Carter's address to the Congress, Cranston said that the treaty had the support of fifty-eight senators, nine short of the two-thirds needed for ratification. Cranston's ability as a vote counter was respected, but at that moment, even fifty-eight votes felt like an optimistic count. Howard Baker, whose support had been indispensable for Carter's foreign policy triumphs, said only that he was leaning against the treaty.

Jackson had been on the offensive against the SALT II treaty for a long time. He had already pronounced the agreement "substantially unequal and unverifiable." Rather than categorically rejecting the agreement, Jackson said there would be a major effort by the Senate to improve the treaty "through amendments and plugging loopholes. The Senate will take seriously its mandate not only to consent but to advise." He did not explain how the Soviet Union would react to major changes in a treaty that had been seven years in negotiation by three U.S. presidents. Amendments and reservations had worked with Panama—barely—but did not make for a promising strategy for dealing with the world's only other superpower.

On June 12, as Carter prepared to leave for Vienna, Jackson unleashed an extraordinary blast in a major speech to the Coalition for a Democratic Majority, an organization formed by many of his closest allies to spearhead opposition to the treaty. Jackson was not an electrifying speaker, but on this occasion, his fiery message more than made up for his plodding style.

"In the seven years since the Moscow summit," Jackson stated, "we have been testing the proposition that despite the lessons of history, it is possible to achieve an accommodation with a totalitarian superpower through a negotiated agreement. The danger is real that seven years of détente are becoming a decade of appeasement." In case any listener missed the central point, Jackson went on: "It is ominously reminiscent of Great Britain in the 1930's when one government pronouncement after another told the British public that Hitler's Germany would never achieve military equality, let alone superiority."

A few days later, Jackson expressed the view that "since the President has taken over in 1977, he has moved from a hard bargaining line with the Russians and on each and every meeting after the first meetings, concessions were made of a substantial nature, and that is appeasement." By mid-June, Baker and Frank Church were talking about the necessity of adding amendments or reservations to the treaty.

Cranston observed that "if Jackson were for [the treaty], there would be no contest." This was obvious, but the real question was whether any treaty could be approved despite Jackson's vocal opposition. By one estimate, Jackson would ensure that thirty senators, mostly Republican, would oppose the treaty. To prevail, the Carter administration would have to win the votes of sixty-seven of the remaining seventy senators. In the best case, any path to victory in the Senate would be torturous and narrow, with numerous potential pitfalls ahead. As the Carter administration began a vigorous national public campaign for the treaty, it also focused intently on the several key senators without whose support ratification would be impossible.

Months of study had led Robert Byrd to favor the treaty. John Culver, one of the leading SALT II advocates, recalled with amazement visiting Byrd's office and seeing the volumes of SALT hearings that Byrd had pored through and highlighted. Byrd had also been impressed, on a trip to Europe, that the European allies regarded SALT II as essential to peace and stability in Europe. At Carter's request, Byrd had visited the Soviet Union to explain to Soviet Premier Brezhnev the role that the Senate would play in the process of treaty ratification. Byrd's commitment was strong, and he stood prepared to do everything necessary to get Senate approval, just as he had on the Panama Canal treaties.

As always, the list of key senators started with Baker. He had demonstrated his statesmanship during the Panama Canal fight; he was also one of a handful of senators who had been on the winning side of every major battle during the Carter years. The White House thought Baker might be willing to play a constructive role, but his price appeared to be high. He had noted that "the Senate will give its advice before it gives its consent." The White House would have been dismayed to know that Baker had received a considerable amount of his SALT briefing materials from Jackson's staff. "His office worked for several months to give me the best information," Baker recalled. "Scoop's staff was far superior to anything else we had seen." Jackson had approached Baker about joining him in formulating amendments, but Baker had declined, indicating that he would work with other Republicans or proceed on his own. Neither possibility boded well for the Carter administration.

Sam Nunn was the undecided Senate Democrat whose support was most pivotal for the administration. Young, thoughtful, and respected, Nunn was a protégé of Richard Russell and House Foreign Affairs Chairman Carl Vinson. He hoped to extend Georgia's powerful influence on national defense issues. Nunn had spent months studying the treaty and related defense issues; he wanted to be a major player on the issue and, if possible, to help the Democratic president from his state.

Nunn had just been reelected by a comfortable margin, so he was in no danger politically, although going against Jackson would not be easy. Nunn seemed willing to consider voting for the treaty if Carter would call for a significant increase in the defense budget, and Carter cared enough about winning Nunn's support for the treaty to endorse the MX mobile missile system and consider a 5 percent increase in the defense budget. Carter agreed to the MX missile with great reluctance. "It was nauseating to confront the gross waste of money going into nuclear weapons of all kinds," he wrote in his diary on June 4. Zbigniew Brzezinski had persuaded him that the green light for the MX was the only hope for gaining Senate approval of the treaty. The maneuver, however, risked forfeiting the support of leading Senate advocates of arms control.

George McGovern, a steadfast leader on such issues, already felt that SALT II did not go far enough in bringing about real reductions in the nuclear arsenals. Back on March 2, McGovern, along with pro-SALT senators Mark Hatfield and Bill Proxmire, had warned Carter that his emphasis on a defense buildup was undermining the purpose of the SALT II treaty. McGovern certainly would not favor the treaty if the price for its passage was an increased defense budget and a potential new arms race. "I don't think [the treaty] is worth fighting for," McGovern said. "I think we should just scrap it."

Despite the daunting challenges, the Carter administration kept plugging away, lobbying senators and working to build grassroots support around the country. By early August, prospects seemed to have brightened somewhat. With major press attention on the Foreign Relations Committee hearings, Baker proved unable to mount a strong case against the treaty and seemed to withdraw from the debate. Jackson's arguments had become more predictable than persuasive. Although he remained the most formidable opponent of the treaty, many senators found his perpetual distrust of the Soviet Union too extreme. Conservatives began to worry that SALT negotiations had gone on so long that the public was not engaged in the issue, which would make a vote for the treaty much easier politically than a vote for the Panama Canal treaties.

The American public may not have been focused on the treaty, but inside the Senate, the intensity was mounting. Byrd believed that the debate on SALT II would be every bit as consequential as the debate on the Panama Canal treaties had been, and he prepared with his customary thoroughness. Byrd and Cranston received significant support from Gary Hart and John Culver, two strong arms control advocates who had sought to serve on the Armed Services Committee because they believed that it should not be dominated by defense hardliners. Culver had a fierce temper and was one of the few senators willing to take on Jackson. He was particularly angry at Jackson's staff members, who he believed were leaking confidential information in order to tilt the public debate against the treaty. Culver prodded John Stennis, the chairman of the Armed Services Committee, to hold a committee meeting to stop the leaks, and when it occurred, the meeting was unusually angry and personal. The stakes were getting very high, and the pressures were building.

Frank Church's strong leadership in the Panama Canal fight had won him few friends in Idaho, where he was facing a strong challenge from Republican Congressman Steve Symms. He was a natural supporter of the SALT II treaty, to the point that it was impossible to conceive of Church opposing the treaty, or the treaty being ratified without Church. At the same time, he understood his precarious political situation as the 1980 election drew nearer, and he was looking for ways to demonstrate his commitment to a strong defense and tough foreign policy. In fact, Church was trying to walk much the same tightrope that Carter was walking. Events would soon show he was working without a net.

In late August, Church's committee staff came to him with the startling news that a brigade of Soviet troops had been found in Cuba. Richard Stone, another committee member, had first surfaced the issue of the Soviet brigade without much fanfare. Church, however, seized the opportunity to take a tough stand. After calling Secretary Vance to forewarn him, Church announced that if the brigade were not removed, the Senate would not approve the SALT II treaty. "The United States cannot permit the island to become a Russian military base, 90 miles from our shores," Church declared at a hastily called press conference in Boise, Idaho, on August 30. "The President must make it clear that we draw the line at Soviet penetration of Latin America."

Church's high-profile position put Jimmy Carter in a nearly impossible position, but the Carter administration's response proved to be a comedy of errors. Carter first pronounced the brigade "unacceptable" and then amended his position to say that "the brigade is certainly no reason to return to the Cold War." Secretary Vance stated on September 5 that the brigade did not represent an increase in the Soviet presence in Cuba; in fact, it soon became clear that an equivalent number of troops had been in Cuba since 1962.

Struggling to salvage the treaty that he had worked so hard for, Vance implored Dobrynin to give him some help:

> Vance: "Anatoly, can't you get them to move some ships around—to move some troops a little bit—so that we could say that it was now acceptable?"
> Dobrynin: "You know after the Cuban missile crisis; there is no way we are going to do that sort of thing; it would be too humiliating."

But, at the same time, while trying to defuse the crisis, the administration moved to prove its toughness toward the Soviet Union. On September 7, the White House announced that the U.S. government would go ahead with the full-scale deployment of a new ICBM missile—the MX.

Byrd and Cranston, working tirelessly to build support for the treaty, were irate about the administration's handling of the Cuban missile brigade, which they regarded, in Byrd's words, as a "pseudo-crisis." On September 23, Byrd went to the White House to tell the president that the White House had to tamp down the brigade issue if the SALT II treaty was to be saved. It was "inappropriate for a mighty nation to go into delirium," Byrd said, "over 2,300 Soviet troops that had neither airlift nor sealift capability to leave Cuba." Byrd urged that the White House and congressional leaders cool their rhetoric. In fact, completely uncharacteristically, Byrd urged that there be no more consultation with the Hill on this issue, because it only tended to hype it further.

After meeting with Byrd, on the advice of White House counsel Lloyd Cutler, Carter convened a group of fifteen "wise men," led by Clark Clifford, to review the situation and report back to him. After grilling representatives of the intelligence community, Clifford and his group concluded that the brigade had in fact been in Cuba since 1962. The issue had only flared up because the intelligence community had somehow lost track of the brigade, and it had now resurfaced.

On October 1, Carter addressed the nation in an effort to put the issue behind him. He stated that he had received assurance from the Soviet Union that the combat brigade did not pose a threat to the United States or Latin America. In his view, the brigade issue was not a reason to return to the days of the Cold War. But continuing to juggle the views of his feuding advisers, Carter still tried to have it both ways, telling the nation that he was not ready to rely completely on the Soviet assurances. Consequently, he was ordering increased surveillance of Cuba and establishing a permanent, full-time Caribbean task force that would increase U.S. ability to respond rapidly to encroachments in the region. It was amateur hour, from start to finish.

Carter would never forgive Church for his willingness to exploit the presence of the Soviet brigade in Cuba in order to make himself look tough to his Idaho constituents. It also disillusioned some of Church's liberal admirers. But the SALT II treaty had been hanging by a thread for a long time. Skepticism about the negotiations process, suspicions about Soviet intentions and actions after the U.S. defeat in Vietnam, deep concern about Carter's commitment to a strong defense, and a darkening international picture presented an impossible combination. On November 9, the dovish Foreign Relations Committee reported the treaty favorably by an unimpressive 9–6 vote. Despite Carter's support on December 12 for Sam Nunn's enormous 5.6 percent increase in the defense budget for 1980, on December 20, the Armed Services Committee voted 10–0, with seven abstentions, that the

SALT II treaty, "as it now stands, is not in the national security interest of the United States."

In fact, the SALT II treaty was dead weeks before the committee votes took place. On November 1, Howard Baker announced his candidacy for president in the Senate Caucus Room where the Watergate Committee hearings had made him famous. Baker said that voters should judge him by his ability to defeat the SALT treaty: "If we defeat the treaty, we will be saying: we intend to be the masters of our own fate again. And we have the confidence to negotiate a new SALT treaty that is safe for this country under a new president who will be safe for this country." Since no one had come up with a scenario by which the Senate would ratify the treaty without Baker's support, his announcement sounded the death knell for SALT II.

Back in June, in an appearance at the National Press Club, Baker had indicated a willingness to serve as a broker between Carter and the Senate hawks, if Carter was willing to bend. However, shortly after Carter returned from Vienna, Baker had announced that he would support the treaty only if significant changes were made—including a requirement that the Soviets dismantle all the SS-9 and SS-18 missile launchers, something the Soviets would never accept. Baker's signals had been increasingly clear: he would not support SALT II. Carter respected Baker so much that he continued to harbor the belief that the "good Baker" who had saved the Panama Canal treaties would do for his arms control treaty what Dirksen had done for Kennedy's Limited Nuclear Test Ban Treaty in 1963. World events would soon reveal this fantasy to be an illusion; in fact, just about everything was different in 1979 than it had been in 1963.

ON DECEMBER 27, THE Soviet Union launched a sudden invasion of Afghanistan. Unlike the brigade in Cuba, this Soviet invasion was sufficient reason to return to the Cold War. The two superpowers promptly did so.

Jimmy Carter finally accepted the inevitable. On January 3, he asked Majority Leader Byrd to defer action on the SALT II treaty. Carter would later describe the "failure to ratify the SALT II treaty and secure even more far-reaching agreements on nuclear arms control" as "the most profound disappointment of my presidency."

The Senate, which had given Carter a great victory in the Panama Canal treaties, had become the graveyard of his dreams for controlling and reducing nuclear arms. On the Panama Canal treaties, the Senate insisted on important reservations, but had generally deferred to Carter's leadership. Although the issue presented huge political problems for many senators, most of them recognized that a new relationship with Panama was in the national interest and grudgingly admired Carter for taking on a long-standing problem that had become our most severe challenge in the hemisphere.

SALT II was a very different matter. There was less inclination to defer to the president, particularly after he got off to a rocky and inconsistent start in dealing with the Soviets. Jackson regarded himself, with some justification, as one of the world's leading experts on defense issues. He undoubtedly disliked and distrusted Carter, but personal animus was not the principal thing driving him. No one doubted that Jackson would have battled Gerald Ford and Henry Kissinger just as fiercely if they had brought the SALT II treaty to the Senate. Younger Democrats on the key committees, such as Nunn and John Glenn, remained unconvinced about the merits of the treaty. A number of arms control supporters, led by McGovern, threatened to jump ship if the price of the treaty was a massive increase in defense expenditures. And no road to Senate ratification existed without Baker, who had decided quite early not to support it.

Ironically, Carter had intuited the situation at the end of 1977. His diary includes this entry: "My sense is that the Republican hierarchy has decided to go along with us on Panama and fight us on SALT."

SALT II had never generated great excitement outside the Beltway, and its demise was barely noticed by the general public. The American people were instead focused on the plight of the hostages in Iran, brought home to them nightly by Ted Koppel, in the news show that would become *Nightline*. The anger and frustration that Americans felt was almost palpable. But the public and its political leaders gave Carter strong support as he tried to resolve this unprecedented situation. The public applauded Carter for shutting off Iranian oil imports and for freezing Iranian assets that were in U.S. banks. Daniel Patrick Moynihan said that Carter was handling the crisis with "great competence, steadiness, and assuredness." Baker offered Carter his "unwavering" support. During the first few weeks of the crisis, Carter was given virtually a free hand to deal with the crisis. Senators said that Carter was helped by Khomeini's "irrationality." One senator stated: "there's not a damned thing you can do when you're dealing with a crazy man."

The year ended on an ironic note. Panama agreed to admit the shah at our request. Senators who had supported the controversial treaties expressed delight, saying it vindicated their votes. "This is the first great friendship dividend to flow from the Panama Canal treaty," Church enthused. Opponents of the treaty—John Tower, Pete Domenici, Jim McClure, and Jesse Helms—said they still didn't like it.

1980

chapter 17

A TOUGH
POLITICAL
CLIMATE

1979 HAD STARTED WITH THE RETURN OF THE AYATOLLAH KHOMEINI and the Iranian Revolution and proceeded with the nuclear accident at Three Mile Island, surging oil prices, gasoline shortages, and the precipitous drop of the U.S. economy. The year ended with U.S. embassy personnel being held hostage in Iran and the Soviet Union invading Afghanistan. A year that had started with the bright promise of peace between Israel and Egypt had turned out to be one of the worst in memory.

Now, 1980 had begun—an election year. Every two years, one-third of the Senate seats are contested. This year, out of the thirty-four Senate seats in play, the Democrats held twenty-four. Two Democratic incumbents, Abe Ribicoff and Adlai Stevenson, were retiring; twenty-two Democratic incumbents would be running. In contrast, only ten Republican seats were in play. For the Democrats, the numbers were bad, and the political climate was even worse.

Gaylord Nelson was one of the Democratic incumbents seeking reelection. Part of the vaunted class of 1962, Nelson had cruised to victory in 1968 and 1974, winning 62 percent of the vote each time. As one reporter noted, Nelson had "a lifelong tendency to loaf or joke his way through the campaign." Nelson had always anticipated that the political environment had to be more difficult than it had been in 1974, when the Republicans had suffered through Watergate and Nixon's resignation. How much more difficult could not have been anticipated.

In January, Nelson received a memo from his pollster, Peter Hart. An old-fashioned politician, Nelson didn't much believe in the importance of polls. Nevertheless, his staff convinced him to commission an initial "benchmark" poll. Hart and his associates polled 617 Wisconsin voters in depth, conducting fifty-five-minute interviews with each.

The news was not good. "There is a widespread feeling throughout the Wisconsin electorate that this nation is in deep and serious trouble," Hart's report began. "About two-thirds of the voters (64%) are of this opinion. This pessimism is more acute among the elderly than among younger voters."

Hart had asked what trends in America constituted a "serious threat to the American way of life." The largest number (37 percent) suggested "moral threats which cut right through the social fabric." This view was shared by younger and older voters alike. They cited "a lack of morality and religion and the breakdown of family structure. They are afraid that people have become too selfish and greedy, that the people are apathetic and just don't care." Hart concluded that their sentiments "suggest a re-emergence of the more traditional approach to life and a turning away from the more publicized free-wheeling attitudes of the 1960's and 70s."

Unsurprisingly, Wisconsin voters were worried that economic conditions "also pose a threat to the American way of life." Inflation and the cost of living was the item mentioned most often. "Other economic threats," Hart noted, "include welfare spending and abuse, credit buying, union power, and big business controls." His bottom line on the economic threats was particularly sobering to a liberal Democrat like Nelson: "These economic threats are more commonly identified with the failures of liberal policies than with the failures of conservative policies."

Wisconsin voters also perceived major threats to the American way of life on the political front. "Leading the list is government's interference in people's lives," Hart noted. "Other threats of a political nature include government spending; bureaucracy and waste; high and unfair taxes; government corruption; lack of unity and patriotism; women's rights; ERA gone too far; liberalism; government leadership, representatives and Communism."

None of this came as a surprise to Nelson. He knew that people were anxious and that 1979 had been a terrible year. He understood the vulnerabilities of an incumbent senator running at a time when voters were disillusioned with government. He had run in 1968, when the country was virtually torn apart by divisions over the Vietnam War and violence in the cities. Still, he believed that Wisconsin voters liked and trusted him, and that his progressive record showed him to be on the cutting edge, part of the solution, not the problem.

But Hart's polling included some troubling indicators about Nelson in particular. He had been a liberal and extraordinarily popular governor. He had won five consecutive statewide elections. He had been an early opponent of the Vietnam War, a tough critic of the automobile and pharmaceutical industries, and the first great environmentalist in the Senate—the father of Earth Day in 1970. Yet, even with those achievements, only 47 percent of those polled said he was doing an "excellent" or "good" job; 41 percent rated his performance as "fair" or "poor." Two-thirds of the voters agreed with Nelson on the issues, but he did not get much credit for his effectiveness. Nelson got high marks in several areas, including work on the environment, but low grades on the issues of most concern to the voters—inflation, energy, welfare, and foreign policy.

Hart was polling for nine other Senate Democrats in 1980, and he offered Nelson at least some encouraging news. Wisconsin was more centrist and more resistant to the rightward trend he was seeing in other states. However, he also pointed out Nelson's special problem: the constant visibility and extraordinary popularity of Wisconsin's senior senator, Bill Proxmire. Nelson had not kept up with his hyperactive colleague. Overall, Hart saw his unimpressive job performance rating, after seventeen years in the Senate, "as a serious liability . . . in light of the voters' generally pessimistic mood." "We cannot overstress," Hart noted, "the necessity of an active, aggressive and hard-hitting campaign to assure Gaylord Nelson of victory."

NELSON WAS HARDLY THE only senator facing a difficult battle. Frank Church, for one, operated under no illusions about how hard his race for a fifth term was going to be. The liberal Church was an outlier in one of the most conservative states in the nation. In 1976, as Jimmy Carter had been elected president, Gerald Ford had crushed Carter in Idaho by a lopsided 60–37 percent margin. The right wing had been gunning for Frank Church for years, particularly since his investigation of the intelligence community. He had further stoked their anger by his leading role in "giving away" the Panama Canal and "selling out" Taiwan.

The National Conservative Political Action Committee (NCPAC), a creation of Jesse Helms's former staffer Charles Black, had targeted Church early, eighteen months before the election. "By 1980," Terry Dolan, the twenty-eight-year-old NCPAC director predicted, "there will be people voting against Church without remembering why." Defeating Church was NCPAC's highest priority, because his chairmanship of the Foreign Relations Committee gave him such high visibility. "Defeating him would send a shiver down the spines of every liberal in the Senate," Dolan observed.

The Republicans had a strong candidate in Congressman Steve Symms, who managed to combine an affable personality and an impressive military record with hard-edged right-wing views and a willingness to do whatever was needed to win. In 1971, Symms had been so disillusioned with America's drift toward socialism that he gave serious thought to moving his family to Australia's Great Barrier Reef. He decided instead to run for Congress, won a seat in 1972, and had become a leading congressional conservative. Church had traditionally shown great political courage on the big issues, such as Vietnam and the Panama Canal. Now, unsurprisingly, he seemed to be looking for ways to placate conservative voters as the election neared. In 1979, he had voted against Carter's two most admired liberal judicial nominees, Congressman Abner Mikva, who was vehemently opposed by the gun lobby, and Patricia Wald, who was not. Columnist Mary McGrory rebuked Church, quoting one of his colleagues who said: "There must be some limit to what a man will do to come back here."

Worse, Church's attempt to take a tough stance on the Cuban brigade had misfired, winning over none of his opponents and disillusioning many of his admirers. "The Soviet brigade," McGrory wrote, "offered him a chance to show that he could stand up to those Commie canal-rustlers." Church's former speechwriter, Bill Hall, said: "It was not a proud moment to have the Senate Foreign Relations chairman from Idaho trying to outdo every right-wing wacko in the Senate." SALT II had failed for many reasons, but Church's bellicose intervention was so visible and striking that many people, starting with Jimmy Carter, would always blame him, unfairly, for its demise.

The campaign showed every sign of becoming vicious. Symms intended to hammer the traditional pocketbook issues of inflation and unemployment, leaving NCPAC and ABC (Anyone but Church) to slam him with an unending series of harsh negative ads. The New Right would also bring to Idaho former intelligence officers and government officials who would rip Church for undermining U.S. security. Retired General John K. Singlaub blasted Church for "emasculating" the CIA. Former ambassador to Chile Edward Korry accused him of suppressing evidence regarding Chile in order to protect the Communists and the Kennedy and Johnson administrations. "I have often stated publicly," Korry noted, "that if I could ever use my voice to . . . remove Frank Church from public office, I would put aside everything to travel to this state." So he did—and Church's race only got tougher as a result.

UNLIKE IDAHO, THE NEW Right did not have a strong presence in the state of Washington. Many people admired Warren Magnuson for his extraordinary legislative accomplishments and his service to the country. But at seventy-six years old, Maggie was slowing, weakened by diabetes and a sore foot that caused him to shuffle rather than walk. A Peter Hart poll of the state showed significant weaknesses, and a particular vulnerability to opponents arguing that it was time for a change. His closest advisers urged him not to seek reelection, sparing himself the strain of an ugly, uncertain campaign. Maggie promised to consider their views, but ultimately decided that he would run again. "You told me that I shouldn't run again last time," he was heard to growl.

"The boss loved his job, loved his work," a former adviser recalled. "He couldn't imagine himself not being a senator," another noted. "It's what I like, what I can do, and what I know," said Maggie. His decision to run again would set up a contest with Washington Attorney General Slade Gorton, a moderate Republican, and a lean, vigorous candidate whose devotion to running contrasted starkly with Maggie's increasing inability to walk.

Magnuson could still raise money; he was, after all, the chairman of the Appropriations Committee and the former chairman of the Commerce Committee. One evening, Ed Muskie had agreed to stop by a fund-raiser at the Mayflower Hotel that Magnuson was doing with corporate lobbyists. Muskie came in and saw Magnuson, aged, exhausted, and unfocused, standing in a receiving line shaking hands automatically with the lobbyists that filed by. After staying a few minutes, Muskie went out to his car, and described the scene to Leon Billings, his administrative assistant. "Don't let me do that," Muskie implored. "Don't let me stay too long."

Jack Javits, one of the only senators whose accomplishments rivaled Magnuson's, spent the early weeks of 1980 wrestling with the same question of whether to run again. Javits had intended to not seek a fifth term, but now, as the time for decision loomed, he vacillated. Politically, he recognized that he might be vulnerable to a challenge from a right-wing conservative in the Republican primary, of the sort that had defeated Clifford Case. He had no independent political operation around the state for he had always relied on the powerful machine of his friend, Governor Nelson Rockefeller. Now Rockefeller was no longer governor. Javits was a Washington and world figure but had done very little in recent years to cultivate his home base.

Much more serious was his deteriorating health. Javits had developed a slackening in his abdominal muscles, which made it difficult for him to walk and climb stairs; the condition was diagnosed as motor neuron disease. He consulted the best doctors, and they told him the ailment tended to be slowly progressive but would in no way affect his mind. Although he did not name the ailment in his autobiography, Javits had amyotrophic lateral sclerosis (ALS), often known as Lou Gehrig's disease, the progressively crippling nerve disorder that would ultimately paralyze and kill him.

By itself, Javits' condition should have decided the issue. Still, he wavered. America was in crisis, and he believed, understandably, that no one could bring his combination of intellect and experience to the problems at hand. In February 1980, he remained inclined not to run. But a State Department briefing convinced him that the effort to bring the hostages home was going badly. As he later wrote in his memoirs, Javits "began to wonder whether the United States was doing all it could." From that question it was only a small step for Javits "to ask whether [he] had any business leaving his post of duty while the troubles of the United States proliferated."

In the last week of February, he made a list of the pros and cons and found it came out perfectly even. He drafted a statement saying that although the decision was "close and agonizing," on balance, he thought he should not run. A close friend advised him that whatever he decided, he should not use a "deathbed statement" like the one he had devised. Javits realized that he would feel terrible leaving the Senate and reversed his decision at virtually the eleventh hour. He announced for reelection and disclosed his affliction with motor neuron disease.

He would write in his autobiography: "I thought I had benefited millions of Americans through my legislation on domestic matters and that I had aided my country by helping to shape foreign policy on some of the greatest events of our time. . . . What took over my thinking was the call of duty and conscience—and the call of what I knew how to do best, which was to be a United States senator. . . . There was no argument to stand up against that."

In truth, Javits, like Magnuson, could not conceive of the Senate without him, or his life without the Senate.

AS THE SENATORS GEARED up for their races, Ted Kennedy was absorbing one devastating blow after another in his challenge to President Carter. In presidential politics, unexpected things happen all the time. Many candidates who look very strong before a campaign can fade in the crucible of the spotlight. Kennedy certainly had weaknesses as a candidate, particularly the vulnerability that Speaker O'Neill had pointed out—the "moral issue," arising out of voters' doubts about his conduct at Chappaquiddick. But even more important, the events of November and December had completely transformed the political landscape.

Jimmy Carter was the president and commander in chief at a time of national crisis. Carter had responsibility for dealing with the hostage crisis, the first challenge from militant Islam, and the Soviet invasion of Afghanistan, a return to the darker days of the Cold War. The White House had skillfully gained political advantage from these very real crises, claiming that Carter could not leave the White House to campaign. The president withdrew from a *Des Moines Register* debate that he had accepted months before. The public understood and supported this decision. They rallied behind Carter. Under the circumstances, Kennedy's challenge to Carter seemed almost unpatriotic. The polls showed Kennedy going from a 2:1 favorite to a 2:1 underdog.

Kennedy struggled to find his footing. His speeches were generally lackluster, as he muted his liberal themes in an effort to build support more broadly. Former senator Dick Clark of Iowa had given up his position as refugee coordinator in the Carter administration in order to join the Kennedy campaign. Clark's son attended Grinnell College in Iowa and was excited that Kennedy would be speaking there. But after the speech, Clark's son expressed disappointment at Kennedy's speech; it was tepid and uninspiring. He advised Clark that all of his friends had felt the same way. The internal workings of the campaign worried Clark as well. Kennedy would sit around with a group of consultants, getting conflicting advice from all of them. At one point, Clark recalled, a lengthy debate took place between the consultants about whether, or under what circumstances, Kennedy should wear glasses.

When Kennedy finally did take a strong position, it seriously backfired. On December 3, in a San Francisco interview, Kennedy said that the shah "ran one of the most violent regimes in the history of mankind—in the form of terrorism and the basic and fundamental violations of human rights, in the most cruel circumstances, to his own people." He also said that the shah had "stolen umpteen billions of dollars from his country." This was a tremendous misstep. Whatever the shah's failings, and they were enormous, critics could now paint Kennedy as giving aid and comfort to the Khomeini regime by focusing attention on the shah. Peter Hart, polling for the Kennedy campaign, found that 54 percent of the public agreed with the statement: "I feel that Edward Kennedy has hurt America by speaking out against the former Shah of Iran."

Meanwhile, the press hammered him on Chappaquiddick. Even the *Boston Globe,* his hometown newspaper, editorialized: "Chappaquiddick was not just an auto accident. Many Americans suspect, not without reason, that Kennedy's handling of its aftermath is another case of a politician stonewalling. And they wonder whether Kennedy would lie to the American people in a more public crisis."

In January, Carter responded to the Afghanistan invasion by imposing an embargo on grain sales to the Soviet Union. Kennedy attacked him, arguing that the embargo would hurt Iowa's farmers but not the Russians, who could easily buy grain elsewhere. It was a transparent attempt to win over the Democratic base in a crucial early primary state—and his criticism had no effect. Iowa's farmers wanted nothing more than to do their part to help Carter stand up to the Soviet Union. On January 21, the Iowa caucuses took place, with an enormous turnout of more than 100,000 people on a freezing winter night. Carter smashed Kennedy, winning 59 percent of the precinct delegates.

Shortly before the Iowa caucuses, Kennedy, sensing defeat, had urged John Culver, Iowa's senator, to abandon his neutrality and endorse him. Culver was not just any Senate colleague; he was one of Kennedy's best friends, a Harvard classmate, and a former Kennedy staffer. However, Culver, facing his own difficult race for reelection, gave it a night's thought, and told Kennedy that he would have to remain neutral.

In fact, beyond the early statements of Jackson and McGovern, Kennedy received very little support for his challenge to Carter from his Senate colleagues. Joe Biden, who maintained close ties with the White House, advised Carter that out of fourteen Democratic senators running for reelection, only one, John Durkin of New Hampshire, favored Kennedy. Kennedy's advisers were embittered that Daniel Patrick Moynihan, who had urged him to make the race and promised to support him, never did.

Kennedy's challenge to Carter presented a difficult choice to Senate Democrats. Overwhelmingly, they liked Ted; he was both a colleague and a friend. They admired the way he worked in the Senate and his resilience in coming back from a series of personal tragedies. Many of them questioned Carter's performance as president and did not have close personal ties to him. Throughout 1979, they certainly did not see Carter as an asset at the top of the ticket.

But even before Kennedy's rocky start and the dramatic change in the political climate, many Senate Democrats had their reservations about his challenge. They understood that the country was moving to the right and recognized the need for Democrats to pursue their longstanding goals through other approaches. Carter's efforts to find the center may not have been successful, but most Senate Democrats doubted that Kennedy's full-throated liberalism pointed the way to success.

Even more fundamentally, Carter was a Democratic president. The senators believed he should be challenged only under certain special circumstances. It had been agonizing but probably necessary in 1968 for Eugene McCarthy and Robert Kennedy to challenge Lyndon Johnson; they responded to a profound moral issue and a disaster for the country: the Vietnam War. In 1980, for many senators, it was difficult to find a similar justification for Ted Kennedy's challenge, even if the liberal wing of the party disliked Carter. And even in 1968, senators remembered that Democratic fratricide took its toll; the divisions in the party did not heal quickly enough and cost Hubert Humphrey the presidency. Overall, the Democratic senators would stay neutral, either because they had their own races, or because they saw no compelling reason to support Kennedy.

JIMMY CARTER HAD SHOWN great restraint in avoiding possible military actions, earning the respect and support of the American people. But by the end of March, the American people were growing frustrated and angry. So was the president. Iranian militants had held more than fifty Americans hostage in the U.S. embassy for almost five months.

In early March, a United Nations mission attempting to resolve the hostage crisis had left Tehran in failure after Khomeini had sided with the militants and refused to allow the UN inspectors unconditional access to the hostages. On March 30, hopes rose that a deal was at hand. That day, Iran's Revolutionary Council voted to take control of the hostages from the militants. The deal required the United States to recognize the role of the Iranian parliament in the hostage crisis and to refrain from taking any propaganda or military action against Iran.

On April 1, Carter felt confident enough to go on national television, suggesting a deal was at hand. His appearance probably influenced some undecided voters in the crucial Wisconsin primary, which he won. But by day's end, the "deal" had begun to fall apart. Abolhassan Bani-Sadr told Carter that his statement accepting the deal did not meet the conditions for transferring the hostages. With that, another opportunity to resolve the crisis and free the hostages had passed. Jimmy Carter faced the question that future presidents would face with Iran and other difficult situations—what happens when steadfast, good-faith efforts at restraint and diplomacy produce no results?

Carter's response was to take a harder line. A week later, he slapped a trade embargo on all U.S. goods to Iran, threw all the Iranian diplomats out of the United States, and asked Congress to allow Americans with claims against Iran to move against $8 billion in blocked Iranian assets. In an April 17 televised news conference, Carter made it clear that the military option was on the table, although any military action would not take the form of invasion or combat.

It was an odd and awkward attempt to combine toughness with continuing restraint. Before too long, it would become clear that Carter's statement foreshadowed the rescue mission that an elite Delta Force unit was training for in North Carolina. The commando unit, under the leadership of Colonel Charles Beckwith, was preparing for the daring mission at a mockup of the U.S. embassy in Tehran. Later, they would practice nighttime desert flying at Yuma, Arizona, while studying Farsi and Iranian customs.

On April 11, Jimmy Carter opened a foreign policy breakfast meeting in the Cabinet Room by saying: "Gentlemen, I want you to know that I am seriously considering an attempt to rescue the hostages." By the end of the meeting, after a full briefing by General David Jones, the chairman of the Joint Chiefs of Staff, and Secretary of Defense Harold Brown, Carter had made the decision to approve the rescue mission, with the strong support of Walter Mondale and all of the senior advisers present. Deputy Secretary of State Warren Christopher, sitting in for Secretary of State Cyrus Vance, said that he could not take a position because he had not yet spoken to Vance.

Vance's subsequent objections did not change the president's determination. Vance later pulled Hamilton Jordan aside to remind him that he had been general counsel at the Pentagon and learned to his regret to be very skeptical of assurances from the military.

Carter's decision to approve the rescue mission was not communicated to any of the Senate leaders, even though Mondale and Vance had been briefing a bipartisan group—Robert Byrd, Howard Baker, Ted Stevens, Frank Church, and Jack Javits—since the early days of the hostage crisis. The briefings had helped keep the Senate's support for the president; Baker, splitting his time between the Senate and the campaign trail, had been particularly supportive.

Another senator, however, virtually stumbled on to the existence of the planned operation. Joe Biden was on a fact-finding mission in the Persian Gulf for the Foreign Relations Committee. Biden was accompanied by Bill Bader, the committee staff director, and John McCain, the popular navy liaison with the Senate. At a stop in Oman, Bader, a former naval officer, asked Biden if he would like to join him on a visit to the aircraft carrier *Nimitz*, anchored off shore. While Biden and McCain watched the sailors of the *Nimitz* conducting drills on the carrier desk, Bader explored the ship's lower decks and was startled to find eight very large Sea Stallion helicopters. When the executive officer of the *Nimitz* found what Bader had discovered, he became extremely agitated and tried to swear Bader to secrecy.

Bader, however, reported to Biden about the helicopters and his belief that they were going to be used for a hostage rescue mission. Bader asked Biden if he should share the information with Church, who was already pressing the administration on whether it planned to take action toward Iran. Biden told Bader that he was absolutely obligated to tell his chairman, and Bader did. Church used the information to press the administration further on whether it had plans for military action to rescue the hostages; in fact, he introduced a resolution saying Congress should be informed of any such military action. This no doubt further worsened Church's relationship with the White House, but the secrecy of the mission remained intact, with apparently no other senators being informed.

On the evening of April 24, Byrd came to the White House for dinner with the president. The eight helicopters were already in the air, heading for the designated landing place in the desert outside Tehran. Carter and Byrd met for nearly two hours. Carter outlined the potential military operation to rescue the hostages. Byrd told him that he should consult with the Senate before approving such an operation, for the president would benefit from having Senate support. It was the obvious moment for Carter to tell Byrd that he had already approved the operation, and it was already under way. He did not do so. Carter would write later that he trusted Byrd completely but concluded that Byrd would prefer to be informed at the same time as other congressional leaders.

The rescue mission failed tragically. Damage to three helicopters reduced the number of operational craft to only five, when six were needed to carry off the mission successfully. One of the helicopters collided with a C-130 transport that had transported the Delta Force rescue troops, killing eight of the men aboard. Carter consented to abort the mission and went on television at 7 a.m. the next day to explain what had happened and to take responsibility.

The next day, Byrd heard the devastating news that the rescue mission had been tried and failed. He was enraged, understandably, that Carter had not told him that the rescue mission was under way. It was not Carter's first mistake in dealing with the proud and complicated majority leader, but this was the one that tore their relationship irreparably. Byrd had played a central role in virtually every domestic and foreign policy achievement of the Carter administration; it was impossible to overstate how much he had done for Carter. Byrd undoubtedly believed that Carter should have brought together the small core group of Senate leaders to be briefed about the mission, if not consulted before Carter had made the decision. But to meet with Byrd for nearly two hours without telling him that the mission was under way was unforgivable.

Byrd held his regular weekly press conference the next day. Saying that Carter had outlined the rescue plan for him on Wednesday night, Byrd said that he was "puzzled" that Carter didn't tell him that the operation was under way even though they spent one hour and forty-five minutes in the Oval Office together: "I don't know what his reason was. I was under the impression that it was not something that was imminent."

Byrd also said that he had advised Carter to delay a covert action until the Europeans had agreed to new sanctions and to consult with a minimum number of senators in advance of any covert action. "I thought that there would be support (among senators) and that the burden would be spread around," Byrd noted, "and that such support in the event of failure would be comforting." Byrd bolstered Carter by expressing the view that the War Powers Act did not require prior consultation because the raid was not intended to take territory, kill Iranians, or threaten the government. But he also offered the view, somewhat gratuitously, that he would not have given the operation a 50–50 chance of success, but hadn't had all the details.

Other senators expressed mixed reactions. Dole said he respected "the president's honest and understandable desire to bring the crisis to a successful close. He has manfully accepted responsibility for the mission's failure, and he has access to information not yet available to the rest of us." Baker offered unqualified support for Carter: "The plan was well-conceived, well-planned and a well-guarded secret. The only quarrel I have with the president is that we should have done it a long time ago."

Jackson was angry that he could not get a clear answer from the Defense Department on whether the administration had "reasonable assurance" that the mission could have succeeded. He called the outcome "nothing short of a disaster." Church suggested that launching the operation without consulting Congress violated the War Powers Act, a claim that Muskie and Cranston ridiculed.

Secretary of State Vance had never been able to overcome his objections to the rescue mission. Worn down from the challenges of the job, and endless bureaucratic warfare with Zbigniew Brzezinski, Vance had threatened to resign several times previously. Now he tendered his resignation to the president, and Carter accepted it. Two days later, Carter surprised and pleased the Senate by nominating Muskie to be secretary of state.

In the immediate aftermath, the failed attempt to rescue the hostages seemed to bring a kind of relief to Americans. Carter stated at his press conference: "There is a greater failure than that of incomplete success. That is the failure to attempt a worthy effort, a failure to try." Talk shows and newspapers picked up the theme. A poll by Pat Caddell showed that the operation "had lanced the festering boil."

But for friends and foes around the world, the damage to America's prestige was clear. Yitzhak Rabin, the former Israeli prime minister and army chief of staff, spoke for many when he asked sarcastically: "America doesn't have enough helicopters?"

On May 4, Carter ended his pledge to refrain from campaigning while the hostages remained imprisoned. Jackson said that Carter was doing the "sensible" thing and should have done it sooner. He also said that Carter needed to break his own and the nation's obsession with the hostages and move on to the nation's larger economic and foreign policy problems. Exactly six months had passed since the hostages were taken. The failed rescue mission marked the end of a period when Carter benefited from national unity and operated almost free from criticism. It had been a long, dark period, and no end was realistically in sight. It was time to resume business and politics as usual.

TED KENNEDY SUFFERED A crushing defeat in the Illinois primary on March 18, but rallied to win crucial victories in New York and Connecticut a week later. After Carter's victory in Wisconsin on April 1, Kennedy managed to capture Pennsylvania narrowly on April 22. Momentum turned drastically against him in May, when Kennedy lost eleven out of the twelve primaries contested, winning only in the District of Columbia, losing key states all across the country, such as Indiana, Nebraska, Maryland, and Oregon.

The delegate count was now running against him, yet Kennedy battled on, finding his voice and benefiting from public discontent with Carter as the hostages remained in Tehran and the economy continued to weaken. On June 3, Kennedy won convincingly in California, New Jersey, and three smaller states, while Carter narrowly won Ohio and two smaller contests. The primary season ended with the president having clinched the number of delegates needed for the nomination, yet with Kennedy still in the race, having finished strongly.

Most Democratic leaders believed that it was time for the Democrats to mend fences. Kennedy's campaign repeatedly requested a debate with Carter as a condition of pulling out. The president and the senator met in the White House on June 5 to discuss the matter, but it did not go well. Carter asked Kennedy to promise to support the Democratic nominee, and Kennedy avoided the question. They argued about whose ads had been harsher. The next day, Carter told his staff that he had decided to debate Kennedy, but Mondale argued against it, saying such a debate would be demeaning. Carter mulled it over and decided that Mondale was right.

Striking similarities exist between the Carter-Kennedy contest and the battle between Barack Obama and Hillary Clinton in 2008. Like Kennedy, Clinton started the race as the overwhelming favorite. She had a campaign that was over-confident, top-heavy with consultants, and absolutely profligate in its spending. She suffered a shocking defeat in Iowa, putting her on the ropes, fell behind in delegates, lost most of the primaries and caucuses, found her voice, and rallied strongly in the large states late in the campaign. She stayed in the race longer than many Democrats thought appropriate.

But there was one major difference: Kennedy was running against a Democratic president. Once the primaries were over, the hard decision to acknowledge defeat should have followed. Instead, he stayed in the race, demanding a debate with the president, fighting for his views to be reflected in the Democratic platform, calling for an open convention, and, seemingly, waiting for some lightening to strike that would reverse the tide. When he finally had to bow out, it was little surprise.

Carter would be the Democratic nominee, but his weaknesses had been exposed—and Ronald Reagan, riding a building Republican wave, would soon put Carter and the Senate Democrats to the test.

chapter 18

AMERICA'S
LAST FRONTIER

IN COMPARISON TO THE PREVIOUS THREE YEARS, THE LEGISLATIVE agenda of 1980 looked sparse. One major legislative challenge remained—a matter of historic magnitude. The Senate would decide on the future of Alaska and resolve the clashing interests of those who wanted to preserve its natural beauty and those who saw its oil, mineral wealth, and timber as vital to the state, and the country's economic future.

The debate about the disposition of Alaska lands dated back to when President Dwight Eisenhower signed the Alaska Statehood Act on July 7, 1958, allowing Alaska to become the nation's forty-ninth state on January 3, 1959. The legislation gave Alaska 104 million acres of formerly federal territory to be its economic base. The statehood act did not address the claims by native Eskimo, Indian, and Aleut tribes that they still legally owned the whole of Alaskan territory. In 1971, the native claims were resolved when Congress and the Nixon administration, moving rapidly to give oil companies access to the rich Prudhoe Bay oil strike, passed legislation giving the tribes their choice of 44 million acres. Under pressure from conservationists, Congress and the Nixon administration also agreed to specify a deadline of December 18, 1978—seven years—for setting aside roughly 80 million acres for conservation. The deadline had passed, and it was now time to make the difficult decisions.

Starting in 1974, Congress began to consider how to translate the conservation mandate into law. Initially, members began producing a number of bills, each dealing with a particular park or monument to be established, chipping away at the 80 million acre mandate project by project. In 1975, the National Park Service (NPS) and conservationists conceived the idea of incorporating all the new parks and monuments into one massive piece of legislation. Working out that legislation would be a staggering task, but it made sense to face all the decisions, and the difficult trade-offs, in a single stroke.

Alaska was literally the last frontier of the United States. Its awesome magnitude defied the imagination of most Americans, including members of Congress. Not only was Alaska one-fifth as large as the entire lower forty-eight states, it contained America's highest mountains, wildest rivers, largest glaciers, vastest wilderness and forests, and stunning amounts oil, gas, and mineral wealth. As the congressional debate would progress, members would find themselves routinely discussing the future of pieces of Alaska as big as the state of Indiana or Virginia.

Jimmy Carter was the first president to come to office having made a strong commitment to environmental protection and conservation in his campaign. That was good politics, because of the popularity of the environmental cause and the rising strength and activism of the environmental movement. But it also reflected Carter's deep personal commitments; he was passionate about the natural beauty of his own state and of the rest of the country. As governor, he had made protecting the environment a high priority, and he saw conservation and environmental protection as a fundamental part of his stewardship as president. Consequently, the Carter administration would be determined to protect as much of Alaska as possible. Eighty million acres was the target set by the 1971 legislation for conservation, but a later Congress, and a president committed to conservation, could up the ante if they so chose.

The action started early in Carter's term. On April 25, 1977, Interior Secretary Cecil Andrus, the former governor of Idaho, put a high priority on preserving Alaska lands but indicated he would wait until autumn of 1977 to make a recommendation on how much land should be protected. That was not fast enough for seventy-nine members of the House, led by Congressman Morris "Mo" Udall of Arizona, who moved immediately to introduce legislation that would designate 115 million acres as federal wilderness. Udall, who had proven to be Carter's strongest opponent in the contest for the Democratic nomination, was a great conservationist. He was also the brother of Stewart Udall, the legendary secretary of the interior in the Kennedy and Johnson administrations, who had probably done more to conserve America's natural resources than any man since President Theodore Roosevelt. On May 19, 1978, the House approved a version of the Alaska Lands legislation, sponsored by Udall, by an overwhelming vote.

By contrast, there was no danger of the Senate rushing to judgment. The oil and gas industries had demonstrated their influence in the Senate clearly enough over many years, most recently throughout the debate over Carter's energy proposals. Alaska was rich in minerals, so the mining industry would be deeply involved in any discussions. Moreover, Alaska's astonishing forests were both great natural resources and extraordinarily valuable to wood and paper industries. The western Republicans who had come to the Senate in the 1970's generally were part of the "Sagebrush Rebellion," which was hostile to the federal government and came down on the side of exploiting the resources of the West to spur the economy, rather than preserving them.

However, the environmental movement had developed into a strong and sophisticated legislative force, starting with the Clean Air Act of 1970 and the fight over the Supersonic Transport in 1971. The fate of Alaska was by far the biggest environmental issue that had arisen during the Carter administration—in terms of conservation, it was the biggest issue that had ever arisen—and the environmentalists were ready for a major battle. They could count on some stalwart environmentalists in the Senate, including Ed Muskie and Gaylord Nelson, the longtime leaders, and some recently elected senators with a strong commitment to the environment—John Chafee, Paul Tsongas, and Gary Hart.

THE STAKES WERE ENORMOUS, which ensured a tough and protracted struggle. The extraordinary animosity between Alaska's two senators injected an element of unusual, personal bitterness.

Ted Stevens was a pugnacious, combative World War II transport pilot who moved to the territory of Alaska at the age of twenty-nine, quickly becoming a visible and effective U.S. Attorney. Moving to Washington to serve as legal counsel to the Interior Department, Stevens had played a central role in drafting and securing passage of the legislation that granted Alaska's statehood. He ran for the Senate in 1968 and lost in the Republican primary. But when the incumbent Alaska senator died, Stevens was appointed to fill his term, arriving in the Senate in December 1968.

In later years, Stevens liked to describe himself as a "mean, miserable SOB." He often intimidated opponents through his power on the Appropriations Committee, his explosive temper, and his long memory for those who crossed him. But in 1980, he was the Republican whip, relatively moderate in his views, and respected for his willingness to make deals and stand by them. He had worked with Warren Magnuson on historic legislation to protect the nation's fisheries, and as a former government lawyer, he often stood up for the interests of federal workers. He had real friends across the aisle. He and his wife, Ann, were part of the Nelson social circle. The night that Tom Eagleton was dropped from the Democratic ticket by McGovern in 1972, Stevens cheered up a somber gathering of Eagleton and his closest friends by arriving unexpectedly with Alaskan salmon.

Alaska's junior senator, Mike Gravel, was elected to the Senate in 1968 and took his seat just ten days after Stevens. Gravel leaped to national prominence in June 1971 by holding a midnight meeting of his Public Works Subcommittee in order to read tearfully from the Pentagon Papers while the country waited for the Supreme Court decision on whether the Nixon administration could stop the *New York Times* from publishing the papers. The next year, Gravel again caught the national eye through an unorthodox campaign to become the Democratic vice presidential nominee, which included nominating himself at the Democratic convention. A University of Alaska professor later said: "Loose cannon is a good description of Gravel's Senate career. He was an off-the-wall guy, and you weren't really ever sure what he would do."

Senators from the same state sometimes encountered difficulties working together, but Stevens and Gravel truly hated each other. A historic decision about Alaska's future, which would have been momentous and difficult under any circumstances, would play out against the backdrop of their enmity.

The Senate had made an effort in 1978 to pass legislation on the Alaska lands, but had failed. Looking at the December 18 deadline for action set seven years before, Carter said on July 31, 1978, that if Congress was not willing to act to save Alaska lands, he might have to do so through administrative action. Carter's authority to act by executive order gave him leverage in negotiations, but using the authority risked the possibility that the state of Alaska might sue, and the ensuing litigation would create uncertainty lasting for years.

In September 1978, even as the natural gas legislation dominated the time of the Senate Energy Committee, the committee staff worked on generating new options for Alaska. By September 17, the committee was looking at a bill that nominally set aside 121 million acres for conservation, though in fact, much of the land would actually be open to mining, drilling, and other development. A coalition of conservation and environmental organizations vehemently opposed this bill, instead supporting the House's far more generous version of the same legislation. On September 20, the Energy Committee reached a tentative agreement to set aside 100 million acres for national parks and conservation areas. Jackson defended it as a strong compromise, but Stevens protested that it cancelled concessions that he had won earlier in the committee.

Jackson led the Energy Committee in one more effort to produce legislation beginning in July. On October 4, the committee agreed on a 95-million acre Alaska lands bill with fewer conservation restrictions than the House's bill. However, Gravel used an obscure provision of the Senate rules to block the committee action, and they had to reconvene and again approve the legislation. Jackson had begun talking to his House counterparts about the general shape of a conference bill, if he could get the Senate bill to the floor. He was not able to surmount the objections of Gravel and Stevens, and on October 15, the Alaska Lands Act had died, to be taken up in the next Congress.

The post-mortems indicated how much was at stake and the level of acrimony between the key players. Stevens accused Gravel of sabotaging the bill in an ad hoc meeting with the House by pushing extreme amendments even after he had told Stevens he would not do so. The House members, agreeing with Stevens, also blamed Gravel for "torpedoing" the bill. Jimmy Carter, however, blamed both senators for the breakdown, since they had aligned themselves with the oil industry and other commercial interests. He decided to wait no longer.

On November 16, Interior Secretary Andrus announced that 110 million acres of Alaska land would be closed to development for three years. The next day, Carter rejected a request from Alaska's Governor Jay Hammond that he refrain from issuing executive orders to protect Alaska lands from development. Hammond had offered not to challenge in court any federal actions on the land for one year if Carter would refrain from naming any part of the land a national monument, which would prohibit all drilling, mining, logging, and hunting. Carter refused, saying that he wouldn't agree to take anything off the table.

Two weeks later, on December 1, Carter used the authority granted to the president under the Antiquities Act to designate 56 million acres of Alaska lands as national monuments by executive order. "Because of the risks of immediate damage to those magnificent areas," Carter said, "I felt it was imperative to protect all of these lands. These areas contain resources of unequaled

scientific, historic and cultural value, and include some of the most spectac-
ular scenery and wildlife in the world." He called passage of Alaska lands legislation in the next Congress his highest environmental priority.

Carter's decision triggered a fierce reaction in independent, frontier
Alaska, which always had an intensely ambivalent relationship with the federal government and the lower forty-eight. (Alaskans cherished their freedom and wanted Washington to stay the hell away, other than providing the
massive amounts of federal funds on which its citizens and corporations relied.) Carter was burned in effigy in Fairbanks. Residents in the Cantwell
area organized a major act of civil disobedience, known as the Great Danili
Trespass, in which they entered the park and violated laws by lighting camp-
fires and firing guns. The towns of Eagle and Glennallen, located in the
shadow of newly designated monuments, issued official proclamations that
they would not respect National Park Service regulations, would not enforce
them, and would shelter those who violated them. Even months later, Carter
would express concern about landing in Anchorage on the way to Japan, because of "the uproar." When he landed, Governor Jay Hammond gave the
president a mule driver's whip, just in case he needed it.

Senator Stevens, accompanied by his wife, flew home to help restore calm
by reassuring angry Alaskans that he would protect their interests. That was
how it came to pass that, on December 4, 1978, they were on a Learjet that
crashed at the Anchorage International Airport, killing five people. Senator
Stevens survived, but his wife did not. Alaska's huge size made reliance on
private airplanes commonplace, and Alaska's harsh weather and mountainous
terrain made air travel much more hazardous. Hale Boggs, the popular House
Majority Leader, had perished in a small plane in Alaska just seven years before. But none of that made Ann Stevens's death any less stunning to the Senate, where she had so many friends.

Like John McClellan and Joe Biden before him, Ted Stevens would deal
with his devastating loss by throwing himself even more completely into his
Senate work. But Stevens would always blame Gravel for his wife's death: if
not for Gravel's filibuster, Carter would not have resorted to issuing the Executive Order, and Ted and Ann Stevens would not have had to be on that plane.

THE YEAR 1980 HAD become the time for decisive action, and presidential
politics would inevitably color the debate. On February 12, acting on Carter's
orders, Secretary Andrus ordered strict environmental protection for one-

tenth of Alaska for the next twenty years. Andrus said he "deeply regret[ted]" the action but believed it was necessary if Congress was not going to move legislation.

On May 3, Stevens, Jackson, and Tsongas met and exchanged proposed amendments for a floor debate that was scheduled to begin on July 21. They agreed on what amendments would be allowed: a substitute from Tsongas, and three amendments each from Stevens, Gravel, and Jackson. This represented an extraordinary effort by the Senate to reach a unanimous consent agreement that would ensure floor consideration and prevent a filibuster, nearly three months before the scheduled debate.

On July 21, the Senate began the long-anticipated debate on the Alaska Lands bill. President Carter called it "the environmental vote of the century" and promised conservationists that he would veto a bill that did not protect enough of Alaska's lands. The Senate Energy Committee version protected 102 million acres, about the size of California and Maine put together. The Carter-backed version protected 125 million acres, an area the size of California, Maine, and Indiana and was generally more restrictive of development of oil, gas, and timber. Dan Tate, the respected White House liaison with the Senate, advised Carter that the prospects for the legislation were "quite poor."

Stevens made his position clear in advance of the debate. Saying that Alaskans should have "the right to continue our lifestyle and traditional means of access," Stevens contended: "This measure doesn't go as far as extremists want, but it will double the area of the national parks, and do the same with the wildlife refuges, triple the existing wilderness. . . . Eight out of the 10 largest parks in the country will be in Alaska."

The Alaska Coalition of environmentalists had mounted their strongest lobbying effort in memory in support of the House version. It announced its backing of five Tsongas-sponsored amendments to restore restrictive "wilderness" and "wildlife refuge" designations to many areas the committee bill left more open. If the amendments failed to pass, Tsongas and Bill Roth would offer a substitute in an effort to accomplish the same thing. Stevens warned that he would oppose the legislation if any of the Tsongas amendments passed. He blamed Gravel for not getting votes for the committee bill or making his intentions clear.

Jimmy Carter, deeply committed on the merits, and with the presidential election less than four months away, hosted a rally of environmentalists in the East Wing of the White House. "On behalf of Americans who care about progress, beauty and the wilderness," Carter said, "preserving Alaska's price-less natural resources is my number one environmental priority . . . Alaska's beauty, diversity and resources are absolutely irreplaceable. We cannot afford to be short-sighted. We owe our children and our country so much more."

The next day, the environmentalists won a series of test votes on an amendment by Hart and Chafee to add 14 million acres of wildlife refuge to the 43 million included in the Senate Energy bill. Votes to table the amendment and to weaken it were all defeated by roughly 2 to 1 margins. Chafee, a passionate environmentalist, implored the Senate: "Never before and never again will we be able to set aside vast tracts of wildlife-rich lands for the enjoyment of future generations." The debate quickly become acrimonious, with Stevens warning that passage of the amendments could produce a "revolt" in the western states, although Secretary Andrus and Senator Hart were also westerners. Stevens also charged that the oil reserve maps being used by the Interior Department were falsified.

That explosion was just a prelude to the shouting match that took place on the third day of debate. Stevens was particularly upset with a Hart amendment that would designate 2.5 million additional acres as wildlife refuge that Stevens thought had been set aside for state control. He threatened a prolonged delaying action if compromise was not found. Both sides agreed to take the bill off the floor for several days in an effort to find common ground. Staff discussions went all evening on July 23, with the senators continuing to talk the next day in Robert Byrd's office.

Jackson, Stevens, and Mark Hatfield defended the Senate Energy Committee bill against conservationists Hart, Chafee, Tsongas, and Cranston. The environmental side had more votes, but faced the threat of a filibuster by Stevens if agreement could not be reached. Gravel moved in and out of the talks, opposing everything and suggesting opponents might prefer to wait for a Republican administration. Alaska governor Hammond reportedly favored asking Stevens to join a filibuster rather than accepting any Tsongas amendments or even a much-weakened version of the House bill. Environmentalists were leaning against making concessions to Stevens, because they essentially had everything they wanted protected through the executive order. But Stevens, Jackson, and Byrd said that they were still making progress and believed a compromise would be possible.

Five days later, on July 29, that crucial moment had arrived where failure looked all too possible, even likely. Governor Hammond, Stevens, and Gravel seemed to have given up on compromising with the environmentalists and urged defeat of the compromise bill that seemed to be emerging. Stevens acknowledged that the other side "came more than halfway" in meeting his demand for additional timbering rights in southeast Alaska, "but anything short of 450 million board feet is not enough." He said Tsongas and Cranston had also offered some additional mining land, but not enough to win his support. Probably near exhaustion, he contradicted himself, saying, "I have argued and argued and argued and won no concessions." Tsongas observed that because of the filibuster threats by Stevens and Gravel, the Senate should pass legislation close enough to the House bill that a conference could be avoided.

But too much was riding on the outcome to give up; a historic accomplishment remained within reach. And Stevens was not only a consummate dealmaker, but he had been so deeply involved in the founding of the state that he had a unique stature and credibility to speak for, and balance, all of Alaska's competing interests. He was very attentive to the energy, mining, and forestry industries, which were vital to Alaska's economy, but he also cared deeply about protecting Alaska's extraordinary natural beauty. If he were making the decision alone, he would undoubtedly strike the balance somewhat differently than Carter and the environmentalists would, but he believed that Alaska's future required a legislative solution, which meant reconciling diverse views through principled compromise. He also recognized and respected the fact that the whole country had a stake in Alaska's future, and that the Senate had emphatically backed the environmentalists' position.

On August 4, the negotiators announced that they had reached a compromise, which involved wrapping Tsongas' amendment into one substitute. Stevens said that he could not support the substitute but considering the strength that Tsongas had shown on test votes, he appreciated that Tsongas had been patient in listening to his objections. In contrast to Stevens and Tsongas' mutual respect in a tense situation, Jackson and Gravel were at each other's throats all day. Gravel accused Jackson of trying to railroad the bill through; Jackson accused Gravel of dilatory tactics. At one point, Tsongas yielded Gravel some time to speak. Gravel made a "scathing response," prompting Tsongas to observe that "every time I try to be reasonable, I end up pulling a stiletto out of my back." Gravel effectively filibustered with repeated quorum calls and motions related to the bill's strict time requirements, which had been agreed to specifically for the purpose of frustrating a filibuster. The Senate left town without finishing the bill.

Two weeks later, the Senate gave "all but final approval" to the Alaska Lands bill by approving a new substitute by a 72–16 vote. Tsongas, the principal author of the substitute, characterized the substitute compromise "as pretty much down the middle" between the House version and the Senate Energy version. Stevens said that the bill was "the best job we can accomplish under the circumstances" and said that Alaska had won 5.5 of its 7 major points and 81 percent of the concessions it had sought. He said that he still voted against the compromise and would try to improve it in the next Congress—not a likely prospect. On August 19, the Senate gave final approval to the bill by a 78–14 vote. Jackson urged the House to accept the Senate bill; "any substantive changes in this bill, in my judgment, will kill it." Stevens said that any concessions from the Senate bill would force him to filibuster; "that's not a threat; that's a promise." Mo Udall and the other House leaders seemed reluctant to go along.

On August 27, Gravel became the first sitting senator defeated in a primary challenge in 1980. Clark Gruening, the son of the legendary Alaska senator Ernest Gruening, whom Gravel had defeated twelve years before, had avenged his father's defeat. Gravel's defeat was welcomed by nearly everyone: Republicans, Democrats, environmentalists. His feckless and untrustworthy behavior during the negotiation process had rendered him one of the least-respected members of the Senate.

The Senate would adjourn early for the fall elections, leaving no time to finish the landmark measure. Its fate would depend on the outcome of the presidential election, now fiercely contested between Carter, Reagan, and a strong and respectable independent candidate, former Illinois Congressman John Anderson. Twenty-two Democratic senators, including some of the most famous names in the party, left Washington to go back to their home states, fighting for their political survival.

chapter 19

FIGHTING TO SURVIVE

BIRCH BAYH SAT IN HIS OFFICE IN AUGUST 1980, RUEFULLY CONTEM-
plating his prospects. Bayh had intensely enjoyed chairing the new Senate
Intelligence Committee, but no one could have predicted this assignment.
With only a few months left before the election in which both the president
and he would be running, it looked as though he would have to take on
Jimmy Carter in a most awkward and embarrassing way: by investigating
the activities of the president's brother. However, just like Gaylord Nelson
with the ethics code, Howard Baker with the Panama Canal, or Scoop Jackson with the natural gas legislation, Bayh understood that great senators did
not always get to pick and choose their defining issues.

Bayh had originally won his Senate seat from Indiana in 1962, with an
upset victory against veteran senator Homer Capehart. Elected at thirty-four,
a lawyer and a farmer who had only served in the Indiana state legislature,
Bayh came to the Senate with an "aw shucks," wide-eyed freshness that was
as genuine as it was rare. He was stunned one night in his first year in the
Senate, on the presidential yacht *Sequoia*, when Everett Dirksen, the Republican leader from the neighboring state of Illinois, spent an hour telling Bayh
what he had to do to get reelected. Plainly, he had made it into the Senate
club.

His first term was solid but unspectacular. Nationally, he became best
known for dragging his friend Ted Kennedy to safety when the small plane
carrying them had crashed on the night after the vote on the Civil Rights Act

of 1964. But serving on the Judiciary Committee, he also played an important role in the adoption of the Twenty-fifth Amendment to the Constitution, dealing with the thorny problem of presidential disability and succession.

Once safely reelected in 1968, Bayh naturally envisioned taking a more prominent role in the Senate. Like other liberal Democrats, Bayh detested Judiciary chairman James Eastland's views on everything, but like surprisingly many other liberal Democrats, he got along well with Eastland personally. In 1969, this relationship paid off when Eastland informed Bayh that he would be named chairman of the Subcommittee on the Constitution. Given the subcommittee's jurisdiction, which included the inflammatory issues of gun control, school prayer, and busing, Bayh joked that he was not sure whether Eastland was trying to do him a favor or end his career.

It proved to be a favor; Bayh's new assignment brought him national attention within months. Richard Nixon was intensely committed to remaking the Supreme Court "in his own image." After securing quick confirmation of Judge Warren Burger to replace Earl Warren as Chief Justice, the Nixon White House and Attorney General John Mitchell pressured Justice Abe Fortas, bloodied from Johnson's effort to elevate him to Chief Justice, to resign from the Court. With a new vacancy to fill, Nixon looked to the South for his next nomination and selected Judge Clement Haynesworth, a respected conservative judge from the U.S. Court of Appeals for the Fourth Circuit.

It looked like an unbeatable nomination, but the Senate Democrats, still angry about the treatment of Fortas, were itching for a fight. As subcommittee chairman, Bayh quickly took the lead of the coalition to oppose Haynesworth. He relished the constitutional issues involved and loved working with the unions, civil rights organizations, and other liberal groups that were major forces in the Democratic Party nationally. The judge's opinions in labor and civil rights cases provided ample ammunition to oppose him, and he had opened himself to criticism by adjudicating several cases involving companies in which he held stock. On November 21, 1969, the Senate rejected the nomination of Clement Haynesworth by a vote of 55–45, with seventeen Republicans joining thirty-eight Democrats, making Birch Bayh a bright new star among national Democrats.

During the Haynesworth fight, Bayh visited Bill Fulbright to make the case that Haynesworth should be rejected. After hearing out Bayh's argument, Fulbright protested, "I know this president. If we reject this nominee, the next one will be worse."

Fulbright was right. Incensed by the Senate's action but determined to continue advancing his "southern strategy" of rebuilding a Republican majority, Nixon quickly nominated another southerner, Judge G. Harrold Carswell, who also served on the Court of Appeals for the Fifth Circuit. Clear signs existed that Carswell lacked Haynesworth's stature as a judge, but Nixon gauged that the Senate would not be up to a second bruising confirmation battle.

Initially, it appeared that Nixon had guessed correctly. *Los Angeles Times* bureau chief Robert Donovan wrote that "Senators are mostly in no mood for another such donnybrook." However, damning press reports soon emerged about Carswell's past. *CBS Evening News* reported that in 1948, running for the Florida state legislature, Carswell told an American Legion rally that he would be "the last to submit to any attempt" to end segregation. This comment alone might have been dismissed as a youthful indiscretion of a sort not unknown to senators. But Carswell's statement went on to say: "I yield to no man . . . in the firm, vigorous belief in the principle of white supremacy, and I shall always be so governed."

Talented, energetic, empowered staff members provided some of the lifeblood of the Senate, and occasionally, those staff members would get out ahead of their principals, knowing (hopefully) how much rope they had to play with. On January 23, 1970, just four days after the nomination, Jim Flug, Ted Kennedy's subcommittee staff director, stepped forward to lead the opposition. Flug sat down with aides to Bayh, Phil Hart, Joseph Tydings, and civil rights and labor lobbyists. Most of the people in the room thought it was important just to make an effort against Carswell. Flug argued that the nomination could actually be defeated. He sent Senator Kennedy a memo entitled "How to Beat Carswell" that said, "I smell blood. I think it can be done if we get the full civil rights apparatus working, which it's beginning to do."

Overcoming his initial reluctance, Bayh again assumed leadership of the opposition to Nixon's nominee. When the floor debate ensued, Bayh declared that Carswell's "incredibly undistinguished career as an attorney and jurist is an affront to the Supreme Court. . . . I do not think we can let our standards sink to the low level suggested by the present nominee." Republican Senator Roman Hruska of Nebraska, the ranking member on the Judiciary Committee, gave a response that would become one of the most famous in Senate history. "Even if he were mediocre," Hruska huffed, "there are a lot of mediocre judges and people and lawyers. They are entitled to a little representation, aren't they, and a little chance. We can't have all Brandeises and Frankfurters and Cardozos and stuff like that there."

Even after that less-than-glowing defense, the Carswell nomination remained in doubt until the day of the vote. But on April 8, 1970, the Senate rejected the nomination by a vote of 51–45, with thirteen Republicans joining thirty-eight Democrats. Flug, the staff architect of Carswell's defeat, sat in the back of the Senate, laughing with tears of joy, saying "I just can't believe it. It's too good to believe."

Nixon had become the first president since Grover Cleveland to have two Supreme Court nominations rejected. Enraged, Nixon went to the White House Press room where he told the country, "A confirmation was not possible for a judge on the Supreme Court of any man who happens to believe in the strict construction of the Constitution, as I do, if he happens to come from the South." Under those circumstances, Nixon said he would ask the attorney general to give him the name of a northern jurist who was a strict constructionist.

The next week, Nixon nominated Judge Harry Blackmun, who served on the Court of Appeals for the Eighth Circuit, a friend of Warren Burger's since childhood and best man at his wedding. The Senate, delighted by Blackmun's credentials and weary of confirmation battles, confirmed him by a 94–0 vote.

In the ongoing war over the makeup of the Supreme Court, Nixon won the first round: preventing Fortas from being elevated, getting Burger confirmed as Chief Justice, and forcing Fortas off the court to create another vacancy. The Senate had won the second: defeating Haynesworth, defeating Carswell, and confirming Blackmun, who would prove to be an independent thinker, quickly evolving into a stalwart of the Court's liberal wing and authoring the *Roe v. Wade* decision in 1973. There would be a decisive third round almost immediately, and again Bayh would play a leading role.

The age and infirmity of Justices Hugo Black and John Harlan gave Nixon two more seats to fill in 1971. After much deliberation, including flirtations with the idea of Howard Baker and Robert Byrd as possible nominees, Nixon chose Lewis Powell, a superb Virginia lawyer esteemed in the bar, and William Rehnquist, a relatively unknown lawyer from Arizona, who had served for two years as assistant attorney general for legal policy in Nixon's Justice Department.

Plainly, Rehnquist was a brilliant legal mind. He had graduated first in his class from Stanford Law School and served as a clerk for Justice Robert Jackson before entering law practice. But Rehnquist, unlike Powell or Burger, was not mainstream conservative. In Rehnquist, Nixon had found a right-wing legal thinker who could, over time, change the direction of the Supreme Court. Nixon recognized that he was nominating "a guy who's there for thirty years, and also, if a Republican is around, a potential chief justice."

Rehnquist had compiled a lengthy paper trail as assistant attorney general. Taken together, the memoranda he had written constituted a blueprint for a radical reversal of Supreme Court jurisprudence in the areas of criminal law and the First Amendment. The Senate Judiciary Committee, with Bayh again taking the lead, wrote to Rehnquist requesting any memoranda that he had written, but Rehnquist declined the request, citing attorney-client privilege. Amazingly, the Judiciary Committee accepted this assertion of privilege, rather than precipitate a Constitutional clash. The clear majority of the committee either favored Rehnquist's nomination or had simply tired of fighting Nixon's nominees.

With the written expression of his legal views well hidden, Rehnquist got through his confirmation hearings by saying as little as possible. Evidence emerged that he had challenged African American and Hispanic voters at the polls in Phoenix, but it had little impact. There was ample reason to believe that Rehnquist was more radical than either Haynesworth or Carswell, but Bayh saw no way to stop the nomination without a "smoking gun."

At the eleventh hour, with the nomination already on the Senate floor, the smoking gun materialized. Bayh's staff received a 1952 memorandum that Rehnquist had written while clerking as the Supreme Court began to consider the issue of schools that were segregated by race. Rehnquist's memo urged Justice Jackson to reaffirm the holding of *Plessy v. Ferguson* that the doctrine of "separate but equal" was Constitutional. To those who believed the Constitution protected individual rights, the memorandum contained frightening reasoning. "In the long run," Rehnquist had written, "it is the majority who will determine what the constitutional rights of the minority are."

Bayh understood what the memo meant, and went immediately to the Senate floor, making an impassioned argument against Rehnquist's confirmation. This time, he did not prevail. Exhausted and testy, the Senate was ready to adjourn for Christmas, and it was tired of fighting the president over

Supreme Court nominees. William Rehnquist was confirmed by a vote of 68–26 on December 10, 1971. Nixon had won a decisive battle over the future of the Supreme Court.

Even so, Bayh, just forty-three, was now one of the Democrats' leading stars, with powerful admirers in the labor and civil rights communities. Bayh also became the Senate's most visible leader on the emerging, powerful issue of equal rights for women. He played an important part in Congress's approval of the Equal Rights Amendment in 1972. Although the ERA, as it was known, would not win the requisite approval from two-thirds of the state legislatures, Bayh went on to play a central role in the enactment of Title IX to the Civil Rights Act of 1964, establishing the right of women to equal rights in colleges and universities. Title IX changed the rules of intercollegiate sports, and provided powerful impetus for women in sports throughout the nation. He also played a key role in the adoption of the Twenty-Sixth amendment to the Constitution, lowering the voting age to eighteen.

Bayh considered seeking the Democratic presidential nomination in 1972, but decided against it, in large part because his wife, Marvella, had been diagnosed with breast cancer. In 1974, Bayh won his third term in the Senate, defeating Richard Lugar, the mayor of Indianapolis, an extraordinarily strong candidate who would reach the Senate two years later.

In 1975, with his wife's cancer in remission, Bayh sought the Democratic nomination. Bayh's liberal coalition would be based on the strong support of the labor, civil rights, and women's groups with whom he had worked closely for the previous seven years. Unfortunately, like Jackson and Church, Bayh underestimated the difficulty of running for president while serving in the Senate and the damaging effect of having several senators, plus Mo Udall, seeking the nomination against one Washington outsider. Bayh fell out of the race quite early and returned to his highly productive Senate career.

The Chairmanship of the Intelligence Committee enabled Bayh to broaden his responsibilities in the foreign policy and defense areas. He contributed to the Foreign Intelligence Surveillance Act, operating at the intersection of his old interests in civil liberties and his newer expertise in national security. He shaped the Intelligence Committee in a bipartisan way, sharing the most sensitive secrets with a small group of senators including Walter "Dee" Huddleston of Kentucky and his former opponent, Richard Lugar, whom he now trusted completely. He devoted many hours to shaping an agreement on a new charter for the intelligence agencies. He had continued his effort to convince the Congress of the need to amend the Constitution in order to require the direct election of the president.

Throughout 1979 and 1980, Bayh continued throwing himself into his Senate work, in an effort to overcome grief following his wife's death. He prepared for a tough reelection campaign, expecting to run against popular Governor Otis Bowen. Surprisingly, however, Bowen decided not to run, leaving the Republican nomination to a young, handsome Indiana Congressman, Dan Quayle, regarded as a far less formidable challenger. Bayh's race would soon be interrupted by unexpected breaking news about the president's family.

ON JULY 15, THE news exploded in front-page headlines across the country that Billy Carter, the president's brother, had accepted $220,000 from Libyan friends and agreed to register as a foreign agent. This wasn't the first time Billy Carter's connection to the Libyan government had come to light. The year before, he had taken a trip to Libya and returned to help set up a Libya-Arab-Georgia Friendship Society. When criticized for his pro-Libyan activities, the president's brother had responded: "There's a helluva lot more Arabians than there is Jews," and referring to his Jewish critics: "They can kiss my ass."

On February 27, 1979, the president had publicly disassociated himself from his brother's remarks: "I don't have any control over what brother says or what he does, and he has no control over what I say or do." Saying he loved his brother, he described him as seriously ill, and shortly thereafter, Billy entered an alcoholic rehabilitation center where he stayed for seven weeks. But now, eighteen months later, the American people discovered that the president's brother had received a large amount of money from the Libyan government, one of the world's leading state sponsors of terrorism, which presumably had sought his friendship to cultivate a channel to the president.

Jimmy Carter had come through the Bert Lance debacle and an investigation of his peanut warehouse with his image for rectitude intact. But the prospect of his brother's Libya connection posed a serious threat. The issue became much more serious for the White House when it came to light that Zbigniew Brzezinski, the president's national security adviser, had asked Billy to use his friendship with the Libyans to get Muammar al-Gaddafi to lean harder to Ayatollah Khomeini to free the hostages.

The press coverage turned into a feeding frenzy. A long and detailed cover story in *Time* began: "Once again, high drama in Washington. Television's glaring floodlights may switch back on as early as next week in the Senate hearing room. . . . Driven by the pressures of election-year politics, the case of Billy Carter's Libyan connections ballooned rapidly last week into a full-fledged Senate inquiry and a political cause célèbre." Seven years after the work of the Senate Watergate Committee, senators were again asking Howard Baker's famous question: "What did the president know, and when did he know it?"

Byrd and Baker met frequently over a period of several days, and on July 24, without mentioning Billy's name, announced the formation of a nine-member panel to look into Billy's Libya connection. Senate Democrats wanted to reduce the analogy to Watergate and resisted creation of a special committee. But Byrd acknowledged that "this is a matter that will not go away."

Under the resulting compromise, a special subcommittee of the Judiciary Committee would conduct the investigation into "activities relating to individuals representing the interests of foreign governments." Bayh would chair, and Strom Thurmond would be the ranking Republican. The leaders filled out the committee with two members of the Foreign Relations Committee, Claiborne Pell of Rhode Island and Lugar. The new chairman pledged to "pursue the truth wherever it may lead, and let the chips fall where they may." Both the majority and minority had authority to issue subpoenas at the committee's direction.

Halfway through the press conference announcing the formation of the subcommittee, a reporter asked Byrd why Billy's name had not been mentioned. Byrd responded: "There's no necessity for it. It might not be confined to Billy Carter." Asked if there was a chance that the investigation would not focus on Billy, Bayh responded: "Not unless you don't read the newspaper clippings."

Baker stated, "We want to resist the temptation to demagogue, witch hunt, to destroy people's characters. But we will pursue the truth." The Senate charged the panel with submitting either a final or interim report by October 4, a month before the election—an almost impossibly short time frame in which to conduct any investigation, but one that would allow the voters to have the facts and judge the importance of Billy Carter's connection to Libya.

The White House immediately pledged full cooperation with the investigation, including the willingness of First Lady Rosalynn Carter and Brzezinski to testify. Clearly the Carter administration had learned the fundamental lesson of Watergate: the cover up is almost always worse than the crime.

Always eager to score partisan points, Bob Dole could not resist giving a speech comparing Watergate to "Billygate." Dole claimed the only real difference between the two situations was that this time, both the president and the Congress were Democratic.

At the time, Bayh and Dole were working closely together on important legislation to improve American innovation by getting the results of university research in the hands of business more expeditiously. But that legislation reflected the "good Dole," a legislator who operated in a substantive, nonpartisan way. Billygate and a high-stakes election year got Dole's political juices flowing, bringing out his slashing, partisan side familiar to the country from the 1976 campaign. Bayh, obviously irked at Dole, pointed out that, unlike Nixon, Carter had pledged full cooperation and did not plan to invoke executive privilege.

Bayh had no illusions about the job: "It's going to be like walking through a minefield." He said that his aides had urged him to turn it down and concentrate on his campaign. He deserved praise for stepping up to a tough assignment like the distinguished senator he was. Nevertheless events would prove that his staff was probably right.

ON AUGUST 4, A line of 300 would-be spectators snaked through the halls of the Dirksen Senate Office Building, as Bayh gaveled the start of the hearings. Both Democrats and Republicans questioned the wisdom of the White House using Billy to urge Gaddafi to lean on the Iranians early in the crisis. Bob Dole asked sarcastically if, after Billy left Tripoli, "something happened that was useful besides the burning of the U.S. embassy."

However, by the second day, despite the presence of eleven television cameras and sixty reporters, senators on both sides of the dais seemed uncertain whether the hearings were even worthwhile. There appeared to be no White House impropriety. Patrick Leahy, a first-term senator also in a tough reelection battle, commented: "I'd just as soon no one [in Vermont] knows I'm on the subcommittee. They'd wonder why I wasn't doing my other duties instead." Max Baucus commented: "The basic feeling of the American people is this may not be 'much ado about nothing,' but it's a lot to do about not very much.' People are saying 'Poor Billy'! They think the media has made a lot of this." Even Dole observed: "A lot was smoke—I'm not sure there was a flame."

Bayh, who had taken the political risk of chairing the panel, said: "In the end, it may not amount to a hill of peanuts." Indianans were worried about other things. "Autoworkers are on unemployment. Farmers are suffering from the grain embargo. People couldn't care less about the Libyans." Bayh also observed: "There's a lot of disenchantment with confrontation between the president and Congress. My constituents are saying 'why can't you fellows get along?'"

Jimmy Carter remained committed to bringing out the full truth. In the White House briefing room in early August, he said that he was "willing and eager to respond in person" to any questions from the special committee and "the sooner the better." He said that he would send the committee "a full and complete report" on the subject this week, make it public at the same time, and answer questions from reporters in a prime-time press conference.

"The complete disclosure of the facts will clearly demonstrate that at no time did my brother influence me in my decisions toward Libya or the policies of this government toward Libya," Carter insisted. "And neither I nor anyone acting in my behalf ever sought to influence or interfere in the investigation of my brother by the Justice Department."

On August 21, Billy Carter began his testimony before the special committee. "I'm not a buffoon, a boob, or a whacko," Billy said. He portrayed himself as an ordinary southerner who had been victimized by the increased scrutiny that came with being the president's brother. "I never offered or did anything for the benefit of Libya or the government of Libya in relation to American government policy or actions." Billy said that he had told the Libyans: "If the people and the government of Libya want to treat me as a friend, that was fine with me. If the people and the government of Libya want to deal with me as a man of potential influence, they had chosen the wrong person, and I so informed them."

Pressed by several senators about whether he regretted his actions, Billy said: "I don't know if I would do it over again. Before I do anything again with Libya I'd talk real long and hard with my lawyers."

Billy said that he had spoken casually with the president about the Libya visit. "He has never been there and we had family talks just as you would tell a member of your family about a trip you may have taken to a foreign land." His bottom line undoubtedly struck the committee as convincing: "I never asked my brother to do anything for the benefit of Libya. I also know he would not do it even if I had been foolish enough to try. . . . Neither Jimmy Carter nor I believe that the government can or should be used for the financial benefits of the president's family."

Unsatisfied, Dole wanted the investigation to go deeper. "We're involved in it now. We have our reputations to worry about. We've got to get the facts,"

Dole said. "We can't have a situation that, when it's all over, the *Post* or the *New York Times* says why didn't you bring this or that out. Once you get into it you've got to be careful or you'll get hit with a falling object."

Nevertheless, Bayh remained quite certain that the hearings had been underwhelming because there was nothing there. He told reporters: "I'll wager that 90 percent of everything we will hear, you have already written about." But, "until you stir the pot, you can't say whether you have a mouse or a dinosaur."

The committee essentially agreed. Once Billy completed his testimony, the drama was over. On September 24, the panel members decided in executive session that there were no questions remaining that required President Carter's testimony or even a sworn statement in response to questions. The committee's interim report came in on October 4, as required, and in time it became the final report. Billygate had ended with not a bang, but a whimper.

THE SENATE HAD HANDLED a difficult political issue about as well as could be expected during the heat of a presidential campaign. The initial over-heated comparisons between Billygate and Watergate were way off the mark. The Republican senators played straight and avoided demagoguery. Even Dole acknowledged, in between partisan zingers, that there was nothing to the controversy.

The senators had grasped the central truth early on: the Carters occupied a special place as the nation's First Family, but they were certainly not the first family with sibling problems. From the beginning, the most likely ex-planation seemed to be that Billy Carter, a troubled man with financial prob-lems, sought to capitalize on the fact that he was the president's brother; Gaddafi wanted to secure influence in high circles in Washington, or alter-natively, to embarrass the president; Jimmy Carter had an understandable reluctance to come down too hard on his brother, and every reason to avoid being involved in the situation at all. Brzezinski's initiative seemed ill con-ceived, but a full array of diplomatic efforts—conventional and unconven-tional—had already failed to free the hostages. The Republicans were loath to pass up a good opportunity to nail the already weakened president, but they also worried about overplaying their hand and risking a backlash that would help the president. After all, with Ronald Reagan as their nominee and antigovernment fervor on the rise, by August 1980, the Republicans had every issue, domestic and foreign, going their way. They did not need to beat up Jimmy Carter because he had a troubled brother.

Carter's forthright handling of his brother's problems at the very least helped him lock up the Democratic nomination. He also benefitted from the help of Abe Ribicoff. Despite his long friendship with Kennedy, Ribicoff thought it was fundamentally unfair for the senator to try to change the convention rules after Carter had won the delegates that he needed for the nomination. Hamilton Jordan, Carter's chief of staff, heard about Ribicoff's views, sought a meeting with him, and asked if the senator would speak at the convention. Ribicoff agreed, taking the lead of the Carter forces on the first night of the convention to defeat the effort by Kennedy's campaign to bring about an open convention. The Carter forces prevailed by a comfortable margin; Kennedy finally acknowledged defeat, and on Tuesday night, made one of the most memorable speeches of his career. On Thursday, the convention came to an end, as Carter, Kennedy, and many Democrats milled about on stage, and Kennedy did not raise the president's arm in the traditional unity pledge, even though he had rehearsed doing so.

More than two months had passed since the end of the primaries. Why had Kennedy stayed in so long? Without a doubt, many Kennedy supporters hoped that something would cause Carter to step aside—perhaps his brother's intensely publicized problems. But it also seems that several of the senators were actively encouraging him to stay in the race. Still stinging from when Carter deceived him about the ill-fated mission to rescue the hostages in Tehran, Byrd continually made positive statements about Kennedy, never missing a chance to criticize Carter, and repeatedly called for an open convention. Carter believed that Byrd was secretly angling for the nomination. Muskie may also have been intrigued by the possibility that the prolonged battle between Carter and Kennedy might result in the convention turning to him as an alternative choice. Jackson apparently had the same thoughts. Several of the greatest senators had demonstrated, yet again, that the siren song of the presidency transfixed them, robbing them of their usual good judgment.

IN OCTOBER, WITH THE Billy Carter investigation done, Bayh could finally hit the campaign trail. He had always been a terrific campaigner, as comfortable on a farm in southern Indiana as he was in a union meeting in Gary. He had won three Senate races against more formidable opponents than Dan Quayle. But he had always been much more liberal than his state, and now Indiana, more conservative than Wisconsin or Minnesota, was moving hard to the right along with the rest of the country.

Perhaps busy with Billygate, perhaps caught up in the insulated environment of the Senate, Bayh had failed to get ahead of the country's changing politics. Republican staffers on the Appropriations Committee had begun keeping track of his absences from committee meetings, using them as campaign fodder. Moreover, the single-issue groups, which had not existed six years earlier, had become forcefully and stridently involved in the Indiana Senate race. "It's been vitriolic," Bayh observed in October. "The outsiders have come here in force."

In his pitch to voters, Bayh stressed his seniority and what he had done for the steel industry, for coal, and for agriculture. His campaign literature touted his accomplishments on national security and inflation and showed him target shooting and talking with National Guard troops. To counter, Quayle's consultants came up with a clever line: "Bayh suffers from the two George's syndrome. He sounds like McGovern in Washington and like Wallace in Indiana."

Elsewhere, Wisconsin's polls had Nelson still comfortably ahead of former Congressman Robert Kasten, but the numbers felt wrong. In late summer, Eagleton called me to his office. When I came in, he looked like a whirling dervish: tearing articles out of the papers, working the phones, scribbling notes, smoking like a chimney.

"We gotta help Gaylord," he told me.

"Why, what's happening?" I asked.

"He just did a west coast fund-raising swing," Eagleton told me.

Nelson hated fund-raising with a passion. "That's good," I ventured.

"No," Eagleton retorted. "He lost money."

Nelson seemed to lack energy. He stunned his staff by cancelling some of his Labor Day campaign events, missing the opportunity to go before traditional Democratic audiences that had been bedrock supporters in the past. Howard Paster, a prominent Democrat, recalled running into Nelson on a September weekend in Washington, shopping at Safeway—far from the re-election battle. Later that month, Carrie Lee Nelson, the senator's wife, went back to Wisconsin to do her first solo campaigning. A former First Lady of Wisconsin, she had always generated great affection around the state. Now, however, as she went from nursing homes to PTA meetings, the mood seemed different—familiar faces but a lack of warmth.

In early October, Kasten released a poll showing that the race was a dead heat. Nelson privately agreed. By virtue of having to run in a primary, Kasten was "much better organized. We're late. There's no question about it," Nelson acknowledged. Kasten recognized the challenge of running against Nelson, conceding that the senator was a living legend in the state: "There is a problem in hitting at Nelson personally. [Wisconsin voters] feel he is basically a good person." Still, Kasten hammered at Nelson hard, charging that he was liberal, out of touch, soft on defense, and unable to economize. "I'm hitting hard on the 'Nelson gap,'" Kasten said, "the difference between what he says and what he does."

Once Congress adjourned in October, Nelson began to campaign intensively. "Gaylord is busting his ass," one staffer happily reported. "He takes it as a personal affront, and an affront to the people of Wisconsin that Kasten is taken seriously." Speaking at the University of Wisconsin at Madison, Nelson chastised Kasten for his opposition to nuclear arms limitations: "Anyone who aspires to high political office and does not understand the awesome consequences of an accelerated nuclear arms race simply is not qualified to hold office."

But he did not seem to be connecting the way he had in the past. "This was a different Nelson on the campaign trail," said a *Capital Times* reporter who had covered him for years. At a state bricklayers' convention, Nelson received a standing ovation from many members, but not the younger ones, who confined themselves to polite applause. To the new generation of voters, Nelson was simply a name in the news, whose accomplishments were ancient history, not an old friend who fought for the issues they cared about.

When Vice President Walter Mondale, his close friend, came to Wisconsin for him, he felt that Nelson was not campaigning well: "I don't know what it was, but the spark and charm wasn't quite there. . . . I could tell it wasn't clicking." A columnist warned Nelson in print, "Most people have forgotten who Gaylord Nelson is or what he's like, and your more frequent appearances in the state during the last six months haven't sufficiently established your personal presence."

Nelson had always been a "happy warrior," in the great Humphrey tradition. Harsh campaigning did not come naturally to him, but now his campaign hit Kasten hard, charging that he had been a "do-nothing congressman who had never passed a bill and didn't show up to work half the time." The negative ads took a toll on Kasten, and Nelson opened up a wide lead in the polls; the race seemed to be over. A *Washington Post* survey, on the eve of the election, predicted that Nelson would be "a comfortable winner." Nelson did not believe that "the country has turned as conservative as some people think." But a strong anti-incumbent, anti-liberal, anti-spending, anti-tax current was running, even in Wisconsin, keeping the race in doubt.

In the closing days, Kasten, a bare-knuckled campaigner, unleashed a series of powerful, negative ads. Nelson had tried to capitalize on his chairmanship of the Small Business Committee, but Kasten now charged that Nelson had missed 63 percent of the hearings of the committee that he had chaired, and that only 2 percent of his bills had become law. The National Federation of Independent Business (NFIB) had always opposed Nelson, despite his work on behalf of small business. Now it weighed in heavily for Kasten.

A few days before the election, a Kasten surrogate pointed out, accurately, that Nelson didn't even have a residence in Wisconsin—a devastating charge in a year when Washington was in particularly ill repute. It was true: Nelson had started to rebel against the demands of traveling back to the state. He still loved Wisconsin but his center of gravity had become Washington. There was a sense that he had lost touch, and to some extent, perhaps he had.

Nelson had tried to fight the conservative tide, even though he did not always do so convincingly. Across the border, in far more conservative South Dakota, McGovern did not really seem to try. McGovern had seriously considered not running for reelection, but got into the race out of anger against the right, who described him as a "Castro lover" and a "baby killer." McGovern had become a national and international celebrity. Six years before, he had done penance in South Dakota for "going national," and during Watergate, having run against Richard Nixon provided a powerful credential. Now, six years later, McGovern had no such cover.

McGovern recognized that he was trailing badly. Publicly, he noted, "it wouldn't be the first time that I was this far behind and won. They always overdo the attack . . . I haven't been in politics this long to peter out now." But when his opponent, Lieutenant Governor James Abdnor, claimed that he was more in tune with South Dakota than the incumbent, McGovern privately agreed. On Labor Day, after a full weekend of campaigning before audiences ranging from indifferent to hostile, McGovern actually wrote the concession speech that he would give in case of the defeat he already anticipated.

In contrast to Nelson and McGovern, Tom Eagleton, only fifty years old, seeking his third term, threw himself into his reelection campaign with his characteristic intensity and energy. Eagleton understood and navigated the shifting currents of American politics as well as anyone. It was partly a result of representing Missouri: at the very center of the country, with major cities, declining industries, and large farming areas, it was the classic swing state, almost evenly divided between Democrats and Republicans, and a microcosm of America. In August 1978, Eagleton had surprised Carter by urging him to finish all his liberal proposals by the end of the year and spend the last two years of his term on a limited legislative program, emphasizing moderate to conservative issues. Eagleton also seized the opportunity to take the lead on legislation creating inspectors general in the major departments of government to lead the fight against "fraud, waste and abuse" to counter the expected charge that he was a big-spending liberal. His stalwart efforts to rescue Chrysler earned him headlines and plaudits around the state.

Eagleton artfully dodged a political bullet from his chairmanship of the District of Columbia Subcommittee. The Washington region's Metrorail system had opened in March 1976 with five stations downtown, and by 1978, the system had expanded into suburban Maryland and Virginia. Everywhere it went, Metro's modern rail cars and futuristic, vaulted-ceiling stations had excited residents and tourists alike. But there was considerably less excitement about finding the money to pay for the full 101-mile system that was on the drawing board. The federal government had to fund 80 percent of the construction, with the various localities, negotiating among themselves, to put up the other 20 percent. The House of Representatives had passed legislation in early 1979 to authorize $1.7 billion for the federal share, but that was before the economy moved into recession, and budget cutting became a mantra on Capitol Hill. As subcommittee chairman, Eagleton was the key player who would decide the fate of the legislation in the Senate.

His staff advised him that it would be politically disastrous to find the money for the Washington, D.C., Metro at a time when federal funds for bus service in St. Louis and Kansas City were being slashed. Eagleton was torn, agreeing with their political judgment, but knowing how much the full Metro system would mean to the Washington region. So he took a page from Proxmire's book and added some embellishments.

He asked Mac Mathias, who was the ranking Republican on the D.C. subcommittee, to meet with him. They had a strong bond, having been elected to the Senate in the same turbulent year, 1968, and having collaborated on D.C. home rule legislation. Where Eagleton exuded intensity, Mathias was relaxed, slow-moving, and sometimes appeared dreamy-eyed. He drove an old battered station wagon from his farm in Frederick and often brought his dog into the office. But he had a keen intellect, and had been a powerful supporter of civil rights and opponent of the Vietnam War, locking arms with Gloria Steinem and Bella Abzug in well-publicized parades. As a Maryland senator with hundreds of thousands of constituents in the Washington suburbs, Mathias was deeply committed to completion of the Metrorail.

Mathias came to Eagleton's office and sank comfortably into a big armchair opposite Eagleton's desk.

"Mac, I've decided to oppose the Metro," Eagleton said abruptly.

"Then it's dead," Mathias said in a deep voice.

"No Mac," Eagleton said hastily. "We've got a plan." He told Mathias he would personally oppose the legislation but wouldn't kill it. In fact, he would help orchestrate its passage in the Senate, lending his staff director to the Maryland senators, Mathias and Paul Sarbanes, and enlisting freshman Carl Levin to manage the legislation in committee. Mathias nodded, and visibly relaxed.

The plan went off like clockwork. Eagleton criticized funding a "gold-plated subway system" for the Nation's Capitol. He alerted John Danforth, his Missouri colleague and close friend, so that Danforth could also oppose the legislation. With Mathias, Sarbanes, and Levin taking the lead, the Senate passed the funding legislation by a comfortable margin. It became law on January 3, 1980.

As the fall campaign heated up, Eagleton's polls showed him running very strongly with his opponent, Gene McNary, a St. Louis county supervisor, generating little excitement. But Eagleton faced one more unusual challenge. He had a troubled niece who had joined the Church of Scientology. Early in 1980, she had tried to extort money from Eagleton, threatening to expose some alleged embarrassing action if he did not pay her. Eagleton refused to be extorted and went to law enforcement authorities. In October 1980, while Eagleton was campaigning for reelection, he was also forced to testify against his niece in her trial for extortion. Eagleton's friends were understandably nervous, wondering how Missouri's voters would feel about this melodrama playing out during the last weeks of the campaign. Ultimately, however, the voters seemed to admire Eagleton for not giving in to extortion—brushes with a troubled family member are all too familiar and served to humanize Eagleton even further. He seemed to maintain a large lead over McNary as the election drew near.

ACROSS THE COUNTRY, A number of Democratic senators who had prepared for tough races were moving toward comfortable victories. In California, despite being targeted by NCPAC, Alan Cranston had amassed a large lead over Republican Paul Gann, who had helped spearhead the adoption of Proposition 13 two years earlier. In South Carolina, Fritz Hollings, who had pledged that "no one would run to the right" of him, was heading toward a landslide victory. In Louisiana, where only the Democratic primary mattered, Russell Long had dispatched his primary opponent handily. Dale Bumpers, John Glenn, Wendell Ford and Daniel Inouye were similarly unassailable. However, a number of other senators, ranging from rising stars to distinguished veterans, were facing unexpectedly tough campaigns.

Gary Hart's movie star looks and rapid rise to national prominence while managing a presidential campaign that lost forty-nine states had evoked some skepticism when he arrived in the Senate in 1975. But Hart had made close friends with some of the young senators focused on defense issues, like Bill Cohen and John Culver. He had impressed many people with his serious work on the sensitive and contentious Church Committee, as well as SALT II, and a range of energy and environment issues. Now suddenly, Hart, whose political future had seemed unlimited, faced the distinct possibility of being a one-term senator. He had come to the Senate on the Democratic tide after Watergate, but that tide had run out. Bill Armstrong's defeat of Floyd Haskell two years earlier augured badly for Hart; Colorado seemed to have ended a brief experiment with progressivism. The Republicans nominated Mary Estill Buchanan to run against Hart, and the still-novel notion of a woman senator seemed to capture the fancy of Colorado voters.

Hart campaigned furiously, battling uphill. But at a key juncture in the campaign, Barry Goldwater came to Colorado. The visit by the legendary Republican should have helped Buchanan. But Goldwater and Hart had served together on the Church Committee, and Hart had deeply impressed his senior colleague, even though they disagreed on issues constantly. When asked about Hart during an interview, Goldwater described him as "the most honest and most moral man" that he had ever met in politics. The headline in the *Denver Post*—"Goldwater Praises Hart"—was a huge boon to the Hart campaign.

Many Washington observers had found John Culver to be a formidable first-term senator, combining great intelligence with a forceful personality and strongly held convictions. Elizabeth Drew, one of Washington's most distinguished reporters, had profiled Culver in a laudatory book, *Senator.* He had built expertise on defense issues, playing a critical role in Carter's decision to kill the B-1 bomber.

Despite his strong start in the Senate, Culver had given serious thought to retiring. He had already been a Senate staffer and served ten years in the House. Educated at Harvard, he was an unabashed, unreconstructed New Deal/Fair Deal Democrat, who would have been more comfortable representing Massachusetts than Iowa. He did not like where the politics of the country were going, and he did not feel well suited to six more frustrating years. But after Roger Jepsen upset Dick Clark in 1978, Culver decided that he had to run again. "He knew he could lose. He wasn't like Talmadge and the others who didn't think they could lose," John Podesta, then Culver's Judiciary Counsel, recalled. "But he thought he was the strongest candidate, and he couldn't give in to the right." Culver decided to run as the liberal he was, making no compromises with the prevailing political climate. He drew a tough opponent in Representative Charles Grassley, an Iowa farmer turned legislator, who could not be mistaken for a Harvard liberal. The National Conservative Political Action Committee targeted Culver from the beginning, running hard negative ads right through Election Day.

In the last week of the campaign, Culver and Grassley squared off in a major debate on a university campus. A gadfly third-party candidate, determined to crash the debate, first disrupted it by yelling from the audience, then charged up onto the stage and came at Culver. Culver wrestled him to the ground, and when his opponent grabbed his tie, Culver wrenched his head back so hard that the tie snapped. The unusual debate attracted some national press attention, but whether it would help Culver in Iowa remained to be seen.

Herman Talmadge, the chairman of the Agriculture Committee, had been in the Senate since his election in 1956. He had followed in the footsteps of his father, Eugene Talmadge, who had been elected governor of Georgia in 1932. Being a Talmadge in Georgia compared to being a Kennedy in Massachusetts: seemingly a life ticket to the Senate. Talmadge was one of smartest senators, as he demonstrated in his performance on the Watergate Committee. "With Watergate," he wrote, "I not only became a nationally known politician but a star of daytime television as well." But after his twenty-nine-year-old son drowned in May 1975, a grief-stricken Talmadge turned heavily to drink. He and his wife had a bitter divorce, in which she charged him with stealing money from his Senate office accounts. His administrative assistant, Dan Minchew, was convicted of misappropriating funds. The Senate Ethics Committee recommended that Talmadge be "denounced" for his conduct, and the full Senate did so.

Still Talmadge remained a formidable politician. He faced a tough Democratic opponent, Zell Miller, a future Georgia governor and senator, and crushed him in the Democratic primary in late August. Miller was the only serious threat to the veteran senator; there seemed to be no way that Mack Mattingly, a pleasant IBM salesman running on the Republican ticket, could possibly challenge Talmadge. But politics had changed in Georgia, just as they had all over the nation. The Republicans sensed Talmadge's over-confidence and vulnerability and poured money into harsh negative TV ads.

In Washington state, an aging Magnuson ran precisely the campaign his staff had feared. At one point, with the television cameras on, Maggie had walked slowly down the steps disembarking from an airplane, waiting on each step and eventually stumbling. The film footage led to a devastating television ad, showing Magnuson on the steps, with a clock in the background timing just how long it took to get down. He looked like the old, frail, crippled man that he in fact was. Slade Gorton, his energetic, attractive opponent, struck exactly the right note, suggesting that Maggie be given a gold watch for retirement. "I'm not saying Maggie hasn't done some good for the state," Gorton told *Time* magazine. "He has. I'm saying he has now become part of the problem of inflation, and I'm part of the solution." The *Seattle Times* called Maggie "the candidate of nostalgia, highly expensive nostalgia."

Javits's last campaign had likewise become painful to watch. On September 9, Nassau County Supervisor Alphonse D'Amato beat him decisively in the Republican primary. It was "a stunning defeat," in the words of the *New York Times*. Javits had made a terrible decision in choosing to run, and now he compounded it, struggling to find the money to stay in the race as a third-party candidate. Many of his friends and admirers feared that if he stayed in the race, he would cause the defeat of the Democratic nominee, Elizabeth Holtzman, the liberal congresswoman who had distinguished herself on the House Judiciary Committee during consideration of Nixon's impeachment. An October 30 *New York Times* editorial stated that it still considered Javits the best candidate of the three, but that "with this last hurrah, [Javits] may lose even more than the seat he has held with distinction for twenty four years. He may also weaken the progressive causes to which he devoted his political life." The *Times* called on Javits "to complete a brilliant career with a selfless, principled withdrawal." Javits stayed in the race.

THESE SENATE RACES WERE uncertain in part because the presidential race seemed to remain too close to call. Reagan had come out of the Republican convention with a large lead over Carter, and all the issues going his way. But the race had tightened after the conventions. The Democrats took advantage of some of Reagan's most extreme views, working effectively to paint him as out of the mainstream. Four years earlier, Gerald Ford had made just such a comeback against Jimmy Carter, because of uncertainty about the newcomer. Now that he was president, Carter benefited from some of the same unease that voters felt about his challenger. There were hints that the hostage crisis could be resolved before the election, creating an "October surprise" that would allow America a sense of relief and boost the beleaguered president.

Sitting on a comfortable lead, the Reagan campaign had avoided a debate with Carter by insisting that any presidential debate should include John Anderson, the former Illinois congressman, running a principled and effective independent candidacy. With Reagan's lead vanishing, his campaign reversed its position, calling for one head-to-head debate. Patrick Caddell, Carter's pollster and principal political adviser, fought the proposal, fearing Reagan's skill on television, but Hamilton Jordan and other Carter aides believed that the president's intellect and grasp of the substantive issues would more than offset Reagan's ability as a performer. The Carter campaign agreed to the debate, which was scheduled for October 28, in Cleveland, just one week before the election. Polls and press reports indicated that many voters remained undecided, waiting to watch the debate and then make up their minds.

Sadly for Carter, Caddell was right. In the debate, the president showed his mastery of the issues, but seemed tight and uncomfortable. He tried to humanize himself by saying that he had asked his ten-year-old daughter, Amy, what she thought the most important issue facing the country was. Her supposed response, "Nuclear weaponry and the control of nuclear arms," was widely ridiculed.

Reagan, on the other hand, came across as a calm, friendly man who had a good grasp of the substance—not at all the extreme right-winger that the Democratic campaign had tried to portray. Reagan deflected Carter's sallies with ease and amusement, saying things like "there you go again."

Then in his closing statement, Reagan, looking straight into the camera, unleashed what might still stand as the most devastating and effective closing statement in the history of presidential debates: "Are you better off than you were four years ago? Is it easier for you to go and buy things in the stores than it was four years ago? Is America respected around the world as it was?" Ronald Reagan won the debate hands down, and the press reporting of the debate, replaying Reagan's best lines and Carter's gaffe, magnified his victory.

After listening to Reagan debate Carter, Gaylord Nelson turned to Kevin Gottlieb, his administrative assistant, and said, "It's over." Gottlieb assumed that Nelson was predicting a Reagan victory. "Yes, but that's not what I'm talking about," Nelson said. "Ronald Reagan proved to the American people tonight that he's not a crazy man, not someone to be feared. If he wins it will bring out people who normally don't vote. That means I'm done."

Jimmy Carter tried to rally, but Election Day, November 4, happened to be the anniversary of the hostage taking. The television news focused again and again on reviewing the key events of this agonizing national experience. *Time, Newsweek,* and *US News and World Report* all had cover stories on the hostage crisis. Pat Caddell's daily polling showed massive slippage in Carter's position, as virtually all the undecided voters broke to Reagan.

The night before the election, on the way to Plains, Georgia, to vote, Jimmy Carter was told he was going to be defeated. In his diary, he wrote: "It was hard for us to believe the dimension of what Pat was telling us, but it later proved to be accurate."

ON ELECTION DAY 1980, I got up early to read the *Post* and the *Times* and drove five minutes to the voting place at Wayside Elementary School in Potomac, Maryland, soon after it opened. In front of the school, the candidates for local office and their supporters had set up their tables and were passing out campaign literature and sample ballots, making one last effort to sway the undecided or uninformed voters. Because it was early, there was almost no line; only a few minutes passed before I got to cast my vote for Jimmy Carter and Walter Mondale and then split my ticket to support Republican Mac Mathias for the Senate.

That special Tuesday, nothing demanded my attention at the Senate subcommittee where I worked. I could just as easily be nervous, imagining what was happening across the country, without going in. I had decided to take the day off, to hang out with Nancy, my wife, play with Susanna, our four-year-old daughter, and just think about the election: what it meant for the country, and, of course, what it might mean for me.

It was a cool, cloudy day. The temperature was in the mid 40's, and there was a slight drizzle of rain. By the afternoon, I was restless and went to the Jewish Community Center in Rockville, Maryland, to relieve the stress by swimming laps. As I walked to my car afterward, I was struck by a feeling that the Republican landslide building across the country was coursing through my veins. I lived and breathed politics in those days, but even for me, this was unusual.

To begin with, I had no doubt how the presidential election would turn out. My view had been consistent all year. As early as April 1980, in a memorandum to Eagleton, I had written that "the polls show a close race between Carter and Reagan, but it isn't and it won't be." I predicted that Reagan would win in a landslide.

I had resigned myself to a Reagan presidency long ago. I rationalized that the country had survived the Nixon presidency, and we would get through the Reagan years, too, as long as we had a Democratic Senate. I had been Tom Eagleton's subcommittee staff director on the Governmental Affairs Committee. When I went to work for him in June 1979, Abe Ribicoff had just announced his decision to retire, putting Eagleton in line to become chairman of the full committee if he won his reelection. He asked me to take charge of the subcommittee and to run the full committee when he became chairman. His only caveat was that he had to be reelected. At the time, the possibility that the Senate might not remain Democratic did not cross our minds.

But by October 1980, as the election grew nearer, with the Reagan landslide I had predicted coming into sharper relief, I began, for the first time, to worry about the Senate. The Democrats had a 58–41 seat majority (with one independent)—seemingly insurmountable. But if Reagan won a landslide, his coattails would help Republican Senate candidates all across the country. I began telling friends that we were going to lose the Senate.

Exit polls did not exist in 1980, so insiders were not able to pass around numbers and rumors during the day as they do now. The seemingly endless day finally over, Nancy and I got into the car at 8 p.m. to go to the party hosted by the Democratic National Committee. I switched on the radio news, and right away the reporter said that the polls had just closed in Indiana. Birch Bayh had decisively lost to Dan Quayle.

Clearly it was over for the stalwart Democratic liberals. I turned to Nancy and said, "They're all going down."

By the time we got to the DNC party at the Hilton, Reagan had a ten-point lead over Carter, and networks were describing a national landslide. A shocked crowd of Democrats milled around and tried to comfort each other.

We left quickly, heading for the Capitol Hill home of our friends Claudia and George Ingram. Both Claudia and George were Hill staffers, and their party was the place where most of our friends would be meeting to spend the election night.

The townhouse was packed, with people on all levels, overwhelmingly Democrats, absorbing one shocking report after another as the polls closed. Across the country, the veteran senators went down one after another.

In Georgia, Herman Talmadge, despite having defeated Zell Miller in the Democratic primary, fell to Mack Mattingly, his undistinguished challenger. Georgia was going strongly Republican; it stayed with Jimmy Carter, its native son, but felt no similar special loyalty to Talmadge, despite his famous name and long service.

Iowans may have appreciated John Culver's candor about his proud liberalism—nevertheless they preferred Charles Grassley's homespun conservatism. The Republican won decisively.

In New York, Jacob Javits, the foremost Republican liberal, found out what many third-party candidates have discovered over the years: once the voters decide that the race is between two other candidates, they don't waste their vote on the third candidate. One of the greatest senators in history, Javits received only 11 percent of the vote, just enough to ensure that Alphonse D'Amato would defeat Elizabeth Holtzman, a nightmare scenario for Democrats in New York and around the country.

In South Dakota, George McGovern delivered the concession speech that he had written two months earlier. He would say later that he knew the race was lost when a South Dakota woman ripped into him for his vote on the Panama Canal, while buying groceries with the food stamps that McGovern had made possible. His state turned on him with a vengeance. James Abdnor defeated McGovern by a 58–39 landslide, the only landslide defeat suffered by an incumbent senator that night. The margin was virtually identical to the national defeat that Nixon had inflicted on McGovern years earlier.

Politically insensitive as ever, Jimmy Carter conceded early, even before the polls closed in the western states, outraging Democrats in close races. They would always believe that thousands of their voters decided to stay home after Carter threw in the towel.

In Washington, Slade Gorton beat Warren Magnuson by a comfortable margin. Gorton's message had worked: the people of Washington could appreciate Maggie's great works but retire him just the same. He was still an icon in his state, but he had run one time too many.

The New Right claimed its most coveted victory in Idaho, as Frank Church went down to Steve Symms. Church had gone through probably the ugliest campaign in the country, hit by every weapon in the right wing's political arsenal. Despite Church's sometimes erratic course over the previous two years, respect for his courage, independence, and sheer stature plainly remained high in Idaho. Reagan carried Idaho by an astonishing margin, 67–25 percent, the second widest margin in the country, but Church lost by only 4,200 votes, in one of the closest races of the night.

Watching a stunning national blowout unfold, Democrats took some solace from the comfortable victories of Christopher Dodd and Alan Dixon, who won the open seats in Connecticut and Illinois created by the retirements of Ribicoff and Stevenson. The best news for Democrats on a grim night was that Patrick Leahy in Vermont and Gary Hart in Colorado both won reelection, squeaking through by identical 50–49 margins. Hart would always credit his narrow victory to Barry Goldwater's unexpected endorsement.

At 11 p.m., I called Senator Eagleton in St. Louis. He had won his election, although it had been much closer than expected. I congratulated him, but he focused on the losses of his friends. "Culver, Church, Maggie, Bayh, Talmadge, Javits defeated," Eagleton said. "I don't want to go back to the Senate. It's going to be awful."

Eagleton cut me off before I could respond. "What are you hearing about Gaylord?" "Too close to call so far," I answered.

At 2:00 a.m., Nelson's race in Wisconsin was the only one that had not been decided. The television coverage of the landslide came to an end. I tried to reach someone at the *Milwaukee Journal* but got no answer. We went home, and I tried to sleep. A few hours later, I called Milwaukee again, and was advised that Nelson had lost narrowly to Kasten.

Democrats' worst nightmare had been realized. Altogether, nine Democratic senators had been defeated, and twelve seats had changed hands. The Senate would turn Republican, for the first time in twenty-six years, and the Great Senate was all but ended.

ON NOVEMBER 4, RONALD Reagan won a landslide victory over Jimmy Carter. Reagan won 51 percent of the popular vote to Carter's 41 percent with

John Anderson polling 7%. Reagan won 489 electoral votes to Carter's 49; at the time, it was the third largest landslide in American history, surpassed only by Franklin D. Roosevelt's victory in 1936 and Richard Nixon's crushing of George McGovern in 1972. Reagan won 44 states, including every one of the 10 largest states in the nation. It was a rout of stunning proportions.

In the Senate, the Democrats lost twelve seats; their 58–41 majority turned into a 53–46 Republican majority, giving the Republicans control of the Senate for the first time since 1955. The election marked the largest swing in the Senate since 1958, the off-year election in which the foundation of the liberal Senate was poured. In 1972, when Nixon had an unprecedented forty-nine-state sweep against McGovern, his landslide had no effect on the Senate races; indeed, the Democrats picked up two Senate seats. But in 1980, Reagan's coat-tails were long and strong and probably had a significant effect in most of the elections.

In political terms, Carter and the Democrats of the Senate had met their perfect storm. Years later, historians and many Americans would give Carter credit for some courageous decisions, particularly with respect to the Camp David accords, the Panama Canal treaties, and a far-sighted policy mix that increased energy production and conservation. Many would praise his restraint in bringing the hostages home from Iran without going to war. But in November 1980, most Americans viewed Jimmy Carter as a failed president, a symbol and constant reminder of a troubled period and America's uncertain and slipping place in a world where events felt out of control. Kennedy's challenge undoubtedly further weakened Carter's position, but it strains credulity to think that Carter would have won reelection if Kennedy had not challenged him. Americans judge their presidents as either having succeeded or failed, based, actually, on a version of Reagan's famous questions "Are you better off?" and "Is the country better off?" than when this president took office? In 1980, most of the voters saw the answer clearly enough, and wanted no more of Jimmy Carter.

But the election represented much more than just a rejection of Carter. The American electorate had taken its time getting comfortable with the idea of Ronald Reagan as president, but ultimately, turned to someone who was a very familiar figure. The former actor, already well known, had burst on to the political scene in 1964, supporting Barry Goldwater's disastrous bid for the presidency. He won two terms as governor of California and sought the presidency in 1968 and 1976. He stood clearly for certain core principles: smaller government, lower taxes, stronger national defense.

His views had looked extreme in 1964, but by 1980, the world had come around to him. Most Americans, including most Democrats, favored smaller government, lower taxes, and a stronger national defense. Carter supporters might believe that he could fashion the best policies to accomplish those goals, using a scalpel rather than a meat axe. But he epitomized a Democratic party struggling to accommodate their longstanding commitments and beliefs with the changing realities facing the country. Most Americans really were not interested in that type of tortured balancing act. They preferred Reagan's clarity, consistency, and simplicity.

By Election Day, the political community anticipated Reagan's victory, although not the magnitude of the blowout. House Speaker Tip O'Neill described it as an unforeseen tidal wave. The Senate outcome shocked virtually everyone. One labor leader commented: "The swing in the Senate is probably even greater, in ideological terms, than the shift in the White House." The reaction of the Senate leaders reflected the political world turned upside down, and the strong right-wing tide. Robert Byrd expressed regret at the defeat of so many Democrats, but said it may turn out to be a "healthy shock" for the party. "I think we need to regroup and unify and come up with a program of our own." Byrd allowed that the Senate would be more conservative but said "as the world of reality is faced up to . . . perhaps it won't be as conservative as it might seem."

Historian Sean Wilentz would later describe the 1980 election as "a major advance in the absorption of the [Republican] party by the new right. The White House would now become firmly attached to the conveyor belts of proposals and personnel built by the conservative counterestablishment. And the Republicans on Capitol Hill would tilt more strongly rightward than ever." Howard Baker described the election as "not only a landslide, but a political earthquake." Even while celebrating the Republican triumph, he commented: "If the New Right leaders think Howard Baker is going to roll over and play dead for them, they are mistaken." He anticipated the political currents that would dominate his party when the new Senate convened in 1981.

Washington Post columnist David Broder captured the moment in an election analysis entitled "A Sharp Right Turn":

Not only did Reagan hand Carter the first defeat an elected president has suffered in a reelection bid since Herbert Hoover went down in 1932 but a host of Senate Democratic invincibles joined him.

A Magnuson of Washington and a Talmadge of Georgia were discarded as if their seniority and committee chairmanships did not count. Alabama elected its first Republican and its first Catholic, Florida its first woman senator. The voters of Idaho and Indiana told Frank Church and Birch Bayh that they would tolerate their deviations from conservative policy through the '60's and '70's—but not into the '80's. It certainly had all the appearance of an era ending—and a new one beginning.

chapter 20

THE LAME-DUCK SESSION

EVERY LAME-DUCK SESSION HAS AN EDGY, QUERULOUS FEEL TO IT—THE members would much rather be at home, savoring their victories or licking their wounds. The one that began on November 12 bordered on the full-on surreal. The Democrats were still in the majority, but a dozen of them had been dispatched. Those who had lost had only weeks remaining to organize their papers and the records of their eighteen, twenty-four, or even thirty-six years of Senate service. Their staff members worked long days to help them, while simultaneously circulating their resumes frantically, hoping to find work in a Capitol about to become dominated by Republicans.

At the same time, the Senate office buildings echoed with the laughter and excitement of triumphant Republicans, who seemed to party endlessly. At the end of one day, the elevator opened in front of me to reveal a group of elderly Republicans, men and women, dressed in formal wear. They poured out of the elevator, filled with exuberance and laughter. One woman, quite heavy, and wearing too much purple eye makeup, but still very striking, caught my eye. In an instant, I realized that it was Senator John Warner's wife—better known as Elizabeth Taylor.

A top Senate Democratic aide said, "[the senators who lost] still don't know what hit them. It's sinking in a lot faster on the rest of us. There are several thousand Democratic staffers up here who thought this was a way of life. It's not an easy time for used and bruised Democratic staffers." Jackson's aggressive staff on the Permanent Subcommittee on Investigations refused to vacate their offices; the Capitol police had to be summoned. Senator Glenn's subcommittee staff director handed out pink slips at the staff party.

McGovern gave the impression of being the calmest of the losers. He said that he was receiving more speaking invitations than he had since his presidential run. Bayh, licking his wounds, gave thought to seeking to become the chairman of the Democratic National Committee, if only to hit back at the right-wingers who had defeated him. Magnuson showed no interest in even coming back for the lame duck.

George Cunningham, McGovern's administrative assistant, said: "Most of us don't feel this lame duck should deal with anything very important. The mood of the country has changed so dramatically. It wouldn't even be proper to do anything other than the housekeeping chores. It's somebody else's ballgame now."

Yet against the odds, the lame-duck session proved to be remarkably productive. The Congress completed action on many of the legislative matters that had been left hanging: a budget resolution and reconciliation bill; five appropriations bills; a three-year extension of revenue sharing; changes in military pay and benefits; a measure making disposal of low-level nuclear waste a state responsibility; and a landmark environmental cleanup bill to deal with toxic waste sites, thereafter to be known, simply, as "Superfund." The Great Senate may have been felled by Reagan's landslide, but it still had work to do.

Ted Kennedy had only one real objective for the lame-duck session. In discussions about his endorsement, general election campaign, and fundraising, Kennedy had asked President Carter to nominate Stephen Breyer to a judgeship on the U.S. Court of Appeals for the First Circuit. Despite the bitterness between the two camps after the election, Carter did so, and given Breyer's stellar credentials, he quickly gained the approval of the judicial selection commission.

Contemporary observers might ask: why would the Republicans permit a Democrat like Breyer a lifetime federal judgeship when they would be in control of the White House and the Senate just weeks later? The answer quickly became clear—and it was characteristic of how the Great Senate had always operated. Personal friendships and mutual respect still trumped ideological differences. Breyer had established a great relationship with Emory Sneeden, Strom Thurmond's chief counsel on the Judiciary Committee. They had breakfast together every morning and devised a uniquely successful way of processing judicial nominations, despite the fact they agreed on few issues. The Judiciary Committee quickly voted to approve Breyer's nomination by a 17–0 vote, while letting twenty other Carter judicial nominations die.

On December 9, the Senate confirmed Breyer to be a federal judge on the First Circuit Court of Appeals. Fourteen years later, the Senate confirmed Bill Clinton's nomination of Judge Breyer to the Supreme Court where he continues to serve. Breyer's colleagues at Harvard Law School, who had once questioned his judgment in taking a job in the Senate, would be reading his judgments for decades to come.

Birch Bayh badly wanted one more legislative accomplishment before leaving the Senate: the legislation reforming patent policy that he had been pushing along with Dole. With the lame-duck session approaching its end, one senator—Russell Long—was preventing Senate passage of the legislation. Long believed that if the taxpayers had paid for the university research, the results belong to the federal government and shouldn't be shared. But on the last day of the session, Bayh got a call from Long. "Take the patent bill," Long said. "You're entitled to it. You earned it."

Once Long lifted his hold, the Bayh-Dole Act became law. In 2002, an article in the *Economist Technology Quarterly* entitled "Innovation's Golden Goose" described Bayh-Dole as "perhaps the most inspired piece of legislation to be enacted in America in the past half century." The article contended that "together with amendments in 1984 and augmentation in 1986, [Bayh-Dole] unlocked inventions and discoveries that had been made in laboratories throughout the United States with the help of taxpayers' money. More than anything, this single policy measure helped to reverse America's precipitous slide into industrial irrelevance." The president of the NASDAQ would estimate that 30 percent of the value of the companies listed came from university research that was commercialized only because of Bayh-Dole.

The time had come for the Senate to finish its historic effort to resolve the issue of Alaska Lands. When it still remained in doubt whether Carter would hang on to the presidency for a second term, many environmentalists contended that Alaska would be better preserved through executive orders rather than legislation that compromised on their most ambitious objectives. Reagan's landslide brought a quick end to that line of reasoning. "There's a lot of feeling that we'd better be realistic and take what we can get," said a House committee staffer. "We're at the mercy of the Senate."

Ted Stevens now urged the House to accept the Senate bill, even though he had previously voted against it. "This bill is the best that can be done. It gives everyone 80 percent of what they were after"—if this was accurate (or, for that matter, mathematically possible), it would be the very definition of a great compromise. The House passed the Senate bill four days later.

An exultant Jimmy Carter signed the landmark legislation on December 2. Mo Udall said that "no president, with the possible exception of Theodore Roosevelt, had ever done more for conservation." It was no hyperbole. Carter's personal commitment to the issue had been extraordinary and effective. He had constantly insisted on protecting as much of Alaska as possible, using his presidential authority to do so, while pushing the Congress toward legislation. With his passion for the issue and his love of details, Carter had spent countless hours poring over maps of Alaska, understanding and making decisions on virtually every national park, monument, and wilderness area to be created. This was presidential leadership of the highest order, and a fitting accomplishment to finish off an otherwise beleaguered term.

But the Senate, too, deserved enormous credit. It was the forum for fierce, extended debate of a magnitude appropriate for the issue. It was the place where sharply conflicting interests clashed and were ultimately reconciled through principled compromise. Neither the politics of an election year nor the fundamental differences between environmentalists and the energy, mining, and forest industries was allowed to prevent the successful resolution of an enormous issue.

The Alaska National Interest Lands Conservation Act set aside for conservation an area larger than the state of California, including four national forests, ten national preserves, sixteen national wildlife refuges, and seven national parks. The legislation doubled the size of our national parks, tripled our wilderness areas, and protected twenty-five free-flowing rivers in their natural state. At the same time, it opened 95 percent of Alaska for unrestricted oil and gas exploration while providing special protection to an area known as the Arctic National Wildlife Refuge and prohibiting oil exploration within the refuge unless the president and both Houses of Congress agreed to allow it. The *Washington Post* editorial page called it "the most important piece of conservation legislation in decades . . . a notable, perhaps stupendous, step forward in preserving a part of the original America for future generations to enjoy and use."

The monumental Alaska Lands Act would stand as the last great accomplishment of a Senate shattered by the election that had just taken place.

THOSE WHO LEFT THE Senate would take vastly different paths. Abe Ribicoff would become counsel to a major New York law firm, splitting his time between New York and Washington. Satisfied by his forty-five-year career in government service, he did not take on the kind of assignments that often go to former senators. Birch Bayh would become a Washington lawyer and lobbyist, but with a relatively low profile. He would have the pleasure of seeing his son, Evan, follow in his footsteps, elected to the Senate in 1998 after having been governor. Ed Muskie eased into senior statesman status, serving as chairman for the Center for National Policy, a Democratic think-tank, and accepting President Reagan's request to investigate the White House role in Iran-Contra, along with John Tower and Brent Scowcroft.

Frank Church would join a New York–based international law firm, but would live only a short time before a second battle with cancer caused his death at fifty-nine. His legacy would generate more controversy than any of his Senate colleagues. Throughout the decade after 9/11, the impact of the Church Committee investigation of the intelligence agencies would continue to provoke fierce debate.

Gaylord Nelson made the fastest and best transition. In February 1981, Bernie Koteen, one of Nelson's closest friends, heard that the Wilderness Society was considering strengthening its leadership structure. "What about Gaylord," Koteen suggested to William Turnage, the organization's president, and the match was made almost immediately. Nelson became the organization's chairman, its chief spokesman and public face around the country. Nelson, the great conservationist of the 1950's and environmental activist of the 60's and 70's, would continue his extraordinary work to safeguard the environment, in the United States and globally, for more than another twenty-five years—through the 80's, the 90's, and into the twenty-first century, until his death in 2005.

Despairing about the country's move to the right, George McGovern never stopped regretting his loss to Nixon or thinking of himself as a potential president. To the chagrin of many of his admirers, he sought the Democratic nomination in 1984 and flirted with another run in 1992. He tried to stay in the forefront of Democratic politics, writing frequently, including an article calling for the impeachment of George W. Bush and Dick Cheney ("Nixon Was Bad. These Guys Are Worse.") In 1996, while grieving over his daughter's death from alcoholism, he wrote an anguished memoir that captured national attention.

At the same time, he continued his life's work of fighting hunger in the United States and internationally. In 1998, President Clinton named McGovern the U.S. Ambassador to the UN Food and Agriculture Organization in Rome, where he served until 2001. In 2001, he became the UN Global Ambassador on World Hunger. In 2008, McGovern, along with Bob Dole, received a World Food Peace Laureate. His fifty-year effort to combat hunger paralleled Nelson's half-century of work on environmental issues.

Jack Javits would be confined to a motorized wheelchair as his ALS worsened. His mind nevertheless reminded sharp, and he continued to fight on for causes that he cared about. Ken Duberstein, a former Javits staffer who later directed congressional relations in the Reagan administration and became Reagan's last chief of staff, remembered Javits lobbying him repeatedly to get the Medal of Freedom awarded to the actor Douglas Fairbanks Jr. Duberstein did not tell Javits that, in fact, President Reagan was actually planning to award Javits himself the Medal of Freedom. Javits was deeply moved to receive this high honor, but at the memorial service following Javits's death on March 7, 1986, Warren Rudman pulled Duberstein aside and said: "He told me to remind you about the Medal of Freedom for Douglas Fairbanks."

Duberstein visited Javits periodically as the ALS took its toll. On one of his last visits Duberstein told Javits that the White House was trying without success to get Senator Pete Domenici to support a 7 percent increase in the defense budget, rather than 5 percent. What could he say to get Domenici's support, Duberstein wondered.

Javits, paralyzed and confined to a wheelchair, could only speak with great difficulty. But he still answered like a great senator: "Ken, you have to understand," Javits said. "When Pete thinks about the decision, what comes first is the state of the nation. Second is the institution of the Senate. If those two factors work, then he might go with the president."

EPILOGUE

GARY HART ONCE DESCRIBED THE SENATE AS A "KIND OF CONTROLLED madhouse." Anyone who ever served there, either as a senator or a staff member, recognized that they were operating on a narrow ledge between paralysis and chaos, working without much margin of error. Many times, when deadlock seemed insurmountable and failure seemed inevitable, senators would come together to find solutions. The senators understood, and they made their staffs understand, Mike Mansfield's wisdom: their individual agendas did not ultimately matter; it was the Senate, and the country, that mattered. It was not the rules that made the Senate work; it was mutual respect, good faith, self-restraint, and a commitment to both the institution of the Senate and the national interest that enabled the senators to reach principled compromise.

Senator Chris Dodd, the Connecticut Democrat, beautifully captured the essence of the Senate at its best in his farewell speech on November 30, 2010:

> Politics today seemingly rewards only passion and independence, not deliberation and compromise as well. It has become commonplace to hear candidates for the Senate campaign on how they are going to Washington to shake things up—all by themselves. . . . The United States Senate does not work that way, nor can it, or should it. Mayors, governors, and presidents can sometimes succeed through the sheer force of their will. But there has never been a Senator so persuasive, so charismatic, so clever, or so brilliant that they could make a significant difference, while refusing to work with other members of this body. Simply put, senators cannot ultimately be effective alone.

From 1977 through 1980, that was how it worked, continuing the mode of operation that began in the early 1960's. Perennially described as the "most exclusive club," the Senate functioned more in the spirit that Javits best captured: as a team. The constraints on partisanship remained strong, fraying only at the end. The Senate included a few members who were determined obstructionists, but they were vastly outnumbered by those who believed that the Senate had to work its collective will. Operating in that way, large legislative accomplishments that seemed unattainable still occurred routinely. For those who worked there, we did not realize that ours was a unique period until it had come to an end.

The 1980 election brought about more than a change in party control in the Senate. Coming after two consecutive elections, 1976 and 1978, in which thirty-seven new senators had been elected, the 1980 tsunami essentially shattered the Senate ecosystem. When the new Senate convened in January 1981, it included fifty-five members who had been in the Senate six years or less. The stalwart veterans who had served three, four, and even six terms—Magnuson, Church, Ribicoff, Muskie, Javits, Nelson, Bayh, McGovern, Talmadge—men Don Riegle recalled as "the tall trees"—were gone, retired or defeated. In their place stood what may have been the weakest group of first-termers to ever walk the Senate floor. Many combined an absence of political experience with a New Right ideology, an aversion to compromise, and a lack of interest in, if not outright contempt for, the institution they were joining.

John Sears, the respected Republican consultant, spoke for many Republicans when he quipped several years later: "If we had known that we were going to win the Senate, we would have found some better candidates." Former Javits and John Heinz aide John Rother recalled a meeting among Republican veterans about slotting some of the weakest of the partisans in committee assignments where they could do the least damage. Paula Hawkins, Jeremiah Denton, Mack Mattingly, James Abdnor—these were senators who came out of nowhere, arrived without political accomplishments, and left six years later with their records intact. Their only legacy was a diminished Senate.

The new Senate differed from its twentieth-century predecessors in another way. Traditionally, the House reflects the popular passions and political swings of the moment. This time, however, the House remained strongly Democratic, while it was the Senate that reflected the Reagan landslide. Senators would be the "foot soldiers in the Reagan revolution." Bipartisan comity and considered judgment were less important than driving the Reagan program, particularly in the early 1980's.

In September 1982, less than two years after the Republican takeover, a major article in *Congressional Quarterly* captured the new and dispirited mood. "In the Senate of the '80's, team spirit has given way to the rule of individuals," journalist Alan Ehrenhalt wrote. "Every man is an island."

The article included a famous 1954 photo of Senators Jack Kennedy, Scoop Jackson, and Mike Mansfield playing softball. "[The picture] seems to stand for a Senate that has disappeared in the years since," Ehrenhalt wrote, "one whose members knew each other well, worked and played together and thought of politics as a team game. Today's Senate, many of its own members complain, is nothing like that. It is seen from within as a place where there is little time to think, close personal relationships are rare, and individual rights, not community feeling, is the most precious commodity." John Tower lamented: "Every year the Senate seemed to be a less congenial place. The professionalism and dedication that had once been characteristic of the institution were ebbing away."

Still, it was not yet unreasonable to expect that the Senate could rebuild and recover from its 1980 shattering. There were plenty of strong senators in both parties. The very weakest fell by the wayside quickly, soon to be replaced by promising new additions. In fact, the Senate did make a noticeable comeback in the mid-to-late 1980's, marked by some significant bipartisan achievements. But the comeback was brief, and the Senate thereafter reentered a downward spiral, which has only continued to accelerate.

In seeking an explanation for the Senate's precipitous decline, the evidence points unequivocally in one direction. Certainly, many times the actions of Senate Democrats, individually or collectively, have frustrated or disappointed supporters like me. I can also recall many instances in which Senate Republicans acted as superb legislators and statesmen. Neither party has ever had a monopoly on fine senators. But overall, today's fractured and ineffective Senate is the product of the continuous, relentless movement of the Republican Party further and further to the right, accompanied by a fierce determination to defeat their Democratic opponents and an increased willingness by some to frustrate and obstruct the legislative process and the operation of government by whatever means possible.

Looking back over the past forty years, one finds Senate Democrats willing to work with Republican presidents Nixon, Ford, Reagan, Bush 41, and Bush 43. The Senate Republicans were likewise willing to work with Presidents Kennedy, Johnson, and Carter. But by in the late 1980's and early 1990's, things were changing dramatically, and it would become clear that the veterans who fell to the Reagan revolution were only the first casualties.

ALTHOUGH THE 1980 ELECTION shattered the Great Senate of the previous two decades, the Senate's ultimate fate was not yet determined. Indeed, the Senate was able to mount a seemingly solid comeback in the mid-to-late 1980's thanks primarily to Bob Dole's period as a master legislator and Senate leader. Despite his obvious talents, Dole was not a major figure in the great Senate of the 1960's and 1970's. Rather, he rose rapidly in his party by being chairman of the Republican National Committee; he operated through acerbic speeches, "gotcha" amendments, and slashing partisanship, rather than through constructive deal making. Of course, there were notable exceptions to his partisanship, such as his work on Bayh-Dole and the start of his historic alliance with George McGovern to combat hunger, but they were the exceptions.

But Dole changed his approach in 1981 when he became chairman of the Finance Committee. He put together an impressive staff eventually headed by Sheila Burke, who had been handling health-care issues for him. Burke was a nurse who had moved from caring for patients to advocacy on health policy. When Dole interviewed Burke, she told him that she was a Democrat from California from a union family. Dole responded that her political background did not matter to him; what mattered was that she understood patient care.

As Finance Committee chairman, Dole threw his great talent and energy into legislative heavy lifting, helping to engineer the Reagan tax cuts and the historic 1983 compromise to strengthen Social Security. When Howard Baker carried out his intention to retire after three terms, Dole defeated four other contenders to become majority leader in January 1985. He had come to relish legislating and deal making; he also thought, despite the experiences of Baker, that a successful record as Senate leader could be a good springboard to the White House in 1988.

Working with a more experienced, less ideological White House in Reagan's second term, Dole's Senate helped bring about major legislative accomplishments. Bob Packwood, now chairman of the Senate Finance Committee, worked with Bill Bradley on far-reaching tax reform. Alan Simpson worked with Ted Kennedy to fashion a landmark immigration bill, granting amnesty for 5 million illegal aliens and making it illegal for an employer to hire illegal immigrants. Barry Goldwater and Sam Nunn championed historic reform of the Joint Chiefs of Staff. Orrin Hatch had just completed his collaboration with Henry Waxman, one of the most liberal House Democrats, to give patent protection to research pharmaceutical companies while speeding the process of making generic drugs available—legislation still referred to as "Hatch-Waxman."

Sheila Burke remembers Bob Dole constantly in motion, never happier than when he was moving from meeting to meeting, making deals or creating the environment for other senators to complete them. He turned his scintillating humor on himself and the frequent absurdities of the Senate. "If you're hanging around with nothing to do and the zoo is closed," Dole remarked, "come over to the Senate. You'll get the same kind of feeling and you won't have to pay."

When the Democrats regained the Senate majority in 1986, Dole and Robert Byrd switched responsibilities, but the Senate continued to function in a workmanlike, bipartisan way. When the presidency of Ronald Reagan was shaken to the core by the ill-advised decision to sell arms to Iran in order to raise money to support the Nicaraguan contras, Daniel Inouye and Warren Rudman led the most visible investigation of the presidency since Watergate with good judgment and even-handedness. Significant legislative accomplishments continued, because of strong congressional leadership and Howard Baker's willingness to become Reagan's chief of staff. "Congress regained its voice in the 1987–1988 session," the *New York Times* opined as the Congress closed, "enacting groundbreaking legislation in areas as diverse as trade policy and welfare reform, civil rights and arms control."

The comeback was not to last.

IN RETROSPECT, THE SPIRAL downward for the Senate began in earnest in January 1989, coinciding with the arrival of Republican Trent Lott of Mississippi after an impressive sixteen-year run in the House. The son of a shipyard worker, Lott attended college and law school at the University of Mississippi. After a brief stint in private practice, Lott came to Capitol Hill in 1968, to work for Congressman William Colmer, an extremely conservative Democrat who chaired the House Rules Committee. When Colmer announced his retirement in 1972, Lott, understanding the way the political winds were blowing in the South, decided to run for his seat as a Republican, and won handily, aided by the strength of Nixon's landslide.

In the House, Lott rose to become Republican whip. His influence increased after the 1980 election, as he proved extremely effective in helping the Reagan administration gets its tax and budget cuts through the House. Lott allied himself with Newt Gingrich and other young House Republicans who resented the high-handed treatment they had received from the House Democrats and disliked the go-along attitude of the House Republican leaders. He was deeply involved in Gingrich's successful effort to bring down House Speaker Jim Wright on ethics charges. In 1988, when a Mississippi Senate seat opened up, Lott won easily.

Most newly elected senators come to the institution with a sense of deep respect, if not awe. Lott was an exception. As he describes in his candid and fascinating memoir, *Herding Cats*, he hated the place from the moment he arrived. "After giving up real national power in the House, after winning a score of victories for Ronald Reagan," Lott wrote, "I expected a warm welcome in the Senate." Instead, Lott and the other freshman "found themselves in 'storage' as the Senate machinery creaked to life." Lott viewed many of his fellow senators as "distant, impossible to befriend." The Senate itself was a "confused and disorganized institution," with chaotic and unpredictable hours. He also concluded that "the Democrats had been in power so long they had adopted bullyboy tactics to enforce their power," ignoring the fact that the Republicans had just recently been the Senate majority for six years.

Lott started making lists of things that he would change if and when he got the chance. He decided that he could rely on a "tight conservative clique of young senators," some who had recently arrived and some who would soon follow: "We were conservative, we were hungry, we intended to make a difference and eventually capture the leadership." The goals would be to make the Republicans both more right wing and more unified and to remake the Senate in the House's image—efficient, driven by the leaders, and deeply partisan. Lott made it into the Republican leadership after the 1992 election, on the bottom rung, and started looking upward immediately.

Lott's arrival in the Senate coincided with what would prove to be a major event in recent Senate history. President-elect George H. W. Bush had nominated John Tower to be his secretary of defense. The Senate had never rejected a Cabinet nomination made by a new president, and Tower, the former chairman of the Armed Services Committee and Reagan administration arms negotiator, had defense credentials that were long and strong. But Sam Nunn, the new chairman of the Armed Services Committee, had concerns about what he believed to be Tower's alcoholism and womanizing. Other senators, notably Carl Levin, focused on possible conflicts of interest arising from Tower's representation of defense contractors after he had left the Senate. The investigation of the nomination became protracted and ugly, as

Democratic opponents in the Senate derived further support from right-wing conservative activist Paul Weyrich, who hated Tower for being a defender of abortion rights.

On the floor of the Senate, Rudman, a respected former prosecutor, launched a powerful critique of the Armed Services Committee report against Tower, saying that he had tried hundreds of cases and had never seen anyone "trashed on such flimsy evidence in my entire life." Dole accused the Democrats of using the nomination to bloody the Bush administration in its infancy. John McCain, recently elected from Arizona, and William Cohen both argued passionately on Tower's behalf. (Even today, Cohen still expresses outrage at the treatment that Tower received.) Democrat George Mitchell, who had just become Senate majority leader, made the vote a test of party solidarity, and Tower's nomination was rejected 53–47, virtually along party lines.

The bitter battle did much to change the tenor of the Senate. The grievances of Lott and other younger Republicans about their treatment by Democrats no longer seemed so far-fetched. Two years later, the partisan divide deepened even further as the nation was treated to the extraordinary spectacle of Clarence Thomas's nomination to the Supreme Court and his confirmation despite serious questions about his qualifications and the allegations of sexual harassment by Anita Hill.

When Bill Clinton entered the White House, ending twelve years of Republican presidential rule, the Republican attitude was: "You have the reins of power. You're on your own. Don't count on Republicans for support or votes." None of Clinton's recent predecessors had faced an absolutely unified opposition party on the issues most central to their agenda. Dole, once again showing his partisan side, announced "the good news is that he's getting a honeymoon in Washington. The bad news is that Bob Dole is going to be his chaperone."

"Dole didn't really dislike Clinton," former Clinton aide and author Sidney Blumenthal would write. "But when the whole Republican Party swiveled against Clinton to deny him any victory, Dole rushed to get to its head. He had prided himself on being a master of the Senate and now he turned his legislative skills to the purpose of blocking everything."

The change in the Senate was palpable to the moderate Republicans. Rudman left first, retiring after two terms at the end of 1992, uncomfortable with "the confrontational, take-no-prisoners attitude" that the new Republicans brought to the Senate. In 1994, John Danforth, just months from retirement, joined Democrats in voting for cloture to pass Clinton's crime bill. When Danforth joined Republican colleagues at lunch, he was met with silence. "It was as though someone had pushed a mute button," he recalled. "It was devastating." At the end of an eighteen-year career, Danforth found himself being treated like a pariah.

A year later, Republican leaders pressured Oregon Senator Mark Hatfield relentlessly to support legislation for a constitutional amendment to balance the budget. The Republican caucus, fired up by Rick Santorum and others from the New Right, virtually ostracized Hatfield when he refused to go along. Hatfield, who had a strong moral streak, finally told Dole that he would resign if that was what the caucus wanted, but that he would not vote in favor of a balanced budget constitutional amendment. It failed to get the requisite two-thirds of the Senate by one vote.

There had certainly been countless times in the past where Senate leaders had urged members of their caucus to vote with them on key issues. But if senators told the leader they could not do so, that traditionally ended the matter. Such decisions were regarded as being motivated by the senator's sincere judgment on the merits, or the senator's perception of political imperatives. Putting the screws to senators and treating them like pariahs if they refused to go along—this was a dramatic departure from the way the Great Senate had always worked.

In November 1994, Republicans led by Newt Gingrich took control of both the House and Senate in a rout reminiscent of 1980. In January 1995, Lott, who had gotten on the Republican leadership ladder, challenged Simpson, the popular Republican whip. Although Simpson was well liked and had Dole's strong endorsement, Lott had been building support almost from the day he reached the Senate. When the Republican caucus met to decide, Connie Mack of Florida, a former House member and one of the most conservative senators, spoke for Lott, arguing that his long friendship with Gingrich would give Republicans a more unified front in their battles against Clinton. That type of argument would have cut no ice in the Senate just a few years before—relationships inside the Senate were what mattered—but the mood of the Senate Republicans had changed dramatically. One senator previously pledged to Simpson—Mitch McConnell—changed his mind and gave Lott a narrow margin of victory.

In 1996, when Dole resigned from the Senate to run for president, Lott became majority leader. As Lott noted proudly, for the first time, both the

Republican Senate and the House had leaders from the South, the culmination of the GOP transformation that began with Goldwater.

Lott made his impact felt almost immediately. He ordered the comfortable but casual Republican cloakroom redecorated in a much more formal way. He established a strong whip system to ensure Republican Party discipline. "To bring order to the chaos," Lott wrote, "I commanded the divided Senate through a team of six or seven Republican members. . . . The panel was nicknamed 'The Council of Trent.'"

Few Republican moderates remained in the Senate, and Simpson, Hatfield, Cohen, and Nancy Kassebaum, finding the place much less congenial, decided to retire at the end of 1996. With increasing frequency, the new Republican senators would come from the House, bringing hard-edged, right-wing credentials—one thoughtful academic study described the group as "Gingrich senators." One new Republican senator decidedly not in that group was Susan Collins, who had been a Senate staffer for Cohen from 1979 through 1986 before returning to Maine to serve in the state government. After she was elected to the Senate to replace Cohen in 1996, Collins was amazed to find how much more partisan the Senate had become in the ten years she had been away. In his own characteristically outspoken way, Alan Simpson would later say: "The Senate changed when the battered children from the House arrived, led by Trent Lott."

The change in the Republican ranks would have a profound impact soon enough. In 1998, after the stunning revelation of President Clinton's affair with White House intern Monica Lewinsky, House Republicans moved aggressively to consider impeachment. Clinton's egregious bad judgment and behavior hardly seemed to reach the constitutionally mandated impeachment threshold of "high crimes and misdemeanors," but Republicans plowed ahead, even after polls showed 70 percent of the nation wanted Clinton to stay in office, and as a result of their overreach, the 1998 off-year elections went surprisingly well for the Democrats. In the end, the Senate concluded the tragic farce of Clinton's impeachment. But even with the eyes of the nation upon it, the Senate could not transcend the partisanship that had fueled the fires of impeachment. Only five Republicans voted against the Article of Impeachment charging Clinton with obstruction of justice.

PARTISAN POISON CONTINUED TO plague the Senate during the presidency of George W. Bush. Senator Bill Frist, a Tennessee Republican, took the majority leader's post in 2002 after Lott was forced to resign as Leader following racially insensitive remarks at Strom Thurmond's 100th birthday. For those who believe that the Senate should include exceptional people from diverse walks of life, Frist represented a potentially exciting choice. He was one of the nation's leading heart surgeons, and a humanitarian who continued to make regular trips to Africa to perform heart and lung transplants.

Unfortunately, whether because of inexperience or presidential ambitions, the Senate leadership position did not bring out the best in Frist. It was an unwritten rule that Senators did not campaign against their colleagues. Certainly, Senate leaders, responsible for working closely together every day, did not campaign against each other. Frist ignored that rule, going to South Dakota to campaign harshly against Tom Daschle, the Democratic leader. Daschle lost narrowly, and one more tradition that had previously contributed to Senate comity came to an end.

Many Americans were deeply troubled when the Senate intervened in the case of Terry Schiavo, a Florida woman who had been in a persistent vegetative state for fifteen years after suffering a loss of oxygen to the brain at the age of twenty-six. If there was ever a moment for a wise and brave doctor to be Senate majority leader, this was it. However, purely on the basis of a videotape of Schiavo, Frist challenged the considered opinions of the Florida court that she was in a persistent, vegetative state. Frist's opinion helped justify the congressional rush to action, which flew in the face of basic Republican principles about deference to states' rights.

John Danforth, an Episcopal priest as well as a lawyer, now in private life, had watched the Republicans' march to the right with mounting concern. The Schiavo case pushed him over the edge. Danforth was appalled that his party would inject the federal government into the most personal and agonizing decision a family could face. "This is not a coalition of traditional Republicans and the Christian right in the nature of a merger of equals," Danforth wrote in a book entitled *Faith and Politics: How the Moral Values Debate Divides America.* "This is the takeover of the Republican Party by the Christian Right." Danforth expressed particular contempt for Frist's role, saying he could not "imagine a physician making a medical diagnosis without examining a patient unless he had a special need to appeal to the Christian Right."

Senators still played an important and self-important part in the national debate, appearing on the Sunday talk shows in large numbers. But even as three senators—Barack Obama, Hillary Clinton, and John McCain—battled for the presidency in 2008, many of their colleagues had stopped performing the principal function of senators: exercising wise and independent judgment in the national interest. "We have been miniaturized," Olympia Snowe of Maine said sadly. And the situation was destined to get even worse.

BARACK OBAMA'S ELECTION WAS a moment of great national hope and pride, but it came at a time of near catastrophic economic turmoil. The nation's economy had fallen off the cliff in the weeks before the election with the collapse of Lehman Brothers and AIG. By the time of Obama's inauguration, the economic crisis had deepened. It is a core part of our national narrative that crisis brings out the best in Americans, and there was reason to believe the very real prospect of another great Depression would galvanize politicians from both parties to put aside their differences.

Events soon proved otherwise. The Republicans in the Senate and House quickly made it clear that the Obama administration and Hill Democrats were on their own. They were using the same playbook they had used against the Clinton administration sixteen years before, but this time their obstruction came at a time of absolute crisis for the country. As the Obama administration worked feverishly to put together a major economic stimulus bill, Senate Republicans focused primarily on preventing Obama's appointees from taking office. The constant threat to filibuster made garnering sixty votes to invoke cloture an absolute requirement to accomplish anything. The White House and the Senate Democrats struggled to find Republicans to support the stimulus, finally winning support from Collins and Snowe as well as Arlen Specter, who decided to switch parties. Republican leader Mitch McConnell and members of his caucus put powerful pressure on Collins and Snowe to get with the program. A picture of Collins in the *New York Times*, which showed her walking up a staircase in the Capitol absolutely alone, spoke volumes.

The courage and independence of Collins and Snowe reminds us that today's Senate does represent a real advance over the great Senate of the 1960's and 1970's in one vital respect—it is no longer a Senate that is exclusively made up of men. In 1979, the Senate included exactly one woman—Nancy Landon Kassebaum of Kansas, who had just been elected. Thirty years later, there were seventeen women senators, not yet half of the Senate or even close, but a huge increase from what it had been. From all reports, the seventeen women senators, led by their "dean," Barbara Mikulski, see themselves as a distinct group, and share uncommonly close friendships that transcend party lines. But despite their close ties, the women senators have been unable to alter the overall harsh and partisan climate of the Senate.

As Obama's term continued, the debate about health care grew long, ugly, and bitterly partisan, with no Senate Republican supporting the effort. The anger across the country fueled further anger in the Senate, and vice versa. The enactment of the legislation by a united Democratic majority was made necessary by the unified opposition, but predictably, passage of the legislation did not cool the partisan fires, as the Republicans promptly pledged to seek its repeal and to block funding for it.

By October 2010, the Senate had come to an extraordinary juncture. Against the odds, it had passed three momentous pieces of legislation—the economic stimulus, the health-care legislation, and a sweeping reform of financial regulation—and yet it was universally regarded as dysfunctional. Carl Levin, a thirty-two-year Senate veteran, was struck by the paradox. "It's been the most productive Senate since I've been here in terms of major accomplishments," Levin said, "and by far the most frustrating. It's almost impossible, day to day, to get anything done. Routine bills and nominations get bottled up indefinitely. Everything is stopped by the threat of filibusters—not real filibusters, just the threat of filibusters." In a *New Yorker* article titled "The Empty Chamber," George Packer noted that "the two lasting achievements of this Senate, financial regulation and health care, required a year and a half of legislative warfare that nearly destroyed the body." In August 2011, the Senate did play a more constructive role than the House in narrowly averting a U.S. government default on its debt, but no branch of government acquitted itself well in creating the crisis that brought the country to the brink.

As debate and despair about the Senate intensified, the two most iconic senators, Ted Kennedy and Robert Byrd, passed away. Kennedy succumbed to brain cancer in August 2009; Byrd to old age, in June 2010. Although Kennedy was only forty-eight when he challenged Jimmy Carter in 1980, he never again sought the presidency. Instead, he became, undeniably, one of the greatest senators in the history of country. Everyone who watched him marveled at how Kennedy could combine such passionate commitment to his liberal beliefs with a constant willingness to work successfully with other senators, and presidents, who held dramatically different views.

Byrd, who had written the history of the Roman Senate, as well as the American Senate, had served longer than any senator in the history of the United States. He would always be remembered for his total commitment to

the Senate and its responsibilities in the constitutional system. In the last decade of his life, Byrd would earn the admiration of many Americans for blasting the "supine Senate" for failing to stop the decision to go to war in Iraq.
Kennedy and Byrd each proved that it was possible to be a great senator even
without a great Senate.

IT IS NOW GENERALLY recognized that the 1980 election was a turning
point in American political history, with Ronald Reagan winning the presidency and the Senate changing drastically. Reagan's victory represented more
than the electorate's verdict that Jimmy Carter was a failed president. It was
the triumph of what Dominic Sandbrook has called "the populist right," and
it reflected a significant departure by the Republican Party from its tradition
of moderate conservatism, respect for privacy and individual freedom, and
support for civil rights.

But Reagan's presidency would be followed by a further lurch to the right
by the Republican Party, in 1994–1996, that would make Democrats, and
many Republicans, long for the days of Reagan and George H. W. Bush's relative moderation, pragmatism, and willingness to make deals across party
lines. Those who thought that the Republican Party could go no further right
learned otherwise in 2010, with the advent of the Tea Party. Mike Huckabee,
whose surprisingly successful campaign for the 2008 Republican nomination
drew support from the Christian Right, captured the new mood of today's
Republican Party, saying: "Ronald Reagan would have a very difficult, if not
impossible time, being nominated in this atmosphere." And in this atmosphere, the Senate is our most vulnerable political institution, because bipartisan comity is the oxygen that is needs to function successfully.

The question is—in this atmosphere, can the Senate somehow transform
itself? Critics frequently suggest that the sixty-vote minimum required to cut
off filibusters is the key to the body's dysfunctions, but I remain skeptical that
basic changes can be made in that area. The minority party will never agree
to diminish the power it currently has, and the majority party, after considering it, will decide that it would be disastrous to ram through a change by majority vote. Moreover, as Senator Dodd reminded us: "In a nation founded in
revolution against tyrannical rule . . . there should be one institution that
would always provide a space where dissent was valued and respected."

But the Senate should be able to respect dissent without condemning itself
to paralysis. Certain changes in the Senate rules are absolutely essential. In

2010, the country watched one senator, Kentucky Republican Jim Bunning, block the extension of unemployment benefits for two weeks, when even his Republican colleagues supported the legislation. The country also saw a single senator, Alabama senator Richard Shelby, block the confirmation of seventy Obama administration executive branch nominees, for reasons unrelated to their positions.

This is madness. The Senate needs to agree upon rules changes that protect the minority party, but prevent individual senators from paralyzing the institution or blocking the president from staffing the executive branch. Justice Robert Jackson once wrote: "The Constitution is not a suicide pact." Neither are the Senate rules.

To turn back the current wave of intense partisanship, the most fundamental change must come from senators themselves. The Republican caucus includes a significant number of senators who have been positive and constructive forces in the past, but at some point decided that it was necessary to join a unified Republican minority. In the lame-duck session of 2010, the Republican senators showed how quickly the Senate could change when they returned to exercising their independent judgment—in essence, to being senators. The Senate enacted legislation to end the policy of "don't ask, don't tell" for gays and lesbians in the military because eight Republican senators refused to follow their leader in opposition. The Senate ratified the START treaty limiting nuclear arms because thirteen Republican senators refused to follow the Republican leader. For instance, Republican Lamar Alexander of Tennessee went into a confidential briefing on START opposed to the treaty, listened to the presentation, and came out convinced that he should support it. His change of position was striking, because it happens so rarely these days. But that's the way the last Great Senate worked all the time.

America is adrift in turbulent and dangerous waters. Facing enormous challenges at home and abroad, we urgently need our once-vaunted political system to function at its best, instead of at its worst. To be sure, it is more difficult to be a senator today than it was in the 1960's and 1970's. The increasingly vitriolic political culture, fueled by a twenty-four-hour news cycle, the endless pressure to raise money, the proliferation of lobbyists and demanding, organized interests are all well known, and they take a toll. But all those factors make it more essential that our country has a Senate of men and women who bring wisdom, judgment, experience, and independence to their work, along with an understanding that the Senate must be able to take collective action in the national interest.

This book tells the story of The Last Great Senate. "Last" can be defined to mean that there have been, and can be, no other great Senates. But "last" can also be defined as "most recent," meaning that there can be another Great Senate after all.

The men and women who are senators today, and those who will join them after the next election, have it in their power to begin making the Senate great again. They have the enormous honor and privilege of walking where the giants walked—Humphrey and Javits, Mansfield and Dirksen, Kennedy and Baker, Jackson and Byrd. It is my hope that they will look at the struggles, accomplishments, and lessons of the last Great Senate, and the urgent needs of our country, and make us proud again.

ACKNOWLEDGMENTS

A first-time author, I discovered that the allegedly solitary work of writing a book is not really so solitary. So many friends and acquaintances in the political community expressed their strong belief that this was an exciting book—that the Great Senate of the 1960's and 1970's should not be forgotten. I am enormously grateful for the enthusiastic encouragement that I received over the past three years.

Initial thanks go to five friends with whom I worked in the Senate in 1978—Richard Wegman, Brian Conboy, Alan Bennett, Paul Hoff, and Paul Rosenthal. In 2008, the excitement of the presidential campaign brought us together monthly for breakfast. Inevitably, we also recalled the great times that we had working in the Senate. It was after one of our breakfasts in June 2008 that I decided to write about the Senate when it was great. The instant, unfeigned excitement of my family and closest friends about the book gave me the jumpstart that a major project needs.

My thanks also go to a number of gifted writers and savvy political people who were kind enough to read parts or all of my draft manuscript: Ken Ackerman, Al Crenshaw, Margaret Crenshaw, Mary Eccles, Alan Ehrenhalt, Peter Fenn, Tamera Luzzatto, Edie Mossberg, Walt Mossberg, Carey Parker, Donald Ritchie (the Senate Historian), Matt Seiden, Wendy Sherman, and Bruce Stokes. Special appreciation goes to Ken, because I also benefited greatly from the workshop he teaches on narrative history; to Alan, because he gave me the single best piece of advice that I received—"don't research and interview forever; write as much book as you have time for"; and Wendy, for looking at a proposed eight-word title, crossing out four of the words and leaving "The Last Great Senate" on the napkin in the restaurant. I am also extremely grateful to Heather Moore, the Senate photo historian, for helping me find many of the wonderful pictures included in this book.

Howard Paster, a major political figure in Washington for more than three decades, passed away on August 11. He shared his vivid recollections and great insights about the Senate with me several times, including once just a few weeks before his death. His many friends will miss his wisdom and generosity of spirit.

I benefited immeasurably from the excellent work of Joe Marks, my research assistant, who pored over newspapers, magazines, and congressional proceedings to help me reconstruct the public record. I found Joe through Madeleine Albright;

she recommended him as a former (and future) journalist who was one of her best graduate students at Georgetown. As usual, Madeleine's assessment was unerring.

Kathy Anderson, my agent, has been the wonderful friend and astute adviser that an aspiring author needs. She had built some credibility with me in 2004 when she advised me *not* to write a book about my losing congressional campaign. This time, she loved the idea of a book about the Great Senate, never doubting that it was potentially an important book that could find an eager audience. Based on this track record, I never question her judgment.

I will always feel a great debt of gratitude to Peter Osnos and Susan Weinberg, the founder and publisher, respectively, of PublicAffairs, for giving an unproven author the chance and support to write this book. Our initial meeting in August 2009 was one that I won't ever forget. They encouraged me to tell the story the way I wanted, as long as I promised not to make it a memoir or trudge through the entire 1960's and 1970's year by year. They also gave me a terrific editor in Brandon Proia, who has combined a great gift for narrative and language, deep interest in the subject, tremendous responsiveness, and unfailing humor and warmth. I am grateful to the whole PublicAffairs team, including Martha Whitt, for meticulously copyediting the manuscript, Michelle Welsh-Horst, for pulling together all the pieces and compiling the final version, and Tessa Shanks, for her efforts to create anticipation and interest in the book. Together, they made the publication process an enjoyable adventure, constantly moving forward.

At this point, the author usually apologizes to his or her family because of the time that writing took away from them. That didn't happen in our case. We have four generations living within twenty minutes of each other, and the excitement resulting from the birth of our twin grandsons two years ago—so, we see each other all the time. I will apologize, though, for how much I have talked about the book, and thank everyone for putting up with me.

To my daughter Susanna, my son Brian, my son-in-law Gabe, and my grandsons, Jacob and Zev: I hope that the book can contribute to a national debate that brings about a political system in our country more effective, courageous, and farsighted than what we have today.

Finally, of course, my greatest thanks go to my wife, Nancy. I remember her eyes lighting up when I told her the idea for the book. "It's wonderful," she said. "You have to write it." It wasn't quite the same as the radiant excitement of June 1969 when we started our marriage and I first came to the Great Senate. But it wasn't that different, either.

IRA SHAPIRO
October 2011

A NOTE ON SOURCES

Any book that chronicles history presents formidable research challenges. My book is a little unusual, because it attempts to recount and recapture the working of the U.S. Senate over a four-term period, from January 1977 through December 1980, rather than focusing on the work of one senator, or the development of one piece of legislation. Moreover, the narrative about the four years is "backlit" by the achievements and disappointments of the Senate during the previous fifteen years, and the book concludes with an epilogue that attempts to explain what has happened since the great Senate shattered in 1980. Consequently, the book actually spans close to fifty years. When one casts the net that wide, it goes without saying that it is impossible to research everything, or to know everything, and I certainly don't pretend to have accomplished either.

My basic approach was to rely on the public record of the actions of the Senate and the leading senators of the time. The principal sources fell into two categories. First, there was the Senate's actions and proceedings, in committee hearings and markups and floor statements and debates, and reported through leading newspapers and magazines, most notably, the *Washington Post*, the *New York Times*, *Time*, and *Congressional Quarterly*.

Second, I have drawn heavily on the biographies that have been written about leading senators. Any author who undertakes to write about the Senate labors in the shadow of Robert Caro's brilliant *Years of Lyndon Johnson: Master of the Senate*, and I derived a great deal of insight and knowledge from Caro's book. I am also indebted to the work of other historians and journalists, and while it is dangerous to single out sources that were most helpful, there are several biographies that I found myself returning to repeatedly: J. Lee Annis's biography of Howard Baker, Don Oberdorfer's biography of Mike Mansfield, Francis Valeo's memoir about Mansfield, Robert G. Kaufman's biography of Henry Jackson, Byron Hulsey's biography of Everett Dirksen, Adam Clymer's biography of Ted Kennedy, LeRoy Ashby and Rod Gramer's biography of Frank Church, William Link's biography of Jesse Helms, Bill Christofferson's biography of Gaylord Nelson, Randall Bennett Woods' biography of J. William Fulbright, Karl Campbell's biography of Sam Ervin, Stephen Gillon's biography of Walter Mondale, and Jules Witcover's recently released biography of Joe Biden. Special appreciation goes to Oberdorfer and Valeo, because it is impossible to understand the Senate of the 1960's and 1970's without understanding Mansfield's central role in creating a democratized Senate.

Third, I have benefited greatly from memoirs, or other books, written by the senators. In this category, most valuable to me were the memoirs of Jacob Javits, George McGovern, Paul Douglas, John Tower, Trent Lott, John Danforth, and the very recently released memoirs of Walter Mondale and Gary Hart. While I found Robert Byrd's autobiography to be disappointing, Senator Byrd's superb *Addresses on the History of the Senate*, Vol. 2, more than made up for it, and was extraordinarily valuable. Thomas Eagleton's *War and Presidential Power: A Chronicle of Congressional Surrender* is a vivid study of a senator grappling with an executive branch opposed to Congress's effort to reassert its authority to declare war.

My book also draws on, and benefits from, a number of valuable books about the Senate, including such classics as Donald Matthews, *U.S. Senators and Their World* and Ross Baker's *Friend and Foe in the U.S. Senate*. Lewis Gould's *The Most Exclusive Club* is a wonderful volume about the twentieth-century Senate. I hope that I benefited from several books that capture the complex texture and rhythm of the Senate on a day-to-day basis. In this regard, several wonderful books about the Senate in the 1970's were delights to reread—Eric Redman's, *The Dance of Legislation*, Elizabeth Drew's *Senator*, Bernard Asbell's *The Senate Nobody Knows*, and Senator William Cohen's *Roll Call*—as was Harry McPherson's *A Political Education*, depicting the Senate of the late 1950's. It was great fun to reread Allen Drury's *Advise and Consent*, the 1959 Pulitzer Prize–winner that first hooked me, and countless other Americans, on the Senate, and politics in general.

I must give special mention to Ambassador William Jorden's *Panama Odyssey*, published in 1984. With the possible exception of Caro's masterpiece, no book captures the actions of U.S. senators as vividly as Jorden, once a distinguished *New York Times* diplomatic correspondent, did in describing the epic Senate battle over the Panama Canal treaties. As a former international trade negotiator, I also recommend it as a book that superbly captures the roller-coaster nature of high-stakes international negotiations. Jorden's book provides the major source for my description of the Senate's consideration of the Panama Canal treaties. My chapter on the Chrysler loan guarantee act also draws heavily from the insightful book *New Deals: The Chrysler Revival and the American System*, by Robert Reich and John Donohue.

Because the narrative focuses on the Senate during the years of Jimmy Carter's presidency, I relied heavily on some of the important books about that presidency. President Carter's 1982 memoir, *Keeping Faith*, and his newly released *White House Diary* were indispensable to me, as was Vice President Mondale's memoir, *The Good Fight*. Betty Glad's 2009 book on Carter's foreign policy was also particularly helpful to me.

The Senate of the late 1970's did its work during crisis years for America, at precisely a moment when American politics was changing profoundly. It is well known that the political currents in America were moving strongly to the right, that special-interest groups were turning to new, sophisticated, and targeted lobbying techniques, and that political campaigns were becoming more costly and more vicious. In retrospect, it is quite clear that today's toxic politics were born in the late 1970's and are closely related to the rise of the New Right. Among the sources most helpful to me on these issues were Link's biography of Jesse Helms, Sean Wilentz, *The Age of Reagan*, Adam Clymer, *Drawing a Line at the Big Ditch*, John Judis, *The Paradox of American Democracy*, Alan Crawford's *Thunder on the Right*, Dominic Sandbrook, *Mad as Hell: The Crisis of the 1970's and the Rise of the Populist Right*, and, coincidentally, the work of two of my old friends from Brandeis, where I attended college: Allan Lichtman, *White Protestant Nation*, and Sidney Blumenthal, *The Rise of the Republican Counter-Establishment*.

I would never presume to write the biography of any individual senator without delving deeply into his or her papers, but because of the scope and span of my book, I decided not to rely on senatorial papers. I conducted approximately ninety interviews with senators and staff members of that era. I understand that there is some controversy among historians about the utility and validity of doing interviews, with Dr. Wilentz, among others, suggesting that interviews are potentially unreliable and blur the line between history and journalism. In this case, I was frankly more concerned by the fact that I could never do as many interviews as I would ideally like to do—so many former senators and staff members had wonderful insights and recollections to contribute. I finally resolved the issue by recognizing that the book was not going to be based primarily on interviews; rather, I hope it is animated by them.

INTERVIEWS

Asterisks denote those people who went from the Senate to serve in the Carter administration as well.

SENATORS, FORMER AND CURRENT

Howard Baker	Tom Daschle	Walter Mondale*
Birch Bayh	Gary Hart	Bob Packwood
Dick Clark*	Ted Kaufman	Don Riegle
William Cohen	Paul Kirk	Jim Sasser
Susan Collins	Carl Levin	Alan Simpson
John Culver	Richard Lugar	Joe Tydings
John Danforth	George McGovern	Lowell Weicker

FORMER SENATE STAFF MEMBERS

David Aaron*	Mary Jane Checchi	Alan Holmer
Mark Abels	Bill Cherkasky	Keith Kennedy
Ken Ackerman	Ed Cohen*	Michael Levy
Madeleine Albright*	Brian Conboy	Rob Liberatore
Susan Alvarado	Peter Connolly	Chuck Ludlam*
Marcia Aronoff	Dick D'Amato	Tamera Luzzatto
Brian Atwood*	Jim Davidson	Chris Matthews
Elinor Bachrach	Robert Dove	Marshall Matz
Richard Baker	Ken Duberstein	Michael McCurry
Alan Bennett	John Duncan	Harry McPherson
Jay Berman	Ken Feinberg	Ed Merlis
Michael Berman*	Peter Fenn	Neil Messick
Leon Billings	Bruce Freed	Richard Moe*
Stephen Breyer	Al From	Ralph Neas
Sheila Burke	Mark Gitenstein	Jeff Nedelman
Bert Carp*	Pat Griffin	Carey Parker
Kay Casstevens	Linda Gustitis	Howard Paster

FORMER SENATE STAFF MEMBERS *(continued)*

John Podesta
Hoyt Purvis
Ed Quick
Bill Reinsch
Mark Robertson
John Rother
David Schaefer
Wayne Schley

Sally Shelton*
Bill Shore
Hannah Sistare
Paula Stern*
Joe Stewart
Tom Susman
Bob Szabo
Dan Tate Sr.

Pam Turner
Robert Tyrer
Richard Wegman
Claudia Weicker
Harrison Wellford*
Burt Wides*

OTHERS INTERVIEWED

Jim Blanchard
David Cohen
Stuart Eizenstat

Peter Hart
Joshua Javits
Carrie Lee Nelson

Don Terry

NOTES

PROLOGUE

ix *one of the three people most seriously considered:* Carl Hulse, "Indiana Senator Offers Obama Risks and Rewards," *New York Times*, August 11, 2008.

ix *Evan Bayh made it clear:* Chris Cillizza, "Evan Bayh Won't Seek Re-election, Senate Majority in Play?" *Washington Post*, February 15, 2010.

ix *"There is too much partisanship and not enough progress":* Ibid. Increasing concern about the Senate's diminishing appeal had been expressed the previous year. Carl Hulse, "Despite Prestige, the Senate's Allure Seems to Be Fading," *New York Times*, February 5, 2009.

ix *He battled Richard Nixon:* John W. Dean, *The Rehnquist Choice: The Untold Story of the Nixon Appointment That Redefined the Supreme Court* (New York: Touchstone, 2001), pp. 21, 61, 266. Dean's book is probably the most revealing of many sources that credit Bayh's leadership in opposing three of Nixon's Supreme Court nominees.

x *"perhaps the most inspired piece of legislation":* "Innovation's Golden Goose," *Economist Technology Quarterly*, December 14, 2002.

xi *"a profound sense of crisis":* Lewis L. Gould, *The Most Exclusive Club: A History of the Modern United States Senate* (New York: Basic Books, 2005), p. xiv.

xi *"the empty chamber":* George Packer, "The Empty Chamber: Just How Broken Is the Senate?," *New Yorker*, August 9, 2010, pp. 38–50.

xii *wanted him to look strong:* Don Oberdorfer, *Senator Mansfield: The Extraordinary Life of a Great American Statesman and Diplomat* (Washington, DC: Smithsonian Books, 2003), p. 246; Randall Bennett Woods, *Fulbright: A Biography* (Cambridge, UK: Cambridge University Press, 1995), p. 353.

xii *tired of fighting with President Nixon:* Dean, *Rehnquist Choice*, p. 278.

xii *"To cool it":* Gould, *Most Exclusive Club*, p. 7, is one of many places this famous anecdote is noted.

xiii *"For protracted periods":* Gould, *Most Exclusive Club*, pp. ix–x.

xiv *"their hearts were touched by fire":* Oliver Wendell Holmes, address delivered for Memorial Day, May 30, 1884, in Keene, New Hampshire.

xv *"It is the Senate as one of the rocks of the Republic"*: Francis R. Valeo, *Mike Mansfield, Majority Leader: A Different Kind of Senate, 1961–1976* (Armonk, NY: M. E. Sharpe, 1999), p. 85. Mansfield's speech appears in the *Congressional Record* on November 25, 1963, but was never delivered because of President Kennedy's assassination.

xvii *began to change in the late 1970's:* Gould, *Most Exclusive Club*, pp. 274–275; Adam Clymer, *Drawing the Line at the Big Ditch: The Panama Canal Treaties and the Rise of the Right* (Lawrence: University Press of Kansas, 2008), pp. 106–163; Alan Crawford, *Thunder on the Right: The "New Right" and the Politics of Resentment* (New York: Pantheon Books, 1980), pp. 272–289; Allan J. Lichtman, *White Protestant Nation: The Rise of the Conservative Movement* (New York: Atlantic Monthly Press, 2008), pp. 307–311.

xviii *"We have been miniaturized"*: Carl Hulse, "Policy Agenda Poses Test for Rusty Legislative Machinery," *New York Times*, April 5, 2009.

xix *completely taken over by the Christian right:* John Danforth, *Faith and Politics: How the "Moral Values" Debate Divides America and How to Move Forward Together* (New York: Viking, 2006), pp. 69, 75, 77.

xix *"the battered children from the House"*: Interview with former senator Alan Simpson, February 2, 2010.

xix *his overriding objective is to defeat Barack Obama:* Matt Schneider, "Senator McConnell: Making Obama a One-Term President Is My Single Most Important Political Goal," MediaIte, July 10, 2011.

xix *brilliant portrayal of Johnson's career:* Robert A. Caro, *The Years of Lyndon Johnson: Master of the Senate* (New York: Alfred A. Knopf, 2002).

xix *"Johnson was a noisy summer storm"*: Gould, *Most Exclusive Club*, p. 232.

xx *the legacy of a democratized Senate:* Valeo, *Mike Mansfield, Majority Leader*, pp. 31–47, 83–88; Oberdorfer, *Senator Mansfield*, pp. 171–174; Gould, *Most Exclusive Club*, pp. 233–235. The theme that Mansfield democratized the Senate was voiced in many interviews with former senators, such as Gary Hart and Dick Clark, who remembered being early beneficiaries of important assignments because of Mansfield's view of the Senate.

xx *"the "national mediator"*: Walter F. Mondale, with David Hage, *The Good Fight: A Life in Liberal Politics* (New York: Scribner, 2010), p. 116; interview with Vice President Mondale, September 11, 2009.

CHAPTER 1: THE GRIND

3 *seventeen new senators and sixty-seven new House members*: Mildred Amer, "Freshmen in the House of Representatives and Senate by Political Party, 1913–2008," Congressional Research Service, August 20, 2008.

4 *a singular moment:* 1953 was the only almost comparable moment of change in political leadership, bringing in a new president (Dwight Eisenhower), new Senate leaders (Robert Taft and Lyndon Johnson), and new

Speaker of the House (Joseph Martin). Martin, however, had been Speaker previously, unlike Tip O'Neill in 1977.

4 *Edmund Muskie of Maine and Ernest "Fritz" Hollings of South Carolina:* Robert C. Byrd, *The Senate 1789–1989: Addresses on the History of the United States Senate*, vol. 2 (Washington, D.C.: U.S. Government Printing Office, 1991), pp. 570–572.

4 *a delicate political conundrum:* Byrd, *Senate Addresses*, vol. 2, p. 570; Carl Solberg, *Hubert Humphrey: A Biography* (New York: W. W. Norton, 1984), p. 454; interview with former senator John Culver, April 15, 2010.

5 *no longer responded to him with their customary warmth:* Solberg, *Hubert Humphrey*, pp. 423–424. The biographer notes: "Humphrey found the new Senate less to his liking. The club-like intimacy in which he had basked . . . seemed to have vanished with the passage of men such as Richard Russell."

5 *Byrd took a call from Humphrey:* Byrd, *Senate Addresses*, vol. 2, pp. 571–572.

6 *None of these senators had come further:* Byrd, *Senate Addresses*, vol. 2, pp. 541–555, and Robert C. Byrd, *Child of the Appalachian Coalfields* (Morgantown: West Virginia University Press, 2005) are two of the many sources recounting Byrd's remarkable rise from poverty.

7 *channeled money to his impoverished state:* In *Child of the Appalachian Coalfields*, Byrd recounts numerous examples of his legendary ability to bring federal funds to West Virginia. A humorist once remarked that Byrd would have moved the entire federal government to West Virginia if the Washington Monument could have fit under the bridges on the highway. In 1989, after thirty years in the Senate, Byrd further enhanced his influence by stepping down as Senate majority leader to become chairman of the Senate Appropriations Committee.

8 *Byrd saw an opening:* Byrd noted that "ideology probably played a bigger role in that race than any subsequent race" he was ever in (Byrd, *Senate Addresses*, vol. 2, p. 563).

8 *a swift and stealthy campaign to defeat Kennedy:* Byrd, *Senate Addresses*, vol. 2, p. 567; Adam Clymer, *Edward M. Kennedy: A Biography* (New York: William Morrow, 1999), pp. 171–173.

8 *Byrd chafed at the widespread idea:* Byrd, *Child of the Appalachian Coalfields*, p. 385.

9 *Nixon gave serious thought to nominating Byrd:* Dean, *Rehnquist Choice*, pp. 133–149. Byrd took the possibility seriously as well. Byrd, *Senate Addresses*, vol. 2, pp. 565–566; Byrd, *Child of the Appalachian Coalfields*, pp. 306–308.

9 *His views on civil rights became muted:* Sanford J. Ungar, "The Man Who Runs the Senate: Bobby Byrd: An Upstart Comes to Power," *Atlantic Monthly*, September 1975, pp. 29–35; Clayton Fritchey, "Senator Byrd's

Emergence as a Senate Leader," *Washington Post*, June 2, 1973; Vera Glazer, "Senator Byrd's Political Star Rising," *Charleston Daily Mail*, January 15, 1974.

9 *"the Southerners' time had passed"*: G. Calvin Mackenzie and Robert Weisbrot, *The Liberal Hour: Washington and the Politics of Change in the 1960's* (New York: Penguin Press, 2008), p. 165.

9 *selfless, unending efforts to make the Senate work:* Political reporters have commented frequently on Byrd's rise in the Senate, his mastery of Senate procedures and rules, and his dedication to the institution. For example, "New Congress—Younger, but Less Brash—Convenes, Pick Leaders, Organizes," *Congressional Quarterly*, January 8, 1977, p. 41; "A Bold and Balky Congress," *Time*, January 23, 1978. Nothing captures Senator Byrd's love of the Senate better than his *Addresses on the History of the United States Senate*, noted above.

9 *the idea of Robert Byrd as majority leader:* "Profile: Robert C. Byrd," *Congressional Quarterly*, January 8, 1977, p. 33; Ungar, "Man Who Runs the Senate."

9 *preferred to be called "Robert"*: Interview with Joseph Stewart, June 14, 2010.

9 *his hands frequently trembled:* Byrd conveyed his embarrassment about his tremor to me when I worked for him in 1979.

9 *unexpected discourse on the inevitability of death:* In 1985, while serving as chief of staff to Senator John D. Rockefeller IV of West Virginia, I attended a meeting where Senator Byrd surprised a visiting West Virginia delegation by veering suddenly into a vivid and gloomy rumination on the inevitability of death.

10 *"Turkey in the Straw"*: I had the completely unexpected pleasure of hearing Senator Byrd play the fiddle on one of the first Friday afternoons after I joined his leadership staff at the Democratic Policy Committee in February 1979.

10 *his presidential bid was not taken seriously:* Byrd, *Senate Addresses*, vol. 2, p. 569.

10 *"the South's unending revenge upon the North"*: William S. White, *Citadel: The Story of the U.S. Senate* (New York: Harper & Bros., 1957), p. 68.

11 *He transformed the role of Senate leader*: Caro, *Lyndon Johnson: Master of the Senate*, pp. 562–580; Valeo, *Mike Mansfield, Majority Leader*, pp. 17–18; Randall B. Woods, *LBJ: Architect of American Ambition* (Cambridge, MA: Harvard University Press, 2006), pp. 263–264.

11 *Using Hubert Humphrey as his liaison:* Caro, *Lyndon Johnson: Master of the Senate*, pp. 452–462; Robert Mann, *The Walls of Jericho: Lyndon Johnson, Hubert Humphrey, Richard Russell and the Struggle for Civil Rights* (New York: Harcourt Brace, 1996), pp. 142–148; Woods, *LBJ*, p. 233.

11 *bullied, badgered, and cajoled the Senate:* Johnson's biographers, including Caro, Woods, and Robert Dallek, provide many examples of his abusive treatment of those Democratic senators he disfavored. Paul Douglas was one of his leading targets. Roger Biles, *Crusading Liberal: Paul H. Douglas of Illinois* (DeKalb: Northern Illinois University Press, 2002), pp. 130–131, 170. Unsurprisingly, Douglas was sharply critical of Johnson as majority leader. "As a deliberative body, the Senate degenerated under Johnson's leadership." Paul H. Douglas, *In the Fullness of Time: The Memoirs of Paul H. Douglas* (New York: Harcourt Brace Jovanovich, 1971), p. 234.

12 *The 1958 election was a rout:* Mann, *Walls of Jericho*, pp. 236–237, is one of many sources that emphasize the importance of that off-year election as a turning point for the Senate. The 1958 off-year election began the transformation of the Senate into a liberal institution, but during the first two years of John Kennedy's presidency, Congress was still closely divided between liberal Democrats and progressive Republicans on the one hand, and conservative Republicans and southern Democrats on the other. Consequently, Kennedy's legislative accomplishments in 1961–1962 were modest. The 1962 off-year election, however, shifted the balance to the liberals, particularly in the Senate.

12 *a new challenge from restive liberals:* Caro, *Lyndon Johnson: Master of the Senate*, pp. 1015–1017; Woods, *LBJ*, p. 344; Mann, *Walls of Jericho*, p. 241.

12 *"He told me to go to hell":* Booth Mooney, *LBJ: An Irreverent Chronicle* (New York: Thomas Y. Crowell, 1976), p. 106.

12 *"We were Cuber-ized":* John G. Tower, *Consequences: A Personal and Political Memoir* (Boston: Little, Brown, 1991), p. 163.

13 *the Senate's most towering accomplishment:* Many historians and observers of American politics believe that the 1964 Civil Rights Act was the greatest legislative accomplishment in the history of the country and the Senate's greatest moment. These include Mann, *Walls of Jericho*; Robert Dallek, *Flawed Giant: Lyndon Johnson and His Times, 1961–1973* (New York: Oxford University Press, 1998); Woods, *LBJ*; Oberdorfer, *Senator Mansfield.*

14 *polar opposite of his flamboyant predecessor:* Oberdorfer, *Senator Mansfield*, pp. 170–176, 206–207; Valeo, *Mike Mansfield, Majority Leader*, pp. 19–23.

15 *believed in a democratic, small-d, Senate:* Valeo, *Mike Mansfield, Majority Leader*, pp. 37–42; Oberdorfer, *Senator Mansfield*, pp. 171–173.

15 *a virtual rebellion inside the Senate:* Oberdorfer, *Senator Mansfield*, pp. 205–206; Valeo, *Mike Mansfield, Majority Leader*, 79–82.

16 *"have ranged from a benign Mr. Chips":* Oberdorfer, *Senator Mansfield*, pp. 206–207; Valeo, *Mike Mansfield, Majority Leader*, pp. 82–85.

17 *the "liberal moment" of 1963 through 1966:* my description of the very brief period of explosive liberal legislative activity from 1963 through 1966.

17 *the "liberal hour" of the 1960's:* Mackenzie and Weisbrot, *Liberal Hour*, sets forth the argument that liberal progress through the 1960's was driven from the top down, by the federal government, with the Senate playing a key role.

17 *"awesome patience":* Valeo, *Mike Mansfield, Majority Leader*, p. 36.

17 *His numerous memos were heartbreakingly prescient:* Oberdorfer, *Senator Mansfield*, pp. 185–186,192–193, 198–199 (to President Kennedy), 213–214, 218, 237–241, 254–255, 267–269, 282–283, 290–291, 314 (to President Johnson); 373–374 (to President Nixon, with whom Mansfield met privately twenty-seven times during Nixon's presidency).

17 *gave up on Nixon's commitment to ending the Vietnam War:* "Cambodia tore it": Oberdorfer, *Senator Mansfield*, pp. 376, 380–383.

17 *angered at the evidence of "dirty tricks":* Ibid., pp. 432–433.

17 *Only Mansfield could have picked Sam Ervin:* Valeo, *Mike Mansfield, Majority Leader*, pp. 233–234.

17 *stronger oversight of the intelligence community:* Loch K. Johnson, *A Season of Inquiry: The Senate Intelligence Investigation* (Lexington: University Press of Kentucky, 1985), pp. 10–13, 229–230; LeRoy Ashby and Rod Gramer, *Fighting the Odds: The Life of Senator Frank Church* (Pullman: Washington State University Press, 1994), pp. 471–472.

17 *"There is a time to stay and a time to go":* Oberdorfer, *Senator Mansfield*, p. 453.

17 *"a kind of controlled madhouse":* Gould, *Most Exclusive Club*, p. 293.

18 *a new reluctance to support "big government" programs:* Michael Pertschuk, *Revolt Against Regulation: The Rise and Fall of the Consumer Movement* (Berkeley: University of California Press, 1982), pp. 49–60; *Report to Leadership Participants on 1980 Findings of Corporate Priorities* (New York: Yankelovich, Skelly and White, 1980): p. 13.

18 *"not just a bunch of little Hubert Humphreys":* David S. Broder, "Hart's Theme," *Washington Post*, February 29, 1984.

18 *genuinely uncertain about what Jimmy Carter cared about:* Steven M. Gillon, *The Democrats' Dilemma: Walter F. Mondale and the Liberal Legacy* (New York: Columbia University Press, 1992), pp. 184–185.

19 *Byrd was determined to get out ahead of the issue:* "Senators Nearer Ethics Code and Pay Raise," Associated Press, January 19, 1977.

19 *The 1974 New Hampshire Senate election:* Gould, *Most Exclusive Club*, p. 265.

20 *Allen . . . a new and ingenious version of the filibuster:* Byrd, *Senate Addresses*, vol. 2, p. 154.

20 *the lethal potential of the post-cloture filibuster:* Michael O'Brien, *Philip Hart: The Conscience of the Senate* (East Lansing: Michigan State University

Press, 1995), p. 207. The clear majority of the Senate supported Hart's anti-trust legislation. But "a major force behind the bill's progress," reported the *Wall Street Journal*, "was the desire of many senators to pass it as a farewell monument to Senator Philip Hart."

20 *"The rich and the powerful were there"*: O'Brien, *Philip Hart*, p. 213.

21 *"I am going to get up and walk out:"* Ibid.

21 *far better to have younger members:* Ibid. p. 201.

21 *agonized about the future of Detroit:* Ibid., p. 210.

22 *"he wagered that conscience"*: Ibid., p. 212, quoting from Coleman Mc-Carthy's column in the *Detroit Free Press*, December 28, 1976.

22 *"his integrity, diligence and compassionate humanism"*: quoting from the *Washington Post* editorial, December 28, 1976.

22 *foremost advocate of American military strength*: Caro, *Lyndon Johnson: Master of the Senate*, pp. 179–180.

22 *"a discharge of political passion"*: Ibid., p. 367, quoting Schlesinger and Rovere.

22 *hearings that calmed the nation:* Ibid., pp. 374–381.

22 *"a man who had been electrocuted and lived"*: Byron C. Hulsey, *Everett Dirksen and His Presidents: How a Senate Giant Shaped American Politics* (Lawrence: University Press of Kansas, 2000), p. 2.

23 *Byrd quickly signaled his priorities and aspirations:* Interviews with Hoyt Purvis, March 22, 2010, and January 17, 2011.

CHAPTER 2: THE NATURAL

25 *unable to decide whether to run for Senate minority leader:* J. Lee Annis, Jr., *Howard Baker: Conciliator in an Age of Crisis*, 2nd ed. (Knoxville: Howard Baker Center for Public Policy, University of Tennessee, 2007), pp. 102–103.

25 *The heir apparent for the job was Robert Griffin:* Judith H. Parris, "The Senate Reorganizes Its Committees: 1977," *Political Science Quarterly* 94, no. 2 (Summer 1979), p. 325, refers to Griffin as the "prospective leader"; "New Congress—Younger, but Less Brash" describes the selection of Baker as "a surprise," p. 35.

26 *"You just have to go over there"*: Annis, *Howard Baker*, p. 103.

26 *Baker still remained undecided:* Ibid.

26 *large disappointments had taken a toll on his confidence:* Ibid., pp. 101–102.

26 *if the senators chose the president:* Ibid., p. xix. After *Newsweek* in 1978 asked a sample of Democratic senators off the record who they would like to see elected president in 1980, a reporter told senior Democrat that a plurality of his colleagues privately backed Baker. "You're wrong," the member responded. "He'd win a majority."

26 *a "junior grade Everett Dirksen"*: Annis, *Howard Baker*, p. 32.

26 *surprised Dirksen with the firmness of his position*: Ibid., pp. 33–34.

27 *seeking to become Senate leader*: Ibid., pp. 43–44.

27 *rejected Baker once again*: Ibid., pp. 50–51.

27 *offered Baker a seat on the Supreme Court*: Ibid., p. 52.

27 *frustrating Nixon with his indecision*: Dean, *Rehnquist Choice*, pp. 239–240.

27 *"Funeral homes are livelier than the Court"*: Annis, *Howard Baker*, p. 52.

27 *"the best television personality in the Senate"*: Ibid., p. 62.

28 *He had harbored high hopes*: Ibid., pp. 92–99.

28 *gave serious consideration to running for governor*: Ibid., p. 102.

28 *"I don't have the votes"*: Ibid., p. 103.

29 *"an idea whose time had come"*: Hulsey, *Everett Dirksen and His Presidents*, p. 196; Mann, *Walls of Jericho*, p. 426.

29 *Aiken had breakfasted with Mike Mansfield*: Oberdorfer, *Senator Mansfield*, p. 174.

29 *Cooper's knowledge of the world*: Robert Schulman, *John Sherman Cooper: The Global Kentuckian* (Lexington: University Press of Kentucky, 1976), pp. 26–32, 44–45, 50–53.

30 *The intensity of the Republican right*: Annis, *Howard Baker*, p. 97; Sean Wilentz, *The Age of Reagan: A History, 1974–2008* (New York: Harper, 2008), pp. 51–68.

30 *Helms had followed a unique path to the Senate*: William A. Link, *Jesse Helms and the Rise of Modern Conservatism* (New York: St. Martin's Press, 2008), pp. 45–128.

31 *Helms broadcast 2,732 viewpoints*: Ibid., p. 70.

31 *vehement opposition to the civil rights movement*: Bill Peterson, "Jesse Helms' Lesson for Washington," *Washington Post*, November 18, 1984.

32 *"liberalism, subversion and perversion"*: Link, *Jesse Helms*, p. 84.

32 *an opportunity to run for the Senate*: Ibid., pp. 114–117.

32 *"almost as lib'rul as the other side"*: Ibid., p. 134.

33 *seeking out Allen as a mentor*: Ibid., pp. 135–136.

33 *within weeks of arriving*: Ibid., pp. 136–137.

33 *"Defeats don't discourage me"*: Ibid., p. 136.

33 *began regularly to resort to the filibuster*: Ibid., pp. 138–139.

34 *"only way a minority has"*: Ibid., p. 139.

34 *Helms had already begun to add the "social issues"*: Ibid., pp. 89–92.

34 *appalled when Gerald Ford picked Nelson Rockefeller*: Ibid., pp. 139–140.

34 *refused to meet with Aleksandr Solzhenitsyn*: Ibid., pp. 141–144.

35 *He would work tirelessly*: Ibid., pp. 167–168, 210–215.

35 *a disarming and conciliatory style of bargaining*: Annis, *Howard Baker*, p. 32.

35 *"bring together a boll weevil and a cotton planter"*: Quoted in Annis, *Howard Baker*, p. xxiv.

35 *quickly moved to share the leadership responsibilities:* Michael Malbin, "The Senate Republican Leaders—Life without a President," *National Journal,* May 2, 1977.

35 *emerge as a counterforce:* Ibid.; Annis, *Howard Baker,* p. 104.

36 *enmity of many liberals:* Godfrey Hodgson, *The Gentleman from New York: Daniel Patrick Moynihan: A Biography* (Boston: Houghton Mifflin, 2000), pp. 114–120.

36 *assertive stance at the UN:* Ibid., pp. 243–250, 261.

36 *crafted Nixon's Family Assistance Plan:* Ibid., pp. 160–174.

CHAPTER 3: GREAT EXPECTATIONS, DIFFERENT AGENDAS

39 *grasped several fundamental political realities:* Betty Glad, *Jimmy Carter: In Search of the Great White House* (New York: W. W. Norton, 1980), pp. 229–241; Robert Kaufman, *Henry M. Jackson: A Life in Politics* (Seattle: University of Washington Press, 2000), pp. 319–320.

39 *Four senators ran in the primaries:* Lloyd Bentsen also sought the nomination, but abandoned the race early, before the crucial Iowa and New Hampshire primaries.

40 *"If Scoop Jackson gave a fireside chat":* Michael Kramer, "Visions of Dream Tickets Danced in Their Heads," New York, August 11, 1980, is one of many reporters to repeat that famous quip.

40 *"the little people couldn't reach the levers":* George Will, "Staying the Coarse," *Washington Post,* January 29, 2008, recalled Harris's comment in discussing the populist turn in the 2008 campaign.

40 *a political cartoon in the* Washington Post: Herbert Block, *Herblock on All Fronts* (New York: New American Library, 1980), p. 151, reprinting his cartoon that appeared in the *Washington Post* on June 10, 1976.

40 *the Democrats drew some comfort from Carter's choice:* Gillon, *Democrats' Dilemma,* p. 169, reflects the widely held view that Mondale was a popular choice.

40 *Carter appeared certain to be the next president:* Wilentz, *Age of Reagan,* pp. 69–70, is one of many sources describing the conventional political wisdom in the summer of 1976.

41 *Americans just felt better:* Ibid., pp. 14–15.

41 *whom many senators had personally despised:* It is not an overstatement to say that many senators "despised" Richard Nixon long before he became president, and understanding the intensity of that sentiment is crucial for understanding the mood and workings of the Senate from the time Nixon took office January 1969 through the time he resigned the presidency in August 1974. For example, Sam Ervin was "appalled by Nixon's original red-baiting campaign against Jerry Voorhis that brought him to Congress in 1947." Karl E. Campbell, *Senator Sam Ervin, Last of the Founding Fathers,*

(Chapel Hill: University of North Carolina Press, 2007), pp. 210–211. Mike Mansfield remembered Nixon campaigning against him in an ugly 1952 race in Montana. He also recalled Nixon urging Eisenhower to intervene militarily in Indochina at the time of Dienbienphu, "and thank the Lord we didn't." Oberdorfer, *Senator Mansfield*, pp. 349–350. Albert Gore Sr. detested Nixon, whom he regarded as a dangerously partisan and combative political enemy. Kyle Longley, *Senator Albert Gore, Sr.: Tennessee Maverick* (Baton Rouge: Louisiana State University Press, 2004), pp. 99–100. Richard Russell once confided to a friend that "Mr. Nixon, if he ever assumes the presidency, would be the worst president imaginable." Campbell, *Senator Sam Ervin*, p. 211. Interviews with Birch Bayh, Joseph Tydings, George McGovern, and Walter Mondale indicate that senators who had no history with Nixon before he became president also grew to despise him.

43   *the most influential forces in the Democratic Party:* Gillon, *Democrats' Dilemma*, pp. 188–191; Mondale, *Good Fight*, pp. 192–195; Wilentz, *Age of Reagan*, pp. 79–82; Jimmy Carter, *Keeping Faith: Memoirs of a President* (Toronto: Bantam Books, 1982), pp. 77–78.

43   *rolling back Taft-Hartley Act:* Woods, *LBJ*, pp. 667–678.

43   *Political Washington looked carefully for telltale signs:* Gillon, *Democrats' Dilemma*, pp. 183–184.

43   *"I learned three things about Carter today":* Ibid., p. 184.

43   *the new president disliked political small talk:* Ibid., p. 192; Mondale, *Good Fight*, pp. 187–188; Charles O. Jones, *The Trusteeship Presidency: Jimmy Carter and the United States Congress* (Baton Rouge: Louisiana State University Press, 1988), pp. 1–9. "He thought politics was sinful," Mondale reminisced. Gillon, *Democrats' Dilemma*, p. 201.

44   *power had tilted dramatically toward the presidency:* Arthur M. Schlesinger Jr., *The Imperial Presidency* (Boston: Houghton Mifflin, 1973), is the best known work on the shift of power, which has been discussed by many scholars and participants in government.

45   *to allow Congress to reclaim its authority:* Jones, *Trusteeship Presidency*, p. 47; Thomas E. Mann and Norman J. Ornstein, *The Broken Branch: How Congress Is Failing America and How to Get It Back on Track* (New York: Oxford University Press, 2006), pp. 59–60; Wilentz, *Age of Reagan*, p. 83; and "Bold and Balky Congress" are four of many sources about Congress's new assertiveness.

45   *As professor Nelson Polsby memorably observed:* Anthony King, ed., *The New American Political System* (Washington, DC: The American Enterprise Institute, 1990), quoting Polsby.

45   *would not hesitate to let the president know:* Carter, *Keeping Faith*, p. 71, refers to Congress as having "an insatiable appetite for consultation"; Kauf-

man, *Henry Jackson*, p. 342; Martin Tolchin, "Byrd, Hinting Strained Relation, Says Carter Failed to Seek Advice, *New York Times*, January 27, 1977.

45 *the type of preparation Carter liked best*: Gillon, *Democrats' Dilemma*, pp. 183–184.

45 *confronted a complicated economic picture*: Bruce J. Schulman, "Slouching Toward the Supply Side: Jimmy Carter and the New American Political Economy," in Gary M. Fink and Hugh Davis Graham, eds., *The Carter Presidency: Policy Choices in the Post–New Deal Era* (Lawrence: University Press of Kansas, 1998), pp. 51–61, Mondale, *Good Fight*, pp. 191–192.

46 *listed job creation as its number-one priority*: Schulman, "Slouching Toward the Supply Side," p. 54.

46 *Carter and the congressional leaders came together:* "The Economy: Something for (Almost) Everybody," *Time*, January 17, 1977.

46 *Michael Blumenthal, the new secretary of treasury:* Clyde H. Farnsworth, "Carter Aides Describe $31 Million Package," *New York Times*, January 28, 1977.

46 *the thirty-eight member Republican Conference:* Peter Milius, "President's $50-per-Person Rebate Meets Stiff Opposition in Congress," *Washington Post*, February 3, 1977.

47 *Jimmy Carter delivered his first televised "fireside chat"*: Peter Milius, "Carter Tax Cut Again Assailed at Hill Hearing," *Washington Post*, February 5, 1977.

47 *Carter and his White House team:* "Policy: When More Is Not Enough," *Time*, February 7, 1977.

48 *Carter's call for Americans to make sacrifices:* Milius, "Carter Tax Cut Again Assailed."

48 *On February 19, without previous consultation:* Peter Milius, "Reluctant Hill Panel Passes $50 Rebate," *Washington Post*, March 18, 1977.

48 *the radical ideas of "share-our-wealth":* Robert Mann, *Legacy to Power: Senator Russell Long of Louisiana* (Lincoln, NE: Authors Guild Backinprint.com Edition, 1992), pp. 22–29.

49 *Long could easily be underestimated*: Ibid., p. 331.

49 *as Bill Proxmire once said admiringly*: William Proxmire quotes collected on Thinkexist.com.

49 *Utterly straight with his colleagues*: Mann, *Legacy to Power*, p. 329.

49 *"No question about it"*: Ibid., p. 331.

49 *stopped drinking long ago*: Ibid., pp. 286–291.

49 *not understanding Russell Long*: Ibid., pp. 340–343, 346–347; Carter, *White House Diary*, pp. 43, 97–98, 102, 110, 141–142, 164–165.

49 *By March, emotions were running high in the Senate*: Milius, "Reluctant Hill Panel Passes $50 Rebate."

50 *after meeting with the president and congressional leaders:* Edward Walsh, "Tax Rebate Seen Linked to Dam Projects," *Washington Post*, April 6, 1977.

50 *columnists Rowland Evans and Robert Novak:* Rowland Evans and Robert Novak, "A Self-Constructed Rebate Trap," *Washington Post*, April 11, 1977.

50 *On April 12, Secretary of Labor Ray Marshall:* "Marshall Sees Rebate Aiding Middle Class," Associated Press, April 13, 1977.

50 *on April 14, in a stunning reversal:* Edward Walsh, "He Warns Against New Spending," *Washington Post*, April 15, 1977.

51 *Muskie raged to Charles Schultze:* Interview with Madeleine Albright, August 25, 2010.

51 *Calling Carter's decision "a disappointment":* Editorial, *Washington Post*, April 15, 1977.

51 *"wait until the M's are called":* Bernard Asbell, *The Senate Nobody Knows* (Garden City, NY: Doubleday, 1978), pp. 120–121.

51 *"chicken shit":* Theo Lippman Jr. and Donald C. Hansen, *Muskie* (New York: W. W. Norton, 1971), p. 100.

51 *the least attractive set of committee assignments:* Asbell, *Senate Nobody Knows*, p. 121; Lippman and Hansen, *Muskie*, p. 101.

52 *Muskie became the principal author and architect:* MacKenzie and Weisbrot, *Liberal Hour*, pp. 211–213; Asbell, *Senate Nobody Knows*, p. 5; Annis, *Howard Baker*, pp. 46–48.

52 *acquitted himself extremely well:* Theodore H. White, *The Making of the President 1972* (New York: Atheneum, 1973), pp. 75–76; Lippman and Hansen, *Muskie*, pp. 16–19.

52 *campaign proved to be top-heavy and slow moving:* White, *Making of the President 1972*, pp. 77–78.

52 *dissolved in the snows of New Hampshire:* White, *Making of the President 1972*, pp. 81–83.

53 *the importance for Democrats to discover fiscal responsibility:* Interview with Al From, January 19, 2011.

53 *in a scathing editorial:* Editorial, *Washington Post*, April 15, 1977.

54 *On April 18, in a twenty-minute televised talk:* Text of Carter's address, "Carter: Oil and Natural Gas . . . Are Running Out," *Washington Post*, April 19, 1977.

54 *On April 20, Carter sought the largest audience possible:* Edward Walsh and J. P. Smith, "Back Energy Plan, Carter Urges Hill," *Washington Post*, April 21, 1977.

55 *Humorist Russell Baker noted:* "The Nation: The Energy War," *Time*, May 2, 1977.

55 *Americans were responding positively:* Ibid.

55 *Congressional leaders recognized the difficulties ahead:* Ibid.

55 *O'Neill quickly announced the formation:* Richard L. Lyons, "House Sets Up a Special Energy Panel," *Washington Post*, April 22, 1977.

55 *moved quickly to address a festering problem:* Parris, "Senate Reorganizes Its Committees," pp. 319–337. Parris was on the staff of the Temporary Select Committee to Study the Senate Committee System, and the discussion of the reorganization draws heavily on her paper.

56 *Mansfield's Senate also saw a rapid expansion of staff:* Michael J. Malbin, *Unelected Representatives: Congressional Staff and the Future of Representative Government* (New York: Basic Books, 1979), pp. 10–16; Parris, "Senate Reorganizes Its Committees."

56 *"a male preserve":* Quoted in Harry McPherson, *A Political Education: A Washington Memoir* (Boston: Houghton Mifflin, 1988), p. xxiii. The ranks of women Senate staffers in professional positions greatly increased in the 1970's, although off an extraordinarily small base.

56 *impressed by Stern's academic and journalistic credentials:* Interview with Paula Stern, July 13, 2010.

57 *"women aren't allowed in the cloakroom":* Interview with Mary Jane Checchi, May 13, 2010.

57 *"I think you mean 'gender,' Senator":* Interview with Madeleine Albright, August 25, 2010.

57 *entrusting Dorothy Fosdick with great authority:* Kaufman, *Henry M. Jackson*, pp. 83–85.

57 *if women were not allowed in the meetings:* Interview with Susan Alvarado, October 11, 2010.

57 *the proliferation of committee and subcommittee assignments:* Parris, "Senate Reorganizes Its Committees," pp. 320–321.

58 *who would have jurisdiction over the oceans:* Ibid., pp. 326–327.

58 *Hollings had spent the summers of 1939 and 1940:* Ernest F. "Fritz" Hollings with Kirk Victor, *Making Government Work* (Columbia: University of South Carolina Press, 2008), p. 153.

59 *reversed Stevenson's recommendation:* Parris, "Senate Reorganizes Its Committees," pp. 326–328.

59 *indicated a willingness to support:* Ibid., p. 324. In fact, Nelson, the chairman of the small business committee, only seemed to acquiesce. He encouraged his staff director to keep the small business community apprised of the plan to abolish the committee, which resulted in a predictable flood of political pressure and the committee staying in operation. Interview with Bill Cherkasky, December 3, 2010.

59 *"incremental idealism":* Roger H. Davidson, David, M. Kovenock, and Michael K. O'Leary, *Congress in Crisis: Politics and Congressional Reform*

(Belmont, CA: Wadsworth, 1966), pp. 5–6, used the term, which began as a guidepost for the temporary committee's efforts.

59 *Byrd and Baker could take satisfaction:* Richard E. Cohen, "Byrd of West Virginia," *National Journal,* August 20, 1977, in which Byrd repeated his support and added: "I'd like to see the number of committees and subcommittees further reduced."

59 *chemistry between Carter and Jackson was terrible:* Carter, *Keeping Faith,* pp. 100, 225; Kaufman, *Henry M. Jackson,* pp. 239, 339–344, 366–367.

59 *"We whipped his ass in the Pennsylvania primary":* Kaufman, *Henry M. Jackson,* p. 341, quoting Thomas Foley's recollection of Jordan's statement to him.

CHAPTER 4: HAWK AND DOVE

62 *convince Johnson that he was pursuing a disastrous course:* Oberdorfer, *Senator Mansfield,* pp. 211–347, and Woods, *Fulbright,* pp. 360–452, present the most comprehensive discussions of the dissents of key senators, but the biographies of Frank Church, George McGovern, Albert Gore Sr., Wayne Morse, and others hammer home the same point.

62 *haunted by doubts about the course he had chosen:* Woods, *LBJ,* pp. 677–678, 731; Dallek, *Flawed Giant,* pp. 277–278, 283.

62 *He mocked Mansfield as a weak-kneed professor:* Oberdorfer, *Senator Mansfield,* p. 239.

62 *and Fulbright as a racist:* Woods, *Fulbright,* p. 427.

62 *Johnson coldly told the senators:* Ibid., pp. 374–375.

63 *Kerry brought the human costs of the war home:* Douglas Brinkley, *Tour of Duty: John Kerry and the Vietnam War* (New York: William Morrow, 2004), pp. 370–373.

63 *"You don't see any hawks around here":* Ibid., p. 361.

64 *"[Scoop] had a fixidity of purpose":* Kaufman, *Henry M. Jackson,* p. 17.

64 *twenty-six-year-old Jackson sought the office:* Ibid., pp. 25–30.

64 *The threat posed by the Soviet Union:* Ibid., pp. 53–70, 95–105, 200–223, 242–260, 341–391.

65 *a network of defense experts and scientists:* Ibid., p. 213–214, 259.

65 *Bob Packwood still spoke in awe:* Interview with Senator Bob Packwood, July 19, 2010. The debate between Jackson and Symington took place in an unusual closed session of the Senate on July 17, 1969. Jackson took on Senators Fulbright and Cooper as well, but he directed most of his fire at Symington, the former secretary of the Air Force, whom he disliked intensely. "He upstaged Symington by producing bigger charts than the Missouri senator illustrating the precipitous expansion of the Soviet nuclear buildup." A *Washington Post* editorial called Jackson "far and away the most effective advocate of the Safeguard system as a defense of the U.S. land based missile deterrent." Kaufman, *Henry M. Jackson,* p. 211.

66 *Jackson virtually stymied the Nixon-Kissinger policy of détente:* Kaufman, *Henry M. Jackson*, pp. 242–243.

66 *Kissinger ruefully recognized:* Ibid., pp. 299–300, quoting Kissinger's memoirs, Henry A. Kissinger, *Years of Upheaval* (Boston: Little, Brown, 1982), pp. 984–985, 991. Commenting on the fierce fight with Jackson over détente and the emigration of Soviet Jews, Kissinger stated that "Jackson was not a man to welcome debate over firmly-held convictions; he proceeded to implement his by erecting a series of legislative hurdles that gradually paralyzed East-West policy. He was aided by one of the ablest—and most ruthless—staffs that I encountered in Washington." Kissinger's battles with Jackson made him "long for the relative tranquility of the Middle East.

66 *the moment was at last right:* Kaufman, *Henry M. Jackson*, pp. 301–322.

66 *"not going to elect an anti-Soviet hardliner":* Ibid., p. 316, quoting Senator Moynihan.

67 *Jackson's hopes were dashed:* Ibid., pp. 352–353.

67 *Jackson had known Sorensen since the mid-1950's:* Ted Sorensen, *Counselor: Life at the Edge of History* (New York: Harper, 2008), pp. 95, 97–100, 490.

67 *the most wrong-headed person imaginable:* Kaufman, *Henry M. Jackson*, pp. 358–361. Alan Weisman, *Prince of Darkness: Richard Perle: The Kingdom, the Power and the End of Empire in America* (New York: Union Square Press, 2007), p. 52: "Warnke was the personification of everything Jackson and Perle loathed about the liberal approach to arms control, which was, to their minds, appeasement and accommodation."

67 *"We can be the first off the treadmill":* Paul Warnke, "Apes on a Treadmill," *Foreign Policy*, Spring 1975.

68 *Jackson imagined the Soviet Union as a burglar:* Kaufman, *Henry M. Jackson*, p. 249.

68 *A central aspect of the Nixon-Kissinger policy of détente:* Ibid., pp. 245–253.

69 *Kissinger described the summit:* Ibid., p. 254.

69 *had not been caught up in the general euphoria:* Ibid., pp. 254–258.

69 *Jackson condemned the results of Vladivostok:* Ibid., pp. 288–289.

70 *intensely committed to seeking a new approach:* Betty Glad, *An Outsider in the White House: Jimmy Carter, His Advisors, and the Making of American Foreign Policy* (Ithaca, NY: Cornell University Press, 2009), pp. 43–48.

70 *startled the wily and experienced Russian:* Ibid., pp. 43–48.

70 *"McGovernism without McGovern":* Kaufman, *Henry M. Jackson*, p. 365, quoting Eugene Rostow, after a meeting between Carter and the Committee on the Present Danger.

70 *testified strongly against Warnke:* Pat Towell, "Foreign Relations Approval of Warnke Expected Despite Concerted Opposition Effort," *Congressional Quarterly*, February 12, 1977.

71 *Byrd's comments were much more negative:* "Both Sides Step up Warnke Word War," *Washington Post*, February 12, 1977.

71 *predicting that Warnke would be confirmed by a wide margin:* Norman Kempster, "Overwhelming Confirmation of Warnke Is Seen by Byrd," *Los Angeles Times*, February 18, 1977.

71 *no Republican made the case as powerfully as Jackson:* Kaufman, *Henry M. Jackson*, pp. 360–361.

72 *senators had come to doubt his intellectual honesty:* Pat Towell, "Carter Assurances Secure Victory on Warnke," *Congressional Quarterly*, March 12, 1977.

72 *Warnke had been put on notice:* Kaufman, *Henry M. Jackson*, p. 361.

72 *an opportunity to gain Jackson's support:* Ibid., pp. 361–364; Glad, *Outsider in the White House*, pp. 108–109.

73 *"taken a giant step in cutting back on arms levels":* Kaufman, *Henry M. Jackson*, pp. 365–367.

73 *"everything is in the sunshine":* Murrey Marder and George C. Wilson, "Jackson Lauds U.S. Arms Proposal as 'Sensible,'" *Washington Post*, April 6, 1977.

73 *breakthrough on information sharing:* Murrey Marder, "President Discloses Key SALT Elements," *Washington Post*, May 27, 1977.

73 *"And both are tenuous":* Murrey Marder, "SALT Diplomacy Shifts to Capitol Hill," *Washington Post*, May 30, 1977.

73 *pursuing Jackson was futile:* Kaufman, *Henry M. Jackson*, pp. 364–370; Glad, *Outsider in the White House*, pp. 108–109, make it clear that Carter went to great lengths to try to gain Jackson's support, but the effort was "counterproductive. He would never win Jackson over to a SALT agreement that the Soviets would sign." Glad, *Outsider in the White House*, p. 108.

74 *Jackson's brilliant and hyperactive staff members:* Kaufman, *Henry M. Jackson*, pp. 360, 364, 366; Weisman, *Prince of Darkness*, pp. 51–56. Leaks of confidential briefings by Jackson's staff were an intense concern of Senate SALT II advocates. Interview with Senator John Culver, April 15, 2010.

74 *issued its report on the prospects:* "Senate Delegation Report on American Foreign Policy and Non-Proliferation Interests in the Middle East." The delegation issued its report on the prospects for peace in the Middle East and U.S. policy toward Iran on February 10, 1977. The complete trip report was printed on May 10, 1977, pursuant to S. Res. 167.

74 *The five days spent in Iran:* "Senate Delegation Report," pp. 17–22.

75 *Iran . . . "an essential ally":* Ibid., pp. 17–19.

75 *"the positive goals of the human rights movement":* Ibid., pp. 20–21.

75 *was much too optimistic:* Ibid., additional views of Senators Culver and Eagleton, pp. 23–28.

76 *"a highly personalized relationship":* Culver-Eagleton views, ibid., p. 23.

76   *"emerging from extreme underdevelopment":* Ibid., p. 25.

76   *"Iran is an authoritarian nation":* Ibid., p. 28.

76   *"as other presidents had before me":* Carter, *Keeping Faith,* p. 435.

76   *a serious threat from the liberal wing:* Wilentz, *Age of Reagan,* pp. 78–81; Mondale, *Good Fight,* pp. 192–195.

77   *He did not hold back very long.* George McGovern, "Memo to the White House," *Harper's,* October 1977, pp. 33–35, refers to an earlier speech in April.

78   *McGovern began driving across South Dakota:* George McGovern, *Grassroots: The Autobiography of George McGovern* (New York: Random House, 1977), pp. 53–67. The summary of McGovern's career draws heavily on his autobiography.

78   *"refined in the fires of opposition":* Ibid., p. 54.

78   *"we just cost that nice guy a Senate seat":* Ibid., p. 83.

78   *McGovern won the South Dakota Senate seat by 200 votes:* Ibid., p. 91.

78   *focused a spotlight on hunger in America:* Ibid., pp. 84–87, 270–271; Mondale, *Good Fight,* pp. 34, 50, 91, 95; Marjorie Hunter, "Senators on Hunger Tour See Squalor in Florida," *New York Times,* March 11, 1969.

78   *Select Committee on Nutrition and Human Needs:* Robert Sam Anson, *McGovern: A Biography* (New York: Holt, Rinehart and Winston, 1972), pp. 218–242.

79   *not immediately drawn to him:* Interview with Marshall Matz, May 10, 2010.

79   *expressed his opposition to war in September 1963:* McGovern, *Grassroots,* p. 97.

79   *"This chamber reeks with blood":* Ibid., p.167, from his Senate speech given on September 1, 1970 ("Nearly the entire Senate was there to hear it").

79   *chaired the Democratic Party's commission:* Ibid., pp. 128–154.

81   *suffered the worst loss in the history of presidential elections:* Ibid., pp. 188–249, is his detailed recounting of the 1972 general election campaign. McGovern's campaign, and the choice of Senator Thomas Eagleton to be his running mate, have, of course, been written about widely: for example, White, *Making of the President 1972.*

81   *"letting everyone kick me in the ass":* Ibid., pp. 253–256; interview with John Holum, March 31, 2010.

81   *rousing reception at the Democratic mid-term convention:* McGovern, *Grassroots,* pp. 258–259. Spirits buoyed, McGovern gave thought to seeking the presidency again, but was dissuaded by his advisors. However, several of them came up with a novel plan that he should approach Hubert Humphrey about them running together, with Humphrey as the presidential nominee. McGovern did so, but ultimately, Humphrey, surprised and flattered, but torn about seeking the presidency for the fourth time, decided against it. Ibid., pp. 260–261.

81 *recognized the brilliance of Jimmy Carter's campaign:* Ibid., pp. 262–263.

81 *blistering assault on Carter's first eight months:* McGovern, "Memo to the White House."

CHAPTER 5: THE APPEARANCE OF IMPROPRIETY

84 *a widespread feeling that corruption was rampant in America:* Dominic Sandbrook, *Mad as Hell: The Crisis of the 1970's and the Rise of the Populist Right* (New York: Alfred A. Knopf, 2011), pp. 10–11.

84 *just two out of ten Americans trusted the government:* Ibid., p. 11.

84 *the two leading environmentalists of their era:* Bill Christofferson, *The Man from Clear Lake: Earth Day Founder Senator Gaylord Nelson* (Madison: University of Wisconsin Press, 2004), p. 173; interview with Leon Billings, February 19, 2010.

84 *Nelson was known for his wry wit:* Ibid., pp. 187–196.

85 *he forged his identity as the "conservation governor":* Ibid., pp. 138–147.

85 *He urged Kennedy to make conservation a priority:* Ibid., pp. 176–178.

85 *"rather bored with the whole subject":* Ibid., pp. 183–184.

86 *Nelson was bitterly disappointed:* Ibid., p. 186.

86 *He made friends in the Senate almost immediately:* Ibid., p. 187, 190, 192.

86 *one of Washington's most popular dinner places:* Ibid., pp. 193–195.

86 *he saw the peril the planet was in:* Ibid., pp. 265–281.

86 *"unprecedented environmental disaster":* Ibid., p. 308.

86 *grapple with the pollution:* Asbell, *Senate Nobody Knows*, pp. 76–77.

86 *radical proposals created space:* Interview with Leon Billings February 19, 2010.

87 *Nelson's effort culminated in the first Earth Day:* Christofferson, *Man from Clear Lake*, pp. 301–312.

87 *"the day environmentalism began to emerge":* Ibid., p. 7, quoting Philip Shabecoff, *A Fierce Green Fire* (New York: Hill and Wang, 1993), p. 113.

87 *veto power over foreign arms sales:* Don Oberdorfer, "Senator Seeks to Slow Arms Sales," *Washington Post*, September 8, 1976.

87 *battled the pharmaceutical companies:* Christofferson, *Man from Clear Lake*, pp. 251–264.

87 *"Byrd has asked me to write the god-damn ethics code"; "Obey's smart as hell":* Nelson made these statements to me when he first explained the assignment on January 18, 1977.

88 *"If restored public confidence demands a strong code":* Statement of Senator Gaylord Nelson, *Congressional Record*, March 17, 1977, pp. 8034–8062.

88 *the task quickly proved even more difficult:* Walter Pincus, "Income Curb Splits Senators as Vote Nears on Ethics Code," *Washington Post*, March 14, 1977.

89 *the anger was bipartisan:* Walter Pincus, "Senators Weighing Restriction on Outside Income," *Washington Post*, March 17, 1977; Spencer Rich, "Muskie Hits Honorarium Limitation," *Washington Post*, March 19, 1977.

89 *had even gone to the Common Cause office:* Interview with David Cohen, former president of Common Cause, December 1, 2010.

89 *he had a fierce temper:* Lippman and Hansen, *Muskie*, pp. 202–203 ("No one doubts that Muskie's temper tantrums were genuine. . . . He was raging with true anger. Reporters who have covered Muskie are accustomed to his testy nature."); White, *Making of the President 1972*, p. 76 ("he had a tendency to emotional outburst").

89 *"throwing us to the wolves":* Spencer Rich, "Challenge to Ethics Code Killed by Senate, 62–35," *Washington Post*, March 23, 1977.

90 *"Jeez, Gaylord, he's killing you":* I heard Eagleton's comment to Nelson on the Senate floor.

90 *"an aide to Senator Nelson":* Pincus, "Senators Weighing Restriction." Muskie's anger at this point particularly resonated with me since I was the aide who had been quoted.

90 *Muskie stalked off the floor:* This scene is, obviously, my personal recollection.

91 *"the Senate is panicking":* Rich, "Challenge to Ethics Code."

91 *"I hate this code":* I heard Ribicoff's statement at a meeting of the special committee in March 1977.

92 *passed his entire program virtually intact:* "Policy: Clean Sweep for Jimmy," *Time*, August 15, 1977.

92 *a major decision on whether to fund the B-1:* "Defense: Carter's Big Decision: Down Goes the B-1; Here Comes the Cruise," *Time*, July 11, 1977.

92 *His ultimate decision to kill the B-1:* Interview with Senator John Culver, April 15, 2010.

92 *effort to create a consumer protection agency:* John B. Judis, *The Paradox of American Democracy: Elites, Special Interests, and the Betrayal of the Public Trust* (New York: Routledge, 2001), pp. 139–140.

92 *successfully filibustered Carter's legislation:* Spencer Rich, "Filibuster Kills Public Financing of Senate Races," *Washington Post*, August 3, 1977.

92 *"he will have a stable government":* "The Administration: Working to Reform Welfare," *Time*, August 15, 1977.

93 *asked Ribicoff to be his attorney general:* Arthur Schlesinger Jr., *A Thousand Days: John F. Kennedy in the White House* (Greenwich, CT: Fawcett Crest, 1965), p. 137.

94 *When Howard Baker made his first foreign trip:* Interview with Senator Howard Baker, October 22, 2008.

94 *Ribicoff's greatest moment of fame:* Lewis Chester, Godfrey Hodgson, and Bruce Page, *An American Melodrama: The Presidential Campaign of 1968* (New York: Viking Press, 1969), pp. 584–585; Theodore H. White, *The Making of the President 1968* (New York: Atheneum, 1969), p. 302.

94 *"Ribicoff and his people exuded class":* Interview with Tom Daffron, April 6, 2009.

94 *Younger senators, such as Gary Hart and John Danforth:* Interview with Senator Gary Hart February 1, 2010; interview with Senator John Danforth, March 30, 2010.

94 *he had written a small book:* Abraham Ribicoff, *America Can Make It!* (New York: Atheneum, 1972).

95 *lashed out at Javits:* Jacob K. Javits with Rafael Steinberg, *Javits: The Autobiography of a Public Man* (Boston: Houghton Mifflin, 1981), pp. 268–269.

95 *expanded authority to reorganize executive agencies:* Carter, *Keeping Faith*, pp. 70–71; Burton I. Kaufman and Scott Kaufman, *The Presidency of James Earl Carter, Jr.*, 2nd ed., rev. (Lawrence: University Press of Kansas, 2006), p. 37.

96 *one cloud in the committee's otherwise blue skies:* Interview with Richard Wegman, June 3, 2010.

96 *praise from Republicans and some conservative Democrats:* Kaufman and Kaufman, *James Earl Carter*, p. 73; Helen Dewar, "Ga. Banker to Get Cabinet-Level Post," *Washington Post*, November 25, 1976.

96 *quickly discovered some disquieting facts:* Kaufman and Kaufman, *James Earl Carter*, pp. 73–77; Michael Putzel, "U.S. Probed Lance Campaign, Found No Grounds to Prosecute," *Washington Post*, January 8, 1977; interview with Richard Wegman, June 3, 2010.

96 *Ribicoff and Percy raised their concerns:* "Senate Panel Approves 8 Top Carter Officials," Associated Press, January 19, 1977; Wegman interview.

96 *Lance faced the possibility of an enormous loss:* "Lance Asks Carter for Time to Unload Falling Bank Stock," *Los Angeles Times*, July 9, 1977.

96 *Carter asked the committee to release Lance:* George Lardner Jr., "Carter Backs Lance Delay in Stock Sale," *Washington Post*, July 13, 1977.

96 *committee agreed to do so:* Helen Dewar, "Senate Unit to Give Lance More Time to Sell Bank Stock," *Washington Post*, July 16, 1977.

97 *opened Pandora's box:* Jack Egan, "This Isn't a Good Year for Lance or His Bank," *Washington Post*, July 17, 1977; Kaufman and Kaufman, *James Earl Carter*, pp.73–75.

97 *holding the new administration to high standards:* William Safire, "Carter's Broken Lance," *New York Times*, July 21, 1977.

97 *the first post-Watergate scandal:* "The Administration: The Sharpening Battle over Bert Lance," *Time*, August 1, 1977, summarized the revelations.

97 *"neither a witch hunt nor a whitewash":* "The Big Showdown over Banker Bert," *Time*, August 22, 1977.

97 *"You have been smeared":* Wendell Rawls Jr., "Senators Back Lance and Abandon Inquiry," *New York Times*, July 26, 1977.

97 *Ribicoff regretted his earlier rush to judgment:* Martin Tolchin, "Ribicoff Regrets his 'Mistake' in Backing Lance," *New York Times*, September 7, 1977; Clayton Fritchey, "The Senators, the Media, and the Lance 'Smears,'" *Washington Post*, September 10, 1977; Wegman interview.

97 *Carter's response stunned the senators:* Carter, *Keeping Faith*, p. 132; Wegman interview.

98 *"it would be wise for Bert Lance to resign":* David Broder and Edward Walsh, "Senators Tell Carter That Lance Should Resign," *Washington Post*, September 6, 1977.

98 *"This guy is going to go, no question":* Martin Tolchin, " Ribicoff Regrets His 'Mistake' in Backing Lance," *New York Times*, September 7, 1977.

98 *Lance offered a full-throated defense:* Robert G. Kaiser, "Lance Denies Banking Practices Were Unethical or Illegal," *Washington Post*, September 16, 1977.

98 *Officials from the U.S. Attorney's office:* Robert G. Kaiser, "Lance Probe Figure Allegedly Didn't Want to Make Waves," *Washington Post*, September 15, 1977; *Washington Post*, September 6, 1977.

99 *"like the committee eating its young":* Interview with Richard Wegman, June 3, 2010.

99 *Jody Powell leaked a false story:* Robert G. Kaiser, "New Hill Testimony Contradicts Lance," *Washington Post*, September 14, 1977.

99 *He sought Byrd's advice:* James T. Wooten, "Carter Aides Say Lance's Future Is Still Uncertain After Hearings," *New York Times*, September 21, 1977.

99 *"no one could replace Bert Lance":* William Claiborne, "Lance Resigns; Carter Accepts Decision with 'Regret and Sadness,'" *Washington Post*, September 22, 1977.

99 *the presumption of innocence had been eroded:* Adam Clymer, "Reaction on Capitol Hill Ranges from 'Lynching' Charge to Relief," *New York Times*, September 22, 1977.

100 *"It is impossible to overestimate the damage":* Carter, *Keeping Faith*, p. 127.

CHAPTER 6: THE LIBERAL FILIBUSTER

104 *artificial price ceilings had created a distorted "dual market":* Richard L. Lyons, "Senate Leaders Move to Break Impasse on Natural Gas Pricing," *Washington Post*, September 24, 1977.

104 *Byrd called up the energy legislation:* Ibid.

105   *liberals did not filibuster:* Sarah A. Treul, "Walter F. Mondale and the Fili-buster: The Evolution of Agenda Control in the U.S. Senate," delivered at the Hubert H. Humphrey Institute, May 2, 2007.

105   *Byrd, Baker, and Jackson responded:* George Larder Jr. and J. P. Smith, "Of Cots and Roll Calls," *Washington Post*, September 29, 1977.

106   *Speaking at a rally in Virginia:* Bill McAllister, "President Says He Would Veto a Bill to Deregulate Natural Gas," *Washington Post*, September 25, 1977.

106   *after the Senate voted to invoke cloture:* Richard L. Lyons, "The Case of the Senate's Backward Filibuster," *Washington Post*, September 28, 1977.

107   *humorous, painfully exhausting, and borderline surreal:* Larder and Smith, "Of Cots and Roll Calls."

107   *Dale Bumpers sharply criticized Byrd's failure:* Ibid.

107   *September 28 saw that type of movement:* Richard L. Lyons, "Senate Sleeps on It," *Washington Post*, September 29, 1977.

108   *That position enraged Long:* George Lardner Jr. and Richard L. Lyons, "Sen-ate Leaders Fail to Unblock Gas Bill Tieup," *Washington Post*, September 30, 1977.

108   *Jimmy Carter noted in his diary:* Jimmy Carter, *White House Diary* (New York: Farrar, Straus and Giroux, 2010), p. 110.

108   *On September 30, in a critical test vote:* Richard L. Lyons, "Senators Refuse to Set Aside Gas Deregulation Plan," *Washington Post*, October 1, 1977.

109   *Byrd decided that the filibuster had to end:* Richard L. Lyons, "Mondale Helps Break Gas Pricing Filibuster," *Washington Post*, October 4, 1977.

109   *an avowed enemy of the filibuster:* Mondale, *Good Fight*, pp. 114–134.

109   *Mondale had been chosen by Carter:* Ibid., pp. 161–164; Carter, *Keeping Faith*, pp. 36–37.

109   *Carter accepted Mondale's vision:* Mondale, *Good Fight*, pp. 171–172; Carter, *Keeping Faith*, pp. 39–40.

110   *"living in Holiday Inns":* Gillon, *Democrats' Dilemma*, p. 152; Mondale, *Good Fight*, p. 157.

110   *grave and growing doubts about the Vietnam War:* Mondale, *Good Fight*, pp. 77–82; Gillon, *Democrats' Dilemma*, pp. 122–125.

110   *spearheaded the enactment of the Civil Rights Act of 1968:* Mondale, *Good Fight*, pp. 55–68; Gillon, *Democrats' Dilemma*, pp. 107–111.

110   *worked with Robert Kennedy and Cesar Chavez:* Mondale, *Good Fight*, pp. 52, 93.

110   *powerful role on the Church Committee:* Johnson, *Season of Inquiry*, pp. 105, 124, 153, 156, 229–230; Gillon, *Democrats' Dilemma*, pp. 160–162; Mondale, *Good Fight*, pp. 135–153.

111   *natural liaison with the Senate:* Gillon, *Democrats' Dilemma*, pp. 190–192; Mondale, *Good Fight*, pp. 185–189.

111 *frequently raised concerns with Carter:* Mondale, *Good Fight,* pp. 178–188, 234–237.

111 *"Nah, he wouldn't do that":* "The Nation: Night of the Long Winds," *Time,* October 10, 1977.

111 *Byrd moved in for the kill:* Lyons, "Mondale Helps Break Gas Pricing Filibuster."

111 *the Senate turned to bedlam:* George Lardner Jr., "Bitterness and Resentment," *Washington Post,* October 5, 1977.

112 *flushed with anger at the criticism:* Richard L. Lyons, "Senate Votes to Decontrol Natural Gas Prices," *Washington Post,* October 5, 1977.

112 *They lost heart and ended their effort:* "The Nation: Night of the Long Winds," *Time,* October 10, 1977.

112 *"The Senate is very much like a violin":* "Night of the Long Winds."

112 *Byrd and Mondale "had used the wrong tactics":* Carter, *White House Diary,* p. 116.

113 *Carter put his prestige on the line: Time,* October 31, 1977.

114 *New Year's Eve found him in Tehran:* Carter, *White House Diary,* p. 156.

114 *offered a withering indictment:* David Broder, "The Senate Has No Excuse," *Washington Post,* December 18, 1977.

CHAPTER 7: A YEAR OF LIVING DANGEROUSLY

117 *While battling the disease:* Solberg, *Hubert Humphrey,* pp. 447–456.

117 *spoke memorable words:* Ibid., p. 456.

118 *The* Washington Post *had asked a thousand people:* Ibid. p. 456.

118 *As political scientist Nelson Polsby observed:* Ibid., p. 458, quoting Polsby.

118 *Humphrey might advise new senators:* Ibid., p. 461.

118 *"Can you believe that Minnesota would send such a fool?":* Ibid., p. 136; Caro, *Lyndon Johnson: Master of the Senate,* p. 448.

118 *served as Lyndon Johnson's bridge to the liberals:* Solberg, *Hubert Humphrey,* pp. 161–164, 176–180; Mann, *Walls of Jericho,* pp. 117–120, 141–148; Caro, *Lyndon Johnson: Master of the Senate,* pp. 454–462.

118 *one of the most attractive personalities:* Gilbert C. Fite, *Richard Russell, Jr., Senator from Georgia* (Chapel Hill: University of North Carolina Press, 1991), p. 420; Mann, *Walls of Jericho,* pp. 144–145; Caro, *Lyndon Johnson: Master of the Senate,* pp. 460–461.

118 *"I knew every senator":* Solberg, *Hubert Humphrey,* p. 461.

118 *a movie star—for Nineteenth Century Fox:* Tower, *Consequences,* p. 128.

119 *he would have to be a loyal soldier:* Solberg, *Hubert Humphrey,* pp. 255–256.

119 *Johnson promptly froze Humphrey out:* Ibid., pp. 272–278.

120 *McClellan would meet Joe Biden:* Joe Biden, *Promises to Keep: On Life and Politics* (New York: Random House, 2007), p. 87.

120   *a prodigious worker in what he called the "legislative kitchen":* Shelby Scates, *Warren G. Magnuson and the Shaping of Twentieth Century America* (Seattle: University of Washington Press, 1997), p. 203, 227–238; Eric Redman, *The Dance of Legislation* (New York: Simon and Schuster, 1973), p. 189–197.

120   *the nation's growing commitment to protect consumers:* Scates, *Warren G. Magnuson,* pp. 212–216.

120   *had become a legendary combination:* Ibid., pp. 217–218; Michael Pertschuk, *Revolt Against Regulation,* pp. 24–28.

121   *asked Church to take the lead on the treaties:* Ashby and Gramer, *Fighting the Odds,* p. 541.

121   *His staff implored him to let this dubious honor pass:* Ibid.

121   *Church had spoken for twenty years:* Ibid., pp. 536–539.

121   *helped smooth passage of the 1957 Voting Rights Act:* Ibid., pp. 82–95.

122   *Johnson gave Church a coveted seat:* Ibid., p. 96.

122   *Church made the keynote:* Ibid., pp. 129–132.

122   *came away deeply opposed to the imperialism:* Ibid., pp. 19–26.

122   *in a December 1964 magazine interview:* Ibid., pp. 190–191.

122   *Church's article:* Frank Church, "We Are in Too Deep in Africa and Asia," *New York Times Magazine,* February 14, 1965, quoted in Ashby and Gramer, *Fighting the Odds,* p. 192.

122   *"plunged into these former colonial regions":* Ibid., p. 193.

122   *traveling with Johnson on Air Force One:* Ibid., p. 207.

122   *deepened his critique of the war:* Ibid., pp. 216–217.

122   *"the most un-revolutionary nation on earth":* Ibid., p. 216.

122   *Church went to the Senate floor:* Ibid., pp. 254–256.

123   *with Republican John Sherman Cooper:* Ibid., pp. 293, 299–305.

123   *The investigation was spurred by accusations:* Ibid., pp. 416–433.

123   *had always distrusted big corporations:* Ibid., pp. 422–423.

123   *ridiculed the argument that Allende's election:* Ibid., p. 430.

123   *tackled an even more explosive issue:* Ibid., pp. 436–443.

124   *made public thousands of previously classified documents:* Ibid., pp. 435–436, 441.

124   *plunged into an investigation of bribes:* Ibid., pp. 455–462.

124   *"Lockheedo," as the Japanese press referred to the scandal:* Ibid., p. 464.

124   *articles by* New York Times *reporter Seymour M. Hersh:* Ibid., pp. 470–471.

124   *The Senate created a Select Committee on Intelligence Activities:* Ibid., p. 471.

125   *Mansfield had long been concerned:* Johnson, *Season of Inquiry,* p. 10; Valeo, *Mike Mansfield, Majority Leader,* pp. 267–268.

125   *When Phil Hart turned down:* Ashby and Gramer, *Fighting the Odds,* p. 472; Loch Johnson, *Season of Inquiry,* pp. 13–15.

125 *a fundamental divide on the committee:* Loch Johnson, *Season of Inquiry,* pp. 57, 70, 96, 132, 145, 174, 236, 248, 271; Ashby and Gramer, *Fighting the Odds,* pp. 473–474.

125 *the committee held 21 public hearings:* Ashby and Gramer, *Fighting the Odds,* p. 478.

125 *The committee issued an extensive report:* Ibid., pp. 474, 478.

125 *The committee also revealed:* Ibid., p. 478.

125 *a springboard to a presidential run:* Ibid., pp. 485–487.

125 *vowed to Mansfield that he would finish:* Ibid., p. 486.

126 *He compared himself to an evangelist:* Ibid., p. 477.

126 *told Carter that Ted Kennedy was going to run for president:* Carter, *White House Diary,* p. 167.

127 *armed with a self-deprecating sense of humor:* Edward M. Kennedy, *True Compass* (New York: Twelve, 2009), p. 186; Clymer, *Edward M. Kennedy,* pp. 38–40. Of the several biographies written about Senator Kennedy, I rely principally on Clymer's, as well as Kennedy's memoir.

127 *he gravitated to experienced senators:* Clymer, *Edward M. Kennedy,* pp. 43–47.

127 *the "lion cub of the Senate":* Adam Clymer, "The Lion Cub of the Senate," *New York Times,* August 26, 2009.

128 *Long was a wily and gifted legislator:* Clymer, *Edward M. Kennedy,* p. 131.

128 *see him as the Democratic frontrunner:* Ibid., pp. 135–136, is one of many sources on this point.

128 *declined to take the leadership role:* Ibid., pp. 161–163; Kennedy, *True Compass,* pp. 316–320.

128 *connecting the strands of fund-raising abuses:* Clymer, *Edward M. Kennedy,* pp. 192–194.

129 *Richardson agreed to Kennedy's insistence:* Kennedy, *True Compass,* pp. 334–335; Clymer, *Edward M. Kennedy,* pp. 200–201.

129 *Kennedy running ahead of the new president:* Kennedy, *True Compass,* pp. 343–344; Clymer, *Edward M. Kennedy,* pp. 209–210.

129 *an excellent and aggressive staff:* Clymer, *Edward M. Kennedy,* pp. 154–166, 192–194, 240–241; Kennedy, *True Compass,* pp. 318–327.

129 *Breyer cited the Civil Aeronautics Board:* Clymer, *Edward M. Kennedy,* pp. 227–228.

129 *shocking his faculty colleagues:* Interview with Justice Stephen Breyer, January 13, 2009.

130 *endlessly fascinating opportunity to shape public policy:* Justice Breyer interview.

130 *in "the dance of legislation":* Redman, *Dance of Legislation.*

130 *Like many committee staffers before him:* This discussion of the power of committee staff reflects my personal experience and observations, but also several principal books including; Clymer, *Edward M. Kennedy*; Redman, *Dance of Legislation*; Pertschuk, *Revolt Against Regulation*; Asbell, *Senate Nobody Knows*; Malbin, *Unelected Representatives*.

131 *Senate consideration of a federal criminal code:* Interview with Ken Feinberg, July 11, 2011.

131 *"I'm not sure what my views are on criminal justice":* Clymer, *Edward M. Kennedy*, pp. 240–241; Malbin, *Unelected Representatives*, p. 39.

131 *Kennedy plainly sought to bridge the chasm:* Clymer, *Edward M. Kennedy*, p. 241.

131 *Feinberg went to work on the herculean task:* Ibid., p. 241.

131 *The American Civil Liberties Union wrote to Kennedy:* Ibid., pp. 241, 257.

132 *Kennedy had sharply criticized him:* Ibid., p. 256.

132 *Carter's determination to proceed piece by piece:* Ibid., p. 256; Carter, *Keeping Faith*, pp. 85–87.

CHAPTER 8: THE PANAMA CANAL FIGHT

135 *the ten-mile wide, American-controlled Canal Zone:* William J. Jorden, *Panama Odyssey* (Austin: University of Texas Press, 1984), pp. 21–65; Clymer, *Drawing the Line*, pp. 1–9.

135 *sympathized with the Panamanian position:* Jorden, *Panama Odyssey*, pp. 30–31.

136 *Mansfield spoke for many:* Ibid., pp. 74–75.

136 *Johnson committed to negotiating a new treaty:* Ibid., pp. 82–87, 110–118.

136 *Nixon largely ignored Panama:* Ibid., p. 147.

137 *Senate conservatives soon shot back:* Ibid., pp. 241, 244, 283.

137 *reassured the country's leader:* Ibid., pp. 293–294.

137 *trailing badly until he began attacking:* Clymer, *Drawing the Line*, pp. 27–32.

137 *"Sally Jones sitting at home":* Ibid., p. 30.

137 *his foremost Latin American expert:* Clymer, *Drawing the Line*, pp. 43–44.

138 *Kissinger briefed Carter:* Ibid., p. 43.

138 *the cornerstone of a new relationship with Latin America:* Ibid., p. 44; Jorden, *Panama Odyssey*, pp. 341–342; Carter, *Keeping Faith*, pp. 152–155, 184; Glad, *Outsider in the White House*, pp. 88–89.

138 *constitutional responsibility is to advise and consent:* Article II, section 2 of the Constitution states that the president "shall have Power, by and with the Advice and Consent of the Senate, to make Treaties, provided two-thirds of the Senators present concur."

138 *reflected on bitter experience:* Gould, *Most Exclusive Club*, p. 13.

138 *It was the Senate that ultimately shattered:* Ibid., pp. 73–90.

138 *Americans trusted Kennedy's leadership:* Hulsey, *Everett Dirksen and His Presidents*, pp. 177–180.

139 *Byrd was ambivalent about the treaties:* Byrd, Senate Addresses, Vol. 2, p. 575; Jorden, *Panama Odyssey*, p. 494.

139 *at least half a dozen seminars:* Ibid., p. 481.

139 *Byrd attended several sessions:* Ibid., p. 481.

139 *"had an uphill road to travel":* Ibid., p. 481.

139 *Hollings approached the problem with an open mind:* Hollings and Victor, *Making Government Work*, pp. 183–184.

140 *sent a newsletter to South Carolina:* Ibid.

140 *an outrageous breach of diplomatic protocol:* Jorden, *Panama Odyssey*, pp. 463–464.

140 *testimony from seventy-nine witnesses:* Ibid., p. 468.

140 *Statements by Panama's chief negotiator:* Ibid. pp. 476–477.

140 *U.S. Ambassador to Panama William Jorden:* Ibid. pp. 473–475.

140 *"intervention" in Panama:* Ibid., p. 474.

141 *General Brown had been working on the treaty:* Ibid., pp. 471–473.

141 *would not be able to deliver many Republican votes:* Ibid., pp. 494–495; Annis, *Howard Baker*, p. 131.

141 *gaining the Republican presidential nomination:* Annis, *Howard Baker*, pp. 129–131.

141 *"lends a chilling quality":* Clymer, *Drawing the Line*, p. 78.

141 *Baker would remember his reaction:* Interview with Senator Howard Baker, October 22, 2008.

141 *"Why now, and why me?":* Clymer, *Drawing the Line*, p. 75.

141 *Baker was especially troubled:* Ibid., pp. 78–79.

142 *He invited General Torrijos to Washington:* Jorden, *Panama Odyssey*, pp. 355–385.

142 *Baker and Byrd both applauded the Carter-Torrijos statement:* Ibid., pp. 479, 492.

142 *two of Baker's most senior advisers:* Ibid., p. 482.

142 *Byrd gave the group a thoughtful description:* Ibid., p. 483.

142 *take the measure of General Torrijos:* Ibid., p. 483.

142 *among Panamanians, Torrijos was a hero:* Ibid., pp. 483–485.

142 *Torrijos impressed the senators:* Ibid., pp. 484–486.

143 *Torrijos walked through the dusty town:* Ibid., p. 484.

143 *this delegation was the toughest:* Ibid., pp. 485–486.

143 *"ugly American" occurred to Ambassador Jorden:* Ibid., p. 485.

143 *one senator told a CBS news reporter:* Ibid., p. 486.

143 *offered an important verdict:* Ibid., p. 486.

143 *Baker was getting increasingly irritated:* Ibid., pp. 490–491; Annis, *Howard Baker*, p. 127.

144 *"squirming like a worm on a hot rock":* Annis, *Howard Baker*, p. 127.

144 *subtly suggesting Baker was weak:* Jorden, *Panama Odyssey*, p. 490.

144 *"the Republican Hamlet on the Potomac":* Clymer, *Drawing the Line*, p. 86.

144 *little doubt that Byrd would fully support:* Ibid., p. 491.

144 *staffers came away with the same positive reaction:* Ibid., p. 491.

144 *Baker laid out the political realities:* Ibid., pp. 492–493.

144 *the treaties must explicitly incorporate:* Ibid., p. 492.

144 *provided the Senate insisted on no changes:* Ibid., p. 492.

144 *Torrijos's commitment settled it for Baker:* Ibid., pp. 493–494.

144 *Baker softened his point:* Ibid., p. 493.

144 *an editorial in one of the government-directed newspapers:* Ibid., p. 493.

145 *decided it was time to declare his support:* Ibid., p, 494.

145 *announced his decision to support the treaties:* Ibid., p. 494.

145 *Byrd had captured the central truth:* Ibid., p. 494.

145 *Church had supported a new Panama Canal treaty:* Ashby and Gramer, *Fighting the Odds*, p. 539.

145 *Perennial right-wing suspicion about Church:* Ibid., pp. 536–537.

145 *78 percent of Americans wanted to maintain control:* Ibid., p. 540.

145 *Sol Linowitz approached him:* Ibid., p. 542.

146 *Sarbanes had won plaudits:* Jorden, *Panama Odyssey*, pp. 366, 465–466; Ashby and Gramer, *Fighting the Odds*, p. 542. This point reflects my personal recollection of the positive reaction to Senator Sarbanes' arrival in the Senate, based principally on his work on the House Judiciary Committee on the impeachment of Richard Nixon.

146 *Most Americans still opposed the treaties:* Clymer, *Drawing the Line*, pp. 92–93.

146 *William Buckley and George Will supported the treaties:* Ibid., pp. 72; Annis, *Howard Baker*, p. 126.

146 *"an issue conservatives can't lose on":* Clymer, *Drawing the Line*, p. 56.

146 *"best political issue that could be handed to a party":* Ibid., p. 56.

146 *The personally genial Laxalt:* Ross K. Baker, *Friend and Foe in the U.S. Senate* (New York: Free Press, 1980), p. 210.

147 *refused to grant the "unanimous consent":* Jorden, *Panama Odyssey*, p. 512.

147 *the fire they were lighting at the grass roots:* Clymer, *Drawing the Line*, pp. 53–69.

147 *The Carter administration had launched:* Ibid., pp. 51–52, 93–94.

147 *had given serious thought to supporting the treaties:* Ibid., p. 36; Jorden, *Panama Odyssey*, pp. 320, 532.

147 *decided the Byrd and Baker amendments were too weak:* Clymer, *Drawing the Line,* p. 100.

147 *introduced an amendment on February 9:* Jorden, *Panama Odyssey,* p. 520.

148 *failed to check its other flank:* Ibid., pp. 522–523, 536–544.

148 *Panamanian leaders were enraged:* Ibid., pp. 532–551, 560–567.

148 *"could cause rejection of the treaty":* Ibid., pp. 543–550.

148 *changing the DeConcini reservation was impossible:* Ibid., pp. 543–550.

148 *agreed to go along for the moment:* Ibid., pp. 543–550.

148 *Metzenbaum and Kennedy spoke strongly:* Ibid., pp. 550–551.

149 *Byrd began quoting the words of Shakespeare:* Ibid., p. 553.

149 *"nothing can be morally right":* Ibid., p. 553.

149 *the White House began to understand:* Ibid., p. 560.

149 *lamented not having recognized the danger:* Ibid., p. 560.

149 *incensed by the administration's poor planning:* Ibid., p. 567.

149 *desperately tried to reassure Torrijos:* Ibid., p. 565.

150 *Baker warned Panama on* CBS News: Ibid., p. 573.

150 *an important ally in Mike Kozak:* Ibid., p. 580.

150 *Purvis told Kozak he had been thinking:* Ibid., p. 580.

150 *Church read the statement:* Ibid., pp. 581–582.

151 *Moynihan took the floor:* Ibid., p. 582.

151 *the* Washington Post *ripped Deconcini:* Ibid., p. 590.

152 *The response from Byrd, Church, and others:* Ibid., p. 591.

152 *Byrd, Church, and Sarbanes shuttled:* Ibid., p. 595.

152 *Gravel was not a Senate heavyweight:* Ibid., p. 582.

153 *They gave themselves ninety minutes:* Ibid., pp. 602–603.

153 *Byrd put a copy of the resolution:* Ibid., p. 603.

153 *Byrd finally agreed to the phrase:* Ibid., p. 604

153 *Lewis received word from Torrijos:* Ibid., pp. 606–607.

154 *Byrd told a group of reporters:* Ibid., p. 609.

154 *"It has to be like this, Dennis":* Ibid., pp. 613–614.

CHAPTER 9: VENTURING INTO THE MIDDLE EAST

157 *Javits regularly stayed on the Senate floor:* Interview with Brian Conboy, July 8, 2011.

158 *when he rose to speak in the Senate:* Javits and Steinberg, *Javits,* pp. 229–235, 259–260.

158 *"I don't like you—or your kind":* Caro, *Lyndon Johnson: Master of the Senate,* pp. 102–103.

158 *Universally recognized as the Senate's best lawyer:* I interviewed numerous former senators, Democratic and Republican, who cited Javits as one of

the great senators of the 1960's and 1970's, and/or the most brilliant. The same consensus emerges from the memoirs of senators with diverse political viewpoints, including William Cohen, John Tower, Lowell Weicker, and Paul Douglas.

158   *a master of the committee process:* Javits and Steinberg, *Javits*, p. 253.

158   *no more than fifteen minutes before the Eastern Shuttle:* This description of Javits's mode of operation, his intellect, and his energy in the Senate reflects my personal observation, his autobiography, and the recollections of the Javits staff, a volume put together in 1981 after his defeat, the latter hereafter cited as "Javits staff remembrances."

158   *He had a soft spot for his staff members:* Javits staff remembrances.

159   *"The United States Senate was my home":* Javits and Steinberg, *Javits*, pp. 252–253.

159   *Javits planned to finish his term:* Ibid., pp. 490, 493.

160   *no president had embraced the intractable issues:* Carter, *Keeping Faith*, p. 273.

160   *"a particularly unpleasant surprise":* Ibid., p. 280.

160   *Sadat impressed Carter:* Ibid., pp. 282–284.

160   *dramatically transformed the political situation:* Ibid., pp. 284–285.

160   *adamant about returning any of the West Bank areas:* Ibid., pp. 288, 292.

161   *His optimism about certain leaders:* Ibid., p. 286.

161   *well-known friends of Israel in the Senate:* Ibid., pp. 288–289.

161   *senators Abe Ribicoff, Hubert Humphrey, Ed Muskie, and Scoop Jackson:* Carter, *White House Diary*, p. 64.

161   *"The Israelis were also facing* their *ancient enemy":* Carter, *Keeping Faith*, p. 297.

162   *Fahd expressed a strong view in support:* Carter, *White House Diary*, p. 161.

162   *On February 14, 1978, the Carter administration announced:* Graham Hovey, "U.S. Plans First Jet Sale to Cairo, Reduces Israeli Order for Craft; Saudis Get 60; Debate Is Expected," *New York Times*, February 15, 1978.

162   *announced its vehement opposition to Carter's proposal:* James Reston, "How to Double Trouble," *New York Times*, January 27, 1978.

163   *appeared overwhelmingly opposed:* Bernard Weinraub, "Close Votes Likely in Congress on Mideast Plane Deal," *New York Times*, April 27, 1978.

163   *deeply involved with Israel since 1946:* Javits and Steinberg, *Javits*, pp. 156–158, 170–182, 271–290.

163   *Javits led the fight to convince the Nixon administration:* Terence Smith, "Senate, by 81-14, Votes 500 Million for Israeli Arms," *New York Times*, Nov. 24, 1971.

164   *made his first trip to Saudi Arabia in early 1977:* Edward C. Burks, "Senator and the Prince: The Odd Couple," *New York Times*, August 6, 1977; Javits and Steinberg, *Javits*, pp. 479–481.

164 *the special relationship between the United States and Israel:* Rowland Evans and Robert Novak, "Carter's Dilemma on Saudi Arms Sales," *Washington Post,* February 2, 1978.

165 *Baker made it known to the White House:* Ibid.

165 *"If you want to work this out, I'm willing to try":* Annis, *Howard Baker,* p. 135.

166 *Brown sent a seven-page letter:* Bernard Weinraub, "Brown Says Saudis Will Accept Curbs on the Use of F-15s," *New York Times,* May 11, 1978.

166 *the Foreign Relations Committee met in its hearing room:* Hedrick Smith, "Jet Deal Still in the Balance," *New York Times,* May 12, 1978.

166 *After a passionate debate, the committee stunned the Senate:* James Reston, "Church and State," *New York Times,* May 12, 1978.

167 *Emotions ran high as the Senate met four days later: Congressional Record,* May 15, 1978, pp. 13264–13662.

167 *Gravel criticized AIPAC for turning the vote into a "litmus test":* David Maxfield, "Middle East Plane Sales Backed by Senate Vote in Major Carter Victory," *Congressional Quarterly,* May 20, 1978.

167 *Packwood defended AIPAC's lobbying with considerable heat:* Ibid.

167 *"What do we want to do with the Israelis?":* "Nation: F-15 Fight, Who Won What?," *Time,* May 29, 1978.

168 *"We must have the courage, we must have the guts":* Ibid.

168 *a rationalization of "American nervelessness":* Ibid.

168 *Tom Eagleton, another strong supporter of Israel:* Ibid.

168 *criticized the Carter administration's "skill and competence":* Ibid.

169 *won an extraordinary and unexpected victory:* Bernard Weinraub, "Mideast Plane Conflict: How Carter Won and Implications for Victors and Losers," *New York Times,* May 24, 1978.

CHAPTER 10: AN EPIC BUSINESS-LABOR CLASH

172 *played a strong role in securing Carter's narrow victory:* Kaufman and Kaufman, *James Earl Carter,* pp. 33–34; Gillon, *Democrats' Dilemma,* pp. 188–190.

172 *Organized labor's share of the workforce:* Judis, *Paradox of American Democracy,* p. 138.

172 *uninterested in putting labor resources into funding recruiting:* Ibid., p. 138.

172 *a fierce and concerted campaign:* Ibid., pp. 138, 140–141.

172 *most notorious for anti-labor tactics:* Javits and Steinberg, *Javits,* p. 389.

172 *According to National Labor Relations Board (NLRB) statistics:* Judis, *Paradox of American Democracy,* p. 138.

172 *sought a labor law reform bill:* Javits and Steinberg, *Javits,* pp. 389–390.

173 *the chances of Senate passage seemed good:* Judis, *Paradox of American Democracy,* p. 140; Javits, ibid., p. 390; Orrin Hatch, *Square Peg: Confessions of a Citizen Senator* (New York: Basic Books, 2002), p. 26.

173 *Moss, a western liberal from the class of 1958:* Pertschuck, *Revolt Against Regulation*, pp. 21, 44, 76–77.

173 *Hatch, a self-styled citizen politician:* Hatch, *Square Peg*, pp. 3–5.

173 *startled at being asked to lead the opposition:* Ibid., p. 24.

173 *Hatch agreed to take on the challenge:* Ibid., p. 25.

174 *prosperity made possible a comfortable consensus:* Judis, *Paradox of American Democracy*, p. 101.

174 *their corporate CEOs served on the boards:* Ibid., p. 109.

174 *drastically expand and rename itself the Business Roundtable:* Ibid., pp. 120–122.

174 *At the urging of two powerful intellects:* Ibid., pp. 116–119, 122–127; Lichtman, *White Protestant Nation*, pp. 303–307.

175 *a concerted message, and a new ideology, emerged:* Judis, *Paradox of American Democracy*, pp. 128–129.

175 *By 1978, it had become pervasive:* Ibid., p. 129; Lichtman, *White Protestant Nation*, pp. 337–338.

175 *"Broom Hilda did five comic strips":* Judis, *Paradox of American Democracy*, p. 129.

176 *Gallup Polls registered just how effectively:* Ibid., p. 130.

176 *one of the AFL-CIO's other priorities:* Kaufman and Kaufman, *James Earl Carter*, p. 34.

176 *strike by the United Mine Workers:* Ibid., pp. 97–98.

176 *He did not intend to be beaten:* Javits and Steinberg, *Javits*, p. 391.

177 *not be operating on a "two-track" system:* Ibid., p. 391; Hatch, *Square Peg*, p. 30.

177 *plenty of time to make their case:* Ibid., p. 30.

177 *Hatch received regular counsel from Jim Allen:* Ibid., p. 28.

177 *Hollings made it clear:* Hollings and Victor, *Making Government Work*, pp. 188–190.

178 *Hatch organized the labor law opponents:* Hatch, *Square Peg*, pp. 30–31.

178 *a handful of conservative to moderate Democratic senators would decide the outcome:* Ibid., p. 29.

178 *they were breaking new ground in lobbying:* Ibid., p. 31.

178 *mobilize the grass roots to flood his office:* Ibid., p. 31.

178 *97 percent of the mail:* Judis, *Paradox of American Democracy*, p. 140.

178 *energize small business by frightening them:* Ibid., pp. 140–141.

179 *"It's a different type of lobbying":* Javits and Steinberg, *Javits*, pp. 390–391, quoting *Congressional Quarterly Almanac*.

179 *Hatch heard that one company:* Hatch, *Square Peg*, p. 32.

180 *Javits, Williams, and Byrd put forth a compromise:* Javits and Steinberg, *Javits*, p. 391.

180 *Long approached Hatch on the Senate floor:* Hatch, *Square Peg,* pp. 34–35.

180 *"Russell Long appears to be running the country":* Quoted in Mann, *Legacy to Power: Senator Russell Long of Louisiana,* p. 348.

180 *In a relatively rare moment of public humor:* Ibid., p. 348.

180 *Long repeated an offer made to Hatch:* Hatch, *Square Peg,* pp. 34–35.

181 *Sparkman pushed him away:* Ibid., p. 36.

181 *"I thought you promised to be with us":* Ibid., p. 36.

181 *already openly predicting a Democratic victory:* Ibid., p. 37.

181 *"Orrin, you know you're going to lose today":* Ibid., p. 37.

182 *Hollings had been doing some discreet lobbying:* Hollings and Victor, *Making Government Work,* p. 190.

182 *He caught Zorinsky coming down the hall:* Ibid., p. 190.

182 *Hatch knew that he had his forty-first vote:* Hatch, *Square Peg,* p. 39.

182 *Long said he was so angered:* Ibid., p. 40.

182 *"we have always known it":* Ibid., p. 40.

182 *"if Senator Long is going to cross over":* Ibid., p. 40.

183 *Javits considered the outcome a tragedy:* Javits and Steinberg, *Javits,* p. 392.

CHAPTER 11: SAVING NEW YORK

185 *"always had the luster and magic of a new town":* Javits and Steinberg, *Javits,* p. 435.

185 *"the temptation to seek the mayoralty":* Ibid., p. 434.

185 *When Walter Mondale was a young senator:* Javits staff remembrances, p. 60 (recollection of Ken Gunther).

186 *an infamous front page headline:* Frank Von Riper, "Ford to City: Drop Dead," *New York Daily News,* October 30, 1975; Javits and Steinberg, *Javits,* pp. 434–446.

187 *In February 1978, the Banking Committee had issued:* Edward C. Burke, "Senate Committee Votes Not to Renew Aid to New York City," *New York Times,* February 10, 1978.

187 *"The American people are just plain fed up":* David Broder, "Restless Votes Pave the Way for Youth Movement into Senate," *Washington Post,* June 8, 1978.

188 *Roth began to "noodle" with his staff:* Interview with Neil Messick, June 4, 2010.

188 *Roth found a House Republican counterpart:* Judis, *Paradox of American Democracy,* p. 148.

188 *"no one in Washington took them seriously":* Interview with Neil Messick, June 4, 2010.

188 *California voters, enraged by soaring property taxes:* Sandbrook, *Mad as Hell,* pp. 280–286.

188 *Ohio voters turned down 86 out of 139 proposed school bonds:* "Sound and Fury over Taxes," *Time*, June 19, 1978.

188 *shocked the political world:* Adam Clymer, "Grumpy Voters Send a Disconcerting Message," *New York Times*, June 11, 1978.

189 *Proposition 13 became the talk of Capitol Hill:* Adam Clymer, "Coast Author of the Tax Cut Scouts Capital," *New York Times*, June 20, 1978; "a prairie fire" of opposition: Adam Clymer, "Reagan Urges Party to Support Tax Cuts," *New York Times*, June 25, 1978.

189 *William Proxmire, a noted pinch-penny:* B. Drummond Ayres, "Congress Responds to Frugality Signal," *New York Times*, June 18, 1978.

189 *"It's not some magic word":* Ibid.

189 *The Senate would have to decide the future:* Lee Dembart, "Koch, in Washington, Pleads for Backing on Long Term Bonds," *New York Times*, June 7, 1978.

189 *Proxmire was the original maverick:* Martin Tolchin, "The Perplexing Mr. Proxmire," *New York Times*, May 28, 1978.

190 *"5,669 consecutive roll call votes":* Ibid.

190 *demonstrated his independence from his own party:* Interview with Ralph Neas, April 21, 2010.

191 *"1978 is not the same as 1975":* Statement of Chairman William Proxmire, Hearings Before the Committee on Banking, Housing, and Urban Affairs, on "New York City Financial Aid," June 6, 7, 12, 13, 1978, p. 1.

191 *"these local parties are offering so little":* Ibid., p. 3.

191 *Brooke's opening statement came as a cold splash of reality:* Statement of Ranking Member Edward Brooke, ibid., p. 4.

192 *Moynihan loved to speak:* Statement of Senator Daniel Patrick Moynihan, ibid., p. 6.

193 *"We are where we are because New York is the central city of this country":* Statement of Senator Jacob Javits, ibid., p. 10.

194 *the "woof and warp of the legislative process":* Javits used that phrase with me during the special committee's work on writing the Senate ethics code.

194 *noting "what a good strong job you're doing":* Senate Banking Committee Hearings, p. 25.

195 *implored the Committee to provide the federal loan guarantees:* Statement of New York City Mayor Ed Koch, ibid., pp. 25–32; Lee Dembart, "Koch, in Washington, Pleads for Backing on Long Term Bonds," *New York Times*, June 7, 1978.

195 *Proxmire asked again and again:* Senate Banking Committee Hearings, pp. 2, 77.

195 *showed a new willingness to support seasonal loans:* Ibid., pp. 167, 182.

196 *"Jack Javits and Pat Moynihan did more to change":* Javits and Steinberg, *Javits*, p. 447.

196 *Lugar drafted and circulated a compromise proposal:* Lee Dembart, "Lobbying for City Aid Stepped Up as Proxmire Unit Ends Hearings," *New York Times*, June 14, 1978.

196 *predicted the committee would approve it:* Lee Dembart, "Senate Panel Votes 12-3 to Back Guarantees for New York Bonds," *New York Times*, June 16, 1978.

197 *less than four weeks after the committee hearings: Congressional Record— Senate*, June 29, 1978, pp. 19577–19628.

197 *gave an extraordinary, perhaps unprecedented, performance:* Statement of Chairman William Proxmire, ibid., pp. 19577–19580.

197 *"we are setting a number of undesirable precedents:* Ibid., p. 19580.

198 *"New York Day in the Senate"; "a national blessing":* Statement of Senator Jacob Javits, ibid., pp. 19583–19585.

198 *Moynihan injected an extraordinary personal note:* Statement of Senator Daniel Patrick Moynihan, ibid., pp. 19585–19586.

198 *With a mischievous smile, Baker observed wryly:* Statement of Senator Howard Baker, ibid., pp. 19586–19587.

199 *"if New York has one quality above all, it is that fantastic brass":* Marjorie Hunter, "Senate Votes New York Aid Bill; Carter Expected to Sign in City," *New York Times*, July 27, 1978.

CHAPTER 12: CLOSING DAYS

201 *Byrd had expressed optimism:* Richard L. Lyons, "Senate Leadership Girds for Filibuster on Gas Price Bill," *Washington Post*, August 1, 1978.

202 *described the negotiations with the Senate as a "descent into hell":* Kaufman, *Henry M. Jackson*, p. 346.

202 *declared the energy crisis to be "the moral equivalent of war":* Text of Carter's address, "Carter: Oil and Natural Gas . . . Are Running Out," *Washington Post*, April 19, 1977.

202 *Finally, after eight more months of haggling:* Robert G. Kaiser and J. P. Smith, "Changing Face of 'Centerpiece' Gas Bill," *Washington Post*, September 9, 1978.

202 *A* Washington Post *analysis commented:* Ibid.

203 *Abourezk and Metzenbaum held a news conference:* Richard L. Lyons, "Two Senators Set to Fight Gas Bill Again," *Washington Post*, August 2, 1978.

203 *A coalition of unions and citizens' action groups:* Richard L. Lyons, "Accord on Natural Gas Threatens to Come Unstuck," *Washington Post*, August 4, 1978.

203 *Bennett Johnston, a key architect of the compromise:* Peter Barnes, "Byrd, Jackson Say Compromise Gas Bill Can Still Be Saved," *Washington Post*, August 13, 1978.

203 *he met with key conferees in both houses:* Richard L. Lyons, "In Big Victory, Hill Conferees Clear Gas Bill," *Washington Post*, August 19, 1978.

204 *Long confirmed that he would vote against:* Ward Sinclair, "Senate Opponents See Tide Turning Against Gas Bill," *Washington Post*, August 25, 1978.

204 *On August 31, he invited the critics:* Robert G. Kaiser and Edward Walsh, "Carter Pushes Harder for Gas Measure," *Washington Post*, September 1, 1978.

204 *back from a brief recess for Labor Day:* Robert G. Kaiser, "Senate Showdown on Gas Decontrol Is Set Next Week," *Washington Post*, September 9, 1978.

204 *Long and Clifford Hansen sent a mailgram:* Ibid.

204 *received endorsements from the National Council of Mayors:* Fred Barbash, "Byrd Gaining Hope on Gas Compromise," *Washington Post*, September 10, 1978.

205 *On September 12, the Senate debated for a second day:* Richard L. Lyons, "Lineup on Gas Bill Remains Very Close," *Washington Post*, September 13, 1978.

206 *On September 14, he engineered a breakthrough:* Richard L. Lyons, "Senate Will Begin Voting Tuesday on the Gas Bill," *Washington Post*, September 15, 1978.

206 *On September 19, Jackson, Byrd, and the supporters:* Richard L. Lyons, "Senators Reject Attempt to Scuttle Gas Compromise," *Washington Post*, September 20, 1978.

206 *the Senate approved the natural gas compromise:* Richard L. Lyons, "Senate Approves Compromise Bill on Natural Gas," *Washington Post*, September 28, 1978.

206 *finally claim significant, if incomplete, progress:* Carter, *White House Diary*, p. 258.

207 *Carter noted in his diary:* Ibid.

208 *Eagleton hated the amount of waste and fraud at DoD:* The brief effort to establish a statutory Inspector General at the Pentagon is based on my personal experience handling the legislation for Senator Eagleton and the Governmental Affairs Committee.

209 *"Ira, Chairman Brooks is on the phone for you":* This also reflects personal experience during the frenzied closing days of the Ninety-fifth Congress.

210 *I found Eagleton in the Monocle restaurant with Muskie:* This is one last personal anecdote.

210 *Byrd gave the Ninety-fifth Congress a grade of "A":* Richard L. Lyons, "Congress Quits After All-Night Session," *Washington Post*, October 16, 1978.

211 *Polls showed overwhelming public admiration:* Glad, *Outsider in the White House*, p. 153.

211 *incumbents were extremely vulnerable:* Robert Lindsey, "California Tax Revolt: Lesson for Legislators," *New York Times*, June 12, 1978.

211 *A New York Daily News poll:* "Nation: All Aboard the Bandwagon," *Time*, June 26, 1978.

211 *the GOP launched a seven-state campaign:* Bill Peterson, "GOP Starts Push for Tax Cut Bill," *Washington Post*, September 21, 1978.

211 *trying to atone for the Panama Canal treaties:* Ibid.

212 *Roth observed: "We have helped the rich":* Ibid.

212 *Short won the Democratic primary:* "Nation: To Candidates, Right Looks Right," *Time*, September 25, 1978.

212 *had brushed aside their concerns:* Rowland Evans and Robert Novak, "Percy: The Lessons of '78," *Washington Post*, November 6, 1978.

212 *The number of corporate PACs exploded:* Lichtman, *White Protestant Nation*, p. 303.

213 *Republican operative Lee Atwater later wrote:* Ibid.

213 *the five best-funded independent Political Action Committees:* Ibid., p. 307.

213 *Republicans also benefited from small contributions:* Ibid.

213 *Clark's brother-in-law called him:* Interview with Senator Dick Clark, November 9, 2010; interview with Peter Hart, July 6, 2010.

214 *Loeb had been gunning for McIntyre:* Jorden, *Panama Odyssey*, p. 526, described McIntyre's speech as "the one most likely to be included in anthologies of great Senate speeches. . . . Its central theme was the low level to which American politics had sunk in the recent past. . . . It was a courageous exposure of the tactics used by a handful of vicious and narrow-minded political manipulators whose main weapons were exaggeration, distortion, prejudice and fear."

214 *Helms was reelected by a comfortable margin:* Link, *Righteous Warrior*, pp. 199–200.

214 *he had created a new model for a senator:* Lichtman, *White Protestant Nation*, pp. 310–311.

214 *"the first all purpose Political Action Committee of the right":* Ibid., p. 311.

216 *Kennedy delivered one of the most memorable speeches of his career:* Clymer, *Edward M. Kennedy*, pp. 276–277.

216 *Bill Clinton, the young governor of Arkansas:* Ibid., p. 277.

216 *Hamilton Jordan, the White House chief of staff:* Ibid.

216 *Kennedy had not yet decided to challenge Carter:* Ibid.

216 *the United States would establish diplomatic relations:* Glad, *Outsider in the White House*, p. 119.

216 *events began to spiral out of control in Iran:* Ibid., p. 167.

217 *"This is the month that blood will triumph"*: Ibid.

217 *hit Washington without warning:* Ibid., pp. 168–169.

217 *The Carter administration offered the shah support:* Ibid.

217 *one comprehensive Department of State memo:* Ibid., p. 170.

217 *understood the severity of the situation:* Ibid.

218 *Brzezinski believed that the shah's only option:* Ibid.

218 *Byrd undertook a major trip to the Middle East:* Interview with Hoyt Purvis, January 14, 2011; interview with Joe Stewart, June 14, 2010.

218 *Byrd had a personal interest in Iran:* Byrd, *Senate Addresses,* vol. 2, p. 588; Purvis interview.

218 *Before leaving Washington, Byrd met with Brzezinski:* Byrd, *Senate Addresses,* vol. 2, p. 588; Purvis interview.

218 *bonfires could be seen:* Byrd, *Senate Addresses,* vol. 2, p. 587.

218 *the grim conversation through the long evening:* Ibid., p. 588; Purvis interview.

218 *When Byrd met with the shah:* Byrd, *Senate Addresses,* vol. 2, pp. 588–589.

218 *Having concluded that the Shah's days were numbered:* Purvis interview.

219 *"A single misstep could produce unforeseeable consequences":* Glad, *Outsider in the White House,* p. 170.

CHAPTER 13: BEFORE THE STORM

223 *twenty new senators, a record number:* Amer, "Freshmen in the House of Representatives and Senate."

223 *decided to continue meeting for lunches:* Interview with Senator Alan Simpson, February 2, 2010.

224 *Stevens stopped attending the group's breakfasts:* Interview with Wayne Schley, April 12, 2010.

225 *Levin had rented a bulldozer:* Interview with Linda Gustitis, July 12, 2010.

225 *"We've come of age as a political force":* Bill Peterson, "Foes of Abortion Aim at Hill 'Deadly Dozen,'" *Washington Post,* February 11, 1979.

225 *Bayh headed the group's "Deadly Dozen" list:* Ibid.

225 *scheduled to receive the Hubert H. Humphrey Inspirational award:* Megan Rosenfeld, "Tears and Tributes at Cancer's Society Volunteer Luncheon," *Washington Post,* March 29, 1979.

226 *"Congratulations on your chairmanship":* Ashby and Gramer, *Fighting the Odds,* p. 561.

227 *the subcommittee chairmen had grown accustomed to their power:* Ibid., pp. 562–563.

227 *He and John Glenn were barely on speaking terms:* Ibid., p. 563.

227 *Helms seized upon a provision in the Senate rules:* Ibid.

227 *the atmosphere was so adversarial:* Ibid.

227 *Carter led the former California governor 57–35:* David S. Broder, "1980 GOP Presidential Field Already Crowded," *Washington Post,* January 21, 1979.

227 *"Army surrenders; Khomeini wins. Destroying all classified":* Glad, *Outsider in the White House,* p. 172.

228 *Bani-Sadr expressed astonishment:* Ibid., p. 178.

228 *Khomeini's goal was "to establish an Islamic Republic":* Ibid., p. 177.

228 *many hours talking with the Senate parliamentarians:* Interview with Robert Dove, June 9, 2010.

228 *"I have stayed on the floor more than any other senator":* Statement of Majority Leader Robert Byrd, *Congressional Record—Senate,* January 15, 1979, pp. 143–146.

230 *complimented Byrd for visiting him:* Statement of Minority Leader Howard Baker, *Congressional Record—Senate,* January 15, 1979, pp. 146–148.

230 *the Senate remained on the first legislative day:* Richard L. Lyons, "On Capitol Hill," *Washington Post,* February 3, 1979; David Broder, "Row over Senate Rules," *Washington Post,* February 4, 1979.

230 *another long day of talks failed to reach a compromise:* Richard L. Lyons, "On Capitol Hill," *Washington Post,* February 9, 1979.

231 *the Senate reached its resolution of changes:* Richard L. Lyons, "Senate Strengthens Rule Restricting Filibusters," *Washington Post,* February 23, 1979.

232 *Peking's leaders were consistent in their demands:* Robert G. Sutter, "Congress and Foreign Policy: Congress and U.S. Policy in Asia: New Relationships with China and Taiwan," Congressional Research Service, 1979, pp. 54–71.

232 *A political firestorm swiftly ensued:* David S. Broder and Bill Peterson, "Credibility of U.S. Hurt, Critics Say: But Most Democrats, Ford Rally Behind President's Decision," *Washington Post,* December 16, 1978.

233 *Reagan attacked the administration:* Ashby and Gramer, *Fighting the Odds,* p. 568.

233 *charged Carter with failing to meet:* Broder and Peterson, "Credibility of U.S. Hurt."

233 *"We owe the Taiwanese more than this":* Edward Walsh and Robert G. Kaiser, "Carter Indicates He'll Reject Delay Sought by Baker," *Washington Post,* December 20, 1978.

233 *Carter quickly and publicly rebuffed Baker's request:* Ibid.

234 *Goldwater and fourteen other conservative lawmakers:* Kenneth Bredemeier, "Goldwater, Other Lawmakers File Suit over Repeal of Taiwan Defense Pact," *Washington Post,* December 23, 1978.

234 *Jimmy Carter continued to make clear his view:* John M. Goshko, "Carter's Plan for Taiwan Is Criticized in Congress," *Washington Post,* January 17,

1979; John M. Goshko, "President Warns Hill on Taiwan," *Washington Post*, January 27, 1979.

234 *Taiwan posed the first major issue for Church:* John M. Goshko, "President Warns Hill on Taiwan," *Washington Post*, January 27, 1979.

234 *had already petitioned Congress and the president:* Ashby and Gramer, *Fighting the Odds*, p. 569.

235 *great mutual respect for each other's abilities:* Ibid., p. 570.

235 *On February 5, Church banged the gavel:* Statement of Senator Frank Church, Taiwan: Hearings Before the Committee on Foreign Relations, February 5, 6, 7, 8, 21, and 22, 1979, p. 1.

235 *Javits dismissed the notion:* Statement of Senator Jacob Javits in ibid., p. 11.

236 *Christopher noted that the issue of China renouncing force:* Statement of Deputy Secretary of State Warren Christopher in ibid., p. 24.

236 *On February 8, Church endorsed a Javits resolution:* Robert G. Kaiser, "Woodcock Nomination Is Supported," *Washington Post*, February 9, 1979.

236 *China launched a major cross-border attack into Vietnam:* Robert G. Kaiser, "Taiwan Security Bill Clears Senate Committee," *Washington Post*, February 23, 1979.

237 *differences between the Church-Javits and Percy formulations:* Mary Russell and Robert G. Kaiser, "Bill on Taiwan Ties Survives Early Tests in Senate and House," *Washington Post*, March 9, 1979.

237 *Helms had threatened to filibuster the nomination:* Robert G. Kaiser, "Envoy to Peking Is Confirmed Easily in Senate," *Washington Post*, February 27, 1979.

237 *On March 13, the Senate approved the Taiwan bill:* Robert G. Kaiser, "House and Senate Adopt Taiwan Bills," *Washington Post*, March 14, 1979.

238 *The Carter administration's recognition of the PRC:* John K. Fairbank, "The New Two China Problem," *New York Review of Books*, March 8, 1979.

238 *Although PRC officials objected to the Taiwan Relations Act:* Ashby and Gramer, *Fighting the Odds*, p. 571.

238 *initial rage about the U.S. decision to recognize China:* Ibid.

CHAPTER 14: ENERGY BATTLES
AFTER THE IRANIAN REVOLUTION

241 *Global oil production at the beginning of 1979:* Sandbrook, *Mad as Hell*, p. 295.

241 *Gasoline prices rose 55 percent in the first three months:* Ibid., p. 298.

242 *Theodore White wrote: "There was a contagion of fear":* Quoted in ibid., p. 295.

242 *a pump failed at Three Mile Island:* Ibid., p. 298.

242 *On April 5, saying "the future of the country we love is at stake":* Edward Walsh and J. P. Smith, "Carter Moves to Raise Cost, Cut Use of Oil," *Washington Post*, April 6, 1979.

243 *strongly supported Carter's proposal:* Kaufman, *Henry M. Jackson*, p. 347.

243 *would require oil companies to pay back only $1.7 billion:* Art Pine, "Windfall Tax with Mild Bite Sent to Hill," *Washington Post*, April 27, 1979.

243 *On May 3, Abe Ribicoff jolted the Senate:* Steven R. Weisman, "Ribicoff Decides He Won't Seek a Fourth Term," *New York Times*, May 4, 1979.

244 *Javits was shocked by his friend's announcement:* Interview with Alan Bennett, July 17, 2009.

244 *Billings asked Moore what he thought of the idea:* Interview with Leon Billings, February 19, 2010.

245 *he ripped into the Carter administration officials:* Art Pine, "Windfall Profits Tax Criticized on Hill," *Washington Post*, May 8, 1979.

245 *The Senate, characteristically, worked on a slower track:* Art Pine, "Leaders Plan Prompt Action on Windfall Bill," *Washington Post*, June 8, 1979.

245 *Kennedy's intensified rhetoric, ripping into Carter's proposal:* Martin Schram, "Kennedy's Intensified Rhetoric Fuels '80 Speculation," *Washington Post*, June 11, 1979.

245 *told Kennedy he would make a lot of his friends look foolish:* Ibid.

246 *On June 22, the Americans for Democratic Action:* Bill Peterson, "ADA Panel Pushes Draft of Kennedy," *Washington Post*, June 23, 1979.

246 *Returning from an economic summit in Tokyo:* "Nation: Carter was Speechless," *Time*, July 16, 1979.

246 *most unusual presidential speeches ever given:* Ibid.

247 *Approval of Carter soon plunged to 23 percent:* Ibid.

247 *As Carter reeled, Howard Baker refused to pile on:* Warren Brown, "Bipartisan Support of Energy Proposals Urged by Sen. Baker," *Washington Post*, July 18, 1979.

247 *he decided to challenge Carter for the Democratic nomination:* Clymer, *Edward M. Kennedy*, p. 284.

247 *the last straw for Jackson as well:* John M. Berry, "Kennedy to Win 1980 Nomination, Jackson Predicts," *Washington Post*, July 25, 1979.

247 *another constant thorn in Carter's side:* Steve Gerstel, "McGovern Backs Race by Kennedy," *Washington Post*, July 27, 1979.

248 *On July 26, the Senate Energy Committee:* Art Pine, "Energy Plan Progress on Hill Is Mixed," *Washington Post*, July 27, 1979.

249 *Baker's support for Carter's energy proposals:* Ibid.

249 *Rising oil prices raised the economic stakes:* Art Pine, "Proposed Oil Tax Becomes a Magic Money Machine," *Washington Post*, July 30, 1979.

250 *Vice President Mondale chided Congress:* Edward Walsh and Richard L. Lyons, "Departing Congress Is Chided About Inaction on Energy Plan," *Washington Post*, August 4, 1979.

250 *the administration began to give ground:* Jerry Knight, "Carter Agrees to Slow His Plans for Synthetic Fuels," *Washington Post*, September 12, 1979.

250 *On September 18, Senate Finance unanimously approved:* "Tax Breaks Favored for Alternative Fuel," *Washington Post*, September 19, 1979.

251 *Long warned the members:* Art Pine, "Finance Panel Votes to Double Solar Credits," *Washington Post*, September 20, 1979.

251 *Jimmy Carter told a group of out-of-town editors:* Martin Schram, "Carter: Nature of Job Breeds Unpopularity," *Washington Post*, September 23, 1979.

251 *Danforth could no longer abide the amount of abuse:* Ibid.

251 *On September 25, Senate Finance voted 13–0:* Art Pine, "Senate Panel Strips All New Oil Finds from Windfall Bill," *Washington Post*, September 26, 1979.

251 *The next day, the Finance Committee had made more cuts:* Art Pine, "Panel Votes away More Money Than Oil Tax Would Raise," *Washington Post*, September 27, 1979.

252 *"They just chug-a-lugged it all":* Ibid.

252 *The chairman told the committee:* "Issue of Fuel Aid for Poor Splits Senate Finance Panel," Associated Press, September 29, 1979.

252 *Hart's subcommittee issued its report:* "Synthetic Fuels Not Likely to Become Alternative to Foreign Oil, Congressional Report Holds," Associated Press, September 29, 1979.

252 *October 3, Long put forth a compromise:* Art Pine, "Long Proposes a Compromise on Oil Windfall Profits Tax," *Washington Post*, October 4, 1979.

253 *The Finance Committee bill would capture:* Art Pine, "Oil Windfall Tax Whittle to 29% in Senate Version," *Washington Post*, October 9, 1979.

253 *On October 2, legislation to create:* Mary Russell, "Lines Are Drawn in Senate on Bill for Energy Board," *Washington Post*, October 3, 1979.

253 *Muskie, with his customary passion:* Ibid.

253 *the Senate rejected the Muskie-Ribicoff substitute:* Mary Russell, "Senate Gives White House Energy Package Victory," *Washington Post*, October 4, 1979.

254 *the EMB legislation passed the Senate on October 4:* Mary Russell, "Senate Votes 'Fast Track' Energy Unit," *Washington Post*, October 5, 1979.

254 *Senate Appropriations Committee approved $20 billion:* Mary Russell, "Senate Unit, in Shift, Backs Synfuel Fund," *Washington Post*, October 11, 1979.

254 *the Committee decided to scale back the tax credit package:* Art Pine, "Senate Panel Shifts on Insulation Tax Credits," *Washington Post*, October 18, 1979.

254 *CBS televised an interview of Kennedy done by Roger Mudd:* Clymer, *Edward M. Kennedy*, pp. 285–287.

254 *O'Neill had warned Kennedy in September:* Ibid., p. 285.

255 *Some of his closest friends wondered:* Ibid., p. 287.

255 *"What are you guys going to advise me to do":* Mark Bowden, *Guests of the Ayatollah* (New York: Grove, 2006), p. 19.

255 *students stormed the lightly-guarded U.S. embassy:* Glad, *Outsider in the White House*, p. 176.

255 *The original idea, according to the leader of the students:* David Harris, *The Crisis: The President, the Prophet and the Shah—1979 and the Coming of Militant Islam* (New York: Little, Brown, 2004), p. 200.

255 *Speaking to a conference of northeastern state officials:* "Business: Crude Assaults," *Time*, November 12, 1979.

256 *Kennedy was attacking him:* Martin Schram, "Kennedy Attacks President's Policy on Oil Price Controls," *Washington Post*, November 4, 1979.

256 *Jackson and the Energy Committee pushed:* Mary Russell, "Senate Begins Fight on Rival Energy Bills," *Washington Post*, November 6, 1979.

256 *The Senate rejected the Proxmires version, 57–37:* Mary Russell, "Senate Begins Fight on Rival Energy Bills," *Washington Post*, November 9, 1979.

256 *On November 7, a* Washington Post *article:* Mary Russell, "Senate Wages Energy War with Popgun Legislation," *Washington Post*, November 7, 1979.

257 *finally began floor debate on the windfall profits tax:* Helen Dewar, "Oil-State Senators Lose Surprise Attempt to Cut Tax on Windfall Profits," *Washington Post*, November 17, 1979.

257 *Bumpers introduced an amendment:* Helen Dewar, "Senate Votes to Repeal Controversial Rule Raising Tax on Inherited Property," *Washington Post*, November 20, 1979.

257 *the Senate voted, 53–41, to exempt most independent producers:* Helen Dewar, "Windfall-Tax Break for Independent Oil Approved by Senate," *Washington Post*, November 28, 1979.

258 *Byrd said he favored raising the windfall profits tax:* Spencer Rich, "Byrd Sees a Compromise Hiking Tax on Oil Profits," *Washington Post*, December 2, 1979.

258 *the Senate voted 58–35 for a Bradley-Chafee amendment:* Helen Dewar, "Senate Votes to Increase Oil 'Windfall Profits' Tax," *Washington Post*, December 5, 1979.

258 *On December 5, the Republicans offered a plan:* Helen Dewar, "Senate GOP Narrowly Beaten in Effort to Force Tax Cuts," *Washington Post*, December 6, 1979.

258 *a compromise that would allow the windfall profits tax to pass:* Helen Dewar, "Sen. Long: 'If Missouri Succeeds in Taxing Louisiana, I'll Get Back at Missouri,'" *Washington Post*, December 9, 1979.

259 *as Danforth would write almost thirty years later:* Danforth, *Faith and Politics*, pp. 24–26.

259 *On December 12, the Senate plunged into a filibuster:* Helen Dewar, "Filibuster Stalls Senate Attempts to Toughen Tax on Oil Profits," *Washington Post*, December 13, 1979.

259 *"In about 15 years, I think you'll be a great senator":* Danforth, *Faith and Politics*, p. 25; interview with Senator Danforth, March 30, 2010.

259 *On December 14, the Senate ended a three day filibuster:* Helen Dewar, "Senate Ends Filibuster on Oil Tax with $178 Billion Compromise," *Washington Post*, December 15, 1979.

260 *Years later, the humiliating defeat stayed with him:* Interview with Senator Danforth, March 30, 2010.

260 *On December 17, the Senate gave final approval:* Helen Dewar, "Senate Votes $178 Billion Oil Tax Bill," *Washington Post*, December 18, 1979.

260 *Three days later, the House and Senate split the difference:* Helen Dewar, "Tax on Oil Profits Set at $227.3 Billion," *Washington Post*, December 21, 1979.

260 *Jimmy Carter would later write:* Carter, *Keeping Faith*, p. 123.

261 *The resulting legislation succeeded in reducing oil imports:* Carter, *White House Diary*, p. 490.

261 *Assessing Carter's quest for a national energy policy:* John C. Barrow, "An Age of Limits: Jimmy Carter and the Quest for a National Energy Policy," in Fink and Graham, eds., *Carter Presidency*, p. 172.

262 *"The bipartisanship that I enjoyed":* Carter, *White House Diary*, p. 530.

CHAPTER 15: FIGHTING THE ECONOMIC TIDE

263 *On a trip to Europe, Ribicoff found "geo-politics":* Ribicoff, *America Can Make It!*, p. 225.

264 *He called on the U.S. government to concentrate its efforts:* Ibid., p. 226.

264 *the creation of a new permanent board:* Ibid., p. 216.

265 *Jimmy Carter had come to office an avowed free trader:* Judith Stein, "The Locomotive Loses Power: The Trade and Industrial Policies of Jimmy Carter," in Fink and Graham, eds., *Carter Presidency*, pp. 74–75.

265 *the American steel industry was facing an acute crisis:* Ibid., pp. 76–82.

265 *completion of the multilateral Tokyo Round:* Carter, *White House Diary*, pp. 313–314.

266 *The Senate passed the Trade Amendments Act:* Ibid., p. 347.

266 *they discovered that 28,000 patents:* Interview with Senator Birch Bayh, March 18, 2010.

266 *Gaylord Nelson meanwhile used his chairmanship:* Interview with William Cherkasky, December 3, 2010.

267 *Chrysler Corporation announced it was closing:* Robert B. Reich and John D. Donahue, *New Deals: The Chrysler Revival and the American System* (New York: Penguin Books, 1985), p. 94.

268 *He was customarily a whirling dervish of activity:* many of the observations about Eagleton come from having worked closely with him for nearly seven years.

268 *He was known for his sense of humor and comic timing:* Interview with Ed Quick, May 21, 2010.

269 *advocates of reasserting Congress's power to declare war:* Thomas F. Eagleton, *War and Presidential Power: A Chronicle of Congressional Surrender* (New York: Liveright, 1974).

269 *He had helped Muskie and Howard Baker:* Interview with Leon Billings, February 19, 2010.

270 *Chrysler, the smallest of the companies:* Ibid., pp. 27–29.

270 *The company seemed snake bit:* Charles K. Hyde, *Riding the Roller Coaster: A History of the Chrysler Corporation* (Detroit: Wayne State University Press, 2003), p. 224; Reich and Donohue, *New Deals*, pp. 27–46.

270 *Riccardo asked Eizenstat for temporary relief:* Reich and Donohue, *New Deals*, p. 88.

270 *By the end of June, Riccardo returned to the White House:* "Business: Chrysler Drives for a Tax Break," *Time*, July 16, 1979.

271 *Miller advised President Carter that Chrysler:* Helen Dewar and Art Pine, "White House, Hill React Cautiously to Chrysler SOS," *Washington Post*, August 2, 1979.

271 *The president agreed: "you're absolutely right":* Reich and Donohue, *New Deals*, p. 105.

271 *"Miller just blew us out of the water":* Ibid.

272 *Russell Long, however, said that it was too early:* Dewar and Pine, "White House, Hill React Cautiously."

272 *It was not difficult to envision the UAW:* Reich and Donohue, *New Deals*, pp. 124, 130–131.

272 *"I just don't like you" were Ford's last words:* "Business: Upheaval in the House of Ford," *Time*, July 24, 1978.

272 *Iaccoca met with Treasury Secretary Miller on September 7:* Douglas Williams, "Chrysler Wants $1.2 Billion in Aid," *Washington Post*, September 13, 1979.

272 *Chrysler reported a staggering $460 million loss:* William H. Jones, "Chrysler's Loss Business History's Biggest," *Washington Post*, October 31, 1979.

273 *Carter administration had decided to provide $1.5 billion:* Helen Dewar, "Chrysler Rescue Plan of $3 Billion Proposed," *Washington Post*, November 2, 1979.

273 *the union announced that it would make concessions:* Helen Dewar, "UAW Pledges Concessions If Chrysler Gets U.S. Aid," *Washington Post*, October 20, 1979.

274 *Proxmire gaveled the Banking Committee hearing to order:* "Chrysler Corporation Loan Guarantee Act of 1979," Hearings Before the Committee on Banking, Housing and Urban Affairs, United States Senate, Part I. November 14 and 15, 1979.

274   *"We let 7,000 companies fail last year; we didn't bail them out":* Statement of Chairman Proxmire, Banking Committee Hearings, p. 2.

274   *Garn, the ranking member, further proved Proxmire's point:* Statement of Senator Jake Garn, Banking Committee Hearings, pp. 3–4.

274   *Heinz, bearer of one of the most famous corporate names:* Statement of Senator John Heinz, Banking Committee Hearings, pp. 66–68.

274   *Weicker had earned a reputation:* Statement of Senator Lowell Weicker, Banking Committee Hearings, pp. 77–79.

275   *The task of making the case for helping Chrysler:* Statement of Senator Don Riegle, Banking Committee Hearings, pp. 69–74.

275   *"The United States has not thought to develop":* Ibid., p. 69.

276   *Eagleton honed in on the critics' concern about the precedent:* Statement of Senator Tom Eagleton, Banking Committee Hearings, p. 81.

276   *Chrysler's employees should receive a substantial part:* Statement of Senator Robert Byrd, Banking Committee Hearings, p. 89.

277   *the more liberal House Banking Committee approved:* William H. Jones, "Panel Approves Chrysler Aid," *Washington Post,* November 16, 1979.

277   *broke with the UAW's long tradition of "pattern bargaining":* William H. Jones, "Chrysler Workers Ratify UAW Pact," *Washington Post,* November 17, 1979.

277   *testifying himself on November 19, Doug Fraser told the press:* W. Dale Nelson, "Fraser's Optimism Decreases," *Washington Post,* November 20, 1979.

277   *On November 20, Nader testified in vehement opposition:* Statement of Ralph Nader, Banking Committee Hearings, pp. 1198–1277.

278   *The exchange became unexpectedly infused with emotion:* William J. Mitchell, "Nader, Garn Clash Bitterly," Knight-Ridder, November 21, 1979.

278   *Citicorp Chairman Walter Wriston testified against the bailout:* William H. Jones, "Wriston Opposes Chrysler Aid," *Washington Post,* November 22, 1979.

279   *He predicted that despite his opposition:* Ibid.

279   *He proposed a "pure" $4 billion bailout:* William H. Jones, "Compromise Chrysler Aid Plan Pushed," *Washington Post,* November 28, 1979.

280   *the Senate Banking Committee, by an emphatic 10–5 vote:* William H. Jones, "Panel Votes Chrysler Aid with Wage Roll-Back Plan," *Washington Post,* November 30, 1979.

280   *"Shared sacrifice" had become the watchword of the day:* William H. Jones, "Misery for Many in Senate's Chrysler Bailout Bill," *Washington Post,* December 1, 1979.

280   *Howard Paster, who had worked for Birch Bayh:* Ibid.

280   *Doug Fraser termed the three-year pay freeze "unacceptable":* William H. Jones, "3-Year Chrysler Pay Freeze Unacceptable, UAW Chief Says," *Washington Post,* December 5, 1979.

281 *On December 14, Mondale, speaking for Carter:* Art Pine, "Aid Needed for Chrysler in January," *Washington Post*, November 15, 1979.

281 *Lugar said that he might bend on the wage freeze:* Merrill Brown, "New Bailout for Chrysler Opposed," *Washington Post*, December 12, 1979.

281 *"the brain drain argument is specious":* *Congressional Record—Senate*, December 19, 1979, p. 36999.

281 *the Eagleton-Roth-Biden amendment passed the Senate:* Reich and Donohue, *New Deals*, p. 155.

281 *Weicker punctured the celebratory atmosphere:* *Congressional Record—Senate*, December 19, 1979, pp. 37048–37050; Reich and Donohue, *New Deals*, p. 155.

282 *Byrd summoned the key senators into his office again:* "Nation: Santa Calls on Chrysler," *Time*, December 31, 1979.

282 *Levin and Riegle went to Gerald Greenwald:* Reich and Donohue, *New Deals*, p. 157.

282 *Byrd went the extra mile:* Interview with Mary Jane Checchi, May 13, 2010.

282 *"probably the biggest mistake Congress has made in its history":* Reich and Donohue, *New Deals*, p. 156.

283 *In conference, the Senate and House split the difference:* Art Pine, "Union Has to Forgo $462 Million of Raise," *Washington Post*, December 21, 1979.

283 *Tsongas declared that "he did not want to do to Detroit":* "Nation: Santa Calls on Chrysler."

284 *the UAW would be supporting Ted Kennedy:* Interview with Jim Blanchard, June 9, 2010.

CHAPTER 16: SALT II: DEATH BY A THOUSAND CUTS

285 *the relationship between the superpowers was deteriorating:* Glad, *Outsider in the White House*, pp. 69–79.

286 *Brezhnev was very emotional about the deterioration:* Ibid., p. 56.

286 *authorized Cyrus Vance to explore a summit meeting:* Ibid., p. 59.

286 *decision to recognize the People's Republic of China:* Ibid., p. 61.

286 *they met more than twenty-five times:* Ibid., p. 64.

287 *Carter and Brezhnev signed the SALT II treaty:* Don Oberdorfer, "U.S., Soviets Reach SALT Agreement," *Washington Post*, May 10, 1979.

287 *was a far cry from the ambitious arms reduction agreement:* Glad, *Outsider in the White House*, pp. 67–68.

288 *Carter had been shocked in January in a meeting with senators:* Carter, *White House Diary*, pp. 281–282.

288 *Treaty opponents, led by Scoop Jackson:* "Special Report: To Educate Their Senators," *Time*, May 21, 1979.

288 *His speech received a lukewarm response:* Glad, *Outsider in the White House*, p. 107.

289 *Cranston said the treaty had the support of fifty-eight senators:* Ibid.

289 *Jackson unleashed an extraordinary blast:* Robert G. Kaiser, "Jackson Rips 'Appeasement' of Moscow," *Washington Post*, June 13, 1979.

290 *By mid-June, Baker and Frank Church:* Annis, *Howard Baker*, pp. 152, 156; Ashby and Gramer, *Fighting the Odds*, pp. 592–593; Glad, *Outsider in the White House*, p. 111.

290 *Cranston observed that "if Jackson were for the treaty":* "Nation: Twin Salvos for SALT," *Time*, April 16, 1979.

290 *recalled with amazement visiting Byrd's office:* Interview with Senator John Culver, April 15, 2010.

290 *Byrd had visited the Soviet Union:* Byrd, *Senate Addresses*, vol. 2, p. 586.

291 *thought Baker might be willing to play a constructive role:* "Nation: Signed and Sealed," *Time*, July 2, 1979.

291 *Baker had received a considerable amount of his SALT briefing materials:* Kaufman, *Henry M. Jackson*, p. 384.

291 *Nunn seemed willing to consider voting for the treaty:* Robert G. Kaiser, "White House Moves to Shore Up Support of SALT," *Washington Post*, September 14, 1979.

291 *"It was nauseating to confront the gross waste of money":* Carter, *White House Diary*, p. 323.

291 *McGovern, a steadfast leader on such issues:* "Nation: Signed and Sealed."

292 *He was particularly angry at Jackson's staff members:* Interview with Senator John Culver, April 15, 2010.

292 *a natural supporter of the SALT II treaty:* Ashby and Gramer, *Fighting the Odds*, pp. 591–592.

293 *seized the opportunity to take a tough stand:* George C. Wilson, "SALT Stumbles over Presence of Soviet Troops," *Washington Post*, September 7, 1979.

293 *Carter first pronounced the brigade "unacceptable":* "Nation: Carter Defuses a Crisis," *Time*, October 15, 1979.

293 *Vance implored Dobrynin to give him some help:* Glad, *Outsider in the White House*, p. 191.

294 *Byrd urged that the White House and congressional leaders:* Ibid., p. 192.

294 *Carter convened a group of fifteen "wise men":* Ibid., p. 193.

294 *Carter would never forgive Church:* Carter, *White House Diary*, pp. 422, 424.

294 *reported the treaty favorably by an unimpressive 9–6 vote:* Kaufman, *Henry M. Jackson*, p. 389.

294 *the Armed Services Committee voted 10–0:* Ibid.

295 *Howard Baker announced his candidacy:* David S. Broder, "Baker, Tying His Fate to SALT, Formally Announces 1980 Bid," *Washington Post*, November 2, 1979.

295   the "failure to ratify the SALT II treaty: Carter, *Keeping Faith*, p. 265.

296   Carter had intuited the situation at the end of 1977: Carter, *White House Diary*, p. 152.

296   Carter was handling the crisis with "great competence": "Iran: The Test of Wills," *Time*, November 26, 1979.

296   Carter was helped by Khomeini's "irrationality": Robert G. Kaiser, "Congress Is Giving President Freer Hand at Crisis Helm," *Washington Post*, December 7, 1979.

297   The year ended on an ironic note: Spencer Rich, "Panama Treaty Supporter Delighted at Offer to Shah, but Foes Unmoved," *Washington Post*, December 16, 1979.

CHAPTER 17: A TOUGH POLITICAL CLIMATE

301   Nelson had "a lifelong tendency to loaf or joke his way through the campaign": Christofferson, *Man from Clear Lake*, p. 339.

302   Hart and his associates polled 617 Wisconsin voters: "Survey of Voter Attitudes in the State of Wisconsin," Peter D. Hart Research Associates, Inc., January 1980.

302   "this nation is in deep and serious trouble": Ibid., p. 2.

302   "moral threats which cut right through the social fabric": Ibid.

302   "These economic threats are more commonly identified": Ibid., p. 3.

302   "Leading the list is government's interference in people's lives": Ibid.

303   said he was doing an "excellent" or "good" job: Ibid., p. 11.

303   he also pointed out Nelson's special problem: Ibid., pp. 9–10.

303   "We cannot overstress," Hart noted: Ibid., p. 13.

303   The right wing had been gunning for Frank Church for years: Ashby and Gramer, *Fighting the Odds*, p. 539.

304   had targeted Church early: Ibid., p. 579.

304   "people voting against Church without remembering why": Ibid., p. 599.

304   moving his family to Australia's Great Barrier Reef: Ibid., p. 600.

304   Columnist Mary McGrory rebuked Church: Ibid., p. 584.

304   "The Soviet brigade," McGrory wrote: Ibid., p. 596.

304   Church's former speechwriter, Bill Hall, said: Ibid.

305   Retired General John K. Singlaub blasted Church: Ibid., p. 601.

305   suppressing evidence regarding Chile: Ibid.

305   A Peter Hart poll of the staff showed significant weaknesses: Scates, *Warren G. Magnuson*, p. 313.

305   His closest advisers urged him not to seek reelection: Ibid., pp. 313–314.

305   "The boss loved his job, loved his work": Ibid., p. 314.

305   saw Magnuson, aged, exhausted, and unfocused: Interview with Leon Billings, February 19, 2010.

305 *Javits had intended to not seek a fifth term:* Javits and Steinberg, *Javits*, pp. 490–494.

306 *Much more serious was his deteriorating health:* Ibid.

306 *"whether [he] had any business leaving his post of duty":* Ibid.

306 *He announced for reelection and disclosed his affliction:* Ibid.

306 *"There was no argument to stand up against that":* Ibid.

307 *Kennedy was absorbing one devastating blow after another:* Clymer, *Edward M. Kennedy*, pp. 292–295.

307 *They rallied behind Carter:* Ibid., p. 295.

307 *Clark's son expressed disappointment:* Interview with Senator Dick Clark, November 9, 2010.

307 *a lengthy debate took place between consultants:* Ibid.

307 *When Kennedy finally did take a strong position:* Clymer, *Edward M. Kennedy*, p. 295.

308 *Peter Hart, polling for the Kennedy campaign:* Ibid.

308 *Even the* Boston Globe, *his hometown newspaper:* Ibid., p. 297.

308 *Carter smashed Kennedy, winning 59 percent:* Ibid., p. 300.

308 *told Kennedy that he would have to remain neutral:* Ibid.; interview with Senator John Culver, April 15, 2010.

308 *Joe Biden, who maintained close ties:* Carter, *White House Diary*, p. 362.

308 *Kennedy's advisers were also embittered:* Clymer, *Edward M. Kennedy*, pp. 305, 307.

309 *they certainly did not see Carter as an asset:* Carter, *White House Diary*, p. 364, notes on October 22: "We assessed the prospects for U.S. senators up for re-election next year, and they are dismal. Many are quite weak or very liberal. Bob Byrd and I will see what we can do to help them."

309 *On March 30, hopes rose that a deal was at hand:* Glad, *Outsider in the White House*, p. 185.

310 *His appearance probably influenced some undecided voters:* Clymer, *Edward M. Kennedy*, p. 308.

310 *threw all the Iranian diplomats out of the United States:* Glad, *Outsider in the White House*, p. 186.

310 *the rescue mission that an elite Delta Force unit was training for:* Ibid.

310 *"Gentleman, I want you to know":* Ibid., p. 263.

311 *learned to his regret to be very skeptical:* Ibid., p. 265.

311 *virtually stumbled onto the existence of the planned mission:* Witcover, *Joe Biden*, pp. 144–146.

312 *Carter would later write:* Carter, *Keeping Faith*, p. 514.

312 *this was the one that tore their relationship irreparably:* Interview with Dan Tate, June 2, 8, 2010; interview with Hoyt Purvis, January 14, 2011; interview with Joe Stewart, June 14, 2010.

312 *"under the impression it was not something that was imminent"*: Joanne Omang, "Byrd Knew of Rescue Plan but Didn't Know It was Underway," *Washington Post*, April 27, 1980.

312 *he would not have given the operation a 50–50 chance of success*: Ibid.

313 *Dole said he respected*: Robert G. Kaiser, "In Stunned Congress, Wariness and Concern over the War Powers Act," *Washington Post*, April 26, 1980.

313 *Baker offered unqualified support*: Ibid.

313 *Jackson was angry he could not get a clear answer*: Ibid.

313 *Church suggested that launching the operation*: Ibid.

313 *"a greater failure than that of incomplete success"*: Glad, *Outsider in the White House*, p. 267.

313 *"America doesn't have enough helicopters?"*: Ibid., p. 268.

313 *Carter was doing the "sensible" thing*: Robert G. Kaiser and Michael Getler, "Carter Responds by Returning to the Political Fray," *Washington Post*, May 4, 1980.

314 *Kennedy still in the race, having finished strongly*: Clymer, *Edward M. Kennedy*, pp. 312–313.

314 *The president and the senator met on June 5*: T. R. Reid and Edward Walsh, "Kennedy: Planning to Be Nominee," *Washington Post*, June 6, 1980; Clymer, *Edward M. Kennedy*, pp. 312–313; Carter, *White House Diary*, p. 435; Kennedy, *True Compass*, pp. 378–379.

314 *Carter mulled it over and decided Mondale was right*: Clymer, *Edward M. Kennedy*, pp. 313–314.

CHAPTER 18: AMERICA'S LAST FRONTIER

317 *Congress and the Nixon administration also agreed to specify a deadline*: Alice Bonner, "Deadline Near for Alaska Lands Bill," *Washington Post*, September 17, 1978.

318 *Carter was the first president to come to office*: Jeffrey K. Stine, "Environmental Policy During the Carter Presidency," in Fink and Graham, eds., *Carter Presidency*, pp. 179–180.

318 *made protecting the environment a high priority*: Ibid., p. 181.

318 *On April 25, 1977, Interior Secretary Cecil Andrus*: Margot Hornblower, "Carter Stressing Environment in Fight over Alaska Lands," *Washington Post*, April 26, 1977.

319 *approved a version of the Alaska Lands legislation*: Mary Russell, "Alaska Land Bill Is Approved," *Washington Post*, May 20, 1978.

320 *Tom Eagleton was dropped from the Democratic ticket*: Interview with Ed Quick, May 21, 2010.

320 *A University of Alaska professor later said*: David Westphal, "Mike Gravel, an Anti-War Crusader for Two Generations," McClatchy Newspapers, December 4, 2007.

320 *Carter said on July 31, 1978:* Loretta Tofani, "Fallback Methods Studied for Saving Alaska Lands," *Washington Post*, August 1, 1978.

320 *a bill that nominally set aside 121 million acres:* Alice Bonner, "Deadline Near for Alaska Lands Bill," *Washington Post*, September 17, 1978.

321 *the Energy Committee reached a tentative agreement:* "Panel Votes to Set Aside Alaska Lands," Associated Press, September 30, 1978.

321 *a 95-million acre Alaska lands bill:* "Technicality Voids Senate Units Vote on Alaska Lands," Associated Press, October 5, 1978.

321 *On October 15, the Alaska Lands Act had died:* Richard L. Lyons, "2 Dozen Major Bills Acted on Near End," *Washington Post*, October 16, 1978.

321 *The post-mortems indicated how much was at stake:* Alice Bonner, "Gravel Accused of Sabotaging the Alaska Lands Bill," *Washington Post*, October 19, 1978.

321 *110 million acres of Alaska land would be closed:* Margot Hornblower, "U.S. Moves to Protect Alaska Land," *Washington Post*, November 17, 1978.

321 *designate 56 million acres of Alaska lands:* Margot Hornblower, "Carter Sets Aside 56 Million Acres of Alaska Lands," *Washington Post*, December 2, 1978.

322 *Carter would express concern about landing in Anchorage:* Carter, *White House Diary*, p. 334.

322 *Stevens would always blame Gravel for his wife's death:* Interview with Susan Alvarado, October 11, 2010.

323 *Secretary Andrus ordered strict environmental protection:* Editorial, "An Unsatisfactory Solution," *Washington Post*, February 13, 1980.

323 *Stevens, Jackson, and Tsongas meet:* "Senators Put Forth Amendments for a Debate over Alaska Lands," Associated Press, May 4, 1980.

323 *On July 21, the Senate began the long-anticipated debate:* Joanne Omang, "Energy and Environment Collide on the Senate Floor This Week," *Washington Post*, July 20, 1980.

323 *Jimmy Carter, deeply committed on the merits:* Philip Shabecoff, "Senate Starts Debating Legislation on Future Use of Land in Alaska," *New York Times*, July 22, 1980.

324 *the environmentalists won a series of test votes:* Richard L. Lyons, "Conservation-Minded Senators Survived Test Votes," *Washington Post*, July 23, 1980.

324 *That explosion was just a prelude to the shouting match:* "Senate Sets Aside Alaska Bill to Let Tempers Cool Off," Associated Press, July 24, 1980.

324 *that crucial moment had arrived:* Joanne Omang, "Governor, Senators Shun Alaska Bill," *Washington Post*, July 30, 1980.

325 *On August 4, the negotiators announced:* Richard L. Lyons and Helen Dewar, "On Capitol Hill: Alaska Land Substitute Set for Floor," *Washington Post*, August 5, 1980.

325 *appreciated that Tsongas had been patient:* Ibid.

325 *Jackson and Gravel were at each other's throats:* Ibid.

325 *"every time I try to be reasonable":* Ibid.

326 *the Senate gave "all but final approval":* Joanne Omang, "Historic Alaska Lands Bill Nears Senate Passage," *Washington Post,* August 19, 1980.

326 *On August 19, the Senate gave final approval to the bill:* Joanne Omang, "Senate Approves Alaska Bill," *Washington Post,* August 20, 1980.

CHAPTER 19: FIGHTING TO SURVIVE

327 *Bayh had intensely enjoyed chairing:* Interviews with Senator Birch Bayh, February 25, 2009, March 18, 2010.

327 *spent an hour telling Bayh what he had to do:* Ibid.

328 *like surprisingly many other liberal Democrats:* Ibid. O'Brien, *Philip Hart,* pp. 151–153; Christofferson, *Man from Clear Lake,* pp. 187–190.

328 *Bayh joked he was not sure:* Bayh interview.

328 *committed to remaking the Supreme Court "in his own image":* The phrase is taken from James F. Simon, *In His Own Image: The Supreme Court in Richard Nixon's America* (New York: D. McKay, 1973).

328 *Bayh quickly took the lead of the coalition:* Dean, *Rehnquist Choice,* p. 21.

328 *"I know this president":* Interview with Jay Berman, May 17, 2009.

329 *"in no mood for another such donnybrook":* Clymer, *Edward M. Kennedy,* p. 161.

329 *stepped forward to lead the opposition:* Ibid., pp. 161–163.

329 *a response that would become one of the most famous:* Dean, *Rehnquist Choice,* p. 21.

330 *the Carswell nomination remained in doubt:* Ibid., p. 163.

330 *Enraged, Nixon went to the White House press room:* Ibid., p. 23.

331 *he was nominating a guy "who's there for thirty years":* Ibid., p. 265.

331 *expression of his legal views well hidden:* Ibid., pp. 266–269.

331 *the smoking gun materialized:* Ibid., pp. 274–275.

331 *Bayh understood what the memo meant:* Ibid.

332 *He shaped the Intelligence Committee in a bipartisan way:* Bayh interview.

333 *the news exploded in front-page headlines:* Ed Magnuson, "Nation: The Burden of Billy," *Time,* August 4, 1980.

333 *"There's a helluva lot more Arabians than there is Jews":* "Nation, The Burden of Billy."

333 *the president had publicly disassociated himself:* Ibid.

334 *Byrd and Baker met frequently:* George Lardner, Jr. "Senate Establishes Investigative Panel," *Washington Post,* July 25, 1980.

334 *"There's no necessity for it":* Ibid.

335 *Dole could not resist giving a speech:* George Lardner Jr., "Probe Leaders Want President as Witness," *Washington Post,* July 26, 1980.

335   *Bayh, obviously irked at Dole:* Ibid.

335   *"It's going to be like walking through a minefield":* George Lardner Jr. and Charles R. Babcock, "Panel to Speed Probe Schedule," *Washington Post*, August 1, 1980.

335   *his aides had urged him to turn it down:* Ibid.

335   *On August 4, a line of 300 would-be spectators:* Margot Hornblower, "Probe of Billy, Libya Begins," *Washington Post*, August 5, 1980.

335   *Dole asked sarcastically:* Ibid.

335   *senators on both sides of the dais seemed uncertain:* Margot Hornblower, "Billy Panel: Wondering About the Need," *Washington Post*, August 6, 1980.

335   *Patrick Leahy, a first-term senator:* Ibid.

335   *Max Baucus commented:* Ibid.

335   *Even Dole observed: "A lot was smoke":* Ibid.

335   *"in the end, it may not amount to a hill of peanuts":* Ibid.

336   *"There's a lot of disenchantment with confrontation":* Ibid.

336   *committed to bringing out the full truth:* Walter Isaacson, "Carter: Battling a Revolt," *Time*, August 11, 1980.

336   *"disclosure of the facts will clearly demonstrate":* Ibid.

336   *On August 21, Billy Carter began his testimony:* Margot Hornblower, "Billy: No Crime Committed," *Washington Post*, August 22, 1980.

336   *Dole wanted the investigation to go deeper:* Margot Hornblower, "Billy Hearing: 'Until You Stir the Pot,'" *Washington Post*, August 24, 1980.

337   *"I'll wager that 90 percent of everything you will hear":* Ibid.

338   *heard about Ribicoff's views:* Interview with Dick D'Amato, April 28, 2011.

338   *repeatedly called for an open convention:* Clymer, *Edward M. Kennedy*, p. 315.

338   *believed that Byrd was secretly angling for the nomination:* Carter, *White House Diary*, pp. 451–452.

338   *Muskie may also have been intrigued:* Clymer, *Edward M. Kennedy*, p. 314; Bill Peterson and Ward Sinclair, "Open Convention Plotted by a Group of House Democrats," *Washington Post*, July 26, 1980. Suspicions about Muskie's interest increased because of the leadership in the open convention movement by Congressman Michael Barnes, a former Muskie staffer.

338   *Jackson apparently had the same thoughts:* "Squall Among the Democrats," *Time*, May 19, 1980; Clymer, *Edward M. Kennedy*, pp. 314–315.

338   *He had won three Senate races:* Bayh had reached the Senate after upsetting three-term incumbent Homer Capehart in 1962. In 1968, he defeated William Ruckelshaus, who had been the respected first administrator of the Environmental Protection Agency. In 1974, Bayh defeated Richard Lugar, the mayor of Indianapolis, who reached the Senate two years later and is still there, running for his seventh term.

339   *Republican staffers on the Appropriations Committee:* Interview with Mary Jane Checchi, May 13, 2010.

339 *"It's been vitriolic"*: Ward Sinclair, "Indiana's for Reagan, but Some Nasty Dust-Ups Mark Other Contests," *Washington Post*, October 19, 1980.

339 *Quayle's consultants came up with a clever line:* David Axelrod, "GOP Aiming at Second Indiana Senate Seat," *Chicago Tribune*, September 25, 1980.

339 *"We gotta help Gaylord":* I was working for Eagleton at the time, but was still close to Nelson, my former boss.

339 *Nelson seemed to lack energy:* Interview with Jeff Nedelman, May 21, 2010.

339 *Howard Paster, a prominent Democrat:* Interview with Howard Paster, June 30, 2011.

339 *Later that month, Carrie Lee Nelson:* Interview with Carrie Lee Nelson, August 30, 2010.

339 *Nelson privately agreed:* Christofferson, *Man from Clear Lake*, p. 340.

340 *Kasten recognized the challenge:* Ward Sinclair, "Wisconsin's Senator Nelson Stumps from Dawn to Midnight," *Washington Post*, October 20, 1980.

340 *"I'm hitting hard on the 'Nelson gap'":* Ibid.

340 *"Gaylord is busting his ass":* Christofferson, *Man from Clear Lake*, p. 340.

340 *"This was a different Nelson on the campaign trail":* Ibid.

340 *When Vice President Walter Mondale, his close friend:* Ibid., pp. 340–341.

340 *Nelson opened up a wide lead:* Ibid., p. 341.

340 A Washington Post *survey on the eve of the election:* David S. Broder et al., "A Survey of the Races State by State," *Washington Post*, November 2, 1980.

341 *Kasten, a bare-knuckled campaigner:* Christofferson, *Man from Clear Lake*, p. 341.

341 *A Kasten surrogate pointed out, accurately:* Ibid.

341 *McGovern had seriously considered not running:* Helen Dewar, "McGovern, Trailing Badly, Campaigning Harder Than Ever," *Washington Post*, July 8, 1980.

341 *McGovern recognized that he was trailing badly:* Helen Dewar, "McGovern Trailing Badly," *Washington Post*, July 8, 1980.

341 *McGovern actually wrote the concession speech:* McGovern, "Thoughts on Leaving the Senate," *Congressional Record*, December 13, 1980, pp. S16637–16638.

341 *threw himself into his reelection campaign:* The description of Eagleton's campaign comes from personal knowledge, since the campaign occurred while I was working for him.

342 *Eagleton had surprised Carter by urging him:* Carter, *White House Diary*, p. 211.

342 *Eagleton artfully dodged a political bullet:* This story comes from personal recollection; I was his subcommittee staff director. It is also told in Ira Shapiro, "Senator Eagleton Made Metro System Possible," *Roll Call*, May 21, 2007.

343 *Eagleton faced one more unusual challenge:* This story also comes from personal knowledge.

344 *the distinct possibility of becoming a one-term senator:* Patrick Buchanan, "Skies Dark for Liberals in the Senate," *Chicago Tribune*, June 12, 1980.

344 *Barry Goldwater came to Colorado:* Gary Hart, *The Thunder and the Sunshine: Four Seasons in a Burnished Life* (Golden, CO: Fulcrum Publishing, 2010), pp. 108–109.

344 *Elizabeth Drew, one of Washington's most distinguished reporters:* Elizabeth Drew, *Senator* (New York: A Touchstone Book, 1979).

344 *He had built expertise on defense issues:* Drew, *Senator*, pp. 23–30; Interview with Hoyt Purvis, February 4, 2010.

345 *Culver had given serious thought to retiring:* Interview with John Culver, April 15, 2010.

345 *"He knew he could lose":* Interview with John Podesta, August 19, 2010.

345 *Culver decided to run as the liberal he was:* Robert G. Kaiser, "Wind from the Right Chills Vulnerable Senate Democrats," *Washington Post*, April 10, 1979; Podesta interview.

345 *Culver and Grassley squared off in a major debate:* Culver interview.

345 *"With Watergate," he wrote:* Herman E. Talmadge with Mark Royden Winchell, *Talmadge: A Political Legacy, a Politician's Life* (Atlanta: Peachtree Publishers, 1987), p. 265.

345 *a grief-stricken Talmadge turned heavily to drink:* Ibid., pp. 317–318.

345 *The Senate Ethics Committee recommended:* Ibid., p. 337.

346 *Miller was the only serious threat:* Ibid., pp. 344–346.

346 *The Republicans sensed Talmadge's over-confidence:* Ibid., p. 352.

346 *The film footage led to a devastating television ad:* Scates, *Warren G. Magnuson*, p. 317.

346 *"I'm not saying Maggie hasn't done some good":* Quoted in ibid., p. 316.

346 *"the candidate of nostalgia":* Ibid.

346 *D'Amato beat him decisively:* Javits and Steinberg, *Javits*, p. 503.

346 *Many of his friends and admirers feared:* Ibid., p. 505.

346 *The* Times *called on Javits:* Ibid.

346 *Reagan had come out of the Republican convention:* David Broder, "Republicans Dream of Watershed Year," *Washington Post*, July 13, 1980; Wilentz, *Age of Reagan*, p. 120.

347 *Carter benefited from some of the same unease:* Martin Schram and David S. Broder, "Reagan's Gears Locked as Carter Pulls Even," *Washington Post*, October 17, 1980; Wilentz, *Age of Reagan*, p. 123.

347 *fearing Reagan's skill on television:* Wilentz, *Age of Reagan*, p. 123.

347 *He tried to humanize himself:* Ibid., pp. 123–124.

347 *Reagan deflected Carter's sallies with ease:* Ibid., p. 124.

348 *Nelson turned to Kevin Gottlieb:* Christofferson, *Man from Clear Lake*, p. 341.

349 *In his diary, he wrote:* Carter, *White House Diary*, p. 479.

349 *I had decided to take the day off:* This section is a personal recollection of election day and night 1980.

353 *House Speaker Tip O'Neill described it:* Wilentz, *Age of Reagan*, p. 125.

353 *One labor leader commented:* Helen Dewar, "GOP, with 53 Seats, Claims the Senate," *Washington Post*, November 6, 1980.

353 *Robert Byrd expressed regret at the defeat:* Ibid.

353 *"a major advance in the absorption":* Wilentz, *Age of Reagan*, p. 125.

353 *"If the New Right leaders think":* Dewar, "GOP, with 53 Seats, Claims the Senate."

353 *David Broder captured the moment:* David S. Broder, "A Sharp Right Turn: Republicans and Democrats Alike See New Era in '80 Returns," *Washington Post*, November 6, 1980.

CHAPTER 20: THE LAME-DUCK SESSION

355 *a dozen of them had been dispatched:* Bill Prochnau, "Senate Figures, Once Powerful, Ponder Future," *Washington Post*, November 15, 1980. This section is supplemented by personal recollection of the lame-duck period.

355 *top Senate Democratic aide said:* Ibid.

355 *Jackson's aggressive staff:* Interview with Ken Ackerman, November 16, 2010.

356 *Senator Glenn's subcommittee staff director:* Ibid.

356 *McGovern gave the impression of being the calmest:* Prochnau, "Senate Figures, Once Powerful."

356 *Bayh, licking his wounds:* Ibid.

356 *"It's somebody else's ballgame now":* Ibid.

356 *the lame-duck session proved to be remarkably productive:* Carter, *White House Diary*, pp. 488, 490, 493.

356 *asked President Carter to nominate Stephen Breyer:* Clymer, *Edward M. Kennedy*, pp. 324–325.

356 *a great relationship with Emory Sneeden:* Ibid.

357 *Bayh got a call from Long:* Gene Quinn, "Exclusive Interview: Senator Birch Bayh on Bayh-Dole at 30," http://ipwatchdog.com/2010/11/07/exclusive-interview-senator-birch-bayh-on-bayh-dole/id=13198/ November 7, 2010.

357 *"perhaps the most inspired piece of legislation":* "Innovation's Golden Goose," *Economist Technology Quarterly*, December 14, 2002.

357 *"We're at the mercy of the Senate":* Joanne Omang, "Shift on Hill May Help Alaska Lands Bill," *Washington Post*, November 8, 1980.

358 *"This bill is the best that can be done":* Ibid.

358 *Mo Udall said that "no president":* "Carter Signs Law for Protection of Alaska Lands," Associated Press, December 3, 1980.

358 *spent countless hours poring over maps of Alaska:* Carter, *Keeping Faith,* p. 582.

358 *The* Washington Post *editorial page called it:* "The Alaska Lands Battle Ends," *Washington Post,* November 17, 1980.

359 *Nelson made the fastest and best transition:* Christofferson, *Man from Clear Lake,* p. 344.

360 *remembered Javits lobbying him repeatedly:* Interview with Ken Duberstein, November 10, 2010.

360 *What could he say to get Domenici's support:* Ibid.

EPILOGUE

361 *beautifully captured the essence of the Senate: Congressional Record—Senate,* November 30, 2010, pp. 58277–58280.

362 *John Sears, the respected Republican consultant:* Carl Hulse, "For Republicans, an '80 Déjà vu?," *New York Times,* August 28, 2010.

362 *slotting some of the weakest of the new partisans:* Interview with John Rother, August 11, 2010.

363 *"In the Senate of the '80's":* Alan Ehrenhalt, "In the Senate of the '80's, Team Spirit Has Given Way to the Rule of Individuals," *Congressional Quarterly,* September 4, 1982.

363 *"seems to stand for a Senate that has disappeared":* Ibid.

363 *"the Senate seemed to be a less congenial place":* Tower, *Consequences,* p. 84.

364 *Dole changed his approach in 1981:* Interview with Sheila Burke, October 13, 2010; the discussion of Dole is also based on my personal observations while working in the Senate.

364 *she told him she was a Democrat from California:* Burke interview.

365 *never happier than when he was moving:* Ibid.

365 *led the most visible investigation:* William S. Cohen and George J. Mitchell, *Men of Zeal: A Candid Inside Story of the Iran-Contra Hearings* (New York: Viking, 1988).

365 *"Congress regained its voice in the 1987–1988 session":* Byrd, *Senate Addresses,* vol. 2, p. 606, quoting *New York Times,* October 24, 1988.

366 *hated the place from the moment he arrived:* Trent Lott, *Herding Cats: A Life in Politics* (New York: Regan Books, 2005), pp. 112–118.

366 *"We were conservative, we were hungry":* Ibid., p. 118.

367 *Rudman, a respected former prosecutor:* Tower, *Consequences,* pp. 350–352.

367 *Dole accused the Democrats of using the nomination:* Ibid., 352–357.

367 *Cohen still expresses outrage at the treatment:* Interview with Senator William Cohen, September 27, 2010.

367 *"Dole didn't really dislike Clinton":* Sidney Blumental, *The Clinton Wars* (New York: Farrar, Straus and Giroux, 2003), p. 159.

367 *Rudman left first*: Warren Rudman, *Combat: Twelve Years in the US Senate* (New York: Random House, 1996), pp. 242–243.

368 *"It was as though someone had pushed a mute button"*: Danforth, *Faith and Politics*, p. 143.

368 *finally told Dole that he would resign*: Interview with Keith Kennedy, November 11, 2010.

368 *Connie Mack of Florida, a former House member*: Interview with Senator Bob Packwood, July 19, 2010.

369 *"The panel was nicknamed 'The Council of Trent'"*: Lott, *Herding Cats*, p. 125.

369 *One thoughtful academic study*: Sean M. Theriault and David W. Rohde, "The Gingrich Senators and Party Polarization in the U.S. Senate," http://journals.cambridge.org/action//displayAbstract?fromPage=online&aid=8360400&fulltextType=RA&fileId=S0022381611000752.

369 *Collins was amazed to find*: Interview with Senator Susan Collins, July 19, 2010.

369 *"The Senate changed when the battered children"*: Interview with Senator Alan Simpson, February 2, 2010.

370 *"a takeover of the Republican Party by the Christian Right"*: Danforth, *Faith and Politics*, p. 7.

370 *Danforth expressed particular contempt for Frist's role*: Ibid., p. 76.

371 *From all reports, the seventeen women senators*: Dan Weil, "Women Senators Pick Politeness over Politics," Newsmax.com, February 4, 2011.

372 *struck by the paradox*: Interview with Senator Carl Levin, August 6, 2010.

372 *"the two lasting achievements of this Senate"*: George Packer, "The Empty Chamber," *New Yorker*, August 9, 2010.

373 *blasting the "supine Senate"*: Robert C. Byrd, *Losing America: Confronting a Reckless and Arrogant Presidency* (New York: W. W. Norton, 2004), p. 79.

373 *"Ronald Reagan would have a very difficult"*: quoted in Dana Milbank, "Reagan's New Party," *Washington Post*, July 20, 2011.

374 *came out convinced he should support it*: Manu Raju, "START Appears Set for Final Approval," http://www.politico.com/news/stories/1210/46669.html, December 21, 2010.

BIBLIOGRAPHY

SENATORS' MEMOIRS AND BIOGRAPHIES

Ashby, LeRoy, and Rod Gramer. *Fighting the Odds: The Life of Senator Frank Church* (Pullman, Washington: Washington State University Press, 1994).

Annis, J. Lee, Jr. *Howard Baker: Conciliator in an Age of Crisis*, 2nd ed. (Knoxville: Howard Baker Center for Public Policy, University of Tennessee, 2007).

Bass, Jack, and Marilyn W. Thompson. *Strom: The Complicated Personal and Political Life of Strom Thurmond* (New York: PublicAffairs, 2005).

Bayh, Birch. *One Heartbeat Away: Presidential Disability and Succession* (Indianapolis: Bobbs-Merrill, 1968).

Biden, Joe. *Promises to Keep: On Life and Politics* (New York: Random House, 2007).

Biles, Roger. *Crusading Liberal: Paul H. Douglas of Illinois* (DeKalb, IL: Northern Illinois University Press, 2002).

Bradley, Bill. *Time Present, Time Past: A Memoir* (New York: Alfred A. Knopf, 1996).

Byrd, Robert C. *Child of the Appalachian Coal Fields* (Morgantown, West Virginia: West Virginia University Press, 2005).

———. *Losing America: Confronting a Reckless and Arrogant Presidency* (New York: W. W. Norton, 2004).

———. *The Senate, 1789–1989: Addresses on the History of the United States Senate*, Vol. 2 (Washington, DC: U.S. Government Printing Office, 1991).

Campbell, Karl E. *Senator Sam Ervin: Last of the Founding Fathers* (Chapel Hill: University of North Carolina Press, 2007).

Caro, Robert A. *The Years of Lyndon Johnson: Master of the Senate* (New York: Alfred A. Knopf, 2002).

Christofferson, Bill. *The Man from Clear Lake: Earth Day Founder Senator Gaylord Nelson* (Madison: University of Wisconsin Press, 2004).

Clymer, Adam. *Edward M. Kennedy: A Biography* (New York: William Morrow, 1999).

Cohen, William S. *Roll Call: One Year in the United States Senate* (New York: Simon & Schuster, 1981).

Cohen, William S., and George J. Mitchell. *Men of Zeal: A Candid Inside Story of the Iran-Contra Hearings* (New York: Viking, 1988).

Cox, Patrick. *Ralph W. Yarborough: The People's Senator* (Austin: University of Texas Press, 2001).

Danforth, John. *Faith and Politics: How the "Moral Values" Debate Divides America and How to Move Forward Together* (New York: Viking, 2006).

Daschle, Tom, with Michael D'Orso. *Like No Other Time: The Two Years That Changed America* (New York: Three Rivers Press, 2003).

DeConcini, Dennis, and Jack L. August Jr. *Senator Dennis DeConcini: From the Center of the Aisle* (Tucson: University of Arizona Press, 2006).

Douglas, Paul H. *In the Fullness of Time: The Memoirs of Paul H. Douglas* (New York: Harcourt Brace Jovanovich, 1971).

Drukman, Mason. *Wayne Morse: A Political Biography* (Portland: Oregon Historical Society Press, 1997).

Eagleton, Thomas F. *War and Presidential Power: A Chronicle of Congressional Surrender* (New York: Liveright, 1974).

Ervin, Sam J., Jr. *Preserving the Constitution: The Autobiography of Senator Sam M. Ervin, Jr.* (Charlottesville, Virginia: Michie Company, 1984).

Fite, Gilbert C. *Richard Russell, Jr., Senator from Georgia* (Chapel Hill: University of North Carolina Press, 1991).

Gillon, Steven M. *The Democrats' Dilemma: Walter F. Mondale and the Liberal Legacy* (New York: Columbia University Press, 1992).

Harris, Fred R. *Alarms and Hopes: A Personal Journey, A Personal View* (New York: Harper & Row, 1968).

Hart, Gary. *The Thunder and the Sunshine: Four Seasons in a Burnished Life* (Golden, CO: Fulcrum Publishing, 2010).

Hatch, Orrin. *Square Peg: Confessions of a Citizen Senator* (New York: Basic Books, 2002).

Helms, Jesse. *Here's Where I Stand: A Memoir* (New York: Random House, 2005).

Hodgson, Godfrey. *The Gentleman from New York: Daniel Patrick Moynihan: A Biography* (Boston: Houghton Mifflin, 2000).

Hollings, Ernest F. "Fritz," with Kirk Victor. *Making Government Work* (Columbia: University of South Carolina Press, 2008).

Hulsey, Byron C. *Everett Dirksen and His Presidents: How a Senate Giant Shaped American Politics* (Lawrence: University Press of Kansas, 2000).

Humphrey, Hubert H. *The Education of a Public Man: My Life and Politics* (Minneapolis: University of Minnesota Press, 1991).

———. *War on Poverty* (Toronto, Canada: McGraw-Hill, 1964).

Javits, Jacob K., with Rafael Steinberg. *Javits: The Autobiography of a Public Man* (Boston, Massachusetts: Houghton Mifflin, 1981).

Johnson, Haynes, and Bernard M. Gwertzman. *Fulbright the Dissenter* (London: Hutchinson, 1969).

Kaufman, Robert G. *Henry M. Jackson: A Life in Politics* (Seattle: University of Washington Press, 2000).

Kennedy, Edward M. *True Compass: A Memoir* (New York: Twelve, 2009).

Kirchmeier, Mark. *Packwood: The Public and Private Life from Acclaim to Outrage* (New York: Harper Collins West, 1995).

Laxalt, Paul. *Nevada's Paul Laxalt: A Memoir* (Reno, Nevada: Jack Bacon, 2000).

Lewis, Finlay. *Mondale: Portrait of an American Politician* (New York: Harper & Row, 1980).

Link, William A. *Righteous Warrior: Jesse Helms and the Rise of Modern Conservatism* (New York: St. Martin's, 2008).

Lippman, Theo, Jr., and Donald C. Hansen. *Muskie* (New York: W. W. Norton, 1971).

Longley, Kyle. *Senator Albert Gore, Sr.: Tennessee Maverick* (Baton Rouge: Louisiana State University Press, 2004).

Lott, Trent. *Herding Cats: A Life in Politics* (New York: Regan Books, 2005).

Mann, Robert. *Legacy to Power: Senator Russell Long of Louisiana* (Lincoln, NE: Authors Guild Backinprint.com Edition, 1992).

McGovern, George S. *Grassroots: The Autobiography of George McGovern* (New York: Random House, 1977).

Mondale, Walter F., with David Hage. *The Good Fight: A Life in Liberal Politics* (New York: Scribner, 2010).

Oberdorfer, Don. *Senator Mansfield: The Extraordinary Life of a Great American Statesman and Diplomat* (Washington, DC: Smithsonian Books, 2003).

O'Brien, Michael. *Philip Hart: The Conscience of the Senate* (East Lansing: Michigan State University Press, 1995).

Prochnau, William W., and Richard W. Larsen. *A Certain Democrat: Senator Henry Jackson, a Political Biography* (Englewood Cliffs, NJ: Prentice-Hall, 1972).

Ribicoff, Abraham. *America Can Make It!* (New York: Atheneum, 1972).

Sandbrook, Dominic. *Eugene McCarthy and the Rise and Fall of Postwar American Liberalism* (New York: Anchor Books, 2005).

Scates, Shelby. *Warren G. Magnuson and the Shaping of Twentieth-Century America* (Seattle: University of Washington Press, 1997).

Schlesinger, Arthur M., Jr. *Robert Kennedy and His Times* (Boston: Houghton Mifflin, 1978).

Schulman, Robert. *John Sherman Cooper: The Global Kentuckian* (Lexington: University Press of Kentucky, 1976).

Solberg, Carl. *Hubert Humphrey: A Biography* (New York: W. W. Norton, 1984).

Talmadge, Herman E., with Mark Royden Winchell. *Talmadge: A Political Legacy, a Politician's Life* (Atlanta: Peachtree Publishers, 1987).

Thompson, Fred D. *At That Point in Time: The Inside Story of the Senate Watergate Committee* (New York: Quadrangle/New York Times Book Co., 1975).

Tower, John G. *Consequences: A Personal and Political Memoir* (Boston: Little, Brown, 1991).

Valeo, Francis R. *Mike Mansfield, Majority Leader: A Different Kind of Senate, 1961–1976* (Armonk, NY: M. E. Sharpe, 1999).

Vetterli, Richard. *Orrin Hatch: Challenging the Washington Establishment* (Chicago: Regnery Gateway, 1982).

Weicker, Lowell P., Jr., with Barry Sussman. *Maverick: A Life in Politics* (Boston: Little, Brown, 1995).

Witcover, Jules. *Joe Biden: A Life of Trial and Redemption* (New York: William Morrow, 2010).

Woods, Randall Bennett. *Fulbright: A Biography* (Cambridge, UK: Cambridge University Press, 1995).

ABOUT THE SENATE

Asbell, Bernard. *The Senate Nobody Knows* (Garden City, NY: Doubleday, 1978).

Baker, Ross K. *Friend and Foe in the U.S. Senate* (New York: Free Press, 1980).

Clymer, Adam. *Drawing the Line at the Big Ditch: The Panama Canal Treaties and the Rise of the Right* (Lawrence: University Press of Kansas, 2008).

Drew, Elizabeth. *Senator* (New York: A Touchstone Book, 1979).

Drury, Allen. *A Senate Journal, 1943–1945* (New York: McGraw-Hill, 1963).

Foley, Michael. *The New Senate: Liberal Influence on a Conservative Institution, 1959–1972* (New Haven, CT: Yale University Press, 1980).

Gitenstein, Mark. *Matters of Principle: An Insider's Account of America's Rejection of Robert Bork's Nomination to the Supreme Court* (New York: Simon & Schuster, 1992).

Gould, Lewis L. *The Most Exclusive Club: The History of the Modern United States Senate* (New York: Basic Books, 2005).

Hamilton, James. *The Power to Probe: A Study of Congressional Investigations* (New York: Random House, 1976).

Johnson, Loch K. *A Season of Inquiry: The Senate Intelligence Investigation* (Lexington: University Press of Kentucky, 1985).

Malbin, Michael. *Unelected Representatives: Congressional Staff and the Future of Representative Government* (New York: Basic Books, 1980).

Mann, Robert. *The Walls of Jericho: Lyndon Johnson, Hubert Humphrey, Richard Russell and the Struggle for Civil Rights* (New York: Harcourt Brace, 1996).

Mann, Thomas E., and Norman J. Ornstein. *The Broken Branch: How Congress Is Failing America and How to Get It Back on Track* (New York: Oxford University Press, 2006).

Matthews, Donald R. *U.S. Senators and Their World* (New York: Vintage Books, 1960).

McPherson, Harry. *A Political Education: A Washington Memoir* (Boston: Houghton Mifflin, 1988).

Pertschuk, Michael. *Revolt Against Regulation: The Rise and Pause of the Consumer Movement* (Berkeley: University of California Press, 1982).

Redman, Eric. *The Dance of Legislation* (New York: Simon & Schuster, 1973).

Sinclair, Barbara. *The Transformation of the U.S. Senate* (Baltimore: Johns Hopkins University Press, 1989).

Stern, Paula. *Water's Edge: Domestic Politics and the Making of American Foreign Policy* (Westport, CT: Greenwood, 1979).

Weisman, Alan. *Prince of Darkness: Richard Perle: The Kingdom, the Power and the End of Empire in America* (New York: Union Square, 2007).

AMERICAN POLITICS AND GOVERNMENT
IN THE 1960's AND 1970's

Beschloss, Michael R., ed. *Taking Charge: The Johnson White House Tapes, 1963–1964* (New York: Simon & Schuster, 1997).

———. *The Crisis Years: Kennedy and Khruschev, 1960–1963* (New York: Edward Burlingame Books, 1991).

Blumenthal, Sidney. *The Rise of the Republican Counter-Establishment: The Conservative Ascent to Political Power* (New York: Union Sterling Press, 1986).

Bowden, Mark. *Guests of the Ayatollah* (New York: Grove, 2006).

Brinkley, Douglas. *Tour of Duty: John Kerry and the Vietnam War* (New York: William Morrow, 2004.

Califano, Joseph A., Jr. *The Triumph and Tragedy of Lyndon Johnson: The White House Years* (New York: Simon & Schuster, 1991).

Carter, Jimmy. *Keeping Faith: Memoirs of a President* (Toronto, Canada: Bantam Books, 1982).

———. *White House Diary* (New York: Farrar, Straus and Giroux, 2010).

Chester, Lewis, Godfrey Hodgson, and Bruce Page. *An American Melodrama: The Presidential Campaign of 1968* (New York: Viking, 1969).

Cramer, Richard Ben. *What It Takes: The Way to the White House* (New York: Random House, 1992).

Crawford, Alan. *Thunder on the Right: The "New Right" and the Politics of Resentment* (New York: Pantheon Books, 1980).

Davis, Lanny. *Scandal: How "Gotcha" Politics Is Destroying America* (New York: Palgrave Macmillan, 2006).

Dallek, Robert. *Flawed Giant: Lyndon Johnson and His Times, 1961–1973* (Oxford University Press, 1998).

———. *An Unfinished Life: John F. Kennedy, 1917–1963* (Boston: Little, Brown, 2003).

Dean, John W. *The Rehnquist Choice: The Untold Story of the Nixon Appointment That Redefined the Supreme Court* (New York: Touchstone, 2001).

Drew, Elizabeth. *Washington Journal: The Events of 1973–1974* (New York: Random House, 1974).

Fink, Gary M., and Hugh Davis Graham, eds. *The Carter Presidency: Policy Choices in the Post–New Deal Era* (Lawrence: University Press of Kansas, 1998).

Glad, Betty. *Jimmy Carter: In Search of the Great White House* (New York: W. W. Norton, 1980).

——. *An Outsider in the White House: Jimmy Carter, His Advisors, and the Making of American Foreign Policy* (Ithaca, NY: Cornell University Press, 2009).

Hargrove, Erwin C. *Jimmy Carter as President: Leadership and the Politics of the Public Good* (Baton Rouge: Louisiana State University Press, 1988).

Harris, David. *The Crisis: The President, the Prophet and the Shah—1979 and the Coming of Militant Islam* (New York: Little, Brown, 2004).

Hoff, Joan. *Nixon Reconsidered* (New York: Basic Books, 1994).

Jones, Charles O. *The Trusteeship Presidency: Jimmy Carter and the United States Congress* (Baton Rouge: Louisiana State University Press, 1988).

Jorden, William J. *Panama Odyssey* (Austin: University of Texas Press, 1984).

Judis, John B. *The Paradox of American Democracy: Elites, Special Interests, and the Betrayal of Public Trust* (New York: Routledge, 2000).

Kaufman, Burton I., and Scott Kaufman. *The Presidency of James Earl Carter, Jr.*, 2nd ed. (Lawrence: University Press of Kansas, 2006).

Kissinger, Henry A. *Years of Upheaval* (Boston: Little, Brown, 1982).

Lichtman, Allan J. *White Protestant Nation: The Rise of the American Conservative Movement* (New York: Atlantic Monthly Press, 2008).

Mackenzie, G. Calvin, and Robert Weisbrot. *The Liberal Hour: Washington and the Politics of Change in the 1960's* (New York: Penguin, 2008).

Mattson, Kevin. *What the Heck Are You Up To, Mr. President?: Jimmy Carter, America's "Malaise," and the Speech That Should Have Changed the Country* (New York: Bloomsbury USA, 2009).

Milazzo, Paul Charles. *Unlikely Environmentalists: Congress and Clean Water, 1945–1972* (Lawrence: University Press of Kansas, 2006).

Morris, Kenneth E. *Jimmy Carter: American Moralist* (Athens: University of Georgia Press, 1996).

Mudd, Roger. *The Place to Be: Washington, CBS and the Glory Days of Television News* (New York: PublicAffairs, 2008).

Perlstein, Rick. *Nixonland: The Rise of a President and the Fracturing of America* (New York: Scribner, 2008).

Reeves, Richard. *President Kennedy: Profile of Power* (New York: Simon & Schuster, 1993).

Reich, Robert B., and John D. Donahue. *New Deals: The Chrysler Revival and the American System* (New York: Penguin Books, 1985).

Sandbrook, Dominic. *Mad as Hell: The Crisis of the 1970's and the Rise of the Populist Right* (New York: Alfred A. Knopf, 2011).

Shesol, Jeff. *Mutual Contempt: Lyndon Johnson, Robert Kennedy and the Feud That Defined a Decade* (New York: W. W. Norton, 1997).

Schlesinger, Arthur M., Jr. *The Imperial Presidency* (Boston: Houghton Mifflin, 1973).

———. *A Thousand Days: John F. Kennedy in the White House* (Greenwich, CT: Fawcett Crest, 1965).

Sorensen, Ted. *Counselor: Life at the Edge of History* (New York: Harper, 2008).

Stanley, Timothy. *Kennedy vs. Carter: The 1980 Battle for the Democratic Party's Soul* (Lawrence: University Press of Kansas, 2010).

White, Theodore H. *Breach of Faith: The Fall of Richard Nixon* (New York: Atheneum/Reader's Digest Press, 1975).

———. *The Making of the President 1972* (New York: Atheneum, 1973).

———. *The Making of the President 1968* (New York: Atheneum, 1969).

Wilentz, Sean. *The Age of Reagan: A History, 1974–2008* (New York: Harper, 2008).

Witcover, Jules. *Marathon: The Pursuit of the Presidency, 1972–1976* (New York: Viking, 1977).

Woods, Randall B. *LBJ: Architect of American Ambition* (Cambridge, MA: Harvard University Press, 2006).

INDEX

Abdnor, James, 350

Abortion issue, 34, 35, 211, 213–214, 225

Abourezk, James
    and energy policy (1977), 105, 106–109, 111, 112–113
    and natural gas legislation, 203

ACDA. *See* Arms Control and Disarmament Agency

ADA. *See* Americans for Democratic Action

Afghanistan, Soviet invasion of, 295, 308

AFL-CIO, 43, 176–177, 183
    lobbying power of, 178
    and setbacks, 172
    See also Labor unions

Aiken, George, 29

Airline Deregulation Act, 207, 215

Airline regulation, 129–131

Alaska
    environmental protection and conservation in, 317–319 (*see also* Alaska lands legislation)
    oil, gas, mineral, and timber wealth in, 317, 318, 319
    and statehood act, 317

Alaska lands legislation
    and Alaska's senators, struggle between, 319–322
    and executive orders, 321–322, 322–323

passage of, 357–359
    and Senate compromise, 325–326
    and Senate debate, 323–326

Alaska National Interest Lands Conservation Act, 321, 358–359

Alaska Statehood Act, 317

Albright, Madeleine, 57

Alexander, Lamar, 374

Allen, James, 20, 33, 178–179

Allende, Salvador, 123

Alvarado, Susan, 57

American Enterprise Institute, 175

American-Israeli Public Affairs Committee (AIPAC), 162–163, 164, 167, 168, 169. *See also* Political action committees

Americans for Democratic Action (ADA), 246

Anderson, Wendell, 212

Andrus, Cecil, 318, 322–324

Antiballistic Missile (ABM) Defense System Treaty, 65, 68–69

Antiquities Act, 321–322

Appalachia, 8

ARA. *See* Area Redevelopment Act (ARA)

Arctic National Wildlife Refuge, 358

Area Redevelopment Act (ARA), 7–8

Arms control, and Soviet Union, 64–70, 72–74. *See also* SALT II

Arms Control and Disarmament Agency (ACDA), 67

Ira Shapiro spent twelve years in senior staff positions in the U.S. Senate, including Minority Staff Director and Chief Counsel of the Governmental Affairs Committee, and Chief of Staff to Senator John D. Rockefeller IV. During the Clinton Administration, he served as the General Counsel and trade ambassador in the Office of the United States Trade Representative (USTR) and played a key role in completing the negotiations on the Uruguay Round, which established the World Trade Organization global trade rules, and the North American Free Trade Agreement (NAFTA). His writing has appeared in the *New York Times*, the *Washington Post*, the *St. Louis Post-Dispatch*, the *Brandeis Review*, and the *Harvard Journal of Legislation*. His 2002 campaign for Congress in Maryland's Eighth District was described by the local press as the "antidote to cynicism" that he promised to deliver. He currently practices international trade law in Washington, D.C.

PublicAffairs is a publishing house founded in 1997. It is a tribute to the standards, values, and flair of three persons who have served as mentors to countless reporters, writers, editors, and book people of all kinds, including me.

I. F. STONE, proprietor of *I. F. Stone's Weekly*, combined a commitment to the First Amendment with entrepreneurial zeal and reporting skill and became one of the great independent journalists in American history. At the age of eighty, Izzy published *The Trial of Socrates*, which was a national bestseller. He wrote the book after he taught himself ancient Greek.

BENJAMIN C. BRADLEE was for nearly thirty years the charismatic editorial leader of *The Washington Post*. It was Ben who gave the *Post* the range and courage to pursue such historic issues as Watergate. He supported his reporters with a tenacity that made them fearless and it is no accident that so many became authors of influential, best-selling books.

ROBERT L. BERNSTEIN, the chief executive of Random House for more than a quarter century, guided one of the nation's premier publishing houses. Bob was personally responsible for many books of political dissent and argument that challenged tyranny around the globe. He is also the founder and longtime chair of Human Rights Watch, one of the most respected human rights organizations in the world.

·   ·   ·

For fifty years, the banner of Public Affairs Press was carried by its owner Morris B. Schnapper, who published Gandhi, Nasser, Toynbee, Truman, and about 1,500 other authors. In 1983, Schnapper was described by *The Washington Post* as "a redoubtable gadfly." His legacy will endure in the books to come.

Peter Osnos, *Founder and Editor-at-Large*